Good Housekeeping
Cooking for Today

Good Housekeeping
Cooking for

Today

Octopus Books

First published 1973 by
Octopus Books Limited
59 Grosvenor Street London W1
ISBN 0 7064 0269 3

Printed in Hong Kong by Mandarin Publishers Ltd.

Contents

Introduction

Today's cook is a busy cook; speed and planning are the essence of her work. That's what this book is all about. Cooking for Today sets out to help you enjoy entertaining and everyday cooking.

In the first section 'Basic Recipes and Techniques', all the essential cookery methods are given, as well as a comprehensive collection of recipes from soups to desserts, sauces and cakes. There are also illustrated step-by-step recipes for 13 classic dishes.

'For the Hostess' includes all the information and specially planned time-saving recipes which the busy hostess needs. There are chapters on wines, aperitifs and brandies; suggestions for setting the table; recipes to be cooked in advance, with advice on freezing and meals to cook in a hurry with suggestions for using a pressure cooker, mixer and blender.

'Entertaining' gives a series of menus for specific occasions from dinner parties and informal buffets to children's parties, Christmas and other family occasions, easy weekends and barbecues. As well as complete recipes there are timetables and lots of handy hints.

In 'Information', a selection of helpful advice is given on subjects including planning a party, basic equipment and herbs and spices.

Notes for readers
Cup measures given in lists of ingredients refer to
Australian measures. Where a recipe refers to double and
single cream, Australian readers should add together the
total quantity and use standard cream.

All the recipes in this series have been tested in the Good
Housekeeping Institute kitchens. If you have any queries,
please do not hesitate to contact us at Good Housekeeping
Institute, Chestergate House, Vauxhall Bridge Road,
London SW1V 1HF

Good Housekeeping Institute Principal
Carol Macartney
Assistant Principal
Margaret Coombes

Smoked haddock and cheese flan (page 200)

Basic Recipes
and Techniques

SOUPS

Soups may be thin and clear, thick and creamy, hot, cold, or so full of meat and vegetables that they make a nourishing meal in themselves. Whatever kind of soup you are planning to make, the basis will always be a tasty stock. Nowadays there are many ready-made stock preparations available, the most popular being bouillon cubes, which make an acceptable stock and save an enormous amount of time and trouble. Beware of the strength of the seasoning if using a bouillon cube and don't add more until you have tasted the finished soup; remember, too, that cubes do not give 'body' to a soup in the same way as bone stock. There is nothing to beat a rich home-made stock – a pressure cooker cuts time and if you own a freezer it is easy to keep stock by freezing it in pint or ½-pint quantities.

White stock – which can be made from veal or mutton bones, or poultry carcasses – is used for the pale, delicately flavoured soups. It can also be used for one of the darker soups with the addition of a few drops of gravy browning. However, a brown stock – made from bones and beef first browned in the oven – is really more satisfactory for a dark soup. It is essential for consommé to use a really tasty brown stock. Turn to the end of the section for stocks.

SOUPE A LA PAYSANNE
serves 6

2 oz. carrots
1 oz. turnip
1 oz. celery
2 oz. leeks
1 oz. butter
salt and pepper
2 pints (5 cups) brown stock
bouquet garni, consisting of:
    2–3 parsley stalks, bay leaf,
    sprig of thyme
croûtons

Cut the carrot and turnip into rough squares; thinly slice the celery and leeks. Bring a pan of water to the boil, add the vegetables and blanch for 3 minutes. Refresh under cold running water. Drain. Melt butter in a pan, add the vegetables and cook without colouring until tender.
Pour the stock over them, bring to the boil, skim and add the bouquet garni. Cover and simmer for 20–30 minutes. Remove bouquet

This is a French classic and can almost make a meal in itself

Use up your surplus garden lettuce in this tasty soup

garni and skim well, using absorbent kitchen paper to remove any remaining fat. Adjust the seasoning if necessary. Pour into a pre-heated bowl and serve the croûtons separately.

SUSAN'S GERMAN SOUP
serves 4; this soup is a meal in itself

2 pints (5 cups) household stock
½ lb. potatoes, peeled
2 leeks, cleaned and sliced
½ lb. turnips, peeled and cubed
¼ lb. carrots, peeled and sliced
1 red or green pepper, sliced
2 sticks of celery, sliced
½ lb. piece streaky bacon, rinded
½ lb. Mettwurst

Place the stock in a large pan with the potatoes cut in small pieces. Simmer until the potatoes are tender. Sieve potatoes and stock together or purée in a blender and return to the pan. Add leeks, turnips, carrots, pepper, celery and bacon and simmer gently, covered, for 1½–1¾ hours.
Meanwhile remove the skin from the Mettwurst and cut into oblique slices. Add to the soup and simmer for a further 15 minutes. Adjust seasoning if necessary and cut the

bacon into bite-size pieces before serving.

FRENCH ONION SOUP
serves 4

2 oz. butter
sugar
1 lb. onions, skinned and sliced
1½ pints (3¾ cups) brown stock
salt and pepper
2–3 oz. (½–¾ cup) Gruyère or Emmenthal cheese, grated
4 thin slices French bread, toasted
white wine (optional)

Melt the butter, add a few grains of sugar and fry the onions slowly until well browned and soft. Stir in the stock, bring to the boil and simmer, with the lid on, for 30 minutes. Season to taste.
Pour into flameproof soup bowls. Sprinkle the grated cheese on the slices of French bread and float one on each bowl of soup. Place the bowls under a hot grill or in the oven at 450°F. (mark 8) until the cheese melts and bubbles, then serve immediately, with more grated cheese if required. A dash of dry white wine may be added to the soup just before turning into the bowls, if wished.

MINESTRONE
serves 4–6

½ a leek, cleaned and shredded
1 onion, skinned and finely chopped
1 clove of garlic, skinned and crushed
1 oz. butter
2 pints (5 cups) white stock, preferably home-made
1 carrot, peeled and cut into thin strips
1 turnip, peeled and cut into thin strips
1 stick celery, scrubbed and thinly sliced
1 oz. macaroni
¼ cabbage, washed and finely shredded
3 runner beans, thinly sliced
1 oz. peas, shelled
1 level tsp. tomato paste or 4 tomatoes, skinned and diced
1–2 rashers of bacon, chopped and fried
salt and pepper
Parmesan cheese, grated

Lightly sauté the leek, onion and garlic in the melted butter for 5–10 minutes, until soft but not coloured. Add the stock, bring to the boil, add the carrot, turnip, celery and macaroni and simmer for 20–30 minutes. Add the cabbage, beans and peas and simmer for a further 20 minutes. Stir in the tomato paste or tomatoes, bacon and seasoning to taste. Serve the Parmesan cheese in a separate dish.

MAMA'S LEEK SOUP
serves 3–4

½ lb. leeks
2 oz. butter or margarine
½-pint (1-oz.) pkt. white sauce mix
1 pint (2½ cups) milk
1 oz. (¼ cup) Cheddar cheese, grated
salt and pepper
croûtons

Thinly slice the leeks, wash thoroughly and drain well. Melt the butter, add the leeks, cover and cook gently for about 10 minutes until tender. Off the heat, shower in the contents of the sauce mix packet and gradually add the milk, stirring briskly. Bring to the boil, stirring, and cook for about minutes. Purée in a blender or work through a wire sieve. Add the cheese, reheat and adjust seasoning – add a little more milk if necessary. Serve with toast croûtons.

ROAD BEAN SOUP

rves 3–4

oz. (1 cup) chopped onion
clove of garlic, skinned and crushed
oz. butter
oz. ($\frac{1}{4}$ cup) flour
pint ($2\frac{1}{2}$ cups) chicken or ham stock
lb. shelled broad beans, fresh or frozen
level tsp. dried thyme
emon juice
alt and pepper
laked almonds (optional) for garnish

ry the onion and garlic in the utter until soft but not coloured. tir in the flour, cook for 2 minutes nd then add the stock. Bring to he boil and add the broad beans nd thyme; simmer, covered, until he beans are tender. Blend or sieve he contents of the pan, adding nore stock if necessary to give a hin creamy consistency.

Adjust the seasoning with lemon uice, salt and pepper. If wished, auté a few flaked almonds in utter and add to the soup just efore reheating.

LETTUCE AND ONION SOUP

erves 6

2 oz. butter
1 large onion, skinned and finely chopped
1 large lettuce, washed and finely shredded
2 pints (5 cups) chicken stock
salt and pepper
$2\frac{3}{4}$ fl.oz. ($\frac{1}{3}$ cup) double cream

Heat the butter in a saucepan, add the onion and fry gently until soft, being careful not to allow it to colour. Add the lettuce and cook in the butter for a few minutes, then add the stock and seasoning. Bring to the boil, cover and simmer for 5–7 minutes. Place half the mixture in a blender and purée. Turn into a bowl and repeat with the remaining mixture.

Return to the saucepan. Bring to the boil, remove from the heat and gradually add the cream, stirring all the time. Serve with cheese straws.

COCK-A-LEEKIE

serves 4

1 boiling fowl–about $2\frac{1}{2}$ lb. oven-ready weight
2 pints (5 cups) stock or water
4 leeks, cleaned and sliced
salt and pepper
6 prunes (optional)

An oxtail makes a rich, meaty soup for a cold day

Consommé princesse, the clearest of soups garnished with asparagus

Cover the fowl with stock or water, add the leeks and seasoning and bring to the boil. Simmer gently for about $3\frac{1}{2}$ hours, until tender. Remove the chicken from the stock, carve off the meat and cut into fairly large pieces. Serve the soup with the chicken pieces in it or serve the soup on its own, with the chicken as a main course.

If prunes are used, soak them overnight in cold water, halve and stone them and add to the stock 30 minutes before the end of the cooking time.

CREAM OF CELERY SOUP

serves 4

1 oz. butter
1 head of celery, scrubbed and chopped
1 oz. ($\frac{1}{4}$ cup) flour
1 pint ($2\frac{1}{2}$ cups) chicken stock
1 blade of mace
1 tsp. lemon juice
salt and freshly ground pepper
2 oz. carrots, peeled and finely diced
$\frac{1}{2}$ pint ($1\frac{1}{4}$ cups) milk

Melt the butter, add the celery and fry gently for 5 minutes. Stir in the flour, cook for a few minutes, then gradually add the stock, stirring. Add the mace and lemon juice, season with salt and pepper; bring to the boil, cover and simmer for 20 minutes. Discard the mace. Purée the soup in a blender or work through a sieve, return it to the pan, add the diced carrot and simmer until the garnish is tender –about 15 minutes. Remove from the heat, add the milk and adjust the seasoning if necessary.

POTATO AND ONION SOUP

serves 4

2 oz. butter
$\frac{1}{2}$ lb. onions, skinned and thinly sliced
1 lb. potatoes, peeled and diced
1 pint ($2\frac{1}{2}$ cups) chicken stock
$\frac{1}{2}$ pint ($1\frac{1}{4}$ cups) milk
salt and pepper
$\frac{1}{2}$ lb. tomatoes, skinned and seeded
1 oz. cheese, grated
1 tbsp. chopped parsley

Melt the butter and fry the onions for 10 minutes. Add the potatoes, cover and continue to cook over a low heat for a further 10 minutes. Add the stock and cook until the potatoes are soft and mushy. Add the milk and sieve or purée in a blender. Adjust the seasoning. Slice the tomato flesh in strips and add to the soup, together with the cheese and parsley. Reheat before serving.

OXTAIL SOUP

serves 6–8

1 oxtail, jointed
1 oz. butter or margarine
2 onions, skinned and chopped
1 carrot, peeled and sliced
2 sticks of celery, scrubbed and sliced
3–4 pints ($7\frac{1}{2}$–10 cups) brown stock
1 oz. lean ham or bacon, chopped
bouquet garni
salt and pepper
3 level tbsps. flour
a little port wine (optional)
squeeze of lemon juice

Wash and dry the oxtail and trim off any excess fat. Fry the pieces of oxtail in the butter with the vegetables for 5 minutes, until evenly browned. Just cover with the stock and bring to the boil. Add the chopped ham or bacon, bouquet garni and seasoning, cover the saucepan and simmer for 3–4 hours, until the tail meat is tender. As oxtail is very fatty, it is necessary to skim the soup occasionally with a metal spoon.

Strain the soup, remove the meat from the bones and cut it up neatly. Return the meat and strained liquor to the pan and reheat. Blend the flour and a little water (or port wine, if used) to a smooth cream. Stir in a little of the hot liquid and return the mixture to the pan. Bring to the boil, stirring until it thickens, and cook for about 5 minutes. Add a squeeze of lemon juice and seasoning to taste before serving.

CONSOMME PRINCESSE

serves 4

2 pints (5 cups) home-made brown stock (bouillon cubes will not do for this soup)
$\frac{1}{4}$ lb. lean beef
$\frac{1}{4}$ pint ($\frac{5}{8}$ cup) cold water
1 carrot, peeled and quartered
1 small onion, skinned and quartered
bouquet garni
1 egg white
small tin of asparagus tips
salt
2 tsps. sherry (optional)

Remove any fat from the stock.

Gazpacho, modern-style

Shred the meat finely and soak it in the water for 15 minutes. Put the meat and water, vegetables, stock and bouquet garni into a deep saucepan; lastly add the egg white. Heat gently and whisk continuously until a thick froth starts to form. Stop whisking and bring to the boil. Reduce the heat immediately and simmer *gently* for 2 hours. (If the liquid boils too rapidly, the froth will break and cloud the consommé.)

Scald a clean cloth or jelly bag, wring it out, tie it to the four legs of an upturned stool and place a bowl underneath. Pour the soup through, keeping the froth back at first with a spoon, then let it slide out onto the cloth. Again pour the soup through the cloth and through the filter of egg white. The consommé should now be clear and sparkling. Meanwhile heat the asparagus tips according to directions. Drain, rinse well. Reheat the consommé, adding salt if liked and a little sherry. Add the hot asparagus tips and serve.

SHRIMP CHOWDER

serves 4

1 large onion, skinned and sliced
½ oz. butter
¼ pint (⅝ cup) boiling water
3 medium potatoes, peeled and diced
1 pint shrimps, shelled
1 pint (2½ cups) milk
1–2 oz. (¼–½ cup) cheese, grated
chopped parsley to garnish

Lightly fry the onion in the butter for about 5 minutes, until soft but not coloured. Add the boiling water, potatoes and seasoning. Cover and simmer gently for 15–20 minutes, or until the potatoes are just cooked. Add the shrimps and the milk and reheat. Stir in the grated cheese and parsley and serve with crusty bread or toast.

GAZPACHO, MODERN-STYLE

serves 4

1 lb. ripe, juicy tomatoes, skinned and sliced
1 small onion, skinned and finely chopped
1 small green pepper (capsicum), seeded and chopped
1 clove of garlic, skinned and crushed
1 tbsp. wine vinegar
1 tbsp. olive oil
1–2 tbsps. lemon juice
salt and pepper
small can tomato juice, optional
¼ cucumber, peeled and diced
1 thick slice of toast, diced

Purée the tomatoes, onion, green pepper, garlic, vinegar and olive oil in a blender. Turn into a basin, add the lemon juice and season to taste and chill thoroughly in a refrigerator. If necessary, dilute with canned tomato juice before serving. Serve sprinkled with the diced cucumber and toast.

STOCKS

BROWN STOCK

makes 2½ pints (6¼ cups)

1 lb. marrow bone
2 lb. shin of beef
3 pints (7½ cups) water
2 sprigs parsley
a pinch of thyme
a pinch of marjoram
a small bay leaf, crumbled
1 carrot, peeled and sliced
1 medium onion, skinned and coarsely chopped
1 stick celery, scrubbed and sliced
5 peppercorns
½ level tbsp. salt

Chop the marrow bone and cut the beef into pieces. Put into a large (approx. 7-pint) saucepan with the rest of the ingredients. Bring to the boil and skim. Simmer for 4–5 hours with the lid on the pan. Strain, cool and leave overnight in the refrigerator to jelly. Skim off any fat from the cold stock. Keep in a cool place for not longer than 2–3 days, boiling up each day.

WHITE STOCK

makes 3½ pints

2½ lb. knuckle of veal or meaty veal bones
1 glass white wine
a little lemon juice
5 pints (12½ cups) cold water
4 oz. sliced onion
4 oz. sliced carrot
bouquet garni
1 level tsp. salt
4 peppercorns

Wipe the knuckle with a damp cloth and put into a large (approx. 8-pint) saucepan. Cover with cold water and bring to the boil, removing any scum. Drain and rinse. Return to the pan, pour the wine over and allow to reduce to about 2 tablespoons. Add the lemon juice and 5 pints water and bring to the boil. Skim.

Add the vegetables and bouquet garni, salt and peppercorns. Reboil, partially cover with the lid and simmer for 4 hours. Strain, cool and leave overnight in the refrigerator. Remove the fat from the cold stock before using. Store as for brown stock.

HOUSEHOLD STOCK

makes 4 pints

2 lb. selection of roast meat bones, chicken or turkey carcass, giblets, bacon rinds etc.
1 lb. sliced vegetables, including onion, carrot, leek, celery, mushrooms, celeriac
1½ oz. fat
bouquet garni
salt
peppercorns
water

Chop the bones and carcass. Put in the oven and brown lightly to add flavour. Sauté the prepared vegetables in fat in a large (approx. 10-pint) pan for 10 minutes, add the bones and remaining ingredients and just cover with water. Bring to the boil and skim.

Cover and simmer for 3–4 hours. Strain, cool and treat as for brown or white stock.

Shrimp chowder – a party soup

Minestrone, an Italian soup

PATES & TERRINES

A pâté is essentially a blend of different meats—principally liver and pork—which has been minced finely, well seasoned and cooked slowly. Because of the high proportion of liver used they tend to be very rich and only small portions should be allowed per person—particularly as pâté is generally served as an appetizer accompanied by toast.

The most famous (and the most expensive) of these mixtures is, of course, pâté de foie gras, made from the livers of specially fattened geese, but you can follow our recipes and make your own pâté maison quite simply and inexpensively. Apart from the delicate fish ones, most pâtés will keep quite happily for a week in the refrigerator—in fact, this can even improve the flavour.

Anything that can be prepared and cooked ahead of time is a boon for a busy hostess, so this makes pâté an ideal choice for a formal dinner party.

Terrines are generally more robust than pâtés and of a coarser texture. They are not really suitable—except in minute quantities—as appetisers, because of their richness. However, terrines make a wonderful main course for a lunch or supper, served accompanied by salad. They are also particularly suitable to serve at an informal party when you have been out of doors for most of the day. Serve hot soup first and follow it with a selection of 2–3 rich terrines, accompanied by lashings of crusty French bread and even the heartiest appetite will be satisfied. The essential difference in the cooking of terrines and pâtés is that terrines are cooked in the dish from which they will be served—properly a terrine, but a suitably shaped casserole or loaf tin will do just as well. They are wrapped in fatty bacon and after cooking should be pressed with a heavy weight to compress the layers of meat really tightly together. Pâtés are usually at least partially cooked before moulding and are served either turned out and sliced, or in individual dishes.

COUNTRY PATE
serves 12

2 oz. butter
8 oz. onion, skinned and roughly chopped
8 oz. lean bacon, rinded and chopped
8 oz. belly of pork, rinded and cut into strips
12 oz. pig's liver, diced
12 oz. stewing steak, finely diced
8 oz. pie veal, diced
3 cloves of garlic, skinned and crushed
¼ pint (⅝ cup) red wine
4 tbsps. brandy or port
2 bay leaves
salt and black pepper
dash of Worcestershire sauce
bacon fat
1 egg, beaten

Melt the butter in a large saucepan and fry the onion and bacon until they are light golden brown. Add the rest of the ingredients, except the egg, and bring to the boil. Cover the pan and simmer for 30 minutes.

Strain off the liquor and put the remainder through the mincer twice, using the finest blade. Mix thoroughly with the strained liquor and the beaten egg. Season

again well. Place the mixture in a foil lined, lightly buttered 1-lb loaf tin. Place in a roasting tin with water half way up and cook in the oven at 350°F. (mark 4) for 1½ hours.

Remove from the oven and cool. Chill for at least 12 hours before turning out and serving.

HOME-MADE PATE DE FOIE
serves 6

1 lb. calf's or chicken liver
4 oz. pork fat
1 small clove of garlic, skinned
pinch of mixed herbs
salt and freshly ground pepper
a little water
2 oz. cooked tongue
a little truffle, if available
aspic jelly
truffle or green leek for garnish

Mince the liver and pork fat with the garlic and mixed herbs; season lightly. Heat a thick frying pan, when hot, add the liver mixture and stir well. When the liver has changed colour add a very little water and allow to simmer for 5 minutes. Press through a fine sieve r purée in a blender. Add the ongue, chopped in diamonds, and he truffle, finely chopped. Adjust he seasoning if necessary.

Line the bases of tiny soufflé dishes r ramekins with a layer of aspic nd some decoration cut from thin lices of truffle or blanched leek. When the decoration has set, fill ach dish with pâté, spread evenly, nd chill until firm. To serve, nmould.

THRIFTY PATE
erves 6

¼ lb. lean belly pork
  lb. pig's or ox liver
  lb. lean streaky bacon, rinded
  oz. onion, skinned and chopped
  small clove of garlic, skinned
  level tsp. salt
  reshly ground black pepper
  oz. butter

Remove the rind and any bones rom the belly pork and dice. Rinse the liver under cold running vater and dry on absorbent paper. Cut into largish pieces. Mince the ork, liver, bacon, onion and garlic ogether three times. Work in the alt and pepper.

Turn into a 2-pint terrine or small asserole, cover and place in a mall roasting tin with water half vay up. Cook at 300°F. (mark 2) or about 1½ hours. Remove the lid. Lay a double sheet of foil over the op, add weights and weight down until quite cold, preferably in a efrigerator. Remove weights and overing. Melt butter over a low eat, pour over pâté and chill.

HUNTER'S PATE
erves 16

  lb. rabbit or hare flesh
  lb. belly of pork, trimmed
  lb. pig's liver
  lb. pork sausage meat
  lb. garlic sausage
  oz. (1 cup) onion, skinned and chopped
  tbsps. sherry
  tbsps. chopped parsley
  level tbsps. dried sage
  alt and black pepper
  lb. fat streaky bacon rashers, rinded

Cut the rabbit or hare into small pieces. Put the pork, liver, sausage meat, garlic sausage and onion hrough the mincer. Mix in the abbit pieces, sherry, parsley and age, and season well.

Take a loaf tin or terrine measuring bout 9½ in. by 5½ in. by 3 in. deep,

Chicken liver pâté is a rich starter for a dinner party

and line it with the bacon rashers. Turn the pâté mixture into the prepared tin and fold the bacon edges over the top. Cover with kitchen foil, place in a roasting tin with water to come half way up and cook in the oven at 325°F. (mark 3) for about 3 hours. Allow to cool in the tin.
Turn out and serve in thick slices. If you wish to store the pâté, turn out when cold and wrap in foil.

POTTED BEEF
serves 6

1 lb. stewing steak, cut into ½-in. cubes
¼ pint (⅝ cup) stock
1 clove
1 blade of mace
salt and pepper
2 oz. butter, melted
fresh bay leaves for garnish

Put the meat in a casserole with the stock and seasonings. Cover and cook in the centre of the oven at 350°F. (mark 4) for 2½–3 hours, until tender. Remove the clove and mace and drain off the stock, setting it aside.
Mince the meat twice or place it in a blender and blend for several minutes until smooth. Add 1 oz. melted butter and sufficient of the reserved stock to moisten. Press into ramekins or soufflé dishes, cover with the remainder of the melted butter and chill. Serve garnished with a fresh bay leaf on each portion.

CHICKEN LIVER PATE
serves 10

1½ lb. chicken livers
3 oz. butter
1 medium onion, skinned and finely chopped
1 large clove of garlic, skinned and crushed
1 tbsp. double cream
2 level tbsps. tomato paste
3 tbsps. sherry or brandy

Rinse the chicken livers and dry thoroughly on kitchen paper. Fry them in the butter until they change colour. Reduce heat, add the onion and garlic, cover and cook for 5 minutes. Remove from heat and cool. Add the cream, tomato paste and sherry or brandy. Purée in blender or pass through a sieve. Turn into individual dishes and flood the tops with melted butter if desired. Chill.

SMOKED TROUT PATE
serves 6

8 oz. smoked trout
2 oz. butter
3 oz. (1½ cups) fresh white breadcrumbs
finely grated rind and juice of 1 lemon
salt and freshly ground black pepper
pinch of ground nutmeg
¼ pint (⅝ cup) single cream
¼–½ pint (⅝–1¼ cups) aspic jelly, made from aspic jelly powder

Remove the skin and bones from the trout and finely chop the flesh. Melt the butter in a small pan and pour on to the breadcrumbs with the lemon rind and juice. Season well with salt, pepper and nutmeg. Add the fish to the breadcrumbs and fold in the cream. Spoon into 6 ramekins or small soufflé dishes. Make up the aspic jelly and when on the point of setting, spoon over the pâté. Chill.

FRESH SALMON PATE
serves 8

2 oz. butter
2 oz. (½ cup) flour
¾ pint (2 cups) milk
1 bay leaf
salt and pepper
¼ level tsp. ground nutmeg
½ lb. fresh haddock or cod fillet, skinned
1 lb. fresh salmon, skinned and boned, or 2 7½-oz. cans tuna
grated rind and juice of 1 lemon
1 tbsp. chopped parsley
2 eggs, beaten
melted butter
parsley sprigs and lemon for garnish

Melt the butter in a pan and stir in the flour. Cook for 2–3 minutes, then slowly add the milk, beating between each addition. Add the bay leaf, salt, pepper and nutmeg and boil gently for 2–3 minutes; discard the bay leaf.
Finely chop or mince the haddock and three-quarters of the salmon. Add to the sauce together with the lemon rind and juice, parsley and eggs. Divide between buttered ramekins. Brush the tops with melted butter and decorate with slices of the remaining salmon. Place the dishes in a large roasting tin with water to come half way up the dishes and cook in the oven at 300°F. (mark 2) for about 40 minutes. Chill. Garnish with parsley and lemon.

KIPPER PATE
serves 4

4 oz. kipper fillets
2 tbsps. dry white wine
freshly ground black pepper
4 oz. butter, softened

Skin the raw fillets and marinade in the wine for 12 hours. Work with a pestle in a mortar or purée in a blender until smooth. Season with the pepper and beat into the softened butter. Divide between 4 small soufflé dishes or ramekins. Serve with hot toast.

SMOKED FISH PATE

serves 6–8

7-oz. can smoked codling
    fillets
6 oz. butter
⅛ level tsp. cayenne pepper
2 tbsps chopped capers
2 tbsps. chopped parsley
1 tbsp. medium dry sherry
1 tbsp. lemon juice
salt and freshly ground black
    pepper
pinch of ground nutmeg
1 oz. butter, melted
cucumber slices to garnish

Cook the codling fillets as directed. Drain, remove any dark skin and flake the flesh. Cream the butter well, adding the cayenne by degrees to taste. Beat in the fish, capers, parsley, sherry and lemon juice. Season to taste. Spoon the pâté mixture either into one 6-in. soufflé dish or into small individual dishes. Top with a little melted butter and chill. Garnish with cucumber slices.

TERRINE OF VEAL AND CHICKEN

serves 6–8

¾ lb. chicken meat
1 lb. veal
¼ lb. chicken livers
4 tbsps. dry white wine
1 clove of garlic, skinned and
    crushed
pinch of mixed spice
2 oz. (1 cup) fresh white
    breadcrumbs
salt and freshly ground
    pepper
6 oz. streaky bacon rashers,
    rinded
2 bay leaves
sprig of thyme

Mince together (with the medium cutter) the chicken meat, veal and chicken livers. Stir the white wine into the mixed meats with the garlic, mixed spice and breadcrumbs. Season well.

Stretch the streaky bacon with the back of a knife. Line a 2-pint terrine or oval casserole with overlapping rashers, making sure they are long enough to envelop the meat completely later. Spoon in the meat mixture and cover with the bacon. Lay a bay leaf or two and a sprig of thyme on top. Cover. Place in a roasting tin with water half way up. Cook in the oven at 325°F. (mark 3) for about 2¼ hours. Allow to cool. When cool, pour off the juices. Chill the terrine and juices separately. When jelly is on the point of setting, spoon over the terrine.

TERRINE OF DUCK, LIVER AND PORK

serves 10–12

1 lb. duck meat (approx.
    yield from a 3½-lb.
    oven-ready duck)
3 level tbsps. Marsala
1½ lb. belly pork, boned and
    skinned
1 lb. calf's liver
1 medium onion, skinned
1–2 cloves of garlic, skinned
1 medium orange
1 level tsp. salt
freshly ground black pepper
½ level tsp. dried thyme
½ lb. streaky bacon rashers,
    rinded
4 bay leaves

Cut the duck meat into long strips and marinate in the Marsala for 6 hours in a cool place. Keep any small pieces to one side. Dice the pork and liver and mince together with the duck trimmings, onion and garlic. Into the minced ingredients blend the juice from half the orange, salt, pepper, thyme and Marsala drained from the duck.

Stretch the bacon by drawing the blade of a knife along each rasher two or three times. Line the terrine with rashers, leaving the ends long enough to envelop the terrine mixture completely later. Spoon one-third of the minced meat into the terrine; then lay half the strips of duck meat along the length of the terrine. Repeat the layers, finishing with minced meat. Wrap the bacon over the top of the meat.

Slice the remaining half of the orange and lay over the terrine with the bay leaves. Cover and place in a roasting tin with water half way up the dish. Cook in the oven at 325°F. (mark 3) for about 2½ hours.

When cooked, remove the lid and place a piece of foil over the pâté (leaving the orange slices and bay leaves in place). Press down firmly with a small plate. Add a 2-lb. weight and allow to cool.

LIVER TERRINE

serves 4–6

1 lb. pig's liver
¼ lb. fat bacon
3–4 anchovy fillets
4 eggs, beaten
1 clove of garlic, skinned and
    crushed
½ pint (1¼ cups) thick white
    sauce
salt and pepper
12 rashers of streaky bacon,
    rinded

Many terrines are encased in rashers of streaky bacon

Mince the liver, fat bacon and anchovy fillets finely, three times – or mince the mixture twice and finally purée in the blender. Mix in the beaten eggs, garlic, sauce and seasonings to taste.

Line a shallow ovenproof dish with the bacon rashers, fill up with the liver mixture and place in a roasting tin with water half way up the dish. Cook at 325°F. (mark 3) for 2 hours. Cover the top of the liver mixture with greaseproof paper or foil, put a weight on top and chill.

TERRINE OF DUCK

serves 6

1¾ lb. frozen duck breast
    portions, thawed
2 level tsps. salt
1 lb. belly pork
1 lb. pie veal
¼ lb. pork back fat
¼ pint (⅝ cup) dry white wine
1 clove of garlic, skinned and
    crushed
freshly ground black pepper
1 small orange, washed and
    thinly sliced
aspic jelly to glaze

Place the duck portions in a roasting tin, sprinkle with the salt and cook in the centre of the oven

at 325°F. (mark 3) for 40 minute Meanwhile, trim the surplus fa from the belly of pork and trim th pie veal into neat pieces. Cut 4– thin strips from the pork fat an reserve for a garnish.

Put the belly of pork, the veal an the rest of the pork fat through th mincer twice. Add the wine, garli salt and pepper and mix thorough ly. Take the duck from the ove remove the skin, cut the flesh fro the bones and dice it. Moisten th minced ingredients with some the cooking juice.

Put half this mixture in a 2- o 2½-pint terrine or casserole, ad the duck meat and cover with th rest of the minced ingredient Arrange the strips of pork fat in lattice on top and cover the dis with foil. Stand the terrine in roasting tin with water half wa up the dish and cook in the centr of the oven at 325°F. (mark 3) fo 1½–2 hours.

Remove the terrine from the ove take off the foil and leave for minutes. Then cover the me with folded foil, place some weigh on top and chill thoroughly. Whe chilled, arrange the orange slic in a pattern on top, glaze wit nearly-set aspic and chill again.

Kipper pâté is the simplest to make

GARNISHES

uitable decorations add good looks as well as ...avour to food and drinks—but they must be ...ery fresh, and preferably quite simple and ...omparatively small. The garnish for any par-...cular dish should be decided on beforehand. ...olours should be chosen to tone with both the ...od and the serving dish—two, or at most three, ...olours are sufficient. Sometimes ingredients ...hich are an integral part of the recipe can also ...dd decorative value.

VEGETABLE AND SALAD GARNISHES

Turned mushrooms have a nicely tailored ...ok. You need to use large button mushrooms ...d 'turn' them with a small, sharp-pointed ...nife, by making a series of cuts from the top of ...e cap to the base at intervals. Then repeat in ...e opposite direction to remove each narrow ...llet'. Sauté the mushrooms in butter.

Baby turnips can be 'turned' prettily in the ...me way.

Carrot curls look crisp on open sandwiches, ...d in salads (or served as cocktail nibblers). ...crape raw carrots and slice them lengthwise ...d paper thin, using a vegetable peeler. ...oll up, fasten with a toothpick and put them ... iced water until they curl. Serve on or off the ...cks.

...nother simple way to cut carrots raw is with ... fondant cutter or tiny pastry cutter—simply ...rape and slice the carrot then flute the edges ...y stamping out with a cutter.

Pickle fans always stay fresh, and suit hot or ...ld dishes. Make lengthwise cuts almost to the ...d of each gherkin, from the 'flower' end. ...pread carefully to form an open fan.

Radish roses to garnish open sandwiches or ...ld meat platters are always popular. Cut off ...narrow slice from the root end of each radish, ...en cut thin 'petals' from stem to root. Put into iced water until the cuts open to form petals.

To make radish water lillies, make 4–8 small deep cuts, crossing in the centre of the radish at the root end, and leave in iced water to open out.

Celery curls are made by cutting the celery into strips about ½ in. wide and 2 in. long and then slitting one or both ends in narrow strips almost to the centre. Leave the pieces in iced water for an hour or so until the fringed ends curl.

Spring onions split down the stem and left in cold water will open out in the same way.

ORANGE OR LEMON GARNISHES

Citrus twists look cool on an iced drink or on top of a chiffon dessert. Using a sharp-edged potato peeler, start to remove a strip of peel from the narrow end of a lemon, orange or grapefruit. Work in a continuous spiral, removing only the coloured part of the peel. Let the peel twist naturally as a garnish.

Orange and lemon slices, deftly twisted, suit fish and chicken dishes and may be used wherever these flavours are present in a recipe. Slit the slice through the rind to the centre, then twist in opposite directions. A double twist with 2 slices gives more emphasis.

SAVOURY GARNISHES

Croûtons are small, fancy-shaped pieces of bread which are fried or toasted. Cut the slices of white bread ¼–½ in. thick, remove the crusts and then either cut the bread into ¼–½ in. cubes and fry them, or leave the slices whole and grill them before cutting up. Use as a garnish for soups.

Croûtons cut into larger triangles and crescents are used as a garnish for minced meat or au gratin dishes.

Cheese triangles are good with soups and savouries. Well butter 6 slices of crustless bread and arrange close together on a baking sheet. Sprinkle 1 oz. finely grated cheese over. Bake in the oven at 350°F. (mark 4) for about 40 minutes. Overlap round the edge of a savoury dish or float on puréed soups.

Fleurons Roll out some puff, flaky or rough puff pastry to ¼ in. thickness, then stamp it into shapes with small fancy cutters, or cut with a sharp knife into squares, triangles or diamonds. To make crescents, which are a traditional shape, use a small round cutter; place it about ½ in. on to the edge of the pastry for the first cut, then move the cutter a further ½ in. inwards and cut again, making a crescent. Continue the length of the pastry, moving the cutter ½ in. each time. Place the fleurons on a baking sheet, brush the tops lightly with beaten egg and bake in the oven at 450°F. (mark 8) until well risen, golden brown and crisp—7–10 minutes.

Buttered crumbs Melt 1 oz. butter and add 1 pint fine white breadcrumbs. Let them absorb the fat, forking the mixture several times. Spread out on baking sheets and dry in the oven on its lowest setting. When ready, they are cream-coloured and dry. Stored in a screw-top jar or polythene bag in a cool place, these will keep fresh for 2 months. Use dry for coating rissoles; toss with butter or grated cheese for topping other dishes.

Crunchy topper Fry 2 oz. fresh white breadcrumbs in 1½ oz. butter until golden brown. Sift together 8 oz. self-raising flour, 1 level teaspoon salt, pepper and ½ level teaspoon dried onion powder. Stir in 3 tablespoons cooking oil and enough milk to give a soft dough. Drop tablespoons of the dough into buttered crumbs and roll into balls in the crumbs. Arrange on top of a casserole about 50 minutes before serving. Bake uncovered in the oven at 375°F. (mark 5).

SAVOURY SOUFFLES AND MOUSSES

A traditional soufflé dish is round and straight sided; it is smooth inside and fluted outside. Plain white china is the most common colour, but brown earthenware, coloured china and ovenproof glass are also available. In some classic soufflé recipes it is recommended that a paper band be tied round the outside of the dish to come about 3 in. above the rim. After cooking the paper is peeled away and the soufflé still stands well above the edge of the dish. This is not strictly necessary, though, as a good soufflé will rise well without and looks just as attractive. Simply butter the dish and dust with breadcrumbs or Parmesan cheese. The paper is necessary to give a 'risen' appearance to a cold soufflé.

A hot soufflé is made on a base of a thick white sauce, or panada, flavoured with meat, fish, cheese or vegetables. Egg yolks are beaten in to make it rich and the egg whites are whisked separately until really stiff and then folded gently in with a metal spoon. The amount the soufflé rises depends on the air whipped into the egg whites, the air expands in the oven heat and raises a hot soufflé, and gives bulk to a cold one. Don't beat or stir the egg whites in rapidly.

To cook a soufflé place in the oven at 350–375°F. (mark 4–5) for 30–45 minutes, until well risen and brown on top. Be careful not to open the door of the oven too early in the cooking or your soufflé will collapse! To test when a hot soufflé is ready, open the oven door after 30 minutes and give the dish a slight movement without taking it out. If the crust moves considerably in the centre, leave it a little longer. Serve a hot soufflé straight from the oven – it will spoil if kept for more than a few moments. This unfortunately makes a soufflé an unsuitable choice for a dinner party, when you cannot rely on the guests being precisely on time – but give the family a treat from time to time. Cold soufflés and mousses are less temperamental and ideal party dishes. They are set with gelatine and a mousse may be served in the dish or turned out of a mould on to a flat serving plate – a ring mould is often used. To turn out a moulded mousse, dip the mould quickly into hot water and invert it on to a wet plate; the mou will then slip easily out of mould and will slide into place the plate if it is not quite centr

CHEESE SOUFFLE
serves 4

4 large eggs
1½ oz. butter
1 oz. (¼ cup) plain flour
½ pint (1¼ cups) milk
6 oz. dry Cheddar cheese,
  finely grated
salt and pepper

Butter a 2-pint capacity sou dish. Separate the eggs. Melt butter, stir in the flour and c for 2–3 minutes. Gradually sti the milk, beating the mixture u smooth. Cook for a few minu longer. Add the egg yolks one

Red house soufflé

16

time, beating well, stir in the cheese and season. Stiffly whisk the egg whites, fold these quickly and evenly into the cheese mixture with a metal spoon and turn into the soufflé dish.

Bake in the centre of the oven at 350°F. (mark 4) for about 45 minutes until well risen and brown. Serve immediately.

RED HOUSE SOUFFLE
serves 6

2 oz. butter
8 oz. onions, skinned and thinly sliced
1 small pkt. frozen sweet corn
8 oz. tomatoes, skinned and thickly sliced
2 tbsps. chopped parsley

For the sauce :
4 oz. butter
4 oz. (1 cup) plain flour
1 pint (2½ cups) milk
salt and freshly ground black pepper
6 oz. strong Cheddar cheese, grated
6 eggs, separated

Butter a 3½-pint soufflé dish or casserole. Heat 2 oz. butter in a frying pan, add the onion and sauté until soft but not coloured. Add the corn and continue cooking for 5 minutes. Remove from the heat and add the tomatoes and parsley.

For the sauce, melt 4 oz. butter in a saucepan, stir in the flour and cook for a few minutes. Gradually add the milk, stirring all the time, bring to the boil and simmer for a few minutes. Add half the sauce to the vegetables and check the seasoning. Turn the mixture into the soufflé dish or casserole.

Add the cheese to the remaining sauce in the pan, beat in the egg yolks and adjust the seasoning again. Stiffly whisk the egg whites and fold into the sauce with a metal spoon.

Spoon the mixture over the vegetables and bake in the centre of oven for about 1 hour at 350°F. (mark 4), until well risen and golden.
Serve at once.

BACON AND ONION SOUFFLE
serves 4

1 oz. butter
6 oz. lean bacon, rinded and chopped
8 oz. onion, skinned and chopped
1 tbsp. chopped parsley
salt and pepper

Cold ham soufflé will satisfy the heartiest appetite

For the sauce :
2 oz. butter
1½ oz. (⅜ cup) plain flour
½ pint (1¼ cups) milk
3 egg yolks
4 egg whites

Butter a 2½-pint capacity soufflé dish. Melt 1 oz. butter in a medium pan, add the bacon and fry for 2–3 minutes. Add the onion and continue cooking until the onion is tender. Remove from the heat. Add the parsley and season to taste.

Melt the 2 oz. butter in a saucepan, add the flour and stir well with a wooden spoon. Cook for 2–3 minutes. Add the milk gradually and bring to the boil, stirring continuously. Mix half the sauce with half the bacon and onion mixture and spoon into the soufflé dish.

Beat the egg yolks one at a time into the remaining sauce. Whisk the egg whites until stiff and gently fold, with a metal spoon, into the sauce. Add the remaining bacon mixture.

Turn into the soufflé dish, bake near the top of the oven at 375°F. (mark 5) for about 45 minutes until well risen and golden.
Serve at once.

MARROW SOUFFLE
serves 4

1 lb. marrow, peeled
2 oz. butter
1 oz. plain flour
½ pint (1¼ cups) milk
salt and pepper
2 level tsps. dried summer savory
3 eggs, separated
4 oz. cheese, grated

Butter a 2-pint capacity soufflé dish. Cut the marrow into thick slices and discard the seeds. Cook in boiling, salted water until tender but still firm. Drain well and roughly chop.

Melt the butter and stir in the flour. Gradually stir in the milk and seasoning. Pour half this sauce over the marrow, add the herbs and spoon into the soufflé dish.

Beat the egg yolks and add to the remaining sauce, with the cheese. Adjust seasoning. Stiffly whisk the egg whites and fold in. Spoon over the marrow.

Bake in the oven at 375°F. (mark 5) for about 30 minutes, until well risen.
Serve at once.

SPINACH SOUFFLE
serves 4

4 oz. onion, skinned and sliced
3½ oz. butter
6-oz. pkt. frozen leaf spinach, or 1 lb. fresh spinach, part cooked and roughly chopped
salt and freshly ground black pepper
¼ level tsp. grated nutmeg
1 oz. plain flour
½ pint (1¼ cups) milk
3 large eggs, separated
1½ oz. Parmesan cheese, grated

Butter a 1½-pint capacity soufflé dish. Gently sauté the onion in 1½ oz. butter until tender, add the spinach and cook a little longer. Season lightly with salt, pepper and nutmeg.

Melt the remaining butter in another pan, stir in the flour and cook for 1 minute. Add the milk all at once, stir well and bring to the boil. Season and add half the sauce to the spinach and onion. Turn into the soufflé dish and place on a baking sheet.

Beat the egg yolks and most of the cheese into the remaining sauce, reserving a little cheese to sprinkle over the soufflé. Stiffly whisk the egg whites and fold carefully through the sauce with a metal spoon. Pour on to the spinach base and sprinkle the remaining cheese over the top. Cook in the centre of the oven at 375°F. (mark 5) for about 40 minutes.
Serve immediately.

COLD HAM SOUFFLE
serves 4

1 oz. butter
1 oz. plain flour
½ pint (1¼ cups) milk
4 large eggs, separated
4 level tsps. powdered gelatine
4 tbsps. water
8 oz. cooked ham, finely minced
½ level tsp. chopped tarragon
¼ pint (⅝ cup) single cream
salt and pepper
cress and slices of ham for garnish

Prepare a 1-pint capacity soufflé dish by tying a double band of greaseproof or non-stick paper round the outside, to stand about 3 in. above the rim of the dish.

Melt the butter in a pan, stir in the flour and cook over gentle heat for 2 minutes. Add the milk and bring to the boil, stirring constantly until the sauce thickens. Remove from the heat and beat in the egg yolks 1 at a time.

Dissolve the gelatine in the water in a basin over a pan of hot water; add to the sauce and leave in a cool place, stirring occasionally until it begins to set.

Stir in the minced ham, tarragon and cream. Adjust seasoning according to taste; beware of adding too much salt, as the ham may already be salty.

Whisk the egg whites until stiff. Fold into the ham mixture, turn into the prepared soufflé dish and leave to set.

To remove the paper collar, wet a palette knife under the hot tap and run it carefully between the 2 layers of paper; gently peel the paper away.

Serve garnished with cress and rolled slices of ham round the dish.

Smoked haddock is the basis for this appetizing savoury mousse

SHRIMP RICE MOUSSE
serves 4

3 oz. long grain rice
½ oz. powdered gelatine
½ pint (1¼ cups) warm water
6–8 oz. shelled shrimps (fresh, canned or frozen, thawed) or prawns, roughly chopped
¼ pint (⅝ cup) mayonnaise
4-oz. pkt. frozen peas, cooked
2 sticks of celery, chopped
salt and freshly ground black pepper
¼ pint (⅝ cup) double cream, lightly whipped
sliced cucumber

Cook the rice in boiling salted water for about 12 minutes until tender; drain. Dissolve the gelatine in the water in a bowl over a pan of hot water; allow to cool, stirring from time to time.
Mix most of the shrimps (or prawns) with the mayonnaise, peas, celery, salt, pepper and dissolved gelatine. Fold in the lightly whipped cream and the rice. Allow to cool.
When nearly set, turn the mousse into a wetted mould and chill thoroughly. When set, turn out on to a wetted serving dish and garnish with reserved shrimps and sliced cucumber.

Salmon and asparagus mousse

SMOKED HADDOCK MOUSSE
serves 6

1 small carrot, peeled and halved
1 small onion, skinned and halved
½ pint (1¼ cups) milk
1 bay leaf
3 parsley stalks
6 peppercorns
1½ oz. butter
1 oz. plain flour
½ pint (1¼ cups) aspic jelly made with aspic jelly powder
½ lb. smoked haddock
3 eggs, hard-boiled
1 tbsp. chopped parsley
¼ pint (⅝ cup) double cream, whipped
juice and finely grated rind of 1 small lemon
salt and freshly ground black pepper
parsley sprigs
watercress

Put the carrot, onion and milk in a pan with the bay leaf, parsley and peppercorns, bring to the boil and allow to infuse off the heat for 10 minutes.
Melt the butter, stir in the flour and cook for 1–2 minutes without colouring. Off the heat, stir in strained milk. Return to the heat bring to the boil and cook, stirring, for 30 seconds. Stir all but 3 tablespoons of the aspic into the sauce. Meanwhile, poach the fish in water to cover for 10 minutes. Drain the fish, discard the bones and skin and flake the flesh. Shell 2 of the eggs and chop. Add to the flaked fish with the parsley. Fold the whipped cream into the aspic sauce when it is on the point of setting. Finally fold in the lemon rind and juice, the fish, eggs and parsley. Adjust seasoning. Turn into a 2½-pint soufflé dish and leave in a cool place to set. Slice the remaining egg and arrange over the surface of the mousse with sprigs of parsley. Dilute the remaining aspic with a further 3 tablespoons water and spoon over the decoration. When set, garnish with watercress.

PRAWN MOUSSE
serves 4

¼ pint (⅝ cup) aspic jelly, made from aspic jelly powder
8 oz. shelled prawns
1 pint (2½ cups) milk
1 small onion, skinned and quartered
1 carrot, peeled and quartered
1–2 cloves
1 bay leaf
3–4 peppercorns
1½ oz. butter
1½ oz. (⅜ cup) plain flour
2 eggs, separated
salt and pepper
½ oz. powdered gelatine
¼ pint (⅝ cup) dry white wine or stock

Make up the aspic jelly, pour a thin layer into a 2-pint mould, add a few prawns for decoration and leave to set. Put the milk, onion, carrot, cloves, bay leaf and peppercorns into a covered pan, bring to the boil, turn out the heat and leave to cool for about 15 minutes, until the milk is well flavoured. Melt the butter, stir in the flour and cook for 2–3 minutes. Gradually stir in the strained milk. Bring to the boil and continue to stir until the sauce thickens. Remove from the heat, cool slightly and beat in the egg yolks and seasoning to taste. Dissolve the gelatine in the wine or stock in a basin over a pan of hot water and stir it into the sauce. Add the remaining prawns, roughly chopped, and leave in a cool place until the mixture begins to set.
Whisk the egg whites stiffly, fold them in and turn the mousse into the prepared mould and leave to set.
Unmould and serve with salad.

SALMON AND ASPARAGUS MOUSSE
Do not attempt this recipe unless you have an electric blender; serves 8

2 level tbsps. aspic jelly powder
1 pint (2½ cups) water
1 oz. butter
1 oz. (¼ cup) plain flour
½ pint (1¼ cups) milk
¼ level tsp. dry mustard
pinch of cayenne pepper
salt and pepper
1 tbsp. cider vinegar
3 eggs, separated
2 7½-oz. cans salmon, drained
1½ level tbsps. powdered gelatine
¼ pint (⅝ cup) double cream, lightly whipped
8-oz. pkt. frozen asparagus, cooked and cooled

Make up the aspic jelly with the water as directed on the packet. Leave until beginning to set, then pour a little into an 8¼-in. spring-release cake tin fitted with a plain base or a 3-pint fluted mould. Use the jelly to coat the sides of the tin and place in refrigerator to set.
When this lining is set, pour more aspic jelly into the tin until it is ¼ in. deep. Leave to set.
Meanwhile put the butter, flour, milk and seasonings into the blender and blend for 15 seconds. Turn into a pan, bring to the boil and cook for 3 minutes. Beat in the vinegar, then the egg yolks. Return the mixture to the heat and cook without boiling for a few more minutes. Add the drained salmon to the sauce and check the seasoning. Put 6 tablespoons liquid aspic in a small basin or cup, sprinkle in the gelatine and stand the cup in a little hot water until the gelatine is dissolved. Add to the salmon mixture. Pour half into blender and blend for about 30 seconds, until smooth. Turn out and repeat with remainder. Leave until just setting. Fold in the cream, followed by whisked egg whites. Spoon into the tin.
When set arrange the asparagus spears on top. Spoon the remaining aspic jelly over and leave for about 1 hour to set.
To unmould, hold a warm cloth round the sides of the tin, release the clip and remove the ring. Warm the base and slide the mousse on to a serving plate.

CHEESE AND CHEESE DISHES

When cheese is made, the best and richest part of the milk, the curd, is separated from the whey, the watery part, pressed and allowed to mature. The quality of the milk and the animal from which it came (whether cow, goat or ewe, or even camel or buffalo), give rise to a wide range of different types of cheese. Local conditions of climate and vegetation, different methods of making it and varying storage conditions during ripening affect the cheese so that almost no cheeses taste the same.

Cheese is an important source of protein, fat and minerals in the diet and is one of the tastiest savoury foods, whether eaten in its natural state or cooked and combined with other foods. Remember never to cook cheese for longer than it takes to heat through and melt – over heating makes it tough and indigestible.

BRITISH CHEESES

HARD CHEESES

Blue Vinney (Blue Dorset) Hard cheese made from skimmed cows' milk; white with a blue vein; rather strong flavour.

Caerphilly A soft, crumbly, whole milk cheese, eaten when about 10 days old; white; creamy, mild flavour; best uncooked.

Cheddar Hard, yellow, whole milk cheese; slightly salty and varying in flavour from mild to quite strong; good cooked or uncooked. The cheddaring process is easily mechanized and carried out under factory conditions and the cheese is therefore produced in many parts of the world, notably New Zealand, Australia and Canada. "Farmhouse" Cheddar is still usually considered the best.

Derby Hard, close-textured, white cheese; mild when young but developing a full flavour as it matures; sage leaves sometimes added to give a green cheese known as **Sage Derby**.

Double Gloucester Hard, orange-yellow cheese; close, crumbly texture; rich flavour similar to mature Cheddar.

Dunlop Scottish cheese similar to Cheddar, but more moist and with a closer texture.

Lancashire A fairly hard cheese but crumbly when cut; mild, tangy flavour when new, developing as the cheese matures; excellent for cooking.

Leicester Hard cheese; orange-

Reading clockwise from bottom left : Camembert, Sage Derby, Leicester, Lancashire, Emmenthal, Danish Blue, Edam, Boursin and Brie

19

red colour; mild, slightly sweet flavour.

Stilton Semi-hard, double cream cheese (i.e. made from rich milk to which extra cream is added); white with evenly distributed blue veining caused by a mould inoculated into the cheese; the rind should be a dull, drab colour, well crinkled, regular and free from cracks; best after 6–9 months. Made only during May–September. A milder, white Stilton is also available. Not suitable for cooking.

Wensleydale Double cream cheese originally matured until blue; now usually sold white and unripe, when it is mild and flaky.

SOFT CHEESE

These are no longer given regional names in Britain.

Cream cheese Made from cream only; may be double cream cheese (from cream with a 45–50 per cent fat content) or single cream cheese (made from cream with a 25–30 per cent fat content); made in small quantities as it keeps for only 6–7 days; soft and rich. Available plain or flavoured with herbs, fruit, nuts etc.

Curd cheese Made by the same method as cream cheese, but from milk; soft, but slightly firmer than cream cheese and not so rich.

Cottage cheese Made from the same method again, but using skimmed milk; very soft, loose-textured, rather flavourless cheese. Mixes well with salads and used for making cheesecake. Available plain or flavoured with herbs or fruit.

CONTINENTAL CHEESES

Bel Paese Italian; rich, creamy cheese; mild flavour; made usually from October to June.

Brie French; soft farm cheese made from whole milk and mould-inoculated; creamy-white, with a brownish, slightly mouldy crust; mild, rich flavour; made in flat rounds 1–1½ in. thick and about 14 in. across, but also available, boxed, in wedges; does not keep well. Not good for cooking.

Camembert French; made from creamy cows' milk inoculated with a white mould; creamy-white, with a light crust similar to Brie; delicious at its best, when starting to soften, but if allowed to over-ripen it becomes too soft and generates unpleasant gases. Made in rounds 4–5 in. across and sold boxed; also sold in individually wrapped portions.

Reading clockwise from top left: Cheddar, Jarlsberg, Stilton, Bleu de Bresse, Port-Salut, Windsor Red and Raybier

Danish Blue White, crumbly cheese with blue veining produced by mould; sharp, salty taste.

Demi-sel French; soft cream cheese; sold in small, square, foil-wrapped packs.

Dolcelatte Italian; a milder, creamier form of Gorgonzola.

Edam Dutch; firm, smooth cheese; ball shaped, bright red outside, deep yellow inside; mild flavour. Good for cooking; low in calories. Also made in other countries but only the Dutch has the true flavour.

Emmenthal Swiss (also French, Italian and Austrian); similar to Gruyère but slightly softer in texture, with larger 'eyes'. Excellent for fondues, quiches, etc.

Fontainebleau French; soft, fresh cream cheese.

Fromage à la crème Soft cheese made from soured milk; served softened with a little milk and with caster sugar and cream.

Gorgonzola Italian; semi-hard, blue veined cheese; sharp flavour.

Gouda Dutch; similar to Edam in texture but creamier and with a better flavour, and a yellow skin. Usually made as large rounds but also exported as small cheeses.

Gruyère Swiss (also French and Italian); hard cheese honey-combed with 'eyes' or holes caused by rapid fermentation of the curd; pale yellow; distinctive, fairly sweet taste; good uncooked but also cooked in many classic European dishes.

Havarti Danish; smooth, light yellow cheese with numerous holes, large and small. Full flavoured, with a piquant after-taste. Foil wrapped.

Limburger Belgian (also German and French); semi-hard whole milk cheese; full flavoured and strong smelling.

Mycella Danish; has the golden yellow colour of rich cream, with

green veining.

Mysöst (Gietöst) Norwegian; whey cheese, made principally from goats' milk; hard and dark brown; sweetish flavour.

Parmesan Italian; the hardest of all cheeses; pale straw colour and full of tiny holes, like pin pricks; used finely grated in cooked dishes or sprinkled on top of hot dishes such as pasta, rice and soups.

Petit Suisse (Petit Gervais) French; unsalted cream cheese; very mild; sold in small, cylindrical, foil-wrapped packs.

Pommel French; unsalted double cream cheese; not unlike Petit Suisse.

Pont l'Evêque French; semi-hard cheese, salted repeatedly while maturing; yellow; made in small squares. Somewhat similar to Camembert and should be eaten soft and not too ripe.

Port-Salut French; semi-hard, round cheese; creamy yellow; mild flavour; should be eaten while still slightly soft.

Roquefort French; ewes' milk cheese layered with a culture of moulded breadcrumbs (the same mould as that inoculated into Stilton); made only during the lambing season and only in the Roquefort district; white, curd-like cheese, mottled with blue veins; sharp, peppery taste.

Samsoe Danish; firm in texture with regular holes, and a mild, sweet nut-like flavour. Cuts well into thin slices or cubes.

STORING CHEESE

The drier, harder cheeses will keep well when stored correctly, but softer cheeses deteriorate quickly, so should be bought only as required. To store cheese, wrap it loosely in polythene, aluminium foil or greaseproof paper – trap some air in the package otherwise the cheese will sweat and mould

will grow quickly – then place it in a cool larder or refrigerator. If you keep it in the refrigerator, make sure that it is brought to room temperature for serving. Wrap different types of cheese separately, so that one does not take on the flavour of another. Pre-packaged cheese keeps well in the refrigerator, but once opened it should be re-wrapped and stored as for fresh cheese. Soft cheeses, including Brie, Camembert and cream cheese, freeze well.

Cottage cheese and cream cheeses have a comparatively short life and must be kept covered in the refrigerator.

PRESENTING THE CHEESE BOARD

A cheese board or platter is one of the best ways of finishing a meal; many people prefer the sharp flavour to a sweet, and others will return to cheese after the sweet, to finish off the last of a dry wine or to enjoy a glass of port.

A good cheese board does not have to offer the number of cheeses that might be available in a restaurant, but there should be a good variety. A balance of hard and soft cheeses, mild and full flavoured ones is the most important consideration and the colours and shapes of the pieces make it more interesting visually. A fairly modest but well-balanced board would offer, say, English Cheddar and Caerphilly, Stilton or Roquefort, Brie and Gouda. Many people will be delighted if you offer something new or unusual for them to try; others will be disappointed if their favourite, good, English cheese is not there.

The board itself may be any attractive platter large enough to hold your chosen selection without looking crowded. For a small selection, an old-fashioned china dish with its own cover is ideal – these are usually a pretty shape and they are perfectly designed for keeping the cheese in good condition, covered but airy. For more pieces, a well-scrubbed bread board or a meat dish serves the purpose, and may also be large enough to accommodate a garnish such as celery, or a small bunch of grapes. For a big party use a tray or the top of a trolley; the first has handles, the latter wheels and either will overcome the problem of lifting a very heavy board carrying a large selection of cheeses. Provide 2 or 3 knives so that the person taking Cheddar does not get unwelcome traces of Stilton

Spaghetti con formaggio is covered in melted cheese

with it.

To go with the cheese, offer a selection of plain and sweet biscuits, and a few salty crackers, or a basket of chunky breads or rolls. Several small dishes of fresh, unsalted butter, in small chunks or individual pats, saves endless passing of a single dish.

Nothing looks more attractive or goes better with cheese than a big bowl of fresh fruit. Polished apples and pears, freshly washed peaches and nuts are probably the most popular at this stage of the meal. Again, make sure there are enough small, dessert knives to go round – it is difficult to skin a peach with an ordinary table knife.

For a change, try serving a selection of crisp salad vegetables with the cheese. Quartered lettuce hearts, chunks of celery, chicory leaves, tomato wedges, small whole radishes and carrot sticks all go down well, with the addition of a little salt.

SPAGHETTI CON FORMAGGIO
serves 2

5 oz. spaghetti
½ lb. lean streaky bacon, rinded and chopped
2 oz. onion, skinned and coarsely grated
1 oz. butter
¼ lb. button mushrooms, sliced
salt and freshly ground black pepper
1 tbsp. salad oil
6 oz. mature Cheddar cheese, grated
chopped parsley

Cook the spaghetti in boiling salted water for 10 minutes. Put the chopped bacon in a frying pan and fry gently for 3 minutes, stirring occasionally with a wooden spoon. Add the onion and cook for a further 1 minute. Add the butter and sliced mushrooms, season lightly and cook for 4 minutes, stirring occasionally. Drain the pasta and return it to the pan with the salad oil. Using 2 forks, coat the spaghetti in the oil until it glistens. Light the grill.

Turn the spaghetti into a flame-proof dish and spoon the bacon and mushroom mixture on top. Sprinkle with grated cheese and grill under a fierce heat for about 30 seconds. Sprinkle with chopped parsley before serving.

ASPARAGUS AU GRATIN
serves 6

1 lb. asparagus, fresh or frozen
2 oz. butter
4 level tbsps. flour
1 pint (2½ cups) creamy milk
3 tbsps. port
1 oz. Parmesan cheese, grated
3 oz. Cheddar cheese, finely grated
salt and pepper

Trim fresh asparagus to even lengths. Plunge fresh or frozen asparagus into boiling salted water, bring to the boil again and blanch for 5 minutes. Drain.

Butter a shallow au gratin dish and arrange the asparagus in the base. Melt the butter, stir in the flour and cook for 1–2 minutes. Remove from the heat and whisk in the milk. Bring to the boil, stirring. Stir in the port, Parmesan and 1 oz. of the Cheddar. Adjust seasoning.

Use this sauce to coat the asparagus. Sprinkle remaining Cheddar over the top and bake towards the top of the oven at 400°F. (mark 6) for about 20 minutes.

CAULIFLOWER AU GRATIN
serves 4

2 lb. potatoes
2 eggs, beaten separately
salt and pepper
margarine
2 lb. cauliflower
10½-oz. can condensed cream of celery soup
2 tbsps. milk
4 oz. well-flavoured Cheddar cheese
2 oz. buttered crumbs

Peel potatoes and cook in boiling salted water. Drain and sieve back into the pan, then beat in 2 tablespoons beaten egg. Season. Using a large star vegetable nozzle, pipe the potato round the edge of a shallow au gratin dish, brush with the remainder of the first egg. Brown in the oven at 400°F. (mark 6) for about 20 minutes, or under the grill.

Meanwhile, break the cauliflower into sprigs and cook in boiling salted water until tender but not mushy. Drain well and arrange in the centre of the potato.

In a saucepan, whisk together the soup, the second egg, milk and cheese. Bring to the boil, stirring, adjust seasoning and pour over the cauliflower. Top with the buttered crumbs and return to the oven or grill to reheat.

MUSHROOMS WITH GRUYERE
serves 4–6

1½ lb. firm button mushrooms
2 oz. butter
¼ pint (⅝ cup) water
2 tbsps. lemon juice
1 clove of garlic, skinned
salt and pepper
2 oz. Gruyère cheese, grated
2½ lb. potatoes, freshly boiled
2 tbsps. warm milk
1 oz. butter
pinch of grated nutmeg
1 egg yolk (optional)

Wipe the mushrooms with a damp cloth. In a large saucepan, melt the butter in the water, add the lemon juice, garlic, salt and pepper. Add the mushrooms and cook without covering over a fairly high heat until the moisture has evaporated (about 25 minutes). Remove the clove of garlic.

Sieve the potatoes and cream with the milk, butter, seasonings and egg yolk if used. Use to pipe a border round a flameproof dish. Place in a hot oven or under the grill to brown. Spoon the mushrooms into the centre of the potato border and sprinkle with grated cheese. Return to the heat to melt the cheese. Serve at once.

CORN AND CHEESE OMELETTE
serves 2

4 eggs
2 tbsps. water
salt and freshly ground black pepper
1 oz. butter
7-oz. can sweetcorn with peppers
2 oz. Lancashire cheese, grated

A quick and appetizing supper – asparagus au gratin

To make an omelette for 1 person, beat 2 eggs lightly with 1 tablespoon water. Season to taste. Heat ½ oz. butter in a heavy-bottomed frying pan, tilting the pan to grease the whole surface, and pour in the egg mixture. Stir gently with the back of a fork, from the sides towards the centre, until no liquid egg remains. Stop stirring and cook a little longer to lightly brown the omelette underneath. Meanwhile, heat the sweetcorn in a separate pan.

When the egg mixture has almost set, spread half the corn down the centre and towards one side. Sprinkle with 1 oz. grated cheese. Tilt the pan and let the omelette fold over.

Repeat for the second omelette. Serve at once.

CHEESE WHEEZIES
serves 2

½ lb. pork sausage meat
3 oz. Cheddar cheese
dried breadcrumbs
oil for deep frying
15-oz. can sweetcorn kernels
4 tomatoes, halved
black pepper
watercress, to garnish

Divide the sausage meat into 6 equal-size pieces. Cut the cheese into 6 equal-size cubes and wrap the sausage meat round each one. Roll into balls. Dip them into the breadcrumbs until well coated and then re-shape with your hands.

Heat the oil to 350°F. and fry the sausage balls for about 5 minutes, until golden brown. Turn the wheezies once or twice during cooking so that they cook evenly. Meanwhile put the corn in a saucepan and warm over a low heat. Sprinkle the tomatoes with pepper and grill.

Arrange the wheezies on the corn, on individual plates, and garnish with the grilled tomatoes and watercress.

CHEESE FRITTERS
serves 2

2 oz. butter
1½ oz. (⅜ cup) flour
½ pint (1¼ cups) milk
salt and freshly ground black pepper
½ level tsp. dry mustard
6 oz. Edam cheese, rinded and diced
7½-oz. can button mushrooms, drained
1 egg, beaten with a little salt
2 oz. dried breadcrumbs
oil for deep frying

Melt the butter in a small pan. Remove from the heat and stir in the flour, return to the heat and cook gently for 30 seconds. Pour in the milk, stir thoroughly and bring to the boil. Season well with salt, pepper and mustard, remove from heat.

Add the diced cheese and the mushrooms to the sauce and blend well together. When cool shape the mixture into fritters with a spoon, coat with the beaten egg and roll in breadcrumbs. Pat the crumbs on firmly with a palette knife and carefully shake off any excess.

Heat the oil to 350°F. and deep fry the fritters for 5 minutes. Drain thoroughly on absorbent kitchen paper.

Serve at once, with salad and potato crisps.

Orange cheesecake is a delicious dessert for a special occasion

ORANGE CHEESECAKE
serves 6–8

3 oranges
juice of 1 lemon
2 level tbsps. powdered gelatine
2 eggs, separated
½ pint (1¼ cups) milk
3 oz. (⅜ cup) caster sugar
1 lb. 4 oz. plain cottage cheese
¼ pint (⅝ cup) double cream, whipped
extra whipped cream for decoration

For crumb base :
4 oz. digestive biscuits
2 oz. (¼ cup) caster sugar
2 oz. butter, melted
3 oranges, peeled and segmented

Finely grate the rind of 2 oranges, squeeze the juice from 3 and add the lemon juice. Put 4 tablespoons of the mixed juices in a small bowl and sprinkle the gelatine over.

Whisk together the egg yolks, milk and 2 oz. sugar; turn into a pan and cook without boiling for a few minutes. Add the soaked gelatine and stir continuously until dissolved.

Leave to cool until just starting to set, then add the grated orange rind and 6 more tablespoons mixed juices.

Sieve the cheese and beat it into the jelly mixture, or blend them together in an electric blender. Whisk the egg whites stiffly, add 1 oz. sugar and whisk again until stiff. Fold quickly into the almost set cheese mixture, followed by the whipped cream.

Turn into a 3-pint (9½-in.), deep, sloping-sided cake tin, its base lined with non-stick paper. Crush the biscuits and stir in the sugar and butter. Spread this over the cheese mixture and press lightly with a round-bladed knife. Chill thoroughly.

To serve, turn out and decorate with overlapping segments of orange and a whirl of double cream.

BLUE CHEESE DRESSING

3 tbsps. French dressing
½ oz. blue cheese
1 spring onion, skinned and snipped

Whisk the French dressing to emulsify it thoroughly. Chop the blue cheese as finely as possible and snip the onion with scissors. Mix thoroughly. Serve spooned over lettuce wedges.

CHEESE SCONES AND GHERKIN BUTTER
makes 9

8 oz. (2 cups) self-raising flour
1 level tsp. baking powder
a pinch of salt
1½ oz. butter or margarine
2 oz. strong Cheddar cheese, finely grated
1 level tsp. dry mustard
approx. ¼ pint (⅝ cup) milk

For gherkin butter :
4 oz. butter
a dash of Tabasco sauce
2 small gherkins, chopped
1 level tbsp. very finely chopped capers
salt and pepper

Sift together the flour, baking powder and salt, rub in the fat until the mixture resembles fine breadcrumbs. Stir in the cheese, mustard and enough milk to give a fairly soft, light dough. Roll out on a lightly floured board to about ¾-in. thickness and cut into rounds with a 2½-in. plain cutter. Place the rounds on an ungreased, pre-heated baking sheet and dredge the tops with flour.

Bake near the top of the oven at 425°F. (mark 7) for about 10 minutes. Cool on a wire rack.

To make the gherkin butter, cream the butter, stir in Tabasco sauce, gherkins and capers and season.

VEAL CORDON BLEU
serves 4

4 veal escalopes, unbeaten (6–7 oz. each)
4 slices of lean cooked ham
4 slices Gruyère cheese
2 oz. butter
3 tbsps. cooking oil
½ pint (1¼ cups) rich brown stock
¼ pint (⅝ cup) Madeira
freshly ground black pepper

Bat out escalopes until of even thickness – about ¼ in. Top each with a slice of ham cut to fit. Cover half with a slice of cheese and fold escalopes in 2. Secure with 2 cocktail sticks.

Melt the butter and oil in a large frying pan. Fry the escalopes quickly on each side. Reduce heat and cook for about 6 minutes on each side until tender and golden brown. Add stock and Madeira and simmer on top of the stove for 5 minutes.

Remove the meat and keep hot on a serving dish. Season the juices with black pepper and boil rapidly to reduce. Take the cocktail sticks from the escalopes, cover with the juices and serve.

CHOOSING YOUR MEAT

All meat needs to be hung in a suitable temperature and for the correct length of time before it is sold, otherwise it is tough and tasteless. Any reputable butcher will see that this is done.

A shoulder of lamb has more fat but also more flavour than the leg

BEEF

What to look for

1. The lean should be bright red, the fat a creamy yellow.

2. There should be small flecks of fat through the lean; this fat (called marbling) helps to keep the lean moist and tender when the meat is cooking.

3. There should be no line of gristle between lean and fat–this usually suggests the meat has come from an old animal and it may be tough.

Chuck and blade

Fairly lean with no bone, suitable for stewing and casseroles. Allow 6–8 oz. per person.

Rib

A large joint, sold on the bone or boned and rolled. Usually roasted. With bone, allow 8–12 oz. per person; without bone, allow 6–8 oz. per person. (Wing rib is sirloin without the fillet.)

Sirloin

A large joint including the undercut which is particularly tender. Usually sold on the bone, but also boned and rolled. Almost always roasted. With bone, allow 8–12 oz. per person; without bone, allow 6–8 oz. per person.

Rump

Cut into steaks for grilling and frying; no bone.

Aitchbone

A big joint with a large bone, often boned or partially boned for convenience when carving. Usually roasted, but also boiled and braised. Sometimes salted and boiled. Allow 12 oz. per person.

Topside

A lean joint with no bone; good flavour. Usually slow roasted, but also braised and pot roasted. Allow 6–8 oz. per person.

Silverside

A boneless joint needing long, slow cooking such as braising. Often salted, for boiling. Allow 8–12 oz. per person.

Flank *(the belly–may be thick or thin)*

A boneless cut, rather coarse. Needs slow, moist cooking such as stewing, braising or pot roasting. Allow 6–8 oz. per person.

Brisket

A fatty joint but with a good flavour; sold on and off the bone. Slow roast, braise or stew; often salted for boiling. With bone, allow 8–12 oz. per person; without bone, allow 6–8 oz. per person.

LAMB, MUTTON

What to look for

1. The younger the animal the paler the flesh; in a young lamb it is light pink, while in a mature animal it is light red.

2. A slight blue tinge to the bones suggests that the animal is young.

3. The fat is firm and white, or creamy coloured.

Scrag and middle neck

A high proportion of bone and fat but a good flavour. Suitable for stews and casseroles. Allow 8–12 oz. per person, on the bone.

Best end of neck

A series of tiny cutlets that may be divided up and fried or grilled, or left as a whole joint and roasted. 2 joints, back to back, form a crown of lamb. Allow 12 oz. per person.

Loin

A prime cut sold on the bone or boned, stuffed and rolled for roasting, or divided into chops for grilling or frying. When roasting with the bone, allow 12 oz. per person; without bone, allow 4–6 oz. per person.

Chump

Cut into chops for grilling, frying and casseroles. Allow 1–2 chops per person.

Leg

A good cut for roasting. With bone, allow 12 oz. per person. Cut the meat off the bone for kebabs etc.

Breast

A rather fatty cut, usually boned, stuffed and rolled. Roasted, braised, stewed. With bone, allow 8–12 oz. per person.

Shoulder

A large joint with more fat, but often with more flavour, than the leg. Usually roasted. Allow 12 oz. per person on the bone.

VEAL

What to look for

1. The flesh should be light in colour, fine textured, pale pink, soft and moist; avoid flabby, wet meat.

2. If the flesh looks bluish or mottled it generally means it comes from an older animal or is rather stale.

3. The fat–of which there is very little–should be firm and pinkish or creamy white.

Best end of neck

Sold on the bone, or boned, stuffed and rolled. Suitable for roasting, braising and stewing; if divided into cutlets, suitable for sautéing or frying. With bone, allow about 1 lb. per person.

Loin

A prime cut for roasting, either on the bone or boned, stuffed and rolled. Also used for sautés and braised or divided into chops for grilling or frying. With bone, allow 8 oz. per person.

Fillet

Sold in the piece for roasting (usually boned and stuffed before cooking), or cut into thin slices or escalopes for frying. Without bone, allow 4–6 oz. per person.

Breast

Good flavour; usually boned, stuffed and roasted, best cooked slowly. With bone, allow 1 lb. per person.

Shoulder

An awkward shape but suitable for roasting if boned, stuffed and rolled. Portions of shoulder meat are often sold for pies and stews. With bone, allow 1 lb. per person.

PORK

What to look for

1. The lean should be pale pink, moist and slightly marbled with fat.

2. There should be a good outer layer of firm, white fat, with a thin, elastic skin; if the joint is to be roasted, get the butcher to score the rind.

3. The bones should be small and pinkish (which denotes a young animal).

Spare rib

A fairly lean cut, good for roasting, but can be cut up for braising and stewing. Also divided into chops for grilling and frying. With bone, allow 8–12 oz. per person.

Loin

A prime cut which often includes the kidney. Best roasted, it can be cooked on the bone or boned and stuffed; also divided into chops for grilling. With bone, allow 8–12 oz. per person; without bone, allow 4 oz. per person.

Leg

A prime cut, but rather large, so it is often cut into 2. Roasted on the bone or boned and stuffed. Sometimes pickled for boiling. With bone, allow 8–12 oz. per person; without bone, allow 4 oz. per person.

Belly

A fatty cut, usually sold salted for boiling. May be roasted or braised, cut into strips for frying or minced for pâtés. Allow 4–6 oz. per person.

Hand and spring

The foreleg, a little on the fatty side. Suitable for roasting, boiling and stewing. Hand is good salted and boiled. Allow 12 oz. per person.

CARVING A JOINT

When a joint is well carved, the meat looks nice on the plate and goes further. Carving is an art most people can master, given a good knife. If you tell the butcher how you want to serve the meat, he will prepare the joint the easiest way for carving.

In order to carve successfully, the 1 essential tool is a long-bladed, sharp knife. To maintain the sharpness, use a steel or a patent sharpener every time you carve. (To use a steel, draw each side of the blade in turn smoothly down and across with rapid strokes, holding the blade at an angle of 45° to the steel.) Careless sharpening can inflict permanent damage on the knife or your finger!

Also essential is a sharp 2-pronged fork to hold the meat, with a guard to protect your hand should the knife slip. The final accessory is a meat dish with sharp prongs to hold the meat in place – this is by no means necessary, but it is extremely helpful.

Meat is usually best cut against the grain, except when it is very tender (undercut, for instance is cut with the grain). The grain of the meat runs lengthwise along the carcass, hence joints are carved from the outside to the centre of the animal.

Before you start to carve, examine the structure of the joint, and notice the exact distribution of bone, lean meat and fat. Carve standing up and use long, even strokes, keeping the blade at the same angle throughout, to give neat, uniform slices. As you carve, move the knife to and fro, cutting cleanly without bearing down on the meat, which presses out the juices. Serve the carved slices on to really hot plates.

Beef and veal (except fillet) are carved very thinly, but pork and lamb are cut in slices about ¼ in. thick. If the joint has a bone, take the knife right up to it, so that eventually the bone is left quite clean.

BEEF

Sirloin of beef on the bone
Stand the joint on its back with the fillet uppermost. First carve out the flank, then remove the fillet from the bone and carve both these into thin slices. Then turn the joint so that the upper-cut is on top, making a long slice against the back bone. Further slices will then separate easily.

Rib
Stand the joint on edge on the bone. Slice downwards along the full length of the joint, cutting each slice down to the bone (if necessary, cutting behind the ribs to free the meat) and slanting a little away from the cut edge, so that the bone is left clean. Support the slices with the fork to prevent them breaking.

Boneless joints
Carve against the grain, usually horizontally. In the case of a long piece of roast fillet, carve downwards.

VEAL

Stuffed breast
Cut downwards in fairly thick slices, right through the joint. Remove the string from each part of the joint as it is carved.

Chump end leg
The bone is sometimes removed and replaced by stuffing. Cut across the grain (i.e. horizontally) into medium-thick slices, right across the joint.
If the bone has been left in, cut the meat in long slices following the shape of the bone. When the bone is reached and cleared, turn the joint over and continue carving vertically on the other side of the bone.

Loin
One of the few joints carved with the grain of the meat. Carve long slices down the length of the back, turning the knife to follow the bone and release the slices. Then turn joint round to complete the cut. Take smaller slices from the chump end and turn the joint over and remove smaller slices.

LAMB

Leg
Begin by cutting a wedge-shaped slice from the centre of the meatier side of the joint. Carve slices from each side of the cut, gradually turning the knife to get larger slices and ending parallel to the bone. Turn the joint over, remove the fat, and carve in long flat slices along the leg.

Shoulder
Cut a long thick slice down to the bone from the centre of the meatier side of the joint. Carve small slices from each side of the hump on the blade bone down to the shank until the whole surface is clean.
Turn the joint over, remove the fat and carve in horizontal slices.

Best end of neck
Remove the chine bone then cut down between the ribs, dividing the joint into cutlets.

Saddle
First carve the meat from the top of the joint in long slices, cutting downwards, to and parallel with the backbone. Do this at each side of the bone, taking about 4 slices from either side of the saddle.

Stuffed breast
Cut downwards in fairly thick slices, right through the joint.

PORK

Loin of pork
Sever the chine bone from the chop bones and put to one side. Divide into chops by cutting between the bones.

Boned and rolled
Remove the string from each part of the joint as it is carved. Cut through the crackling where it was scored half-way along the joint. Lift off the crackling and cut into pieces. Carve the meat into slices.

Leg
Use the point of the knife to cut through the crackling; it is usually easier to remove it and then divide it into portions. Carve as for leg of lamb, but medium-thick.

Spring
Remove the rib bones underneath, then turn the crackling back on top. Remove some of the crackling before carving. Distribute fat and lean evenly by cutting alternate slices from either end until the bone is reached. Turn joint over and carve the meat from the other side of the bone.

GAMMON

Joints for boiling are usually boned and rolled. Carve as for boned and rolled beef, but in slightly thicker slices.

HAM

Cold cooked ham is best carved on a ham stand as this supports the awkwardly shaped joint. A specially long thin knife is used. Carve in the thinnest possible slices, as for leg of lamb.

ROASTING

There is no method of cooking meat can give a tastier result than roasting, with so little trouble. Plainly roasted meat, served with fresh vegetables and rich gravy is considered one of the best possible meals.

Meat to be roasted must be prime quality, tender and juicy. Roasting is a quick method of cooking, and will not break down tough, sinewy fibres; joints that are likely to be at all tough should be pot roasted, braised or casseroled instead. Guidance as to which cuts are suitable is given in the section 'Choosing your meat', but be guided by your butcher as well—only roast those joints which he recommends and you will not have cause for complaint.

TRADITIONAL ROASTING

It is traditional to roast in the oven at a high temperature—425°F. (mark 7). This sears the joint quickly on the outside, giving a good meaty flavour, and is the ideal way when you know the meat is of prime quality—well hung and tender. Many people prefer to roast at 375°F. (mark 5). This is the best way if in doubt about quality and for small joints, as it keeps the joint more moist than the higher temperature, there is less shrinkage and the meat is likely to be more tender, though the flavour may not be quite as good. Before starting to cook, arrange the shelves in the oven so that there is room for the joint and so that the meat will be in the centre. Pre-heat the oven; if the meat is placed in a cold oven and heated too slowly, the juices will run too freely, leaving the joint dry and tasteless.

Put the joint in the roasting tin so that the cut surfaces are exposed and the fattest part is on top; this automatically bastes the joint. If the natural fat is meagre, top the meat with some dripping or lard. During the cooking time, spoon the hot fat and juices over the meat from time to time, to keep it moist and juicy. Never pierce the meat with a fork or knife as this will allow the juices to escape, leaving the joint dry.

For those who like less fatty meat, it is a good idea to place the joint on a rack or grid in the roasting tin, so that it is kept free of the dripping. This is particularly convenient if roast potatoes or Yorkshire pudding are being cooked, as they can be placed under the grid and will absorb all the juices and the flavour of the meat.

COVERED ROASTING

Roasting in a covered tin, in aluminium foil or in a transparent roasting bag helps to keep the oven clean. It also keeps the meat moist; because this method is also partly steaming, it breaks down the fibres more thoroughly than conventional roasting, making the meat more tender and rendering the fat almost to nothing. To brown and crisp the outside of the joint, remove the lid or open the foil 30 minutes before the end of the cooking time; transparent roasting bags allow the joint to brown without this.

This is a good method for a joint that you suspect may be slightly tough, or if your family doesn't like any fat at all on meat. It does however tend to destroy some of the true open-roasted flavour. Potatoes cooked with a covered joint will not brown.

FROTHING

If you like a particularly brown, crisp outside to the meat, sprinkle with flour and salt 15 minutes before the end of the cooking time and leave uncovered.

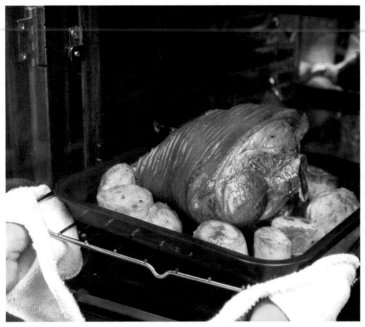

Score the skin of pork to allow the crackling to cook crisply through

Use an evenly shaped joint for successful spit roasting

CRACKLING

The outside skin of pork is left on to form 'crackling'. Make sure this is scored deeply and evenly at $\frac{1}{4}$-in. intervals all over the joint, or it will be extremely difficult to carve. To make the crackling extra crisp and golden brown, rub cooking oil and salt into the skin before cooking.

MEAT THERMOMETERS

A meat thermometer is an infallible guide to when the joint is cooked. Insert it into the thickest part of the joint (but not against the bone) before you start cooking. The thermometer then registers the temperature at the innermost part of the joint and when it shows the correct internal temperature (see chart), the meat is correctly cooked. This is particularly useful with beef, ensuring that you can have it rare, medium or well done, just as you wish. (It is of course necessary to work out the approximate cooking time, so that you know roughly what time to start cooking.)

SPIT ROASTING (OR ROTISSERIE COOKING)

Spit roasting is a development of the original method of cooking meat, in front of an open fire. (The closed-oven method now commonly used should more properly be called baking.) The flavour of spit roasted meat is as different from oven roasted as the latter is from that of meat roasted in a covered tin. Gas and electric cookers are available fitted with a spit, or you can buy a separate, electrically operated model. On a cooker, the spit is best if fitted to the grill unit—spit roasting in the

oven shows very little difference from ordinary oven roasting. But either way the joint browns more evenly than oven roasted meat and needs even less attention, since it is completely self basting.

Any joint, with bone or boneless, that is suitable for quick roasting may be roasted on a spit. It must, however, be shaped as evenly as possible, so that it will revolve steadily (e.g. a shoulder of lamb on the bone is not really satisfactory). If it is not a compact shape, remove the bone, stuff the joint if you wish, roll it and tie with string. Frozen meat must be completely thawed before cooking starts.

First turn on the heat and allow the grill or oven to become very hot. Push the shaft through the meat, push the holding forks into place on either side and secure them, to hold the meat firmly in place. Place the loaded shaft in position and start the motor. Allow the shaft to revolve several times before you leave it, to make sure that there is no obstruction and it is turning evenly. Cook the meat on full heat for 5 minutes or according to the manufacturer's instructions, to sear the surface, then reduce the heat and cook for the appropriate time. Individual manufacturers recommend different cooking times, so follow the instructions given with your model. If you wish, the joint may be basted from time to time with the juices and fat from the drip tray, though this is not strictly necessary. To vary the flavour, try adding fruit juice or cider to the juices, or more conventionally a sliced onion or a clove of garlic.

COOKING TIMES AND OVEN TEMPERATURES

Beef on the bone		425°F. (mark 7)	15 min. per lb. plus 15 m (rare)
		425°F. (mark 7)	20 min. per lb. plus 20 m (medium)
		375°F. (mark 5)	25 min. per lb. (medium-well done)
	boned and rolled	425°F. (mark 7)	20 min. per lb. plus 20 m (rare)
		425°F. (mark 7)	25 min. per lb. plus 25 m (medium)
		375°F. (mark 5)	30 min. per lb. (medium-well done)
Lamb on the bone		425°F. (mark 7)	20 min. per lb. plus 20 m
		350°F. (mark 4)	27 min. per lb. plus 27 m
	boned and rolled	425°F. (mark 7)	25 min. per lb. plus 25 m
		350°F. (mark 4)	35 min. per lb. plus 35 m
Veal on the bone		425°F. (mark 7)	25 min. per lb. plus 25 m
	boned and rolled	425°F. (mark 7)	30 min. per lb. plus 30 m
Pork on the bone		425°F. (mark 7)	25 min. per lb. plus 25 m
	boned and rolled	375°F. (mark 5)	30–35 min. per lb. plus 35 min.

USING A MEAT THERMOMETER

Meat		Temperature of meat	Results
Beef	Rare	140°F.	Very rare when hot, but i when cold.
	Medium	160°F.	Brown meat, but with bl running from it; pale pin tinge when cold.
	Well done	170°F.	Well cooked. Tends to be when cold.
	Very well done	180°F.	Fibres breaking up; fat rendered down.
Lamb		180°F.	Moist, brown meat.
Veal		180°F.	Moist, pale meat.
Pork		190°F.	Moist, pale meat.

CCOMPANIMENTS OR OASTS

ORKSHIRE PUDDING
r beef

oz. (1 cup) plain flour
pinch of salt
egg
pint (1¼ cups) milk or milk and water
oz. lard or dripping

ft together the flour and salt, ake a well in the centre and eak in the egg. Stir in half the uid and beat the mixture until is smooth. Add the remaining uid gradually and beat until ell mixed.

ut the butter in a tin measuring out 7 in. square and heat it in e oven. Pour in the batter and ke at 425°F. (mark 7) for about minutes, until well risen. Cut to squares and serve at once.

ORSERADISH CREAM
r beef

tbsps. grated horseradish
tsps. lemon juice
level tsps. sugar
inch of dry mustard (optional)
pint (⅝ cup) double cream

ix the horseradish, lemon juice, gar and mustard. Whip the eam until it just leaves a trail, en fold in the horseradish ixture.

ORSERADISH SAUCE
r beef

pint (⅝ cup) white sauce
-2 tbsps. grated horseradish
tbsp. vinegar

ix the ingredients thoroughly d serve warm.

INT SAUCE
r lamb

nall bunch of mint, washed
level tsps. sugar
tbsp. boiling water
-2 tbsps. vinegar

rip the mint leaves from the alks and put with the sugar on board. Chop finely. Put in a uce boat, add the boiling water d stir until the sugar is dissolved. ir in the vinegar to taste. Leave e sauce to stand for 1 hour fore serving.

Most people like roast beef slightly rare

MINT JELLY
for lamb

6 lb. cooking apples
2¼ pints (5⅝ cups) water
a bunch of fresh mint
2¼ pints (5⅝ cups) vinegar
6–8 tbsps. chopped mint
green colouring (optional)

Wash and roughly chop the apples, do not peel or core. Put in a large pan with the water and bunch of mint and simmer until really soft and pulpy. Add the vinegar and boil for 5 minutes. Strain through a jelly cloth. Measure the extract and return it to the pan with 1 lb. sugar to every pint of extract. Stir until the sugar has dissolved and boil rapidly until a 'jell' is obtained on testing a few drops on a cold saucer.

Stir in the chopped mint and a few drops of colouring, if required. Skim and turn into warm, dry jars and seal.

RED-CURRANT JELLY
for lamb

3 lb. red-currants
1 pint (2½ cups) water
sugar

Wash the fruit but don't remove the stalks. Put into a pan with the water and simmer gently until the red-currants are really soft and pulpy. Strain through a jelly cloth, measure the extract and return it to the pan with 1 lb. sugar to each pint of extract. Stir until the sugar has dissolved and then boil rapidly until a 'jell' is obtained on testing a few drops on a cold saucer. Skim, turn into warm, dry jars and seal. Cranberry jelly is made in the same way.

APPLE SAUCE
for pork

1 lb. cooking apples, peeled and cored
1 oz. butter
a little sugar (optional)

Slice the apples into a pan, add 2–3 tablespoons water and simmer, covered, until soft – about 10 minutes. Beat to a pulp with a wooden spoon, then sieve or purée in an electric blender if wished. Stir in the butter and add a little sugar if the apples are very tart.

GOOSEBERRY SAUCE
for pork

½ lb. gooseberries, topped and tailed
1 oz. butter
1–2 oz. sugar (optional)

Stew the fruit in as little water as possible, until soft and pulped. Beat well then sieve the fruit or puree in a blender. Add the butter and a little sugar if the fruit is very sour.

CUMBERLAND SAUCE
for ham and mutton

1 orange
1 lemon
4 level tbsps. red-currant jelly
4 tbsps. port
2 level tsps. cornflour
2 tsps. water

Pare the rind thinly from the orange and lemon, cut in strips, cover with water and simmer for 5 minutes. Squeeze the juice from both fruits. Put the red-currant jelly, orange juice and lemon juice in a pan, stir until the jelly dissolves, simmer for 5 minutes and add the port. Blend the cornflour and water to a smooth cream and stir in the red-currant mixture. Return the sauce to the pan and re-heat, stirring until it thickens and clears. Drain the strips of rind and add to the sauce.

SAGE AND ONION STUFFING
for pork

2 large onions, skinned and chopped
1 oz. butter
4 oz. fresh breadcrumbs
2 level tsps. dried sage
salt and pepper

Put the onions in a pan of cold water, bring to the boil and cook until tender – about 10 minutes. Drain well, add the other ingredients and mix well.

PRUNE AND APPLE STUFFING
for pork

4 oz. prunes, soaked and stoned
8 oz. cooking apples, peeled and cored
4 oz. cooked long grain rice
2 oz. shredded suet
2 oz. almonds, blanched and shredded
salt and pepper
juice and grated rind of ½ a lemon
1 egg, beaten

Cut the prunes into quarters and roughly chop the apples. Mix the fruit, rice, suet and nuts. Season to taste, add the lemon rind and juice and bind with beaten egg.

CELERY STUFFING
for pork and lamb

4 sticks celery, scrubbed and finely sliced
1 onion, skinned and finely chopped
2 tbsps. cooking oil
juice and grated rind of 1 orange
salt and pepper
4 oz. fresh white breadcrumbs

Place the celery in a pan, cover with boiling water and simmer for 15–20 minutes, until tender. Heat the oil and sauté the onion until golden.

Drain the celery and put it in a basin; mix with the onion, orange juice and rind. Season well and add the crumbs. Mix carefully with a fork.

GRILLING

Grilling is a primitive method of cooking in which the food is cooked by direct heat from an open flame. One of the best ways of grilling is over charcoal, but this is obviously an outdoor party method now—we normally settle for the more conventional gas and electric grills.

The principle remains the same though. The grill should be turned on well before it is needed, to allow it to get really hot. The meat or fish is brushed with oil or melted butter if it is very lean and placed on the heated grid, in a grill pan. Cooking is then started with the grill on full heat, and if the food starts to burn, the heat is lowered.

GRILLING MEAT

Since grilling is a quick method of cooking, it is suitable only for the best cuts of meat; fresh, under-hung meat and the poorer cuts will remain tough. Many meats benefit from marinading first; for the marinade, mix 2 parts salad oil with 1 part vinegar or lemon juice, add a little chopped onion and some salt and pepper. Keep turning the meat in this marinade for about 2 hours. The remaining marinade may then be used in a sauce to serve with the meat. If you are not marinading, simply sprinkle the meat with salt and pepper (for beef use pepper only), and brush with a little oil or melted butter.

Steak, chops, kidneys, tender liver, sausages, bacon and fish are the foods usually grilled; the only vegetables suitable for this method of cooking are tomatoes and mushrooms.

Steak: Marinade the meat for 2 hours, or brush with melted butter or oil. Cook under fierce heat for 1 minute on each side, then reduce the heat to moderate and cook for the required time, turning the meat from time to time.

Grilling times in minutes:

Thick-ness	Rare	Medium	Well done
¾ in.	5	9–10	14–15
1 in.	6–7	10–12	15
1½ in.	10	12–14	18–20

Chops, lamb and pork: Remove any skin and central bone, and trim neatly. If the chops are un-shapely, tie with string or fasten with a skewer; alternatively, re-move all the bone, roll neatly and tie or skewer into place. Grilling times: 10–15 minutes (lamb), 15–20 minutes (pork).

Liver: Wash, wipe and cut in slices ¼–½ in. thick. Grilling time: 5–10 minutes.

Kidneys: Wash, skin and cut in half. Remove the core and, if liked, thread on to a skewer to make handling easy. Grilling time: minutes.

Bacon and ham: Lean rashers such as gammon, require brushing with oil or melted butter. For thinly cut rashers, cook for 2 minutes, until the fat is transparent on the one side; turn and cook the other side. Thick rashers may take 10–15 minutes.

Sausages: Prick the sausages and grill slowly, under a medium heat, turning frequently until well browned all over. Grilling time: 15–20 minutes.

MIXED GRILL
serves 4

best end of neck lamb chops
½ lb. chipolata sausages
lamb's kidneys
rashers of bacon
tomatoes
mushrooms, washed
salt and pepper
melted butter or oil

Trim the chops, separate the sausages, skin, halve and core the kidneys, trim the rind from the bacon, halve the tomatoes and trim the ends of the mushroom stalks. Brush the chops, kidneys, tomatoes and mushrooms with fat or oil and season. Heat the grill and place the tomatoes (cut side up) and the mushrooms (stalks up) in the grill pan, where they will be basted by the juices from the other food and will cook without further attention.

Put the grill grid in place and put on the chops, sausages and kidneys. Cook them under a medium heat, allowing 14–16 minutes altogether and turning the food on the grid frequently to ensure even cooking. The kidneys will probably be cooked first, so remove these and keep them warm. Replace them by the bacon rashers and cook for a further 3–5 minutes. If the grill is small and all the food has to be cooked separately, heat the oven to a low temperature to keep the food warm as it cooks.

Serve the mixed grill on a large plate, with a simple garnish of watercress and lemon. Traditional accompaniments are chipped or matchstick potatoes, and for more formal occasions maître d'hôtel butter.

Note: Small pieces of fillet or rump steak may be substituted for the lamb chop; a small portion of calf's or lamb's liver is sometimes included.

NOISETTES OF LAMB
These are prepared from a whole best end of neck. Ask the butcher to chine the meat, but not to cut through the rib bones.

Remove the chine bones, skin the meat and remove all the rib bones. Season the inside of the meat with salt, freshly ground pepper and herbs and roll it up tightly, starting from the thick end, rolling towards the flap and wrapping it round. Tie securely at 1½-in. intervals.

Using a sharp knife, cut up in portions, with the string coming in the centre of each one.

Brown quickly on both sides under a hot grill, then reduce the heat and cook for a further 10–15 minutes turning once, until the meat is cooked right through.
Top with pats of savoury butter.

GRILLING FISH
Most fish can be grilled, though the drier types are better cooked in other ways. The fish should be seasoned, sprinkled with lemon juice and (except for oily fish such as herrings) brushed liberally with melted butter. Cutlets should be tied neatly into shape.

Fillets and large fish should be cooked in the grill pan rather than on the grid.

Cutlets and fillets: Grill first on one side for 3–10 minutes, depending on thickness, then turn with a flat, metal draining slice. Brush with fat and grill the second side. Serve very hot with a garnish

Noisettes of lamb topped with maître d'hôtel butter

of grilled tomato halves or parsley sprigs and a sauce.

Whole fish: Wash and scale the fish. Score it with a sharp knife in 3–4 places on each side (this allows the heat to penetrate the thick flesh more quickly), season and brush with melted butter if required. Line the pan with foil if you wish, to catch the juices, place the fish on the grid or in the pan and grill rather slowly, so that the flesh cooks thoroughly without the outside burning.

Turn the fish once or twice, handling it carefully to prevent breaking. To test whether the fish is done, insert the back of a knife next to the bone to see if the flesh comes away easily. Serve with maître d'hôtel butter or melted butter, lemon wedges and chopped parsley.

GRILLED MULLET
serves 4

4 mullet, cleaned
3–4 tbsps. olive oil
3–4 tbsps. vinegar
piece of onion, skinned and finely chopped
few peppercorns
bay leaf or a few parsley stalks

Wash the fish and wipe them well. Put them in a dish with the oil, vinegar, onion, peppercorns and herbs; and leave to marinade for about 1 hour, turning them several times.

Drain the fish and put them on a greased grill grid. Cook under a medium heat for about 10 minutes, basting with some of the marinade and turning them once.
Serve with tomato sauce.

GRILLED HERRINGS WITH MUSTARD SAUCE
serves 4

4 herrings, cleaned
½ pint (1¼ cups) white sauce
1 level tbsp. dry mustard
2 level tsps. sugar
1 tbsp. vinegar

Have the heads cut off and the fish cleaned but left whole. Wash and wipe them and make 2–3 diagonal cuts in the flesh on both sides of the fish and sprinkle with salt and pepper. Brush with oil or melted butter and cook on a greased grill grid for 10–15 minutes under a moderate heat, turning the fish once, until thoroughly cooked on both sides.

Make up the white sauce by using all milk or half milk and half fish stock. Blend the mustard, sugar

and vinegar to a smooth cream and stir into the sauce.

Serve the herrings hot, with the mustard sauce either poured over the fish or served separately in a gravy boat.

ACCOMPANIMENTS FOR GRILLS

SAVOURY BUTTERS
Serve these savoury butters chilled and cut into pats, 1 pat on each portion of meat or fish.

Anchovy butter: Beat 1 part of anchovies (pounded to a paste) with 2 parts butter. A little spice or flavouring may be added, but take care with salt – anchovies are very salty themselves.

Maître d'hôtel butter: Beat 4 oz. butter, mix in 2 tablespoons finely chopped parsley and a squeeze of lemon juice, with salt and cayenne pepper.

Chutney butter: Beat 2oz. butter with 2 oz. chutney and ¼ teaspoon lemon juice, until well blended.

Black butter (for meat): Melt 2 oz. butter in a pan and heat until dark brown. Add 1 tablespoon wine vinegar, a little salt and freshly ground black pepper and 1 teaspoon chopped parsley. Pour over the meat while still hot.

Black butter (for fish): Heat 2 oz. butter until lightly browned. Add 1 tablespoon vinegar, 2 teaspoons capers, cook for a further 2–3 minutes and pour over the fish. Sprinkle with chopped parsley and serve at once.

Garlic butter: Skin and crush a

Whole fish should be scored 2 or 3 times before grilling

large clove of garlic. Beat it well into the butter, to taste, and season lightly with salt and pepper.
Horseradish butter: Soften 4 oz. butter and add 2 tablespoons creamed horseradish. Beat them well together.
Green butter: Wash a small bunch of watercress and dry thoroughly. Chop finely. Beat 2 oz. of the watercress into 4 oz. softened butter until well blended.

MATCHSTICK POTATOES

Peel the potatoes and cut them into very small chips of matchstick size. Leave them to soak in cold water for at least 30 minutes. Drain and dry well on absorbent kitchen paper. Fry in hot deep fat for 3 minutes; drain on absorbent paper. Before serving, re-heat the fat and fry for a further 3 minutes.

SAUTE POTATOES

Peel the potatoes as thinly as possible. Cook in boiling salted water until just tender. Drain thoroughly and cut the hot potatoes into slices ¼ in. thick. Fry slowly in a little hot butter, turning them once so that they are crisp and golden on both sides. Drain well on absorbent kitchen paper and serve sprinkled with a little chopped parsley or chives.

GAME CHIPS

Scrub and peel the potatoes and slice very thinly into rounds using a mandoline slicer. Soak them in cold water and dry.
Fry in hot deep fat for 3 minutes. Remove from the fat and drain on absorbent paper. Before serving, reheat the fat and fry the chips for a further 3 minutes.

MAITRE D'HOTEL POTATOES

1 lb. potatoes
1 tbsp. olive oil
salt and freshly ground black pepper
chopped parsley
1 tbsp. vinegar

Boil the potatoes in their skins and peel the potatoes while still warm. Cut into ¼-in. slices. Heat the oil in a frying pan, add the rest of the ingredients and toss the sliced potatoes in the mixture until well heated. Serve at once.

CRISP FRIED ONION RINGS

4 large onions, skinned and cut into ¼ in. slices
a little milk
a little flour
salt and pepper
fat for deep frying

Separate the onion slices into rings and dip in the milk and then the seasoned flour. Heat the fat so that when one ring is dropped in, it rises to the surface surrounded by bubbles. Gradually add the rest of the rings to the fat and fry for 2–3 minutes until golden brown. Drain on crumpled absorbent kitchen paper, season and serve at once.

CARROTS COWAN

1 lb. carrots
salt
½ oz. butter
2 level tbsps. brown sugar
juice of 1 orange

Trim and scrape the carrots. Slice thinly if old, leave whole if young. Simmer in salted water for about 15 minutes, until cooked. Drain and add a knob of butter, the sugar and orange juice. Heat gently to melt the butter and dissolve the sugar, then simmer for 5 minutes.

GLAZED CARROTS

serves 4

2 oz. butter
1 lb. young carrots, scraped and left whole
3 lumps of sugar
¼ level tsp. salt
a little stock
chopped parsley

Melt the butter in a pan. Add the carrots, sugar, salt and enough stock to come half-way up the carrots. Cook gently without a lid, shaking the pan occasionally, until soft. Remove the carrots from the pan and keep them hot.

Boil the liquid rapidly until it reduced to a rich glaze. Repla the carrots in it a few at a tim turning them until all sides a well coated with glaze.
Serve sprinkled with chopp parsley.

SAUTE CUCUMBER

Peel the cucumber and cut in h lengthwise. Cut into dice and co very gently in butter in a cover pan for 10–15 minutes.
Serve with a white sauce or melt butter.

CREAMED SPINACH

Allow ½ lb. uncooked spinach p person. Wash well in several wate to remove all grit, and strip off a coarse stalks. Chop roughly. Pa into a saucepan with only the wat that clings to the leaves after was ing. Heat gently, turning t spinach occasionally, then bri to the boil and cook gently un soft – about 10–15 minutes. Dra thoroughly. Push through a nyl sieve or purée in a blender. Ac 1–2 tablespoons of cream a some salt and pepper. Rehe before serving.

SAVOURY LEMON SAUCE

rind and juice of 1 lemon
½ pint (1¼ cups) white sauce, (using half milk and half fish or chicken stock)
1–2 level tsps. sugar
salt and pepper
1–2 tbsps. single cream (optional)

Simmer the lemon rind in the mi and stock for 5 minutes, strain, an use the liquid to make a whi sauce. When it has thickened, st in the lemon juice and sugar an season to taste.
If the sauce is too sharp, stir in little single cream just befor serving.
Serve with grilled fish or chicke

BLACK BUTTER SAUCE

2 oz. unsalted butter
1½ tbsps. tarragon vinegar
salt and pepper
2 tsps. finely chopped parsley

Cut the butter into small piece and put in a small strong pan. Hea until it is a golden brown colou then remove from the heat an cool. Meanwhile put the vinegar another small pan and reduce t about half the original quantity Stir in the butter and re-hea Season and add the parsley.
Serve with plaice, sole and skat

Grilled gammon is delicious with a fruit garnish

FRYING

Frying is a quick method of cooking, giving a tasty, succulent result. Natural fat makes an important contribution to the flavour of many foods, and frying fat can add extra flavour where this is lacking in the original.

Only tender cuts of meat – steaks, chops, lambs' or calves' liver and kidney, gammon and bacon rashers. Do not fry the poorer cuts of meat as these need long, slow cooking to break down the tough fibres and if fried will remain hard and tough. Most fish can be fried, and it is a particularly good method of cooking for those with little natural flavour or colour.

Fried eggs and egg dishes such as pancakes and omelettes are traditional favourites and a large selection of vegetables can be fried. Certain sweet foods – doughnuts, fruit fritters – are also fried.

Frying may be done in shallow fat, or by completely submerging the food in deep fat; either way there are certain basic rules for success.

Never add the food to the pan until the fat reaches the correct frying temperature (see chart and individual recipes). If the fat is not hot enough it will soak into the food, instead of sealing the outside crisply, and the result will be soggy and unpleasant.

Do not add too much food to the pan at once, as this lowers the temperature of the fat. Add a small piece at a time. Maintain the temperature by carefully controlling the heat.

Never overload the pan, or foods will start to stew rather than fry.

After frying, drain foods thoroughly on absorbent kitchen paper.

Shallow fat frying

For shallow frying, use a small quantity of fat in a shallow frying pan. This method is suitable for steaks, chops, liver, young chicken, sausages, fish steaks, white fish such as sole, and pancakes – all these need only sufficient fat to prevent them sticking to the pan. Made-up dishes such as fish cakes and rissoles can also be shallow fried, but need enough fat to half-cover them. In this case, most of the foods require a coating of batter or egg and breadcrumbs. Cooking oils, lard, dripping and butter are all suitable for shallow frying. When frying with butter, put a little oil in the pan first to keep the butter from browning; when the oil is hot add an equal quantity of butter, then add more butter as the food starts to colour.

Dip in beaten egg, then press the breadcrumbs on well

Deep fat frying

The food is cooked in sufficient fat to cover it completely. This method is used for batter coated fish, whitebait, chipped potatoes, doughnuts and made-up dishes such as croquettes and fritters. A deep pan and a wire basket are needed, with enough fat to come about three-quarters of the way up the pan; clarified beef fat (for less delicate foods), lard and oil are all suitable. The fat must be pure and free from moisture to prevent spitting or boiling over. After frying, cool the fat and strain it into a basin or wide-necked jar and cover; store it in a cool place for future use.

COATING BATTER – 1

4 oz. (1 cup) flour
pinch of salt
1 egg
¼ pint (⅝ cup) milk or milk and water (approx.)

Mix together the flour, salt, egg, and sufficient liquid to give a stiff batter which will coat the back of a spoon; beat well until smooth. Dip the food into the batter, holding the pieces on a skewer or fork, and drain slightly before putting into the hot fat.

COATING BATTER – 2

4 oz. (1 cup) flour
pinch of salt
1 tbsp. oil
1 egg, separated
2–3 tbsps. water or milk and water

Mix together the flour, salt, oil and egg yolk with sufficient water to give a stiff batter which will coat the back of a spoon; beat until smooth. Just before using, whisk the egg white stiffly and fold it into the batter. Dip the food pieces into seasoned flour before coating them with the batter.

This method gives a lighter, crisper batter than the first recipe.

EGG-AND-CRUMBING

Have a beaten egg on a plate and some fresh white or dry breadcrumbs on a piece of kitchen paper or in a shallow dish. Dip the food in the egg and lift it out, letting it drain for a second or two. Transfer it to the crumbs and tip the paper backwards and forwards until the food is well covered.

Deep fat frying guide

Food	Size	Temperature	Time
Chipped potatoes Fry for 5 minutes at 360°F., remove from pan and raise temperature to 380°F. Fry for a further 3 minutes	¼ in. thick	360°F. 380°F.	5 minutes 3 minutes
Potato croquettes (egg and breadcrumb coating)	3½ in. long	375°F.	3–4 minutes
Scotch eggs (egg and breadcrumb coating)	3½ in. by 3½ in.	325°F.	10 minutes
Chicken Kiev (egg and breadcrumb coating)	4 in. by 2½ in. (approx.)	325°F.	15 minutes
Fritters (using fritter batter)			
pineapple rings	¼ in. thick	350°F.	5 minutes
apple rings	¼ in. thick	350°F.	4 minutes
banana	1 banana cut in half lengthwise	375°F.	2–3 minutes
Rechauffé dishes		360–380°F.	as recipe
Fish fillets (egg and breadcrumb or batter coating)	approx. ½ in. thick	350–360°F.	5–10 minutes
Doughnuts		350–360°F.	5–10 minutes

Press in the crumbs with a small palette knife, then shake the food to remove any surplus.

Alternatively, have the crumbs in a polythene bag and shake the food pieces inside the bag until they are covered.

Do not use this method if the food is likely to break up.

CHICKEN MARYLAND
serves 4

a 3-lb. oven-ready chicken, jointed into 8 portions
2 level tbsps. seasoned flour
beaten egg
4 oz. (2 cups) fresh white breadcrumbs
1 tbsp. cooking oil
3 oz. butter
½ oz. (1½ tbsps.) flour
½ pint (1¼ cups) chicken stock
¼ pint (⅝ cup) soured cream
salt and pepper

For corn fritters:
2 oz. (½ cup) flour
salt and pepper
1 egg, beaten
¼ pint (⅝ cup) milk
8-oz. can sweet corn, drained
fat for frying

For fried bananas:
1 banana per person

Discard the skin from the chicken joints. Dip each piece of chicken into the seasoned flour, then coat with egg and breadcrumbs, patting the crumbs firmly on to the chicken. Heat the oil in a large frying-pan and add the butter. When the butter is melted add the chicken, reduce the heat and cook slowly, allowing 35–45 minutes, until evenly browned and well cooked. Drain and keep warm.

Pour off all but 2 tablespoons of the fat. Add the flour and cook, stirring, for 2–3 minutes. Stir in the stock and soured cream, bring to the boil and check the seasoning. Serve the chicken surrounded by corn fritters and fried bananas, with the gravy in a sauceboat.

Corn fritters

Sift the flour and seasoning into a basin, make a well in the centre and add the beaten egg and 4 tablespoons of milk. Beat until smooth. Add enough milk to give a thick coating consistency, then add the sweet corn. Fry the batter in spoonfuls in shallow fat for about 5 minutes, turning once.

Fried bananas

Peel the bananas and cut into 3–4 pieces. Before you make the gravy, fry the banana in the chicken fat.

Hamburgers – a favourite lunch-time snack

HAMBURGERS
serves 4

1 lb. lean beef
½ an onion, grated (optional)
salt and pepper
melted butter or oil for coating or a little fat for shallow frying

Mince the meat very finely and mix well with the onion and a generous amount of salt and pepper. Shape lightly into 4 round flat cakes.

To cook, shallow fry in a little fat, allowing 4–6 minutes on each side. Hamburgers can be served rare or well done, according to personal preference.

Variations:

Traditionally, hamburgers contain no other ingredients, but they can be varied by adding any of the following when mixing the meat and seasoning:–
2–4 oz. cheese, grated
1 tbsp. sweet pickle
1–2 level tbsps. made mustard
1 level tsp. mixed herbs
1 tbsp. chopped parsley
2 oz. mushrooms, skinned and sliced
2–3 tomatoes, skinned and chopped
Alternatively, when the hamburgers are cooked, top them with a fried or poached egg or with a sprinkling of grated cheese.

Serve in a plain, soft bap with onion rings, slices of tomato and American relish on top, or accompanied by a salad.

MUSTARD STEAKS
serves 4

4 fillet steaks
salt and pepper
1 tbsp. cooking oil
2 oz. butter
¼ pint (⅝ cup) double cream
2 level tsps. French mustard

Sprinkle the steaks with salt and pepper. Heat the oil and butter and fry the steaks for 3–5 minutes on each side. Drain and keep hot. Pour the cream into the remaining butter and meat juices and cook without boiling until thick; stir in the mustard and pour the mixture over the steaks immediately before serving.

PEPPER STEAK
serves 4

1 oz. white peppercorns
1½ lb. rump steak, cut 1 in. thick
1 tbsp. cooking oil
1 oz. butter
2 tbsps. brandy
¼ pint (⅝ cup) dry white wine
2 tbsps. double cream
salt and pepper

Crush the peppercorns roughly and coat both sides of the steak with them. Heat the oil and butter in a frying pan. Fry the steak, turning once, for 6–10 minutes, according to taste. Place on a serving dish and keep hot. Pour off the fat, leaving the peppercorns in the pan. Pour in the brandy and wine, add the cream and warm through. Taste and season; pour over the steak and serve at once.

Note: For a less pungent flavour, try canned green peppercorns.

LIVER, BACON AND MUSHROOMS
serves 4

¾–1 lb. calves' or lambs' liver
seasoned flour
4 rashers of lean bacon, rinded and chopped
1–2 onions, skinned and chopped
fat or oil
4 oz. mushrooms, sliced

Wash and trim the liver and cut into thin strips. Toss in seasoned flour to coat. Fry the bacon until the fat begins to run, add the onion and cook for 5 minutes, or until

soft, then add the sliced mushrooms and strips of liver. Add a little more fat if necessary and continue frying over a gentle heat, stirring from time to time until the meat is just cooked – about 5–10 minutes.

FRIED SWEETBREADS
serves 4

1 lb. lambs' or calves' sweetbreads
juice of ½ a lemon
1 egg, beaten
salt and pepper
2 oz. (1 cup) fresh white breadcrumbs
8 rashers streaky bacon, rinded

Soak the sweetbreads in cold water for 3–4 hours. Drain, put in a pan and cover them with cold water and the lemon juice. Bring the water slowly to the boil and simmer for 5 minutes. Drain and leave the sweetbreads in cold water until they are firm and cold, then strip off any stringy unwanted tissue.

Press the sweetbreads well between sheets of absorbent kitchen paper, slice, season and dip in the beaten egg, then the crumbs. Cut the bacon rashers into strips and fry lightly until just crisp; drain and keep hot. Fry the sweetbreads in the same fat until golden. Toss the bacon and sweetbreads together and serve at once with tartare or tomato sauce.

FRIED SCAMPI
serves 4

8 oz. shelled scampi or Dublin Bay (large) prawns
seasoned flour
4 oz. (1 cup) plain flour
pinch of salt
1 tbsp. oil
1 egg yolk
2–3 tbsps. water or milk and water
fat for deep frying

If fresh scampi or prawns are used discard their heads and remove the dark veins; if frozen, allow to thaw then drain well.

Dip the scampi in seasoned flour. Mix together the flour, salt, oil and egg yolk with sufficient liquid to give a stiff batter which will coat the back of a spoon; beat until smooth. Dip the scampi in the batter. Heat the fat until a cube of bread dropped into it takes 20 seconds to brown. Fry the scampi a few at a time until they are golden brown, drain and serve with tartare or tomato sauce.

Alternatively, fry the scampi coated in egg and breadcrumbs.

FISH CAKES
Serves 2

½ lb. smoked haddock
½ lb. potatoes, peeled and
    quartered
1 oz. butter
1-2 tbsps. chopped parsley
salt and pepper
milk or beaten egg to bind
1 egg, beaten, to coat
dry breadcrumbs
fat for frying

Poach the fish in water until tender, drain, discard the skin and flake the flesh. Boil and drain the potatoes and mash with the butter. Mix the fish with the potato, parsley and salt and pepper to taste, binding if necessary with a little milk or egg. Form the mixture into a roll on a floured board, cut into 8 slices and shape into cakes. Coat with egg and crumbs. Fry in shallow fat until crisp and golden; drain well on absorbent kitchen paper.
These fish cakes are good served with tomato or parsley sauce.

FRIED FILLETS OF MACKEREL
Serves 2

2 mackerel, filleted
oil for frying
a few button mushrooms,
    wiped
1 onion, skinned and thinly
    sliced
1 small clove of garlic,
    skinned and crushed
a little vinegar
grilled tomatoes
parsley, chopped

Fry the fillets quickly in very hot shallow oil, then arrange them on a dish and keep hot. Cook the mushrooms, onion and garlic in the reheated oil, browning them well, and spoon over the fillets. Heat the vinegar until very hot, pour over the fillets and surround with grilled tomatoes. Sprinkle with chopped parsley.

FISH PUFFS
Serves 2

½ lb. potatoes, peeled
½ lb. white fish – haddock or
    cod
½ a small onion, grated
2 level tsps. curry powder
salt and pepper
1 oz. butter, melted
2 eggs, beaten
deep fat for frying

Some of the nicest fritters have a sweet filling

Boil and drain the potatoes and mash them. Poach and flake the fish, mix it with the potatoes and remaining ingredients (except the fat for frying) and beat until smooth.
Heat the fat until it will brown a cube of bread in 40 seconds. Drop the fish mixture into it with a teaspoon, fry quickly until golden, drain on crumpled kitchen paper and serve with a well-flavoured sauce, such as tomato or tartare.

CHIPPED POTATOES

allow 6-8 oz. potatoes per person

Peel the potatoes and cut into ¼-½ in. slices, then into strips ¼-½ in. wide. (For speed, several slices can be put on top of one another and cut together, or use a special 'chipper'.) Place in cold water and leave for at least ½ hour; drain well and dry with a cloth.
Heat oil in a deep fat fryer until when one chip is dropped in it rises to the surface straight away, surrounded by bubbles. Put enough chips into the basket to about quarter-fill it and lower carefully into the fat. Cook for 6-7 minutes, remove and drain on absorbent paper. Repeat this procedure until all the chips have been cooked.
Just before serving, reheat the fat, test to make sure it is hot enough and fry the chips rapidly for about 3 minutes, until crisp and brown. Drain well on absorbent paper and serve at once in an uncovered dish, sprinkled with salt.
Note: The initial soaking helps to remove the excess starch from the potatoes, making the chips crisp.

DOUGHNUTS
makes 10-12

1 level tsp. sugar
4 tbsps. milk (approx.)
¼ oz. dried yeast
8 oz. (2 cups) plain flour
½ level tsp. salt
2 oz. butter or margarine
1 egg, beaten
jam
deep fat for frying
sugar and ground cinnamon
    to coat

Dissolve the sugar in the milk, warm slightly and whisk in the yeast. Leave in a warm place until frothy – about 15 minutes. Mix the flour and salt and rub in the fat. Add the yeast and egg and mix to a soft dough, adding a little more milk if necessary. Beat well until smooth and leave to rise until doubled in size. Knead lightly on a floured board and divide into 10-12 pieces. Shape each into a round, put 1 teaspoon of jam in the centre and draw up the edges to form a ball, pressing firmly to seal them together. Put on a greased baking sheet and leave to prove for about 15 minutes.
Heat the fat until it will brown a cube of bread in 40 seconds. Fry the doughnuts fairly quickly until golden brown – 5-10 minutes, according to size. Drain on crumpled kitchen paper and toss in sugar mixed with a little cinnamon (if liked). Serve really fresh.
Alternatively, shape the doughnuts into rings, removing a small circle from the centre of each ring. In this case, do not add the jam but prove and bake plain. Roll in sugar and cinnamon as for the jam-filled doughnuts.

FRUIT FRITTERS WITH LIQUEUR
Serves 4

8 canned pineapple rings,
    drained
2 tbsps. Kirsch
4 oz. (1 cup) plain flour
pinch of salt
1 egg
¼ pint (⅝ cup) milk
fat for deep frying
caster sugar and ground
    cinnamon

Soak the pineapple rings in the Kirsch. Make up a coating batter by sifting the flour and salt into a basin. Make a well in the centre and break in the egg. Add half the milk gradually and beat the mixture until smooth. Add the rest of the milk and beat until well mixed. Heat the fat until it is hot enough to brown a cube of bread in 1 minute.
Dip the pineapple rings in the batter and fry in the fat until golden. Drain on crumpled kitchen paper, toss in caster sugar and a little ground cinnamon.

CONTROLLED PAN FRYING
There are now available electric frying pans and deep-fat fryers with built-in thermostatic controls. Any food that can be fried in the normal way can be fried in a temperature-controlled pan and they are particularly useful for foods which need a high degree of accuracy in the fat temperature to achieve the correct result. Once the desired temperature is reached, the thermostat maintains it automatically with only small variations.
The deep-fat fryers are most useful if you cook in any quantity, as you can generally cook larger amounts more quickly than by the ordinary deep frying method. These fryers prevent the fat spitting in your face or spattering over the hob. Although they take a rather larger quantity of fat than the normal deep fryers, it can, of course, be used repeatedly.
Shallow-fat frying in a controlled-temperature pan is often more satisfactory than in an ordinary pan, as the heat is evenly spread, giving a more level temperature overall. Dry-frying (i.e. with little or no fat) can be very successful in this type of frying-pan, in particular those with a 'non-stick' or easy-clean finish.
Controlled-temperature pans can also be used for braising, pot roasting and stewing.

33

A casserole can be anything from an inexpensive, tasty meal for the family to the richest of dinner party dishes. The long, slow cooking method breaks down the fibres of the meat and draws out the full flavour.

In the main, casserole dishes use the cheaper, tougher cuts that require long cooking to make them tender, but these cuts often have the most taste. Add vegetables and a rich, home-made stock and the result is a meal to be proud of. For a party dish, add cream or soured cream to the cooking liquid to make a really delicious sauce. For many casserole recipes, the ingredients are fried first. This can either be done in a frying pan, transferring the food to a casserole afterwards, or it can be done in a flameproof casserole, using the same pan for top-of-the-stove and oven cooking.

If you are using 1 pan only, be careful to discard the excess fat before adding liquid.

PAUPIETTES OF PORK
serves 2

2 6-oz. pork escalopes
1 level tbsp. flour
1 tbsp. cooking oil
1 oz. butter
3 oz. onion, skinned and chopped
3 tbsps. dry white wine
¼ level tsp. paprika
½ pint (1¼ cups) chicken stock
1 tbsp. cream

For forcemeat :
1 oz. butter
2 oz. lean streaky bacon, rinded and diced
1 oz. onion, skinned and chopped
2 oz. (1 cup) fresh white breadcrumbs
4 oz. pork sausage meat
¼ level tsp. dried thyme
salt and freshly ground black pepper

Place the escalopes between sheets of non-stick paper and bat out with a meat bat or a heavy knife until fairly thin.

For the forcemeat melt the butter in a small pan, add the bacon and the onion and fry until soft. Allow to cool.

Combine the mixture with the breadcrumbs, sausage meat and thyme; season and spread the forcemeat over the meat. Roll up the meat and tie with string.

Toss the pork rolls in the flour. Heat the oil in a small pan, add the butter and when beginning to colour, fry the pork until evenly browned. Transfer the meat to a small casserole.

Reheat the pan juices and add the onion. Fry until transparent. Stir in the excess flour with the wine, paprika, stock and cream. Bring to the boil and pour it over the meat. Cook in the oven at 350°F. (mark 4) for about 1½ hours. Skim off any excess fat with kitchen paper and remove the string from the meat before serving. Serve with creamed potatoes and green beans.

PORK RIBS WITH SPICED SAUCE
serves 4

2 lb. spare ribs, English cut
1 tbsp. cooking oil
1 oz. butter
½ lb. onions, skinned and finely chopped
1 level tbsp. flour
½ level tsp. ground ginger
½ pint (1¼ cups) chicken stock
2 tbsps. white wine vinegar
8-oz. can cranberry sauce
¼ level tsp. dried rosemary
salt and freshly ground black pepper
chopped parsley for garnish

Trim the spare ribs of excess fat. Heat the oil in a large frying pan, add the butter and on the point of browning add the meat. Fry briskly and brown on both sides. Transfer to a casserole. Add the onions to the pan and fry until tender, stir in the flour and ginger and cook for a minute.

Add the stock, vinegar, sauce,

rosemary and seasoning and bring to the boil, stirring. Pour over the meat. Cover the casserole and cook at 325°F. (mark 3) for about 1½ hours.

Remove the meat from the casserole. Lift off the fat by laying sheets of absorbent paper over the top of the liquid. Reduce the juices by one-third by boiling hard in a pan, or in the casserole if it is flameproof. Return the meat to the casserole and reheat. Sprinkle with fresh parsley before serving.

SCANDINAVIAN PORK
serves 4

4 pork chops
2 fresh herrings (or other small oily fish)
4 medium-sized potatoes, peeled
4 onions, skinned
butter
2 eggs
1 pint (2½ cups) milk
1 oz. (¼ cup) flour
salt and pepper
parsley for garnish

Trim the chops of excess fat and rind. Cut the heads and tails off the herrings and fillet them. Slice the potatoes and onions thinly. Butter a large ovenproof dish, put in a layer of potato, a layer of onion, then 2 chops and 2 herring halves and a further layer of potato and onion. Add the remaining 2 chops and 2 herring halves, then fill in round the sides and cover the top with the rest of the onion and potato. Put a few small knobs of butter on top and cook, uncovered, at 350°F. (mark 4) near the top of the oven for 1 hour. Slake the flour with a little of the measured milk to a smooth cream, beat in the eggs and gradually add the rest of the milk. Season to taste, then pour this mixture over the contents of the casserole. Return the dish to the oven for a further ½ hour, until the savoury custard topping is set. Garnish with parsley.

VEAL AND RICE PAPRIKA
serves 4

1 oz. butter
1 lb. pie veal, cut into small pieces
6 oz. onion, skinned and finely sliced
1 level tsp. paprika
1 level tbsp. tomato paste
¾ pint (1⅞ cups) stock
6 oz. (¾ cup) long grain rice
¼ pint (⅝ cup) soured cream
salt and pepper
chopped parsley for garnish

Melt the butter in a frying pan. When on the point of turning brown, add the veal and fry briskly. Transfer the meat to a casserole and fry the onion until tender. Stir in the paprika, tomato paste and stock. Pour over the veal, cover and cook in the oven at 325°F. (mark 3) for about 1 hour, or until tender. Add the rice, cover and return to the oven for a further 30 minutes.

Gently heat the soured cream in a small pan and fork it through the rice. Season and sprinkle with chopped parsley.

VEAL AND OLIVE CASSEROLE
serves 5–6

2 lb. stewing veal, cubed
1 oz. (¼ cup) flour
1 oz. butter
2 tbsps. cooking oil
1 clove garlic, skinned and finely chopped
2¼-oz. can tomato paste
1 beef bouillon cube
1 pint (2½ cups) boiling water
1 bay leaf
pinch of thyme
pinch of marjoram
12 black olives, stoned
¼ lb. mushrooms, sliced
4–6 oz. (½–¾ cup) long grain rice
12 small stuffed olives
salt and pepper
For glazed onions :
12 small onions, skinned
butter
2 level tbsps. soft brown sugar
2 tbsps. vinegar
2 tbsps. port

Coat the veal cubes with flour and brown on all sides by frying in the mixed butter and oil. Transfer to a casserole. Add the garlic, tomato paste, the bouillon cube dissolved in the boiling water and the herbs. Cook in the centre of the oven at 350°F. (mark 4) for 1½ hours. After the first hour, add the black olives and sliced mushrooms. Adjust seasoning.

To glaze the onions, cook them gently in butter in a pan with the lid on, shaking occasionally. Meanwhile, put the sugar, vinegar, and port in a pan and cook until a thick syrup is formed. When the onions are cooked, put them into the syrup and boil it for a few minutes, until the onions are well coated.

Cook the rice in plenty of boiling salted water for 12–15 minutes. Drain well.

Serve the casserole with the boiled rice and garnish with the stuffed olives and glazed onions.

Veal and rice paprika, finished with soured cream

POULET A L'ORANGE
serves 4

4 chicken portions, halved
2 tbsps. cooking oil
1 pkt. white sauce mix
½ pint (1¼ cups) milk
2 medium oranges
white grapes for garnish

Fry the chicken pieces in the oil until well browned. Remove from the pan and place in a 4-pint casserole. Make up the sauce according to directions on the packet, using the milk. Thinly pare the rind (free of all pith) from 1½ oranges and cut in thin strips. Add these to the sauce, together with the juice of 1 orange. Pour the sauce over the chicken, cover and cook in the oven at 375°F. (mark 5) for about 45 minutes, or until the chicken is tender.

Cut the remaining orange in slices and use it for garnish along with the grapes.

CHICKEN AND WALNUTS
serves 6

3½–4 lb. roasting chicken, jointed and skinned
2 tbsps. sherry
2 level tsps. caster sugar
3 tbsps. oil
8 oz. button mushrooms, wiped and sliced
6-oz. can water chestnuts, drained and diced (optional)
1 pint (2½ cups) chicken stock
2 level tbsps. cornflour
4 oz. halved walnuts
1 oz. butter

Place the chicken joints in a dish, pour the sherry and caster sugar over them and leave to marinade

Chicken, cooked with orange and garnished with grapes

Marinaded beef with olives for a French style casserole

for 1–2 hours.

Heat the oil in a frying pan. Drain the chicken pieces and brown in the oil. Place the mushrooms and water chestnuts in a large casserole and arrange the chicken pieces on top. Pour over the chicken juices and stock, cover the casserole and cook in the oven at 350°F. (mark 4) for 2 hours.

Drain off the liquor, keeping the chicken hot, and thicken it with the cornflour, slaked with a little water. Brown the walnuts in melted butter for 4–5 minutes and drain.

Arrange the chicken, mushrooms and water chestnuts on a serving plate and pour some of the thickened gravy over them. Garnish with the browned walnuts. Serve the remaining gravy separately in a sauce boat.

Rabbit is delicious in a casserole

POULET EN COCOTTE
serves 4

For stuffing :

4 oz. sausage meat
2 level tbsps. fresh white
    breadcrumbs
1 chicken liver, chopped
2 level tbsps. chopped parsley

3–3½ lb. oven-ready chicken
salt and freshly ground black
    pepper
2½ oz. butter
8 oz. lean back bacon, in the
    piece, rinded
1 lb. potatoes, peeled
6 oz. shallots, skinned
1 lb. small new carrots,
    scraped
chopped parsley to garnish

Mix together all the stuffing ingredients in a bowl until well blended. Adjust seasoning. Stuff the chicken at the neck end, plump up and secure with a skewer. Truss the bird as for roasting and season well.

Melt the butter in a large frying pan, add the chicken and fry, turning until browned all over. Place the chicken and butter in a large casserole. Cut the bacon into ¾-in. cubes, add to the casserole, cover and cook at 350°F. (mark 4) for 15 minutes. Meanwhile, cut the potatoes into 1-in. dice.

Remove the casserole from the oven and baste the chicken. Surround with the potatoes, shallots and carrots, turning them in the fat. Season, return to the oven and cook for a further 1½ hours. Garnish with chopped parsley. Have a hot plate to hand for carving the bird, but serve the vegetables and juices straight from the casserole.

FRENCH BEEF AND OLIVE CASSEROLE
serves 4

For marinade :

3 tbsps. cooking oil
1 carrot, peeled and sliced
1 onion, skinned and sliced
2–3 sticks of celery, scrubbed
    and cut in 1-in. pieces
¼ pint (⅝ cup) red wine
¼ pint (⅝ cup) wine vinegar
bunch of fresh herbs
1 clove of garlic, skinned
    and crushed
few peppercorns
salt and pepper

1½ lb. rump steak, trimmed
6 oz. fat bacon, rinded
6 oz. lean bacon, rinded
¼ pint (⅝ cup) red wine
¼ lb. black and green olives
3–4 tomatoes, skinned and
    sliced

Make up the marinade as follows. Heat the oil and add the vegetables. Fry until brown, then add the remaining ingredients, bring to the boil and simmer for 15 minutes. Allow to cool. Cut the meat into thick chunks and cover with the marinade.

Fry the fat bacon to extract the fat, then remove from the pan. Fry the meat on both sides in the bacon fat and put it in a casserole. Dice the lean bacon and add to the casserole with the marinade, wine and olives. Cover with greased greaseproof paper, then with a lid and cook in the oven at 325°F. (mark 3) for 1½–2 hours.

Shortly before serving, remove any excess fat and add the sliced tomatoes. Serve with buttered noodles and grated cheese.

MARINADED STEAK POT
serves 6

2 lb. chuck steak
2 tbsps. garlic vinegar
2 oz. dripping
1½ oz. (⅜ cup) flour
¼ lb. button onions, skinned
¼ lb. button mushrooms,
    wiped and stalked
¼ lb. streaky bacon, rinded
    and diced
1 pint (2½ cups) beef stock
1 bay leaf
1 level tbsp. tomato paste
bouquet garni
chopped parsley

Cut the meat into neat pieces, put it in a polythene bag and add the vinegar. Toss the meat well, place the bag in a deep bowl and leave the meat overnight to marinade.

Melt the dripping in a frying pan. Drain the meat, reserving the juices, and coat with the flour. Fry it until sealed and brown on all sides. Remove the meat from the pan, add the onions, mushrooms and bacon and fry for 5 minutes. Place the mixture together with the meat and juices in a tightly-lidded casserole.

Pour the stock into the frying pan, stir to loosen the sediment and add the bay leaf, tomato paste and bouquet garni. Bring to the boil and pour over the meat. Cover tightly and cook in the oven at 325°F. (mark 3) for about 1½ hours. Discard the bay leaf and bouquet garni and serve sprinkled generously with chopped parsley.

BROWN CASSEROLE OF RABBIT
serves 4

1 rabbit, jointed
2 oz. (½ cup) seasoned flour
2 oz. dripping
1 onion or leek, skinned and
    sliced
1 meat extract cube or 2
    level tsps. powdered meat
    extract
1 pint (2½ cups) stock or water
2 carrots, peeled and diced
1 stalk of celery, scrubbed
    and chopped
bouquet garni
1 tbsp. tomato ketchup
pinch of ground nutmeg
fried croûtons to garnish

Soak the rabbit joints in cold salted water to remove the blood. Dry the pieces and toss in flour, then fry in the dripping, several joints at a time, until lightly browned. Remove from the pan, add the onion or leek and fry gently for a few minutes; add the remaining ɔur and fry until lightly browned. ›dd the meat extract with the ɔquid and stir until boiling. Put ıe rabbit and the vegetables into casserole and pour the sauce over. ›dd the bouquet garni, ketchup ıd nutmeg, cover and cook in the ɛntre of the oven at 350°F. nark 4) for about 2 hours. emove the herbs, adjust season- ıg and serve the casserole gar- ished with fried croûtons.

UMMER LAMB CASSEROLE

rves 4

lb. neck of lamb
level tsps. salt
level tsp. pepper
lb. new carrots, scraped and sliced
lb. small new potatoes, scraped
lb. frozen peas or fresh peas, shelled
level tbsp. tomato paste
resh mint, chopped

lace the meat in a shallow flame- roof casserole, cover with cold ater and bring to the boil. Pour ff the water, rinse the meat and eturn it to the casserole with 1 int ($2\frac{1}{2}$ cups) cold water, to which he salt and pepper has been added. Bring to the boil, add the carrots, over and cook in the oven at 25°F. (mark 3) for about $1\frac{1}{2}$ hours, ntil the meat is fork tender.

›dd the potatoes to the casserole vith the peas, if fresh are used; over and cook for a further 20 ninutes. Remove the meat and trip the flesh from the bones. Cut t roughly and return it to the cas- erole with the peas and tomato aste. Adjust seasoning and return he casserole to the oven for a urther 10–15 minutes.

To serve, sprinkle with chopped nint.

NAVARIN OF LAMB

erves 4

2 lb. middle neck of lamb, trimmed
2 oz. lard or dripping
2 level tbsps. flour
2 level tsps. salt
$\frac{1}{2}$ level tsp. pepper
3 level tbsps. tomato paste
1 pint ($2\frac{1}{2}$ cups) hot water
bouquet garni (including cut clove of garlic)
4 onions, skinned and sliced
4 carrots, peeled and sliced
4 small turnips, peeled and sliced
8 small potatoes, peeled

Cut the meat into serving-size pieces. Melt 1 oz. fat in a pan and brown the meat a few pieces at a time. Dredge with seasoned flour and brown again. Gradually stir in the tomato paste and hot water, add the bouquet garni, bring to the boil, reduce heat, cover and simmer for 1 hour.

Melt 1 oz. fat in a pan and fry all the vegetables except the potatoes. When lightly browned add to the meat and simmer for a further 30 minutes. Discard the bouquet garni, add the potatoes and simmer for a further 30 minutes.

Adjust seasoning and skim off fat.

A fish casserole makes a pleasant change from meat and poultry

LAMB JULIENNE

serves 6

3 level tbsps. flour
1 level tsp. curry powder
2 level tsps. salt
freshly ground black pepper
2 lb. boned shoulder lamb, cubed
oil for frying
$1\frac{1}{2}$ pints ($3\frac{3}{4}$ cups) water or chicken stock
8 small onions, skinned
8 carrots, peeled

For crispy dumplings:
$1\frac{1}{2}$ oz. butter
2 oz. (1 cup) fresh white breadcrumbs
8 oz. (2 cups) self-raising flour
1 level tsp. salt
$\frac{1}{2}$ level tsp. dried onion
3 tbsps. corn oil
milk

Sift together the flour, curry powder, salt and pepper. Toss the lamb cubes in this mixture. Fry the meat in the oil until well browned. Stir in any excess flour. Gradually add the water or stock, stirring, and bring to the boil. Transfer to a casserole and add the onions. Cover and cook in the oven at 325°F. (mark 3) for 1 hour. Cut the carrots into long thick matchsticks and add to the meat. For crispy dumplings, melt the butter in a pan, stir in the crumbs and cook gently, stirring frequently, until golden. Sift together the flour, salt and onion powder. Stir in the oil and enough milk to give a soft but manageable dough. Shape into balls, coat with crumbs and arrange in the casserole. Cover and cook for a further hour.

CIDERED HADDOCK CASSEROLE

serves 4–6

1–$1\frac{1}{2}$ lb. haddock or cod fillet, skinned
$\frac{1}{2}$ lb. tomatoes, skinned and sliced
2 oz. button mushrooms, sliced
1 tbsp. chopped parsley
salt and freshly ground black pepper
$\frac{1}{4}$ pint ($\frac{5}{8}$ cup) cider
2 tbsps. fresh white bread-crumbs
2 tbsps. grated cheese

Wipe the fish, cut into cubes and lay these in an ovenproof dish. Cover with the sliced tomatoes and mushrooms, the parsley and seasonings and pour the cider over. Cover with foil and cook in the centre of the oven at 350°F. (mark 4) for 20–25 minutes. Sprinkle with the breadcrumbs and cheese and brown in a hot oven, 425°F. (mark 7), or under a hot grill.

FISH AND BACON CASSEROLE

serves 6

4 oz. bacon, rinded and chopped
3 onions, skinned and chopped
$\frac{1}{2}$ oz. butter
$1\frac{1}{2}$ lb. white fish, free of skin and bones
salt
cayenne pepper
1 tsp. Worcestershire sauce
$\frac{1}{4}$ pint ($\frac{5}{8}$ cup) tomato sauce
$\frac{1}{4}$ pint ($\frac{5}{8}$ cup) water

Fry the bacon and onion in the butter. Put alternate layers of bacon and onion and the fish into a casserole, sprinkling each layer with salt and very little cayenne pepper.

Mix the Worcestershire and tomato sauces with the water and pour over the fish. Cover and cook in the oven at 350°F. (mark 4) for 45 minutes.

SWEETBREAD HOTPOT

serves 4

1 lb. sweetbreads
1 onion, skinned and chopped
8 oz. peas, shelled
4 oz. mushrooms, wiped and sliced
1 oz. butter
2 oz. ($\frac{1}{2}$ cup) plain flour
1 pint ($2\frac{1}{2}$ cups) white stock
salt and freshly ground black pepper
1 tsp. mixed herbs
toast to garnish

Soak the sweetbreads in salted water until free from blood – about 1 hour. Cover with fresh water, bring slowly to the boil, then pour off the liquid.

In a flameproof casserole, fry the onion, peas and mushrooms slowly for 5 minutes in the butter. Add the flour and stir until cooked. Add the liquid slowly, season, sprinkle in the herbs and bring to the boil.

Chop the sweetbreads and add to the casserole. Cook at 325°F. (mark 3) for about 2 hours. Serve garnished with triangles of toast.

Lamb julienne

BRAISING

Braising is a combination of baking and steaming. It is suitable for both the less expensive roasting cuts and stewing meats – particularly such cuts as leg of mutton, rib, brisket or silverside of beef, best end of neck of lamb or knuckle of veal, pork spare ribs and, of course, poultry and game (especially the tougher, boiling birds). It gives a delicate flavour to the food and a tender, moist consistency. A split calf's foot added to the pan will make it even more succulent. Start with a fairly generous joint, as it will shrink a little in the cooking. Many vegetables can also be successfully braised.

Meat is cooked by laying it on a bed of vegetables (called a mirepoix), just covered with liquid, and is either cooked in the oven at 300–325°F. (mark 2–3), or simmered on top of the stove. The liquid may be stock, wine or cider. The meat may be braised either as a whole joint, or boned and stuffed, or sliced. Prepare the vegetables you plan to use in the mirepoix – e.g. an onion, a carrot, a small turnip, 2 stalks of celery – by peeling and trimming in the usual way and cutting into pieces. Use enough to make a 2-in. layer in the bottom of the pan.

Put about 1 oz. dripping into a flameproof casserole along with a few bacon rinds. Fry the meat in the hot fat until well browned all over. Take out the meat, add the vegetables, seasoning and a bouquet garni to the pan and place the meat on top. Add sufficient stock or water to half-cover the mirepoix. Bring to the boil, cover and simmer gently, basting every 15–20 minutes for half the cooking time until the meat is tender. (For a joint under 3 lb. allow 2 hours.) Slice the meat and serve with vegetables, in the cooking juices. Alternatively, coat the meat in seasoned flour and fry in the melted dripping; remove the meat from the pan before frying the vegetables and continuing as in the first method. Cover, and cook in the oven at 325°F. (mark 3) until the meat is tender.

To serve, the vegetables are usually piled round the meat and the liquor (made into a sauce) is poured over them.

To braise vegetables, fry lightly first, then season, add a little liquid and cook slowly in the oven.

Chicken absorbs the flavours of herbs and vegetables braised with it

BRAISED CELERY
serves 4

**4 small heads of celery,
    trimmed and scrubbed
2 oz. butter
stock
salt and pepper**

Tie each head of celery securely to hold the shape. Fry lightly in 1½ oz. butter for 5 minutes until golden brown. Put in an ovenproof dish, add enough stock to come half-way up the celery, sprinkle with salt and pepper and add the remaining butter. Cover and cook in the centre of the oven at 350°F. (mark 4) for 1–1½ hours.
Remove the string and serve with the cooking liquid poured over.

BRAISED CHICORY
serves 4

**1½ lb. chicory, washed and
    trimmed
1 oz. butter
¼ level tsp. grated nutmeg
juice of ½ a lemon
¼ pint (⅝ cup) chicken stock
1½ level tsps. cornflour
1 tbsp. cold water
2 tbsps. cream
salt and black pepper
chopped parsley**

Plunge the trimmed chicory into boiling water for 1 minute. Drain and rinse with cold water. Drain again. Butter a large casserole. Lay the chicory in the base in a single layer, and dot with butter. Stir the nutmeg and lemon juice into the stock and pour it over the chicory. Cover with buttered foil or a lid and cook at 325°F. (mark 3) for about 1½ hours. Blend the cornflour with the water. Drain the juices from the casserole into a small saucepan, add the cornflour and bring to the boil, stirring; allow it to bubble for 1 minute. Adjust the seasoning and pour the sauce over the chicory. Sprinkle with parsley.

SWEET-SOUR RED CABBAGE
serves 4

**2 lb. red cabbage, shredded
2 medium onions, skinned
    and sliced
2 cooking apples, peeled and
    chopped
2 level tsps. sugar
salt and pepper
bouquet garni
2 tbsps. water
2 tbsps. red wine vinegar
1 oz. butter or margarine**

In a casserole, layer the cabbage with the onions, apples, sugar and seasoning. Put the bouquet garni in the centre.
Pour the water and vinegar over the mixture, cover tightly and cook at 300°F. (mark 2) for about 2½ hours.
Just before serving, add the butter and mix well into the other ingredients.

CHICKEN IN A POT
serves 6

**4 oz. pork sausage meat
2 level tbsps. fresh white
breadcrumbs
1 chicken liver, chopped
2 tbsps. chopped parsley
3½-lb. oven-ready chicken
3 tbsps. cooking oil
salt and freshly ground black
    pepper
4 sticks celery, scrubbed and
    thickly sliced
2 leeks, washed and thinly
    sliced
½ lb. small turnips (or swedes),
    peeled and quartered
½ lb. carrots, peeled and
    roughly sliced
juice of ½ a lemon
bouquet garni
a little stock made from the
    giblets
chopped parsley to garnish**

In a bowl, combine the sausage meat, breadcrumbs, liver and measured parsley. Stuff the chicken with this mixture and truss with skewers or string. Heat the oil in a large pan, season the skin of the bird with salt and pepper and fry lightly in the oil until golden brown on all sides.
Transfer the chicken to a large casserole. Put the celery, leek, turnip and carrot in the oil, cover and cook gently for 5 minutes, stirring often. Drain and pack round the chicken. Add the lemon juice and just enough stock to give a depth of about 1 in. in the base of the casserole. Add the bouquet garni.
Cover tightly, place on a baking sheet and cook in the oven at 350°F. (mark 4) for about 1½ hours, until both the chicken and vegetables are fork tender.
Arrange the chicken and drained vegetables on a large plate. Keep them warm in the oven. Skim off any surplus fat from the juices using a spoon and crumpled kitchen paper and reduce slightly. Adjust the seasoning and sprinkle in the parsley.
Pour the juice over the chicken and serve at once.

BRAISED PORK AND RED CABBAGE

serves 6

2 lb. unsalted belly pork, rinded
½ oz. butter
1 tbsp. cooking oil
1 lb. cooking apples, peeled and cored
1 lb. red cabbage, trimmed and finely shredded
2 level tbsps. flour
3 tbsps. wine vinegar
1 pint (2½ cups) stock
salt and freshly ground black pepper

Cut the pork away from the bone in one piece, then cut it into strips ½ in. wide. Cut each strip in half. In a frying pan, melt the butter with the oil and heat until bubbling. Season the pork and fry until well browned on both sides. Reduce heat and cook for a further 10–15 minutes. Slice the apples roughly.

Place a good third of the red cabbage in a deep casserole, add some apple and half of the meat. Continue to layer up, finishing with the apple. Blend the flour with the vinegar, gradually add the stock until blended and adjust the seasoning. Bring to the boil, stirring, and cook for 2–3 minutes before pouring over the casserole. Cook, covered, at 350°F. (mark 4) for about 2 hours, or until the pork is tender.

BRAISED BEEF WITH SOURED CREAM AND MUSHROOMS

serves 6

3½ lb. thick flank beef, trimmed free of fat
14-oz. can plum tomatoes
2 beef stock cubes
½ lb. onions, skinned and quartered
½ lb. carrots, peeled and halved
1 lb. button mushrooms, washed and stalks removed
2 oz. butter
1 or 2 5-fl. oz. cartons soured cream
chopped parsley for garnish

Cut the lean meat into thin strips. Pour the tomatoes into a large, flameproof casserole and crumble in the stock cubes. Arrange the meat in the centre with the onions, carrots and mushroom stalks round the sides. Cover tightly, preferably with foil and a lid. Cook at 325°F. (mark 3) for about 2 hours.

Remove the lid and gently turn the meat in the juice. Cover, reduce heat to 300°F. (mark 2) and cook for a further hour, or until tender.

Slice the mushrooms. Melt the butter and fry the mushrooms. Discard the vegetables from the casserole. On top of the cooker, add the mushrooms to the beef and stir in the contents from 1 carton of soured cream. Reheat carefully, without boiling. Adjust the seasoning; if wished, stir in another carton of soured cream and garnish with chopped parsley.

BRAISED DUCKLING WITH TURNIPS

serves 4

3½ lb. oven-ready duckling, cut into 4 joints
salt and freshly ground black pepper
2 large onions, skinned and chopped
1 lb. small turnips (or swedes), peeled and quartered
2 stalks celery, scrubbed and chopped
1 level tsp. dried thyme
1 pint (2½ cups) brown stock
1 level tbsp. cornflour
1 tbsp. chopped parsley

Place the duckling joints in a roasting pan and season well. Cook, uncovered, at 400°F. (mark 6) for about 20 minutes, until well browned. Remove from the tin and set on kitchen paper to absorb any excess grease.

Place the onions, turnips and celery in the base of a flameproof casserole. Sprinkle thyme over and lay the joints on top. Pour the stock over the duckling, cover and cook at 375°F. (mark 5) for about 1 hour.

Blend the cornflour to a creamy consistency with a little water. Stir into the casserole juices, bring to the boil and cook for 1 or 2 minutes. Arrange the duckling and vegetables on a hot serving plate, pour the juices over and garnish with chopped parsley.

BRAISED VEAL CUTLETS

serves 4

2½ oz. butter
4 veal cutlets, neatly trimmed
4 oz. cooked ham, chopped
1 tbsp. chopped onion
1 tbsp. chopped parsley
salt and pepper
¼ pint (⅝ cup) red wine

Melt 2 oz. of the butter and in it fry the cutlets until golden brown. Fry the ham and onion, add the parsley and season well. Cover the

Preparing braised chicory

cutlets with this mixture, place carefully in a casserole and add the wine and sufficient water to come halfway up the meat.

Cook in the oven at 350°F. (mark 4) with a lid on for about 45 minutes. Take out the cutlets and keep them hot while boiling the liquid to reduce it slightly.

Just before serving, add the remaining knob of butter to this liquor and replace the cutlets in it.

BRAISED GAMMON

serves 12

½ a gammon, either bottom or knuckle end (about 7 lb.)
1 onion, skinned and halved
1 carrot, peeled and halved
1 turnip (or swede), peeled and halved
bouquet garni
2 pints (5 cups) stock
3 tomatoes, skinned and sliced
a few mushrooms, washed and sliced (optional)
½ pint (1¼ cups) rich brown sauce
¼ pint (⅝ cup) sherry (optional)

Soak the gammon overnight in cold water.

Place it in a large pan with the vegetables and herbs and add just sufficient fresh cold water to cover. Bring to the boil and simmer for half the calculated cooking time. (Allow 15–20 minutes per lb. and 15 minutes over.) Remove the gammon and peel off the rind.

Place the gammon in a braising pan or a deep, flameproof casserole and add the stock, tomatoes and mushrooms. Cover tightly and place in the oven at 350°F. (mark

4) for the remainder of the cooking time.

Place the gammon on a warm dish, strain the stock and reduce to a half-glaze by boiling. Brush over the gammon. Add the sauce and sherry to the remaining stock, boil up and serve as gravy.

BRAISED SWEETBREADS

serves 4

1 lb. frozen lambs' sweetbreads, thawed
1 large carrot, peeled and diced
1 onion, skinned and diced
2 stalks celery, scrubbed and diced
1 tbsp. cooking oil
salt and pepper
½ pint (1¼ cups) white stock
2–3 oz. green streaky bacon rashers, rinded
2 level tsps. cornflour
parsley for garnish

Soak the sweetbreads for at least 4 hours, changing the water several times. Put into fresh cold water and bring to the boil; lift the sweetbreads out and rinse under running cold water. Remove the black veins and skin, wrap lightly in a cloth or muslin and cool pressed between 2 weighted plates. Fry the prepared vegetables in the oil until half cooked. Place them in the base of a casserole which is just large enough to take the sweetbreads. Add the seasoning and stock (just enough to cover the vegetables) and arrange the sliced sweetbreads on top. Overlap the rashers of bacon on top.

Cover and cook in the oven at 375°F. (mark 5) for ½–¾ hour, basting occasionally with the juices

Vermouth is the ideal flavour with this delicious brill

Increase the oven temperature to 425°F. (mark 7) and remove the lid for the last 10 minutes.
Strain the liquor from the casserole. Thicken it with the cornflour and pour over the sweetbreads. Garnish with parsley.

BRAISED PIGEONS WITH GOLDEN SPAGHETTI
serves 4

2 oz. bacon, rinded and diced
1 carrot, peeled and diced
1 piece of turnip (or swede), diced
2–3 sticks of celery, scrubbed and chopped
1 onion, skinned and chopped
4 pigeons, halved
1½ pints (3¾ cups) stock
bouquet garni
salt and pepper
1 level tbsp. cornflour
6 oz. spaghetti
2 oz. butter
tomatoes or watercress to garnish

Put the bacon and vegetables into a flameproof casserole and lay the 8 portions of pigeon on top. Add enough stock to almost cover, the bouquet garni and seasonings, cover tightly and cook on top of the stove for 1 hour until the pigeons are almost tender.
Transfer the casserole to the oven and cook uncovered at 350°F. (mark 4) for 45 minutes until the stock is reduced and the pigeons are browned. Thicken the stock with cornflour if necessary.
Meanwhile, boil the spaghetti in salted water until tender and then drain. Add the butter to the spaghetti in small pieces, making it golden and glistening. Serve the pigeons on a hot dish, surrounded by the spaghetti and garnished with tomatoes or watercress.

BOEUF EN DAUBE
serves 6

2½ lb. top rump of beef
1 oz. butter
2 tbsps. cooking oil
½ lb. onions, skinned and finely sliced
1 lb. carrots, peeled and finely sliced
½ lb. salt pork, rinded and cubed
½ pint (1¼ cups) dry white wine
¼ pint (⅝ cup) beef stock
1 level tsp. dried basil
½ level tsp. dried rosemary
1 bay leaf
½ level tsp. powdered mixed spice
salt and pepper
6 black olives, stoned

Secure the beef firmly with string. Melt the butter with the oil and fry the meat quickly on all sides to seal. Drain on absorbent paper and place in a casserole. Fry the vegetables and salt pork until golden brown, drain and place round the beef. Pour over the wine and stock and stir in the herbs and seasonings. Bring to the boil, cover and cook at 325°F. (mark 3) for 2½–3 hours until fork tender. About ½ hour before the end of the cooking time, add the olives. When cooked, remove the string from the meat and slice. Skim the fat from the juices and serve from the casserole.

ORANGE-BRAISED PORK CHOPS
serves 4

3 oz. butter
½ lb. onions, skinned and sliced
4 pork chops
salt and pepper
1 level tsp. dry mustard
2 level tsps. Demerara sugar
1 level tbsp. plain flour
3 large oranges
¼ pint (⅝ cup) dry white wine

In a frying pan, heat 1 oz. of the butter, add the onions and fry gently until light golden brown. Remove them from the pan. Trim any excess fat from the chops.
In a small bowl, mix together the salt and pepper, mustard, sugar and remaining 2 oz. butter. Spread on one side of each chop. Fry the chops until golden on both sides.

Remove from pan, add flour to the juices and mix well. Coarsely grate the rind from 2 oranges and add to the pan with the onions. Squeeze the juice from 2 oranges and make up to ¼ pint (⅝ cup) with water. Add to the pan, stirring, then add the wine and bring to the boil.
Peel remaining orange and cut it into segments. Arrange the chops in a flameproof pan, add the orange segments. Pour on the sauce. Cover and simmer on top of the stove for 40 minutes.

BRAISED BRILL
serves 4

2¼ lb. brill (or sole or whiting), filleted
salt and pepper
2½ oz. butter
fresh white breadcrumbs
2 shallots, skinned and chopped
1½ tsps. finely chopped parsley
6 tbsps. dry vermouth

Season the brill. Melt 1 oz. of the butter and dip the fillets in it, then coat them with the breadcrumbs. Mix together the chopped shallots and parsley and spread over the base of a greased baking dish. Lay the fillets on top. Melt the rest of the butter and use to glaze the fish. Spoon the vermouth carefully round the fish (not over it).
Cook, uncovered, at 450°F. (mark 8) for 10–15 minutes. Transfer the fish to a hot serving plate and keep warm. Pour cooking juices into a small pan, and boil rapidly to reduce. Pour over the fish.

HERRINGS BRAISED IN WINE
serves 6

½ bottle Mâcon (red)
thick slices of onion, carrot and celery
1 bay leaf
bouquet garni
6 peppercorns
salt and pepper
6 herrings (or other small oily fish), cleaned
sauté button mushrooms, small onions and parsley

Place the wine, sliced vegetables, herbs, peppercorns and seasoning in a saucepan. Cover and simmer for 30 minutes.
Arrange the herrings in a single layer in an ovenproof dish. Strain the liquor over them, adding a little water, if necessary, almost to cover them. Cover and cook at 325°F. (mark 3) for 1 hour.
Garnish with sauté mushrooms, small onions and parsley. ●

Boeuf en daube is a classic braised dish

Ragoût of liver

LIVER

Ox liver has a strong flavour and is often rather tough and coarse-textured. Best used for casseroles.
Calf's liver is very tender and has a delicate flavour. It can be lightly grilled or fried, but over-cooking makes it hard and dry.
Lamb's liver has a slightly stronger flavour than calf's, but is also suitable for grilling or frying.
Pig's liver has a pronounced distinctive flavour and a softer texture. It is best casseroled and makes an excellent pâté.
Allow 4 oz. liver per person.

SAVOURY LIVER

serves 4

1 lb. lambs' liver
2 oz. (1 cup) fresh white breadcrumbs
1 tbsp. chopped parsley
1 level tsp. mixed dried herbs
1 oz. suet, chopped
salt and pepper
grated rind of ½ lemon
little egg or milk to mix
4 rashers streaky bacon, rinded
¼ pint (⅝ cup) stock or water

Wash and slice the liver and arrange it in a casserole. Mix together the breadcrumbs, parsley, herbs, suet, seasoning and lemon rind. Bind with a little egg or milk. Spread the stuffing on the liver and place the bacon on top. Pour in the stock or water and cover.
Cook in the oven at 350°F. (mark 4) for 30–45 minutes, until the liver is tender, removing the lid for the final 15 minutes to crisp the bacon.

RAGOUT OF LIVER

serves 4

1 lb. lambs' liver
4 level tbsps. seasoned flour
1 onion, skinned and sliced
4 rashers of bacon, chopped
1 oz. fat or oil
¾ pint (1⅞ cups) stock
1 oz. sultanas
1 apple, peeled and grated
1 level tsp. tomato paste
8 oz. (1 cup) long grain rice

Wash and trim the liver, cut it into small pieces and coat with the seasoned flour. Fry the liver, onion and bacon in the fat or oil until golden brown. Add the stock to the pan and bring to the boil, stirring constantly. Add the sultanas, apple and tomato paste and simmer for 20 minutes.
Cook the rice in boiling salted water until tender and serve separately.

LIVER MARSALA

serves 4

1 lb. calves' or lambs' liver
lemon juice
seasoned flour
2 oz. butter
3 tbsps. Marsala
¼ pint (⅝ cup) stock
grilled tomatoes, matchstick potatoes and parsley to garnish

Slice the liver, sprinkle with the lemon juice and coat with seasoned flour. Melt the butter in a frying pan and fry the liver quickly on both sides until lightly browned.
Stir in the Marsala and stock and simmer until the meat is just cooked and the sauce syrupy. Arrange the liver on a serving dish and garnish with the tomatoes, potatoes and parsley.

KIDNEY

Ox kidney has a fairly strong flavour. It needs slow, gentle cooking to make it tender. It is usually cooked with steak in casseroles and pies, or curries. Allow 4 oz. kidney to 1 lb. steak.

Calf's kidney is more tender and delicate in flavour than ox kidney but is used in the same ways. One kidney will serve 1–2 people and is usually sold chopped.
Lamb's kidneys are usually the best, being small, well-flavoured and tender enough to grill or fry either whole or in halves. The skin and white 'core' should be removed for cooking. Allow 2 per person.
Pig's and sheep's kidneys are similar to lamb's but are slightly larger and not quite so tender. Pig's kidney has a strong flavour. They can be halved and grilled or fried or used in stews, curries, or casseroles. Allow 1–2 per person depending on size.

KIDNEYS IN RED WINE

serves 4

2 oz. butter
1 onion, skinned and chopped
4–6 sheeps' kidneys
3 level tbsps. flour
¼ pint (⅝ cup) red wine
¼ pint (⅝ cup) stock
bouquet garni
1 level tbsp. tomato paste
salt and pepper
2 oz. mushrooms, sliced

Melt the butter and fry the onion until golden brown. Wash, ski nd core the kidneys and cut them into small pieces; add to the pan nd cook for 5 minutes, stirring ccasionally.

tir in the flour, add the wine and tock and bring slowly to the boil, hen add the bouquet garni, tomato aste and some salt and pepper. immer for 5 minutes. Add the ushrooms and simmer for a further 5 minutes.

emove the bouquet garni before erving and check the seasoning.

KIDNEY ROYALE
erves 4

lambs' kidneys
½ oz. butter
medium-sized onion, skinned and chopped
canned red pimiento caps
alt and freshly ground black pepper
tbsps. Irish whiskey
tbsps. soured cream
oz. (1 cup) long grain rice
chopped parsley

Halve the kidneys, remove and discard the skin and cores, then ut into pieces. Melt the butter in a rying pan and fry the onion gently or about 5 minutes, till transparent ut not coloured. Add the kidneys nd fry for about 10 minutes.

tir in the pimiento, season and immer for a further 5 minutes. Pour the whiskey over and ignite. When the flames have died remove he pan from the heat, stir in the ream and then reheat without oiling.

Cook the rice in boiling salted water until tender. Arrange it ound the edge of a serving dish nd pile the kidneys in the centre. Garnish generously with chopped arsley.

HEART

Ox heart is the largest and tends to be rather tough unless cooked ong and slowly. It can be parboiled whole and then roasted, or cut up and braised or stewed, but n any case it needs strong seasonings and flavourings. An ox heart weighs about 3–4 lb. and serves 4–6 people. It can be bought sliced.

Calf's heart is small and more tender, but still needs slow cooking. It may be roasted, braised or stewed. 1 calf's heart will serve 2 people.

Lamb's heart is more tender than ox or calf's and has a fine flavour. It is usually stuffed and either roasted or braised. Allow 1 per person.

RICH CASSEROLED HEART
serves 4

1 ox heart, 2½–3 lb.
2 oz. fat or oil
2 onions, skinned and sliced
1 oz. (¼ cup) flour
½ pint (1¼ cups) stock
½ lb. carrots, peeled and grated
½ a small swede, peeled and grated
pared rind of 1 orange
6 walnuts, chopped

Slice the heart, removing the tubes, and wash it well. Fry in the fat or oil till slightly brown, then put into a casserole. Fry the onions and add to the casserole. Add the flour to the remaining fat and brown slightly. Pour in the stock, bring to the boil, stirring, and simmer for 2–3 minutes, then strain over the meat in the casserole. Cover and cook at 300°F. (mark 2) for 2½–3 hours. Add the carrots and swede and cook for a further hour.

Shred the orange rind and boil for 10–15 minutes; drain. Add the walnuts and orange rind to the casserole for the last 15 minutes.

STUFFED HEART CASSEROLE
serves 4

4 small lambs' hearts
2 level tbsps. seasoned flour
1 oz. fat or oil
1 pint (2½ cups) stock
1 onion, skinned and sliced
4 sticks of celery, scrubbed and sliced
¼ lb. carrots, peeled and sliced
1 tbsp. cider (optional)

For stuffing :
4 oz. (2 cups) breadcrumbs
1 medium-sized onion, skinned and finely chopped
3 tbsps. melted butter
2 level tsps. mixed dried herbs
salt and pepper

Wash the hearts, slit open, remove any tubes and wash again. Mix the ingredients for stuffing and fill the hearts with it. Tie them into their original shape with string, coat with seasoned flour and brown quickly in the hot fat or oil.

Place in a casserole with the stock, cover and cook in the oven at 350°F. (mark 4) for 2½ hours, turning them frequently. Add the onion, celery, carrots and cider (if used) for the last 45 minutes.

SWEETBREADS

Ox sweetbreads need slow,

Try lambs' kidneys flamed in Irish whiskey – kidney royale

gentle cooking in a casserole.
Calf's sweetbreads are more tender than ox, but are also best stewed or casseroled.
Lamb's sweetbreads are tender, with a fine delicate flavour. They can be fried, or casseroled. Allow 4 oz. sweetbreads per person.

FRIED SWEETBREADS
serves 4

1 lb. lambs' or calves' sweetbreads
juice of ½ lemon
beaten egg
breadcrumbs for coating
oil for deep frying
tomato slices and onion rings

Soak the sweetbreads for 3–4 hours in cold water, then drain and put in a pan. Cover with cold water and lemon juice and bring slowly to the boil. Simmer for 5 minutes. Drain and leave in cold water until they are firm and cold; strip off any stringy unwanted tissues.

Press the sweetbreads well between absorbent paper, slice and dip in the beaten egg and crumbs. Fry the sweetbreads in the hot fat until golden. Serve at once with tartare or tomato sauce and garnished with tomato slices and onion rings.

CREAMED SWEETBREADS
serves 4

1 lb. sweetbreads, prepared (see fried sweetbreads)
½ an onion, skinned and chopped
1 carrot, peeled and chopped
few parsley stalks
½ bay leaf
salt and pepper
1½ oz. butter
1½ oz. (⅜ cup) flour
½ pint (1¼ cups) milk
squeeze of lemon juice
chopped parsley for garnish

Put the sweetbreads, vegetables, herbs and seasonings in a pan with water to cover and simmer gently until tender–about ¾–1 hour. Drain and keep hot, retaining ½ pint (1¼ cups) of the cooking liquid.

Melt the butter, stir in the flour and cook for 2–3 minutes. Remove the pan from the heat and gradually stir in the sweetbread liquid and milk. Bring to the boil and continue to stir until it thickens. Season well and add the lemon juice.

Reheat the sweetbreads in the sauce and serve sprinkled with parsley.

Sweetbreads are delicious coated with egg and breadcrumbs and fried

POULTRY AND GAME

Poultry is the term used for all birds reared specially for the table. It includes chicken, duck, goose and turkey. Game refers to wild birds and animals that are hunted for food, but which are protected by law at certain seasons. The most common game birds are grouse, partridge, pheasant, wild duck, black game and ptarmigan; the only protected animals are deer. Hare, pigeon and rabbit are usually grouped with game although they are not protected. Pigeon and rabbit are sometimes reared specially for the table; both are prepared in much the same ways as game and it is therefore convenient to include them.

CHICKEN

A very young chicken (6–8 weeks old, weighing 1–2 lb.) is known as a poussin and is usually grilled, fried or baked. A broiler (12 weeks old, weighing $2\frac{1}{2}$–$3\frac{1}{2}$ lb.) is cooked in the same way. (Frozen chickens are usually broilers.) There is of course no reason why these birds should not be casseroled or braised. A roaster (4–5 lb.) and a capon (up to 10 lb.) both look and taste very appetizing when stuffed and roasted. Boiling fowl (18 months old, weighing 4–7 lb.) are boiled or casseroled; the meat is too tough to roast.

TURKEYS, DUCKS, GEESE

Whole turkeys are most commonly roasted, stuffed with 1 or 2 kinds of forcemeat. Cut joints may be made into a variety of casserole dishes.

Ducks may be roasted, casseroled or braised. They are rich and are therefore usually served with a sharp-flavoured sauce or accompaniment such as apple sauce or orange salad. Ducklings are more commonly eaten than fully grown ducks. Buy a duck or duckling weighing at least 3 lb., otherwise the proportion of bone is too high.

Geese (average weight 9–10 lb.) are usually roasted, though they can be casseroled. Again they are rich in fat and need something to offset this.

Game birds tend to dry out when roasting, so bard them with bacon

GAME BIRDS

Generally speaking, the more simply game is cooked, the better. For young birds there is no better way than roasting. For older birds that are likely to be tough, braising or casseroling are better. Since game birds lack fat, it is usual to bard the breast before roasting with pieces of fat bacon and to baste frequently with fat during cooking. Sometimes a knob of butter or a piece of juicy steak is put inside the bird before it is cooked, to keep it moist.

HARE AND RABBIT

Hares may be roasted (if young), fricasseed or braised. They are usually hung for 7–10 days before cooking. Rabbits may be cooked almost any way suitable for other kinds of meat, but only young, tender ones should be roasted or fried; they also make a good pie filling and adapt well to jellied moulds.

VENISON

This is the meat of the red deer. The haunch is the prime cut and this and the other better-quality cuts roast and fry well. Venison, which should be well hung, does tend to be rather dry; so bard or

lard it and marinade before cooking. The back and breast may be casseroled or braised.

PREPARATION

Most poultry and game are now sold ready for cooking, that is hung, cleaned or drawn where appropriate, and plucked or skinned. However, since many of the birds are stuffed before cooking, you need to be able to truss them at home (trussing keeps the bird a good shape, so that it looks attractive and is easy to carve).

Note: Poultry are cooked without the feet, but game feet are left on for cooking.

TRUSSING

There are 2 ways of trussing, using either a trussing needle and fine string or a skewer and string. First stuff the bird if required, then fold the neck skin under the body and fold the wing tips back towards the backbone so that they hold the neck skin in position. Make a slit in the skin above the vent and put the tail (the 'parson's nose') through.

If you are using a trussing needle, thread it with fine string and insert it close to the second joint of the right wing; push it right through

the body, passing it out to catch the corresponding joint on the other side. Then insert the needle in the first joint of the left wing, pass it through the flesh at the back of the body, catching the wing tips and the neck skin, and bring it out through the first joint of the wing on the right side. Tie the ends of the string in a bow. To secure the legs, re-thread the needle, insert it through the gristle beside the parson's nose and tie the legs and tail firmly together. If you are using a skewer, insert it right through the body just below the thigh bone and turn the bird over on its breast. Catching in the wing tips, pass the string under the ends of the skewer and cross it over the back. Turn the bird over and tie the ends of the string round the tail, at the same time securing the drumsticks.

FROZEN BIRDS

Both poultry and game are frequently sold frozen. *The bird must be thoroughly thawed before cooking starts.* A single joint of chicken will take 2–3 hours to thaw; a whole chicken or game bird 12–2. hours, depending on size. A large turkey may take up to 3 days.

ROAST CHICKEN

Wipe the inside of the bird with a clean, damp cloth and stuff the neck end. Don't stuff too tightly, as the forcemeat mixture tends to swell and might split the skin. To add flavour if left unstuffed, put a knob of butter with some herbs, an onion or a wedge of lemon in the body. Truss. Brush the chicken with oil or melted butter and sprinkle with salt and pepper. Place a few strips of streaky bacon over the breast if you wish.

Cook at 375°F. (mark 5), allowing 20 minutes per lb. plus 20 minutes. Baste occasionally and put a piece of greaseproof paper over the breast if it seems to be browning too quickly.

Alternatively, wrap the bird in foil before cooking, with the join along the top or use a transparent roasting bag, following the instructions. Allow the same cooking time but open the foil for the final 15–20 minutes to allow the bird to brown.

Serve with roast potatoes and green vegetables or a tossed green salad; also bacon rolls, chipolata sausages, bread sauce and thin gravy made from the giblets.

To roast a very small bird, spread with softened butter and put a knob of butter inside. Wrap in buttered paper and cook for only about $\frac{1}{2}-\frac{3}{4}$ hour, according to size. Remove the paper for the last 15 minutes to brown the breast.

ROAST TURKEY

Stuff and truss and spread with softened butter or dripping. Cover the breast with strips of fat bacon. Cook either at 325°F. (mark 3), basting regularly, or at 450°F. (mark 8) wrapping the bird in foil first and unwrapping it for the last 30 minutes. In either case turn it once, for even browning.

Cooking times – at 325°F. (mark 3)

6–8 lb.	3–3½ hours
8–10 lb.	3½–3¾ hours
10–12 lb.	3¾–4 hours
12–14 lb.	4–4¼ hours
14–16 lb.	4¼–4½ hours
16–18 lb.	4½–4¾ hours

Cooking times – at 450°F. (mark 8)

6–8 lb.	2¼–2½ hours
8–10 lb.	2½–2¾ hours
10–12 lb.	2¾ hours
12–14 lb.	3 hours
14–16 lb.	3–3¼ hours
16–18 lb.	3¼–3½ hours

If preferred, use a large roasting bag and follow directions.
Serve with roast potatoes and brussels sprouts; sausages, forcemeat balls, bacon rolls, thin gravy, bread sauce, cranberry sauce.

ROAST DUCK

Allow 12–14 oz. per person

Stuff at the tail and truss as for chicken, except that the wings are not drawn across the back. Prick the skin all over with a fine skewer and sprinkle the breast with salt and pepper.
Cook at 375°F. (mark 5) for 20 minutes per lb.
Serve with apple sauce, new potatoes, peas and thin brown gravy, or orange salad, or with bigarade sauce.

ROAST GOOSE

serves 8

Stuff and truss. Sprinkle with salt and place in a roasting tin on a wire rack, as goose tends to be fatty. Cover the breast with greaseproof paper or foil. A sour apple put in the roasting tin will add extra flavour to the gravy.
Cook at 400°F. (mark 6) for 15 minutes per lb. plus 15 minutes, without basting. Alternatively cook at 350°F. (mark 4) for 25–30 minutes per lb. Remove the paper for last 30 minutes to brown skin. Serve with gravy and apple or gooseberry sauce.

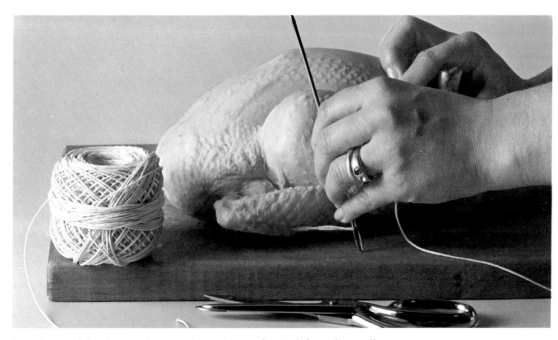

Trussing a chicken for roasting, using fine string and a special trussing needle

ROAST GROUSE

serves 2–3

Truss, season inside and out and lay some fat bacon over the breast. Put a knob of butter inside and place the bird on a slice of toast. Cook at 400°F. (mark 6) for 30 minutes, basting frequently. After 20 minutes, remove the bacon, dredge the breast with flour, baste well and cook for a further 10 minutes. Serve the grouse on the toast on which it was roasted, with thin gravy, bread sauce, fried crumbs and matchstick potatoes.

ROAST PARTRIDGE

serves 1–2

Season the inside with salt and pepper, replace the liver and add a knob of butter. Truss. Cover the breast with pieces of bacon fat. Cook at 450°F. (mark 8) for 10 minutes, then reduce the temperature to 400°F. (mark 6) and cook for a further 10–20 minutes, according to size. Partridge should be well cooked.
Serve with fried crumbs, game chips, clear gravy, watercress, bread or orange sauce and quarters of lemon.

ROAST PHEASANT

serves 4–5

Wipe the bird inside and out and put a knob of butter, flavoured with herbs and lemon juice, inside. Truss and cover the breast with strips of fat bacon. Cook at 450°F. (mark 8) for 10 minutes, then reduce the temperature to 400°F. (mark 6) and continue cooking for 30–40 minutes, according to size. Baste frequently with butter.

15 minutes before the end, remove the bacon, dredge with flour and baste well. Serve as for partridge.

ROAST WILD DUCK

Mallard serves 4–5
Pintail serves 2
Widgeon serves 2
Teal serves ½–1

Truss like a domestic duck and spread with softened butter. Cook at 425°F. (mark 7), basting frequently. Allow 20 minutes for teal, 30 minutes for mallard and widgeon – they should on no account be overcooked. Halfway through the cooking time, pour a little port or orange juice over the bird. Serve with thin gravy, and orange salad or bigarade sauce.

ROAST VENISON

For marinade :

2 carrots, peeled and chopped
2 small onions, skinned and chopped
1 stick of celery, scrubbed and chopped
6 peppercorns
parsley stalks
1 bay leaf
3 blades of mace
red wine

The best joint for roasting is the saddle, but for a small piece use the loin or a fillet cut from the saddle. Place the vegetables and flavourings for the marinade in a large container, put in the venison and add sufficient wine to half cover it. Leave to marinade for 12 hours, turning the meat 2–3 times.
It was traditional to cover the meat with a paste made by mixing flour and water to a stiff dough (allow

about 3 lb. flour to a saddle) and rolling it out to ½-in. thickness. Nowadays, however, the meat is usually brushed generously with oil and wrapped loosely in foil. Roast in the centre of the oven at 325°F. (mark 3), allowing 25 minutes per lb.; 20 minutes before the end of cooking time, remove foil or paste, dredge joint with flour and return to oven to brown. Serve hot with thick gravy and redcurrant or cranberry jelly.

GAME CHIPS

Scrub and peel the potatoes and slice very thinly into rounds. Soak the slices in cold water, dry them and fry in deep fat for about 3 minutes (fill the frying basket only ¼ full). Remove the chips from the fat and drain well.
Just before serving, reheat the fat and fry the chips rapidly for a further 3 minutes, until crisp and brown. Drain well on kitchen paper and serve in an open dish.

FRIED CRUMBS

2–4 oz. fresh white breadcrumbs
1 oz. butter

Fry the crumbs in the butter until golden brown.

BREAD SAUCE

1 medium onion, skinned
2 cloves
¾ pint (2 cups) milk
salt
a few peppercorns
¾ oz. butter
3 oz. fresh white breadcrumbs

The richness of duck can be offset by the sharp orange tang of bigarade sauce

Stick the onion with the cloves and place in a saucepan with the milk, salt and peppercorns. Bring almost to boiling point and leave in a warm place for about 20 minutes to infuse.

Remove the peppercorns and add the butter and the breadcrumbs. Mix well and allow to cook very slowly for about 15 minutes, then remove the onion. Serve hot.

BIGARADE SAUCE

3 oranges (use bitter ones, e.g. Seville, when available)
1 lemon
1 level tbsp. sugar
1 tbsp. vinegar
2 tbsps. brandy
1 level tbsp. cornflour

Grate the rind from 1 orange and squeeze the juice from all of the oranges and the lemon. Melt the sugar in a pan with the vinegar and heat until it is a dark brown caramel. Add the brandy, orange and lemon juice to the caramel and simmer gently for 5 minutes. Drain the excess fat from the tin in which the duck was roasted and add the grated rind and the orange sauce to the sediment. Stir in the cornflour blended with a little water, return the tin to the heat, bring to the boil and cook for 2–3 minutes, stirring.
Adjust seasoning.

ORANGE SALAD

2 oranges, peeled
chopped tarragon or mint
French dressing
endives or crisp lettuce
leaves, washed

Divide the oranges into segments, removing all the skin, pith and pips. Alternatively, cut across in thin slices, using a saw-edged knife.
Put the orange into a shallow dish, sprinkle with tarragon or mint and pour the dressing over; allow to stand for a short time.
Spoon the orange on to a bed of endives or lettuce to serve.

VEAL FORCEMEAT
for turkey

8 oz. lean veal, trimmed and diced
6 oz. lean bacon, rinded and diced
2 onions, skinned and finely chopped
2 oz. butter
6 oz. fresh white breadcrumbs
2 large mushrooms, wiped and chopped
2 tsps. finely chopped parsley
salt and freshly ground black pepper
pinch of cayenne pepper
pinch of ground mace
2 eggs, beaten
milk (optional)

Mix the veal and bacon and pass twice through a mincer, then beat them well in a bowl. Fry the onion lightly in a little of the butter until soft but not coloured – about 2–3 minutes. Add to the meat.
Add the breadcrumbs, mushrooms, remaining butter, seasoning and spices and bind with the beaten eggs. Mix well together; if the mixture is too stiff, add a little milk.
Use as required.

APPLE AND CELERY STUFFING
for duck; use double the quantity for goose

2 oz. bacon, rinded and chopped
1 oz. butter
2 onions, skinned and chopped
2 sticks of celery, scrubbed and chopped
4 medium cooking apples, peeled and cored
3 oz. fresh white breadcrumbs
2 tbsps. chopped parsley
sugar to taste
salt and pepper

Fry the bacon in the butter for 2–3 minutes until golden brown and remove from the pan with a slotted spoon. Fry the onions and celery for 5 minutes and remove from the pan with a slotted spoon. Slice the apples into the pan and fry for 2–3 minutes until soft. Add the breadcrumbs, parsley, sugar and seasoning and mix well together.

APRICOT STUFFING
for chicken; make double this quantity to stuff the neck end of a turkey

3 oz. dried apricots
3 oz. fresh white breadcrumbs
¼ level tsp. mixed spice
¼ level tsp. salt
¼ level tsp. pepper
1 tbsp. lemon juice
1 oz. butter, melted
1 egg, beaten

Soak the apricots overnight in cold water. Drain off the liquid, chop the fruit, stir in the remaining ingredients and bind with the egg.

POULET AU GRAND MARNIER
serves 4–6

For stuffing:
3 oz. butter
4 oz. onions, skinned and finely chopped
4 oz. celery, scrubbed and finely chopped
1 level tsp. dried marjoram or oregano
½ lb. cooked ham, minced or finely chopped
½ level tsp. grated orange rind
6 oz. fresh white breadcrumbs
1 tbsp. Grand Marnier
salt and freshly ground black pepper

3½–4 lb. oven-ready chicken
½ oz. butter
salt and pepper
juice of 2 medium oranges
2 tbsps. Grand Marnier
½ lb. cherries, stoned
2 oz. (¼ cup) caster sugar
1 level tbsp. flour
½ pint (1¼ cups) water
parsley sprigs

Melt 1 oz. butter in a large pan. Add the onion and celery, cover with a lid and simmer for 10 minutes. Add remaining 2 oz. butter and allow it to melt. Stir in the herbs, ham, orange rind, breadcrumbs and Grand Marnier. Mix well together, adjust seasoning and use this to stuff the bird, then truss in the usual way.
Smear the ½ oz. butter over the bird. Sprinkle with salt and pepper. Put the chicken and its washed giblets in a roasting tin. Pour the juice of 1 orange over the bird. Roast at 375°F. (mark 5) for about 1½–2 hours. 15 minutes before the end of cooking time spoon 2 tablespoons Grand Marnier over the breast and complete the cooking.
Meanwhile squeeze the juice from the remaining orange and put it in a small pan with the cherries and the sugar. Cook over gentle heat. Remove the bird from the roasting pan. Discard the trussing string and keep the bird warm on a serving dish.
On top of the stove, reduce the pan juices to about 2 tablespoons by boiling rapidly. Stir in the flour and add the water. Bring to the boil and let it bubble for 1–2 minutes. Season well.
Drain the cherries and arrange them round the bird. Add the cherry juice to the thickened pan juices. Pass all through a sieve. Garnish with parsley and serve the gravy separately.

Poulet au Grand Marnier, generously garnished with cherries

GROUSE A L'AMERICAINE
serves 4

2 young grouse
2 oz. butter
salt and pepper
4 oz. fresh breadcrumbs
cayenne pepper
4 rashers of bacon, rinded
4 tomatoes, halved
1 lb. button mushrooms,
    washed
watercress

Slit the grouse down the back and flatten. Brush them with melted butter and dust with salt and pepper. Grill lightly for 5 minutes under a medium heat, sprinkle with the breadcrumbs and dust sparingly with cayenne. Continue to grill for about 20 minutes, turning the birds frequently. Roll the bacon and grill, with the tomatoes and mushrooms, for 3–5 minutes, until cooked. Serve round the grouse on the serving dish.

SALMI OF PARTRIDGE OR PHEASANT
serves 4

2 partridges or 1 pheasant,
    lightly roasted
1 shallot, skinned and
    chopped
1 orange, peeled and
    segmented
¼ pint (⅝ cup) stock
½ pint (1¼ cups) espagnole
    sauce
¼ pint (⅝ cup) red wine
a few white grapes, skinned
    and pipped
red-currant jelly

Remove the skin from the birds; cut off the breast and leg joints; set aside. Break up the remaining carcasses into small pieces and put in a pan with the shallot, orange rind and stock. Simmer together for ½ hour. Strain the stock from the pan, put it together with the espagnole sauce, wine and joints into a saucepan and simmer until the meat is heated through–about 10 minutes. Arrange the joints on a serving dish and boil the sauce until it is reduced to a syrupy consistency. Pour it over the game and garnish with the grapes, orange segments and red-currant jelly.

HUNTER'S CASSEROLE
serves 4

3½-lb. rabbit, skinned and
    jointed into small pieces
    (2½ lb. meat when skinned)
salt and freshly ground black
    pepper
2 tbsps. cooking oil
½ oz. butter
¼ pint (⅝ cup) dry white wine
1 clove of garlic, skinned and
    crushed
3 tbsps. chopped parsley

Season the rabbit joints. Heat the oil and butter in a heavy pan and fry the rabbit briskly on all sides until golden brown. Remove the rabbit pieces and place in a casserole. Drain the excess fat from the pan juices and add the wine, garlic and 2 tablespoons chopped parsley. Adjust the seasoning and heat for a few minutes. Pour the sauce over the rabbit and cook in the centre of the oven at 375°F. (mark 5) for about 45 minutes, until the flesh is tender. Remove the flesh from the bones; return to the sauce and cook for a further 15 minutes. Sprinkle with remaining chopped parsley.

CHICKEN CHASSEUR
serves 4

4 chicken joints
seasoned flour
1 tbsp. cooking oil
1 oz. butter
1 onion, skinned and chopped
2 oz. mushrooms, washed and
    sliced
2 tomatoes, skinned and
    seeded
½ pint (1¼ cups) espagnole
    sauce or rich gravy
4 tbsps. dry white wine
salt and pepper
chopped parsley

Coat the chicken joints in seasoned flour and fry until golden in the oil and butter. Arrange in a casserole in a single layer. Add the onion and mushrooms to the pan and fry gently for 5 minutes. Drain off the fat. Dice the tomatoes and add to the onion and mushrooms, and add the espagnole sauce or gravy, the wine and seasoning. Pour over the chicken. Cover and cook in the oven at 350°F. (mark 4) for about 1¼ hours, until tender. Sprinkle with chopped parsley before serving.

TURKEY A LA KING
serves 4

8 oz. button mushrooms
1 small green pepper
    (capsicum), seeded
2 oz. butter
1½ oz. (⅜ cup) flour
6½-oz. can pimiento (sweet
    red pepper), drained and
    diced
¼ pint (⅝ cup) turkey stock
¼ pint (⅝ cup) milk
Tabasco sauce
12 oz. cooked turkey, diced
salt and pepper
1–2 tbsps. sherry

Wipe the mushrooms and remove the stalks but do not peel. Slice thickly. Slice the pepper thinly. Melt the butter and sauté the mushrooms and pepper for 10 minutes. Stir in the flour and cook for 2–3 minutes. Add the pimiento caps, and slowly stir in the stock and milk. Bring to the boil, reduce heat, add a few drops of Tabasco and the turkey. Season and simmer for 15 minutes. Add sherry, reheat and serve with rice.

PIGEONS IN CREAM
serves 6

6 pigeons
4 oz. butter
¼ pint (⅝ cup) stock
2 tbsps. red-currant jelly
½ pint (1¼ cups) double cream
1 tbsp. brandy
chopped parsley

Wash the pigeons and trim away the claws and undercarriage bones. Fry in the butter until well browned. Place in a casserole, breast side down in the butter and juices; add the stock and cover tightly. Cook in the oven at 325°F. (mark 3) for about 2 hours until really tender. Remove the birds from the casserole and keep warm. Boil the juices rapidly to reduce by half. Stir in the red-currant jelly and cream. Adjust seasoning. Bring to the boil and reduce the heat. Warm the brandy, ignite and pour flaming over the sauce. Pour the sauce over the birds, and sprinkle with chopped parsley.

Grilled grouse à l'américaine makes a quick 'company' dish

COOKING WITH VEGETABLES

Vegetables add interest and flavour to the day's meals and many of them are also a good source of vitamins and minerals. For example, a helping of potatoes and a green vegetable will supply most (if not all) of the daily Vitamin C requirements.

Storing and preparation

Buy vegetables in prime condition and store in a cool, airy place – a vegetable rack in a well ventilated larder is ideal, or the vegetable compartment of a refrigerator. Green vegetables should be used as soon as possible after gathering, while their Vitamin C value is at its highest.

All vegetables should be prepared with care and as near to the time of cooking as possible, to retain both flavour and Vitamin C content.

Serving

Serve vegetables as soon as they are cooked – they tend to deteriorate when they are kept hot and some develop unpleasant, strong smells. Serve them slightly under- rather than over-cooked. and drain them well if they have been boiled. Serve all vegetables really hot, especially if fried. Don't cover them with a lid or they will become soggy.

A sprinkling of salt and pepper improves most vegetables – especially fried ones, where no salt is used in the cooking process. Add a knob of butter to boiled or steamed vegetables when serving.

JERUSALEM ARTICHOKES

Scrub the artichokes; using a stainless steel knife or peeler, peel them quickly and immediately plunge them into cold water, to prevent discolouration. A squeeze of lemon juice or a few drops of vinegar added to the water helps to keep them a good colour.

Cook in boiling salted water to which a little lemon juice or vinegar has been added for about 30 minutes, until just soft. Drain, garnish with finely chopped parsley and serve with melted butter or a white, cheese, or hollandaise sauce.

Allow 6–8 oz. per person.

GLOBE ARTICHOKES

Cut off the stem close to the base of the leaves and take off the outer layer of leaves and any others which are dry or discoloured. Soak the artichokes in cold water for about 30 minutes to ensure they are clean; drain well (upside-down).

Cook them in boiling salted water until the leaves will pull out easily – about 20–40 minutes, depending on size – and drain upside-down. Serve them with melted butter or hollandaise sauce. Globe artichokes may also be served cold, with a vinaigrette dressing.

Allow 1 artichoke per person as a starter.

ASPARAGUS

Cut off the woody end of the stalks and scrape the white part lightly, removing any coarse spines. Tie in bundles with all the heads together and place upright in a deep saucepan or special asparagus pan of boiling salted water. Boil for 10 minutes, then lay them flat and continue cooking until just soft – further 10–15 minutes (this do not apply when cooking in special pan).

Alternatively, lay the bundles the bottom of a saucepan with t heads all pointing in the sam direction and have one side of t pan slightly off the heat, so th the heads are in the cooler pa allow about 15 minutes.

Drain well and untie the bundl before serving with melted butt or hollandaise sauce.

Don't overcook asparagus – it better to have to discard more the stem part than to have the ti mushy.

Allow 8–12 stems per person.

AUBERGINE (EGGPLANT

Aubergines should be of a unifor purple colour, free from bler ishes. Cut off the stem and sm 'leaves' which surround it; wa the vegetables but do not pe them.

Aubergines are usually fried stuffed and baked. If frying, sli the aubergines, spread them o

n a plate and sprinkle with salt. Leave for 30 minutes, then dry with kitchen paper and dip in flour, if wished, before frying. Allow about 6 oz. per person.

BROAD BEANS

Shell and cook the beans in boiling salted water until soft – 20–30 minutes. Serve with butter or parsley sauce. When broad beans are very young and tender – that is, when the pods are only a few inches long and the beans inside very small – the whole pods may be cooked and eaten.
Allow 8–12 oz. per person (weight including pods).

FRENCH AND RUNNER BEANS

Top and tail the beans. String runner beans if they seem coarse. Slice runner beans thinly; French beans may be left whole or broken in half. Cook in boiling salted water for about 10–15 minutes, until soft. Remove any scum that rises to the top with a spoon. Drain and toss with pepper and a knob of butter before serving. French beans may be cooked and served cold, with vinaigrette dressing.
Allow 6 oz. per person.

BEETROOT

Cut off the stalks 1 in. or so above the root, then wash the beetroots, taking care not to damage the skins or they will 'bleed' while boiling. Boil in salted water until the skin will rub off easily with your thumb – the time depends on age and freshness, but 2 hours is about average. When they are ready, peel off the skin and cut the beets into cubes or slices. Serve hot, coated with a white sauce, or cold plain or in a little vinegar.
Allow 4–6 oz. per person when served as an accompaniment.

GLAZED BEETROOTS

Serves 4

12 small beetroots, cooked
1 oz. butter
1 level tsp. sugar
salt and pepper
grated rind of 1 lemon
1 tsp. chopped chives
2 tsps. chopped parsley
juice of ½ lemon
1 tbsp. capers

Remove the skin, stalks and root end from the beetroots. Melt the butter in a saucepan and add the beetroots, sugar, salt, pepper and lemon rind. Toss the beetroots in the pan over a medium heat

Sauté courgettes and tomatoes, finished au gratin

until they are well coated; add the remaining ingredients, heat through and serve.

BROCCOLI

(purple-headed or Cape and sprouting)

White and purple-headed broccoli are cooked like cauliflower, but take only 15–20 minutes. Serve plain, buttered, or with hollandaise sauce.
Cook sprouting broccoli as for asparagus – set upright in the pan and boil for about 15 minutes.
Allow 6–8 oz. per person.

BRUSSELS SPROUTS

Wash the sprouts, removing any discoloured outer leaves, and cut a cross in the stalks. Cook in boiling salted water until tender – 8–10 minutes. Drain, return them to the pan and reheat with pepper and a knob of butter.
Allow 6–8 oz. per person.

SAVOY AND DUTCH CABBAGE

Remove the coarse outer leaves, cut the cabbage in wedges and take out the hard centre stalk. Wash thoroughly and cook rapidly in about 1 in. of boiling salted water for about 12 minutes. Take care

not to overcook. Drain well, chop roughly if wished and toss with a knob of butter, sprinkling of pepper and a pinch of grated nutmeg (optional). Serve at once. Allow 4 oz. prepared cabbage per person.

Spring greens

Separate the leaves and discard any thick stems. Wash well and shred roughly. Cook as for cabbage.
Allow ½ lb. per person.

Red cabbage

Wash and shred the cabbage and braise with apple and onions, until tender.

CARROTS

New

Trim off the leaves and any root, wash, then scrape lightly with a sharp knife. Boil the whole carrots in salted water for about 15 minutes, or until tender. Serve tossed with a little butter, pepper and chopped parsley.

Old

Peel thinly and cut into ¼- or ½-in. strips, lengthwise, or into strips and then across into small squares, or into thin rounds. Cook and serve as for new carrots, but simmer for about 20 minutes.
Allow 4–6 oz. per person.

CAULIFLOWER

Remove the coarse outside leaves, cut a cross in the stalk end and wash the cauliflower. Boil it stem side down in salted water for 20–30 minutes, depending on size. Drain well and serve coated with white or cheese sauce.
The cauliflower can be divided into individual florets and cooked in fast-boiling salted water for about 10 minutes. Drain well and serve tossed with butter and a sprinkling of pepper or coated with sauce.
A medium-sized cauliflower serves 4 people.

CELERIAC

(the root of turnip-rooted celery)

Cut away leaves and root fibres. Do not peel. Boil in salted water for 40–60 minutes. To serve, drain, peel and slice; add butter, salt, pepper and parsley. Celeriac may also be served raw, cut into julienne strips and mixed with other salad vegetables.
Allow 4–8 oz. per person.

CELERY

Wash, scrub and cut the stalks into even 1½–2 in. lengths. Cook in boiling salted water until tender – about 20 minutes, depending on the coarseness of the celery. Add a stock cube for extra flavour. Drain well and serve with a white, parsley or cheese sauce. Celery is also very good braised.
Allow 1 head of celery per person if small, 2–3 sticks if large.

CHICORY

Generally eaten raw as a salad plant, but chicory may also be cooked. Cut off a thin slice from the base. Pull away any damaged outer leaves and wash quickly under cold water.
To cook, plunge the whole heads into boiling water and blanch for 5 minutes. Drain and cook in the minimum of water with a knob of butter, lemon juice and seasoning for about 20 minutes. Serve sprinkled with chopped parsley or a little paprika.
Allow 1–2 heads per person when chicory is being cooked.

CORN ON THE COB

Choose the cobs when they are plump, well formed and of a pale golden yellow colour. Remove the outside leaves and silky threads, put the cobs into boiling unsalted water (salt toughens the corn) and cook for about 15 minutes, depending on their size.

Drain well and serve with melted butter, salt and freshly ground pepper.

Allow 1–2 cobs per person.

COURGETTES (ZUCCHINI)

Cut away the stalk end and ¼ in. from the rounded end; do not peel. If small, blanch whole, otherwise slice thickly; blanch in salted water for 5 minutes. Drain, then sauté in a little butter, lemon juice and chopped parsley for a few minutes. Season before serving.

Allow ¼ lb. per person, when served as an accompaniment.

courgettes. Cook gently until soft and slightly transparent and put them in an ovenproof dish. Melt the remaining ½ oz. butter and cook the tomatoes, parsley, garlic, pepper and sugar until a thickish purée forms.

Re-season the mixture if necessary and pour it over the courgettes. Sprinkle with the cheese and breadcrumbs and grill until golden brown.

LEEKS

Remove the coarse outside leaves and cut off the roots and most of the green. Wash very thoroughly,

dripping round the meat or stuffed and baked, either whole or in rings.

Allow 8 oz. per person when served as an accompaniment.

ONIONS

Onions vary considerably in both size and flavour from the small white 'cocktail' onion to the large, mild Spanish onion.

Both the leaves and the bulbs of the young plants, known as spring onions, may be eaten in salads, but in the case of the ordinary mature onions the stems and skin are discarded.

Chop the centres finely, mix with the crumbs, seasoning and 1 oz. cheese. Fill the onions and place them in a greased ovenproof dish. Put small knobs of butter on top and sprinkle with the remaining cheese. Bake in the centre of the oven at 400°F. (mark 6) for 20–30 minutes, till the onions are cooked and browned.

Serve with tomato sauce.

PARSNIPS

Wash the parsnips, peel, quarter and remove the hard centre core if the parsnips are at all woody. Quarter or slice and cook in boiling salted water for 20–40 minutes, until soft. Drain and toss in butter, salt, pepper and a little grated nutmeg.

To roast parsnips, par-boil them (halved or quartered) for 5 minutes in salted water, drain and cook as for roast potatoes for about 1 hour. Allow 6–8 oz. per person.

PEAS

The season for fresh peas lasts for about 6 weeks only, but they are sold preserved in various ways—canned, dried, dehydrated and frozen. Frozen and dehydrated peas are very similar to fresh ones when they are properly cooked and presented.

Allow 8–12 oz. fresh peas (as bought), 3 oz. drained canned or frozen peas, or 2 oz. dehydrated peas, per person.

Fresh peas

Shell and wash, place in boiling salted water with about 1 level teaspoon sugar and a sprig of mint and cook until tender – 15–20 minutes. Drain them, remove the mint and toss the peas with a knob of butter before serving.

Frozen, dehydrated and canned peas

Follow the manufacturer's directions.

Onions, stuffed with cheesy crumbs, baked and served with tomato sauce

COURGETTES (ZUCCHINI) WITH TOMATOES

serves 4

1 lb. courgettes (zucchini), cut into ¼-in. slices
salt
2½ oz. butter
½ lb. tomatoes, skinned and chopped
1 tbsp. chopped parsley
1 small clove of garlic, skinned and crushed
pepper
½ level tsp. sugar
2 oz. cheese, grated
1 oz. (½ cup) fresh white breadcrumbs

Put the courgette slices into a colander, sprinkle with salt and allow to drain for about an hour; dry them well. Melt 2 oz. butter in a frying pan and put in the

splitting them down the centre to within 1 in. or so of the base, to ensure that all grit is removed. Cook whole in salted water until soft – 15–20 minutes. Drain very thoroughly. Serve coated with a white or cheese sauce.

Small leeks are excellent boiled and served cold with a vinaigrette dressing.

Allow 1–3 leeks per person, or 8–12 oz., depending on the amount of waste.

VEGETABLE MARROW

Large marrows must be peeled, the seeds removed and the flesh cut into even-sized pieces. Cook in boiling salted water until tender – about 20 minutes – and drain well. Serve coated with a white or cheese sauce.

Marrow can also be roasted in the

Chopped onions are included in many savoury dishes as flavouring. As a separate vegetable, they are best braised, fried, or stuffed and baked.

BAKED STUFFED ONIONS

serves 4

4 medium-sized onions, skinned
2 level tbsps. fresh white breadcrumbs
salt and pepper
2 oz. cheese, grated
butter

Cook the onions in boiling salted water for 15–20 minutes, removing them before they are quite soft; drain and cool. Scoop out the centres, using a pointed knife to cut the onion top and a small spoon to remove the centres.

SAUTE OF PEAS

serves 4

few spring onions, trimmed
1 oz. butter
2 lb. peas, shelled
salt and freshly ground black pepper
¼–½ pint (⅝–1¼ cups) white stock
1 tsp. chopped parsley

Lightly fry the onions in the butter for about 2 minutes, then add the peas, salt and pepper and just enough stock to cover the peas. Cover with a tightly fitting lid and cook gently for 15–20 minutes, until the peas are tender

move the lid after 10–15 minutes to allow the cooking liquid to evaporate.
Sprinkle with chopped parsley just before serving.

POTATOES
Peel old potatoes as thinly as possible; new potatoes are scraped, or brushed and cooked with the skins on and peeled before serving. Cook the potatoes as soon as possible after peeling. Allow 6–8 oz. per person.

Boiled potatoes
Cut the prepared potatoes into even-sized pieces (leave new potatoes whole), put into cold water, add ½ level teaspoon salt per lb., bring to the boil and simmer until tender but unbroken – 15–20 minutes for new potatoes, 20–30 minutes for old.
Drain well, add a knob of butter and serve sprinkled with chopped parsley.

Creamed potatoes
Boil old potatoes as above; using a fork or potato masher, mash with a knob of butter, salt and pepper to taste and a little milk. Beat them well over a gentle heat with a wooden spoon or hand-held electric mixer until fluffy.
Serve in a heated dish, mark with a fork and sprinkle with chopped parsley.

Baked or 'jacket' potatoes
Choose even-sized old potatoes, free from 'eyes' and blemishes. Scrub well, dry and prick all over with a fork. Bake near the top of the oven at 400°F. (mark 6) for about ¾–1 hour for small potatoes, 1–1¼ hours for larger ones, or until soft when pinched. Cut a cross in the top of each potato and put in a knob of butter or a spoonful of soured cream.

Roast potatoes
Using old potatoes, peel in the usual way and cut into even-sized pieces. Cook in boiling salted water for about 7 minutes and drain well. Transfer them to a roasting tin containing 4 oz. hot lard or dripping, baste well and cook near the top of a hot oven – 425°F. (mark 7) – for about 20 minutes; turn them and continue cooking until soft inside and crisp and brown outside – about 40 minutes altogether. Alternatively, place potatoes in the tin round a roasting joint. Drain well on kitchen paper and serve uncovered, sprinkled with salt.

LYONNAISE POTATOES
serves 4

½ lb. onions, skinned and sliced
1–2 tbsps. cooking oil
1 lb. sauté potatoes
chopped parsley

Fry the onions slowly in the oil until golden brown – about 10 minutes. Serve in layers with the potatoes and sprinkle with chopped parsley.

SEAKALE
Wash well, cut off ends and tie into neat bundles. Cook for 20–

This is a hot curry and is good served with boiled rice

30 minutes in boiling salted water to which a squeeze of lemon juice has been added. Drain well and remove the strings before serving. Serve coated with béchamel or hollandaise sauce.
Seakale may also be braised or served au gratin, served cold with a vinaigrette dressing or eaten raw with cheese and in salads.
Allow 4–8 oz. per person.

SPINACH
Wash well in several waters to remove all grit and strip off any coarse stalks. Pack into a saucepan with only the water that clings to the leaves after washing. Heat gently, turning the spinach occasionally, then bring to the boil and cook gently for 5–15 minutes until soft. Drain thoroughly, chop roughly or purée and reheat with

a knob of butter and a sprinkling of salt, pepper and nutmeg.
Allow 6–8 oz. per person.

SWEDES
(Swedish turnips)
Peel thickly and slice, dice or cut into julienne strips. Keep covered with water and cook as soon as possible after peeling. Boil in a little salted water with the lid on for about 20 minutes, according to size and age. Drain well, and mash them with a little salt, pepper, grated nutmeg and a knob of butter.
Alternatively, cut them in chunks or fingers and roast them round the joint allowing 1–1¼ hours.
Allow 4–6 oz. per person.

SWEET PEPPERS (CAPSICUMS)
Both red and green peppers can be sliced or chopped and eaten raw in a salad. Small amounts of raw or blanched peppers may be included in savoury dishes made with rice and macaroni. Peppers may be fried or stuffed and baked. To prepare them, remove stem, seeds and membrane. For stuffing and baking, leave whole, parboil for 5 minutes and bake at 350°F. (mark 4) for 25–30 minutes. Or cut in rings and sauté in butter for 5 minutes.
Allow 1 medium-sized pepper per person for cooked dishes such as stuffed or fried peppers.

SWEET PEPPERS WITH TOMATOES
serves 4

2 tbsps. cooking oil
½ an onion, skinned and chopped
1 clove of garlic, skinned and crushed
4 tomatoes, skinned and sliced
2 level tbsps. tomato paste
¼ pint (⅝ cup) dry white wine
4 medium-sized peppers, seeded and thinly sliced
salt and pepper

Heat the oil and lightly fry the onion and garlic for 5 minutes without colouring. Add the tomatoes, tomato paste and wine and simmer for 5 minutes. Add the peppers, cover and simmer for 30 minutes. Adjust seasoning.

TURNIPS
Peel thickly to remove the outer layer of skin and put under water to prevent discolouration. Young turnips can be left whole, older ones should be sliced, diced or cut in strips. Cook whole in salted water for 20–30 minutes, if sliced or diced cook for 15–20 minutes. Toss young turnips in butter or a little top of the milk, with added seasoning, or serve in white sauce. Mash old ones with salt, pepper, nutmeg and a knob of butter.
Allow 4–6 oz. per person.

VEGETABLE CURRY
serves 4

1 cauliflower, cut in large sprigs
6 tomatoes, skinned and sliced
6-8 small potatoes, peeled and quartered
¼ lb. shelled peas
¼ lb. French beans, sliced
1 level tbsp. turmeric
1½ level tbsps. mild curry powder
½ level tsp. salt
2 oz. butter
6 small onions, skinned
1 clove of garlic, skinned and crushed
½ pint (1¼ cups) stock

Place the raw cauliflower, tomatoes, potatoes, peas and beans on a large plate. Mix the spices and salt and sprinkle over the vegetables. Melt the butter in a heavy pan and sauté the small onions and garlic. Add the spiced vegetables, then the stock; cover, bring to the boil and simmer for about 20 minutes, until all the vegetables are tender. Serve with boiled rice.

SALADS

Serve crisp, cool salads for
main courses, starters and
accompaniments. Full of vitamins
and minerals for your family, quick
and easy to prepare for guests—
salads are the answer to many
a 'what shall we eat?' situation.
Above : Dutch salad, based on
cheese, apples and spinach.

MAIN COURSE SALADS

PORK AND BEAN SALAD
serves 4

2 tbsps. chopped parsley
1 small onion, skinned and
    very finely chopped
1 level tsp. dry mustard
1 level tsp. French mustard
1 level tsp. paprika pepper
1 level tsp. salt
freshly ground black pepper
$\frac{1}{4}$ level tsp. grated nutmeg
2 level tsps. caster sugar
juice of 1 orange
4 tbsps. salad oil
2 tbsps. tarragon vinegar
7-oz. can red kidney beans,
    drained
2 large cooked potatoes, diced
1 lb. cold, cooked pork
    sausages
2 eating apples, cored and
    diced
2 tomatoes, skinned and
    seeded

Put the parsley, onion, seasonings,
spices, sugar, orange juice, oil and
vinegar in a lidded container, close
and shake to make a dressing.

In a bowl, lightly toss together the
beans, potatoes, sausages (cut into
$\frac{1}{4}$-in. slices) apples and chopped
tomatoes. Fold the dressing
through and leave to marinade for
30 minutes, giving the mixture an
occasional stir. Turn into a salad
bowl for serving.

CHICKEN SALAD
serves 6

3½-lb. oven-ready boiling fowl
1 small onion, skinned
2-3 strips of lemon rind
2 tbsps. lemon juice
blade of mace
2 sprigs of parsley
6 peppercorns
2 cloves
salt
4 oz. ($\frac{1}{2}$ cup) long grain rice
2 oz. sultanas
1 oz. seedless raisins
8 oz. white and black grapes,
    skinned and pipped
$\frac{1}{4}$ pint ($\frac{5}{8}$ cup) mayonnaise
1 tomato, sliced, for garnish
1 egg, hard-boiled and sliced,
    for garnish
watercress for garnish

Put the fowl in a casserole with the
onion, lemon rind and juice, the
herbs and spices, tied in muslin,
salt to taste and sufficient water to
cover; cook slowly on top of the
stove or in the oven until tender –
about 3 hours.
Remove all bones and skin from
the fowl and dice the flesh. Boil the
rice in the strained chicken stock

until tender, drain if necessary and
leave until cold. Mix the diced
fowl, rice, dried fruit and half the
grapes, adding the mayonnaise.
Pile high in a deep dish and garnish
with a border of alternating black
and white grapes; on top place a
few tomato and egg slices and a
tuft of watercress.

SWEDISH CHICKEN SALAD
serves 6

3½-lb. oven-ready chicken,
    roasted
6 oz. ($\frac{3}{4}$ cup) long grain rice
1 green eating apple
1 red eating apple
2 bananas
lemon juice
$\frac{1}{4}$ pint ($\frac{5}{8}$ cup) double cream
7 fl. oz. ($\frac{7}{8}$ cup) mayonnaise
1 level tsp. curry powder
salt and pepper
watercress for garnish

Allow the chicken to cool. Meanwhile cook the rice in boiling,
salted water for about 12 minutes,
drain and cool. Carve the chicken
into slices and cut these into strips.
Halve and core the apples and slice
thinly. Peel the bananas and slice
thickly. Sprinkle both with lemon
juice.
Whip the cream to the same consistency as the mayonnaise and
fold it in. Add the curry powder.
Fold in the chicken, apple and
banana. Add more lemon juice
and adjust the seasoning. Pile on a
bed of rice, or combine with the

rice. Garnish with watercress.

BEEF SALAD
serves 4

8 oz. (1 cup) long grain rice
2-3 tomatoes, skinned and
    sliced
8 oz. cold, cooked beef, thinl
    sliced and cut in strips
1 tbsp. finely chopped onion
1 level tsp. made mustard
3 tbsps. French dressing
1 lettuce, washed and
    separated
4 tomatoes, sliced, to garnis

Cook the rice in boiling, salt
water for about 12 minutes a
allow to cool. Mix with the
matoes, meat and onion.
Add the mustard to the Fren
dressing and stir into the sala
ingredients. Serve with the lettu
and remaining sliced tomatoes.

CHEESE SALAD BOWL
serves 4

1 lettuce, washed and
    separated
bunch of watercress, washed
    and trimmed
$\frac{1}{2}$ lb. tomatoes, skinned and
    sliced
4 oz. small, new potatoes,
    boiled and diced
6-8 oz. Cheddar cheese, dice
$\frac{1}{4}$ pint ($\frac{5}{8}$ cup) mayonnaise
a little made mustard
chopped chives or parsley

Line a salad bowl with lettuce ar

watercress. Combine the tomatoes, ...otatoes and cheese. Mix the ...ayonnaise with a little mustard ...nd combine with the potato ...ixture. Put into the centre of the ...alad bowl and sprinkle with ...hives or parsley.

...ALAMI SALAD
...rves 4

...oz. Danish salami, thinly
   sliced
...oz. Samsoe cheese, diced
...rench dressing
...mall bunch of radishes,
   trimmed and sliced
...clove of garlic, skinned and
   cut
...lettuce, washed and roughly
   shredded
...cucumber (or 1 small, ridge
   cucumber), thinly sliced
...unch of watercress, washed
   and trimmed
...oz. Gruyère cheese, thinly
   sliced

...ut 8 slices of salami to one side ...nd cut the rest into strips, using ...cissors. Toss the Samsöe cheese ...n 2 tablespoons of the dressing, ...ix in a bowl with the salami and ...adishes. Add the garlic. Leave for ...little time for the flavours to ...ellow.
...ut half way through each slice of ...he reserved salami and curl into ...ones.
...o serve, remove the garlic, lightly ...oss the lettuce, cucumber and ...alf the watercress in a little ...ressing. Arrange in a shallow flat ...ish. Tuck in the slices of Gruyère ...ound the edge and pile the ...ressed cheese and salami mixture ...n the centre. Surround with ...alami cones and watercress sprigs.

...IQUANT EGG SALAD ...ITH YOGHOURT ...RESSING
...rves 4

For dressing:
...pint (1¼ cups) low-fat
   natural yohourt
...level tsp. paprika pepper
...level tsp. sugar
...tbsp. lemon juice
...tbsp. orange juice
...epper
...tbsp. finely chopped parsley

...head of celery, scrubbed
   and finely sliced
...eggs, hard-boiled and
   sliced
...carrots, peeled and grated
...few radishes, washed and
   sliced
...cucumber (or 1 whole,
   small, ridge cucumber)

Salami salad, served continental style on a wooden board

For the dressing combine the natural yoghourt with the paprika pepper, sugar, strained lemon and orange juices, a little pepper and the finely chopped parsley.
Fold the celery through half the dressing and spoon into a salad bowl. Arrange the eggs on top, cover with the grated carrot and surround with sliced radishes and cucumber.
Spoon the remaining yoghourt dressing over the top. Chill before serving.

TIVOLI SALAD
serves 8

1 large crisp lettuce
2 12-oz. cans pork and ham,
   or equivalent in thickly
   sliced cooked ham
8 oz. Samsoe cheese
11-oz. can whole sweet corn
   kernels
3 tsps. finely chopped onion
chopped chives to garnish

For dressing:
4 tbsps. mayonnaise
2 tbsps. cream
1½-2 tbsps. lemon juice
freshly ground black pepper

Wash and separate the lettuce. Cut the meat and cheese in thick slices, then into small cubes. Drain the corn and add to the meat and cheese, with the onion.
Blend the mayonnaise and cream with lemon juice to sharpen; season with pepper. Fold the mayonnaise mixture through the meat and cheese.
Arrange a bed of lettuce on a dish and pile the mixture on top. Garnish with chopped chives.

SIDE SALADS

DUTCH SALAD
serves 6

1½ tbsps. lemon juice
3 firm, green, eating apples
8 oz. Edam cheese, rinded
7-oz. can pimientos (sweet
   red peppers), drained
¾ lb. spinach

For dressing:
1½ tbsps. cider vinegar
3 tbsps. corn oil
salt and freshly ground black
   pepper
½ level tsp. dry mustard
½ level tsp. caster sugar

Put the lemon juice in a bowl. Dice the apples, discarding the core; turn at once in the lemon juice. Cut the cheese into dice the same size as the apples. Cut the pimiento into small strips. Carefully wash the spinach and remove all the stems; roughly break the drained leaves into manageable pieces.
Whisk together the dressing ingredients and toss the spinach in the dressing until it glistens. Drain, and arrange round the edge of the salad bowl. Toss the apple, cheese and pimiento in the remaining dressing and pile in the centre of the spinach.

TUNA-FILLED TOMATOES
serves 4

4 large tomatoes
2 oz. butter
1 onion, skinned and chopped
4 oz. button mushrooms,
   wiped and sliced
7-oz. can tuna, drained and
   flaked
2 tbsps. chopped parsley

Remove the top from each tomato, cutting in a zig-zag fashion with a small, sharp-pointed knife. Using a teaspoon, scoop out the soft core and seeds and discard. Put the tomato cases on a baking sheet. Heat the butter in a frying pan, add the onion and cook until soft, without colouring. Add the mushrooms, continue cooking for a few minutes. Add the flaked tuna, together with the parsley. Mix well together and divide the filling between the tomatoes. Cover with kitchen foil and bake in the centre of the oven at 350°F. (mark 4) for 20–30 minutes.

BEAN AND CELERY SALAD
serves 4

½ lb. French beans, trimmed
   and halved
1 celery heart, scrubbed and
   finely sliced
½ dill cucumber, roughly
   chopped
7½-oz. can butter beans,
   drained
3–4 tbsps. well-seasoned
   French dressing
chopped chives to garnish

Cook the French beans in boiling salted water for about 5 minutes, drain and leave to cool. Toss the celery, dill cucumber, butter beans and French beans in enough dressing to moisten them.
Chill slightly and serve sprinkled with chopped chives.

SPINACH SLAW
serves 4

½ lb. fresh spinach
6 oz. white cabbage, washed
   and trimmed
2 oz. seedless raisins
4 tbsps. lemon juice
3 tbsps. salad oil
salt and freshly ground black
   pepper
caster sugar
1 dessert apple, cored and
   chopped but not peeled

Remove any coarse stems from the spinach and wash thoroughly; pat the leaves dry on a clean cloth. Finely shred the spinach and cabbage. Soak the raisins in half the lemon juice until soft and swollen, then add to the spinach and cabbage.
Whisk together the oil, remaining lemon juice, salt, pepper and sugar to taste. Add the apple and pour over the spinach and cabbage. Blend with 2 forks until the vegetables glisten with the dressing.

TOMATO AND ANCHOVY SALAD

serves 6

rind of ½ a lemon
3 tbsps. lemon juice
3 tbsps. salad oil
½ level tbsp. caster sugar
salt and freshly ground black
  pepper
2-oz. can anchovy fillets,
  drained and finely chopped
1½ oz. shallots, skinned and
  chopped
1½ lb. tomatoes, skinned and
  sliced

Using a potato peeler, thinly pare the lemon rind, free of the white pith, and chop it. Whisk together the chopped rind, juice, oil, sugar and seasoning. Add the anchovies and shallots. Turn the tomatoes in this dressing and leave in a cool place for 1–2 hours.

SALADE BASQUE

serves 4

6 eggs, hard-boiled and sliced
7-oz. can tuna, drained and
  flaked
2 dill cucumbers, finely sliced
8 tomatoes, skinned and
  sliced
2-oz. can anchovy fillets,
  drained
3–4 tbsps. salad oil
1 tbsp. wine vinegar
1 level tsp. French mustard
2 level tbsps. tomato ketchup
1 level tsp. dried mixed herbs

Layer the sliced eggs, flaked tuna, cucumber and tomatoes in a salad bowl. Split the anchovy fillets in half lengthwise and arrange in a lattice over the tomato layer.
Whisk the remaining ingredients together to make a dressing and pour over the salad. Chill.

RED CABBAGE AND SWEET CORN SALAD

serves 8

1½ lb. red cabbage
⅛ pint (⅓ cup) French dressing
½ a cucumber (or 1 small
  ridge cucumber), diced
salt and freshly ground black
  pepper
11-oz. can sweet corn kernels,
  drained
¼ level tsp. finely grated
  lemon rind
2 tsps. clear honey

Quarter the cabbage, discarding any coarse stems, and shred the leaves very finely. Place in a large bowl with the dressing, toss and leave for 2 hours.
Put the diced cucumber in a bowl, season with salt and pepper and leave for 2 hours. Drain off any excess moisture, and add the cucumber, corn, lemon rind and honey to the cabbage. Toss thoroughly in the dressing.

RICE SALAD, GREEK STYLE

serves 12

1 lb. (2 cups) long grain rice
⅛ pint (⅓ cup) French dressing
4 oz. onions, skinned and
  finely chopped
½ a green pepper (capsicum),
  seeded and chopped
½ a red pepper, seeded and
  chopped
2 sticks celery, scrubbed and
  finely sliced
7-oz. can pimientos (sweet
  red peppers), drained and
  chopped
stoned black olives to garnish

Cook the rice in boiling, salted water for about 12 minutes. Drain, and while the rice is still hot, pour the dressing over and mix well. Add the onion and peppers, celery and pimientos. Brush a 2½-pint plain ring mould with oil, carefully spoon in the rice mixture. Cool, then turn out on to a flat plate just before serving. Garnish with olives.

SALAD DRESSINGS

FRENCH DRESSING

¼ level tsp. salt
⅛ level tsp. pepper
¼ level tsp. dry mustard
¼ level tsp. sugar
1 tbsp. vinegar or lemon juice
2–3 tbsps. salad oil

Put the salt, pepper, mustard and sugar in a bowl, add the vinegar and stir until well blended. Whisk in the oil gradually with a fork.
The oil separates out on standing, so if necessary whisk the dressing again immediately before use. Alternatively, make a larger quantity and store it in a salad cream bottle, shaking it up vigorously just before serving.
Note : The proportion of oil to vinegar varies with individual taste, but use vinegar sparingly. Wine, tarragon or other herb flavoured vinegar may be used.

MAYONNAISE

1 egg yolk
½ level tsp. dry mustard
½ level tsp. salt
¼ level tsp. pepper
½ level tsp. sugar
¼ pint (⅝ cup) salad oil
1 tbsp. vinegar or lemon juice

Celery and beans make a sophisticated side salad

Put the egg yolk into a basin with the seasonings and sugar. Mix thoroughly, then add the oil drop by drop, stirring briskly with a wooden spoon the whole time, or using a whisk, until the sauce is thick and smooth. If it becomes too thick, add a little of the vinegar. When all the oil has been incorporated, add the vinegar gradually and mix thoroughly.

FOAMY MAYONNAISE

2 egg yolks
salt and pepper
¼ pint (⅝ cup) salad oil
2 tbsps. lemon juice
1 egg white, stiffly whisked

Cream the egg yolks and seasonings and add the oil drop by drop, stirring hard all the time, until the mayonnaise is thick and smooth, then stir in the lemo[n] juice.
Put in a cool place until require[d] just before serving, fold in th[e] egg white.

THOUSAND ISLANDS MAYONNAISE

¼ pint (⅝ cup) mayonnaise
1 tbsp. finely chopped stuffed
  olives
1 tsp. finely chopped onion
1 egg, hard-boiled and
  chopped
1 tbsp. finely chopped green
  pepper (capsicum)
1 tsp. chopped parsley
1 level tsp. tomato paste

Mix all the ingredients togethe[r] until evenly combined.
This is a popular American sala[d] dressing.

A moulded rice salad, with onion, peppers, celery and olives

ork and bean salad

SAVOURY SAUCES

A good sauce can make a dish. It enhances the flavour of the food and adds new dimensions of texture and moisture. A sauce is not difficult to make, either, once the basic principles are mastered – the right amount of flour to liquid and careful regulation of the heat while blending are probably the two factors that have the greatest bearing on the texture of the finished sauce.

Most savoury sauces are thickened with either flour or egg. Flour sauces are based on a roux, made by melting the butter (or other fat), adding the flour, mixing thoroughly and cooking until they are well combined. For a brown sauce the roux is cooked until it is an even golden brown colour; the roux for a white sauce is not allowed to colour. The liquid is then added gradually and the sauce is stirred and cooked after each addition until it reaches the required consistency. (Beginners will find it easier if they take the pan off the heat to add the liquid.)

For white sauces the liquid used is usually milk or milk and white stock. For brown sauces, meat stock or vegetable water give a good flavour (stock made from a bouillon cube is adequate for most

but beware of over-seasoning) and for fish sauces you can use the bones from the fish to make a stock, combining this with milk for a sauce.

If you are entertaining, it helps the last minute rush if you can make the sauce earlier in the day – but the one thing worse than a lumpy sauce is one with a skin on top. If you make a sauce well in advance, press a piece of damp greaseproof paper on to its surface to stop this happening, and reheat it when needed. The basic white sauce recipes given here show how to vary the proportion of flour and fat to liquid to give sauces of different consistencies for different purposes.

WHITE SAUCES

1 *Pouring consistency*
¾ oz. butter
¾ oz. (approx. 2 level tbsps.) flour
½ pint (1¼ cups) milk or milk and stock
salt and pepper

Melt the fat, add the flour and stir with a wooden spoon until smooth. Cook over a gentle heat for 2–3

minutes, stirring until the mixture begins to bubble. Remove from the heat and add the liquid gradually, beating and stirring rapidly after each addition to prevent lumps forming. Bring the sauce to the boil, stirring continuously, and when it has thickened, cook for a further 1–2 minutes. Add salt and pepper to taste.

2 *Coating consistency*
1 oz. butter
1 oz. (3 level tbsps.) flour
½ pint (1¼ cups) milk or milk and stock
salt and pepper

Make the sauce as for pouring consistency.

3 *Binding (panada) consistency*
2 oz. butter
2 oz. (6 level tbsps.) flour
½ pint (1¼ cups) milk or milk and stock
salt and pepper

Melt the fat, add the flour and stir well. Cook gently for 2–3 minutes, stirring. Add the liquid gradually, beating well. Bring to the boil, stirring all the time, and cook for 1–2 minutes after it has thickened. Add salt and pepper to taste. This thick sauce is used for binding mixtures such as croquettes.

There are many variations on basic white sauce – those give here are perhaps the most popula These may also be made wit béchamel.

MUSHROOM SAUCE Was and slice 2–3 oz. button mush rooms. Fry in ½–1 oz. butter unt soft but not coloured and fold int ½ pint (1¼ cups) white sauc Season to taste.
Serve with fish, meat and eggs.

PARSLEY SAUCE Make ½ pin (1¼ cups) white sauce, using ha milk and half stock, if availabl When the sauce thickens, stir i 1–2 tablespoons chopped parsle and a little salt and pepper. Don reboil or the parsley may turn th sauce green.
Serve with fish, boiled or braise bacon, or vegetables.

SHRIMP SAUCE Simmer th rind of 1 lemon and a bay leaf fo 5 minutes in ½ pint (1¼ cups) liqui from which the sauce is to be mad (milk or milk and fish stock). Strai and use to make the white sauc When it thickens, stir in 2 o frozen, canned or potted shrimp season to taste and reheat for 1– minutes. Serve with fish.

ANCHOVY SAUCE
Make ½ pint (1¼ cups) white sauce with half milk and half fish stock. When it thickens, remove it from the heat and stir in 1–2 teaspoons anchovy essence (to taste), then a squeeze of lemon juice. (Anchovy essence is very salty and you will not need extra seasoning.) If you wish to tint the sauce a dull pink, add a few drops of red colouring. Serve with fish.

CAPER SAUCE
Make the white sauce using ½ pint (1¼ cups) milk, or ¼ pint (⅝ cup) milk and ¼ pint cooking liquid from the meat. When the sauce thickens, stir in 1 tablespoon capers, and 1–2 teaspoons vinegar from the capers or lemon juice. Season well. Reheat for 1–2 minutes.
Serve with boiled mutton or lamb.

BECHAMEL SAUCE
A classic, rich, white sauce

½ pint (1¼ cups) milk
1 shallot, skinned and sliced (or a small piece of onion, skinned)
a small piece of carrot, peeled and cut up
½ a stick of celery, scrubbed and cut up
½ a bay leaf
3 peppercorns
1 oz. butter
1 oz. (¼ cup) flour
salt and pepper

Put the milk, vegetables and flavourings in a saucepan and bring slowly to the boil. Remove from the heat, cover and leave to infuse for about 15 minutes. Strain the liquid and use this with the butter and flour to make a white sauce. Season to taste before serving.

AURORE SAUCE
½ pint (1¼ cups) béchamel sauce
1–2 level tbsps. tomato paste
1 oz. butter
salt and pepper

Make the sauce and when it has thickened stir in the tomato paste. Add the butter a little at a time and season to taste.
Serve with egg dishes, chicken or fish.

MORNAY SAUCE
½ pint (1¼ cups) béchamel sauce
2 oz. Parmesan, Gruyère or mature Cheddar cheese, grated
paprika pepper
salt and pepper

Chicken chaudfroid, garnished with radishes, angelica and lemon rind

White sauce, made to a pouring consistency

Make the béchamel or plain white sauce and when it thickens, remove from the heat and stir in the cheese and seasonings. Do not reheat or the cheese will become overcooked and stringy.
Serve with eggs, chicken or fish.

WHITE CHAUDFROID SAUCE
¼ pint (⅝ cup) normal strength liquid aspic made from aspic jelly powder
¼ oz. (1½ level tsps.) powdered gelatine
½ pint (1¼ cups) béchamel sauce
⅛–¼ pint (⅜–⅝ cup) single cream
salt and pepper

While the aspic is still warm stand it, in a basin, in a pan of hot water. Sprinkle in the gelatine and stir until it has dissolved, taking care not to overheat the mixture. Stir in the warm béchamel sauce, beat well and add the cream. Adjust the seasoning.
Strain the sauce and leave to cool, stirring frequently so that it remains smooth and glossy. Use when at the consistency of thick cream, for coating chicken, fish or eggs.

SOUBISE SAUCE
½ lb. onions, skinned and chopped
1 oz. butter
a little stock or water
½ pint (1¼ cups) béchamel sauce
salt and pepper

Cook the onions gently in the butter and a small amount of stock or water until soft—about 10–15 minutes. Sieve and stir the purée into the sauce, with seasoning to taste; reheat for 1–2 minutes.
Serve with lamb or veal.

VELOUTE SAUCE
¾ oz. butter
¾ oz. (2 level tbsps. approx.) flour
¾ pint (1⅞ cups) chicken or other light stock
2–3 tbsps. single cream
a few drops of lemon juice
salt and pepper

Melt the butter, stir in the flour and cook gently, stirring well, until the mixture is a pale fawn colour. Stir in the stock gradually, bring to the boil, stirring all the time. Simmer until slightly reduced and syrupy. Remove from the heat and add the cream, lemon juice and seasoning.
Serve with poultry, fish and veal.

TOMATO SAUCE
(made from fresh tomatoes)

1 small onion, skinned and chopped
1 small carrot, peeled and chopped
1 oz. butter
½ oz. flour
1 lb. cooking tomatoes, quartered
½ pint (1¼ cups) chicken stock (made from a cube)
½ a bay leaf
1 clove
1 level tsp. sugar
salt and pepper
2 level tsps. tomato paste (optional)
1–4 tbsps. white wine or sherry (optional)

Melt the butter in a pan and lightly fry the onion and carrot in the butter for 5 minutes. Stir in the flour and add the tomatoes, the stock and flavourings. Bring to the boil, cover and simmer for about 30 minutes, or until the vegetables are cooked. Sieve, reheat and reseason if necessary.
Tomato paste may be added to give a fuller flavour and a better colour. The wine or sherry may be added just before serving. Adjust seasoning after rather than before adding these optional ingredients.
Serve with croquettes, cutlets, réchauffés or any savoury dish.

TOMATO SAUCE
(made from canned tomatoes)

½ an onion, skinned and chopped
2 rashers of bacon, rinded and chopped
½ oz. butter
½ oz. flour
15-oz. can of tomatoes
1 clove
½ a bay leaf
a few sprigs of rosemary (or 1 level tsp. mixed dried herbs)
salt and pepper
pinch of sugar (optional)

Melt the butter in a pan and fry the onion and the bacon in the butter for 5 minutes. Stir in the flour and gradually add the tomatoes, also the flavourings and seasonings. Simmer gently for 15 minutes, then sieve and re-season if necessary. Add sugar if the flavour is too acid.
Serve with made-up meat dishes such as rissoles or stuffed peppers, and with cutlets.

HOLLANDAISE SAUCE

2 tbsps. wine or tarragon
    vinegar
1 tbsp. water
2 egg yolks
3–4 oz. butter
salt and pepper

Put the vinegar and water in a small pan and boil until reduced to about 1 tablespoon. Cool slightly.

Put the egg yolks in a small basin and stir in the vinegar. Put over a pan of hot water and heat gently, stirring all the time, until the egg mixture thickens (never let the water go above simmering point or the sauce will curdle). Divide the butter into small pieces and gradually whisk into the sauce; season to taste.

If the sauce is too sharp add a little more butter–it should be slightly piquant, almost thick enough to hold its shape and warm rather than hot when served.

Serve with salmon and other fish dishes, asparagus or broccoli. (The vinegar may be replaced by lemon juice–this tends to give a slightly blander sauce.)

MAYONNAISE

makes about ⅓ pint (¾ cup)

1 egg yolk
½ level tsp. dry mustard
½ level tsp. salt
¼ level tsp. pepper
½ level tsp. sugar
¼ pint (⅝ cup) oil
1 tbsp. white vinegar

Make sure that all ingredients are at room temperature. Put the egg yolks into a basin with the seasonings and sugar. Mix thoroughly, then add the oil drop by drop, beating briskly with a wooden spoon the whole time, or use a whisk. Continue adding oil until the sauce is thick and smooth –if it becomes too thick too quickly, add a little of the vinegar. When all the oil had been added, add the vinegar gradually and mix thoroughly.

TARTARE SAUCE

¼ pint (⅝ cup) mayonnaise
1 tsp. chopped tarragon or
    chives
2 tsps. chopped capers
2 tsps. chopped gherkins
2 tsps. chopped celery
1 tbsp. lemon juice or
    tarragon vinegar

Mix all the ingredients well, then leave the sauce to stand at least 1 hour before serving, to allow the flavours to mellow. Serve with fish.

Add oil very gradually for a mayonnaise, whisking all the time

BROWN SAUCES

GRAVY

A rich, brown gravy is served with all roast joints–thin with roast beef and thick with other meats. If the gravy is properly made in the roasting tin, there should be no need to use extra colouring. Remove the joint from the tin and keep it hot while making the gravy.

THIN GRAVY

Pour the fat very slowly from the tin, draining it off carefully from one corner and leaving the sediment behind. Season well with salt and pepper and add ½ pint (1¼ cups) hot vegetable water or stock (stock made from a bouillon cube is adequate but extra seasoning will not be required). Stir thoroughly with a wooden spoon until all the sediment is scraped from the tin and the gravy is a rich brown. Return the tin to the heat and boil for 2–3 minutes. Serve very hot.

This is the 'correct' way of making thin gravy, but some people prefer to make a version of the thick gravy given below, using half the amount of flour.

THICK GRAVY

Leave 2 tablespoons of the fat in the tin, stir in 1 level tablespoon flour (preferably shaking it from a flour dredger, to give a smoother result). Blend well and cook over the heat until it turns brown, stirring continuously. Carefully mix in ½ pint (1¼ cups) hot vegetable water or stock and boil for 2–3 minutes. Season well, strain and serve very hot.

ESPAGNOLE SAUCE

This classic brown sauce is used as a base for many savoury sauces

1 oz. streaky bacon, chopped
1 oz. butter
1 shallot, skinned and
    chopped (or a small piece
    of onion, chopped)
1 oz. mushroom stalks,
    washed and chopped
1 small carrot, peeled and
    chopped
¾–1 oz. (2–3 level tbsps.) flour
½ pint (1¼ cups) beef stock
a bouquet garni
2 level tbsps. tomato paste
salt and pepper
1 tbsp. sherry (optional)

Melt the butter in a pan and fry the bacon in the butter for 2–3

minutes. Add the vegetables and fry for a further 3–5 minutes, or until lightly browned. Stir in the flour, mix well and continue frying very slowly until it turns brown. Remove from the heat and gradually add the stock (which if necessary can be made from a stock cube). Stir after each addition.

Return the pan to the heat and stir until the sauce thickens. Add the bouquet garni, tomato paste, salt and pepper. Reduce the heat, cover and allow to simmer very gently for 1 hour, stirring from time to time to prevent it sticking (an asbestos mat under the pan is a good idea). Alternatively, cook in the centre of the oven at 300°F. (mark 1–2) for 1½–2 hours. Strain the sauce, reheat and skim off any fat, using a metal spoon. Re-season if necessary.

If required, add the sherry just before the sauce is served, to give extra flavour.

Serve with beef dishes.

DEMI-GLACE SAUCE

¼ pint (⅝ cup) clear beef gravy
    or jellied stock from under
    beef dripping
½ pint (1¼ cups) espagnole
    sauce

Add the gravy to the sauce and boil (uncovered) until the sauce has a glossy appearance and will coat the back of the spoon with a shiny glaze.

Serve with dishes made from beef.

BROWN CHAUDFROID SAUCE

¼ pint (⅝ cup) normal strength
    liquid aspic, made from
    aspic jelly powder
¼ oz. (1½ level tsps.) powdered
    gelatine
¾ pint (1⅞ cups) espagnole
    sauce
Madeira, sherry or port to
    taste
salt and pepper

While the aspic is still warm stand it, in a basin, in a pan of hot water. Sprinkle in the gelatine and stir over a gentle heat until it dissolves. Warm the espagnole sauce and beat in the aspic and gelatine mixture. Add Madeira, sherry or port to taste and extra salt and pepper if necessary.

Strain the sauce and allow to cool, beating it from time to time so that it remains smooth and glossy. When it reaches the consistency of thick cream, use to coat game, duck or cutlets (see illustration for chicken chaudfroid, previous page).

SWEET SAUCES

Add a delicious sweet sauce to your dessert, to give it new dimensions. Whether you are serving a hot, steamy pudding or a smooth, icy sorbet a sauce will provide added flavour and texture. For a quick dessert, nothing can beat a bought ice cream with a helping of your own favourite sauce.

A true custard sauce, made with eggs, for fruit sweets

CUSTARD SAUCE

makes ½ pint (1¼ cups)

1½ level tbsps. custard powder
1½–2 level tbsps. sugar
½ pint (1¼ cups) milk

Blend the custard powder and sugar with a little cold milk to a smooth cream. Boil the rest of the milk and stir into the blended mixture. Return the sauce to the boil, stirring all the time until it thickens.
Serve hot, with puddings or pies.

EGG CUSTARD SAUCE

makes approx. ½ pint (1¼ cups)

1½ eggs or 3 egg yolks
1 level tbsp. sugar
½ pint (1¼ cups) milk
a few strips of thinly pared lemon rind

Whisk the eggs and sugar lightly. Warm the milk and lemon rind and leave to infuse for 10 minutes. Pour the milk on to the eggs and strain the mixture into the top of a double boiler or into a thick-based saucepan. Stir over a very gentle heat until the sauce thickens and lightly coats the back of the spoon. Serve hot or cold, with fruit sweets.

CHOCOLATE SAUCE

makes ½ pint (1¼ cups)

level tbsp. cornflour
level tbsp. cocoa powder
level tbsps. sugar
pint (1¼ cups) milk
a knob of butter

Blend the cornflour, cocoa and sugar with 1 tablespoon of the milk. Heat the remaining milk with the butter until boiling and pour on to the blended mixture, stirring all the time to prevent lumps forming. Return the mixture to the pan and bring to the boil, stirring until it thickens; cook for a further 1–2 minutes. Serve with steamed or baked sponge puddings.
Note: The cornflour and cocoa may be replaced by 2 level tablespoons chocolate blancmange powder.

JAM SAUCE

makes approx. ¼ pint (⅝ cup)

3 rounded tbsps. jam
¼ pint (⅝ cup) water or fruit juice
2 level tsps. arrowroot
2 tbsps. cold water
a squeeze of lemon juice (optional)

Warm the jam and water or fruit juice and simmer for 5 minutes. Blend the arrowroot and cold water to a smooth cream and stir into the jam mixture. Return the sauce to the heat, stirring, until it thickens and clears. Add the lemon juice and sieve into a sauce boat.
Serve hot with steamed or baked puddings, or cold over ice cream.
Note: A thicker sauce is made by just melting the jam on its own over a gentle heat and adding a little lemon juice.

SYRUP SAUCE

makes approx. ¼ pint (⅝ cup)

3–4 tbsps. golden syrup
3 tbsps. water
juice of ½ lemon

Warm the syrup and water, stir well and simmer, uncovered, for 2–3 minutes; add the lemon juice. Serve with steamed or baked sponge puddings.

FRUIT SAUCE

makes approx. ½ pint (1¼ cups)

15-oz. can fruit (e.g. apricots), drained
2 level tsps. arrowroot
squeeze of lemon juice or 1 tbsp. rum, sherry or fruit liqueur (optional)

Sieve the drained fruit or purée in a blender, make up to ½ pint (1¼ cups) with juice and heat until boiling. Blend the arrowroot with a little more juice until it is a smooth cream, then stir in the puréed fruit. Return the mixture to the pan and heat gently, continuing to stir, until the sauce thickens and clears. A squeeze of lemon juice or 1 tablespoon rum, sherry or a fruit liqueur may be added just before the sauce is served.
Good with meringue sweets, cold soufflés, hot baked puddings, steamed puddings and ice cream.

LEMON OR ORANGE SAUCE

makes ½ pint (1¼ cups)

grated rind and juice of 1 large lemon or orange
1 level tbsp. cornflour
2 level tbsps. sugar
1 egg yolk (optional)

Make up the fruit rind and juice with water to give ½ pint (1¼ cups). Blend the cornflour and sugar with a little of the liquid to a smooth cream. Boil the remaining liquid and stir into the mixture. Return it to the pan and bring to the boil, stirring until the sauce thickens and clears. Cool, add the egg yolk (if used) and reheat, stirring, but do not boil.
Serve hot or cold, as for fruit sauce.

BUTTERSCOTCH NUT SAUCE

makes approx. ¼ pint (⅝ cup)

1 tbsp. golden syrup
1 level tbsp. brown sugar
½ oz. butter
2 level tsps. custard powder
¼ pint (⅝ cup) water
lemon essence
2 tbsps. nuts, chopped

Put the syrup, sugar and butter in a pan and heat gently until melted. Remove from the heat and mix in the previously blended custard powder and water. Bring the mixture to the boil, stirring, and mix in a little essence and the nuts. Serve hot or cold, with baked or steamed puddings.

MOUSSELINE SAUCE

makes approx. ¼ pint (⅝ cup)

1 egg
1 egg yolk
1½ oz. sugar
1 tbsp. sherry
4 tbsps. single cream

Place all the ingredients in a basin over a pan of boiling water and whisk with a rotary whisk or electric mixer until pale and frothy and of a thick creamy consistency. Serve at once, over light steamed or baked puddings, fruit, fruit sweets or Christmas pudding.

SABAYON SAUCE

makes approx. ¼ pint (⅝ cup)

2 oz. (¼ cup) sugar
4 tbsps. water
2 egg yolks
rind of ½ lemon, grated
juice of 1 lemon
2 tbsps. rum or sherry
2 tbsps. single cream

Dissolve the sugar in the water over gentle heat and boil for 2–3 minutes, until syrupy. Pour on to the beaten yolks and whisk until pale and thick. Add the lemon rind, lemon juice and rum or sherry, and whisk for a further few minutes. Fold in the cream and chill well.
Serve with cold fruit sweets.

RUM BUTTER

3 oz. butter
3 oz. (½ cup) soft brown sugar
2–3 tbsps. rum
grated rind of ½ a lemon
1 tsp. lemon juice

Cream the butter and beat in the other ingredients carefully, as for brandy butter.

Serve with Christmas pudding and mince pies.

BRANDY BUTTER

3 oz. butter
3 oz. (⅜ cup) caster or icing
    sugar
2–3 tbsps. brandy

Cream the butter until pale and soft. Beat in the sugar gradually and add the brandy a few drops at a time, taking care not to allow the mixture to curdle. The finished sauce should be pale and frothy. Pile it up in a small dish and leave in a cool place to harden before serving.
Traditionally served with Christmas pudding and mince pies.

CHOCOLATE SAUCE

2 oz. plain (dark) chocolate
½ oz. butter
1 tbsp. milk
1 tsp. vanilla essence

Melt the chocolate and butter in a basin standing in a pan of hot water. Stir in the milk and vanilla essence and serve straight away, over ice cream.

COFFEE SAUCE

4 oz. (⅔ cup) Demerara or
    granulated sugar
2 tbsps. water
½ pint (1¼ cups) strong black
    coffee

Put the sugar and water in a heavy-based pan and dissolve over a gentle heat, without stirring. Bring to the boil and boil rapidly until the syrup becomes golden in colour. Add the coffee and stir until the caramel has dissolved. Boil for a few minutes, until syrupy. Allow to cool, and serve poured over ice cream.

MELBA SAUCE

4 level tbsps. red-currant
    jelly
3 oz. (⅜ cup) sugar
¼ pint (⅝ cup) raspberry purée
    (from ½ lb. raspberries or a
    15-oz. can)
2 level tsps. arrowroot
1 tbsp. cold water

Mix the jelly, sugar and raspberry purée and bring to the boil. Blend the arrowroot with the cold water to a smooth cream, stir in a little of the raspberry mixture, return the sauce to the pan and bring to the boil, stirring with a wooden spoon until it thickens and clears. Strain and cool.
This sauce is traditionally served

Add a little extra to ice cream with a rich, home-made sauce

Brandy butter is a traditional 'hard' sauce for mince pies

over fresh peaches and ice cream.

APRICOT SAUCE

Mix some sieved apricot jam with a little lemon juice and 2 teaspoons sherry; pour it over ice cream and sprinkle with dessicated coconut or other decoration.

BUTTERSCOTCH SAUCE

1 oz. butter
1 oz. (⅙ cup) soft light brown
    sugar
1 tbsp. golden syrup
1 oz. nuts, chopped
a squeeze of lemon juice
    (optional)

Warm the butter, sugar and syrup until well blended. Boil for 1 minute and stir in the nuts and lemon juice. Serve straight away, over ice cream.

PECAN RUM SAUCE
makes ¾ pint (1⅞ cups)

6 oz. (1 cup) soft brown sugar
2 level tsps. instant coffee
6 tbsps. single cream or
    evaporated milk
1 oz. butter
1 tbsp. golden syrup
1 tbsp. rum
2 oz. shelled pecans (or
    walnuts)

Combine in a saucepan the sugar, coffee, cream or evaporated milk, butter and golden syrup. Cook over a low heat to dissolve the sugar, bring to the boil and boil gently, stirring, for 2–3 minutes, or until thickened. Stir in the rum and nuts. Serve either cold or warm, with vanilla ice cream.
This sauce may be bottled and stored for a short time.

CHERRY SAUCE
makes approx. ¾ pint (1⅞ cups)

½ lb. black or dark red
    cherries
2 oz. (¼ cup) sugar
2 level tsps. arrowroot
almond essence
2 tsps. cherry brandy

Stone the cherries and cook in a little water with the sugar until fairly tender. Drain the fruit; make the juice up to ½ pint (1¼ cups) with water if necessary. Blend the arrowroot with a little juice, return it with the rest of the measured juice to the pan, and cook until transparent. Pour over the cherries and add a little almond essence and the cherry brandy.
Allow to cool. Serve with ice cream.

FLAMBE SAUCE
makes approx. ⅓ pint

8-oz. can fruit cocktail
grated rind of ½ lemon
3 oz. (⅜ cup) sugar
1½ oz. butter
3 level tsps. cornflour
2 tbsps. brandy

Gently heat the fruit cocktail with the grated lemon rind, sugar, butter and cornflour, stirring until the mixture thickens. Add the brandy, but do not stir. Ignite the brandy and spoon into the sauce. Pour the sauce at once over vanilla ice cream.

MARSHMALLOW SAUCE
makes ½ pint (1¼ cups)

4 oz. (½ cup) sugar
3 tbsps. water
8 marshmallows, cut up
    small
1 egg white
½ tsp. vanilla essence
red colouring (optional)

Dissolve the sugar in the water and boil for 5 minutes. Add the marshmallows and stir the mixture until they have melted. Whip the egg white stiffly and gradually fold in the marshmallow mixture. Flavour with vanilla and if you like, add a drop or two of colouring to tint it pink. Serve at once, over coffee or chocolate ice cream.

HONEY SAUCE

2 oz. butter
1½ level tsps. cornflour
4–6 oz. clear honey

Melt the butter in a pan and stir in the cornflour. Gradually add the honey. Bring to the boil and cook for a minute or two.

HOT DESSERTS

Brown sugared peaches with soured cream

ALMOND FRUIT PUFF
serves 6
For filling :
2 oz. butter
2 oz. (¼ cup) caster sugar
½ tsp. almond essence
1 egg, beaten
1 oz. (1½ tbsps.) flour
2 oz. (½ cup) ground almonds
2 oz. maraschino cherries,
   halved
8-oz. can prunes, drained
8-oz. can sliced peaches,
   drained
8-oz. can apricot halves,
   drained
1 small apple, peeled and
   chopped
1 lb. frozen puff pastry,
   thawed
1 egg, beaten

Cream the butter and sugar until
pale and fluffy. Beat in the essence,
egg, flour and almonds and then
lightly fold in the cherries, canned
fruits and apple.
Roll out a quarter of the pastry
very thinly and trim to an 8-in.
diameter circle. Place on a baking
sheet, prick well with a fork and
brush round the rim with beaten
egg. Divide the remaining pastry
in half. Roll out one piece and
trim it into a 9-in. circle, for the

lid. Roll out the remainder into a
strip 1 in. wide by about 14 in.
long. Divide this strip in half and
lay the strips over the egg-glazed
rim to form a 'wall'. Leave pastry
in a cool place to relax for 30
minutes.
Pile the fruit mixture inside the
'wall'. Brush the 'wall' with beaten
egg, place the pastry lid on top and
press the edges together lightly.
Roll out the trimmings thinly and
cut into thin, narrow strips. Arrange on the lid like the spokes of a
wheel and glaze the pastry with
beaten egg.
Bake at 450°F. (mark 8) for 15
minutes. Cover the puff with
dampened greaseproof paper and
cook for a further 45 minutes at
350°F. (mark 4). Serve warm in
wedges with whipped cream.

BROWN-SUGARED
PEACHES WITH SOURED
CREAM
serves 4

4 large fresh peaches
2 level tbsps. soft brown sugar
½ level tsp. powdered
   cinnamon
½ pint (1¼ cups) soured cream
4 level tbsps. caster sugar

Heat the grill before starting.

Dip the peaches into boiling water,
count 10, then plunge them into
cold water. Skin, stone and slice
them. Arrange the slices evenly in
individual soufflé dishes or
ramekins.
Blend the soft brown sugar with
the cinnamon and sprinkle the
mixture over the peaches.
Spoon the soured cream over the
peaches. Sprinkle each with 1
tablespoon of caster sugar and
place them under a hot grill until
the sugar melts and caramelizes.
It is important that the grill is very
hot, otherwise the cream will melt
before the sugar forms a crust.
If practical, chill before serving;
otherwise, serve straight from the
grill.

HOT GINGER SOUFFLE
serves 4

1½ oz. butter
1½ oz. (⅜ cup) plain flour
½ pint (1¼ cups) milk
3 oz. (⅜ cup) caster sugar
1 tbsp. brandy (optional)
⅛ level tsp. powdered ginger
2 oz. preserved stem ginger,
   chopped
4 large eggs, separated

Butter a 7-in. (2-pint) soufflé dish.
Melt the butter in a saucepan,

stir in the flour and gradually
add the milk. Bring to the boil,
reduce the heat and cook for 2
minutes. Stir in the sugar, brandy
and ginger and beat in the egg
yolks one at a time. Stiffly whisk
the egg whites and fold into the
mixture in the pan.
Turn the mixture into the soufflé
dish and bake at 350°F. (mark 4)
for about 40–45 minutes, until it
is well risen and just firm to the
touch.
Serve at once with ginger syrup
and cream.

APPLE AND BRAMBLE
PLATE PIE
serves 6

2 lb. cooking apples, peeled
   and cored
6 tbsps. water
½ level tsp. dried grated
   orange rind
3 oz. (⅜ cup) sugar
8 oz. shortcrust pastry
   (i.e. made with 8 oz. flour)
3–4 tbsps. bramble jelly
milk and sugar for glazing

Slice the apples fairly thickly and
place in a shallow layer on the base
of a large saucepan. Cover with
the water and bring gently to the
boil.

Reduce heat and cook for a few minutes until some of the fruit begins to break up – most of it should remain in slices and there should not be any extra juice. Stir in the orange rind and sugar and leave to cool.

Divide the pastry in half. Roll out one part into a large circle and use to line a 1¾-pint clear ovenproof glass flan dish or an 8-in. fluted flan ring placed on a baking sheet. Spread the base with bramble jelly and spoon the part-cooked apple on top.

Roll out the remaining pastry to make a lid. Damp the pastry edges, lift the lid into position and press the edges together. Knock up the edges with the back of a knife, make a slit in the lid, brush with milk and dredge with granulated sugar.

Place the flan dish on a pre-heated baking sheet. Bake in the centre of the oven at 400°F. (mark 6) for about 35–40 minutes or until the pastry is a good colour.

Serve warm with clotted cream.

APPLE DUMPLINGS WITH WALNUT SAUCE
serves 4

**12 oz. shortcrust pastry
   (i.e. made with 12 oz. flour)
4 large cooking apples,
   washed and cored
6 level tbsps. mincemeat
1 egg, beaten**

For sauce :
**2 oz. butter
2 oz. (⅜ cup) Demerara sugar
1½ tbsps. cream
2 oz. (½ cup) walnuts,
   coarsely chopped**

Divide the pastry into 4; knead lightly and roll each piece out into a large enough circle to wrap round an apple. Place each apple on to a pastry round and fill the centres generously with mincemeat.

Brush the pastry edges with egg and completely enclose the apples with the pastry, sealing the join. Place the dumplings on a baking sheet, join side down, and brush all over with beaten egg. Bake in the oven at 400°F. (mark 6) for about 35 minutes until golden brown.

Meanwhile make the walnut sauce by melting the butter and stirring in the sugar; when dissolved, add the cream and nuts and bring to the boil.

Serve the sauce separately in a jug to pour over the dumplings.

Golden apple dumpling, served with hot walnut sauce

APPLE FLAN
serves 6

For pastry case :
**3 oz. (¾ cup) plain flour
3 oz. (¾ cup) self-raising flour
2 oz. butter
2 oz. margarine
1 oz. (¼ cup) icing sugar,
   sifted
water**

For filling :
**4 tbsps. apricot jam
2 tbsps. water
juice of 1 small lemon
1¼ lb. eating apples
1–2 level tbsps. caster sugar**

Place the flours in a bowl, rub in the fats to resemble fine bread-crumbs. Stir in the icing sugar. Mix to a firm but pliable dough with cold water. Knead lightly on a floured board. Roll out and use to line a 9–9½ in. loose-bottomed French fluted flan tin.

Boil together the jam and water for 2–3 minutes, stirring. Sieve into a cup or small bowl. Cool, then spread half over the flan base. Squeeze the lemon juice into a bowl. Peel, core and thinly slice the apples straight into the lemon juice – for speed slice on the chisel edge of a grater. Turn apple slices in the juice to prevent discolour-ation. Spoon apple into the flan case, keeping the surface level. Sprinkle with sugar.

Place on a baking sheet and cook in the oven at 400°F. (mark 6) for about 35 minutes. Whilst still hot brush with the rest of the apricot glaze to which any excess lemon juice has been added.

Serve warm rather than hot, with thick cream.

RICE AND FRUIT TART
serves 8

**7 oz. (⅞ cup) long grain rice
1¼ pints (3 cups) milk
6 oz. (¾ cup) caster sugar
2 eggs, beaten
3 firm pears, peeled and
   cored
12 apricots, halved and
   stoned
3 peaches (or large plums),
   halved and stoned
½ lb. apricot jam**

Simmer the rice in boiling water for 3 minutes and drain well. Put the milk and 2½ oz. (⅓ cup) of the sugar on to boil and when boiling add the rice. Stir well, and simmer gently until the rice is tender and most of the liquid has been absorbed.

Meanwhile, using a shallow pan, dissolve the remaining sugar in ⅓ pint (⅞ cup) water, bring to the boil and boil for 2 minutes.

Beat the eggs into the rice, then mould the mixture into a well buttered 10-in. shallow ovenproof dish, covering the base and the sides. Place the dish in the centre of the oven at 350°F. (mark 4) for 10 minutes.

Remove the dish from the oven, remould the sides if necessary and return it to the oven for a further 20 minutes, or until the rice is firm and set.

Quarter the pears and simmer them gently in the sugar syrup for about 10 minutes. Add the apricots and peaches and continue to simmer for 5 minutes until all the fruits are tender but not soft. Drain them well, and arrange them in the rice case. Keep everything warm.

Melt the apricot jam in the remaining syrup and boil until reduced by one-third. Strain and spoon a little over the fruits – just enough to glaze them.

Put the rest in a sauce boat and serve as an accompaniment to the hot tart.

CHERRY-WALNUT UPSIDE DOWN PUDDING
serves 6

For topping :
**1 oz. butter
2 oz. (4 tbsps.) soft light
   brown sugar
3 oz. glacé cherries, halved
3 oz. walnuts, coarsely
   chopped
1 tbsp. coffee essence**

For sponge base :
**4 oz. butter or margarine
4 oz. (½ cup) caster sugar
2 eggs, lightly beaten
2 tbsps. coffee essence
6 oz. (1½ cups) self-raising
   flour**

Lightly grease a 6-in. round cake tin. Melt the butter and brown sugar for the topping and stir in the cherries, walnuts and coffee essence. Spread the mixture evenly over the base of the cake tin.

Cream the butter and sugar until light and fluffy; beat in the eggs one at a time and stir in the coffee essence. Fold in the sifted flour, turn into the tin, level and bake at 350°F. (mark 4) for 50–55 minutes until the sponge is firm but springy to the touch and shrinks slightly from the tin.

Turn out the pudding on to a heated serving plate and serve hot with whipped double cream or clotted cream.

PEACH COBBLER

erves 4

oz. (1½ cups) dried peaches
oz. (½ cup) granulated sugar

or topping:

oz. butter
oz. (2 cups) self-raising flour
oz. (2 tbsps.) caster sugar
pint (⅝ cup) milk, approx.
egg, beaten
)emerara sugar

oak the peaches for 2–3 hours n 1 pint (2½ cups) cold water. Put he peaches, sugar and water into a aucepan, bring to the boil and hen simmer for about 30 minutes, r until the peaches are tender. Arrange in a 1½-pint pie dish.
Rub the fat into the flour until he mixture resembles fine bread-rumbs. Stir in the sugar and nough milk to give a soft but nanageable dough. Knead the cone dough lightly on a floured oard and roll out to approxi-nately ½-in. thickness. Cut out ½-in. diameter rounds with a luted cutter. Arrange over the eaches.
Brush the scones with a little eaten egg or milk and sprinkle vith Demerara sugar. Bake at 50°F. (mark 8) for 15 minutes ntil well risen and golden brown.

.EMON LAYER SPONGE

erves 4

eggs, separated
oz. (¾ cup) caster sugar
oz. butter
oz. (½ cup) flour
pint (1¼ cups) milk
tbsps. lemon juice
rated rind of 1 lemon

Beat the egg yolks with the sugar nd the softened butter in a large asin. Stir in the flour, milk, lemon uice and rind. Whisk the egg vhites until stiff and fold evenly nto the mixture. Turn into a uttered 2-pint pie dish and place n a roasting tin with water to ome half-way up the dish. Bake n the oven at 350°F. (mark 4) for 0–50 minutes until lightly set.

EMON CANDY ALASKA

rves 4

oz. butter
oz. (⅞ cup) caster sugar
oz. cornflakes, crushed
pint (1¼ cups) vanilla ice cream
sour lemon sweets, finely crushed
egg whites
ice of ½ a lemon

Melt the butter in a saucepan, stir in 3 oz. (⅜ cup) of the sugar, heat gently until dissolved and then toss the cornflakes in the syrup.
Use to line a 7-in. pie plate and chill. Soften the ice cream in a basin and beat in the lemon sweets. Refreeze. Whisk the egg whites until stiff, add half the remaining sugar and whisk again until stiff. Fold in the rest of the sugar. Scoop the lemon ice cream into the chilled pie shell, sprinkling it with lemon juice.
Pile the meringue over the ice cream, covering it completely. Cook on the top shelf of a pre-heated oven at 450°F. (mark 8) for about 5 minutes until light brown. Serve at once.

BAKED ALASKA

serves 4

1 7-in. round sponge cake
11-oz. can fruit (e.g. raspberries), drained
17-fl. oz. block of ice cream
3–4 egg whites
4–6 oz. (½–¾ cup) caster sugar

Pre-heat the oven to 450°F. (mark 8). Place the sponge cake on a flat ovenproof dish and spoon over it just enough canned fruit juice to moisten the cake. Put the ice cream in the centre of the cake and pile the fruit on top.
Whisk the egg whites stiffly, whisk in half the sugar, then fold in the remaining sugar. Pile this meringue mixture over the cake, completely covering the cake, ice cream and fruit. Be sure to take the meringue right down to the dish, sealing the sides completely. Place in the oven immediately, near the top, and cook for 2–3 minutes or until the outside of the meringue just begins to brown. Serve at once.

PEAR AND ALMOND CREPES

For batter:

4 oz. (1 cup) plain flour
pinch of salt
1 egg
½ pint (1¼ cups) milk
1 tbsp. brandy
½ oz. butter, melted

For filling:

4 oz. butter
2 oz. (⅜ cup) icing sugar
2 oz. (½ cup) ground almonds
¼ tsp. almond essence
grated rind of 1 lemon
15-oz. can pears, drained and diced
melted butter
lemon wedges

Pancakes with a difference filled with pear and almond

Sift the flour and salt into a bowl. Break the egg into the centre, add 2 tablespoons of milk and stir well. Gradually add the rest of the milk, stirring. Beat until the batter has the consistency of single cream, then add brandy and melted butter. Heat a 7-in. frying pan and brush the surface with a little butter. Raise the handle side of the pan slightly and pour in the batter from the raised side so that a very thin skin of batter flows over the pan. Place pan over a moderate heat and leave until the pancake is golden brown; turn it and repeat. Turn the pancake out on to a plate and keep warm. Make 8 pancakes, stacking them up as you go, separated with sheets of greaseproof paper.
Cream the butter and sugar until light and fluffy. Stir in the ground almonds, almond essence, lemon rind and diced pears. Spread a little of the filling over one half of each pancake; fold the other half over and then in half again to form a triangle.
Arrange the pancakes in an ovenproof dish overlapping each other; brush lightly with butter and quickly flash under a hot grill. Serve with lemon wedges.

BANANAS EN CROUTE

serves 4

4 large bananas, peeled
grated rind and juice of 1 lemon
1 level tbsp. caster sugar
½ level tsp. powdered cinnamon
8 slices brown bread
1½ oz. butter
1 oz. (¼ cup) walnuts, chopped

Halve bananas lengthwise and leave to soak in lemon juice for 1 hour. Blend together caster sugar, lemon rind and cinnamon. Remove crusts from the bread. Melt ½ oz. butter in a frying pan and fry bananas on both sides until golden. Toast and butter the bread; sprinkle with cinnamon sugar. Lay banana on top and sprinkle with the chopped nuts.

A simple apple flan, served warm, is always popular

PARTY PUDDINGS

PISTACHIO APPLE FLAN

serves 6

For flan case :

2 large eggs
2 oz. (¼ cup) caster sugar
2 oz. (½ cup) plain flour

For filling :

½ pint (1¼ cups) milk
2 oz. (¼ cup) caster sugar
1 oz. (¼ cup) plain flour
¼ oz. cornflour
1 large egg
1 oz. butter

For decoration :

2 sharp eating apples
½ pint (1¼ cups) water
juice of ½ lemon
2 oz. (¼ cup) caster sugar
5 tbsps. apricot jam
**1½ oz. pistachio nuts, peeled
  and chopped**

Grease an 8½-in. sponge flan tin well, placing a disc of greased greaseproof paper on the raised base to prevent any sticking. Put the eggs and sugar in a large deep bowl, stand this over a pan of hot water and whisk until light and creamy – the whisk should leave a trail when lifted from the mixture. Remove from the heat and whisk until cool. If an electric mixer is used, do not place over hot water. Sift half the flour over the mixture and fold in very lightly, using a tablespoon. Add the remaining flour in the same way. Turn the mixture into the flan tin and bake towards the top of the oven at 425°F. (mark 7) for 12–15 minutes, until well risen and golden brown.

Turn out carefully and cool on a wire rack.

Meanwhile heat the milk in a pan. Mix the sugar, flour, cornflour, egg and a little milk and stir in the hot milk. Allow the mixture to thicken and just come to the boil, then add the butter and beat well. Cover and cool.

Peel, core and slice the apples in rings. Poach until soft but not broken in a light syrup made from the water, lemon juice and sugar. Drain the apple rings and leave to cool.

Brush the outside and top rim of the flan case with warm sieved apricot jam to which a little water has been added. Coat the outer edges with pistachio nuts. Fill the flan case with pastry cream and arrange apple ring on top. Glaze with more jam and chill before serving.

STRAWBERRY PALMIERS

makes 6 pairs

**8 oz. frozen puff pastry,
  thawed**
sugar to dredge
¼ pint (⅝ cup) double cream
4 tbsps. (⅜ cup) single cream
1 tbsp. orange liqueur
2 level tsps. icing sugar
¾ lb. strawberries

Roll the pastry into a rectangle 12 in. by 10 in. Dredge with caster sugar. Fold the long sides to meet in the centre and dredge again; fold in half lengthwise. Press light-ly with a rolling pin. Cut into 12

equal slices, place well apart on a baking sheet, cut-side down. Open the tip of each.

Bake near the top of the oven at 425°F. (mark 7) for about 8 minutes, until the sugar is a light caramel colour. Turn each one over and bake for a further 4 minutes. Cool on a wire rack.

Whip the creams together until light and fluffy. Add the liqueur and icing sugar and use to sandwich the palmiers in pairs. Tuck halved strawberries into each.

TRANCHE AUX FRUITS

serves 6

For pastry case :

5 oz. (1¼ cups) plain flour
3 oz. butter or margarine
1½ level tsps. caster sugar
1 egg yolk
4 tsps. cold water (approx.)

For filling :

**1 small eating apple, peeled,
  cored, quartered and
  thinly sliced**
**1 medium orange, peeled and
  sliced**
1 banana, peeled and sliced
**7½-oz. can prunes, drained
  and stoned**
3 tbsps. Grand Marnier

For confectioner's custard :

½ pint (1¼ cups) milk
2 oz. (¼ cup) caster sugar
1 oz. (¼ cup) plain flour
½ level tbsp. cornflour
1 large egg
icing sugar
2 tbsps. apricot jam

Sift the flour, rub in the fat a sprinkle the sugar over the mi ture. Blend the yolk with the wat and stir into the rubbed-in ingre ents. Add a little more water necessary to give a firm doug Knead lightly and roll out on floured surface.

Use this dough to line a 14 in. 4½ in. tranche frame, or a 9 loose-bottomed French flut flan tin. Bake blind, using dri beans, at 400°F. (mark 6) for abo 20 minutes. Remove the bear then cook for a further 5 minute Leave the pastry case to cool or wire rack.

Meanwhile prepare the app orange, banana and prunes. Mac rate them in separate bowls, ea containing ½ tablespoon Gra Marnier.

Prepare the confectioner's cu tard by bringing the milk to t boil; whisk together the suga flour, cornflour and egg, stir ha the milk into the whisked i gredients then pour the whe back into the pan. Bring to the bo stirring constantly.

Remove from the heat and stir 1 tablespoon Grand Marnier. C slightly and pour into the past case. Dust with icing sugar prevent a skin forming.

When completely cold, arran the fruits in alternate rows ov the surface.

Heat the apricot jam with the le over fruit juices and liqueur, in small pan. Bubble until thickene Sieve and brush the glaze over t fruit. Serve with thick cream.

BLACKBERRY AND PINEAPPLE BRIOCHE

serves 6–8

oz. (2 cups) strong plain
  flour
level tsp. salt
oz. (1 tbsp.) caster sugar
oz. fresh baker's yeast
½ tbsps. warm water
eggs, beaten
oz. melted butter, cooled
  but still liquid
egg, beaten with 1 tsp. water
  for glaze

For filling :
6-oz. can pineapple pieces
tbsps. Kirsch
pint (⅝ cup) single cream
pint (⅝ cup) double cream
level tbsp. icing sugar
lb. blackberries or
  raspberries

Sift together the flour, salt and sugar. Blend yeast with the water and add to the dry ingredients, together with the eggs and butter. Work into a soft dough and knead well for about 5 minutes. Place in an oiled polythene bag and allow to rise at room temperature for –1½ hours, until the dough has doubled in size.
Brush a 2-pint fluted brioche mould with oil. On a lightly floured surface, thoroughly knead the risen dough. Make a ball with three-quarters of it and place in the bottom of the mould. Press a hollow in the centre and place the remaining piece of dough in the middle. Put the mould in a large polythene bag and stand it in a warm place to let the dough rise again until light and fluffy – about hour.
Brush with egg glaze and bake at 450°F. (mark 8) for 15–20 minutes, until brown. When cooked, the brioche should sound hollow when tapped on the base. Allow to cool, then cut a thin slice from the top and scoop out some of the crumb. Drain the pineapple and mix 3 tablespoons of the juice with 3 tablespoons of Kirsch; spoon the liquid over the inside of the brioche and let it soak for 5 minutes. Whip the creams until they just hold their shape, then beat in the sugar. Reserve a little for decoration. Fold in the pineapple, reserving a few pieces for decoration.
Spoon layers of the cream mixture and blackberries into the brioche, again reserving some for decoration, and decorate the top with piped cream, blackberries and pieces of pineapple and, if liked, top with the lid of brioche.

MELON AND PINEAPPLE SALAD

serves 6

1 honeydew melon
2 16-oz. cans pineapple
  chunks, drained
4 tbsps. Cointreau or curaçao
caster sugar (optional)
few glacé cherries

Slice the melon in half lengthwise, scoop out and discard the seeds. Scoop out the flesh in large pieces and keep to one side. Using scissors or a sharp knife serrate the edge of one of the melon halves. Cut the melon flesh into chunks and pile these and the drained pineapple chunks into the decorated melon half.
Sprinkle over the liqueur and sugar, if used. Decorate with glacé cherries.

MANDARIN LIQUEUR GATEAU

serves 8

3 large eggs
3 oz. (⅜ cup) caster sugar
3 oz. (¾ cup) plain flour
2 11-oz. cans mandarin
  oranges, drained
2 tbsps. maraschino liqueur
8-oz. can red cherries,
  drained
apricot glaze
½ pint (1¼ cups) double cream,
  lightly whipped
icing sugar
angelica

Grease and line a 10-in. by 1½-in. deep sandwich tin. Put eggs and sugar in a bowl over a pan of hot water and whisk until thick and pale in colour. If using an electric mixer do not place over hot water. Sift the flour over the whisked eggs and fold in lightly and quickly with a metal spoon. Turn the mixture into the prepared sandwich tin and bake at 375°F. (mark 5) for about 30 minutes. Cool on a wire rack.
Macerate the oranges in maraschino for 30 minutes. Remove stones from all but 12 of the cherries. Split the cake in two and place one half cut side up on a serving plate. Spoon over the strained maraschino and spread with a little apricot glaze.
From the centre of the second half, stamp out 3 2-in. circles, close to each other. Brush remaining surface with apricot glaze. Arrange groups of mandarins round the edge; chop the remainder. Spread most of the cream over the first half and top with chopped mandarins and stoned cherries.

A brioche loaf filled with pineapple and blackberries

Carefully lift the second half on top of the first. Fill the holes with the remaining cream and top with the sponge circles, dredged with icing sugar. Finish with a cluster of whole cherries and angelica leaves.

NUTTY CARAMEL PIES

serves 4

4½ oz. (⅝ cup) caster sugar
¼ pint (⅝ cup) milk
1 egg
1 egg yolk
¼ pint (⅝ cup) double cream,
  lightly whipped

For base :
3 oz. (¾ cup) plain flour
2 oz. butter
2 oz. plain (dark) chocolate

For decoration :
¼ pint (⅝ cup) honey sauce
2 oz. broken walnuts

Dissolve 2 oz. sugar in a heavy pan and allow to caramellize to a pale golden brown. Remove from the heat and pour on 3 tablespoons of boiling water, very slowly. Return to the heat, simmer to dissolve the caramel, add the milk and stir.
Beat the whole egg and yolk with 1½ oz. sugar, add the caramel-milk and strain back into the saucepan. Cook very gently until the custard coats the back of a spoon. Pour into a basin and allow to cool. When it is cold, transfer the custard to a freezing tray and freeze it to a slush in the ice-making compartment of the refrigerator or a home freezer. Beat well, and fold in the cream. Return to the tray and freeze until firm.
Knead the flour, butter and remaining 1 oz. of sugar to a manageable dough. Roll out thinly

Caramel ice cream on a pastry base, with nuts and a honey sauce

Strawberry galette and whipped cream

and line 4 3½-in. shallow patty pans. Bake blind for 15 minutes at 375°F. (mark 5) until light golden brown. Allow to cool.
Melt the chocolate in a bowl over hot water and dip the edges of the pies into soft chocolate.
To serve, pile ice cream into the pastry shells, and spoon over honey sauce and walnuts.

ICED CHARLOTTE RUSSE
serves 12

For ice cream layers:
½ pint (1¼ cups) milk
15 oz. (1⅞ cups) sugar
1 vanilla pod
2 eggs, beaten
½ pint (1¼ cups) double cream
1 pint (2½ cups) water
1 lb. raspberries
8 tbsps. lemon juice
½ pint (1¼ cups) hazelnut yoghourt

For sponge case:
3 level tbsps. sugar
4 tbsps. water
4 tbsps. sherry
28 boudoir biscuits or sponge fingers (2 packets)

Heat the milk with 3 oz. sugar and the vanilla pod and pour on to the beaten eggs, stirring. Return to the saucepan and cook over a low heat, stirring, until the custard thickens. Strain and remove the vanilla pod. Allow to cool.
Half-whip the cream and fold into the cold custard. Pour the mixture into an ice tray and freeze until slushy. Turn into a chilled bowl and whisk thoroughly. Freeze again until slushy.
For the raspberry layers, dissolve 12 oz. sugar in the water, bring to the boil and reduce by boiling to 1 pint. Cool. Sieve the berries to remove the pips and make a purée; add the lemon juice, yoghourt and sugar syrup, turn into an ice tray and freeze to a slush.
Screw up some kitchen foil and make it into a collar to fit inside the base of an 8½-in. round cake tin, leaving a small gap between the tin side and foil to support the biscuits.
Dissolve the 3 level tablespoons of sugar in the water in a small pan and simmer for 5 minutes. Blend with the sherry in a flat dish, then soak the biscuits briefly in the mixture, removing them before they become soggy. Place the biscuits side by side in the gap made by the foil. Chill the tin.
Layer the vanilla and raspberry ice cream, starting with half the vanilla. Lift the foil ring as the vanilla layer is spooned in, but leave it in position above the vanilla layer to give support to the biscuits. Freeze the vanilla layer until solid; remove the foil.
Continue by adding half the raspberry ice cream, freezing, then repeating with the remaining vanilla and raspberry. Leave in the freezer until required. Turn out on to a serving dish, leave in a cool place to soften a little, then cut with a knife dipped in warm water.
Note: This large iced charlotte is best made in a home freezer; if you are using the ice-making compartment of a refrigerator, make the mixture in 2 lots.

A frozen sponge, sandwiched with coffee ice cream

PUDDING GLACE
serves 8–10

For coffee ice:
10 egg yolks
12 oz. (1½ cups) caster sugar
½ pint (1¼ cups) water
1 pint (2½ cups) double cream, whipped
3 level tbsps. instant coffee
4 tsps. water

For whisked sponge:
2 large eggs
2 oz. (¼ cup) caster sugar
2 oz. (½ cup) plain flour
3 tbsps. rum
juice of 1 small orange

For decoration:
glacé fruits (e.g. cherries and angelica)
¼ pint (⅝ cup) double cream, whipped

For coffee sauce:
½ pint (1¼ cups) water
8 oz. (1 cup) sugar
4 tbsps. instant coffee
2 level tbsps. cornflour

First make the ice cream. Beat the yolks thoroughly. Dissolve the sugar in the water in a small saucepan and boil to 217°F. – about 5 minutes. Cool slightly, beat the egg yolks in a deep bowl then pour the syrup slowly on to the egg yolks in a thin stream, beating. Place the bowl over a pan of hot water and continue to beat until thick. When cold, fold in the whipped cream and the coffee blended with the water. Pour into ice trays and freeze until slushy.
Meanwhile, grease and line the base of a shallow 8½-in. cake tin. Whisk together the whole eggs and caster sugar for the sponge until pale and fluffy and the whisk leaves a trail. Sift the flour over the mixture and fold in with a metal spoon. Pour the mixture into the prepared cake tin and bake a 375°F. (mark 5) for about 1 minutes. Turn out and cool on wire rack; remove the paper.
Split the cake in half. Blend together the rum and orange juic and spoon over the sponge halve. Line either a 4-pint charlott mould or an 8-in. deep cake ti with greaseproof paper. If necessary, trim half the sponge to fit th base of the mould and ease int place. Spoon the slushy ice crear over this half of the sponge.
Top with the remaining spong half and return to the freezer com partment until firmly set – about hours. Unmould and decorat with whipped cream and glac fruits.
To make the coffee sauce, dissolv the sugar in the water in a smal saucepan over gentle heat. Sti in the coffee. Blend the cornflou to a thick cream with a little col water, pour on some of the coffe syrup, stirring, and return to th pan. Stir over the heat to thicken Serve the sauce separately.

STRAWBERRY GALETTE
serves 8

9 oz. (2¼ cups) plain flour
6 oz. butter
3 oz. (⅜ cup) caster sugar
1–1½ lb. strawberries, hulled
6 oz. red-currant jelly
3 level tsps. arrowroot

Stand a 9-in. plain flan ring on a baking sheet. Sift the flour, rub in the butter and add the sugar Lightly knead the mixture unti it forms a dough.
Roll out the dough and use to line the flan ring, drawing the sides u to make a wall. Press into shap with the fingertips and crimp th edge with finger and thumb Prick the base and bake at 350°F (mark 4) for about 30 minute until lightly browned.
Allow to cool for 15 minutes o the tray, then remove the ring an with a palette knife lift on to a wire rack. Leave until cold.
Cut strawberries in half. Brush th base of the galette with red-currant jelly and arrange strawberries cut side uppermost ove the red-currant jelly.
Make up a glaze by heating ¼ lb red-currant jelly with ¼ pint (⅝ cup) water. Bring to the boil sieve and blend in the arrowroo mixed with a little water. Retur to the pan and cook until th arrowroot clears.
Coat the strawberries with th warm glaze and leave to set. Serve with lightly whipped cream.

HOME-MADE ICES

Although bought ices are very good, the variety achieved by making your own is well worth the little extra trouble.

The only equipment necessary is an ordinary domestic refrigerator with a frozen food compartment, or a home freezer, and a rotary whisk. An electric ice cream machine makes the process easier still, but is not essential. There are several varieties of both cream and water ices. The most common types are:

Cream ices These are seldom made entirely of cream, but any of the following mixtures give good results: equal parts cream and custard (egg custard, made with yolks only); cream and fruit purée; cream and egg whites. The cream may be replaced by unsweetened evaporated milk and flavouring and colouring ingredients are added as required.

Water ices The foundation is a sugar and water syrup, usually flavoured with fruit juice or purée; wine or liqueur is frequently added.

Sherbets A true sherbet is a water ice with whipped egg white added, to give a fluffy texture.

Sorbets Semi-frozen ices, sometimes flavoured with liqueur.

Because they are soft, they are not moulded but served in tall glasses or goblets.

Bombes Iced puddings frozen in a special bomb-shaped mould; bombes may be made of a single ice cream mixture known as a parfait or of two or more. They are often elaborately decorated after unmoulding.

MAKING ICE CREAM

To obtain the best results, use a rich mixture, with plenty of flavouring. A flavour that tastes quite strong at room temperature will become much less so when frozen. See that the mixture is well sweetened, too, as this helps to accentuate the flavour of the frozen ice. But don't go to the other extreme and over-sweeten, as too much sugar will prevent the mixture freezing properly (too much alcohol used as flavouring will also prevent freezing). Colouring is not affected by freezing, so use sparingly, a drop at a time.

FREEZING

If you are using the frozen food compartment of a refrigerator, set the dial at the lowest setting about 1 hour before the mixture is ready. Put the mixture into a polythene ice cube tray and place in the frozen food compartment. To improve the texture, either stir the mixture at 20-minute intervals until it is half frozen and then leave it undisturbed until frozen, or allow it to half-freeze, turn it into a cool bowl and whisk thoroughly with a rotary whisk, then replace it in the freezing compartment and leave until hard. The time required will vary with the refrigerator, but usually it takes several hours. Once the mixture is frozen the temperature may be returned to normal storage temperature. The ice cream develops a better, more mellow flavour if left for a while. If you have a home freezer, use the same method, but the mixture will of course freeze much more quickly.

USING AN ELECTRIC ICE CREAM MAKER

An electric ice cream maker (like the one pictured above) will give you a more even-textured ice more quickly. It has a central motor attached to 2 paddles, which move continually while it is freezing. Put the whole machine in the refrigerator or freezer, making sure that the contact between the base and the freezer shelf is good.

Shut the door—you will find that the flex will not seriously affect the seal—plug in and switch on. If you intend making much ice cream this is well worth the small investment.

RICH VANILLA ICE CREAM
serves 4

$\frac{1}{4}$ pint ($\frac{5}{8}$ cup) milk
1$\frac{1}{2}$ oz. sugar
2 egg yolks, beaten
$\frac{1}{2}$–1 tsp. vanilla essence
$\frac{1}{4}$ pint ($\frac{5}{8}$ cup) double cream, partially whipped

Heat the milk and sugar and pour on to the egg yolks, stirring. Return the mixture to the pan and cook it over a very gentle heat, stirring all the time until the custard thickens; strain it and add the vanilla essence. Allow to cool, fold in the partially whipped cream, pour into a polythene ice cube tray and freeze.

ORANGE ICE CREAM
serves 4

$\frac{1}{2}$ pint (1$\frac{1}{4}$ cups) double cream
$\frac{1}{2}$ pint (1$\frac{1}{4}$ cups) orange juice
caster sugar
mandarin orange sections
wafers

Serve strawberry liqueur ice cream with luscious strawberry sauce

Whip the cream until it holds its shape. Stir in ¼ pint orange juice and add remaining ¼ pint a little at a time. Add sufficient sugar to make the mixture taste slightly over-sweet. Pour into a polythene ice cube tray and freeze. Serve with mandarin sections and wafers.

FRUIT ICE CREAM
serves 4

small can evaporated milk
8 oz. fresh raspberries or a 15-oz. can, drained, or other fruit such as strawberries, pears, bananas
2 oz. sugar (if fresh fruit is used)

Place the unopened can of milk in a pan of boiling water and keep on the boil for 15 minutes. Remove from the pan, cool and chill thoroughly for several hours. Sieve the fruit to make ¼ pint purée; add the sugar if required. Open the can of milk and whip until stiff. Fold in the purée. Pour into a polythene ice cube tray and freeze.

STRAWBERRY LIQUEUR ICE CREAM
serves 4

¼ pint (⅝ cup) double cream, lightly whipped
8 oz. strawberries, puréed
½ tsp. vanilla essence
1 tbsp. rum or maraschino
2 oz. (¼ cup) sugar

Mix the cream with all the other ingredients, pour into a polythene ice cube tray and freeze for ¾–1 hour. Turn out and whisk until smooth. Return mixture to the tray and freeze until firm.

CHOC-DE-MENTHE

Make up the basic vanilla ice cream recipe, replacing the vanilla essence by 2 teaspoons crème de menthe and a few drops of green colouring. When the mixture is half frozen, turn into a chilled bowl and whisk. Crumble a small bar of flake chocolate and fold in. Return to the tray and freeze.

BERRY ICE CREAM
serves 8

2 level tsps. powdered gelatine
2 tbsps. water
15-oz. can strawberries or raspberries, puréed or 1 lb. fresh fruit, puréed
1–3 oz. soft brown sugar
1½ tbsps. lemon juice
¼ pint (⅝ cup) single cream
2 oz. biscuit crumbs
½ pint (1¼ cups) double cream

Dissolve the gelatine in the water in a basin held over a pan of hot water. Pour the fruit pulp into a bowl, add sugar to taste and the lemon juice. Stir in the dissolved gelatine, single cream and crushed biscuit crumbs. Two-thirds fill a polythene ice cube tray and freeze until fairly stiff. Beat again and fold in the whipped double cream. Freeze again.

TOASTED ALMOND ICE
serves 4

½ pint (1¼ cups) milk
3 oz. (⅜ cup) sugar
a pinch of salt
4 egg yolks
¼ pint (⅝ cup) double cream
vanilla essence
2 oz. crushed praline (see below)
2 egg whites
3 level tbsps. icing sugar
1 tbsp. chopped toasted almonds

Boil the milk. Mix the sugar, salt and egg yolks and stir in the milk. Cook over a very gentle heat, stirring constantly, until thick, then allow to cool. Pour into a polythene ice cube tray and freeze for 20–30 minutes.
Turn the mixture out, whip until creamy and add the cream, a little vanilla essence and the crushed praline. Pour the mixture back into the freezing tray and freeze until firm, stirring it after the first half hour.
Serve with a sauce made by whipping the egg whites and icing sugar together until just stiff enough to drop from a spoon, then adding the chopped nuts.

PRALINE

2 oz. (¼ cup) caster sugar
2 oz. chopped toasted almonds

Heat the sugar in a pan until a deep amber colour, stir in the chopped almonds and pour the mixture on to a greased tin or slab. When it is cool, pound in a mortar or crush with a rolling pin.

HONEY ICE CREAM
serves 8

1 lb. raspberries
¼ pint (⅝ cup) double cream
¼ pint (⅝ cup) plain yoghourt
3 egg whites
2 tbsps. lemon juice
10 level tbsps. clear honey
a pinch of salt

Sieve the raspberries to give ½ pint purée. In a bowl, blend together the raspberry purée,

Pear sorbet with meringue is light and refreshing

ream, yoghourt, lemon juice, oney and salt. Turn the mixture nto a polythene ice cube tray and reeze until firm. Turn out into a owl and beat until smooth.
stiffly whisk the egg whites and old in. Return the mixture to the ray and freeze.

EMON ICE CREAM
erves 6

pint (1¼ cups) double cream
eggs
rated rind and juice of 2 lemons
0 oz. (1¼ cups) caster sugar
pint (1¼ cups) milk

Beat together the cream and eggs until smooth. Add the lemon rind, he juice, sugar and milk and mix horoughly. Pour into polythene ce cube tray and freeze for about hours. Do not stir while freezing.

EMON SHERBET
erves 4

oz. (1 cup) caster sugar
pint (2½ cups) water
ind and juice of 3 lemons
egg white

Dissolve the sugar in the water over a low heat, add the thinly pared lemon rind and boil gently for 10 minutes; leave to cool. Add he lemon juice and strain the mixture into a polythene ice cube ray. Half-freeze, then turn into a owl, whisk the egg white and old it in, mixing thoroughly. Return to the tray and freeze.

ORANGE SHERBET
erves 4

4 oz. (½ cup) caster sugar
½ pint (1¼ cups) water
1 tbsp. lemon juice
rind of 1 orange, grated
rind of 1 lemon, grated
juice of 3 oranges and 1 lemon
1 egg white

Dissolve the sugar in the water over a low heat, bring to the boil and boil gently for 10 minutes. Add 1 tablespoon lemon juice. Put the grated fruit rinds in a basin, pour the boiling syrup over and leave until cold. Add the mixed fruit juices and strain into a polythene ice cube tray.
Half-freeze the mixture then turn t into a bowl, whisk the egg white and fold it in, mixing thoroughly. Return to the tray and freeze.
Other flavours of sherbet may be made by adding ½ pint (1¼ cups) fruit purée and the juice of ½ a emon to ½ pint syrup.

A crunchy cornflake crust coats this lemon freeze

FRUIT SORBET

Follow the recipe for lemon sherbet but add 2 egg whites, which will give a much softer consistency. Freeze the mixture only until it is stiff enough to serve. Spoon into glasses.

LEMON FREEZE
serves 8

2 oz. cornflakes, crumbled
5 level tbsps. caster sugar
1 oz. butter, melted
2 eggs, separated
small can of sweetened condensed milk
4 tbsps. lemon juice

Blend together the cornflake crumbs, 2 tablespoons sugar and butter until well mixed. Press all but 4 tablespoons into the base of a polythene ice cube tray.
Beat the egg yolks in a deep bowl until really thick and creamy. Combine with the condensed milk. Add the lemon juice and stir until thickened. Beat the egg whites until stiff but not dry. Gradually beat in remaining sugar; fold through the lemon mixture. Spoon into the polythene tray and sprinkle with the remaining cornflake crumbs. Freeze.

PINEAPPLE SORBET
serves 6

2¾-lb. pineapple
6 tbsps. lemon juice
4 tbsps. orange juice
¼ pint (⅝ cup) water
11 oz. (1⅜ cups) sugar
whipped cream, for serving

Peel the pineapple, remove the core and discard. Pulp the flesh in a blender. Put the pineapple pulp through a sieve to give ¾ pint (2 cups) purée. Mix the purée with the lemon and orange juice, water and sugar, stirring until the sugar has completely dissolved. Pour into polythene ice cube trays and freeze without stirring until crystals have formed but the spoon still goes in.
Serve accompanied by whipped cream, either in sundae glasses or returned to the empty shell.

PEAR SORBET MERINGUE
serves 6

15½-oz. can pears, drained
12 oz. (1½ cups) caster sugar
½ pint (1¼ cups) water
3 tbsps. lemon juice
3 egg whites
1 fresh pear, sliced and cored
melted chocolate

Place the pears in a measure and make up to ½ pint with some of the juice. Purée in a blender or put through a sieve. Dissolve half the sugar in the water, bring to the boil and reduce to ½ pint (1¼ cups) syrup. Pour on to the pear purée, add the lemon juice and stir well. Freeze until firm.
Meanwhile, draw a 9-in. circle on a sheet of waxed paper; divide into 6 segments. Whisk the egg whites until stiff, add 3 oz. sugar and whisk again until stiff. Fold in the remaining 3 oz. sugar.
Spoon the meringue into a forcing bag fitted with a large star vegetable nozzle. Following pencilled lines as a guide, pipe a scalloped edge round the circle indenting each section. Fill in the base with more meringue, then build up the scalloped edge and outline each section. Dry in the oven on the lowest setting for 3–4 hours, until crisp and firm. Cool and remove the paper.
To serve, spoon the sorbet into the meringue nests. Arrange slices of fresh pear dipped in lemon juice between them and drizzle with melted chocolate.

APRICOT SHERBET
serves 4

2 eggs, separated
1 oz. caster sugar
16-oz. can of apricots, puréed
pinch of ground nutmeg
4 tbsps. single cream

Beat the egg whites until stiff and continue whisking while gradually adding half the sugar. Fold in remaining sugar. Mix the puréed fruit, egg yolks, nutmeg and cream. Fold carefully into the egg whites, then pour immediately into a polythene ice cube tray and freeze for 3–4 hours.

APRICOT BOMBE
serves 4

1 recipe quantity vanilla ice cream
1 oz. finely chopped blanched almonds
7½-oz. can apricots
2 tbsps. brandy

Allow the ice cream to soften a little, stir in the almonds.
Spoon two-thirds into a chilled ½-pint pudding basin and press it against the sides to form a shell. Pile the drained apricots with a tablespoon juice and the brandy into the centre and top with a lid of the remaining ice cream. Cover with foil and freeze until firm. Unmould to serve.

Gâteaux and Pâtisserie

Continental gâteaux and pâtisserie are made from traditional basic mixtures. Many of the decorations are also traditional. If you long for the lovely things that fill the windows of French and Viennese pastry shops, try your hand at some of these.

BASIC GENOESE SPONGE
this sponge is used as a base for many gâteaux

1½ oz. butter
2½ oz. (⅝ cup) plain flour
½ oz. cornflour
3 large eggs
3 oz. (⅜ cup) caster sugar

Grease and line a 9-in. straight sided sandwich tin or a 7-in. square cake tin.

Heat the butter gently until it is melted, remove it from the heat and let it stand for a few minutes. Sift together the flour and cornflour. Place the eggs in a large deep basin over a saucepan of hot water, whisk for a few seconds, add the sugar and continue whisking over the heat until the mixture is very pale in colour and a trail forms when the whisk is lifted.

Remove from the heat and whisk for a few seconds longer. Resift half the flour over the egg and carefully fold it in, using a metal spoon. Then pour in the melted butter (cooled until it just flows) round the side, folding it in alternately with the remaining flour. Turn the mixture into the prepared tin and bake near the top of the oven at 375°F. (mark 5) for about 30 minutes, or until well risen and just firm to the touch. Turn out carefully and leave to cool on a wire rack.

CREME AU BEURRE

3 oz. (⅜ cup) caster sugar
4 tbsps. water
2 egg yolks, beaten
4-6 oz. unsalted butter

Place the sugar in a heavy based saucepan; add the water and leave over a very low heat to dissolve the sugar, without boiling. When the sugar is completely dissolved bring to boiling point and boil steadily for 2–3 minutes, to 225°F. Pour the syrup in a thin stream on to the egg yolks, whisking all the time. Continue to mix until the mixture is thick and cold.

Gradually beat the egg yolk mixture into the creamed butter and flavour as desired.

Chocolate: Put 2 oz. chocolate dots in a small bowl with 1 tablespoon water. Leave to stand over hot water until the mixture is

...nooth and the chocolate melted. ...ool slightly and beat into the ...asic crème au beurre.
...offee: Beat in 1–2 tablespoons ...ffee essence to taste.

GATEAU CENDRILLON

...-in. Genoese sponge
...tbsp. coffee essence
...offee crème au beurre
...pricot glaze
...offee fondant icing or glacé
  icing
...2 hazel nuts, lightly toasted

...o the basic recipe for Genoese ...dd the coffee essence at the ...whisking stage. Bake in the usual ...ay and cool.
...plit the cold sponge in half and ...andwich the halves together with ...wo-thirds of the crème au beurre. ...rush the top with apricot glaze, ...oat with icing and leave to set.
...o decorate, pipe with whirls of ...rème au beurre and top each ...whirl with a hazel nut.

GATEAU MONT BLANC

...or sponge base:
...oz. (¼ cup) caster sugar
...large eggs
...oz. (½ cup) plain flour

...or filling:
...½-oz. can sweetened chestnut
  purée
...pint (1¼ cups) double cream,
  lightly whipped
...cing sugar

...rease and line the raised base of ...n 8½-in. sponge flan tin. Whisk ...ogether the sugar and eggs until ...hick and creamy – the whisk ...hould leave a trail when lifted. ...ift the flour over the surface and ...ightly fold it in with a metal spoon. ...urn the mixture into the pre-...ared tin, level with a palette knife ...nd tap the tin once or twice on ...he table top.
...ake the sponge flan above the ...entre of the oven at 425°F. ...mark 7) for about 15 minutes. ...urn out carefully on to a wire ...ack to cool.
...o finish, place the chestnut ...urée in a forcing bag fitted with a ...arge plain icing nozzle. Lightly ...whip the cream until it just holds ...ts shape.
...pread a little of the whipped ...cream over the base of the flan and ...pipe the chestnut purée in a net ...over the cream, gradually working ...it into a dome shape. Using a large ...star vegetable nozzle, pipe the ...remainder of the whipped cream ...n a shell pattern round the edge. ...ightly dust the whole with icing ...sugar.

Gâteau Mont Blanc, with piped chestnut purée

GATEAU ROXALANNE

5 oz. (1¼ cups) self-raising
  flour
1 oz. (¼ cup) cornflour
4 oz. (½ cup) caster sugar
1 level tsp. baking powder
½ level tsp. salt
2 fl. oz. (¼ cup) corn oil
¼ pint (⅝ cup) cold water
1 level tsp. grated lemon rind
1 tsp. lemon juice
2 egg yolks
4 egg whites
¼ level tsp. cream of tartar

For icing and decoration:
8 oz. plain (dark) chocolate
6 oz. butter
12 oz. (2⅝ cups) icing sugar
2 egg yolks
flaked almonds

Grease a 7-in. tube cake tin. Sift all the dry ingredients into a mixing bowl. Whisk together the corn oil, water, lemon rind, lemon juice and egg yolks. Add to the dry ingredients and beat to form a smooth, slack batter.
Whisk the egg whites and cream of tartar until stiff and dry, then fold into the batter mixture. Turn into the prepared tin and bake in the centre of the oven at 350°F. (mark 4) for about 1 hour. When the cake is cooked, invert it on to a wire rack until the cake slips out of the tin.
Melt the chocolate in a basin over hot, not boiling, water. Cream the butter and sugar together until light and creamy. Beat in the egg yolks and melted chocolate. When the cake is cold, spread the sides with this chocolate icing. Coat the edges in flaked almonds. Cover the top with more icing and pipe on a decoration.

GATEAU CARAQUE

4 oz. (½ cup) caster sugar
4 large eggs
4 oz. (1 cup) plain flour

For filling and decoration:
apricot glaze
chocolate crème au beurre
grated plain (dark) chocolate
chocolate caraque (see below)
icing sugar

Grease and base-line 2 oblong shallow tins 12 in. by 4½ in. In a deep bowl whisk together the sugar and eggs until really thick and creamy – the whisk should leave a trail when lifted from the mixture. Sift the flour over the surface and lightly fold in, using a metal spoon. Divide between the 2 prepared tins. Level the surface with a palette knife and bake just above the centre of the oven at 425°F. (mark 7) for about 25 minutes, until well risen, golden and spongy to the touch. Turn out and cool on a wire rack.
Sandwich the sponges together with apricot glaze and brush the top with the same glaze. Spread the chocolate crème au beurre round the sides and coat with coarsely grated chocolate. Arrange the chocolate caraque pieces side by side over the apricot glaze. Dust the centre with sifted icing sugar.
Chocolate caraque: Shred or grate 4 oz. plain (dark) cooking chocolate on to a plate and place over a pan of hot (not boiling) water. When melted, spread thinly over a marble slab or other cool surface. When just on the point of setting, run the edge of a sharp knife across the surface of the chocolate, so that it forms curls.

LINZER TORTE

6 oz. (1½ cups) plain flour
1 level tsp. ground cinnamon
a pinch of ground cloves
1½ level tsps. cocoa
½ level tsp. baking powder
3 oz. blanched almonds,
  finely chopped, or use
  nibbed almonds
6 oz. butter
5 oz. (⅝ cup) granulated sugar
2 eggs, beaten
raspberry jam
icing sugar
whipped cream (optional)

Grease a 9-in. spring-release cake tin.
Sift together the flour, spices, cocoa and baking powder. Put the almonds in a bowl, add the butter (straight from the refrigerator and coarsely grated). Stir in the sugar, eggs and flour mixture, in that order. Work together and shape into a roll. Wrap in greaseproof paper and chill for about 1 hour.
Roll out about two-thirds of the dough to line the base of the tin; press the dough up the sides to form a ½-in. wall. Fill with a thick layer of jam. Roll out the remainder of the dough, cut into strips and use to cover the jam in an open lattice. Bake in the centre of the oven at 350°F. (mark 4) for about 1 hour.
Leave the torte to cool in the tin, then remove the sides of the tin. Mature for 1–2 days before cutting. Fill in the lattice with fresh jam and serve dusted with icing sugar.

GATEAU NOUGATINE

For Genoese sponge:
3-4 oz. butter, melted
4 oz. (1 cup) plain flour
2 oz. (½ cup) cornflour
6 large eggs
6 oz. (¾ cup) caster sugar

For nougat:
5½ oz. caster sugar
4 oz. blanched almonds,
  finely chopped
a whole lemon

For filling and topping:
crème au beurre
2 tsps. Tia Maria
2 tbsps. apricot glaze
6 oz. plain (dark) chocolate
  cake covering

Grease and base-line 2 9-in. round sandwich tins.
Make up the Genoese mixture, divide it between the 2 tins and bake 1 above the other in the oven at 425°F. (mark 7) for 10 minutes. Reduce the temperature to 375°F. (mark 5) and bake for about a

further 15 minutes. Turn out and cool on a wire rack.

For the nougat, put the sugar in a heavy based pan and dissolve over a very low heat. When it is caramel coloured, add the almonds a little at a time, stirring gently with a metal spoon. Turn quickly on to an oiled surface then use a whole lemon to roll out the nougat thinly. Using a warmed cutter, quickly stamp out 12–14 leaf shapes. Leave the remainder of the nougat to set, then roughly crush it. (Should the nougat become too set before all the leaf shapes are cut, put it in a warm oven for a few minutes.)

To finish the cake, make up the crème au beurre, adding the Tia Maria, and sandwich the layers of Genoese together with it. Spread the remainder round the edges and coat evenly with the crushed nougat. Brush the cake top with apricot glaze.

Make up the chocolate covering and spread over the glazed surface, easing it to the edge with a knife. When it is nearly set, mark the chocolate into serving portions with a warmed knife. Arrange the nougat leaves in position before the chocolate completely sets, or fix with a little crème au beurre.

DOBOS TORTE

4 eggs
6 oz. (¾ cup) caster sugar
5 oz. (1¼ cups) plain flour
4 oz. (½ cup) caster sugar for caramel
a few toasted hazel nuts

For chocolate butter cream :
5 oz. butter or margarine
8 oz. (1¾ cups) icing sugar, sifted
2 oz. cooking chocolate, melted

Draw 5–6 rectangles, 10 in. by 4½ in., on non-stick paper. Place the papers on baking sheets.

Whisk the eggs and sugar together in a basin over a pan of hot water until very thick and fluffy. Sift the flour over the top and carefully fold it in with a metal spoon. Divide the mixture between the rectangles in thin, even layers. Bake towards the top of the oven at 375°F. (mark 5) for about 10 minutes, until golden brown.

Peel off the papers and if necessary trim the edges of the rectangles with a sharp knife to neaten them. Cool on wire racks.

Select the layer with the best surface and lay it on an oiled baking sheet or on non-stick paper. Put the caster sugar for the caramel in

Profiteroles, filled with cream and served with chocolate sauce

a wide based saucepan and place it over a low heat to dissolve, without stirring. Shake the pan occasionally. When it is completely dissolved, cook gently to a golden brown. Pour the caramel evenly over the selected cake layer, so that the surface is completely covered. Quickly mark it into 8 sections with the back of an oiled knife.

To make the butter cream, cream the butter and gradually beat in the icing sugar. Beat in the cool but still soft chocolate. Sandwich together the layers of cake with butter cream and place the caramel covered layer on top.

Cover the sides of the Torte with butter cream and mark decoratively with a fork. Pipe the remainder in whirls on the caramel surface and top each whirl with a toasted hazel nut.

GATEAU AMANDINE

4½ oz. (⅝ cup) caster sugar
3 large eggs
3 oz. (¾ cup) plain flour

For filling and decoration :
apricot glaze
4 oz. whole blanched almonds
½ pint (1¼ cups) double cream or coffee crème au beurre
icing sugar

Grease and base-line a 9½-in. (top measurement) moule à manqué cake tin.

Whisk together the sugar and eggs until thick and creamy – the whisk should leave a trail when lifted. Sift the flour over the surface and lightly fold in with a metal spoon. Turn the mixture into the prepared tin and bake just above the centre of the oven at 375°F. (mark 5) for about 30 minutes, until well risen and golden brown. Turn out and cool on a wire rack.

When the cake is cold, split and sandwich with apricot glaze. Using a sharp knife, split the nuts in half and cut in thin slices. Whip the cream and lightly sweeten with icing sugar. Completely mask the cake with the cream and cover with sliced nuts. Dust lightly with icing sugar and chill. Eat the same day.

BELGIAN TORTE

8 oz. butter
2 oz. (¼ cup) caster sugar
2 tbsps. corn oil
vanilla essence
1 large egg, beaten
1 lb. (4 cups) plain flour
2 level tsps. baking powder
a pinch of salt
½ lb. stiff apricot jam
icing sugar

Grease an 8-in. round cake tin. Beat the butter until creamy, add the sugar and beat again. Add the oil, a few drops of vanilla essence and the egg. Beat well. Sift the flour with the baking powder and salt and gradually work it into the mixture. Then, using the finger tips, knit the mixture together as for a shortbread dough.

Divide the dough into 2 pieces and knead lightly until smooth. Coarsely grate half the dough into the cake tin in an even layer. Cover with warm jam nearly to the edge. Coarsely grate the remainder of the dough over the top.

Bake the cake just above the centre of the oven at 300°F. (mark 1–2) for about 1½ hours, until the surface is lightly browned. While hot dredge heavily with icing sugar. Cool in the tin and when cold turn out carefully.

PROFITEROLES
makes about 20

2½ oz. choux pastry–i.e. made with 2½ oz. (⅝ cup) flour etc.
¼ pint (⅝ cup) double cream
1 egg white
icing sugar

For chocolate sauce :
4 oz. chocolate dots
½ oz. butter
2 tbsps. water
2 level tbsps. golden syrup
vanilla essence

Lightly grease 2 baking sheets. Spoon the choux pastry into a fabric forcing bag fitted with a ½-in. plain vegetable nozzle. Pipe out about 20 small bun shapes on the baking sheets; hold the nozzle upright while piping and lift it away with a sharp pull to release the mixture.

Bake the choux buns just above the centre of the oven at 425°F. (mark 7) for about 25 minutes until well risen and golden brown. If correctly cooked, the insides should be hollow and fairly dry. Make a hole in the base of each bun with a skewer or knife and cool them on a wire rack.

Shortly before the profiteroles are required, make the chocolate sauce. Melt the chocolate dots with the butter in a small pan over a very low heat. Add the water, syrup and 2–3 drops of vanilla essence; stir well until smooth and well blended.

Put the double cream and egg white into a bowl and whip them together until thick and standing in peaks. Spoon into a fabric forcing bag fitted with a small plain nozzle and pipe into the centre of each bun, through the hole in the bottom.

Dust with icing sugar and serve with the chocolate sauce spooned over or served separately.

CREAM PUFFS
makes about 16

2½ oz. choux pastry – i.e. made
  with 2½ oz. (⅝ cup) flour etc.
¼ pint (⅝ cup) double cream
2½ fl. oz. single cream
icing sugar

The characteristic light, crisp texture and crazy-paving tops of cream puffs are achieved by baking the pastry in its own steam. For this you will need large, shallow tins with tightly fitting lids, or heavy, flat baking sheets with roasting tins inverted over them, sealing the joint with a flour and water paste if necessary.

Spoon the choux pastry into a forcing bag fitted with a ½-in. plain vegetable nozzle and pipe into small rounds on the tins or baking sheets. Leave plenty of space between them.

Cover the piped choux with the lids or roasting tins and bake just above the centre of the oven at 400°F. (mark 6) for 40–50 minutes. It is important that the puffs are left undisturbed during cooking, or the steam will escape and cause the buns to collapse. Estimate the end of the cooking time by giving the tin a gentle shake – if the buns are cooked they will rattle on the base. Cool on a wire rack.

Just before the puffs are required, make a hole in the base of each. Whip the 2 creams together and fill the puffs, piping with a small plain vegetable nozzle. Dust with icing sugar.

PETITES FEUILLETEES

puff or flaky pastry
1 egg white, lightly broken
  with a fork
apricot jam
double cream, whipped
chopped nuts

Roll out the pastry thinly and cut into 3-in. squares. Fold the corners of each square to the centre and join them with a tiny cut-out shape of pastry. Brush with egg white and bake in the centre of the oven at 450°F. (mark 8) for 10–15 minutes.

Cool on wire racks. Sieve the apricot jam and brush it over each pastry to glaze. Decorate with piped whipped cream and chopped nuts.

BASIC PATE SUCREE
This French flan pastry is traditionally used in pâtisserie and larger gâteaux

4 oz. (1 cup) plain flour
a pinch of salt
2 oz. (¼ cup) caster sugar
2 oz. butter at normal room
  temperature
2 egg yolks

Sift together the flour and salt on to a pastry board or, better still, a marble slab. Make a well in the centre and into it put the sugar, butter and egg yolks.

Using the fingertips of 1 hand, pinch and work the sugar, butter and egg yolks together until well blended.

Gradually work in all the flour and knead lightly until smooth. Put the paste in a cool place for at least 1 hour to relax, then roll out and use according to the recipe.

BATEAUX AUX FRUITS
makes 6 ; for this and the following recipes, make up the basic quantity of pâte sucrée given above and use a third of the dough for each variation

⅓ quantity pâte sucrée recipe
apricot glaze
11-oz. can mandarin oranges,
  drained
6 glacé cherries

Roll out the pastry thinly and use to line 6 4½-in. boat shaped patty tins, pressing it lightly into shape. Bake blind, without baking beans, towards the top of the oven at 375°F. (mark 5) for 5–7 minutes, until just tinged brown. Cool on a wire rack.

Warm the apricot glaze slightly and brush it over the insides of the pastry boats.

Arrange the fruit neatly in the boats and brush with more warm apricot glaze.

BATEAUX SAINT ANDRE
makes 6

⅓ quantity pâte sucrée recipe
½ lb. cooking apples, peeled
  and cored
1 oz. sugar
1 tbsp. water
½ egg white
4 oz. (⅞ cup) icing sugar

Roll out the pastry and use to line 6 4½-in. boat shaped patty tins, pressing it lightly into shape.

Slice the apples into a pan and stew with the sugar and water until pulpy; then continue to cook until the purée is thick enough to hold its shape; leave until cold.

Make petites feuilletées from flaky pastry

Divide the purée between the uncooked pastry boats and spread it evenly.

Make up an icing, using the egg white and icing sugar and spread a thin layer over each boat. Roll out the pastry trimmings and cut into short strips; place 2 across each boat. Bake in the centre of the oven at 375°F. (mark 5) for about 10 minutes, until the pastry has set and the topping is tinged brown. Leave to cool in the moulds for a few minutes, then turn out carefully and cool on a wire rack.

BATEAUX DE MIEL
makes 6

⅓ quantity pâte sucrée recipe
4 oz. butter
4 oz. (½ cup) caster sugar
4 oz. ground almonds

3 tsps. thick honey
coffee essence
coffee glacé icing

Roll out the pastry thinly and use to line 6 4½-in. boat shaped patty tins, pressing it lightly into shape. Bake blind, without baking beans, towards the top of the oven at 375°F. (mark 5) for 5–7 minutes, until just tinged brown. Turn out and cool on a wire rack.

Cream the butter and sugar until light and fluffy. Beat in the almonds, honey and 2 teaspoons coffee essence.

Divide the creamed mixture between the boats, piling the mixture up to a ridge and smoothing the surface on either side. Chill.

When firm, coat with icing and decorate with a wavy line of stiffer piped icing.

Bateaux aux fruits, on a base of pâte sucrée

PERFECT PASTRY

Many people consider good pastry the mark of a good cook—so make sure of your results by checking a few general rules before you start. The first requirements for success are cool working conditions and a hot oven—and the richer the pastry, the hotter the oven. To help keep the pastry cool, handle it as little as possible and use only your fingertips for rubbing in the fat. Always use cold water for mixing (except for choux pastry and hot water crust). The rich pastries—flaky and puff—will be improved if you leave them in a cool place between rollings and again before baking.

The proportion of ingredients is vital to the texture of the finished pastry, so add the water cautiously, using only enough to make the mixture bind without becoming sticky—sticky dough leads to hard pastry. Use the barest minimum of flour on the rolling pin and working surface, or you will alter the proportions, giving you dry pastry.

Always roll pastry lightly and as little as possible. Avoid stretching it when you are lining a flan case or covering a pie, or it will shrink back during cooking and spoil the finished shape.

INGREDIENTS

Pastry ingredients are simple, basic foodstuffs, so make sure you use good quality brands for the best results.

Flour Plain flour is best, though for shortcrust pastry you can use self-raising with quite good results.

Fat Butter, margarine and lard are generally used, though nowadays proprietary vegetable shortenings (both blended and whipped) and pure vegetable oils are often used as well, with excellent results. If you are using one of these, remember to follow the directions on the packet, as the proportion of fat to flour may vary slightly.

Liquid As a rule, allow 1 teaspoon of liquid per ounce of flour for shortcrust pastry and 1 tablespoon per ounce to bind suet or flaky pastries to an elastic dough.

BAKING BLIND

Flans and tarts are often 'baked blind' when they are to be filled with a cold or soft uncooked filling, as with lemon meringue pie. To do this, line the pie dish or flan ring with the pastry. Cut out round of greased greaseproof paper slightly larger than the pastry case and fit this, greased side down, inside the pastry. Half-fill the paper with uncooked haricot beans or rice or with stale bread crusts. Bake the pastry as directed in the recipe for 10–15 minutes until it has set. Remove the paper and beans, rice or crusts from the pastry case and return it to the oven for another 5 minutes or so to dry out. It is now ready to use. Alternatively, line the pastry case with kitchen foil, which does not need filling with beans.

Small tartlet cases can be baked blind without lining. Line the tartlet tins with pastry, prick well with a fork and bake as directed in the recipe.

SHORTCRUST PASTRY

Quick and simple, using the 'rubbing-in' method. Forms the basis of a wide range of sweet and savoury dishes.

6 oz. (1½ cups) plain flour
pinch of salt
1½ oz. lard
1½ oz. margarine
6 tsps. water (approx.)

Sift the flour and salt together into a wide, shallow bowl. Cut the fat into small knobs and add it. Using both hands, rub the fat into the flour between finger and thumb tips. After 2–3 minutes there will be no lumps of fat left and the mixture will look like fresh breadcrumbs.

Add the water, stirring with a round-bladed knife until the mixture begins to stick together. With one hand, collect it together and knead lightly for a few seconds, to give a firm, smooth dough. The pastry can be used straight away, but is better allowed to 'rest' for 15 minutes. It can also be wrapped in polythene and kept in the refrigerator for a day or two. Alternatively store at the rubbed in stage. Allow dough to return to room temperature before rolling out.

When pastry is required, sprinkle a very little flour on a board or table and roll out the dough evenly, turning it occasionally. The usual thickness is about ⅛ in.; do not pull or stretch it. Use as required. The usual oven temperature is 400–425°F. (mark 6–7).

This quantity of shortcrust pastry will line a 6–7-in. flan ring or top a 1½–2 pint fruit pie.

FLAN PASTRY

Slightly richer than shortcrust, made in the same way. It is usually sweetened and ideal for flan cases, tartlets and other sweet pastries. For savoury dishes, omit the sugar.

5 oz. (1¼ cups) plain flour
3 oz. butter or margarine and lard, mixed
1½ level tsps. caster sugar
1 egg, beaten
4 tsps. water

Sift the flour and salt together into a bowl and rub in the fat with the finger tips, as for shortcrust pastry, until the mixture resembles fine breadcrumbs. Mix in the sugar. Add the egg and water, stirring until the ingredients begin to bind, then with one hand collect the mixture together and knead very lightly to give a firm, smooth

dough. Roll out as for shortcrust pastry and use as required.
This pastry should be cooked in a fairly hot oven–400°F. (mark 6). This quantity of pastry will line a 7–8-in. flan ring.

CHEESE PASTRY

A savoury pastry, suitable for pies, tarts and flans. This is a simple version, not so rich as that given below.

4 oz. (1 cup) plain flour
pinch of salt
2 oz. butter or margarine and lard (mixed)
2 oz. (½ cup) Cheddar cheese, finely grated
a little beaten egg or water

Sift the flour and salt together into a bowl and rub in the fat, as for shortcrust pastry, until the mixture resembles fine crumbs in texture. Mix in the cheese. Add the egg or water, stirring until the ingredients begin to stick together, then with one hand collect the dough together and knead very lightly to give a smooth dough. Roll out as for shortcrust pastry and use as required.
The usual temperature for cooking cheese pastry is fairly hot–400°F. (mark 6).
This quantity of pastry will fill 8 boat moulds, 12 patty tins or a 7-in. flan ring.

RICH CHEESE PASTRY

Requires rather more care in making than the simpler version. Suitable for party and cocktail 'nibblers'–not suitable for flan cases.

3 oz. butter or margarine and lard (mixed)
3 oz. (¾ cup) Cheddar cheese, finely grated
4 oz. (1 cup) plain flour
pinch of salt

Cream the fat and cheese together until soft. Gradually work in the flour and salt with a wooden spoon or a palette knife until the mixture sticks together; with one hand collect it together and knead very lightly until smooth. Cover with greaseproof or waxed paper and leave in a cool place. Use as required.
Cook at 400°F. (mark 6).

SUETCRUST PASTRY

A traditional pastry, quick and easy to make and can be used for both sweet and savoury dishes. It can be baked, but steaming and boiling give much more satisfactory results.

Almonds and fruit for a frangipan flan

8 oz. (2 cups) self-raising flour
½ level tsp. salt
4 oz. shredded suet
8 tbsps. cold water (approx.)

Sift together the flour and salt into a bowl. Add suet and enough cold water to give a light elastic dough and knead very lightly until smooth. Roll out to ¼-in. thickness and use as required.
This quantity of pastry will be sufficient for a 1½-pint steak and kidney pudding.

FORK-MIX PASTRY

Made with oil, this is more suitable for savoury dishes than sweet.

2½ tbsps. corn oil
1 tbsp. cold water
4 oz. (1 cup) plain flour
pinch of salt

Put the oil and water into a basin and beat well with a fork to form an emulsion. Add the sifted flour and salt gradually to the mixture to make a dough. Roll this out on a floured board or between greaseproof paper.
Bake in a fairly hot oven–400°F. (mark 6). This quantity of pastry is sufficient to line a plate pie.

CORNISH PASTIES

makes 4

12 oz. chuck or blade steak
4 oz. raw potato, peeled and diced
1 small onion, skinned and chopped
salt and pepper
12 oz. shortcrust pastry–i.e. 12 oz. (3 cups) flour, etc.

Cut the steak into small pieces,

To line pastry into small moulds, ease the pastry to the shape of the moulds and then roll the rolling pin over the top

add the potato and onion and season well. Divide the pastry into four and roll each piece into a round about 8 in. in diameter. Divide the meat mixture between the pastry rounds, damp the edges, draw the edges of the pastry together to form a seam across the top and flute the edges with the fingers.

Place on a baking tray and bake in the oven at 425°F. (mark 7) for 15 minutes to start browning the pastry, then reduce the heat to 325°F. (mark 3) and cook for about 1 hour. Serve hot or cold.

FRANGIPAN FLAN

serves 4

6 oz. shortcrust pastry – i.e. made with 6 oz. (1½ cups) flour, etc.
For frangipan cream:
¾ oz. cornflour
¾ pint (2 cups) milk
4 egg yolks
1 oz. caster sugar
3 oz. (¾ cup) ground almonds
vanilla essence
For fruit layer:
¼ lb. white grapes, skinned and halved
2 oranges, peeled
1 banana, peeled and sliced
For topping:
caster sugar
2 oz. (½ cup) flaked almonds, toasted

Roll out the pastry and use to line a 7½-in. plain flan case. Bake blind at 425°F. (mark 7) for 20 minutes. Cool.

Mix the cornflour with a little of the cold milk, blend in remaining milk and bring slowly to the boil, stirring all the time.

Remove from the heat and beat in the egg yolks one at a time. Add the caster sugar, ground almonds and a few drops of vanilla essence. Cook for about 1 minute until the sauce thickens. Stir well, cover and leave until cold.

Meanwhile, remove the pips from the grape halves and cut the oranges into segments. Arrange the grapes, oranges and banana slices in the pastry case. Spread the frangipan cream over the fruit, piling it into a pyramid shape. Dust thickly with caster sugar.

Stand the flan on a serving plate. With a red-hot skewer (held in a cloth) brand the sugar until it caramellizes. Reheat skewer between brandings. Sprinkle the sugar with almonds. Use within a few hours of making.

Place the butter on the dough in small pieces, using a round bladed knife

CREAM CHEESE BOATS

makes 16

4 oz. cheese pastry – i.e. 4 oz. (1 cup) flour, etc.
3 oz. cream cheese
1 oz. lean ham, finely chopped
2 tsps. top of the milk
salt and pepper
4 slices processed cheese

Line 16 3½-in. boat shaped moulds with the pastry. Prick the bottom of the pastry well and bake blind just above the centre of the oven at 400°F. (mark 6) for about 10 minutes or until golden brown. When cool, remove from the moulds. Beat the cream cheese until smooth, add the ham and top of the milk. Season well. Pipe the cheese into the pastry boats and decorate with triangular 'sails' cut from the sliced processed cheese. Use within a few hours of making.

STEAK AND KIDNEY PUDDING

serves 4

8 oz. suetcrust pastry – i.e. 8 oz. (2 cups) flour, etc.
½–¾ lb. stewing steak, cut into ½-in. cubes
¼ lb. kidney, skinned and cored
2 level tbsps. seasoned flour
1 onion, skinned and chopped

Half-fill a steamer or large saucepan with water and put it on to boil. Grease a 1½-pint pudding basin. Cut off a quarter of the pastry to make the lid. Roll out the remainder and use to line the basin.

Slice the kidney and coat both the steak and the kidney with seasoned flour. Fill the basin with the meat, onion and 2–3 tablespoons of water. Roll out the remainder of the pastry to a round the size of the basin top and damp the edge of it. Place on top of the meat and seal the edges of the pastry well.

Cover with greased greaseproof paper or foil and steam over rapidly boiling water for about 4 hours, refilling the pan as necessary with boiling water.

The meat can be prepared and stewed with the onion for about 2 hours earlier in the day or the previous night before being used for the filling. In this case, reduce the steaming time to 1½–2 hours.

RICH PASTRIES

Always handle flaked pastries lightly and as little as possible.

The fat to be used should be worked on a plate with a knife before you start to make the pastry. This softens it, as it needs to be about the same consistency as the dough with which it is going to be combined.

Remember to allow these richer pastries to 'rest' during the making as well as after shaping and before baking. Cover the pastry and leave in a cool place for 15 minutes or so. This prevents the fat becoming oily and spoiling the flaked texture of the finished pastry.

Roll out the pastry lightly, evenly and as quickly as possible.

FLAKY PASTRY

The commonest of the flaked pastries, used for both savoury and sweet dishes.

8 oz. (2 cups) plain flour
pinch of salt
6 oz. butter or butter and lard
8 tbsps. cold water to mix (approx.)
squeeze of lemon juice
beaten egg to glaze

Mix together the flour and salt. Soften the fat by working it with a knife on a plate; divide it into 4 equal parts. Rub one quarter of the softened fat into the flour with the fingertips and mix to a soft,

elastic dough with the water and lemon juice. On a floured board, roll the pastry into an oblong 3 times as long as it is wide.

Put another quarter of the fat over the top two-thirds of the dough in small flakes, so that it looks like buttons on a card. Fold the bottom third up and the top third down and give the pastry half a turn, so that the folds are now at the sides. Seal the edges of the pastry by pressing with the rolling pin. (On a warm day, allow to rest at this stage before continuing.) Re-roll into the same oblong shape as before.

Continue with the remaining two quarters of fat in the same way. When all the fat is used, wrap the pastry loosely in greaseproof paper or a polythene bag and leave it to rest in a refrigerator or a cool place for at least ½ hour before using. Sprinkle a board or working surface with a very little flour. Roll out the pastry ¼–⅛ in. thick and use as required.

The usual oven temperature for flaky pastry is hot – 425°F. (mark 7).

This quantity of pastry will line 2 8-in. pie plates or will make 16 Eccles cakes or cream horns.

ROUGH PUFF PASTRY

Similar in appearance and texture to flaky pastry, though generally not so even. Quicker and easier to make, and can be used as an alternative for flaky in most recipes.

8 oz. (2 cups) plain flour
pinch of salt
6 oz. butter or margarine and lard mixed
8 tbsps. cold water to mix (approx.)
squeeze of lemon juice
beaten egg to glaze

Sift the flour and salt into a bowl; cut the fat (which should be quite firm but not hard) into cubes about ¾ in. across. Stir the fat into the flour without breaking up the pieces and mix to a fairly stiff dough with the water and lemon juice. Turn on to a floured board and roll into a strip 3 times as long as it is wide, using firm, sharp movements. Fold the bottom third up and the top third down, then give the pastry a half-turn so that the folds are at the sides. Seal the edges of the pastry by pressing lightly with the rolling pin. Continue to roll and fold in this way 4 times altogether. Leave to rest in a cool place wrapped in greaseproof paper or polythene

ag for about 30 minutes before
sing. Roll out and use as for
aky pastry.

he usual oven temperature for
ooking rough puff pastry is 425°F.
mark 7).

UFF PASTRY

*he richest of all pastries,
iving the most even rising, the
ost flaky effect and the crispest
exture. Requires very careful
andling, allowing plenty of time
o rest before the final rolling
nd shaping.
lthough most cooks will want to
e able to make it, the standard
f bought puff pastry is very high.
n our recipes we refer to the
nished weight of pastry so that
eady-made pastry may be used
s an alternative.*

oz. (2 cups) plain flour
inch of salt
oz. butter (preferably
  unsalted)
tbsps. cold water to mix
  (approx.)
queeze of lemon juice
eaten egg to glaze

ift the flour and salt into a bowl.
Vork the fat with a knife on a plate
ntil it is soft, then rub about ½ oz.
f it into the flour.
Aix to a fairly soft, elastic dough
vith the water and lemon juice
nd knead lightly on a floured
oard until smooth.
orm the rest of the fat into an
blong and roll the pastry out
ato a square.
lace the fat on one half of the
astry and enclose it by folding
ne remaining pastry over and
ealing the edges firmly with the
olling pin.
urn the pastry so that the fold
to the side, then roll out into a
trip 3 times as long as it is wide.
old the bottom third up and the
op third down and seal the edges
vith the rolling pin. Cover the
astry and leave it to rest in a cool
lace (preferably the refrigerator)
r about 20 minutes.
urn the pastry so that the folds
re to the side and continue rolling,
olding and resting until the se-
uence has been completed 6
imes altogether.
fter the final resting, shape the
astry as required. Always brush
ne top surfaces with beaten egg
efore cooking, to give the charac-
eristic glaze of puff pastry—add a
inch of salt if a really rich glaze is
equired.
he usual oven temperature for
ooking puff pastry is 450°F.
mark 8).

Puff pastry, cream, jam and glacé icing for a mille-feuilles slice

This quantity of pastry will make
12 cream slices or a flan case 12 in.
by 6 in.

BAKEWELL TART
serves 4

4 oz. flaky or rough puff
  pastry—i.e. 4 oz. (1 cup)
  flour, etc. (or 8 oz. frozen
  puff pastry, thawed)
1–2 tbsps. raspberry jam
2 oz. butter or margarine
2 oz. (¼ cup) caster sugar
grated rind and juice of ½
  lemon
1 egg, beaten
3 oz. (1 cup) cake crumbs,
  sieved
3 oz. (¾ cup) ground almonds

Roll out the pastry thinly and
line a deep 7-in. or 8-in. pie plate.
Spread the bottom of the pastry
case with the jam.
Cream the fat and sugar with the
lemon rind until pale and fluffy.
Add the eggs a little at a time and
beat after each addition. Mix
together the cake crumbs and
ground almonds, fold half into
the mixture with a tablespoon,
then fold in the rest, with a little
lemon juice if necessary to give a
dropping consistency.
Put the mixture into the pastry
case and smooth the surface with a
knife. Bake near the top of the
oven at 425°F. (mark 7) for about
15 minutes, until the tart begins
to brown; transfer to the centre
of the oven and reduce the temperature to 350°F. (mark 4) and
cook for a further 20–30 minutes,
until the filling is firm to the
touch.
Serve hot or cold.

HOT CHICKEN PIE
serves 6

4 lb. oven-ready chicken
1 small onion, skinned and
  halved
1 carrot, peeled
1 leek, washed and trimmed
  or 1 stick of celery,
  scrubbed
6 peppercorns
salt

For the sauce :
2 oz. butter
6 oz. (¾ cup) onion, skinned
  and chopped
½ lb. sweet red peppers,
  seeded and finely chopped
2 oz. green chillies, halved
  and seeded
4 level tbsps. flour
1 pint (2½ cups) chicken stock
4 oz. (1 cup) mature Cheddar
  cheese, grated
salt and freshly ground black
  pepper

6 oz. puff pastry (i.e. made
  with 6 oz. flour) or 13 oz.
  frozen puff pastry, thawed
1 egg, beaten

Simmer the chicken in sufficient
water to cover with the vegetables—onion, carrot, leek or
celery—peppercorns and salt, for
about 2 hours. Remove chicken,
reduce the liquor to 1 pint by
rapid boiling and then strain.
Melt the butter in a saucepan, fry
the chopped onion, peppers and
chillies for 10 minutes; if wished,
the chillies may be removed at
this stage.
Carve the chicken, cutting it into
fork-size pieces, and discard the
skin. Place the meat in a 3-pint

pie dish with a funnel. Blend the
flour into the fried vegetables
and slowly add the strained stock,
stirring continuously. Bring to the
boil.
When the liquid has thickened,
add the cheese and adjust the
seasoning. Spoon over the chicken
and allow to cool.
Roll out the puff pastry and use to
cover the filled pie dish. Knock up
and scallop the edge and score the
top of the pastry into diamonds
with a knife, glaze with beaten egg,
place on a baking sheet and cook
in the oven at 450°F. (mark 8) for
30 minutes. Reduce heat to 325°F.
(mark 3) and cook for a further
30 minutes.

MILLE-FEUILLES SLICES
makes 6

4 oz. puff or rough puff pastry
  —i.e. 4 oz. (1 cup) flour, etc.
  (or 8 oz. frozen puff pastry,
  thawed)
raspberry jam
whipped cream
glacé icing
chopped nuts

Roll the pastry into a strip ⅛ in.
thick, 4 in. wide and 12 in. long.
Brush the baking tray with water,
lay the pastry on it and cut it
from side to side in strips 2 in.
wide, but don't separate the slices.
Bake near the top of the oven, at
450°F. (mark 8) for 10 minutes.
Separate the strips and cool them.
Split each into two and sandwich
them together in threes or fours
with jam and cream. Cover the
tops with glacé icing and sprinkle
a few chopped nuts at each end.

CHOUX PASTRY

A rich pastry that swells in cooking to a crisp, airy texture. It is traditionally used for sweet pastries such as éclairs and profiteroles, and occasionally for special savoury dishes.

$1\frac{1}{2}$ oz. butter or margarine
$\frac{1}{4}$ pint ($\frac{5}{8}$ cup) water
$2\frac{1}{2}$ oz. ($\frac{5}{8}$ cup) plain flour, sifted
2 eggs, lightly beaten

Melt the fat in the water and bring to the boil. Remove from the heat and quickly tip in the flour all at once. Return the pan to the heat and beat the paste until it is smooth and forms a ball in the centre of the pan. (Take care not to over-beat or the mixture becomes fatty.) Allow to cool slightly. Beat in the eggs gradually, adding just enough to give a smooth, glossy mixture of piping consistency. Use as required.

The usual oven temperature is 400°F. (mark 6).

This quantity will make 10–12 éclairs or 20 profiteroles.

Fill each éclair with cream and dip in melted chocolate

CHOCOLATE ECLAIRS

makes 10–12

$2\frac{1}{2}$ oz. choux pastry–i.e. $2\frac{1}{2}$ oz. ($\frac{5}{8}$ cup) flour, etc.
whipped cream or crème pâtissière
chocolate glacé icing made with 4 oz. ($\frac{7}{8}$ cup) icing sugar etc., or 3–4 oz. melted chocolate

Make up the choux pastry and spoon into a fabric forcing bag fitted with a $\frac{1}{2}$-in. diameter plain round nozzle; pipe fingers $3\frac{1}{2}$–4 in. long on to a baking tray. Keep the lengths even and cut the paste off with a wet knife against the edge of the nozzle. Bake the éclairs near the top of the oven at 400°F. (mark 6) for 30–35 minutes, until well risen, crisp and of a golden brown colour.

Remove from the tray, make a slit in the side to allow the steam to escape and leave on a wire rack to cool.

When the éclairs are cold, fill with the whipped cream or crème pâtissière, then ice the tops with a little chocolate glacé icing or dip them in melted chocolate.

HOT-WATER CRUST PASTRY

Used for raised pies, as the hot water used to mix the pastry makes it pliable enough to mould easily.

1 lb. (4 cups) plain flour
2 level tsps. salt
4 oz. lard
$\frac{1}{4}$ pint ($\frac{5}{8}$ cup) plus 4 tbsps. milk or milk and water

Sift the flour and salt together. Melt the lard in the liquid, then bring to the boil and pour into a well made in the dry ingredients. Working quickly, beat with a wooden spoon to form a fairly soft dough. Turn it out on to a lightly floured board and knead until smooth. Use as required, keeping the part of the dough not actually being used covered with a cloth or upturned bowl to prevent it hardening.

The usual oven temperature is 425°F. (mark 7) for the first 15 minutes, reduced to 365°F. (mark 4) for the remainder of the time.

SHAPING A RAISED PIE BY HAND

Roll out $\frac{2}{3}$ of the prepared dough to a round 12 in. in diameter. Take a straight-sided container 4 in. in diameter (e.g. a large jam jar), dredge with flour and turn upside down. Lift the round of dough with the rolling pin and place over the base of the container. Mould dough round the container by pressing firmly to the sides, keeping the edge even.

Cut a double thickness of greaseproof paper or kitchen foil to fit round the pie. Wrap the paper round the pastry and tie with string. Leave in a cool place until the pastry is firm enough to stand in the 'raised' position without a mould.

Turn the container the right way up and gently ease it out of the pastry case, twisting it gently to loosen. Leave the paper in position. Place the pastry case on a baking sheet, and fill with the prepared meat mixture. Pack the filling well down at the sides to hold the shape of the pie. Brush the edge with water. Roll out the remaining pastry to make a lid. Place on top of the pie and press the edges together to seal. Trim away the surplus pastry and paper with scissors.

Make a hole in the centre of the lid and decorate the top with pastry leaves cut from the trimmings. Brush with beaten egg white or water and bake as directed.

MAKING A RAISED PIE IN A CAKE TIN OR MOULD

Grease a 6-in. round cake tin–preferably one with a loose bottom, which makes it easier to remove the pie after baking. Roll out $\frac{2}{3}$ of the dough and use to line the sides and bottom of the tin, making sure that the pastry is free of creases and splits. Add the filling, cover with the remaining dough, rolled out to form a lid, and decorate. Bake as directed in the recipe.

RICH RAISED PIE

serves 6–8

1 lb. hot-water crust pastry i.e. 1 lb. (4 cups) flour, etc.
veal bones
$2\frac{1}{2}$-lb. oven-ready chicken, boned
salt and pepper
$\frac{1}{2}$ lb. lean pork
$\frac{1}{2}$ lb. lean streaky bacon rashers, rinded
$\frac{1}{2}$ lb. shoulder veal
2 tbsps. chopped parsley
1 lb. pork sausage meat

Chop the veal bones and use them together with the chicken bones skin and giblets, to make a well-seasoned, concentrated jellied stock; leave to cool in the refrigerator.

Separate the chicken breasts and cut into pieces; mince the remainder of the flesh, together with the pork and half the bacon rashers. Dice the veal. Blend the parsley into the sausage meat. Cut the remaining bacon rashers in half, stretch each piece with the back of a knife, spread a thin layer of sausage meat on to each rasher and roll up.

Make the pastry and use two-thirds of it to line an 8-in. oval fancy pie mould, placed on a baking sheet. Press the pastry well into the base and the pattern. Use three-quarters of the remaining sausage meat to make a lining over the pastry. Fill the centre alternately with bacon rolls, minced pork mixture, veal and chicken breasts, piled well up. Season well and cover with the remaining sausage meat.

Damp the edges of the pastry, roll out the remaining piece and use for a lid. Trim the edges and seal. Decorate with pastry trimmings, and make a hole in the centre of the pie. Brush well with beaten egg.

Bake at 400°F. (mark 6) for 3 minutes, reduce the heat to 350°F (mark 4) and cook for a further hours. Cover with foil once the pastry is a good golden brown.

When the pie is quite cold, fill with cool but not cold liquid stock through the hole in the centre of the lid. Leave for several hours.

CAKES FOR THE FAMILY

Most cakes are straightforward to make if you follow the recipe carefully. Always use the ingredients specified, as substituting granulated sugar for caster, or self-raising flour for plain, will alter the texture considerably and could be disastrous. Always make sure eggs are at room temperature when you use them and don't use butter or margarine straight from the refrigerator either; let them soften a little first, unless you are using one of the 'soft' margarines.

Oven temperature is critical in cake baking, so always pre-heat the oven before you start and don't open the door until after two-thirds of the cooking time given in the recipe has elapsed. If the cake seems to be browning too quickly, lower the temperature towards the end of the time. To test whether a light textured cake is cooked, press it lightly with the tip of a finger – it should be spongy, give only very slightly to the pressure,

then rise again immediately. With a fruit cake, lift it gently from the oven and listen to it carefully; if there is a sizzling sound, the cake is not yet cooked through. Alternatively, insert a warm skewer (never a cold knife) into the centre of the cake. It should come out perfectly clean; if any mixture is sticking to it, the cake requires longer cooking.

WHISKED SPONGE

2 eggs
4 oz. (½ cup) caster sugar
4 oz. (1 cup) plain flour, sifted

Grease and base-line an 8-in. sandwich tin.

Whisk the eggs and sugar in a bowl over hot water until thick and leaving a trail. Remove from the heat. Sprinkle the sifted flour over the egg mixture and carefully fold in, using a metal spoon, until the flour is evenly distributed. Pour into the prepared tin and bake just above the centre of the

oven at 350°F. (mark 4) for 25–30 minutes

Turn out and cool on a wire rack and use as required.

VICTORIA SANDWICH CAKE

4 oz. butter or margarine
4 oz. (½ cup) caster sugar
2 large eggs
4 oz. (1 cup) self-raising flour
grated rind of 1 lemon (or other flavouring)

Grease and base-line 2 7-in. sandwich tins or line 1 8½-in. straight sided sandwich tin with paper to come a little above the rim.

In a bowl, cream together the butter and sugar until light and fluffy. Add the eggs one at a time, beating well after each addition. Add the lemon rind or other flavouring.

Lightly beat in the flour. When well mixed, divide the mixture evenly between the 2 tins and level off the surface of each. Bake

the cakes (side by side, if possible) at 350°F. (mark 4) for about 25 minutes (30 minutes for a single deeper cake).

Turn the cakes out on to a wire rack to cool. To prevent marking the top surface if the cakes are to be left un-iced, first cover the rack with a clean tea towel, or turn them on to the hand and quickly reverse on to the rack. Sandwich the cakes (or split and sandwich the large cake) with jam or butter cream; ice the top with glacé icing or dust with icing sugar.

COFFEE NUT CAKE

6 oz. butter or margarine
6 oz. (⅔ cup) caster sugar
3 large eggs
6 oz. (1½ cups) plain flour
¾ level tsp. baking powder
pinch of salt
coffee butter cream
chopped and whole walnuts to decorate
coffee glacé icing

Grease and line 2 7-in. sandwich tins.

Cream the butter and sugar until light and fluffy, then beat in the eggs one at a time. Sift the flour, baking powder and salt and fold in a little at a time.

Divide the mixture equally between the prepared tins and bake in the centre of the oven at 350°F. (mark 4) for about 30 minutes, until golden brown and firm to the touch. Turn out the cakes and cool on a wire rack.

Make some butter cream with 3 oz. butter and 6 oz. (1 cup) sifted icing sugar and add sufficient coffee essence to give a good flavour.

Sandwich the layers together with the butter cream and use the remainder to coat the sides of the cake. Roll the sides in chopped walnuts and coat the top with glacé icing flavoured with coffee essence; decorate with the whole walnuts.

GRASMERE CAKE

12 oz. (3 cups) plain flour
1 level tsp. mixed spice
1½ level tsps. bicarbonate of soda
6 oz. butter or margarine
½ pint (1¼ cups) milk plus 1 tbsp.
1 tbsp. lemon juice
6 oz. (1 cup) Demerara sugar
6 oz. currants, cleaned
3 oz. sultanas, cleaned

Line a 9¾-in. by 5¾-in. loaf tin (top measurement) with greased greaseproof paper.

Sift the flour, spice and bicarbonate of soda into a wide bowl; cut the fat into small pieces and add to the bowl. Using the tips of the fingers, rub the fat into the flour until the mixture resembles fine breadcrumbs.

Add the lemon juice to the milk (the milk will clot and turn sour). Add the sugar, currants and sultanas to the dry ingredients and mix well. Gradually add the soured milk, stirring with a wooden spoon, until a dropping consistency is reached.

Leave the mixture covered for several hours or overnight.

Turn the mixture into the prepared tin. Level off the surface of the mixture with a spatula or knife. Place the tin on a baking sheet and bake in the centre of the oven at 325°F. (mark 3) for about 2 hours.

The Grasmere cake should be evenly risen and have a smooth surface. Leave it for a few minutes

Grasmere cake to cut and keep

in the tin before lifting it out on to a wire rack to cool. Carefully remove the paper.

Grasmere cake can be stored satisfactorily for about 1 week. Wrap it in kitchen foil when cold, or else wrap it in greaseproof paper and store in an airtight tin.

Note : If you prefer, omit the milk and lemon juice and use an equivalent quantity of buttermilk.

FROSTED APPLE CAKE

4 oz. butter or margarine
4 oz. (½ cup) caster sugar
2 large eggs
4 oz. (1 cup) self-raising flour
vanilla essence

For topping :
1 level tbsp. caster sugar
2 level tsps. powdered cinnamon
2 oz. flaked almonds
1 large cooking apple
icing sugar

Grease and line an 8-in. double sandwich tin.

Cream together the butter and sugar and beat in the eggs one at a time. Lightly beat in the flour, with a few drops of vanilla essence. Turn the mixture into the prepared cake tin.

Toss together the sugar, cinnamon and nuts. Cover the surface of the cake evenly with peeled, cored and very thinly sliced apple, and sprinkle with the nut mixture. Bake in the centre of the oven at 350°F. (mark 4) for about 30 minutes.

Cool slightly, then turn out carefully on to a wire rack covered with a clean tea towel. Reverse with the apple side uppermost and cool.

FARMHOUSE CAKE

4 oz. (1 cup) wholemeal flour
4 oz. (1 cup) self-raising flour
½ level tsp. mixed spice
½ level tsp. bicarbonate of soda
3 oz. lard
4 oz. (½ cup) caster sugar
2 oz. stoned raisins, cleaned
2 oz. sultanas, cleaned
1 oz. chopped mixed peel
1 egg, beaten
milk to mix (approx. 4 fl. oz., ½ cup)

Grease and line a 6-in. round cake tin, or a 8¼-in. by 4¼-in. loaf tin (top measurement).

Sift together the flours, spice and bicarbonate of soda, and rub in the lard. Add the sugar, fruit and peel. Mix with the beaten egg and sufficient milk to give a soft dropping consistency.

Put into the prepared cake tin and bake in the centre of the oven at 350°F. (mark 4) for about 1 hour. Turn out and cool on a wire rack.

SPICY DATE AND NUT CAKE

12 oz. (3 cups) plain flour
6 oz. butter or margarine
6 oz. (¾ cup) caster sugar
2 level tsps. ground cinnamon
6 oz. nuts, chopped
6 oz. stoned dates, chopped
14½-oz. can apple purée
1½ level tsps. bicarbonate of soda
1 tbsp. milk (approx.)

For topping :
2 tbsps. chopped dates and nuts
2 level tsps. caster sugar
½ level tsp. ground cinnamon

Grease and line a 9¾-in. by 5¾-in. loaf tin (top measurement).

Sift the flour into a bowl and rub in the fat; add the sugar, cinnamon, nuts and dates. Make a well in the centre and add the apple purée. Dissolve the bicarbonate of soda in the milk and add to the mixture; mix well and put into the prepared tin.

Mix together the ingredients for the topping, sprinkle over the surface of the cake and bake in the centre of the oven at 375°F. (mark 5) for about 1¼ hours. Carefully remove and cool on a wire rack.

RICH FRUIT CAKE

suitable for Christmas and celebration birthday cakes

8 oz. (2 cups) plain flour
½ level tsp. ground ginger
½ level tsp. ground mace
8 oz. butter
8 oz. (1⅓ cups) soft dark brown sugar
4 large eggs, beaten
1-2 tbsps. brandy
grated rind of 1 lemon
8 oz. currants, cleaned
8 oz. stoned raisins, cleaned and roughly chopped
8 oz. sultanas, cleaned
4 oz. small glacé cherries, halved
4 oz. mixed chopped peel
2 oz. nibbed almonds

Choose either a 7-in. square or an 8-in. round cake tin. Cut a double strip of greaseproof paper long enough to line the sides of the tin and 2 in. deep. Make a 1-in. fold lengthwise and snip at intervals. Cut 2 paper squares or rounds for the base.

Grease the tin. Fit 1 paper square or round into the bottom of the tin, line the sides, fitting the snipped edges into the corners and overlapping them smoothly at the base.

Fit in the other square or round and grease the lining. Either tie a band of brown paper round the outside of the tin, or place it inside a slightly larger tin.

Sift the flour with the spices. Cream the butter and sugar together in a bowl using a wooden spoon; beat well until the mixture is pale in colour, light and fluffy in texture and about twice its original volume. Add 1 tablespoon egg at a time, beating well. If the mixture shows signs of curdling, beat in 1-2 tablespoons sifted flour.

Using a metal spoon, lightly fold in the flour, alternately with the brandy and followed by the lemon nd, fruit and nuts. Mix thoroughly to distribute the fruit evenly. Then spoon all the mixture into the prepared tin, pushing it well into the corners. Use a rubber spatula to get all the mixture from the bowl.

With the back of a spoon, make a slight hollow in the centre of the mixture to prevent uneven rising. Put the tin on a newspaper-lined baking sheet. Bake below the centre of the oven at 300°F. (mark 2) for about 3¾ hours. If the cake shows signs of browning too quickly, cover the top with a sheet of greaseproof paper and reduce the heat to 275°F. (mark ½) for the last hour of the cooking time. Test by sticking a warmed skewer into the centre of the cake. If no uncooked mixture adheres to it, remove the cake from the oven. Allow it to cool for a few minutes in the tin, then turn it out on to a wire rack. When it is cold, remove the papers.

DEVIL'S FOOD CAKE

o oz. (2½ cups) plain flour
level tsps. bicarbonate of soda
level tsp. salt
oz. butter or margarine
oz. (1½ cups) soft light brown sugar
large eggs
oz. unsweetened chocolate, melted
fl. oz. (1 cup) milk
tsp. vanilla essence

For butter filling :
oz. butter
oz. (1 cup) icing sugar
tbsp. top of the milk

For frosting :
oz. chocolate dots
lb. (3½ cups) icing sugar
tbsps. hot water
egg yolks
oz. butter, melted

Grease and line 2 8½-in. sandwich tins, keeping the greaseproof paper round the sides above the rims.
Sift together the flour, bicarbonate of soda and salt. Cream together the fat and sugar until pale and fluffy, then gradually add the eggs, one at a time, beating well after each addition. Add the melted chocolate and beat well. Then add the flour alternately with the milk and vanilla essence. Turn the mixture into the tins and bake at 350°F. (mark 4) for about 40 minutes. Cool on a wire rack.
To finish, sandwich the cakes together with butter filling and coat with the frosting; finish in swirls

A light, fluffy gâteau for tea-time

using a round-bladed knife. Leave to set, preferably until the next day, before slicing.
Butter filling:
Cream the butter until soft then gradually beat in the sifted icing sugar with the milk.
Frosting:
Melt the chocolate dots in a bowl over warm, not boiling, water. Off the heat, stir in the sifted icing sugar and hot water. Gradually beat in the egg yolks, one at a time, followed by the melted butter, a little at a time. Continue to beat until of a spreading consistency.

GATEAU A L'ORANGE

4 eggs, separated
4 oz. (½ cup) caster sugar
grated rind of 1 orange
4 tbsps. orange juice
3½ oz. (⅞ cup) plain flour

For filling and decoration :
4½ oz. butter
5 oz. (⅝ cup) caster sugar
1 egg
1 egg yolk
grated rind of 1 orange
4 tbsps. orange juice
1 tbsp. orange liqueur
2 oz. almonds, flaked and toasted
1 whole orange

Grease and base-line a 9-in. straight sided sandwich tin.
Place the egg yolks and sugar in a basin and whisk until pale and thick. Beat in the orange rind and juice. Fold in the flour. Beat the egg whites stiffly and fold into the mixture. Turn it into the prepared tin and bake above the centre of the oven at 350°F. for about 30 minutes.
Turn out and cool on a wire rack. Meanwhile prepare the filling. Put 1½ oz. butter in a bowl with the caster sugar, egg, egg yolk, orange rind and juice and liqueur. Place over a pan of hot water and

whisk until smooth and thick. Leave until completely cold. Split the cake in 2 and sandwich together with a little of the butter cream. Cream the remaining butter and beat it into the rest of the filling. Use this thickened butter cream to cover the top and sides of the cake. Press the toasted almonds into the cream round the sides of the cake. Peel remaining orange free of all white pith; divide into segments to decorate the top.

FRUIT AND ALMOND SLICES
makes 12

3 oz. (¾ cup) plain flour
1 oz. (2 tbsps.) caster sugar
2 oz. butter
1 oz. currants
12 glacé cherries, halved

For topping :
2 oz. butter
2 oz. (¼ cup) caster sugar
1 large egg, beaten
2 oz. (½ cup) ground almonds
almond essence
icing sugar

Grease a shallow oblong tin measuring 12 in. by 4 in. and line the base with greased greaseproof paper.
In a bowl, mix together the flour and 1 oz. caster sugar. Lightly work in the butter, using the fingertips, until the mixture begins to bind together. Spoon it into the tin and press into an even layer over the base, using a round-bladed knife. Scatter the currants over, then arrange the cherries at intervals in between.
For the topping, cream the butter and sugar together until light and fluffy. Add the egg gradually and beat thoroughly. Stir in the ground almonds and 1–2 drops almond essence. Spread carefully over the fruit layer and bake the cake just below the oven centre at 375°F. (mark 5) for about 40 minutes,

until just set and golden brown. Loosen the edges, turn out and cool on a wire rack. Dredge with icing sugar and cut into bars.

MADEIRA CAKE

6 oz. butter
6 oz. (¾ cup) caster sugar
3 large eggs
5 oz. (1¼ cups) self-raising flour
4 oz. (1 cup) plain flour
juice and grated rind of ½ lemon
citron peel to decorate

Grease a 7-in. round cake tin.
Cream the butter and beat in the sugar until light and fluffy. Add the eggs one at a time, beating well after each addition.
Sift the flour and fold it in alternately with the lemon juice and rind. Turn the mixture into the prepared tin, add a few slices of thinly cut citron peel on top. Bake in the centre of the oven at 325°F. (mark 3) for about 1 hour and 10 minutes.
Cool for a short time in the tin, then turn it out on to a wire rack to cool thoroughly.

UNCOOKED CHOCOLATE CAKE

4 oz. sweet biscuits
2 oz. digestive biscuits
2 oz. shelled walnuts or seedless raisins
3½ oz. butter or margarine
1 oz. (2 tbsps.) caster sugar
3 oz. golden syrup
2 oz. (½ cup) cocoa

For icing :
2 oz. cooking chocolate
1 tbsp. hot water
2½ oz. (½ cup) icing sugar
knob of butter

Place a 7½- or 8-in. flan ring on a flat serving plate.
Roughly crush the biscuits with a rolling pin. Coarsely chop the walnuts or raisins and mix with the biscuits. Cream together the butter, sugar and syrup. Beat in the sifted cocoa and work in the biscuits and walnuts or raisins. When the ingredients are well mixed, press evenly into the flan ring and leave to refrigerate overnight. The next day remove the flan ring, spread the icing over the top of the cake and leave to set.
To make the icing, put all the ingredients in a small saucepan and stir together over a very low heat until the chocolate has melted. Spread over the cake when of a coating consistency.

Devil's food cake

CAKE DECORATING

Many of the nicest cakes are also the simplest to make, but they often require a little filling or decoration with a simple icing to turn them into something special. A sponge or Victoria sandwich would be nothing without its touch of glacé icing, jam filling or butter cream. None of these is a specialist decoration, anyone can make an attractive finish with a very little practice, and even beginners' mistakes are not too expensive!

Icings are not merely decoration, of course. They add moisture and a contrast of texture and flavour to the cake itself. So ring the changes and add to your repertoire. There is very little special equipment you need. For piped decorations you will want a forcing bag and a few nozzles, but even if you don't possess a piping set, that needn't deter you. Butter cream,

glacé icing and fondant icing can all be poured over the top of the cake or spread on with a palette knife. There are just a few simple rules to follow in order to achieve a perfect result.

First, allow the cake to cool thoroughly before you start. While it is cooling, prepare any decorations you plan to use – chop walnuts, cut glacé cherries or angelica into small pieces, grate chocolate, cut up crystallized fruit, etc. When you are ready to start, brush any crumbs off the top of the cake. If you are planning to ice the top, it must be level, so if necessary level the top, turn the cake over and use the flat underside. Most cakes can be left on the wire cooling rack while you are icing, but a soft sponge should be placed on a flat plate, as moving it would crack a soft icing. Do the filling

first, then decorate the sides and finally the top.

If you are going to pipe some icing on to the cake, you may find the large fabric forcing bags are rather large for icing nozzles – so here's how to make your own paper icing bag.

Fold a 10-in. square of greaseproof paper in half to form a triangle and then roll it up along the longest edge, so that it looks like an ice cream cone. Snip off the tip of the bag, drop in the icing nozzle (preferably one without a screw band) and fill with the required amount of icing. Be careful to avoid overfilling. Fold the top flap down, enclosing the front edge until the bag is sealed and quite firm.

To decorate the sides of a cake with jam, coconut, nuts and so on, first brush apricot glaze round

the sides of the prepared cake, or spread it on with a knife. Either put the chosen decoration on greaseproof paper and, holding the cake carefully on its side, roll it through the decoration, or press the nuts etc. a little at a time on to the cake with a round-bladed knife. Continue until the sides are evenly and completely coated. Do this before icing the top.

BUTTER CREAM OR ICING
This amount will coat the sides and top of a 7-in. cake or give a topping and a filling

4 oz. butter
**6–8 oz. (1½–1¾ cups) icing
    sugar, sifted**
**a few drops of vanilla essence
    or other flavouring**
1–2 tbsps. milk

Cream the butter until soft and

Many attractive decorations can be made using only a palette knife

gradually beat in the sugar, adding a few drops of essence and the milk.

As a filling Spread the butter cream evenly over the lower half of the cake with a round-bladed knife, taking it right to the edges, then put the top half of the cake neatly in place.

As a side covering Spread the butter cream evenly round the sides of the cake, using a round-bladed knife and making sure all the cake is coated. Then, using the flat blade of the knife, pat chopped nuts or chocolate vermicelli on to the sides.

As a topping Pile the butter cream on top of the cake and spread it out smoothly and evenly to the edges until it completely covers the surface. To give a more interesting effect, the surface of the butter cream can be patterned by using a fork or knife before being decorated with crystallized fruits, nuts, glacé cherries, chocolate drops, or extra butter cream piped in whirls, etc.

ALMOND BUTTER CREAM

Substitute almond essence for vanilla and add 2 tbsps. very finely chopped toasted almonds; mix well. This is not suitable for piping.

APRICOT BUTTER CREAM

Omit the vanilla essence and milk. Add 3 tbsps. sieved apricot jam and a squeeze of lemon juice.

BUTTERSCOTCH BUTTER CREAM

Omit the vanilla essence. Melt 1 level tbsp. soft brown sugar and 1 oz. butter together and heat for a few minutes. Cool slightly and beat well into the basic butter cream.

CHOCOLATE BUTTER CREAM

Add either $1-1\frac{1}{2}$ oz. melted but not hot chocolate or chocolate dots, or 1 level tbsp. cocoa blended to a paste with a little hot water.

COFFEE BUTTER CREAM

Omit the vanilla essence and flavour instead with 2 level tsps. instant coffee powder or 1 tbsp. coffee essence.

COFFEE AND WALNUT BUTTER CREAM

Omit the vanilla essence. Add 1–2 tsps. coffee essence and 1 level tbsp. chopped walnuts. This is not suitable for piping as the nuts will block the nozzle.

GINGER BUTTER CREAM

Omit the vanilla essence. Add 3 oz. preserved ginger, very finely chopped. This is not suitable for piping.

LIQUEUR BUTTER CREAM

Omit the vanilla essence and milk. Add 1–2 tsps. liqueur, and colouring according to the flavour of the liqueur.

MOCHA BUTTER CREAM

Omit vanilla essence and milk. Blend 1 level tsp. cocoa and 2 level tsps. instant coffee powder with a little warm water; cool before adding to the mixture.

ORANGE BUTTER CREAM

Omit vanilla essence and milk. Beat in 2 tbsps. orange juice, the grated rind of 1 orange and 1 tsp. Angostura bitters.

RASPBERRY BUTTER CREAM

Omit the milk. Beat in 2 tbsps. raspberry purée or sieved jam.

WALNUT BUTTER CREAM

Add 2–3 level tbsps. very finely chopped walnuts. This is not suitable for piping.

GLACE ICING

This amount is sufficient to cover the top of a 7-in. cake or 18 small buns. If the sides are also to be iced, make twice the amount

4 oz. ($\frac{7}{8}$ cup) icing sugar, sifted
1–2 tbsps. warm water colouring and flavouring (see below)

Put the icing sugar in a basin and gradually add the warm water. The icing should be thick enough to coat the back of a spoon quite thickly. Add a few drops of colouring or flavouring essence as required and use immediately. For icing of a finer texture, put the sugar, water and flavouring into a small pan and heat, stirring, until the mixture is warm – don't make it too hot. The icing should coat the back of a wooden spoon and look smooth and glossy.

If the sides of the cake are to be decorated, other than with glacé icing, do this before icing the top. To coat the whole cake, place the filled or plain cake on a wire cooling rack over a large sheet of greaseproof paper. Pour the icing evenly from the bowl on to the centre of the cake and allow it to run down the sides, guiding the flow with a palette knife. Keep a little of the icing in reserve in the bowl to fill any gaps.

If only the top of the cake is to be coated, pour the icing on to the centre of the cake and spread it, using a round-bladed knife and stopping just inside the actual edge to prevent the icing dripping down the sides. Decorate with cherries, angelica and so on and leave to set, or leave the plain icing to set and add piped decoration later.

Adding decorations Put these in place quickly before the icing sets – this holds them firmly and prevents the icing from cracking, as it would do if they were added later. Allow the icing to set firmly before attempting to do any piped decoration.

Small cakes These can be iced either by pouring the icing over them as above, or by holding them lightly in the fingers and dipping them into it.

Note: Glacé icing should not be runny, but should coat the back of a spoon quite thickly.

CHOCOLATE GLACE ICING

Dissolve 2 level tsps. cocoa in the measured water.

COFFEE GLACE ICING

Blend 1 tsp. coffee essence or 2 level tsps. instant coffee in a little water.

LEMON GLACE ICING

Substitute 1–2 tbsps. strained lemon juice for the water.

LIQUEUR GLACE ICING

Replace 2–3 tsps. of the water by the required liqueur.

Feather icing – simple but pretty

Butter cream and chopped walnuts turn a plain cake into a glorious gâteau

MOCHA GLACE ICING

Add 1 level tsp. cocoa and 2 level tsps. instant coffee to a little water.

FEATHER ICING

Before you start, make up a small amount of icing in a contrasting colour (e.g. chocolate on plain or lemon glacé icing); it should be of a slightly thicker consistency than the basic icing. Ice the cake with glacé icing in the usual way. Immediately, while the original icing is still wet, using a writing nozzle or a paper piping bag with the tip cut off, pipe parallel lines $\frac{1}{2}-\frac{3}{4}$ in. apart across the cake. Quickly draw a skewer or the sharp point of a knife through the icing at right angles to the piping, in alternate directions. Wipe the point clean after drawing each line.

FONDANT ICING

Makes sufficient icing to give a thick coating to a 7-in. cake

¼ pint (⅝ cup) water
1 lb. lump or granulated sugar
1 oz. glucose or a good pinch of cream of tartar

Choose a strong, heavy pan large enough to avoid the syrup boiling over. Put the water into the pan, add the sugar and let it dissolve slowly without stirring. When the sugar has dissolved, bring the syrup to the boil, add the glucose or cream of tartar and boil to 240°F. Pour into a heat-resistant bowl and leave to cool until a skin forms on top.

Beat the icing until it thickens, then work the fondant with a knife and finally knead with the hands until it is smooth. Colouring and/or flavouring (e.g. lemon, coffee, chocolate) may be worked in at this stage. The icing may now be used at once, or stored.

To use Place the icing in a basin over hot water and heat until it is the consistency of thick cream (don't over-heat or the texture will be spoilt). If necessary, dilute with sugar syrup or water.

To ice small cakes or pastries Spear them on a fork or skewer and dip them in the prepared fondant.

To ice a large cake Put the cake on a wire rack with a plate below and pour the icing quickly all over the cake. Don't touch the icing with a knife, or the gloss finish will be spoilt. Add any decoration and leave the icing to set.

To give a thick topping Pin a band of double greaseproof paper

Marzipan shapes like these teddy bears are favourites with the children

closely round the cake so that it comes 1 in. above the top. Prepare the fondant from 8 oz. sugar and the thinning syrup from 4 oz. sugar. Pour the fondant over the top of the cake. When the icing has set, ease off the paper collar, using the back of a knife blade dipped frequently in hot water. This method can also be used with glacé icing. *Note:* Cakes to be coated with fondant icing should first be coated completely with apricot glaze and then covered with almond paste.

APRICOT GLAZE

Place ½ lb. apricot jam and 2 tbsps. water in a saucepan over a low heat and stir until the jam softens. Sieve the mixture, return it to the pan, bring to the boil and boil gently until the glaze is of a suitable coating consistency. This glaze can be potted, as for jam, and kept for future use.

ALMOND PASTE
(Marzipan)
yield: 1 lb.

4 oz. (⅞ cup) icing sugar, sifted
4 oz. (½ cup) caster sugar
8 oz. (2 cups) ground almonds
1 tsp. lemon juice
almond essence
beaten egg to mix

Blend together the sugars and ground almonds, add the lemon juice, a few drops of almond essence and enough beaten egg to bind the mixture together to give a firm but manageable dough. Turn it out on to a sugared board and knead lightly until smooth. Almond paste can be used to make many simple yet attractive decor-

ations for a cake. There are two basic methods to achieve this.

1 For flat decorations, roll out the paste on a sugared board and cut out the required shapes. This can be done either with a pastry cutter, if this will give the shape you want; or with a sharp knife drawn carefully round a template of stiff card. Don't choose anything too complicated to begin with – stars, candles, engines or boats all have straight sides and clear, simple outlines.

2 For animal figures, roll the paste in the hands to form small balls or sausage shapes and use these to make up the animal. It is a good idea to draw the figure first to give you an idea of the proportions. Make the body first, then stick on the arms, head, legs, etc. Paint on a face with food colouring, using a very fine brush. Simple shapes to start with are cats, teddy bears, Santa Claus (coloured red where appropriate) and snails (made from one long 'sausage' wound round and round).

To give more variety, almond paste may be coloured if wished – Santa Claus, as we've already suggested, can be a nice bright red and holly or ivy leaves to decorate a Christmas cake could be a good, strong green. But be careful to colour only as much paste as you need, or the rest will be wasted. As you gain more confidence, you will find the ideas are almost inexhaustible. Almond paste shapes and figures are particularly good for children's party cakes – a clown, rocket ships, a 'magic roundabout', trains and houses can all be made from a basic cake shape and imaginative use of almond paste. Colour some paste

with a very little black treacle or caramel colouring and cut out witches and broom sticks for a Hallowe'en cake.

Leaves – particularly good for decorating a Christmas cake – can be made by drawing round a real leaf on to a piece of white card and using that as a template for cutting the shape from the almond paste. Draw in the veins with the point of a skewer and leave the paste to dry lying over a piece of crumpled foil, to give it a naturalistic curve. To make holly leaves, cut strips of thinly rolled green almond paste, ½ in. wide and 1–1¾ in. long. Using a tiny round cutter (the reverse end of a piping nozzle may be suitable) cut curves out of the sides to make the holly leaf shape. And, of course, almond paste is the traditional decoration for an Easter-time simnel cake. You can make miniature coloured Easter eggs for the top of the cake and cut out little chick shapes to go round the edge.

AMERICAN FROSTING

Makes sufficient frosting for a 7-in. cake. This is the traditional finish for a walnut cake

8 oz. (1 cup) sugar
4 tbsps. water
1 egg white

Gently heat the sugar in the water, stirring until dissolved. Then, without stirring, heat to 240°F. Beat the egg white stiffly in a deep bowl. Remove the sugar syrup from the heat and when the bubbles subside, pour it on to the egg white, whisking continuously. When the mixture thickens, is almost cold and starts to look opaque, pour it quickly over the cake. With a palette knife, quickly swirl the frosting into peaks. Add any required decorations. *Note:* To make this frosting properly, it is necessary to use a sugar-boiling thermometer.

CARAMEL FROSTING

Substitute Demerara sugar for the white sugar.

COFFEE FROSTING

Add 1 tsp. coffee essence to the mixture while beating.

LEMON FROSTING

Add a little lemon juice while beating the mixture.

ORANGE FROSTING

Add a few drops of orange essence and a little orange colouring to the mixture while it is being beaten.

MORE ADVANCED CAKE DECORATING

Most rich fruit cakes for celebration occasions are decorated with almond paste and royal icing. Royal icing is not so easy to handle as glacé or fondant, but the results can be so delightful that it is well worth a little practice. It makes economic sense too, since most confectioners charge quite highly to ice even a birthday cake. Practice on family birthday cakes, before you tackle something for a big party; or try out one or two designs on paper (it's cheaper than cake!).

QUANTITIES OF ICINGS FOR A FORMAL CAKE

Cake size		Almond Paste	Royal Icing
	6 in. ●	¾ lb.	1 lb.
6 in. ■	7 in. ●	1 lb.	1¼ lb.
7 in. ■	8 in. ●	1¼ lb.	1½ lb.
8 in. ■	9 in. ●	1¾ lb.	2 lb.
9 in. ■	10 in. ●	2 lb.	2¼ lb.
10 in. ■	11 in. ●	2¼ lb.	2¾ lb.
11 in. ■	12 in. ●	2½ lb.	3 lb.
12 in. ■	13 in. ●	3 lb.	3½ lb.

ALMOND PASTE

Make up a quantity of paste, according to the size of your cake. With a piece of string, measure round the outside of the cake. Take two-thirds of the almond paste and roll it out on a surface dredged with icing sugar to a rectangle half the length of the string and in width twice the depth of the cake. Trim with a knife and cut in half lengthwise. Knead the trimmings into the remaining paste and roll out to fit the top of the cake. Check at this stage that the surface of the cake is absolutely level.

Brush the sides of the cake with apricot glaze. Put the 2 strips of almond paste round the cake and smooth the joins with a round-bladed knife, keeping the top and bottom edges square. Brush the top with apricot glaze, place the rolled-out top paste in position and roll lightly with a sugar-dusted rolling pin. Make sure the joins adhere well. Run a straight-sided jam jar round the edge to smooth the paste and stick it firmly to the cake. Leave the

Break up a spray of artificial flowers to make a delicate decoration

almond paste for a week before icing, loosely covered.

ROYAL ICING

4 egg whites
2 lb. (7 cups) icing sugar, sifted
1 tbsp. lemon juice
2 tsps. glycerine

Whisk the egg whites until slightly frothy. Stir in the sugar a spoonful at a time with a wooden spoon. When half the sugar is incorporated, add the lemon juice. Continue adding more sugar, beating well after each addition until you reach the right consistency.

It is this initial beating that gives it a light texture; skip it and the result will be disappointing, often heavy and difficult to use. The mixture is right for coating if it forms soft peaks when pulled up with a wooden spoon; it should be a little stiffer for piping and thinner for flooding.

Lastly stir in the glycerine, which prevents the icing becoming too hard. If you use an electric mixer, take care not to overbeat. If royal icing becomes too fluffy, it gives a rough surface and breaks when piped. It helps to allow it to stand for 24 hours in a covered container before using. Gently beat by hand and if necessary adjust the consistency before using.

Note: powdered albumen is available commercially and avoids the problem of large quantities of left over egg yolks.

EQUIPMENT

Before starting to decorate with icing you will need the following equipment:

1. A turntable – this enables you to get a smooth finish all over and round the sides of the cake. It is possible to work without a turntable, using an upturned basin instead, but it makes it much more difficult to obtain a good finish.

2. An icing ruler, or a long, straight bladed knife longer than the diameter of the cake – this is for flat icing.

3. An icing nail or a cork fixed to a skewer. This serves the same function as a turntable, in miniature, for piping flowers and other small designs.

4. Plain writing nozzles in 3 sizes, to make lines, dots or words.

5. Star nozzles for rosettes, zigzags and ropes.

6. Shell nozzles.

7. Petal and leaf nozzles.

8. A forcing bag. Preferably make one yourself from greaseproof paper and use with icing nozzles without a screw band. If you use a fabric bag, attach a screw adjustment and use nozzles with a screw band.

FLAT ICING

To ice the cake, place it on a silver cake board 2–3 in. larger than the cake. With the cake and board on a turntable, spoon on an ample quantity of icing then use a palette knife to work it evenly over the top, using a paddling motion to remove any air bubbles. Roughly level the surface.

Draw an icing ruler (or a knife longer than the width of the cake) steadily across the cake top at an angle of 30° to smooth the surface. Be careful not to press too heavily. Neaten the edges, removing surplus icing by holding the knife

parallel with the side of the cake. Leave to dry for about 24 hours. Cover the sides the same way, still using a paddling motion. Hold a small palette knife or plain edged icing comb in one hand to the side of the cake and at a slight angle towards it. Pass the other hand under and round the turntable so that a little more than a complete revolution can be made. Keeping the knife quite still in one hand, revolve the turntable with the other, smoothly and fairly quickly. Towards the end, draw the knife or comb away without leaving a mark. Remove any surplus from the edge with a knife. If you prefer ice the sides before the top.

To achieve a really professional looking finish (and this is a must with a tiered wedding cake), give the cake a second coating with slightly thinner icing, about 2 days after the first. Trim off any rough edges from the first coat with a sharp knife or fine clean sandpaper and brush off the loose icing before starting the second coat.

PIPING TECHNIQUES

When using a forcing bag, avoid over filling. Small sized bags are easier to handle especially when using a writing nozzle – it is much better to refill frequently. Insert the appropriate nozzle in the end of the bag, spoon the icing in and fold the top flap down, enclosing the front edge until the bag is sealed and quite firm. Hold the bag in one hand with the thumb on top, the first finger resting down on the side of the bag and the second finger curved underneath. Use your other hand to steady the bag while you are piping.

To pipe lines use a writing nozzle. Make contact with the surface of the iced cake and squeeze out just enough icing to stick to the surface. Continue squeezing and at the same time raise the bag and pull towards you; hold the bag at an angle of about 45°. Lift the nozzle and the line of piped icing from the surface, to keep a sagging line. The icing can then be guided and lowered into the required design.

To pipe stars and scrolls use a star nozzle. For stars, hold the nozzle almost upright to the flat iced surface, pipe out a blob of icing and withdraw nozzle with a quick up and down movement. For scrolls, hold the bag at an

Piping random lacework to fill in the scallops

angle, as for a straight line. With the nozzle almost on the iced surface, pipe out a good head and then gradually release the pressure on the bag and pull away with a double or single curve; the whole operation is one movement.

Trellis work can be very effective. Use a writing nozzle to pipe parallel lines across the space to be covered; when these are dry pipe more lines on top of them in the opposite direction. For a really good finish, pipe a third layer, using a very fine nozzle. If any 'tails' are left at the ends of lines, trim them off while still soft.

Flowers and leaves Leaves are piped with a special leaf nozzle directly on to the surface of the cake. Flowers are made up in advance on paper and fixed to the cake after they have dried out. Stick a 2-in. square of non-stick paper to an icing nail with a small blob of icing (or to a cork fixed to a skewer). Work on this surface and leave the flowers to dry on the paper. When dry, peel away the paper and fix the flowers to the cake with a small blob of icing.

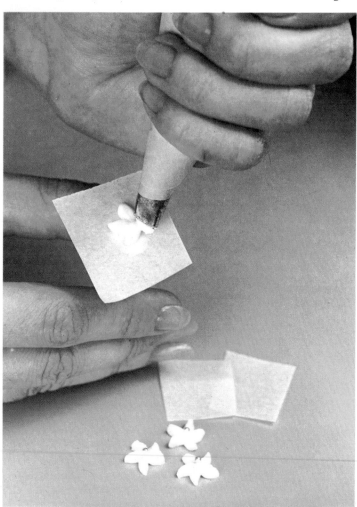

Making daisies separately to be fixed on the cake later

'**Run out' designs,** may either be piped directly on to the cake and flooded, or on to non-stick paper and fixed on the cake when dry. For separate 'run outs', draw out the design first on card, quite clearly. Cut a piece of non-stick paper to cover it and fix it with a spot of icing at each corner. Trace the outline of the design with a medium-fine writing nozzle; thin the icing to a 'just-flowing' consistency with unwhisked egg white and pour it into a small paper forcing bag. Cut the tip off the bag and flood the icing into the outline; if it is the correct consistency it will run smoothly into place. Leave flat for several days before peeling off the paper.

To pipe a 'run-out' directly on to the cake, prick the design out first with a fine pin and work as above.

TO DECORATE OUR WEDDING CAKE

Before starting any piping, place the pillars in position and prick round them with a pin. This will ensure that there is still room for them when everything else is done!

SCALLOPS

For each cake in turn, cut a circle of greaseproof paper the diameter of the cake. Fold the large one into 8, the middle one into 8 and the small one into 6, then for each cake proceed as follows.

Either free-hand or with compasses mark in the scallops (about 1 in. deep at the widest point) between the folds in the paper. Place the paper on the cake and secure with pins. Prick the outline of the scallops on to the flat iced surface. Remove and, using the prick marks as a guide, pipe the scallops in with a No. 2 writing nozzle. Pipe a second scallop $\frac{1}{4}$ in. outside the first, using a No. 3 writing nozzle, and a third line using the No. 2 nozzle again.

To make the scallops on the side of the cake, measure the depth of the cake and cut a band of greaseproof paper to size. Place it round the cake and secure with a pin at a point where one of the top scallops comes to the edge of the cake. Mark the points of the scallops right round the cake, remove the paper and draw in the scallops as for the top. At the same time draw corresponding scallops $\frac{1}{2}$ in. deep at the base. Secure the paper round the cake and prick out the design. Tilt the cake slightly and rest it on a firmly wedged, shallow tin, so that you can work on the sides. A

damp cloth under the tin helps to prevent movement. Pipe in the scallops round the top and base as for the flat surface.

LACE

Fill in the scallops – top, sides and base – with 'lace'. This is done with a No. 2 writing nozzle, almost resting on the surface. Pipe a wriggly line with no obvious set pattern, but keep it looking neat.

FLOWERS

The easiest flowers to pipe are daisies. Fix a square of paper to an icing nail or cork and use a medium petal nozzle. Pipe one petal at a time by squeezing out a small amount of icing, withdrawing the nozzle with a quick down and up movement. Pipe 5 petals, almost touching in the centre. Fill in the centre of each daisy either with a silver ball or with a small dot or several tiny dots from a No. 2 nozzle.

FERN SHAPED LINES

The fern shaped lines have to be piped on the side of the cake free-hand. Tilt the cake as for the scallops and pipe the lines $\frac{1}{4}$ in. from the side scallop, using a No. 3 nozzle. Repeat with a No. 2 nozzle $\frac{1}{4}$ in. below the first line. The vertical line is done with a No. 2 nozzle. Finish with a bold dot from a No. 3 nozzle at the apex of the lines. This pattern may be piped as a fine line or as a series of small dots, which are easier to control.

FINISHING

Neaten the base of each cake with a series of dots in the angle between the cake and the board; for the large cake using a No. 3 nozzle, for the smaller cakes a No. 2 nozzle. Where the scallops meet at the base, bring a line of 3 dots up the side of the cake, with a No. 2 nozzle, using varying degrees of pressure to obtain different sizes. Position the pillars within the guide lines previously pricked out. Check that they are level, to ensure that the tiers stand level when positioned. Ideally use a spirit level for this. Fix each pillar in position with icing, using a little extra if the height needs adjusting at all. Ensure that none of the icing creeps out from under the base of the pillars. Allow to dry.

Mount the tiers carefully on the pillars to make sure that everything fits together properly, and decide on the decoration for the top. Then dismantle the cake again and keep the tiers separately until the day.

BREAD MAKING AT HOME

For centuries bread has been a symbol of all that is good in life. Even today, when commercially baked bread is so readily available, there is something peculiarly satisfying about baking your own. Perhaps it is the special flavour and smell of bread that has just come out of the oven, perhaps it is working with live yeast that causes it – either way it is a joy not to be missed.

There is nothing unduly difficult about yeast cookery, provided you realise that yeast, unlike other raising agents, is a living plant, requiring gentle warmth in order to grow. Like any other plant, yeast also requires food and water; it obtains these from the flour itself and from the moisture used in mixing the dough. Given these conditions, yeast grows rapidly and as it grows carbon dioxide is formed. The bubbles of this gas are responsible for the spongy texture of the bread. The growing yeast also gives the characteristic smell of bread.

Not all breads use yeast as the raising agent; baking powder and bicarbonate of soda are also used. Breads made with these raising agents, except for soda bread, are usually slightly sweetened and are used as tea breads rather than as general purpose breads.

YEAST

Dried yeast can be stored for up to 6 months if kept in a tightly sealed container. It comes in the form of small, hard, light brown granules and instructions for activating it are usually given on the package.

Fresh baker's yeast looks rather like putty and has faint 'winey' smell. To keep it fresh, store it in a loosely tied polythene bag in a cold place – it will keep for 4–5 days in a larder, up to a month in the refrigerator; it can also be

Cheese loaf, floury Scotch bap and morning rolls

frozen, in which case it will keep for up to a year if tightly wrapped.

FLOUR

For the best results when making a basic white bread, use 'strong' plain flour. This has a higher gluten content than household plain flour, so it absorbs more water, giving a larger volume and a lighter texture. 'Soft' flour, which absorbs fat but less water, is suitable for some types of richer fancy breads.

BASIC WHITE LOAF

this quantity of flour makes about 2½ lb. dough, giving 1 large loaf or 2 small loaves, or about 18 rolls

1½ lb. (6 cups) strong plain
    white bread flour
1 level tbsp. salt (½ oz.)
½ oz. lard
½ oz. fresh baker's yeast (for
    dried yeast, see note below)
¾ pint (1⅞ cups) water

Grease a 2-lb. loaf tin or 2 1-lb. tins, or 2 baking sheets if making rolls.

Sift the flour and salt into a large bowl and rub in the lard. Blend the yeast with the water. Mix the dry ingredients with the yeast liquid, adding the liquid all at

once. Stir in with a wooden fork or spoon. Work it to a firm dough, adding extra flour if needed, until it will leave the sides of the bowl clean.

Turn the dough on to a floured surface and knead thoroughly, to stretch and 'develop' it. To do this, fold the dough towards you, then push down and away with the palm of your hand. Continue kneading until the dough feels firm and elastic and no longer sticky – about 10 minutes. Shape it into a ball.

Put the dough in a lightly oiled polythene bag to prevent a skin forming (the bag must be large enough to allow the dough to rise), tie it loosely and allow to rise until it is doubled in size and will spring back when pressed with a floured finger.

Allow time for the rising of the dough to fit with your day's arrangements, but the best results are achieved with a slow rise. Allow ¾–1 hour in a warm place, 2 hours at average room temperature, up to 12 hours in a cold larder or up to 24 hours in the refrigerator.

Refrigerated risen dough must be allowed to return to room temperature before it is shaped.

Turn the risen dough on to a

lightly floured surface, flatten it firmly with the knuckles to knock out the air bubbles, then knead to make it firm and ready for shaping (do not use too much flour or the colour of the crust will be spoilt.) Stretch the dough into an oblong the same width as the tin, fold it into 3 and turn it over so that the 'seam' is underneath. Smooth over the top, tuck in the ends and place in a greased 2 lb. loaf tin. (For 2 small loaves, divide the dough into 2 and continue as above; for rolls, divide the dough into 2-oz. pieces and roll each into a ball, place on the baking sheets about 1 in. apart.)

Place the tin inside a lightly oiled polythene bag and leave to rise again until the dough comes to the top of the tin and springs back when pressed with a floured finger.

Leave for 1–1½ hours, or longer in a refrigerator. Leave rolls until doubled in size.

Remove the polythene bag, place the tin on a baking sheet and put in the centre of the oven. Put a pan of boiling water on the oven bottom. Bake at 450°F. (mark 8) for 30–40 minutes (15–20 minutes for rolls), until well risen and golden brown. Rolls will double in size. When the loaf is cooked it will shrink slightly from the sides of the tin, and will sound hollow if you tap the bottom of the tin. Turn out and cool on a wire rack.

Note: If dried yeast is used, dissolve 1 level teaspoon caster sugar in ¾ pint (1⅞ cups) water warmed to 110°F.; sprinkle on 2 level teaspoons dried yeast and leave in a warm place until frothy–about 10 minutes. Then continue as for fresh yeast.

WHOLEMEAL LOAF

makes 2 large or 4 small loaves; the detailed technique is the same as for a basic white loaf

2 oz. fresh baker's yeast (for
    dried yeast see note below)
1½ pints (3¾ cups) water
3 lb. (12 cups) plain
    wholemeal flour
2 level tbsps. caster sugar
2 level tbsps. salt
1 oz. lard

Blend the yeast with ½ pint of the measured water.

Mix together the wholemeal flour, sugar and salt. Rub in the lard. Stir the yeast liquid into the dry ingredients, adding sufficient of the remaining water to make a firm dough that leaves the bowl clean.

Turn the dough on to a lightly floured surface and knead as for white bread. Shape it into a round ball, place in an oiled polythene bag and leave to rise. When risen, knock the dough down with the knuckles to knock out the air bubbles and shape to fit 2 2-lb. tins or 4 1-lb. tins, greased. Put aside to rise again, wrapped in oiled polythene bags.

Bake the loaves in the centre of the oven at 450°F. (mark 8) for 30–40 minutes. Cool on a wire rack.

Note: When using dried yeast, dissolve 1 level teaspoon caster sugar in ½ pint (1¼ cups) of the water warmed to 110°F. and sprinkle 2 level tablespoons dried yeast on top. Leave until frothy–about 10 minutes.

FLOURY SCOTCH BAPS AND MORNING ROLLS

½ oz. fresh baker's yeast (for dried yeast see note below)
½ pint (1¼ cups) milk and water, mixed
1 lb. (4 cups) strong plain white flour
1 level tsp. salt
2 oz. lard

Blend the yeast with the liquid. Sift together the flour and salt and rub in the lard. Stir in the yeast liquid and work to a firm dough, adding extra flour if needed, until the dough leaves the bowl clean. Turn on to a lightly floured surface and knead for about 5 minutes. Place the dough in an oiled polythene bag and tie loosely. Allow to rise at room temperature for about 1½ hours, or until the dough springs back when pressed lightly with a floured finger.

Use two-thirds of the dough to make a large bap. Shape it into a ball and roll out with a floured rolling pin to about ¾–1 in. thick. Place on a well floured baking sheet and dredge the top with flour.

Divide the remaining dough into 3–4 equal-sized pieces, shape each into a ball and roll out to about ½ in. thick. Place on the baking sheet and dredge the tops with flour. Cover with an oiled polythene bag and allow to rise at room temperature until doubled in size–about 45 minutes.

Press each bap and roll gently in the centre with 3 fingers, to prevent blisters forming. Bake just above the centre of the oven at 400°F. (mark 6) for 20–30 minutes for the large bap, 15–20 minutes

Sally Lunn is a traditional tea bread from Bath

for the morning rolls. Cool on a wire rack.

Note: when using dried yeast, dissolve ½ level teaspoon caster sugar in ¼ pint (⅝ cup) warm milk and water. Sprinkle 2 level teaspoons dried yeast on top and leave in a warm place until frothy – about 10 minutes.

CHEESE LOAF
makes 2 1-lb. loaves

1 lb. (4 cups) strong plain white flour
2 level tsps. salt
1 level tsp. dry mustard and pepper, mixed
4-6 oz. Cheddar cheese, grated
½ oz. fresh baker's yeast (for dried yeast see note below)
½ pint (1¼ cups) water

In a large bowl, sift together the flour, salt, mustard and pepper. Add nearly all the cheese, reserving a little for the tops of the loaves.

Blend the baker's yeast in the water until smooth. Add to the dry ingredients and work to a firm dough, adding extra flour if needed, until the dough leaves the bowl clean. Turn the dough out

on to a lightly floured surface and knead until elastic and no longer sticky – about 10 minutes. Put into a lightly oiled polythene bag, tie loosely and leave to rise until the dough doubles in size (see basic white loaf).

Turn the dough on to a board and flatten firmly with the knuckles to knock out the air bubbles, then knead to make a firm dough. Halve the dough and shape to fit 2 greased 1-lb. loaf tins (shape as for basic white loaf).

Place the tins in an oiled polythene bag and put in a warm place to rise until the dough reaches the top of the tin and springs back when lightly pressed with a floured finger–about 45 minutes. Remove the bag.

Sprinkle the remaining cheese on top of the loaves. Place the tins on a baking sheet and bake in the centre of the oven at 375°F. (mark 5) for about 45 minutes – take care not to over-bake. Cool on a wire rack.

Note: If dried yeast is used, dissolve 1 level teaspoon sugar in ½ pint (1¼ cups) water warmed to 110°F. and sprinkle 2 level teaspoons dried yeast on top. Leave in a warm place until frothy – about 10 minutes.

SALLY LUNN
makes 2

2 oz. butter
¼ pint (⅝ cup) milk plus 4 tbsps.
1 level tsp. caster sugar
2 eggs, beaten
½ oz. fresh yeast or 2 level tsps. dried yeast
1 lb. (4 cups) strong plain white flour
1 level tsp. salt
sugar glaze, made by boiling 1 tbsp. water with 1 tbsp. sugar for 2 minutes

Melt the butter slowly in a pan remove from the heat and add the milk and sugar. Add the warm milk mixture and the eggs to the yeast; blend well. Sift together the flour and salt, add the liquid, mix well and knead lightly. Divide the dough between 2 well greased 5-in. round cake tins and leave to rise in a warm place for about ¾-1 hour until the dough fills the tins. Bake just above the centre of the oven at 450°F. (mark 8) for 15–20 minutes.

Turn the loaves out on to a wire rack. Make up the sugar glaze and glaze the loaves while they are hot.

CROISSANTS
makes 12

1 oz. fresh baker's yeast (for dried yeast see note below)
½ pint (1¼ cups) water, less 4 tbsps.
1 lb. (4 cups) strong plain white flour
2 level tsps. salt
1 oz. lard
1 egg, beaten
4-6 oz. hard margarine

For glaze:

1 egg, beaten with a little water
½ level tsp. caster sugar

Blend the yeast with the water. Sift together the flour and salt and rub in the lard. Add the yeast liquid and the egg and mix well together. Turn the dough on to a lightly floured surface and knead until the dough is smooth – 10-1 minutes. Roll the dough into a strip about 20 in. by 8 in. and ¼ in thick, taking care to keep the edges straight and the corners square. Soften the margarine with a knife, then divide it into 3. Use 1 portion to dot over the top two-thirds of the dough, leaving a small border clear. Fold the dough in 3 by bringing up the plain (bottom) third first, then folding the top third over. Turn the dough so that the fold is on the

Keep the malt fruit bread for a few days before cutting it

right-hand side and seal the edges with a rolling pin.
Reshape the dough to a long strip by gently pressing at intervals with a rolling pin. Repeat with the other 2 portions of margarine.
Place the dough in an oiled polythene bag and allow to rest in the refrigerator for 30 minutes. Then roll out as before and repeat the folding and rolling (but without fat) 3 more times. Place in the refrigerator for at least 1 hour.
Roll the dough out to an oblong about 23 in. by 14 in. Cover with lightly oiled polythene and leave for 10 minutes. Trim with a sharp knife to 21 in. by 12 in. and divide in half lengthwise. Cut each strip into 6 triangles, each 6 in. high and with a 6 in. base.
Mix together the egg and caster sugar for an egg glaze and brush this over the dough. Roll up each triangle loosely from the base, finishing with the tip underneath. Curve into a crescent shape. Put the shaped croissants on to ungreased baking sheets. Brush the tops with more egg glaze and put each baking sheet inside a lightly oiled polythene bag. Leave at room temperature for about 30 minutes, until light and puffy.
Brush the croissants again with egg glaze before baking in the centre of the oven at 425°F. (mark 7) for about 20 minutes. Eat while warm.
Note: If you are using dried yeast, warm the water to 110°F. and add 1 level teaspoon caster sugar, then sprinkle 1 level tablespoon dried yeast over it. Leave in a warm place until frothy–about 10 minutes.

Swedish tea ring–try it with coffee

APRICOT AND WALNUT LOAF

4 oz. (1 cup) brown flour
4 oz. (1 cup) strong white flour
1 level tsp. salt
1 level tsp. caster sugar
good knob of lard
1 oz. (⅛ cup) caster sugar
4 oz. dried apricots, chopped
2 oz. walnut halves, broken
¼ oz. fresh baker's yeast
¼ pint (⅝ cup) water

For topping:
1 oz. butter
1 oz. (⅛ cup) caster sugar
1½ oz. plain flour

Line the base and grease a 1-lb. loaf tin.
Mix together the flours, salt and sugar, into a large bowl. Rub in the lard, add the sugar, apricots and walnuts. Blend the yeast with the water and add all at once to the flour. Mix to a soft, scone-like dough that leaves the bowl clean (adding more flour if necessary). Two-thirds fill the prepared tin and put it inside a polythene bag until the dough rises to within ½ in. of the top of the tin.
Lightly rub together the butter, sugar and flour until the mixture resembles coarse breadcrumbs and cover the loaf with this mixture. Bake in the centre of the oven at 400°F. (mark 6) for 40–45 minutes. Cool in the tin for 10 minutes, then turn out on to a wire rack.

MALT FRUIT BREAD

12 oz. (3 cups) plain flour
½ level tsp. bicarbonate of soda
1 level tsp. baking powder
2 level tbsps. Demerara sugar
4 level tbsps. golden syrup
4 level tbsps. malt extract
¼ pint (⅝ cup) milk
2 eggs
9 oz. sultanas, seedless raisins or chopped dates

Grease a loaf tin measuring 9 in. by 5 in. by 2⅝ in. (top measurements).
In a large bowl, sift together the flour, bicarbonate of soda and baking powder. Add the sugar. In a small pan, warm together the syrup, malt and milk–do not overheat as this will cause curdling. Cool.
Beat the milk, eggs and fruit into the flour until evenly mixed. Turn into the prepared tin. Bake just below the centre of the oven at 300°F. (mark 2) for 1½ hours.
Turn out and cool on a wire rack. Store, wrapped in kitchen foil, for several days before serving sliced and buttered.

SWEDISH TEA RING

For dough:
8 oz. (2 cups) strong plain white flour
½ level tsp. caster sugar
1 level tsp. dried yeast
4 oz. warm milk
½ level tsp. salt
1 oz. margarine
½ egg, beaten
½ oz. butter, melted
2 oz. (⅓ cup) brown sugar
2 level tsps. powdered cinnamon

For decoration:
4 oz. icing sugar, sifted
water
lemon juice
4 glacé cherries
angelica
½ oz. almonds, blanched

In a large bowl, blend together 2½ oz. of the flour, the sugar, yeast and milk. Set aside in a warm place until frothy–about 20 minutes. Sift the remaining flour with the salt and rub in the margarine. Add the egg and the flour mixture to the yeast batter and mix well to give a fairly soft dough that will leave the sides of the bowl clean. Turn the dough out on to a lightly floured surface and knead until it is smooth and no longer sticky–about 10 minutes. Place the dough in a lightly oiled polythene bag, tie loosely and leave as for a basic white loaf.
When risen, turn out the dough on to a lightly floured surface and roll to an oblong 12 in. by 9 in. Brush with melted butter then mix together the brown sugar and the cinnamon and sprinkle it over the dough. Roll up tightly from the long edge and seal the ends together, to form a ring. Place the ring on a greased baking sheet.
Using scissors, cut slashes at an angle, 1 in. apart and to within ½ in. of the centre. Twist each section slightly so that it lies at an angle. Cover with a lightly oiled polythene bag and put to rise in a warm place for about 30 minutes.
Bake just above the centre of the oven at 375°F. (mark 5) for 30–35 minutes.
Blend the icing sugar with a squeeze of lemon juice and just enough water to give a thick coating consistency. While the ring is still warm, coat it with the icing. Decorate with halved cherries, angelica and flaked almonds.

LOBSTER THERMIDOR

Lobster is the most delicious of shellfish, and is popular even in parts of the world where it is comparatively commonplace. Lobster thermidor is a classic way of preparing it as a hot main dish for 2.

When buying lobster, choose one that weighs heavy in proportion to its size. If you are buying a live one, make sure it is lively, too, as one that seems tired may have been around for a day or two and grown thin inside its shell. A good 2-lb. lobster should yield about 12 oz. meat.

The smaller, hen lobsters are the more tender and delicate and the coral, or spawn, from the hen is an extra delicacy. If you are making a dish such as lobster thermidor, which does not require the coral, save it for a sauce or soup the next day. (You could add it to the thermidor sauce, but the subtle flavour would be lost with the cheese.)

Most people buy lobsters ready boiled, but if you have a live one, wash it, place in cold salted water, bring slowly to the boil and boil fairly quickly for 15–25 minutes, according to size. When the water is brought slowly to the boil like this, the warmth penetrates the central nervous system gradually and the lobster apparently experiences no discomfort.

Do not over-cook it as the flesh tends to become hard and thready. An alternative method of killing a lobster for this dish, so that you don't cook it twice, is to pierce the brain with the sharp point of a knife. To do this, lay the lobster out flat on a wooden board, hard shell uppermost. Have the head toward your right hand and cover the tail with a cloth. Hold it behind the head and pierce through the little cross marking on the head – this is the brain and the lobster will be killed instantly.

a 2 lb. lobster (cooked)
2 oz. butter
1 small onion, skinned and finely chopped
1 oz. ($\frac{1}{4}$ cup) flour
$\frac{1}{4}$ pint ($\frac{5}{8}$ cup) milk
1 oz. Cheddar cheese
1 tbsp. white wine
pinch of paprika pepper
salt and pepper
Parmesan cheese, grated
lettuce, watercress and lemon to garnish

serves 2

Cut the cooked lobster down the centre back, and open out

Crack the claws with a rolling pin and take out the flesh

Using a large, sharp-pointed knife cut the lobster carefully down the centre back; open out the two halves and take out all the flesh. Discard the intestine, which looks like a small vein running through the centre of the tail, the stomach, which lies near the head, and the spongy gills, which are not edible. Clean the shells thoroughly and rub them with oil to make them shine. Twist the large and small claws from the shells and, using a rolling pin, crack the large claws and carefully remove all the flesh using a small, pointed knife and a skewer.

Cut all the flesh into pieces about $\frac{1}{2}$ in. long (you will find it easier if you cut the meat at an angle). Heat half the butter in a small frying pan and add the lobster meat. Sauté gently, turning occasionally.

Sauté the lobster and start to make the thermidor sauce

Meanwhile, in a small pan, heat the remaining butter. Add to it the onion and sauté until soft. Add the flour and blend thoroughly. Add the milk, stirring, and bring to the boil. Simmer for a few minutes. Grate the Cheddar cheese finely and add to the sauce. Mix thoroughly over a low heat, add the wine and paprika; season.

Pour the sauce over the lobster in the frying pan and mix well. Cook over a low heat for a few minutes. Place the cleaned lobster shells on a grill rack, then spoon the lobster mixture into them.

Add grated cheese, wine, paprika and seasoning to the sauce

Pour the sauce over the lobster and cook over gentle heat

Fill the mixture into the shells, sprinkle with Parmesan and grill

Sprinkle thickly with grated Parmesan cheese and place under a pre-heated grill. Cook until the sauce is bubbling and golden brown. Place on an oval platter on a bed of lettuce. Garnish with watercress and lemon slices.

serves 6-8

3½-4 lb. oven-ready chicken
1 onion, skinned
1 carrot, peeled
3 parsley stalks
1 bay leaf
6 peppercorns
½ lb. pork sausage meat
½ lb. lean pork, minced
2 shallots, skinned and chopped
salt and pepper
4 tbsps. Madeira
3 oz. cooked ham, sliced
3 oz. cooked tongue, sliced
2 oz. sliced bacon fat
½ oz. pistachio nuts, blanched
6 black olives, stoned

For finishing :

1 pint (2½ cups) aspic jelly,
   made from aspic jelly
   powder and chicken stock
¾ pint (1⅞ cups) béchamel
   sauce
salt and pepper
2-3 tbsps. double cream
¼ oz. powdered gelatine
cucumber, radishes and black
   olives for garnish

Lay the bird on a board, breast side up. Using a sharp boning knife, cut off the wings at the second joint and the legs at the first. Turn the bird over and make an incision down the centre of the back. Keeping the knife close to the carcass and slightly flattened, to avoid damaging the flesh, carefully work the flesh off the rib cage—scrape just enough to expose both of the wing joints.

Take hold of the severed end of 1 wing joint. Scrape the knife over the bone backwards and forwards, working the flesh away from the bone. Continue until both wing and socket are exposed. Sever all the ligaments and draw out the bone. Repeat for second wing.

Carry on working the flesh off the carcass until the leg and socket are reached. Sever the ligaments attaching the bone to the body flesh and break the leg joint by twisting it firmly in a cloth. Hold the exposed joint firmly in 1 hand and scrape away all the flesh down to

the broken leg joint. Working fro the opposite end of the leg, ea out the bone, scraping off t flesh until the bone is complete exposed. Pull the leg bone fre repeat for the other leg. Contin working the flesh cleanly off t body and breast, being careful n to break the skin.

Lay the boned chicken, skin si down, on the board and turn t legs and wings inside out. Ma a stock using the chicken bone giblets, onion, carrot, parsley, b leaf, peppercorns and enou water just to cover.

Work together the sausage me: pork, shallots, salt and pepper a bowl. Moisten with the Made wine. Slice the ham, tongue a bacon fat into long strips abo ¼ in. wide.

Spread half the farce over t boned out chicken. Lay along t bird, in alternate lines, strips ham, tongue and bacon fat, pi achio nuts and the olives. Cov with the remaining farce. Dr the sides of the chicken togeth

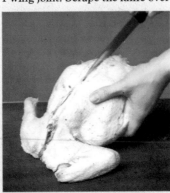

Turn the chicken on its breast and cut down the centre back

Scrape the flesh off the leg bone, down to the broken joint

Good Housekeeping Classic
Chicken Galantine

d sew up, using a trussing
edle and fine string.
rap the galantine in a double
ickness of muslin and tie the
ds to make a neat shape. Strain
e stock, pour it into a large pan
d immerse the galantine in it.
ver well and simmer for about
hours. Drain, reserving the
ck.
ace the galantine, still wrapped
muslin, on a plate; cover with
other plate and top with a
ight. When nearly cold, remove

ork the flesh cleanly off
carcass without breaking the skin

the muslin, and when thoroughly
cold carefully remove the trussing
string.
Make up 1 pint aspic jelly using
some of the strained chicken stock.
To make a chaudfroid sauce, make
up ¾ pint (1⅞ cups) béchamel
sauce, cover with damp grease-

Flatten the bird and arrange the
stuffing ingredients on it

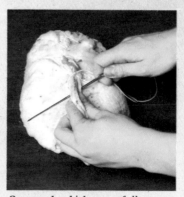

Sew up the chicken carefully,
using a trussing needle

proof paper to prevent a scum
forming and allow to cool. Dissolve the gelatine in 4 fl. oz.
(½ cup) of the prepared aspic and
stir into the cold béchamel sauce.
Strain the sauce and beat well.
Place the chicken on a wire rack
with a board or baking sheet

underneath. When the chaudfroid
sauce is on the point of setting,
pour it over the chicken to coat it
thoroughly.
When the chaudfroid sauce is set,
decorate the galantine with cucumber, radishes and olives and
spoon over the remaining aspic
jelly. Put in a cool place to set.

Coat the cooked galantine in a
rich chaudfroid sauce

Creamy white chicken breasts, filled with rich garlic butter, coated in breadcrumbs and crisp fried in deep fat–chicken Kiev is another perfect choice for a special dinner for two, and relatively easy for four, as it can be kept hot for a short while. Warn your guests what is in the middle of the golden ball on their plates–if they attack it too ferociously the butter will spurt! As you want the breasts only of two chickens for this dish, why not use packaged chicken portions? Or if you prefer to use whole birds, save the legs for a delicious casserole for the family. Make your breadcrumbs freshly to give a real soft-and-crispy outside to the chicken. If you use ready-made crumbs (your own or bought) you will find that they brown long before the chicken is cooked and in the full cooking time will become unpleasantly brown and hard. For the best results, use a day-old sandwich loaf and either grate it or crumb in a blender. A frying thermometer is essential for chicken Kiev, as the temperature of the oil is critical. If it is too hot, the outside will brown before the inside is cooked. If it is not hot enough, the oil will soak right through coating and chicken before the outside is brown, making it soggy and oily.

Good Housekeeping Classic

CHICKEN KIEV

4 chicken breasts (about 8 oz. each with bone)
4 oz. butter
grated rind of ½ a lemon
4 tsps. lemon juice
salt and pepper
1 large clove of garlic
2 tbsps. chopped parsley
1 oz. (¼ cup) seasoned flour
4 eggs, beaten
12 oz. fresh white breadcrumbs
oil for frying

serves 4

If the chicken breasts are frozen allow to thaw completely. Using a small, sharp knife, carefully

Beat out the chicken breasts with a heavy knife or meat bat

work the flesh off the bone. very careful not to split the fle Place each piece of chicken fl between 2 sheets of silicone (n stick) kitchen paper and beat with a heavy knife or meat until quite thin. Put aside i cool place.

In a bowl, beat together the but and lemon rind. When the but is soft, add the lemon juice slow beating all the time. Add the

ream the butter with lemon juice

rush the garlic before adding it

Roll a portion of butter in each

and pepper and mix well in. Skin and crush the garlic and add to the butter with the parsley and mix well together. Turn the butter out on to a sheet of non-stick paper, roll up and chill.

When the butter is firm, divide it into 4, placing 1 piece in the centre of each piece of chicken. Fold the chicken round and secure with cocktail sticks. Dip each piece of chicken in seasoned flour, brush with beaten egg and then with breadcrumbs. Brush with

Coat well with egg and fresh white breadcrumbs

egg and roll in the crumbs a second time, to give a thorough coating. Chill for 1–2 hours. (The chicken *may* be fried immediately, but a short time in the refrigerator helps to make the breadcrumb coating firm.)

In a large saucepan or deep fat fryer, heat the oil to 325–350°F. Place 2 pieces of chicken in the frying basket and lower into the oil. Fry for 12–15 minutes, de-

Fry the chicken Kiev 2 at a time in deep fat, and keep hot

pending on size, until golden brown. Take out of the fat, remove cocktail sticks, drain on absorbent kitchen paper and keep warm in the oven at 350°F. (mark 4) while you fry the remaining portions.

Serve with new potatoes and tomato and chicory or celery salad.

Veal à la Crème Flambé

This is a dinner party dish using a choice cut of veal. With a delicious creamy flavour, and a light hint of herbs, you'll find it a treat by any standard.

Serve it with a white Burgundy and your guests will remember your cooking with pleasure.

Just a hint before you start – you will need a really sharp knife to skin the veal neatly and economically; if you don't have one that you think will be up to the job, it is better to ask the butcher to do it for you.

2 lb. leg of veal, boned
4 oz. butter
1 onion, skinned
bouquet garni
1 clove of garlic, skinned and crushed
½ pint (1¼ cups) veal stock
½ pint (1¼ cups) white wine
salt and pepper
8 oz. button mushrooms
1 tbsp. lemon juice
8 oz. button onions
1 tsp. sugar
beurre manié (made from 1½ oz. flour and 2 oz. butter)
4 tbsps. double cream
2–3 tbsps. brandy
watercress

serves 6

To trim the meat, loosen the skin with a knife. Take hold of the skin with a cloth in one hand and work in towards the meat with the blade close against the fatty tissue. Cut

Cut the skin and fatty tissue away from the meat

Fry the cubes of veal a little at a time to brown them all over

the meat into 1-in. cubes.

Melt 2 oz. butter in a pan, allow it to sizzle, then fry the meat quickly on all sides to seal. Fry the meat in 2 lots, so that all the meat in the pan can rest on the bottom. When it is well sealed, remove the meat from the pan and place in a casserole.

Add the whole onion, the bouquet garni and the crushed garlic.

Make a bouquet garni by tying the herbs in a piece of muslin

Bring the stock and wine to the boil together and pour over the meat. Season well.

Cover and cook in the oven at 325°F. (mark 3) for about 1 hour, until tender.

Meanwhile, wipe the mushrooms but do not peel. Using a small knife, 'turn' the mushrooms by removing tapering fillets from the caps, all the way round; insert the blade into the dome of the caps and draw the knife in a spiral,

Pour boiling stock over the meat and seasoning in the casserole

turning the mushrooms towards you until the knife rests horizontally.

Put the mushrooms in a small pan and just cover them with water. Add the lemon juice and 1 oz. butter and cook until the water has evaporated. Keep warm.

Soak the button onions for 5 minutes in warm water, then peel them quickly.

Place in a small pan, just cover with water, add a pinch of salt, sugar and 1 oz. butter. Cook for 5 minutes, raise the heat and quickly

evaporate all the water. Add to the cooked mushrooms and keep warm.

When the veal is cooked, remove the bouquet garni and onion from the casserole and strain off the liquid. Keep the veal warm.

Reduce the liquid to ¾ pint (2 cups) by boiling fast. Whisk in the beurre manié little by little, bring to the boil and simmer for 5

'Turn' the button mushrooms to make an attractive garnish

Button onions soaked in warm water are easy to peel

minutes. Stir a spoonful of sauce into the cream and return all the cream to the pan. Reheat carefully, without boiling, and adjust seasoning.

Warm the brandy in a soup ladle or small pan, ignite and pour over the meat. Add the meat to the sauce.

Serve on a pre-heated dish, with the glacé onions, mushrooms and a watercress garnish.

Add beurre manié a little at a time and whisk into the liquid

COLONI
GOOSE

Colonial goose is a New Zealand classic, stemming presumably from a time when goose was hard to come by, but lamb was plentiful. The apricot and honey stuffing is delicious and the flavour of the meat itself is enhanced by marinading.

Of course, you don't have to bone the meat yourself if you order it from the butcher in advance. If you do attempt it yourself, use a really sharp knife and keep the blade close to the bone. That way it is comparatively easy. For the marinade, a polythene bag is not essential but it is a convenient way of keeping the wine and vegetables close to the meat so that the flavour penetrates thoroughly.

4½ lb. leg of lamb

For stuffing :
1 oz. butter
1 tbsp. clear honey
4 oz. dried apricots
2 oz. onion, skinned and quartered
4 oz. fresh white bread-crumbs
¼ level tsp. dried thyme
1 egg, beaten
¼ level tsp. salt
freshly ground black pepper

For marinade :
½ lb. carrots, peeled and sliced
6 oz. onion, skinned and sliced

1 bay leaf
3 parsley stalks, crushed
¼ pint (⅝ cup) red wine

serves 6–8

Place the meat on a wooden board. Using a small, sharp knife, work

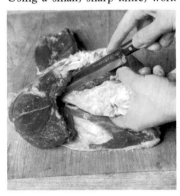
Draw out the bone, carefully severing all the ligaments

the meat away from the bone, from the top of the leg down to the first joint. Now cut along the line of the bone from the opposite end of the leg, just enough to release the bone. Work the flesh away from the bone, being careful not to puncture the skin in any other place. Sever the bone from all the flesh and ligaments. Draw out the bone, working from the top of the leg.

Put the butter and honey in a small pan, melt over a low heat. Grate the onion and add to the bread-crumbs in a basin with the melted butter, honey, thyme and egg.

Start to work the meat away from the bone with a sharp knife

Apricots and honey make this stuffing pleasantly unusual

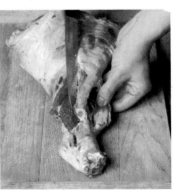
Next, cut along the bone from the opposite end of the leg

Snip the apricots with scissors into the basin and season well. Bind all the stuffing ingredients together. Wipe the lamb with a clean, damp cloth, trim off the excess fat from the top of the leg and spoon the stuffing into the cavity from which the bone was removed. Force the stuffing well down into the leg with the back of the spoon. Sew up with a trussing needle and fine string. Do not sew it too tightly, or the skin may split while the meat is roasting.

Lift the meat into a polythene

bag placed inside a large deep bowl. Add the marinade ingredients and leave in a cool place for about 6 hours, turning the meat occasionally in the juices. Remove from the marinade and weigh the stuffed joint. Roast at 350°F. (mark 4) for 25 minutes per lb. If

Fill the lamb with as much stuffing as it will hold

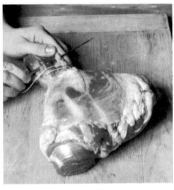
Sew up the joint with a trussing needle, but not too tightly

the meat starts to over-brown, cover it with foil. Remove the string and place the joint on a serving dish. Keep hot.

Pour off the fat from the roasting tin and stir a little flour into the juices. Cook for a few minutes. Add 2–3 tablespoons of the strained marinade and a little water. Adjust seasoning. Bring to the boil, stirring, and simmer for a further 5 minutes. Serve the gravy separately.

A large polythene bag helps when marinading the joint

These delicious steaks are served on slices of fried aubergine and accompanied by a rich sauce of tomatoes, onions and herbs. Serve them with creamed potato and sauté mushrooms. Tournedos are thick slices of beef cut from the heart of the

Cut strips of pork fat and flatten with a knife

fillet and tied into rounds. In England they are lean, but in France the butchers make them up with a small piece of fat tied round each steak. We show you how to add the fat for this classic dish from southern France. For a more economical recipe you could substitute noisettes of lamb, in which case there is no need to wrap the meat in fat.

serves 4

6 oz. pork fat in a piece
4 6-oz. tournedos, 1½ in. thick
2 medium-sized aubergines
salt
1 lb. ripe tomatoes
4 oz. onion
1½ oz. butter
¼ pint (⅝ cup) water
bay leaf
¼ level tsp. dried basil
1 clove of garlic
1 tbsp. cooking oil
freshly ground black pepper

Cut the pork fat through the skin into strips as wide as the tournedos are thick. Now slice thinly along each strip and flatten by drawing the blade of a knife along each

Wrap a strip round each steak and tie with string

slice. Trim the edges. Wrap a strip of fat round each steak; press the steaks down slightly and secure the fat with string. Do not tie too tightly.

Slice the aubergines thickly and at an angle. Each slice should be roughly the same diameter as the tournedos, so that each steak will sit comfortably on a slice of aubergine. Place in a single layer on a plate and sprinkle with salt. Insert the point of a small knife into the stem of each tomato; give 1–2 sharp twists. Bring a small pan of water to the boil and blanch 1 tomato at a time for 10 seconds, then place it immediately in cold water. Skin the tomatoes, reserving the skins, and halve them. Scoop out the seeds with a spoon and roughly dice the flesh. Melt ½ oz. butter in a pan with a tightly fitting lid. Skin the

Skin the tomatoes and scoop out the seeds with a spoon

Tie the tomato seeds and skin in muslin and add to the pan

onions, slice them finely and sauté in the butter until tender. Tie the tomato seeds and skin in a double thickness of muslin and add to the pan with the tomatoes, water, bay leaf and basil. Bring to the boil, cover and simmer for about 15 minutes until reduced to a thick pulp. Season and keep hot. Meanwhile, skin the garlic, cut off 1 end and push it on to the prongs of a fork to rub the cut edge over the surface of a frying pan. Heat the oil in this pan. Add the remaining butter and when it

is on the point of turning brown add the tournedos, using tongs. Cook over medium heat for about 14 minutes (see chart below), turning the meat half way through. When the meat is turned, dry the aubergine slices on absorbent paper and fry on both sides in the

Cook the provençal sauce until it is thick and pulpy

same pan for the remaining time. Arrange the aubergine on a hot serving plate, snip the string from the tournedos and sit each on a slice of aubergine. Garnish with sauté mushrooms and watercress. Remove the muslin bag, squeeze it to extract all the juice and serve the sauce separately.

Cooking times in minutes

Thickness	Rare	Medium	Well-done
¾ in.	5	9–10	12–15
1 in.	6–7	10	15
1½ in.	10	12–14	18–20

Rub the frying pan with a cut clove of garlic

Fry the steaks in oil and butter, handling them with tongs

FILET DE BOEUF EN CROUTE

This succulent, rich French way with fillet of beef is a delectable main course for a special occasion dinner party. The finest, tenderest cut of beef is coated with a rich pâté de foie and encased in crisp puff pastry. The contrasting textures and flavours will delight any palate. Be sure to choose your best Burgundy to go with it! When buying the beef for this dish it is essential to ask for the best quality. Ask the butcher to cut a 2-lb. fillet about 8–9 inches long – this will be the right thickness for the cooking times given in this recipe. The pâté used must also be a good one – firm and fine textured. Beat it well with a wooden spoon to make it soft and easy to spread.

We start by tying the fillet with string to keep its shape – fillet tends to shrink and curl when cooked and this is the only way to keep it in a long narrow roll – so whatever you do, don't try to take short cuts. Filet de boeuf en croûte is at its best served piping hot straight from the oven. Make sure the vegetables match the standard of the meat – asparagus and broccoli are a suitable choice in season, and creamed potatoes offer a better contrast of texture with the pastry than roast. Any leftover beef will still be good served cold, with a tossed green salad and new potatoes.

2 lb. fillet of beef
salt and pepper
2 oz. butter
1 tbsp. cooking oil
8 oz. liver pâté
11-oz. pkt. frozen puff pastry, thawed
1 egg, beaten
watercress and 1 tomato for garnish

serves 6

Place the meat on a board and, using a sharp knife, trim off all excess fat and sinewy parts from the meat. Sprinkle all over with salt and pepper.

Tie some fine string round the meat at intervals to form it into a neat shape. Carry the string round the ends and across to the other side as for a parcel. Tie firmly.

Heat half the butter with the oil in a frying pan and fry the meat until browned all over, turning frequently. Put the meat in a roasting tin and dot with the remaining butter. Cook at the top of the oven at 400°F. (mark 6) for 10 minutes. Remove, leave until cold and then untie the string.

Mix the pâté well in a small basin until smooth. Season to taste. Using a small palette knife, spread pâté over the top and sides of the meat. Roll out the pastry about $\frac{1}{8}$ in. thick, to a rectangle large

Brown the fillet in hot oil and butter to seal

Soften the pâté and spread it all over the meat

Brush the edge of the pastry with egg to help it seal

enough to cover the meat completely. Place the meat pâté side down in the centre of the pastry. Spread pâté over the rest of th

im the ends at an angle and cut
close to the meat

ush the trimmed ends with egg
d fold diagonally across

eat. Brush one long side of the
stry with egg.
old the unbrushed side over the
eat, fold up the second side and
ess together. Trim the ends of
e pastry at an angle, cutting it
aight off close to the meat.
serve these trimmings for decor-
on. Brush the upper surfaces of
e trimmed ends with beaten egg
d fold diagonally across the ends
the parcel. Raise the oven tem-

Decorate the croûte with leaves cut
from pastry trimmings

perature to 425°F. (mark 7). Roll
out the pastry trimmings and cut
into leaf shapes. Brush the pastry
surface with beaten egg, arrange
the leaves in the centre and brush
those with egg. Bake in the centre
of the oven for 40 minutes until
the pastry is golden.
Serve on a flat platter with a
garnish of watercress and tomato.

Crème Caramel

Rich and creamy, smooth and delicately flavoured – that is our vanilla flavoured custard. Topped with the burnt flavour of caramel it becomes the most delicious sweet ever, a favourite from nursery to adult dinner parties.

The recipe is basically simple, but it is not always easy to turn out successfully, so follow our step by step instructions and pictures for perfect results every time.

The traditional moulds to use are individual dariole moulds, for which you can substitute tea cups so long as they will withstand the heat of the caramel (boiling sugar is much hotter than boiling water). Alternatively you can make it in a single 2-pint capacity mould (in this case, extend the cooking time to about 1 hour).

This is one of the best examples of the use of a bain marie for

cooking; it is vital that the custards should not get too hot in the oven, or they will curdle, so a bain marie is used to ensure an even, low temperature.

Crème caramel is an ideal recipe for the busy hostess to prepare – it can be made well in advance and kept in a cool place.

For caramel :
2 tbsps. cold water
5 oz. (⅝ cup) caster sugar
3 tbsps. boiling water

For custard :
1 pint (2½ cups) milk
1 vanilla pod
4 large eggs
2 egg yolks
1½ oz. caster sugar

serves 8

Pour the cold water into a small, thick based frying pan. Stir in the sugar, using a wooden spoon.

Dissolve the sugar in the water, then bring to the boil

Place over a low heat to dissolve the sugar, stirring occasionally. When the sugar has dissolved, bring to the boil and boil without stirring until the sugar turns a dark, golden brown. Remove at once from the heat and slowly spoon in the boiling water, stirring to loosen the caramel. Lightly oil

The caramel is ready when it is a rich, golden brown

8 ¼-pint (⅝ cup) capacity dariol moulds. Spoon some of the carame into each mould and leave in a co place until set.

Meanwhile, make the custar Pour the milk into a saucepan, ad the vanilla pod and bring slowly the boil. Leave to infuse for abo

...train the custard before ...ouring into the moulds

Spoon a little caramel into each mould before filling with custard

Cook the crèmes caramels au bain marie to prevent them boiling

Ease the custard away from the mould with a knife

...o minutes. Crack the 4 eggs into a ...eep bowl and add the extra egg ...olks. Add the caster sugar and ...hisk with a rotary whisk until ...ell blended and pale in colour. ...emove the vanilla pod from the ...ilk, rinse and dry it and store in a ...r of caster sugar for further use.

Pour the milk on to the eggs, stirring, and strain into a measuring jug. Skim off the froth from the top, or leave it to subside. Divide the custard between the caramel based moulds. Place in a large roasting tin, in ½ in. cold water. Cover with a double sheet of kitchen foil, to prevent a skin forming on the surface of the custards.

Cook in the centre of the oven at 325°F. (mark 3) for about 45 minutes until set. To test whether the custards are cooked, insert a fine skewer two-thirds of the way through each one; if it comes out clean, the custard is cooked. Remove the moulds from the water and, while still warm, ease the custard away from the side of the mould with a small, sharp knife. Shake once and invert into an individual glass dish. Ease the mould away and allow to cool completely before serving.

Cool, rich bavarois is the smoothest dessert you can offer. Make it in an old-fashioned mould like the copper one we have used to make it even more interesting.

A bavarois (or Bavarian cream as it is sometimes called) is a rich egg custard mixture set with gelatine and flavoured either with chocolate, as here, or with coffee, or just vanilla.

Don't try to hurry the making, or you are likely to curdle the custard or to get a stringy gelatine mixture. Work at it gently and slowly, stirring all the time when necessary, until it is setting.

As a change from this moulded dessert, make the cream in small individual soufflé dishes and flavour individual portions differently, say 2 chocolate, 2 coffee and 2 vanilla.

serves 6–8

3 large eggs, separated
¾ pint (1⅞ cups) milk
1 vanilla pod
3 oz. (⅜ cup) caster sugar
5 tbsps. water
1½ level tbsps. powdered gelatine
3 oz. chocolate dots, or plain (dark) block chocolate, grated
½ pint (1¼ cups) double cream

Make sure the egg whites are at room temperature; this makes whisking easier.

Ladle some of the warmed milk on to the creamy yolks and sugar

Stir custard over gentle heat, without boiling, until it thickens

Put the milk in a pan with the vanilla pod and heat gently until it just reaches boiling point. Whisk together the egg yolks and sugar in a bowl until the mixture is pale and fluffy.

Ladle about one-third of the warm milk on to the creamy yolks and

Dissolve the gelatine in a small basin over a pan of warm water

Pour the gelatine steadily into the custard, stirring constantly

sugar, scrape down the sides of the bowl with a spatula and blend in well.

Remove the vanilla pod (if this is rinsed under running water and dried thoroughly it may be stored in a jar of caster sugar for future use).

Blend the egg custard with the remaining milk in the saucepan and stir over gentle heat to thicken. This will take 15–20 minutes. Do not allow it to boil or the mixture will curdle. If you find it difficult to control the heat sufficiently, put the custard in a basin over a pan of hot water to thicken it.

Stir the chocolate dots or grated block chocolate into the hot custard until completely dissolved and evenly mixed.

Measure the water into a bowl and sprinkle in the gelatine. Place it over a pan of hot water and dissolve the gelatine slowly. Allow to cool for 1–2 minutes.

Stir 1–2 tablespoons of the chocolate custard into the dissolved gelatine and pour this blend in a thin stream into the remainder of the custard, stirring continuously

with a spoon.

Turn the custard into a bowl and place it in a larger basin of ice cubes and water and stir continuously until thick but still flowing.

Lightly whip three-quarters of the cream and whisk the egg whites until stiff but not dry. Spoon a little of the chocolate custard into the cream, then add all the cream to the custard, blending thoroughly.

The chocolate mixture should now be on the point of setting. Pour it on to the whisked egg whites and fold it in quickly and lightly with a tablespoon, until no pockets of egg white are visible. Do not fold in too much as this will beat out some of the air in the mixture, and the bavarois will be small and solid.

Pour into a lightly oiled 2½-pint

In a bowl over ice, stir cream and custard together until blended

capacity mould and put in the refrigerator to set.

To serve, remove the moulded bavarois from the refrigerator and allow it to stand for 15 minutes. Then ease the bavarois away from the side of the mould by tilting at a slight angle and rotating the mould. Unmould it on to a wet serving plate and slide it into the centre of the plate.

Whip the remaining cream and pipe rosettes round the base of the bavarois with a large star vegetable nozzle. Decorate with caraque chocolate.

When almost setting, pour the mixture into a mould and leave to set

CREPES SUZETTE

If you have a chafing dish, let your guests enjoy watching you finish this delicious flambé dish of pancakes in orange butter sauce. If you don't have a pan pretty enough for public scrutiny (or if you're not sufficiently extrovert to want to display your skills), simply heat the pancakes and sauce in the oven and pour the flaming brandy over when you take it to the table. Either way you can do the main preparation the day before if you wish.

For pancake batter :
4 oz. (1 cup) plain flour
pinch of salt
grated rind of ½ a lemon
1 egg
½ pint (1¼ cups) milk or milk and water
½ oz. butter, melted
butter for frying
For orange butter sauce :
5–6 lumps of sugar
2 large oranges
3 oz. butter
2 oz. (¼ cup) caster sugar
1 tbsp. orange juice
1 tbsp. cointreau
2–3 tbsps. brandy
serves 4

Beat in the liquid gradually to obtain a smooth batter

Sift the flour and salt together and mix in the grated lemon rind. Make a well in the centre and break in the egg. Gradually add half the liquid, beating well until the batter is smooth. Add the remaining liquid and the melted butter and beat until well mixed. Heat a little butter in a 7-in., thick-based frying pan. When it is really hot, tilt the pan so that the butter runs round and completely coats the sides of the pan; pour off any surplus. Pour in just enough batter to cover the base of the pan thinly and cook quickly until golden brown underneath. Turn with a palette knife or by tossing and cook the second side until golden. The pancakes for this dish should be really thin and lacy. As the pancakes are cooked, stack

flat on a plate with a sheet of greaseproof paper between each one. Cover and, if you are cooking ahead, keep in a cool place until required; if using straight away, keep warm.

Remove the zest from the oranges by rubbing the lumps of sugar over the rind until they are soaked in oil. Crush the sugar lumps and add them to the butter with the caster sugar. Beat the butter and sugar until soft and creamy and then add the orange juice and cointreau.

The pancakes should be thin and lacy for this dish

Remove the zest from the oranges by rubbing with lump sugar

Work again until thoroughly mixed. Keep in the refrigerator until required.

If you have a chafing dish, put it ready on a trolley or sideboard before the meal. Have ready also the brandy, some matches, a tablespoon and fork. Half an hour before serving, put the stack of pancakes, covered with a second plate or foil, in the oven at 300°F. (mark

Work the butter and sugar with a wooden spoon until soft

2). Melt the orange butter over a gentle heat and leave in a warm place. To serve, pour half the orange butter sauce into the chafing dish and light the flame underneath. Take one pancake at a time and place it in the dish, spoon over the sauce, fold the pancake in half and in half again. Push to one side of the dish while you repeat with more pancakes until the pan is full. You will have to do this in two batches. Make sure that all the pancakes are well soaked with sauce. Pour brandy into the tablespoon, heat the bowl of the spoon

Add orange juice and cointreau to the orange butter

Fold the pancakes and soak in the warm butter sauce

with a lighted match, pour over the pancakes in the chafing dish and ignite. Serve at once. Repeat with remaining sauce and pancakes.

To prepare without using a chafing dish, place a little of the orange butter in the middle of each pancake, fold the pancakes into four and arrange them in a shallow ovenproof serving dish. Melt the remaining orange butter in a pan on top of the stove and pour over the pancakes. Put the dish in the oven at 300°F. (mark 2) and leave while the first course is eaten (about ½ hour).

To serve, uncover the dish and take it to the table. By this time the orange butter will have melted and thoroughly soaked the pancakes. Warm the brandy gently as above, pour it over the pancakes and ignite.

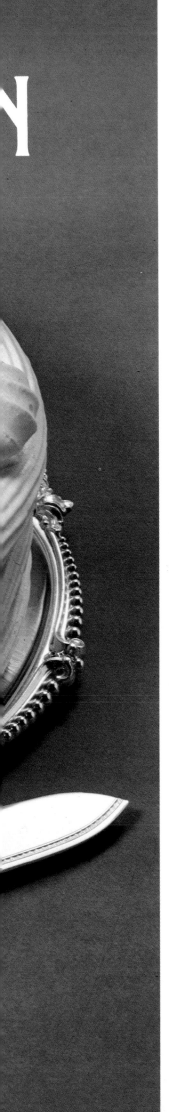

This is a classic French sweet made of mouth-watering meringues and cream flavoured with chestnut purée. Although it looks and tastes so luscious it is quite easy to make and because of its exotic appearance it is sure to gain you many compliments from your guests at a dinner party or buffet. For a party, make the meringue rounds and shells well in advance and store them in airtight tins until you require them.

To whip the maximum amount of air into meringues, the egg whites must be at room temperature and they should be whisked by hand with a balloon or rotary whisk. It will help if you use a really large, deep bowl.

An electric mixer works too fast and tends to produce a flat, close-textured meringue.

serves 8–10

6 large egg whites
12 oz. (1½ cups) caster sugar
½ pint (1¼ cups) double cream
2 tbsps. milk
8¾-oz. can sweetened chestnut purée
1 tbsp. dry sherry
3 marrons glacés
1 oz. chocolate dots

Cover 3 baking sheets with non-stick paper. Invert a 9-in. sandwich tin on to each one and draw a

Pipe out 3 9-in. circles of meringue on to non-stick paper

whisked egg white. Whisk well, drawing all the meringue into the centre of the bowl.

Using a forcing bag fitted with a large vegetable star nozzle, fill the meringue into the bag. Pipe

When the meringue is cooked the paper should peel off easily

Whisk the egg whites in a large bowl until stiff and frothy

line round the tin. Ensure that the eggs are at room temperature by taking them out of the refrigerator at least 1 hour before you start.

Place a large mixing bowl (6-pint capacity) on a damp cloth to stop it slipping and use a rotary whisk to whisk the whites. (A balloon whisk is even better.) Draw the whites continually from the sides of the bowl into the centre and whisk until they stand stiffly in peaks and cling around the whisk, looking dry like cotton wool.

Gradually whisk in all the sugar a spoonful at a time, sprinkling it over the whole surface of the

Layer the meringue discs with chestnut flavoured cream

meringue circles to fill the pencil circles on the non-stick paper, starting from the centre and working out. Use slightly less than a third of the meringue for each circle. With the remaining meringue pipe 6 shell shapes on to the paper in the corners of the baking sheets.

Dry the meringues in the oven set at its lowest for about 4 hours. Half way through the cooking time, reverse the top and bottom baking sheets in the oven so that one meringue does not colour more than either of the others. When they are dry, remove from the oven

and cool slightly. Then turn the meringue discs over on to the palm of your hand and peel away the paper.

Cool on wire racks. Place 1 meringue disc on a flat serving plate. Whip the cream with the milk until it just holds its shape and put 7 dessertspoons cream to one side. Fold the chestnut purée and sherry into the remaining cream.

Spoon half the chestnut cream around the meringue base. Spread to the edges with a palette knife. Place the second meringue disc on top. Repeat this process with the remaining cream and the third disc. Position the meringue shells evenly round the top of the vacherin.

Removing one shell at a time, dab

Fix the meringue shells in position with plain whipped cream

a little of the reserved plain cream under each with a palette knife and press back into position. Drop more reserved cream from a dessertspoon between the meringue shells. Place the marrons glacés directly on the meringue in the centre.

Melt the chocolate dots in a bowl over a pan of hot water. Spoon into a small greaseproof paper piping bag and snip off the tip

Spoon cream between the shells and drizzle with melted chocolate

with scissors. Press the bag firmly and evenly and drizzle the chocolate over each spoonful of cream, drawing the bag from side to side. Chill 1–2 hours before serving.

Classic

u
horé

For pastry base:
4 oz. (1 cup) plain flour
salt
2 oz. butter
1 oz. (⅛ cup) caster sugar
1 egg yolk
¼ tsp. vanilla essence

For choux pastry:
2 oz. butter
¼ pint (⅝ cup) water
2½ oz. (⅝ cup) plain flour
pinch of salt
2 eggs, beaten

For filling:
¼ pint (⅝ cup) double cream,
whipped, optional

For glaze:
8 oz. (1 cup) granulated sugar
8 tbsps. water

For pastry cream:
1 pint (2½ cups) milk
4 oz. (½ cup) caster sugar
2 oz. (½ cup) plain flour
½ oz. cornflour
2 large eggs
2 oz. butter

For decoration:
1-lb. 13-oz. can apricot
halves, drained
angelica

serves 8

For the pastry base, sift the flour and salt on to a working surface. Make a well in the centre, add the butter and sugar and work them together with the fingertips of 1 hand. Add the egg yolk and

Mix the pastry on a flat surface with the fingers of one hand

vanilla essence and mix to a soft dough with the heel of 1 hand. Wrap in greaseproof paper or polythene and chill for ½ hour. Roll out to a round 8½ in. in diameter. Place the round on a baking sheet, prick with a fork and crimp the edge with the fingers. Bake in the oven at 350°F. (mark 4) for about 20 minutes. Cool on the baking sheet until beginning to firm, then lift carefully on to a wire rack. Meanwhile, place the butter and water in a pan and melt over a

low heat. Sift the flour and salt on to a piece of greaseproof paper. Bring the butter and water to the boil, remove from the heat and tip the flour quickly into the pan. Beat the mixture to a paste until it starts to leave the sides of the pan. (Take care not to over-beat or the

Crimp the edge of the pastry base with the fingers

mixture become fatty). Add the eggs slowly, beating hard between each addition until it is a smooth piping consistency.

Grease a baking sheet. Press the rim of an 8½-in. diameter flan ring in flour and place the ring on the baking sheet, to make a floured imprint. Spoon the choux paste into a forcing bag fitted with a large plain nozzle. Using the floured ring as a guide, pipe two-thirds of the paste in a circle.

With the remaining choux, pipe out 16 small buns on to another greased baking sheet. Bake buns

Pipe out a choux ring, using the flour circle as a guide

Pipe 16 small buns, taking care to keep them all the same size

and ring in the oven at 450°F. (mark 8) for 15 minutes. Reduce the heat to 375°F. (mark 5) and cook for about a further 20 minutes. When cooked, pierce the bases of buns and ring to release the steam, and cool on a wire rack. If you wish, split the buns when cold and pipe in whipped cream. For the glaze, dissolve the sugar with the water over gentle heat, then bring to the boil and boil rapidly to 260°F. (when a drop of syrup will harden in cold water). Dip the tops and sides of the buns into the syrup, using tongs to hold them. Place the pastry base on a flat plate, position the ring on top and arrange the glazed buns round the ring, dipping your fingers in iced water as you do so, so that the hot syrup does not stick.

To make the pastry cream, heat the milk in a pan. Mix together the

Use tongs to dip the choux buns in hot sugar glaze

sugar, flour, cornflour and eggs and stir in a little of the hot milk. Pour all the mixture into the saucepan of milk and stir over gentle heat until it thickens and just comes to the boil. Add the butter and beat well.

Arrange all but 6 apricot halves in the centre of the gâteau. Spoon over the warm (not hot) pastry cream, brush with apricot juice and decorate with the remaining apricot halves and the angelica. Serve cold on the same day.

Arrange the choux ring and buns on the flat pastry base

Baba au Rhum

Rum babas are favourites both at tea time and as a dessert. Traditional French pâtisserie, the dough is light and fluffy because of the yeast used to raise it. Spoon over it the warm honey and rum syrup and the result is delicious indeed. French pastry shops sell them heavily glazed with apricot to give a really rich, glowing appearance.

Babas are difficult to serve if you pour over too much syrup initially,

Blend together yeast, milk and 2 oz. flour until smooth

as they become wet while standing, but if you serve a small jug of syrup separately, the extra syrup is good added just before eating. Alternatively, some people will appreciate an extra spoonful of rum spooned over at the last minute.

makes 8–10

1 oz. fresh baker's yeast (or 1 level tbsp. dried yeast)
6 tbsps. warm milk
8 oz. (2 cups) plain strong flour
½ level tsp. salt
1 oz. (⅛ cup) caster sugar
4 eggs, beaten
4 oz. butter, soft but not melted
4 oz. currants
For honey and rum syrup :
4 tbsps. clear honey
4 tbsps. water
rum
For apricot glaze and decoration :
3 tbsps. apricot jam
2 tbsps. water
whipped cream
glacé cherries

Grease 8–10 3½-in. ring moulds with lard.

In a bowl, blend together the yeast, milk and 2 oz. (½ cup) of the flour, until smooth. Allow to stand in a warm place until frothy—about 20 minutes for fresh yeast, 30 minutes for dried. During this period the yeast is growing and as it does so it forms carbon

Leave the yeast mixture in a warm place until frothy

Add all the ingredients to the original dough

Beat thoroughly with a wooden spoon for 3–4 minutes

dioxide. The bubbles of this gas are responsible for the spongy texture of the finished cake.

Add the remaining flour, the salt, sugar, eggs, butter and currants, and beat thoroughly for 3–4 minutes. This develops the dough so that it will rise well.

Half fill the tins with the baba dough, cover with oiled polythene to prevent a skin forming and allow to rise until the moulds are two-thirds full.

Bake near the top of the oven at

400°F. (mark 6) for 15–20 minutes. Cool for a few minutes and turn out on to a wire rack, placed over a plastic tray to catch the drips of syrup.

Warm the honey and water together and add rum to taste. While the babas are still hot, spoon over them sufficient warm honey and rum syrup to soak each baba well.

Half fill the baba moulds and cover with oiled polythene

Spoon honey and rum syrup over the babas while they are hot

Heat the jam and water together, sieve it, brush the babas with the apricot glaze and leave to cool.

Pipe a whirl of whipped cream into each baba with a large star vegetable nozzle, and top with a cherry. Transfer to serving plates and serve extra syrup and/or whipped cream separately if you wish.

When cold, fill the centre of each with piped cream

For the Hostess

A hot, puff-topped chicken pie (page 77)

THE WINE TO GO WITH IT

If you are serving good food you owe it the justice of a good wine. Precisely which wine you serve with which food is largely a matter of personal taste and pocket; the suggestions we give with our dinner party menus are by no means the ultimate and some connoisseurs would doubtless have quite different ideas. There are, however, certain guidelines that it is as well to follow; just as some foods don't mix well, so some wines are better than others with certain foods.

Fish is always better with a white wine; for some reason, when fish is eaten with red wine both tend to take on a metallic taste which ruins them. Very oily fish can do this even to white wine and the only answer then is to stick to beer. Meats will take red, white or rosé. Beef and lamb tend to have the most pronounced flavours and do justice to the finest of clarets and Burgundies–but if mint sauce, garlic or other strong herbs are in the dish you are wasting your money if you drink anything too expensive, as the flavour will be drowned.

A vinegary salad dressing will also kill any wine; if you wish to serve a dish accompanied by salad and wine, make the dressing with white wine or lemon juice in place of vinegar. Pork, veal or chicken are good with white wines (though not with a sweet Sauternes), but are equally good with a light red or rosé. The really sweet, heavy wines are best with desserts, especially cakes and pastries. Any dish cooked in wine should of course be accompanied by the same type of wine.

Most of our recommendations refer to French or the better known European wines because few of the better Australian, South African or Californian wines are exported at sensible prices. It is, however, well worth experimenting with these if you get the chance.

Serving wine

There is a lot of nonsense talked about different glasses for different types of wine. To enjoy wine, your glass should be large enough to hold a generous helping without being more than half full, and the bowl should be roundish, tapping in towards the top so that the bouquet of the wine doesn't escape the instant it is poured out (that is also why you don't fill it more than half full). It should be stemmed so that the temperature of your hand does not affect the temperature of the wine, and it

Draw the cork firmly but gently

FOOD AND WINE

Clear soup, consommé, oxtail soup, smoked salmon or eel	Dry or medium dry sherry
Meaty and savoury hors d'oeuvre	Red Burgundy or Bordeaux or rosé
Other soups and most starters	Dry sherry or the wine chosen for the main course
Oysters, shellfish, fine fish plainly cooked	Chablis, Muscadet
Turbot, trout, bass, sole, salmon	White Burgundy, Moselle, Hock
Fish with sauces, cold meat	White Alsace
Pasta and pizza	Red Chianti Valpolicella, Bardolino
Paella	White Italian (eg. Soave) or Spanish
Chicken, veal, pork	Red or white Bordeaux (dry), Alsace, hock, Graves or rosé
Lamb, beef, roast chicken, ham, game, pork, duck	Red Bordeaux or Burgundy, Côtes du Rhône (choose a fine wine for, say, a plain roast sirloin; something less demanding if there is a rich sauce with the meat).
Light sweets, gâteaux, ices	Sweet White Bordeaux
Cheese, nuts and dessert fruit	Port, Madeira, Marsala or cream sherry
	Champagne or a sparkling hock or Moselle can be served throughout a meal

should be clear so that you can see the true colour of the wine. Tall stemmed hock glasses are very good for a chilled wine as they keep your hand well away from the bowl, and a long flute encourages Champagne bubbles to rise. But a glass that is right for one wine is just as right for any other and the range shown are all a good shape; 2–3 sizes could see you through from sherry to port, whatever you serve in between.

The temperature at which wine is served is most important, as a fine wine can be ruined if it is over-heated; equally if it is too cold you will not be able to appreciate the full flavour. Red wine should be drunk at room temperature and should be left standing in a warm room for several hours before serving. It should be opened an hour or so before serving to give it time to breathe. If you have left it too late for that, pour it into a warmed decanter, or warm the glass with your hands, but never stand it in front of the fire, on a radiator, or hold it under a warm tap–the sudden warmth ruins the wine and it will never recover. When red wine has been brought to room temperature it is better to drink it all as it will probably spoil if allowed to go cold again. White wine is rather less sensitive–you just lie it down in the refrigerator for half an hour or so, or if the refrigerator is full stand it in a bucket of cold water and ice cubes for 20 minutes, until it is just chilled but not iced.

It may be a good idea to decant a red wine if it is more than 5–6 years old. Wine gradually forms a sediment which makes it cloudy if the bottle is shaken at all. A bottle that has lain on its side for a while will have all the sediment lying along the one side of the bottle, so when you take it out of the rack, either keep it on its side in a cradle while you bring it to room temperature and open it, or stand it upright for a few *days* so that the sediment can settle to the bottom of the bottle out of harm's way, or

Choose stackable racks to store your wines so that you can add to them as your cellar grows. A dozen or so bottles will meet the demands of most occasions if you choose a wide selection of wines. Our selection includes a light, sparkling French wine, red and white Burgundies, a good red Chianti, a lighter white from Alsace and 2–3 cheap, lesser known wines to experiment with ▶

ecant it carefully, leaving the sediment behind.

Drawing the cork is not difficult. The easiest way is to use a levered cork-screw. This will enable you to do it without jerking the bottle—particularly useful if you are trying to keep the bottle on its side in a cradle. If you use a traditional cork-screw you will certainly have to raise the neck of the bottle a little, but if you keep it tilted as our expert has, the sediment will remain together and just slide gently down the side of the bottle. Don't panic if the cork breaks and you cannot get it out—just push it through and strain the wine if necessary.

Starting a cellar

People who do much entertaining, or like to open a bottle fairly regularly for family gatherings, will find it worth starting their own small cellars. If bottles are bought by the dozen they are, like most things, cheaper. You will also find that somehow the wine tastes better if you have kept it a while.

intends that you should keep them for 2–3 months at the very least before opening them—the trouble is unless you know him he probably won't tell you that! Merchants like to sell quickly because storage space is expensive and short term storing cannot affect the price they can charge to the customer; but wines suffer a sort of shock when transferred from barrel to bottle, almost like a bruising, which only time will heal.

If you have to buy in a hurry you are as well off with a brand-name wine; these are blended wines whose characters do not alter much with time and which will go down much the same as vin ordinaire does in France—enjoyable but not exactly select. Try several until you find one you like. Being less subtle in the first place, these wines also suffer less noticeably from being moved around. They are not meant for long term keeping.

When it comes to choosing wine, the novice often looks a bit blankly at the label. There is no need to be put off, though, if you are willing

The French laws of Appellation Controllée mean that French wine labels must tell you exactly what you're getting—which vineyard, what year and whether home bottled. Though not obliged to by law, the Germans often go into even more detail about whether they were early or late grapes, first pressing or second—all sorts of information which does mean something to an expert. Unfortunately other countries are less scrupulous and labels tend to be less helpful—you have to feel your way round and get to know those that are good from those that are not so good. From the label on a single vineyard French or German wine bottle, an experienced merchant can tell you whether the wine will be a full flavoured Burgundy or a lighter one, whether the white you are buying will be smooth, heavy and rich flavoured, or fresh and young tasting, and what degree of dryness or sweetness to expect. With these carefully labelled wines, it's not a question of good or bad, but a question of what you're after. At the other end of the scale, if you buy something labelled 'Spanish Chablis' or 'Australian Burgundy' you still know what you are getting—something that doesn't deserve a name of its own, but which vaguely resembles something else. Australian and Californian vineyards are now beginning to label their wines more carefully, to tell the customer in more detail what he is getting.

The date on the bottle is not necessarily an indication of a good or bad vintage, more of the age of the wine. Wines of really poor vintages are rarely exported anyway, and many growers will sell off their poorer wine for blending rather than put their own label on it. There *are* special vintages for certain wines, but only a connoisseur could be expected to remember, or pay for, these.

What you do need to know is how old a particular type of wine should be before it is likely to reach its best. Most white wines are very good after as little as 3 or 4 years—some people will lay them down for longer but it is debatable whether it is worth the trouble. Rosés and a very few red wines are similar (the more recent the date on a Beaujolais bottle the better it should be; outside France it is rarely sold less than 2 years old, but beware of any that has more than 4 years under its belt).

The wines that are usually better for age are the red table wines (and port of course, but that's a subject in itself). No claret or red Burgundy will ever be bottled at much less than two years old. The best are then probably worth keeping in the bottle for 10 years to mature—if you pay a high price for a good single vineyard claret and then drink it while it is only 3–4 years old, you are wasting money; these are made to be kept and if drunk sooner are no better than a cheaper wine.

Financially it is sound to buy some young wines to lay down for a few years, as when they are ready to drink they will be much more expensive to buy—but do buy some for drinking sooner as well or you'll be miserable while you wait! Whatever you buy it will be a good investment in terms of enjoyment for yourself and your friends.

Use glasses with a rounded bowl and a longish stem; 2–3 sizes will serve most occasions

'Cellar' may sound a very grand word, but that cupboard in the spare room may be an ideal place for storing wine. Anywhere that is dark, has an even temperature (preferably on the cool side) and is not subject to vibration, will do. It needs to be deep enough to take the bottles lying down, and a store of a dozen will see most families through most occasions. Wine needs to be kept lying on its side, otherwise the cork will dry out and shrink, and there are many types of rack available. It is probably best to buy stackable racks, that you can add to as your stock increases; the traditional wood and galvanised metal racks as shown in our picture are as good as any.

If you are used to buying wine in single bottles, when required, you will have had some pleasant experiences and some nasty surprises. This is because very few wines are at their best when newly lugged home from the corner shop; they need time to settle again before you drink them. Another reason is that many wines are sold when freshly bottled and the merchant

to admit your ignorance and let the wine merchant help you. The first thing you can tell from the label is whether you have a wine from a particular area, blended and bottled on the estate or by an established shipper; whether it is an out and out mix up, aimed simply at producing an acceptable drink with no pretensions (this usually applies to branded wines, which often are blends not only from different areas, but even from different countries); or whether it is a wine from a single vineyard and a single year's growth—in which case the grower will have put his own name on it because he believes it is something to be proud of.

Nobody drinks fine wines every day, just as nobody eats fillet steak every day. Blended wines are often very good and are definitely not to be sneezed at (all except the most exceptional vintages of Champagne are blended, and nobody queries the quality then). If you decide to go for something better, though, ask your merchant for help.

An apéritif is the liquid equivalent of an appetizer. It stimulates the appetite and livens the palate; it also serves a social function of 'breaking the ice' during the first half hour of a gathering before a meal (in the last century, when they hadn't caught on to the idea of before-dinner drinks, they used to call this the black half hour). Many people at this stage of the evening will drink their favourite form of refreshment regardless of what is to follow—which often means a spirit or spirit-based mix. But a real food lover shuns spirits, for nothing deadens the palate more quickly.

The best apéritifs are wine-based and on the dry side. Often a glass of the wine to be drunk with the meal is a perfectly good start, particularly if it is a light white wine or perhaps a Beaujolais; a full claret is rather heavy going without food, though. Champagne is the perfect apéritif, as it is perfect at any other stage of the meal.

Sweet drinks of any sort are to be avoided since sweetness tends to dull the appetite. (Having said that, one should add that many people nevertheless do take sweet sherry before a meal and you should always have it available to offer.) The most common and acceptable apéritifs, though, are the dry or medium dry sherries, vermouths and certain patent apéritifs which usually have a wine base and some bitter additive such as herbs or quinine, or both. The French particularly specialize in patent apéritifs, though they hardly know what sherry is.

SHERRIES & APERITIFS

SHERRY

'Sherry' is an anglicization of the name Jerez de la Frontera, a small, triangular, coastal area of Spain. Situated on the far western coast, just south of the southern tip of Portugal, it is bounded on two sides by the great rivers Guadalquivir and Guadalete, on the third by the Atlantic dunes. The vineyards are no more than 20½ miles long and less than 15 miles wide; from this area comes the world's entire supply of genuine sherry. The English are the great sherry drinkers of the world and have been since the 16th century; the celebrated 'sack' of Elizabethan days was the same type of wine as today's sherry, though sweeter than most. 70

per cent of the entire produce of Jerez is today exported to England.

There are no 'vintage' sherries, as there are wines. The produce of different years is slowly blended together and fortified with brandy, until in time certain characteristics develop which determine the type of sherry in a particular cask. There are two main divisions of type: *fino*, the drier sherries, and *oloroso*, the fuller or sweeter types.

As a general rule, the drier the taste of a sherry the paler the colour.

Finos are pale, delicate and dry.

Manzanillas come from an area on the coast which is said to account for their sharp, almost salty flavour. These are the palest of all sherries. When a manzanilla is taken away from its home district it tends to lose its characteristic flavour and become just a very good fino—it is therefore rare for sherry to be exported under a manzanilla label.

Amontillados develop a darker colour and a distinctive 'nutty' flavour early in the maturing process and the wine is then left to mature with no more blending. Amontillados are usually stronger than other sherries, containing up to 25 per cent alcohol. They need to age in the wood for at least 8 years, and there is always the chance that the wine will go off instead of maturing properly. This is the reason that amontillados are more expensive than other sherries. An amontillado is often known as a 'medium' sherry, indicating that its flavour

somewhere between a fino and an oloroso–but should never be 'medium' in quality.

The *cream* and *golden* sherries based on *oloroso* wine are darker in colour and considerably sweeter than the finos. The term 'oloroso' means fragrant, and the wine starts its life just as dry as the finos; the sweetness comes in the blending with other wines.

Amoroso is particularly rich and usually slightly darker than the cream sherries.

The sweetest, darkest sherry of all is *East India Brown*–so called from the 17th century habit of sending barrels of sherry on a round trip to India in the hold of sailing ships to speed the maturing process.

These brown sherries, because of their full, rich flavour, are essentially dessert wines as their sweetness defeats the object of an apéritif. They are more suitably served as an alternative to liqueurs or port at the end of a meal.

There are certain characteristics of sherry that make it very different from other wines. One is that that new wine is totally unpredictable. When 2 lots of a table wine are made from the same type of grape, grown on the same slopes, it will be possible for the grower to predict certain characteristics long before the wine is tasted. 2 casks of sherry made from exactly the same harvest of grapes, picked in neighbouring rows of vines, can be entirely different; not until the taster opens the cask can he tell whether it is going to develop into fino, amontillado, oloroso or a 'raya', which will never be anything much and may either serve as a blending wine or may even be turned into vinegar if it is really mediocre.

The distinguishing mark of a fino in the making is its tendency to grow a thick 'flor'. This is caused by a wild yeast carried in the air, which when it settles on the wine produces a thick, white scum which totally excludes all other yeasts and bacteria that normally attack wine. Whereas growers of other wines try to exclude air from the new wines to avoid contact with these bacteria, sherry growers leave several inches space at the top of their casks to allow the flor to take hold. A good fino has a delicacy and freshness of taste that is largely imparted by this bacteriological action.

All sherries are blends, the newer wines readily taking on the flavour and characteristics of the more mature. Sherry growers have elaborate systems of barrels called 'solera', which enable them to add newer wine progressively to older and to top up the first barrel with a newer one still. Apart from their own special blends they will also make up blends for a shipper who asks for a wine with certain characteristics. This is why many sherries are known by the name of the shipper rather than the grower.

Each shipper has his own system of classifying the sherries within the broad categories, so it is possible to give only general guide-lines on how to choose sherries for your own use. The best method is to find one or two sherries that suit your personal taste and stick to them. When you are giving a party you can always widen the selection so as to be able to offer your guests a

Left to right : very pale dry fino; pale dry fino; amontillado; golden oloroso; pale cream

choice–and by buying from the same shipper's range you will have a very good idea of what to expect by way of dryness and richness.

Many other parts of the world produce a fortified wine known as sherry, notably South Africa, Australia and Cyprus. Most of these wines are poor substitutes for true sherry; the soil and climate of the Jerez area have indisputably marked its produce as unique. South African sherries are the closest to the original since they are made from the same type of grape and with the same solera system of blending; the climate of the vineyards and their closeness to the sea are also similar to Jerez. The result is a range of extremely good sherries, particularly on the medium-to-sweet side, which tend to

sell more cheaply than the Spanish.

The traditional sherry glass is smaller than an ordinary wine glass, but proportionally rather taller; it should never be more than half filled or the scent of the wine is lost. Dry sherry is often drunk very slightly chilled.

OTHER APERITIFS

Of apéritifs other than sherry, the best known is vermouth. This is another fortified wine, this time blended with herbs and spices, the principal flavouring agent being wormwood (German 'Wermut'). Although still often referred to merely as 'French' (dry) or 'Italian' (sweet), both kinds are made in either country. There are three different types of Italian vermouth–dry white, sweet white and sweet red– the best known brand names being Cinzano and Martini. French vermouths are generally drier than the Italian, the best known being Noilly Prat. One particularly good French vermouth is Chambéryzette–a light, slightly pink drink made from wild strawberries.

A slice of lime, a twist of lemon peel or a cherry on a stick can garnish most apéritifs

Vermouth may be served either neat over ice or diluted with soda; a twist of lemon is usually added to dry vermouth, a cherry to sweet. In addition, vermouths are often mixed with spirits: dry vermouth with dry gin to make a dry martini; sweet red vermouth with rye whisky to make a manhattan; sweet white vermouth also mixes well with gin or vodka.

There are many other well known wine-based apéritifs, such as Dubonnet, St. Raphael, Byrrh and Punt e Mes. In addition to a blend of herbs, all of these drinks contain a little quinine which gives them a distinctive flavour. They are usually served in a similar way to vermouth–over ice, with soda and with a twist of lemon or lime.

Although hard spirit does not make a good apéritif, there is available a variety of spirit-based apéritifs, generally known as 'bitters'. The best known of these is Angostura Bitters, which should be used literally in drips. When added to gin, this makes a pink gin; it can also be added to the water in your ice trays, to make pink ice. A popular Italian bitters is Campari, usually served with ice and soda and a twist of lemon. The equivalent French drink is Amer Picon, which is dark and has a very bitter flavour; it is usually mixed with Grenadine and soda and served over ice. Fernet Branca and Underberg, also quinine-flavoured apéritifs, are medicinal and said to be good for clearing the head as well as clearing the palate!

The last category is the aniseed based apéritifs, which come from all round the Mediterranean, and there are several brands available. Pernod and Ricard are probably the best known, and they should all be served well diluted with water and ice. They taste quite gentle but are much stronger than brandy.

RED WINES

The most and the best of the world's red wines are made in France. The Bordeaux and Burgundy areas alone produce something like 2,500 different red wines and several other, smaller, wine areas of France also produce quite large quantities. Italy and Spain are the only other European red wine producers of any consequence. Portuguese red wines, though very good, are little known; in Germany, Hungary and Yugoslavia what few are made are not very good. California, Australia and one or two of the South American countries are the only other areas that export much, and these are not yet well known.

Red wine is always made from black grapes, and from grapes that have been ripened in really hot sun so that they have lost all trace of acidity. To give the wine the 'lift' it needs (that made from the juice of totally sweet grapes can be rather flat and dull), the skins and sometimes the pips and stalks are used as well as the juice. The skins, pips and stalks contain tannin which by itself is harsh tasting but which is a vital ingredient in red wine. White wine is made from the juice only of rather less fully ripened grapes.

Bordeaux Wines

Almost half the production of the vast Bordeaux wine area is red. These are the wines that in Britain are known as claret, and have been the favourite table wines for centuries. Many clarets are the finest possible wines, and there is at present a speculative market in them, so expensive have they become.

The chief geographical areas within Bordeaux are Médoc, Pomerol, St. Emilion and Graves. The finest of these wines are traditionally classified into 'growths' (e.g. premier cru, etc.); the not-so-great are expressed in different ways. There are several hundred 'bourgeois' growths, more 'artisan' growths and even 'paysan' growths. It is the bourgeois growths that most of us drink most of the time, and they are considerably better than their rather derogatory sounding name implies – extremely good wines at generally very reasonable prices.

Wines which carry the district names on their label will be either a blend of wines from that area, or a wine from the local co-operative, from a specific village or from a specific vineyard. You can be sure with Bordeaux that wine with any pretensions at all will claim on its label the highest level to which it is legally entitled, indicated at the lower levels by the words Bordeaux and Bordeaux Supérieur (blends, the latter with a minimum 10·5 per cent alcohol content), then a district

Burgundy, bread and cheese – what could be better for a quick lunch?

name (Médoc, Pomerol, St. Emilion), then at the top a commune or village name. These all fall within the laws of appellation controllée. Beyond this are some 2,000 estates, all of which sell under their own château name – on the labels of these the appellation controllée is usually in small type.

The Médoc area supplies a large number of good clarets, usually at a sensible price; they are comparatively light and are usually ready to drink after 3–4 years. Haut-Médoc wines are rather better and include those from the communes of St. Estèphe, Pauillac, Margaux and St. Julien, all of which are appellations controllées. The number of excellent châteaux wines from this area makes it impossible to list them. All you can do is to try some of them and remember the names of those that particularly appeal. As for age, none of these is ready to drink at less than 6 years old and many, depending on the particular château and vintage, will go on improving the longer they are kept – 10 years is not too long for

most, 15 is not unusual and longer can produc the most exquisite drinks if you have th patience to wait.

Pomerol is a small area containing dozens o very small châteaux, from which come som of the finest first growth wines. They are or the whole lightish, almost slightly sweet wine compared with the rest of Bordeaux and ar good at about 4–5 years old. A lesser vintag may even be ready to drink at 3 years old, ye no Pomerol will spoil for keeping longer.

By contrast, the neighbouring area of St Emilion, one of the largest districts in the Bor deaux area, is usually better represented on win lists than the others. These are full, savoury strong wines, often ready to drink at only years old. Again the number of châteaux make it impossible to list them.

It comes as a surprise to many people to kno that Graves produces any red wine at all, fo the name never in fact appears on the bottles the area is much better known for its whit wines which do carry the name. Reds from th

Claret in an attractive decanter to complement a rich roast pork joint

covering many names; nearly all will need something like 10 years in the bottle before they are ready for drinking.

The Côte de Beaune, which includes Beaune, Pommard and Volnay, produces wines that are marginally less good than those from the Côte de Nuits; but it does produce, in far greater quantities, wines that need only 6–7 years in the bottle – they therefore tend to appear on the wine list more frequently.

It is worth remembering that the simple label Beaune is rather more specific, and therefore better, than Côte de Beaune, and Hospices de Beaune (the wines made at the hospital and whose proceeds support the hospital) are better still. Otherwise the names to look for are Corton (preferably on its own but also in combination with other names), Pommard (Epenots and Rugiens) and Volnay (especially Caillerets or Santenots), Chassagne-Montrachet and Santenay.

Beaujolais

In the southern tip of the Burgundy area are 3 districts that produce wines rather different from the rest of Burgundy. These are the Côte Chalonnaise, a small area, Mâcon, producing many reasonable wines but nothing great, and Beaujolais. Beaujolais produces large quantities of lightish, lively wine. It is cheap both because there is lots of it and because it is best drunk young – locally and in Paris it is drunk as 'vin de l'année', when it is very light indeed. Outside France it tends to be 2–4 years old and therefore slightly heavier, but it should still not be a strong wine – if it is it has probably been doctored.

Rhône

Most Rhône wines are rather dark coloured and strong tasting unless they are kept for a long time to mature (10–15 years), and few are honoured with this treatment. Probably only Hermitage and Côte-Rôtie come into this category. Much better known is Châteauneuf-du-Pape. This is a strong, warm tasting wine that needs only 2–3 years in the bottle and is often cheaper than Burgundy.

Red Wines from Italy and Spain

The red wines most exported from Italy are Chianti, Valpollicella, Soave and Barolo. There are many other good ones grown, but unfortunately very few of the rest are exported. To really appreciate how good they can be, one has to drink them in Italy. The best are matured in cask rather than the bottle, sometimes for as long as 7–8 years, and are then ready to drink as soon as they are bottled.

One of the best red wines made in Spain is Rioja, which is frequently exported. Young Rioja is an excellent, cheap vin ordinaire much better than its French equivalents. Rioja that has been allowed to mature is smooth and velvety; it may become light and slightly sweet, or be stronger yet still somewhat fresh tasting. These mature wines are known as Rioja Reservas; they may be 15 or more years old and are certainly very good indeed. They deserve to be better acknowledged on the world's wine lists.

Graves area bear the name of a château or village rather than area. The best known of all, one that has been classed as a first growth for over a century, is Château Haut-Brion; this wine needs a really long time in the bottle to bring out the best in it. Following that are some 20 or so wines of classed growths, all of which are extraordinarily good. They have a strong, full flavour excellent with plain roast meat or game.

Burgundy

Burgundy wines tend to be rather more robust than clarets, without becoming in any measure strong or coarse. In fact the two are much more similar than most people make out – it is the stronger wines of Italy, Spain and the southern hemisphere that really stand out as different. There is no system of classification in Burgundy such as that used in the Bordeaux area, each wine is sold purely on the reputation of the village or vineyard name it bears; it therefore becomes possible to buy rather inferior wines

because they seem to bear the right name, which is a trap for the unknowing. What in fact happens is that village, vineyard and market town names become hyphenated to each other in a mammoth effort at identification, and it is a question of knowing precisely which combination is the best of several which sound similar – unfortunately a task for the merchant or connoisseur rather than the ordinary wine drinker.

The finest Burgundies are grown on the hills known as the Côte de Nuits. The names to watch for here are Fixin, Chambertin (notably Gevrey-Chambertin and Chambertin Clos de Bèze), Morey-St.-Denis, Chambolle-Musigny (if you find something labelled just Musigny it is the best from here), Clos de Vougeot, Vosne-Romanée and Nuits-St.-Georges. The last named village produces more wine than most in Burgundy but is also particularly subject to blending with cheaper wines, so should be approached with circumspection. These are very broad categories,

Supreme amongst white wines is Champagne. It is a party drink; its bubbles and fine golden colour make it look gay, its delicate balance of tart and sweet flavours, its delicious bouquet and the speed with which its alcohol takes effect (also the gentleness with which it lets you down again) make it ideal for celebrations of all kinds.

All Champagnes are blends and it is therefore the shipper's name that appears on the bottle. There are 12–20 of these, all of whom are well known and whose non-vintage Champagne (wine blended from different years as well as different vineyards) will always be good. The Champagne that is sometimes not so good is that sold by the retailer under his own brand name. This is often recommended for parties, but unless it is one you know it may be a rather unexciting drink and may disappoint many newcomers to Champagne. On the other hand, a good one is the best value for money, so shop around.

Vintage Champagne is an animal rarely seen at large parties – it needs reserving for quiet celebrations amongst a few friends, for the price tends to be prohibitive. This is still a blended wine from several different vineyards, but all from the same year's grapes. The growers declare a special vintage only occasionally, usually a hot year when the grapes have come early to a full, sweet ripeness. French law prevents shippers selling as 'Vintage' more Champagne than was made in that year, so it is virtually impossible to be fooled.

Before we go on to other white wines, the table wines that we drink more often, it would perhaps be as well to be technical for a moment and point out how white wine is made. It is basically a simpler process than red wine. Only the juice of the grapes is used, the skins being discarded, so both black and white grapes can be made into white wine (very few black grapes have dark flesh as well and all have clear juice). The grapes are lightly pressed, instead of being squeezed as for red, and left to ferment until the required amount of sugar is converted into alcohol. If a sweeter wine is required, fermentation is stopped sooner than for a medium or dry wine – this is done by various methods, the most common being filtering off the yeast or adding sulphur dioxide. For the very sweet white wines, such as those of Sauternes, the grapes need to be really sweet and ripe before they are picked; for the dryer wines this is not so important. Once the fermentation stops, white wines are usually ready to drink. They may improve with a little time in the bottle but there is rarely any point in laying down white wines as you would red. Their quality often lies in their freshness of flavour.

German wines

Whereas France undoubtedly takes first place for red wines, first place for white is a contest between France and Germany. More French wines are drunk because they are cheaper than the good German wines, but it would be impossible to judge which are actually best. The reason German white wines are so good, and so expensive, is that the growers are meticulous about not mixing wines from different casks, even if they are from the same vintage and vineyard. Whereas a French grower harvests all his grapes virtually at once, presses them, then the following year blends wines from different casks to make what he thinks will be the best wine he can achieve, a German grower picks his grapes in several different stages, from when they are just ripe enough right up to the time when they are shrivelling on the stem. All the wines made from these are kept separately throughout their development, and labelled on the bottle to show exactly what they are. Thus 'Spätlese' means late-gathered grapes; 'Auslese' means selected picking of the best and the ripest bunches of grapes; 'Beerenauslesen' means individually selected ripe grapes off the best bunches; 'Trockenbeerenauslesen' means

the grapes have been left so long that they hav shrivelled and the juice has concentrated to rich syrup – the wine produced from these is vir tually a liqueur. There is no wonder with thi elaboration that the product is expensive – on should perhaps point out that even the Ger mans drink these wines only on speci occasions and can get very cheap brande wines for everyday drinking.

The main wine producing areas in German are the Moselle and the Rhine. Moselle wine are fresh tasting and light coloured, with tendency to an almost 'hard' taste that i characteristic. The best are made in the village of the middle Moselle – Piesport, Brauneber Bernkastel, Graach, Wehlen, Zeltingen, Uerzi and Erden; all are made from the Rieslin grape. So labels on a fine Moselle wine wi read first the name of the village (or excep tionally the name of a very famous vineyard then the name of the vineyard – e.g. Bernkastle Doktor – finally come the words or phrase describing quality and when the grapes wer gathered. The later the grapes were gathered and therefore the sweeter the wine, the bette the quality is assumed to be.

Also on the label will be the name of the growe and where the wine was bottled ('original abfüllung' or 'orig.-abf.' indicates that it wa bottled on the estate). To a connoisseur th grower's name is important, for some can b utterly relied upon to produce the best wine possible from the grapes of a given year.

To return to the humbler, blended wines tha are more readily available, there are a numbe available that are first class blends, for exampl the one known as Moselblümchen. Th standard usually depends on the shipper and i also indicated in the comparative prices.

Rhine wines (hock) are a richer, more golde colour than those from the Moselle and ten to be fuller and softer. The two wines can b distinguished easily without even opening th bottle, as Moselle wine is in tall elegant gree bottles, while Rhine wines go into similarl shaped brown bottles. On the Rhine the Ries ling grape is again the most commonly grown for it is very hardy as well as producing goo wine, but other grapes are also grown. On hoc bottles the label therefore bears the name o the grape between the vineyard name and th description of quality. More often than not

White Wines and Dessert Wines

ommercial blend of Rhine wines is labelled
Liebfraumilch – the name on its own meaning
imply Rhine wine. The quality of the blend
lepends on the shipper's name (Sichel, Dein-
ard, Langenbach and Hallgarten are among
he best known).

The Rhine includes 4 main areas which
roduce excellent wines – the Rheingau, the
Nahe, Rheinhessen, and the Palatinate. Wines
rom these areas are all known as hock and are
roadly better or worse, usually depending on
he amount of Riesling grape used.

French white wines
Among the French white wines the Burgundies
re considered by many to take first place.
Typically, a white Burgundy is still and dry.
Burgundy includes a number of the names that
re familiar to all wine drinkers. Perhaps the
most famous, not only because of its own wine
ut because it is much imitated, is Chablis.
Chablis wines are very dry, delicately scented,
lightly stony flavoured wines with a fresh,
risp taste. The cheap Chablis that are very
opular tend to be young, very fresh and rather
ard, and there are about 30 vineyards that
roduce wines under their own names. The
etter known, because they are the largest,
re Les Fourchaumes, Vaillons and Montée de
Tonnerre. Wines from all these vineyards can
e found labelled with the vineyard name, or
imply the terms Chablis Grand Cru or
Chablis Premier Cru.

The next most important part of Burgundy is
Côte de Beaune, from where come Corton-
Charlemagne, Montrachet and Meursault.
Different as these wines are, they are similar
when compared together against Chablis. In
ifferent degrees they are soft, smooth, full
vines with a delicate scent. Montrachet, if
ood, can be equal to the best white wine
Burgundy produces.

The last of the well known areas is Mâcon,
roducing Mâcon Blanc, the white Burgundy
quivalent of Beaujolais, cheap and drunk
oung, Mâcon Supérieur, the next cheapest
nd a yellowish, general purpose carafe wine,
nd Pouilly Fuissé. This last has the virtue of
roducing in quantity a wine of great character
hat is excellent with fish and chicken. Bur-
undy of course produces many other white
vines, too numerous to cover in this space.

From Bordeaux, the great claret area, come
Sauternes, Barsac, Graves and Médoc. Ordinary
Sauternes is a sweet table wine, very popular in
Britain as it is lightish and not too expensive.
But the great châteaux of Sauternes – Yquem
nd others close by – produce a wine that comes
nto an altogether different category. Château
vines from Sauternes are made from what the
Germans would call Spätlese or Auslese –
elected bunches of grapes that have ripened
ntil they are almost rotten, so that the juice is
o sweet and concentrated that it will go on and
n fermenting and when it can ferment no more
here will still be sugar left in the wine, leaving
so sweet and rich that it is really only suitable
s an after dinner wine (the ordinary Sauternes
ave to be stopped from fermenting artificially
n order that there should be some sugar
emaining). Compared with the German wines

A selection of dessert wines

of this type, though, Sauternes is very good
value. While the better Sauternes are perhaps
only twice the price of the lesser ones, the best
German wines are ten times the price of their
lesser brethren. Barsac is similar to Sauternes,
but perhaps not quite so rich and sweet.

The best known dry white wine from Bordeaux
is Graves. Unlike the red wines from this area,
the white does not bear any distinguishing
village names but simply calls itself Graves or
Graves Supérieur. At its best, Graves is dry,
full and mellow; the lesser ones tend to be a
little sweeter. Graves is classed with Sauternes
as being one of the most popular basic white
table wines in Britain. There are half a dozen
châteaux in Graves that export under their own
names, and whose produce is superb. The
other main area is Entre-deux-Mers which
produces large quantities of a medium wine
that is very popular locally, served with oysters
and other seafoods.

One of the links between Burgundy and
Bordeaux is the river Loire. The six hundred
miles of this valley naturally produce some very
diverse wines, some much akin to white
Burgundies, others more like those from
Bordeaux, yet others with a character all of their
own. The names to watch for particularly are
Muscadet, Pouilly-Fumé and Sancerre. These
are all likely to be reasonably priced and
pleasant.

The other well known white wine comes from
the border between France and Germany –
Alsace. Though thoroughly French now,
Alsace has many German traditions from the
days when it belonged to the German empire.
This shows to some extent in the typical bottles
of Alsace wines – long thin green bottles, taller
still than the German bottles.

The wines from this area are dry and full
flavoured. They are similar to German wines
in some ways, usually fresh and young tasting,
occasionally sparkling, but on the whole they
are fuller. Identified by grape variety, the
Riesling, Sylvaner and Traminer (a spicy,
aromatic wine) are the best and the most
common; Muscat is rather sweeter and more

flowery scented, while Sylvaner grapes give
the local carafe wine.

Dessert wines
We have already covered some of the best wines
for serving after dinner when talking about
hock and Sauternes. Although these are
generally drunk as table wines throughout the
meal, the best, and the sweetest, are good only
with the dessert. At their best they need to be
drunk alone, when all the food is finished. They
are so sweet that they take the edge off the
appetite and both wine and food would lose
their pleasure if consumed together. These
wines are extremely expensive, though, and
most people will turn instead to port, Madeira
or Marsala to drink with their cheese and fruit.
Not that these fortified wines are of a lesser
breed than the first but they are made differently. Port starts as a dark red, strong wine
from the Oporto district of Portugal. It is a
blended wine made from sweet grapes and in
the old days these were allowed to go on
fermenting until all the sugar was converted to
alcohol, giving a very strong, dry wine. Then
somebody thought of stopping the fermentation by adding a little brandy (the extra
alcohol is what does the trick) – and the result
was a rich, strong wine but a sweet one. The
wine improves enormously by ageing in cask
or bottle.

Ordinary, cheap port is called Ruby Port. It is
aged in barrels and bottled only when it is ready
to drink. It is then sold quite cheaply for
drinking young. Tawny Port is also kept in
barrels, but for a much longer time. It spends
perhaps 10–15 years in the barrel, until its
colour lightens from red to tawny, and the
flavour is correspondingly mellower. This is
the most popular of ports, combining smooth-
ness of flavour with a comparatively reasonable
price.

Vintage port is a little like Champagne – it
only happens in special years. When a shipper
declares a 'vintage' he bottles the wine 2 years
after the vintage and leaves it to age in the
bottle, where it forms a considerable deposit
and finally a crust which means it has to be
treated with the greatest respect. Usually only
merchants, clubs and large restaurants have
the facilities for laying down vintage port and
leaving it undisturbed for the appropriate
length of time.

Madeira is made on a similar principle, the
difference being the grapes from which it is
made. The sweetest Madeira and the best for
after dinner are Malmsey and Bual. Others
are not quite so sweet and are often drunk,
chilled, as apéritifs. Equally, because they are
not so sweet, they are sometimes more acceptable to the unaccustomed palate.

Marsala unfortunately rarely appears except
in zabaglione. It is nevertheless an extremely
good fortified wine not unlike a cream sherry,
but with the rather more burnt, caramelly
taste of Madeira. Coming from the flat area on
the west coast of Sicily it is of course drunk
more in Italy than anywhere, but there have
been periods when it has been fashionable in all
parts of the world. Certainly it is good enough
to serve after all but the grandest meals.

MIXING DRINKS

All mixed drinks are greatly improved by being really cold, so use plenty of ice, or chill the bottles thoroughly in the refrigerator beforehand. The correct garnish makes all the difference to the appearance of a drink and adds a really professional finishing touch to a cocktail. Many of the cocktail recipes given in our chart can be made with other spirits — in particular, gin and vodka are virtually interchangeable, a vodka martini being a very popular drink. Try making a gimlet with gin or vodka — you'll find it very refreshing. A Collins can be made with any of the spirits as a base and a Rickey or a Manhattan can also be mixed using any of the spirits.

GIN

Perhaps the most popular of all bases for mixed drinks. Don't use Dutch gin — this is not really suitable.

Martini
5–6 ice cubes
1 part dry vermouth
3 parts gin
1 large olive

Put the ice cubes in a glass jug, pour in the vermouth and gin and stir vigorously. Strain the drink into a martini glass and decorate with an olive.

Pink gin
2–3 drops Angostura bitters
1 part gin
2–3 parts iced water

Put the bitters into a glass and turn it until the sides are well coated. Add the gin and top up with iced water to taste.

Gibson
5–6 ice cubes
1 part very dry sherry
5 parts gin
1 pearl cocktail onion

Put the ice cubes in a glass jug, pour in the sherry and gin and stir well. Strain the drink into a chilled martini glass and add the onion on a stick.

Negroni
2–3 ice cubes
½ part Campari
1 part sweet vermouth
2 parts gin
1 slice orange
soda water

Put the ice cubes into a tumbler and pour over them the Campari, vermouth and gin. Float the slice of orange on top and then top up with soda water to taste.

VODKA

An increasingly popular drink which can be successfully used as an alternative to gin in many recipes.

Moscow mule
3 ice cubes
2 parts vodka
ginger beer or lemonade
lemon and cucumber slices

Put the ice into a mug or tall glass and add the vodka. Top up with ginger beer or lemonade and garnish with lemon and cucumber. Stir lightly.

Bronx
1 part dry vermouth
1 part sweet vermouth
juice of ½ orange
3 parts vodka

Put 4–5 ice cubes into a shaker and pour in the vermouths, orange juice and vodka. Shake well till a frost forms and strain into a chilled martini glass.

Bloody Mary
1 part vodka
2 parts tomato juice
squeeze of lemon juice
dash of Worcestershire sauce

Put some ice into a shaker with vodka, tomato juice, lemon and sauce. Shake and strain into a tumbler. Tabasco, salt and pepper may be added.

Screwdriver
1 part vodka
juice of 1 orange
Angostura bitters (optional)

Put some ice cubes into a tall glass and pour in the vodka and orange juice. Add the bitters and stir lightly.

WHISKY

Scotch, Irish, Canadian, rye or Bourbon all have different tastes. Where necessary we have specified which type should be used.

Old fashioned
1 lump of sugar
1–2 dashes Angostura bitters
1–2 ice cubes
1 part whisky
½ slice orange

Put the sugar cube in a glass and shake the bitters onto it; mix round the glass to dissolve the sugar. Put in the ice, pour over the whisky and float the orange on top.

Whisky sour
juice of ½ a lemon
1 level tsp. sugar
1 tsp. egg white
1 part rye whisky

Put all the ingredients in a shaker and stir together, then add cracked ice and shake well. Strain into a chilled glass and decorate with a twist of lemon.

Virginia mint julep
9 sprigs of mint
1 tsp. sugar or sugar syrup
crushed ice
3 parts Bourbon whisky

Put 6 sprigs of mint into a cold glass. Add the sugar and crush the 2 together. Fill the glass with crushed ice and pour in the whisky, stirring well.

Tom Collins
juice of 1 lemon
1 tbsp. sugar or sugar syrup
3 parts whisky
soda water

In a shaker, mix 6 ice cubes, lemon, sugar and whisky until a frost forms. Pour into a glass and add a slice of orange. Top with soda water and stir.

RUM

A sugar-based drink with a wide range of flavours. There are three basic colourings — dark, golden and white.

Cuba libré
2 parts golden or dark rum
3 parts Coca Cola
juice and peel of ½ lime
 or lemon

Put 3–4 ice cubes into a tall glass and pour in the rum, Coca Cola and fruit juice. Stir gently and drop in the lemon or lime peel.

Gimlet
3–4 ice cubes
1 part lime juice
3 parts white or golden rum

Put the ice into a jug and pour in the lime juice and rum. Stir well and strain into a chilled martini glass.

Manhattan
4–5 ice cubes
1 part sweet vermouth
3 parts white or golden rum
1 maraschino cherry

Put the ice cubes into a glass jug and pour in the vermouth and rum. Stir vigorously and strain into a chilled martini glass. Drop in the cherry.

Daiquiri
cracked ice
juice of 2 limes
1 tsp. sugar or sugar syrup
3 parts white rum

Put lots of cracked ice in a shaker and add the lime juice, sugar and rum. Shake well till a frost forms and then strain into a chilled martini glass.

BRANDY
Don't use your best brandy for mixed drinks – it should be drunk on its own. Use a younger, cheaper one instead.

Brandy Rickey
1 lime
½ tsp. sugar
3 parts brandy
maraschino cherry
soda water

Put 4–5 ice cubes in a shaker and add the lime juice, sugar and brandy. Shake well and pour into a tall glass. Drop in the cherry and lime peel and top up with soda water.

Brandy fizz
4–5 ice cubes
juice of 1 lemon
1 tsp. sugar or sugar syrup
1 part yellow Chartreuse
2 parts brandy
soda water

Put the ice cubes in a shaker and pour in the lemon, sugar, Chartreuse and brandy and shake until a frost forms. Pour without straining into a tall glass, top with soda and stir lightly.

Brandy Alexander
4–5 ice cubes
1 part cream
1 part crème de cacao
3 parts brandy

Put the ice cubes into a shaker and add the cream, crème de cacao and brandy. Shake until a frost forms and strain into a glass.

SHERRY
The classic before-dinner drink in a new, exciting guise – these recipes may shock the purists but they're delicious.

Sherry cobbler (makes 2)
ice
¼ pint sherry
1 level tsp. sugar
2 tsps. fresh orange juice
slices of orange
few strawberries

Put a few pieces of ice in a glass jug and add the sherry, sugar and orange juice. Stir well. Pour without straining into 2 chilled tumblers and decorate with the fruit. Serve with a drinking straw.

Sherry refresher (makes 4–6)
3 grapefruit
6 tbsps. sweet sherry
soda water
ice

Squeeze the juice from the grapefruit and strain into a jug. Add the sherry and chill. Serve in goblets with a little ice and soda water to taste.

Sherry cocktail
4–5 ice cubes
1 part dry vermouth
3 parts very dry sherry
1 slice lemon rind

Put the ice in a glass jug and pour in the vermouth and sherry. Stir well and strain into a chilled martini glass. Drop in the twisted lemon rind.

WINE
Ideal for warm days, a wine cocktail, whether based on Champagne or a cheap rosé, is light and refreshing.

Spritze (approx. 3½ pints)
1 bottle white wine
2 pints soda water

Chill the wine and soda water thoroughly. Just before serving, combine in a large glass jug.

Sangria (approx. 2½ pints)
1 bottle red wine, chilled
1 pint fizzy lemonade, chilled
1 slice of lemon
1 liqueur glass brandy
slices of apple and orange
caster sugar

Shortly before serving, mix the chilled wine and lemonade in a large bowl and add the lemon slice and brandy (optional). Float the apple and orange slices on top and add caster sugar to taste.

Alfonso
1 lump of sugar
2 dashes Angostura bitters
1 tbsp. Dubonnet
Champagne, well chilled

Put the sugar in the base of a champagne glass and drop on the bitters. Add the Dubonnet and, if liked, an ice cube as well. Top up with champagne.

Vin blanc cassis
4 parts dry white wine
1 part crème de cassis

Chill the wine. Pour the crème de cassis into a claret glass and top up with wine.

PORT
Not your favourite vintage port, of course, but a good ruby or tawny one – and white port looks especially refreshing.

Port flip
1 egg
1 level tsp. icing sugar
1 wineglass port
2–3 ice cubes
nutmeg

Break the egg into a shaker or an electric blender and add the sugar, port and ice. Shake or blend well. Strain into a goblet and sprinkle with a little nutmeg before serving.

Tawny sparkler (3½ pints)
juice of 1 lemon
1 whole lemon
1 bottle tawny port
4 tbsps. curaçao
soda water

Put the lemon juice in a bowl and add the port and curaçao. Slice the whole lemon, float it on top and leave for 20 mins. Fill glasses two-thirds full and top up with chilled soda water.

Port cocktail
4–5 ice cubes
2 drops Angostura bitters
1 tsp. curaçao
3 parts port

Put 4–5 ice cubes in a jug and pour in the bitters, curaçao and port. Stir vigorously and strain into a chilled martini glass.

Note: Whatever you use as a measure, be sure to use the same measure for all the ingredients in a drink, so that the proportion of one ingredient to another is accurate.

LITTLE KNOWN WINES

When the names of wines from France, Germany and Italy are not known outside their own region, it is usually because that country has better things to offer. But other parts of the world, Europe and elsewhere, suffer from a certain lack of development in the wine trade, which means that many perfectly acceptable wines are simply not marketed widely.

In Europe the prime example of this is probably Portugal, which produces quite large quantities of good wine as cheap as any going. There are 2 main types of Portuguese table wine–vinho verde, which is drunk young and is light and refreshing (it may be either red or white), and vinho maduro which is more mature and fuller. Both are blended and sold under brand names rather than local or grape names. In the first group come such brands as Casal Garcia and Casal Mendes; these are slightly sweet compared with some vinho verde, but seem to be more popular abroad than the very dry wines drunk locally. Among the vinhos maduros there are a number of good blends and brands–Almada, Arealva, Justina, Estoril, Serradayres, Allegro, Campo Grande, Solar, Serrador, Realeza and so on. These are usually interesting blends, and cheap relative to wines of comparable quality from other countries. The best wines of Portugal (known as Reservas and Garrafeiras) are rarely exported.

Switzerland and Austria seem to specialize in white wines, but rarely export them in any quantity. The Swiss Visperterminen, Sion and Lavaux are all light, pleasant wines, while Valais is very good indeed. Neuchâtel is light and slightly tart, almost like a Portuguese vinho verde. There are 3 areas of Austria that produce good wine. Wachau produces a variety of white wines, the best known probably being Schluck, a dry one. Wien is the Vienna 'vin ordinaire', light but highly drinkable. Gumpoldskirchen provides slightly sweet, light wines.

Austrian wines are very similar in type to Hungarian and Yugoslav wines, largely because of the geographical proximity and geological similarity of the vineyards. The best known Hungarian wine is Egri Bikaver, or Bull's Blood; this is a rich, dark red wine which matures well. Amongst Hungarian white wines, Tokay is unusual in that it resembles the sweetest and best of German fine wines, or a Château d'Yquem from Sauternes; the rest still have a faint flavour of rich sweetness, but are much lighter and more versatile when it comes to what to eat with them. The names worth learning to recognise, if not to pronounce, are Badacsonyi, Szurkebarat and Debroi Harslevelu. Meanwhile, simple Hungarian Riesling, like Yugoslav Riesling, is a cheap, ordinary and usually acceptable wine.

Among the Yugoslav wines the only name that has achieved any recognition other than just Riesling is Lutomer–an area that produces exceptionally good Rieslings. Yugoslav Riesling is similar in character to Hungarian or Alsace, but the price is generally a good reason for preferring the Yugoslav! Other, more southerly areas of Yugoslavia produce wines of varying quality, but they are not exported in any great quantity.

The largest, up-and-coming wine areas of the world are outside Europe, notably in California and Australia. Both these countries pean stock, and some new varieties are being developed as well. The best wine that California has produced so far is probably from the old European Pinot Chardonnay grape, but there are many others worth trying and promise of yet better to come.

Australia has been hampered not only by the unfortunate habit of using European names for non-European wines but also by a poor distribution set-up that seemed at one time to doom Australian wine to the home market for ever. These difficulties are now disappearing as the grape names become the current identification and distribution improves; but a further difficulty arises as some of the names that are the same as European names are for different grapes. For example, an Australian

Some of the lesser known wines come as pleasant surprises

entered the wine trade with unfortunately imitative labels on their bottles–Chablis, hock, claret and so on. This meant that drinkers used to European wines automatically compared the new product with the old, and it must be said that on that basis, the old usually won. Nevertheless, if these wines do not try to be anything else, they are often extremely good in their own right. There is a trend now away from the imitative names, towards the use of grape and district names.

The Californian climate is more completely reliable than anywhere in Europe, and the quality of wines from year to year is therefore more consistent. Semillon, Sauvignon, Pinot Chardonnay and Cabernet Sauvignon are the best known grapes used, all grapes from Euro-Riesling label indicates what is known in Europe as Semillon; if you really want Riesling, you have to ask for Rhine Riesling. It is to be hoped that these difficulties will disappear as some of the better wine estates (known as wineries) start to use their own names on the labels.

There is an enormous amount of fun to be had trying new wines, and the lesser known ones are usually comparatively inexpensive. Something that is particularly rewarding is to drink a local wine when you are cooking foreign dishes. The Greek favourite Retsina may be somewhat unpalateable in normal circumstances, but serve it with dolmades and loukomades and it will take you right back to that Greek holiday!

Brandy and Liqueurs

When the eating is over, when all the wine has gone and the dishes have been cleared away, then is the time to serve coffee and to offer brandy or liqueurs. This habit probably started as a precaution against the ill effects of over-eating, for many spirit based drinks, especially those that include herbs, act as aids to digestion. But medicine is forgotten now and we enjoy a wide range of after dinner drinks for the pleasure of their flavours alone.

Liqueurs are expensive but are served in very small glasses, so they need not be extravagant.

BRANDY

Brandy is the most widely known and widely made of these drinks. A spirit distilled from wine, it is made in every country that grows wine, the character of the wine being reflected in the brandy. It is not, however, the 'best' wines that provide the most palatable brandy. This is illustrated by the history of Cognac, which comes from a region in the west of France which used to produce a rather poor grade wine. Yet the grape grown and the type of soil in that region yield a brandy recognised as the finest in the world.

The grapes for brandy are picked before they are fully ripe, so that they retain a certain degree of acidity. The wine is made in the early autumn and distilled as soon as fermentation stops, before the winter is over.

The wine is heated in a still, the alcoholic vapour is driven off, recaptured and condensed into liquid spirit. In the Cognac region the stills used are old-fashioned pot-stills, operated by craftsmen. Different constituents of the wine vapourize at different temperatures, and pot-stills give a very fine control over just which part of the vapour, containing the desirable amount of alcohol and flavour, is retained. The wine is distilled twice to give a high alcohol content. Other areas use different types of still which give varying, usually less fine, control.

The spirit obtained is of course clear and colourless. Much of the colour is drawn from the oak barrels in which the brandy is left to mature, and the flavour is affected by the wood too. Freshly distilled Cognac is about 70% alcohol; for sale it is normally diluted to about 40% and the sweetness and colour are adjusted with sugar and caramel – different shippers using different amounts of both but usually keeping to a constant style.

Brandy is as much affected by the treatment it receives after distillation as by the wines from which it is made. This can clearly be seen if Cognac is compared with Armagnac – another very fine brandy coming from an area in western France not far from the Cognac country.

In Armagnac a different type of still is used, in which the wine is distilled only once; the alcohol content is therefore lower (about 53%) but the flavour and smell are correspondingly

many on brandy. They are flavoured with all kinds of different fruits, herbs, nuts, roots, seeds, leaves and flowers, sometimes a combination of these, and are nearly all heavily sweetened with sugar. Many are known by their chief ingredient (such as cherry brandy, crème de menthe, crème de cacao), others such as Bénédictine or Chartreuse are sold under a brand name and the ingredients are secret.

The most common liqueur bases are brandy, whisky, gin and rum, but some are based on a spirit with very little flavour, distilled from potatoes or a grain; this provides the alcohol content, the other ingredients providing all the flavour. Many liqueurs are not coloured by their ingredients, others are deliberately given brilliant or rich colours which add to their

Bénédictine
This is one of the secret recipes. It originated with the Benedictine monks at Fécamp in Normandy, in the 16th century, and is still made in that area. It is very sweet and highly aromatic, suggesting that its main flavouring ingredients are spices and herbs.

Calvados
An apple brandy, made in Normandy from cider. The best comes from the Vallée d'Auge. Old Calvados can be a magnificent brandy.

Cassis
A blackcurrant liqueur mainly drunk in France, where it is sometimes diluted and served as a long drink. The base is brandy.

Chartreuse
Another of the secret recipes, again originating from a monastery in France, this time in the 17th century at a Carthusian monastery near Grenoble. There are 2 types of Chartreuse, one is green and has a very high alcohol content, the other yellow, much sweeter and not so strong.

Cherry brandy
The best is made from a base of distilled cherries. Cherries are then macerated in the brandy to give it colour and flavour. Cheaper cherry brandies are made by macerating cherries in a neutral spirit.

Crème de cacao
A very sweet, colourless liqueur, flavoured with cocoa.

Crème de menthe
A very sweet liqueur flavoured with fresh mint. It is available both colourless and coloured.

Crème de moka
A very sweet, coffee-flavoured liqueur.

Curaçao
A colourless liqueur flavoured with oranges and based on either brandy or gin. There are many different brands of curaçao the best known being Grand Marnier and Cointreau.

Drambuie
A whisky based liqueur flavoured with honey.

Fruit brandies
There are many brandies distilled directly from fruits and berries other than grapes. The prime example is Kirsch, made from cherries, but popular liqueurs are also made from raspberries, (crème de framboise, Himbeergeist) plums (quetsch, Zwetschenwasser), apricots (abricot, Aprikosengeist), gentiane (Enzian) and many others.

Kirsch
A colourless liqueur distilled from the small black cherries native to Switzerland, Germany and Alsace.

Kummel
A liqueur with definite medicinal properties. It is based on a highly distilled spirit made from grain or potatoes, and flavoured with cumin and caraway seeds. Some brands are sweeter than others. It is always colourless.

Maraschino
A cherry liqueur distilled from marasca cherries, on the Dalmatian coast in Yugoslavia.

Van der Hum
A South African liqueur based on Cape Brandy. The main flavouring ingredient is naartje, the South African tangerine, with other fruits and spices.

Rich, sweet, spirit-based liqueurs for after dinner

stronger. The brandy is then matured in barrels made of black oak, a rather soft, moist wood which gives the brandy a darker colour and stronger flavour than the lighter oak used for Cognac. Sugar is not normally added, so the final product is much dryer. Cognac and Armagnac are always matured for at least 2 years, usually up to 5. If kept for as much as 20 years the flavour becomes increasingly fine, but the alcohol content decreases as it evaporates through the porous wood. The letters VSOP on a label stand for Very Special Old Pale and indicate that it has been kept for at least 5 years.

LIQUEURS
Liqueurs are all based on a spirit of some sort,

appeal – crème de menthe is an obvious example. (Where the word 'crème' occurs in the name, this usually indicates that the liqueur is particularly sweet.) Below is a list of the commonest liqueurs, their characteristics and ingredients (where known).

Advocaat
A thick, yellow liquid, the texture of double cream. Made from brandy and egg yolks.

Anisette
Colourless, very sweet liqueur flavoured with aniseed.

Apricot brandy
A brandy base, flavoured with dried apricots; the very best may be distilled from fresh apricots and their kernels (see fruit brandies).

COFFEE

Devoted coffee drinkers tend to be fanatical about their favourite blend and their favourite method of preparing it. However, it is all a matter of personal taste and what is right for one can well be quite wrong for another. There are nevertheless some golden rules about coffee, without which you cannot hope to produce a good, refreshing brew.

The first requirement is for fresh coffee. If you have a grinder, buy the coffee beans freshly roasted and store them in an airtight container. Never keep beans for more than a month, and preferably use them up in a shorter time than that. If you do not have a grinder, buy your coffee either freshly ground or pre-ground and packed in a vacuum-sealed package. Once the pack has been opened, only keep it for a week – it quickly gets stale. If you drink so little coffee that you can't use up reasonable quantities in this time, it is much better to keep a jar of a good brand of instant coffee in the cupboard, and buy the fresh only when you know you are entertaining and will require it. Alternatively you might consider the 1-cup size filters with the coffee built in; these come in packs of 8 and, since each is individually sealed, do not get stale quickly.

Always keep coffee-making utensils sparklingly clean. This sounds obvious – you always do the washing up – but unless you scrub and rinse the pot thoroughly, as soon as it is empty, the stale coffee will cling and spoil the next brew.

Always drink coffee while it is fresh – never make a bigger quantity than you need and save it for later. Stale coffee becomes bitter-tasting and is unpleasant to drink. Equally, although you should make coffee with freshly boiled water, never boil the coffee itself as this will also make it bitter.

Be sure that the coffee is correctly ground for your particular method. For instance, if you make it in a jug, it is very difficult to make finely ground coffee settle, and the result will be powdery; conversely, if you use coarsely ground coffee with a paper filter, the water stays on the grounds for such a short time that the coffee will be very weak – it needs grinding finely to release its full strength.

Finally, never use boiled milk. Heat the milk

These coffee-makers all give a good brew

to just below boiling point, or serve cream.

JUG METHOD

Warm a jug of which you know the capacity and measure out 1½–2 oz. medium-ground coffee for every pint of water. Put the coffee in the jug, pour on boiling water, stir and cover. Leave to infuse for 4–5 minutes, then strain the coffee into another warmed jug or straight into the cups.

If you draw a metal spoon across the surface of the coffee just once while it is infusing, the grounds should settle and you may not need to strain it.

CONA OR SYPHON METHOD

For this method a special Cona or similar syphon-type of coffee-maker is needed. Allow 1½–2 oz. medium-ground coffee per pint of water, and always fill the machine to capacity. Beware of coffee that is too finely ground, as the grounds will creep down the valve into the coffee to be served, making it powdery. Put cold water in the lower container and heat it. Place the upper container, with its valve in position, in the neck of the lower container and add the coffee. When the water boils it will rise on to the coffee. Lower the heat, stir gently once or twice and allow the coffee to infuse for 1–2 minutes, then remove from

the heat. The coffee will then filter back into the lower container.

The particular advantage of this method is that the coffee itself is never in direct contact with the heat and therefore cannot boil, however careless you may be. Many people also like the result obtained using a glass container in preference to metal.

FILTER METHOD

For a metal or china filter, allow 1½ oz. medium ground coffee per pint of water. For the more modern paper filters, allow 1 oz. finely ground coffee.

Warm the coffee pot and place the filter containing the coffee in position. Pour boiling water through the filter. When the water has all gone through, remove the filter and serve the coffee.

This method is particularly easy and economical if you are making only 1–2 cups at a time.

PERCOLATOR METHOD

Use a top-of-the-stove percolator, or an electrically heated model. Allow 1½–2 oz. medium or coarsely ground coffee per pint of water. Pour the cold water into the percolator, put the coffee in the metal basket and put this in position. When the water boils it is forced up the centre tube and filters over and down through the coffee grounds. Allow the water to circulate for 8–10 minutes. Most electric percolators can be pre-set to switch off after the required length of time.

ESPRESSO METHOD

Espresso machines make a strong brew. Allow 1 oz. finely ground coffee per pint of water. Put the cold water in the machine and the coffee in the special container. When the water boils it is forced under steam pressure through the grounds and into a separate jug.

PLUNGER METHOD

Allow 1½–2 oz. medium-ground coffee per pint of water. Place the coffee in the bottom of the special jug, pour on the boiling water and insert the plunger. The air escapes through a vent in the centre of the plunger and the coffee is pressed through the filter manually.

HOW DO

Some of the most delicious foods are difficult to eat tidily, but you can at least present your guests with the right equipment or prepare the food as helpfully as possible. If you are in doubt about the best things to provide, here is a brief check list for the foods that cause most embarrassment.

Globe artichokes The outer leaves are pulled away with the fingers, and the fleshy base of each leaf dipped in melted butter or dressing and sucked. When setting the table, provide individual small plates or bowls for the discarded leaves. Finger bowls are a help (use small glass or pottery fruit bowls if you don't have special bowls). A small knife and fork are needed for the 'choke'.

Asparagus If served as a separate course, asparagus is eaten in the fingers, each spear being dipped in melted butter, sauce or dressing, which is poured on the side of the plate. It helps if you leave part of the firm stalk on when you trim the asparagus for cooking, to serve as a 'handle'. Lay a small knife and fork

to be used to retrieve any of the tips which may break off. Finger bowls are a help, again, or thick napkins.

Avocados Serve on a small plate (or special avocado dish), with a teaspoon. You use your spare hand to steady the avocado while eating.

Corn on the cob It is easier to eat this vegetable tidily with special holders to spear into each end of the cob, instead of grasping it with the fingers. If you do not have special holders, use your smallest skewers. A small knife and fork should also be laid, the knife to spread the butter and the fork to help gather up the last bits of corn. Bear in mind that it is difficult to eat this elegantly, even with the proper equipment!

Melon Your guests will find it much easier to eat melon if it has been cut beforehand into bite-size pieces and arranged back on the skin. Provide a fruit knife and fork, which is also the best equipment if you have not pre-cut the melon. For small Charentais or Ogen melons, which are served cut in halves, provide a teaspoon.

Chicken in a basket This is eaten wit fingers only, so have plenty of thick pape napkins and finger bowls.

Gulls' and quails' eggs Serve hard-boile and in their shells, for your guests to peel th eggs themselves. Dip them in salt or celery sa and eat in the fingers.

Spaghetti Lay a spoon, fork and a knife, s that guests can choose whether they twist th strands round the fork in the bowl of the spoo Italian style, or cut it up more conventionall even those who cut it up will probably want spoon for the last pieces of spaghetti and sauc For other pastas (cannelloni, lasagne) a spoo and fork are sufficient.

Lobster It is sensible to serve lobster alread removed from its shell, in a salad. If you d leave it in the shell, you must provide lobste picks, and there is no good substitute for th specially designed implement. If you dress th lobster and return it to its shell for servin provide a fish knife and fork.

Mediterranean prawns It is easiest to pu the shell off the prawns in the fingers and the

SERVE IT?

at the flesh with the help of a small fish fork, but provide a fish knife as well, to meet all references. Provide finger bowls.

Mussels (Moules marinières) These are best eaten from a bowl or soup plate, with a fork to get the mussel out of the shell (holding the shell in your fingers) and a spoon for the liquor. Provide a plate for discarded shells. Finger bowls are a help.

Oysters A small fork is all that is needed.

Prawn or lobster cocktail Put a teaspoon on the plate under the cocktail glass – this is the easiest implement to eat it with.

Soups Most soups of course are simply served in an open soup plate or double handled cup, with a soup spoon. Some of the more substantial soups – bouillabaise, cock-a-leekie, etc. – contain more solid foods. If you wish, drain off the liquor, serve it separately in a soup cup with a spoon, and serve the meat or more solid foods separately, with a knife and fork.

Snails Serve the snails in their shells, preferably in a special snail dish which will hold the shells upright and prevent the butter running

out. Provide long, thin snail forks for extracting the snails from the shells and special tongs to hold the shell.

Whelks and winkles Serve in the shells, like snails. Unfortunately there are few forks made that are thin enough to go into these shells, and the usual alternative is to provide your guests with sterilized hat pins with which to prise out the fish. Sturdy, plastic cocktail sticks might serve as a substitute if elegant pins are not to be found.

Grapefruit Cut the fruit in half and carefully cut round between the flesh and the skin with a curved, serrated knife. Then cut either side of each membrane, so that the segments can be lifted out completely free of membrane. Provide long, tapering grapefruit spoons for eating.

Serrated spoons for grapefruit are available; if you have these, the halved grapefruit do not need any preparation.

Smoked trout Remove the skin from the body of the fish but leave the head and tail intact. Provide fish knives and forks.

Smoked salmon Just cut as thinly as possible. If it is really tender it should be possible to cut and eat it with a fork only, but check this first and provide a knife as well, if in doubt.

Swiss cheese fondue Provide a basket full of cubes of crusty bread and long-handled forks. Each guest spears a cube of bread on a fork and dips it into the fondue.

Chinese food The Chinese traditionally do not serve separate courses. All the food is set out at once in serving dishes in the centre of the table, with the exception of rice – each person has an individual bowl of rice. The hot dishes are usually kept on a hot plate. Each person takes a mouthful of food from one dish (using chopsticks, or a fork) and either eats it direct or puts it in his rice bowl; he may dip it in one of the sauces on the way. A mouthful of rice is taken between each helping from the central dishes. The diners go to each dish in turn, to mingle the flavours and textures. Apart from the rice bowl and chopsticks, provide each person with a plate for discarded bones, shells and so on.

etting the table is a gracious art that should not be allowed to die. Whatever anybody says about looks not counting, they ost definitely do count when it comes food. The look of the food itself somehow fects the way it tastes and an elegant or etty table-setting, depending on the mood the meal, will help your party off to a od start and maintain the atmosphere right rough to the cheese.

you are slightly nervous about the forthming meal (though you have no need to be you follow our timetables!) a carefully anned table-setting can reassure you. This is e one place where nothing can go wrong at e last minute. You can set the table hours in lvance if you wish and, provided you can ep the children out, it will still be perfect hen guests arrive – leaving you free to give all ur last minute attention to the food.

he basis for your table-setting will be the nen or mats you choose. Individual place ats can be right even for a formal occasion if u have a really super table to show off. A ord of warning, though, to those with mperamental table surfaces – if you are going supply enough mats to protect the table oroughly from heat and scratches from all ossible sources, the effect will be lost; you ed to be able to leave large areas of wood xposed to achieve an uncluttered look.

o both protect your table and set off your est china and cutlery, the answer is an ficient heat-proof covering and a crisply undered linen cloth. It is possible to buy to rder protective cork mats that will exactly fit ur table and fold away when not in use. This voids the ugly lumps made by individual mats nder a cloth. Alternatively, use a length of eavy green baize.

he traditional white damask cloth is still alid as a perfect formal setting for fine tableare, but if you prefer something a little more nusual, any plain colour to tone with your aina will give the right effect; patterned oths are better kept for informal occasions hen plain earthenware plates and dishes are use. And whatever your cloth, guests will ppreciate really large linen napkins that roperly cover even the most ample lap.

n general, keep your setting as simple as ossible. Use colours sparingly and base them n the tones predominant in the china, bearing mind that when the food arrives that should ke the centre of attention. Silver, glass, andles (white or to match the china) and few flowers will complete the picture.

would be so nice if we could all have a choice f china for different occasions. To have fine nina for formal dinners and chunky earthenare for less formal occasions would be ideal (as ould a choice of silver or stainless steel utlery) – but of course we have to make do ith what is available. The rule, though, is not try to make your tableware do something for hich it is not designed. If all you have is studio ottery, don't try to be formal with it.

lasses add lustre to a table, and if you can rovide two for each guest (one for wine, one r water) it will add luxury to the occasion. If ou intend serving a second wine with the

Mix and match your tableware in style

dessert you absolutely *must* have fresh glasses for that.

Glasses go to the right of the place setting, above the knives. If you are putting out more than one glass, arrange them so that the one to be used first is on the right, and work inwards. Although it looks attractive to set out different shaped glasses, don't worry too much about having the correct glasses for each wine as the rules are much less strict now than they used to be. A large, stemmed glass with a rounded bowl, cupping in towards the top, is suitable for all wines.

Conventions about different glasses for different wines may have disappeared as irrelevancies, but those about arranging cutlery are still very much in existence. The principle of a place setting is that it should form a neat square, with the inside knife and fork the width of the plate apart and the dessert spoon and fork the same distance from the table edge. All the items should be as close together as possible without actually touching. This produces a much tidier result, especially if all the handles are lined up a consistent $\frac{1}{2}$ in. from the edge of the table.

Knives (blades pointing inwards) and spoons always go on the right, forks on the left (left-handed people have to juggle for themselves – sorry). Exceptions are the dessert spoon and fork in neat alignment across the top (spoon handle to the right, fork handle to the left) and fruit knife, if it is needed, under the dessert fork, also with its handle to the right. These can just as correctly go to the sides, but it's a matter

of how much space you can afford – the more you build the setting sideways, the more widely you have to space the chairs.

The oft-quoted advice 'start at the outside and work your way in' should come out right with a properly laid table, which is doubtless why the rules have survived. A menu of soup followed by fish, then meat and finally the dessert, should have a left-to-right place setting as follows: fish fork, meat fork, space for plate, meat knife, fish knife, soup spoon. Dessert spoon and fork above the plate gap would logically be left to the end by anyone following this rule. The item that presents the most difficulty is the bread and butter knife, theoretically the last knife to be used but one that is needed throughout the meal. This may be placed either inside or outside the meat knife, or vertically across the side plate – the latter, incidentally is a good way of holding a springy linen napkin in position. Small spoons for starters or for desserts in glasses can be brought in with the dish.

For a buffet, even a formal one, the rules for positioning the tableware are thrown totally to the winds. The prevailing need at a buffet is to display the food to advantage and to put plates, cutlery and napkins where they will least hinder people coming to the table for serving. This usually means grouping them at one end of the table, where guests can collect them before moving on to gather their first course without getting in each other's way. Another solution, ideal if your room space will allow it, is a side table or trolley for these things. Positioning of utensils aside, the rules for setting a buffet table remain similar to those for any other table. Simplicity is again the key, the more so here as the display of all the food together at once imparts its own festive atmosphere. A plain cloth is the perfect background for elaborate trays of salads, cold joints and sumptuous desserts, and one big centrepiece of flowers, set well back where it can't be knocked over by reaching hands, will complete the scene.

For all the delights of displaying all the foods at once, it is better not to over-crowd the table. If you have a large number of guests and only an average-size table, it may be worth leaving the desserts off the table until most people have eaten their main course. You can then whisk away the empties and refurnish the table with desserts, refreshing the eye as well as tempting the palate.

Feel free to mix formal and informal styles. Any style followed through too precisely becomes stiff, and it is the unexpected touches that give individual flair. A formal table setting should logically have formal flowers, but simple garden flowers, like daises or sweet peas, arranged casually in a pottery jug, may just bring the table to life. Conversely, an informal setting with pottery and multi-coloured linen could become magnificient with the help of a silver candelabra.

'Mix and match' is therefore the key. Bear this in mind when you are buying tableware and it will be much easier when you come to actually set the table. A little planning and imagination go a long way!

Informal Table Settings

To make the best of informal occasions, go for natural finishes – wood, earthenware, chunky glasses, coarse linen napkins and cloth or mats. Straw mats are attractive, inexpensive and protect the table well. Use of colours in the green/brown range helps to accentuate the casual feeling and these tones will always complement wooden and earthenware dishes; they are also good colours to put beside food. If your casual tableware is of the decorated earthenware type, maybe white with a brightly coloured pattern, follow through the colours of the dishes into the cloth and napkins, but choose coarse linen or cotton; wooden bowls and stainless steel cutlery fit the mood better than silver and fine glass.

This is the ideal time, too, to bring out odd bits

more than 1 plate, and choose a lightweight material so that it is easy to handle. Tray cloths have gone rather out of style now, and with easy-clean surfaces it is probably easier to do without. But a pleasant arrangement of dishes, a fresh, bright napkin and perhaps a single flower in a small jug or an egg cup will add savour to any meal. If your tray does not clean too easily or if the surface is smooth and slippery, use a linen table mat or tray cloth that matches the napkin.

The secret of setting a tray is two-fold; never over-load it so that it looks overcrowded or precarious; but do include on it everything that is needed for the meal – cruet, side plate, cream jug, depending on what you are serving. This means of course that you have to plan the right

are all of a similar style. For instance, several variations on straight-sided cups in plain pastel colours can mix very well, or curvy cups in different flower patterns, perhaps some with scalloped edges. Serving plates can also be pretty pieces of china that you have collected over the years – often you can find single dishes that are a better shape for sandwiches than the conventional, round plates usually supplied with a tea service. The teapot can match the cups or not, as you please, though it is nicer if the teapot, milk jug and sugar basin match. All that you need otherwise are napkins, teaspoons, tea knives and perhaps cake forks if you are serving a squashy gâteau. Knives must be small, otherwise they overbalance off the small tea plates and become an embarrassment. If you don't have special cake forks, small fruit forks will serve the purpose and are better than leaving people to fight the cream with their bare fingers. The napkins for tea should be small – they are really only for wiping fingers, since tea-time food is usually cut to small sizes for eating easily.

For most trolleys, cloths are essential. The glass trolley in our picture is an exception, since the surfaces clean easily with a damp cloth and look much better with no covering, but a wooden trolley should be protected. Use pretty or plain cloths to match the napkins and the style of the china.

Set the afternoon tea trolley with fine china and linen

and pieces of pottery and glass that you have collected just because you liked them – they don't have to match anything else so long as the mood is right. Be flexible about the purpose of certain utensils. If you have only 1 set of bowls and you want to use these for the sweet course, bring out some pottery mugs for the soup; or if you're not serving soup but need the bowls for a side salad, serve the sweet in wine glasses – or on the pottery side plates if they are more suitable. Bring out your odd jugs for sauces and salad dressings, and a really old fashioned, chunky glass jug looks just right for holding celery sticks alongside the cheese.

MEALS ON A TRAY

Whatever the reason for a meal on a tray, it is a luxury for most of us. An invalid tray in bed, when you are starting to recover from 'flu, or just tea by the fire, either way it is really rather pleasant. To make it even more pleasant it is worth setting the tray properly.

Use a large tray if possible, to give room for

sort of meal for a tray. This should preferably be a 1-dish meal, and only a single course. It rather detracts from the luxury if you have to get up in the middle to take out the dirty dishes and fetch another course. (For an invalid of course it's different; there's somebody else to see to such details!)

THE TEA TROLLEY

It is rather sad that afternoon tea is disappearing from the social scene. For one thing, it is a far less expensive way of offering hospitality than a dinner party. Nevertheless the opportunity to indulge does still arise and it is worth making an occasion of it.

This is without doubt the time to bring out the wedding-gift china tea service. Although tea doesn't really taste any different out of a mug or an earthenware cup, somehow a fine china cup is one of the niceties. If you haven't a complete service of matching plates, cups and saucers, a harlequin set made up from different services is just as pretty, so long as the pieces

COFFEE MORNINGS

Coffee mornings fall into 2 groups. Some are large gatherings, perhaps in aid of a charity or local association, in which case the table should be set on much the same lines as for a buffet. Cups and saucers should be laid at one end of the table, with space for the coffee pot. A good supply of coffee is the central point of the occasion, and for this you must have several coffee pots at the ready, hot milk or cream and 2–3 bowls of sugar on the table for people to help themselves. Serving plates and teaspoons are usually the only other equipment needed; if you are serving fruit breads or open sandwiches you will need to put out small plates, but if it is biscuits only, most people will find it easier to use their saucers.

A casual coffee morning for a few friends is a much different affair. Again the trolley comes into its own, but it would be a mistake mid-morning to use the fine china that is suitable for tea. Chunky earthenware cups and plates are the best at this time of day, and the coffee cups should of course be full size – tiny coffee cups are for after dinner only.

It is unlikely that you will serve anything for which knives will be needed, but your guests will almost certainly be sitting down, so provide plates, and small napkins may be a help. Again, have at least 2 pots of coffee available, with a choice of cream or warm milk. Use plain trolley cloths in the morning, to encourage the informal atmosphere. There is not usually room for flowers on a loaded trolley, so put 1–2 bowls around the room instead.

The rules for any occasion may of course be bent to suit your own taste. Nevertheless any hostess will feel more relaxed if the setting is right, and designed to complement the food.

FLOWERS FOR THE TABLE

Flowers bring any table setting to life. Before the meal, when all the linen and tableware are set out but there is no food, the table seems dead until flowers are added. Between courses, flowers help to distract from the bare table mats.

Arranging flowers for the table is a special art, something over and above the normal skills of producing an artistic arrangement. In this context, the choice of flowers is crucial to the success of the arrangement – you can't necessarily just make use of the flowers you have available, as you would in a normal room setting. Just as linen and china are chosen to tone together and to match the mood of the food, the flowers must do the same. Their colours must also tone with or complement the colours of the tableware.

Other considerations also come into your choice of flowers. At a dinner party, or any sit-down meal, the flowers should never be so tall that they obscure one guest's face from another, or that they run the risk of being knocked over as dishes are passed around. Strong-smelling flowers should be avoided as these distract from the pleasure of the food smells and can even conflict with them unpleasantly. On the other hand, flowers for the buffet table benefit from height as the guests are usually standing anyway and the height of a flower arrangement can give shape to an otherwise flat arrangement of foods. Choose your containers for table flowers care-

fully. Keep them low, fairly flat and if they have any height at all, be sure they are heavy based and therefore stable. Collect together old pottery dishes, copper or brass pans, large glass ashtrays even – all these are ideal containers for table flowers.

The arrangement shown at the head of this page was made in a copper gratin dish, the handles showing to break up an otherwise rather formal arrangement of red roses, dahlias and briony berries. This particular arrangement is designed for a formal dinner table setting on a white cloth or dark, polished wood surface – the colour is strong, the arrangement low and the shape very compact, the outline merely broken by a few straying dahlia buds. This red on a coloured cloth could be quite wrong unless it tied in very closely with the colours of the cloth and china.

Try fixing a small pin holder to one side of a large glass ashtray, using plasticine or florist's clay; make a posy of 2–3 cabbage roses, clematis heads or other wide flowers to cover the pin holder only, leaving the gleaming glass and water exposed alongside. This is an elegant, small arrangement that cannot obstruct the dinner table conversation.

Alternatively, twine a few trailing flowers and leaves round the holder of a tall candle – the candle will be sufficiently firmly wedged not to tip, and the flowers will serve to soften the shape of the holder. (Please don't let the wax drip on them though – there's nothing more dismal

than scorched, dying flowers.) If you particularly like candles, you may like to buy a special candle holder with a flower holder in the base – these make it much easier to provide the flowers with water.

It is rarely advisable to go for a strictly formal arrangement at the table, even if the setting is a formal dinner. Fine china and silver can become somehow sterile if a stark arrangement of flowers is used, and something soft and casual, added as if an afterthought (but a planned afterthought please) will be more pleasing.

When it comes to choosing flowers, your choice does of course depend largely on what grows in your garden or what you can afford to buy from the florist. Roses are nearly always suitable – either arranged with other flowers as here, or casually plonked in a small pottery jug for the supper table. Daisies of all sorts, marigolds and any small flowers lend themselves well to table arrangements. Don't neglect scabious, Christmas roses or the little early gladioli and even the common nasturtium, with its pretty, round leaves. Large flowers are difficult unless you have a table like a football pitch – guests sit so close to the blooms that the arrangement disappears behind one single flower head. And do be careful to shake dahlias well before you bring them to the table – they are rather prone to hiding earwigs within their curly petals and it is not very appetizing to see an insect emerge and wander across the dinner table.

...rctotis, early gladioli, dianthus and chincherinchees will stay fresh for days

...se height and width for a buffet table arrangement

It is of course possible to use large flower heads by simply floating a single head in a dish of water – take this a stage further and place a small finger bowl by the side of each place, with a flower head floating in it. Big tea roses are ideal for floating in a bowl, though they do need to be fully out to look effective. Hydrangeas also look well in this way and can be used quite late in the year when they are fading to lovely tapestry reds, blues and greens.

Failing finger bowls, use oyster or scallop shells with 1–2 small flower heads fastened with plasticine – pinks and carnations are very good for this but they need a little extra foliage.

To present a striking splash of colour in the centre of the table, arrange a mass of tulip heads in a flatish white, or glass, bowl – cut the heads really short and be generous with the quantity so that they are packed tightly in. Another attractive mass arrangement can be made simply with 4–5 pots of African violets in full bloom, grouped in a shallow, square casserole or similar container. This is not as extravagant as it sounds because the violets will go on as pot plants for months or even years.

At times when flowers are short, use wild berries, hips, spindle, old man's beard, or leaves from variegated plants like peperomia, tradescantia or begonia. Alternatively, use an arrangement of fruit and leaves. Make a base of wide leaves in a dish – ivy, rhododendron, even rhubarb well polished with oil – and make an arrangement of different shapes and colours. Aubergines and grapes go together well, or polished apples and copper beach leaves. Gourds are particularly helpful in this context and it is well worth trying to cultivate an ornamental gourd plant in your garden or on a balcony; they make an extremely attractive base for a table arrangement. Failing this a common marrow makes a good colour base, as long as you cover part of the large shape with something more interesting.

For a buffet table, long stems and an abundance of flowers become an advantage. Tone the colours with the china and linen again but for a buffet you can be much freer with shape. Use either a single, large display or several tiny posies. All the flowers shown in the two biggest arrangements are good buys from the florist as they last well. In the white bowl, spray chrysanthemums, day lilies and chincherinchees with moluccella (bells of Ireland) should keep fresh looking for days. The pink and white arrangement of arctotis (South African daisies), early gladioli, dianthus and chincherinchees should keep similarly well. Remember even for a buffet table to stick with delicately scented flowers – freesias and strongly scented lilies are for the living room only.

If you want an arrangement which does not take up too much room on a buffet table, use tall candlesticks with a special holder that fits where the candle normally goes. The flowers are arranged in the holder, secured in plastic foam and wire, so that they stand above the food while the candlestick itself takes up very little table space. This is a good arrangement for a wedding buffet where the cake takes pride of place. Choose delicate flowers like dianthus, white early gladioli and trails of stephanotis.

China, glass, cutlery and table linen can turn a meal into a banquet. They can transform the atmosphere of something quite ordinary into a really special occasion. Perhaps this is why people so love to give them as wedding presents. But to keep them in good condition does require just a little effort.

The easiest to care for is china. Most china and earthenware will keep its good looks with simple washing in hot water and detergent. It is best rinsed in very hot water after washing and left to drain in a plastic covered rack, then put away as soon as it is dry – drying on a tea towel is a miserable job and not terribly hygienic unless you use a clean cloth every time.

Glasses take a little more effort. These really do need polishing with a soft, dry, fluff-free cloth while they are still hot, otherwise they will not have that lovely shine that sets off your table. If your glassware does develop a film – in the bottom of a decanter, for instance – it can be removed with a solution of 1 tablespoon salt in $\frac{1}{4}$ pint ($\frac{5}{8}$ cup) vinegar. When shaken, this acts as a gentle abrasive that will not harm the surface. Stubborn, stuck-on food should be removed from china or glass first by soaking in cold water then, if necessary, rubbing gently with a nylon scourer. Never use a metal scourer, as this will damage the surface.

A dish washer is still regarded as something of a luxury in most households, despite the acceptance of clothes washing machines. But if you have a large family or do a lot of entertaining – or even if you have a small family but are out at work all day – it can save more time than almost any other appliance. The important things to remember if you have a dish washer are to use the correct amount of powder and to stack things carefully in the machine. And don't use it for non-stick pans, or for knives that have bone, wooden or plastic handles that might come loose or warp and discolour in very hot water. If you have any difficulties, such as film forming on the china, try adjusting the amount of powder – this is usually the reason for the film. If the trouble persists contact the supplier of your dish washer, who will usually be able to give you a simple answer depending on the model and type of powder you are using.

Cutlery is very important. Nothing is less inviting than a fork that does not look thoroughly clean – however sure you are that it has actually been washed. Stainless steel is by far the easiest to keep good-looking. All it requires is careful washing in hot water with an ordinary washing up liquid, and drying and polishing to retain its shine. If you leave cutlery to drain you will find it retains the water spots and these cannot be removed once it is dry. Treat stainless steel bowls and vegetable dishes the same way.

If your stainless steel does become marked, perhaps because you have inadvertently left a dish with something in it for too long, use one of the patent stainless steel cleaners, which are usually either a powder or a paste. Never touch it with a tarnish remover intended for silver – this will severely damage the surface. The second common enemy of stainless steel is salt – if allowed to come into contact with stainless steel in hot water it may very quickly

Caring for tableware and linen

There are several proprietary cleaners for silver

Crisp, home-laundered linen

cause pitting. Another is electrolysis – if food is left in a stainless steel dish with a silver or nickel plated spoon in it, or covered with aluminium foil, the two metals set up an electrolytic action and subsequent corrosion that is extremely difficult to remove – and the food is also contaminated.

Silver is much more tedious to keep in good condition, though most people think the result is worth any amount of trouble. Ordinary, everyday cutlery doesn't tarnish as readily as one might think, as the constant washing and drying up polishes it. It will want a thorough clean from time to time though. For any silver there are many proprietary cleaners on the market. Liquid dips are extremely useful in an emergency particularly for items with a difficult

shape like a fork, but silver cleaned this wa tarnishes again fairly quickly. Paste or semi liquid polish or an impregnated pad is mor effective for long-term cleaning, and there ar some preparations that give a truly long lastin shine. Whatever preparations you choose, d use a very soft cloth – cheese cloth is ideal – o you will risk scratching the silver. For decora tive ware a soft brush is useful, to remove th polish from the cracks.

After cleaning always wrap any silver that i not on display in tissue paper and a polythen bag as excluding air delays the tarnishin action (specially treated tarnish preventin cloths are available). Silver cared for like thi may need thorough cleaning perhaps onl twice a year. Copper, brass and pewter are th same in this respect, and there are speci; cleaners for all of them.

When it comes to special table cloths an napkins, there is a lot to be said for sendin them to a professional laundry. The finis your linen will receive there is much bette than you can give at home unless you enjo ironing and are prepared to spend a lot of tim and effort achieving a good finish. Laundrie are also experienced in stain removal and ar much less likely to damage a badly staine article than you are if you tackle it yourself.

But for everyday cloths and some made fror easy-care fabrics, home laundering is just a effective. Courtelle and Terylene are particu larly good as they need only light ironing cotton seersucker is pretty for a breakfast c supper cloth and even looks better for no being ironed! Rayon is difficult to keep lookin good however you treat it – it needs as muc ironing as linen but will not take starch an loses its 'body' very quickly. The only re; disadvantage of synthetic fabrics for the tabl is that stain removal can be difficult, thoug some do have a special stain-resistant finisl Most synthetics do not react well to very hc water and some will not withstand the use c chemical solvents. Wherever possible, tak some corrective action over a stain as soon a possible, though not at the expense of you guests' comfort and peace of mind! Rinse c sponge any stain with cold water first (hc water will often set a stain like a dye), then soa the cloth in a washing powder solution fc several hours before washing.

White linen is usually not much of a problem normal washing will remove most stains, an a mild solution of bleach can be used for any thing that is particularly stubborn. Coloured are more difficult as the colours may not b fast – whatever treatment you intend using, d test a small corner first. For grease marks use grease solvent before normal washing – an failing all else send the article to the laundry Try to keep your tablecloths flat – a speci; linen cupboard or drawer helps. Nothing i more frustrating than to find that a beautifull laundered cloth has been pushed up to a corne and needs ironing all over again. It helps t preserve the colour of linen that is not use often if you cover it with tissue paper or a piec of sheeting. Do not leave white table linen i the airing cupboard once it is thoroughly dry either, as the warmth may discolour it.

COOK AHEAD FOR YOUR PARTY

Dinner party menus that can be prepared in advance. These are menus for working wives, or for the day when you are expected to be out with your guests all day and return in the evening to provide a splendid feast.

MENU *serves 4*

TOMATO JUICE
BEEF OLIVES
BUTTERED RICE, GREEN SALAD
SHERRY TRIFLE

Timetable *for dinner at 8.00 p.m.*
Day before: *Cook beef olives, cool and store in a cool place. Boil and drain rice. Cool and cover. Store in a cool place. Wash and dry salad ingredients. Prepare French dressing.*
In the morning: *Prepare sherry trifle, cover and store in refrigerator.*
7.00 *Put tomato juice in refrigerator. Put beef olives to warm in oven at 325°F. (mark 3) turning after 20 minutes.*
7.45 *Sauté mushrooms. Toss rice in melted butter until hot. Dish up beef olives and keep warm. Toss salad. Remove trifle from refrigerator.*
8.00 *Serve tomato juice.*

BEEF OLIVES

**8 slices of topside, cut about
$\frac{1}{4}$ in. thick and $2\frac{1}{2}$ in. by 3 in.**
$\frac{1}{4}$ lb. button mushrooms
**1 large tomato, skinned and
seeds removed**
**1 small onion, skinned and
quartered**
**2 oz. (1 cup) fresh white
breadcrumbs**
2 tsps. chopped parsley
1 level tsp. mixed fresh herbs
1 oz. suet, shredded
salt and pepper
1 egg yolk
dripping, for frying
**$\frac{3}{4}$ pint (2 cups) stock or
tomato juice**
1 level tbsp. flour
parsley, to garnish

Remove all the fat from the beef.

Sherry trifle is a traditional English dessert

Veal fricassee can be prepared well in advance and re-heated

Wipe and peel the mushrooms an trim the stalks level with the cap Chop tomato finely. Mince th fat with the mushroom skins an stalks and the onion. Add th breadcrumbs, herbs, suet an tomato; mix well, season and bin with the egg yolk.

Flatten each piece of beef b beating with a rolling pin or meat bat. Divide the stuffing int 8 and place a portion in the centr of each piece of steak. Roll u carefully and secure with fin string or cocktail sticks.

Brown the olives in a little melte dripping then arrange in a ca serole. Pour over the hot stock tomato juice and cook in the ove at 325°F. (mark 3) for about hours until tender. Meanwhi sauté the mushrooms in a litt butter and keep warm.

Strain off the gravy and thicke Remove the string or cockta sticks from the olives. Dish u and garnish with mushrooms an parsley. Serve with buttered ri and a green salad.

SHERRY TRIFLE

4 trifle sponge cakes
strawberry jam
16-oz. can sliced peaches
**2 tbsps. syrup from canned
peaches**
2 tbsps. sherry
**1 tbsp. finely chopped,
blanched almonds**
**$\frac{3}{4}$ pint (2 cups) pouring
custard, cold**
$\frac{1}{3}$ pint ($\frac{3}{4}$ cup) double cream
1 egg white
**small macaroons, for
decoration**
**toasted almonds, for
decoration**

Split the sponge cakes in ha lengthwise. Sandwich the halv together with strawberry jam an cut into $\frac{1}{2}$-in. slices. Arrange the base of a shallow glass dis Drain the peach slices and arran in pairs, alternating with spon cake so that the peach slices sta above the sponge cake. Reser some slices for decoration. M together the syrup and sherry a sprinkle over the cake and peache Scatter the chopped almonds ov and pour on the cool custard.
Whisk together the cream and e white until just thick enough hold its shape. Spoon over th custard and shape into swir with a knife.
Decorate with small macaroor chopped, toasted almonds a remaining peach slices. Chill for short while before serving.

CHILLED MELON
(CANTALOUP)
VEAL FRICASSEE
BAKED TOMATOES AND
DUCHESSE POTATOES
CHEESE BOARD
FRESH FRUIT

Timetable *for dinner at 8.00 p.m.*
Day before: *Prepare veal
fricassee, except for garnish. Cool
and keep in refrigerator.*
7.15 *Cut melon and chill. Set oven
at 350°F. (mark 4) and put veal
to reheat, adjusting sauce
consistency if necessary. Bake
tomatoes and fill. Boil and cream
potatoes, add ½ a beaten egg and 1
tbsp. cream. Season well and pipe
out in rosettes on a baking sheet.
Glaze with remaining beaten egg
and brown in the oven.*
7.30 *Prepare croûtes to garnish
veal.*
8.00 *Serve first course.*

VEAL FRICASSEE

1–1½ lb. stewing veal
¼ lb. back bacon, cut in 2 thick
  rashers
1 oz. butter
1 tbsp. oil
1 small onion, skinned and
  finely chopped
½ pint (1¼ cups) veal stock or
  water
salt and pepper
kneaded butter (¾ oz. flour
  worked into ¾ oz. softened
  butter)
1–2 tbsps. lemon juice
2 slices white bread
parsley, for garnish

Cut the veal into even 1-in. cubes.
Rind and trim the bacon and cut
as for the veal. Melt the butter,
add the oil and fry the veal and
bacon until pale brown. Remove
the meat and place in a large
casserole. Add the onion to the
fat, fry and add to the casserole.
Pour over the stock or water,
season and cover. Cook in the
oven at 350°F. (mark 4) for 1½
hours.
Strain off the liquor into a small
pan, keeping the meat hot in the
casserole. Drop small pieces of
the kneaded butter into the warm
liquor, stir well to thicken, bring
to the boil and boil for 2–3
minutes. Add the lemon juice and
adjust seasoning. Pour the sauce
over the veal.
Toast the bread slices, cut into
triangular croûtes and use to
garnish the veal, with the parsley.

BAKED TOMATOES

8 large, firm tomatoes
1 oz. butter
2 oz. long grain rice
salt and pepper
2 oz. frozen peas, cooked

Cut a thin slice from the rounded
end of each tomato, scoop out a
little of the seed and core. Put a
knob of butter on each and bake
in the oven at 350°F. (mark 4) for
about 10 minutes. Meanwhile cook
the rice for about 12 minutes in
boiling, salted water and drain.
Season the rice, spoon into the
tomatoes and top with peas.

A glazed baked salmon has a really festive air about it

MARINADED
MUSHROOMS
GLAZED BAKED SALMON
GARNI
FRENCH BEANS,
TOMATOES, ASPARAGUS
LEMON MERINGUE PIE

Timetable *for dinner at 8.00 p.m.*
Day before: *Prepare mushrooms
and leave in refrigerator to
marinade. Prepare salmon, but
not vegetable garnish.*
Bake flan case.
In the morning: *Finish lemon
meringue pie if to be served cold.*
5.30 *Garnish salmon.*
6.30 *Finish pie if serving warm.*
7.00 *Take mushrooms out of
refrigerator.*
8.00 *Serve first course.*

MARINADED
MUSHROOMS

1½ lb. button mushrooms
juice of 1 large lemon
12 fl. oz. (1½ cups) wine
  vinegar
1 small clove of garlic, skinned
  and crushed
2 medium onions, skinned
  and chopped
1 bouquet garni
1 level tsp. salt
freshly ground black pepper
¼ pint (1¼ cups) olive oil
1½ level tbsps. tomato ketchup
chopped parsley, to garnish

Wipe the mushrooms. Put them in
a pan with the lemon juice and
enough water to cover and bring
to the boil. Boil for 5 minutes
then leave until cold.
Meanwhile, put the wine vinegar
into a saucepan and add the
garlic, chopped onion, bouquet
garni, salt and pepper. Bring to the
boil and boil, uncovered, for 5
minutes. Remove the garlic and
cool the liquor. Add the olive oil
and tomato ketchup.
Drain the mushrooms well and
put into a deep bowl. Pour the
dressing over and leave to marinade
for several hours, or overnight, in
the refrigerator.
To serve, lift out the mushrooms,
place in a shallow dish, sprinkle
with the chopped parsley, and
pour over them the dressing,
strained through a sieve.

GLAZED BAKED SALMON
GARNI

1½ lb. piece middle cut fresh
  salmon (or fresh tuna)
butter
½ pint (1¼ cups) aspic jelly,
  made from aspic jelly
  powder
black olives, for garnish
cucumber slices, for garnish
12 very small tomatoes,
  skinned
½ lb. French beans, cooked
  and cooled
16-oz. can asparagus tips,
  drained
¼ pint (⅝ cup) French dressing

Generously butter a large piece
of foil. Lay the prepared fish in
the centre, join the edges carefully
together to form a loose package.
Place on a baking sheet and bake
in the oven at 300°F. (mark 2) for
about 1 hour. When the fish is
cooked it should show signs of
coming away from the bone. Unwrap the fish while still warm and
remove the skin. Leave to cool.
When completely cold, coat with
a thin layer of aspic jelly and
decorate with halved olives and
cucumber slices. Place on a serving
dish and garnish with a little
chopped aspic. Surround with
the tomatoes, beans and asparagus
tips and spoon a little French
dressing over the vegetables.

LEMON MERINGUE PIE

For pastry case:
4 oz. (1 cup) plain flour
pinch of salt
3 oz. butter
1 level tsp. caster sugar
1 egg, beaten

For lemon filling:
½ pint (1¼ cups) water
grated rind and 2–3 tbsps.
  juice from 1 large lemon
2 oz. (¼ cup) sugar
2 level tbsps. cornflour
2 egg yolks
½ oz. butter

For meringue topping:
2 egg whites
4 oz. (½ cup) caster sugar

First make the pastry case. Sift
the flour and the salt together and
rub in the butter with the fingertips until the mixture resembles
fine crumbs. Mix in the sugar. Add
the egg, stirring until the ingredients begin to stick together, then
with one hand collect the mixture
together and knead very lightly to
give a firm, smooth dough. Roll
out and use to line a 7-in. plain
flan case. Line with foil and bake

blind at 400°F. (mark 6) for 15 minutes. Cool on a wire rack. Place the water, grated lemon rind and 2 oz. sugar in a pan and heat gently to dissolve the sugar. Blend the cornflour with the lemon juice, strain on the hot syrup and stir. Return to the pan and bring to the boil; boil for 3 minutes. Remove from the heat and beat in the egg yolks and butter. Set aside. Whisk the egg whites until stiff, add 2 oz. caster sugar and whisk again. Fold in a further 1½ oz. sugar. Pour the lemon filling into the flan case and pile the meringue on top, making sure that the meringue meets the pastry edge. Dredge with remaining sugar. Bake at 300°F. (mark 2) for about ½ hour, until the meringue is crisp and lightly browned. Serve warm or cold.

MENU *serves 4*
SPRING VEGETABLE SOUP
PORK-STUFFED PEPPERS
ORANGES A LA TURQUE

Timetable *for dinner at 8.00 p.m.*
Day before: *Blanch peppers, make stuffing and sauce. Keep separately, covered, in a cool place. Prepare oranges and refrigerate.*
In the morning: *Prepare soup from a packet.*
7.30 Fill peppers, pour over sauce and heat in oven at 375°F. (mark 5) for about 30 minutes. Take oranges out of refrigerator. Reheat soup.
8.00 Serve first course.

PORK-STUFFED PEPPERS

4 large or 6 small green peppers (capsicums)
1 onion, skinned and finely chopped
1 oz. lard
2 oz. (¼ cup) long grain rice
¾ pint (2 cups) beef stock, made from a cube
1 lb. pork ring
2 tbsps. chopped parsley
salt and pepper
1 lb. tomatoes, skinned and seeds removed
1 level tbsp. flour
½ level tsp. sugar

Remove a thin slice from the stem end of each pepper, scoop out the seeds and membrane. Blanch the peppers and tops in boiling water for 2 minutes.
Fry the onion in half the lard. Add the rice, stir and continue to cook gently until opaque. Stir

Whole oranges in caramel sauce – nothing could be more delicious

in half the stock, cover and simmer for 12 minutes until liquid is completely absorbed.
Skin and coarsely mince the pork ring. Stir into the rice with the parsley and season mixture well. If the mixture looks rather dry, 1–2 tbsps. water can be added. Stuff the peppers and replace the lids. Put in an ovenproof dish. To make the sauce, fry the remaining onion in the remaining lard until soft but not coloured. Chop the tomatoes and add to the onion and cook to a pulp. Sprinkle with the flour, pour on the remaining stock and simmer until thickened. Season well, stir in the sugar. Pour the sauce over the peppers, cover and cook in the oven at 375°F. (mark 5) for about 30 minutes.

ORANGES A LA TURQUE

4 large juicy oranges
¼ pint (⅝ cup) water
½ lb. (1 cup) caster sugar
1 clove

Thinly pare the rind from 2 of the oranges free of white pith, cut into very thin strips with a sharp knife or scissors. Put into a small pan, cover well with water and cook until peel is tender; strain.

Cut away all the white pith from the oranges and the rind and pith from the remaining 2. Hold the oranges over a bowl to catch the juice, and slice carefully into rounds. Reassemble each orange and secure with cocktail sticks. Dissolve the sugar in the ¼ pint water with the clove. Bring to the boil and boil until caramel coloured. Remove from the heat, add 3 tablespoons water, return to a very low heat to dissolve the caramel and add the juice from the oranges. Arrange the oranges in a serving dish, top with the shredded orange rind and pour the caramel over. Leave in the refrigerator, turning occasionally.

MENU *serves 4*
MELON COCKTAIL
CHICKEN BEAUJOLAIS
GREEN SALAD,
FRENCH BREAD
SYLLABUB

Timetable *for dinner at 8.00 p.m.*
Day before: *Cook chicken Beaujolais but do not add tomato quarters, cool and store in refrigerator. Wash and dry salad ingredients. Prepare French*

dressing.
Make syllabub and store in a cool place, but not the refrigerator.
7.30 Put chicken to reheat with tomatoes in oven at 350°F. (mark 4). Toss salad. Prepare melon cocktail and chill briefly.
8.00 Serve first course.

CHICKEN BEAUJOLAIS

4 rashers of back bacon, rinded and cut up
cooking oil
4 chicken portions, skinned
2 oz. onion, skinned and finely sliced
¾ oz. plain flour
¼ pint (⅝ cup) Beaujolais
¼ pint (⅝ cup) water
1 chicken stock cube
salt and pepper
4 tomatoes, skinned and quartered
chopped parsley, to garnish

In a shallow, flameproof casserole (large enough to take the chicken in a single layer), gently fry the bacon snippets until beginning to brown. Drain from the fat. Add just enough oil to the casserole to cover the base. Brown the chicken evenly and lightly, remove from the casserole and strain off all but 1 tablespoon fat. Add onion; when beginning to colour stir in the flour and cook for 1–2 minutes. With the casserole still over the heat, slowly stir in the wine, water and crumbled stock cube. Loosen the residue from the pan base and bring to the boil, stirring. Adjust the seasoning, replace the bacon and chicken, flesh side down, and tuck the tomato quarters into the corners. Cover and cook for about 1¼ hours. Serve the chicken with the sauce spooned over and garnished with chopped parsley.

SYLLABUB

thinly pared rind of 1 lemon
4 tbsps. lemon juice
6 tbsps. white wine or sherry
2 tbsps. brandy
2–3 oz. caster sugar
½ pint (1¼ cups) double cream
grated nutmeg or chopped nuts

Place the lemon rind, juice, wine and brandy in a bowl and leave for several hours, or overnight. Strain into a large bowl, add the sugar and stir until dissolved. Add the cream slowly, stirring all the time. Whisk until the mixture forms soft peaks. Spoon into glasses and sprinkle with nutmeg or nuts. Serve with sponge fingers.

COOK AHEAD - WITH A FREEZER

Freezing is fast superseding bottling, canning and drying as the most important means of preserving food. Unlike other forms of preserving, freezing does not destroy or alter anything contained in the food. The natural cycle of life is not destroyed, but held in 'suspended animation'; equally, enzymes and micro-organisms in the food (which cause normal deterioration) are not destroyed.

The food will therefore come out of the freezer as good (or as bad) as it went in. There is only one proviso – that it is wrapped and sealed correctly.

Frozen food, then, is as fresh as fruit and vegetables from the greengrocer. Indeed, it is often fresher and in better condition, as stock at the shop has probably been in transit for several days, whereas fruit and vegetables from your own garden (and commercially frozen) are frozen within hours of picking – with the result that they will have lost far fewer vitamins.

Almost any food can be frozen, but whatever it is, it should, of course, be in first class condition. Fruit and vegetables should be ripe, firm and freshly picked; meat and poultry must be good quality and suitably hung. Cooked foods need to be cooled as rapidly as possible before going into the freezer. Everything should be clean and done as quickly as possible – food deteriorates quickly if it is left lying around and may become contaminated.

USING THE FREEZER

To freeze food successfully, retaining its appearance, taste and food value, it must be frozen quickly so that the ice particles that form are tiny. If you freeze slowly, the ice particles are large and damage the cell structure of the food. This means choosing a freezer with a special low freezing temperature and freezing in smallish quantities so that the fresh food going in doesn't raise the temperature in the cabinet too much and slow the freezing process (a maximum of $\frac{1}{10}$ the freezer's capacity in any 24 hours is recommended by most manufacturers). Once the food is frozen, raise the temperature to the normal 0°F. (−18°C.) for storage.

PACKAGING

Packaging food for your freezer is all-important. Solids should be packed as tightly as possible, excluding all the air. Aluminium foil is best for moulding difficult shaped objects, like chickens or joints, but it tears easily on jagged bones, so it is safest to overwrap with polythene (again squeezing out as much air as you can) afterwards.

Fruit and vegetables can either be packed in rigid containers (imperative for delicate whole fruits) or simply in sealed polythene bags. In this case, if you are having problems removing the air, dip the bag into a bowl of water – this pushes all the air out and moulds the bag snugly round the vegetables. Alternatively, suck the air out through a straw. Seal the bag immediately, and don't forget to dry the outside before putting it into your freezer.

If you can't fill a rigid container completely, use crumpled greaseproof or waxed paper to fill up the remaining space. Liquids expand when frozen, so always allow at

Frozen fruit salad in a solid block

least ½ in. headspace when sealing a polythene bag or a container with a lid. Alternatively, leave the container open until the liquid is frozen – but don't forget to seal it when it *is* frozen, or it will dehydrate rapidly. If you are using a polythene bag for liquids, it helps to fit the bag into a pre-former – any straight-sided carton or plastic box – before pouring in the liquid. Freeze the liquid in the pre-former and when it is solid just slip it out and pack it away – and your carton is ready to be used again.

If you're freezing a combination of solids and liquid – such as fruit in syrup, or a casserole – do be sure the solid pieces are all below the level of the liquid. A piece of crumpled greaseproof paper over the top will generally be sufficient to keep the pieces down. Aluminium foil is the best material in which to freeze casseroles, again because it moulds so closely; you can freeze them in a casserole dish, but this slows the freezing and thawing processes and also puts one of your dishes out of action. The best way is to cook and cool the casserole; line an ovenproof dish with foil and spoon the meat and sauce into it, making sure the meat is completely covered. Put it in the freezer and when it is solid lift the foil out of the dish, wrap it over the top and overwrap in polythene. To use the casserole, simply remove the polythene and foil and pop the food into the same ovenproof dish to reheat.

There are available foil dishes in various shapes and sizes which are invaluable for use in freezing, as they can go straight from the freezer to the oven. With care they can be used more than once, which needn't make them an extravagance. Many small containers used for commercial products, such as ice cream and yoghourt, can be re-used in home freezing and are a great help for freezing small quantities of sauces, herbs and breadcrumbs.

Remember to package food in the quantities you will want to use. It's no good freezing a pâté for 10 if you are going to need only 4 slices from it; so slice it *before* you freeze it, put a sheet of waxed paper or polythene between each piece and then wrap the whole thing in foil. The same applies to cakes, meat, or anything that you freeze in quantity but use only in small amounts. If you make up a sauce, freeze it in ½-pint or pint containers, not in 1 solid block.

Another idea is to freeze stock and sauces in an ice-cube tray. When solid, turn out the cubes and put them in a polythene bag. A little soda water squirted into the bag will prevent the cubes sticking together. This is also an ideal way to freeze a variety of foods used in small quantities – concentrated mint sauce, tomato sauce, chopped herbs in a little water and so on. Finally, do label everything you put in the freezer. You may think that you'll remember what each package is, but after a while you may find it a problem – especially if you have a number of packages all much the same shape. Serving a dish of mashed potato instead of shepherd's pie, or a second course of chicken pie instead of blackberry and apple could be embarrassing! So tie or stick a label on to each package as it goes into your freezer and put on the date as well as the contents. A list of everything you freeze, kept handy inside the lid of the freezer, will ensure a steady rotation of stock.

PREPARING FOOD FOR THE FREEZER

FRUIT should be just ready for eating; over-ripe fruit can be puréed and frozen for use in fools, mousses, etc. Rinse all but soft fruits (such as raspberries) in ice-cold water and drain very thoroughly. To prevent discolouration, keep fruits such as apples and pears covered in water and lemon juice during preparation.

Fruit may be frozen in 3 ways – as a dry pack, in sugar, or in syrup.

Dry packing is suitable for fruit that is to be used for pies or preserves and for small whole fruit, so long as the skin is undamaged. Pick over, wash, dry on absorbent kitchen paper and use a rigid container to prevent damage during handling and storage.

Free-flow dry packing is suitable for small fruit or pieces of fruit such as strawberries or grapefruit segments. Pick the fruit over and prepare as necessary; spread it out on a baking sheet and freeze until firm. Then pack (preferably in a rigid container) for storage.

Dry sugar packing is particularly suitable for soft fruits. Pick over the fruit but don't wash it unless really necessary. The sugar and fruit can either be put into rigid containers in layers, or else mixed together before being packed. The fruit is more likely to retain its shape if layered, because when it is mixed with sugar the juice is

Freeze small quantities of stock or sauces in ice-cube trays

drawn out and leaves the fruit almost in purée form. Use caster sugar.

Syrup is best for non-juicy fruits or for those which discolour during preparation and storage. The strength of the syrup varies according to the particular fruit being frozen – refer to the chart for the correct strength.

20 % syrup is 4 oz. sugar dissolved in 1 pint water
30% syrup is 8 oz. sugar dissolved in 1 pint water
40% syrup is 10 oz. sugar dissolved in 1 pint water
50% syrup is 1 lb. sugar dissolved in 1 pint water.

Dissolve the sugar in the water by heating gently and bringing to the boil; cover and allow the syrup to become quite cold before using. Normally you will find ½ pint syrup is enough to cover 1 lb. fruit. Leave about ½ in. space at the top of the container to allow for expansion during freezing. If the fruit tends to float above the level of the syrup, hold it down with a piece of crumpled waxed or greaseproof paper.

VEGETABLES

Speed is particularly important when dealing with vegetables.

These should be frozen as soon as possible after picking. They need to be blanched before freezing, to kill some of the microorganisms which cause discolouration and 'off' flavours. Of course, this also drives off some of the vitamins, but don't think it ruins the nutritional value of the vegetables – after all, when you cook them fresh, some of the vitamins are still lost.

For blanching you need a very large pan and a wire basket. Place the vegetables in the basket and immerse in boiling water (approximately 6 pints to 1 lb. of vegetables). When the water re-boils, cook for the recommended blanching time (see chart), then plunge the vegetables into ice-cold water. Drain and pack immediately. Don't try to do too large a quantity – 1 or 2 lb. at a time is about right, in successive batches. Pack the vegetables in rigid containers or polythene bags, allowing a little space for expansion for vegetables which pack tightly, such as peas.

MEAT

If you are going to home-freeze meat, do be absolutely sure the meat is fresh. Many butchers now

Extracting air from the package is essential for successful freezing

provide meat ready-packed for the home freezer and this is probably a better bet than trying to butcher half a carcass yourself. If you buy jointed fresh meat to freeze yourself there are 1 or 2 points to watch for. Very lean meat tends to dry out during freezing, so look for a good 'marbling' of fat, which helps to prevent this. On the other hand, too much fat tends to go rancid after a while, so trim some of it off if you think it's excessive.

It is generally better to freeze meat off the bone whenever possible – the bones slow down freezing and thawing and take up a lot of space in your freezer. If, however, you leave the bone in place – such as in a leg of lamb or pork chops – pad it well to avoid puncturing the wrapping. Separate steaks and chops with waxed paper or polythene so that you can remove just one or two.

POULTRY AND GAME
Truss the bird as for the table, but *do not* stuff it. Pad the protruding bones before you wrap it. Game must be hung before freezing, for the same length of time as if you were going to eat it immediately. Then proceed as for poultry.

FISH
Fish should be frozen only if you can get it to your freezer within 12 hours of the catch. Clean the fish as usual, leaving small fish whole but removing the heads and tails of larger ones. Skin and fillet flat fish. Salmon, trout and similar fish can be frozen whole in a sheet of ice; dip them in cold water, leave them in the freezer until frozen and then repeat the process several times until the ice glaze is about $\frac{1}{8}$ in. thick. Wrap individual fish in polythene and pack in cartons or overwrap with heavy-duty polythene.

COOKED DISHES
One of the great advantages of a freezer is that you can cook when you feel like it and store whole meals for future use. You can make 3 or 4 pies at once (particularly useful if you have a glut of fruit in your garden), eat 1 now and freeze the rest; or make up a casserole using double your normal quantity – eat half and freeze the rest.

In general, the foods can be prepared and cooked as if they were to be served immediately,

A well stocked freezer, with each package clearly labelled

but it is wise to reduce the amount of seasoning. Take care not to over-cook the food, particularly if it is to be reheated for serving. Chill food quickly after cooking and wrap and freeze it carefully. When you are freezing stock or soups, remember that liquid expands when frozen, so allow some space for this.

THAWING AND REHEATING
Ideally, food should be thawed very gently in the refrigerator – but this can take up to 6 hours *per lb.*, and most people simply don't have that amount of time in hand. There are some foods, though, that *must* be thawed right through before they are cooked – in particular poultry. Whole fish retain their flavour and texture better if thawed out slowly and whole fruit that is to be eaten with no further preparation will retain its shape more readily. Leave the food in its original wrapping while thawing.

If you don't have quite so much time in hand, thaw at room temperature, but don't let it stand too long. Once food thaws out, the micro-organisms start working again and it will deteriorate much more quickly than if the food were fresh.

Luckily, a lot of the real standbys you keep in the freezer can be cooked straight from frozen. Stews, casseroles, cooked meat in gravy, fruit pies will all reheat appetizingly from frozen – but if the dish the food is in isn't one of the freezer-to-oven type, do allow it at least 30 minutes at room temperature. Anything in a foil

container, of course, can go straight into the oven.

Chops, steaks, small fish and other small items can be cooked without thawing. The only point to watch is that the food is thoroughly hot right through – and not burnt to a cinder on the outside at the same time. A joint of meat can equally well be thawed or cooked straight from the freezer – either way is quite satisfactory. Again, you must ensure that it is cooked through to the centre.

Soups and sauces are best thawed slowly, though if you're in a hurry you can turn the frozen lump into a saucepan and heat it very gently. Cakes, pâtés, sweets and so on also need slow, gentle thawing (though, of course, if you've followed our advice and sliced them before freezing they won't take more than an hour).

Finally, vegetables should never be thawed. Pop them straight into a little boiling water, or toss them gently in butter in a heavy lidded pan.

DO NOT FREEZE . . .
Eggs in their shells (they crack) or hardboiled (they turn rubbery). The solution is simple – freeze the whites and yolks separately.

Boiled old potatoes (they go leathery); mash them with butter – but not milk – and they will be fine.

Fully-cooked chips (they go soggy); the answer is to part-cook them, freeze, and just crisp them up in deep hot fat straight from the freezer.

Salad stuffs – lettuce, watercress, celery, chicory – all go limp, soggy and unattractive. If you have a

glut in the garden you can freeze a soup made from one of these ingredients.

Single cream – of less than 40 per cent butterfat (it separates). Double cream is fine.

Mayonnaise (it curdles).

Custards (they tend to separate) – so freeze them *before* cooking.

Moulds – anything containing a high proportion of gelatine.

Anything flavoured with garlic (it develops an unpleasant, musty flavour) – if possible, add garlic at point of reheating or use it very sparingly.

GOLDEN RULES
1. Always start with good-quality foods and freeze them at peak freshness.
2. Keep handling to a minimum and make sure everything is clean.
3. Pay special attention to packaging and sealing. Exposure to air and moisture damages frozen foods.
4. Cool food rapidly if it's been cooked or blanched; never put anything hot – or even warm – into your freezer.
5. Freeze as quickly as possible, and in small quantities.
6. Freeze in the coldest part of the freezer, and don't pack the food to be frozen too closely.
7. Transfer newly added items to the main part of the cabinet once they've been frozen.
8. Remember to return the switch from 'accelerated' to 'normal' once newly added foods have been frozen – i.e. after 24 hours.
9. Maintain a steady storage temperature of −18°C. (0°F.) and don't do anything that will cause temperature fluctuations within the freezer.
10. Label and date food to ensure a good rotation of stock.
11. Defrost the freezer at a time when stocks are low.
12. Be prepared for emergencies. Make sure you know what to do in case of breakdown or powercuts.

And for freezing cooked foods
1. Go lightly with the seasoning and preferably omit garlic entirely.
2. Use shallow rather than deep dishes.
3. Cool everything as rapidly as possible and freeze at once.

Note : Polythene bags or film *must* be removed before food is put into the oven.

Raw meat (do not stuff):	lamb, veal, pork – 6 months; beef – 8 months; mince, offal, sausages – 3 months
Cooked meat:	roasts (whole or sliced) – 2–4 weeks; meat loaves, pâtés – 1 month; casseroles, curries, etc. – 2 months
Poultry and game:	giblets – 3 months; duck, goose – 4–6 months; turkey, game birds – 6–8 months; chicken, venison – 12 months
Raw fish and shellfish:	salmon – 4 months; white fish – 6 months. *Not advisable unless within 12 hours of catch*
Cooked fish:	pies, fish cakes, croquettes, kedgeree, mousse, paellas – 2 months
Liquids:	highly seasoned sauces, etc. – 2 weeks; other sauces, stocks, soups – 2–3 months; fruit juices – 6–8 months
Pizza:	baked – 2 months; unbaked – 3 months
Pastry, uncooked:	pies – 3 months; shortcrust – 3 months; flaky and puff – 3–4 months
Pastry, cooked:	meat pies – 3–4 months; fruit pies – 6 months; empty cases – 6 months
Pancakes:	filled – 1–2 months; unfilled – 2 months
Desserts:	mousses, fruit creams – 2–3 months; home-made ice cream, cooked sponge puddings – 3 months; double cream – 4–6 months
Cakes:	uncooked – 2 months; cooked, iced – 2 months; sponge flans, Swiss rolls, layer cakes – 6 months
Scones and biscuits:	unbaked Danish pastries – 6 weeks; baked and unbaked biscuits, baked scones and teabreads – 6 months
Bread:	baked – 1 month; sandwiches – 1–2 months; bought part-baked bread and rolls – 4 months
Butter:	salted – 3 months; unsalted – 6 months
Commercially-frozen:	ice cream – 1 month; other – 3 months
Fruit and vegetables:	10–12 months

Freezing fruit

Fruit	Preparation	Pack
Apples; raw sliced purée	Blanch slices 2–3 min., cool in ice-cold water. Pack. Peel, core and stew in minimum amount of water – sweetened or not. Sieve or liquidize. Cool before packing	Mix 4 oz. sugar to 1 lb. fruit or mix with 20% syrup. Pack in rigid containers
Apricots (and Nectarines)	Plunge into boiling water for 30 secs. to loosen skins. Peel, leave whole, or cut in half or slice into syrup	Mix with 30% syrup plus ascorbic acid
Blackberries (and Blueberries)	Wash in chilled water, drain. Dry pack or dry sugar pack – lightly crush and mix with sugar till dissolved. Can also be frozen in cold syrup – leave a headspace	Dry sugar pack – 4 oz. sugar to 1 lb. fruit. Syrup – 50%
Cherries *(best used for pie filling)*	Remove stalks, wash and dry. Dry pack or dry sugar pack *stoned* cherries or cover with cold syrup – leave headspace	Dry sugar pack – 4 oz. sugar to 1 lb. fruit. Syrup – 30%
Citrus fruits (Grapefruit, Orange, Lemon and Lime)	(a) Squeeze out juice and freeze, sweetened or not, in ice cube trays. Remove when frozen and pack for storage. (b) Peel, segment and pack in cold syrup (including juice from fruit) or dry sugar pack – sprinkle sugar over fruit until juices start to run. (c) Mix grated peel with a little sugar for pancakes, etc. (d) Freeze slivers of peel, free of pith, to add to drinks. (e) Slice peel into julienne strips, blanch for 1 min., cool and pack. Use for garnish	(a) Pack cubes in polythene bags. (b) Syrup – 50%. Dry sugar pack – mix 8 oz. sugar to 1 lb. fruit. In rigid containers. (c–e) Wrap in foil.
Currants (Black, red)	Wash and trim. Either dry pack for whole fruit or cook to a purée with very little water and brown sugar	Pack whole in rigid containers or polythene bags
Figs	Wash gently, remove stems. Freeze unsweetened, whole or peeled; or peel and pack in cold syrup; or leave whole and wrap in foil – suitable for dessert figs	Syrup – 30%. Pack whole in polythene bags or in rigid containers
Gooseberries	Wash and dry. Dry pack whole fruit for pie filling, or pack in syrup; purée, sweetened to taste, for fools, etc.	Pack in polythene bags or rigid containers. Syrup – 45%
Grapes	Seedless grapes can be packed whole; others should be skinned, pipped and halved. Pack in cold syrup	Syrup 30%. Use rigid containers
Greengages *(skins tend to toughen during freezing)*	Wash and remove stones. Pack in syrup with ascorbic acid. Don't open till required, as fruit discolours rapidly	Syrup – 30% plus ascorbic acid. Use rigid containers
Melon (Cantaloup and honeydew)	Halve, seed, and cut into balls, cubes or slices. Put straight into syrup. Or use dry pack – sprinkle over a little sugar	Syrup – 30%. Pack in polythene bags
Peaches	Skin, stone, brush with lemon juice. Pack halves or slices in cold syrup. Or purée with 1 tbsp. lemon juice and 4 oz. sugar to 1 lb. fruit – use for sorbets, soufflés, etc.	Syrup – 30% plus ascorbic acid. Use a rigid container
Pineapple	Peel and core. Pack unsweetened slices in boxes, separated by waxed paper. Pack cubes in syrup (including any juice). Pack crushed pineapple with sugar	Syrup – 30%. Sugar pack – 4 oz. sugar to ¾ lb. fruit. Use rigid containers.
Plums (and Damsons)	Wash, halve and stone. Stew with a little sugar and pack as a purée, or pack whole fruit uncooked in syrup (stew later)	Syrup – 30% plus ascorbic acid. Use polythene bags
Raspberries (and Loganberries)	Choose firm, clean, dry fruit. Use dry method, dry sugar method, or purée – sweetened to taste	Dry sugar pack – 4 oz. sugar to 1 lb. fruit. Freeze in small quantities
Rhubarb	Wash, trim, slice. Blanch for 1 min., cool quickly. Pack in syrup, or dry pack, to use for pies, crumbles, etc.	Syrup – 50%. Use rigid containers
Strawberries	Choose firm, clean, dry fruit; remove stalks. Pack by dry method, dry sugar method, or as purée – sweeten to taste	Dry sugar pack – 4 oz. sugar to 1 lb. fruit. Use small containers
Unsuitable for freezing:	Bananas. Pears discolour and go mushy – not very satisfactory	

Freezing vegetables

Vegetable	Preparation	Blanching time
Asparagus	Grade into thick and thin stems (for asparagus tips, cut off stalks). Wash, blanch, cool and drain. Tie into *small* bundles, separated with waxed paper. Pack in rigid containers	Thin stem – 2 min. Thick stem – 4 min.
Artichokes (Globe)	Trim, wash in cold water, add a little lemon juice to blanching water. Cool and drain upside-down. Pack in rigid containers	Blanch a few at a time in a large pan for 7–10 min.
Aubergines (Eggplant)	Peel and slice roughly. Blanch, chill and dry on absorbent paper. Pack in layers, separated by waxed paper	4 min.
Avocados	Peel; mash with 1 tbsp. lemon juice per avocado and pack	—
Beans – French, runner and broad	Select young, tender beans; wash thoroughly. French – trim ends and blanch; cool, drain and pack. Runner – slice thickly and blanch; cool, drain and pack. Broad – shell and blanch; cool, drain and pack	3 min. 2 min. 3 min.
Beetroot (short blanching and long storage can make beetroot rubbery)	Choose small beets. Wash well, blanch and rub off skin. Beetroot under 1-in. diameter may be frozen whole; large ones should be sliced or diced. Pack in cartons	Small whole – 5–10 min. Large – cook until tender (45–50 min.)
Broccoli	Trim off any woody parts and large leaves. Wash in salted water, and cut into small sprigs. Blanch, cool and drain well. Pack in boxes in 1 or 2 layers, tips to stalks	Thin stem – 3 min. Medium stem – 4 min. Thick stem – 5 min.
Brussels sprouts (pack those of equal size together)	Use small compact heads. Remove outer leaves and wash thoroughly. Blanch, cool and drain well before packing	Small – 3 min. Medium – 4 min.
Cabbage (red and green)	Use only young, crisp cabbage. Wash thoroughly, shred finely. Blanch, cool and drain. Pack in small quantities	1½ min.
Carrots	Scrape and dice. Blanch, cool, drain and pack	3–5 min.
Cauliflower	Heads should be firm, compact and white. Wash, break into small sprigs. Add lemon juice to the blanching water. Blanch, cool, drain and pack	3 min.
Celery (goes soft when thawed)	Trim, scrub well. Cut into 1-in. lengths. Use in cooked dishes	3 min.
Celeriac (Celery root)	Wash and trim. Cook until almost tender, peel and slice	—
Corn on the cob (there may be loss of flavour and tenderness after freezing)	Select young yellow kernels, not starchy, over-ripe or shrunken. Remove husks and 'silks'. Blanch, cool and dry. Pack individually in freezer paper or foil	Small – 4 min. Medium – 6 min. Large – 8 min.
Courgettes (Zucchini)	Choose young ones. Wash, cut into ½-in. slices. Blanch, or sauté in a little butter. Cool, drain and pack	1 min.
Fennel	Cut into short lengths. Blanch, cool, drain and pack	3 min.
Kohlrabi	Use small roots, 2–3 in. diameter. Cut off tops, peel and dice. Blanch, cool, drain and pack	1½ min.
Marrow (young ones only)	Peel, slice and blanch. Pack with ½ in. headspace	3 min.
Mushrooms, small button large	Leave whole; wipe clean and sauté in butter. Cool and pack in polythene bags. Slice and use only in cooked dishes	Sauté in butter 1 min.
Onions, large small	Skin, finely chop and blanch. Pack in small plastic containers and overwrap to prevent the smell filtering out. Blanch whole to use later in casseroles	2 min. 4 min.
Parsnips (young)	Peel and cut into narrow strips. Blanch, cool and dry	2 min.
Peas (young, sweet ones)	Shell and blanch. Cool, drain and pack in polythene bags	1 min.
Peppers, sweet (Capsicums)	Freeze red and green separately. Wash well, remove stems, seeds and membranes. Blanch as halves for stuffed peppers, or in thin slices for stews and casseroles	3 min.
Potatoes, old new	Fry chips in deep fat, cool and freeze in polythene bags for final frying. Or freeze as croquettes or duchesse potatoes. Scrape, cook fully with mint and cool	Fry for 2 min.
Spinach	Select young leaves. Wash very thoroughly; drain. Blanch in small amounts, cool quickly, press out excess moisture. Pack, allowing ½ in. headspace	2 min.
Tomatoes, purée or juice	Skin, core and quarter. Simmer in their own juice 5–10 min. until soft. Push through a nylon sieve or purée in a blender and season with salt. Cool and pack in small quantities	—
Turnips (small, young ones)	Peel, cut into ½-in. dice. Blanch, cool, drain and pack. Can be fully cooked and mashed before freezing – allow headspace	2½ min.

Unsuitable for freezing:	Chicory, endive, kale, lettuce, radishes, watercress. Jerusalem artichokes are suitable only as purées and soups	

Packing a selection of foods for the freezer

BORTSCH
serves 6

6 small raw beetroot (approx. 2 lb.), peeled
2 medium-sized onions, skinned and chopped
4 pints (10 cups) seasoned beef stock

Grate the beetroot coarsely and put it, together with the onion, in a pan with the stock. Bring to the boil and simmer without a lid for 45 minutes. Strain.

To pack and freeze: Allow to cool. Pour into a rigid plastic container, label and seal. Alternatively, pour into a polythene-lined preformer and when frozen solid remove the polythene bag from the pre-former, label and seal.

To use: Defrost overnight in the refrigerator, or allow 8 hours at room temperature. (Stand a preformed package in a basin.) Bortsch is best served chilled.
When it is fully defrosted, add 2 tablespoons lemon juice and 6 tablespoons dry sherry. Adjust seasoning and serve in bowls, with a whirl of soured cream and a few chopped chives floating on top.

QUICHE LORRAINE
serves 4–6 as a starter or 3 for a buffet party

6 oz. shortcrust pastry – i.e. 6 oz. (1½ cups) flour, etc.

For filling :

6 rashers of bacon, rinded and chopped
2 medium-sized onions, skinned and chopped
1 oz. butter
2 oz. Gruyère cheese, thinly sliced
equal quantities milk and single cream, to make ¼ pint (⅝ cup) – 4 tbsps. each
2 large eggs
salt and pepper

Set an 8-in. flan ring on a baking sheet and line it with the pastry. Leave in the refrigerator to rest.

Scallops and duchesse potato – a good starter from the freezer

Bortsch – Russian beetroot soup served with a swirl of soured cream

Fry the bacon and onion in the melted butter for a few minutes, till the onion is transparent and the bacon cooked through; allow to cool. Place the thinly sliced cheese in the base of the pastry-lined flan ring. Spoon the onion and bacon mixture over. Make a custard by whisking the milk, cream, eggs and seasoning together and pour it over the filling in the flan case.

To pack and freeze: Put the uncooked and unwrapped flan in a level area of the freezer until firm. When frozen, cover the top of the flan with a round of non-stick or freezer paper. Remove the flan ring if you like, but don't forget to replace it before the flan is cooked. Lift the frozen flan from the baking sheet, using a palette knife or a fish slice. Wrap in foil to make a neat parcel. Several flans can be stacked on top of each other, before being wrapped in foil. Overwrap, seal and label.

To cook: Unwrap and place on a baking sheet (replace the flan ring if necessary). Cover loosely with foil. Bake from frozen just above the oven centre, at 375°F. (mark 5) for ¾ hour, then remove foil and cook for a further 15 minutes, until golden on top. Serve hot or cold, garnished with chopped parsley.

COQUILLES ST. JACQUES
serves 6

½ lb. fresh scallops, shelled
¼ pint (⅝ cup) dry white wine
¼ of a small onion, skinned
a sprig of parsley
1 bay leaf
1 oz. butter
2 oz. button mushrooms, sliced
6 small natural scallop shells, washed
duchesse potatoes (optional – made with 1½ lb. mashed potato)

For sauce :

2 oz. butter
2 oz. (½ cup) plain flour
¾ pint (1⅞ cups) milk
2 oz. (½ cup) cheese, grated
salt and pepper

Rinse and slice the white parts of each scallop into 4; leave the coral whole. Place in a pan with the wine, onion, parsley and bay leaf. Bring to the boil and simmer for 5 minutes. Drain, keeping the strained liquor to one side. Melt the butter and sauté the mushrooms for 5 minutes.
Melt the butter for the sauce in

a pan, add the flour and cook over a gentle heat without browning for 1 minute; stir in the strained liquor and the milk. Return the pan to the heat and bring to the boil, stirring till the sauce is smooth and thickens. Cool slightly, then stir in the sautéed mushrooms, cheese and scallops, with seasoning to taste.

To pack: Divide the mixture between the scallop shells (or 6 individual ovenproof dishes). Pipe duchesse potato mixture round the shells and brush with beaten egg.

To freeze: Freeze uncovered, so as not to damage the piped potato. Place inside 2 polythene bags for storing.

To thaw: Remove the seal and packaging and if a potato border was not added before freezing, pipe it on now. Set the coquilles on a baking sheet, loosely covered so as not to damage the potato. Leave in the refrigerator for about 8 hours.

To serve: If taken straight from the freezer, remove the outer wrapping. Place the coquilles on a baking sheet, cover loosely with foil and place in the oven at 425°F. (mark 7) for 50–60 minutes. If thawed, reheat for 15 minutes. Uncover, brush with beaten egg and cook for a further 10–15 minutes until golden. Garnish with a wedge of lemon or parsley sprigs.

COURGETTES (ZUCCHINI) A LA GRECQUE
serves 4

2 small onions, skinned and thinly sliced
3 tbsps. olive oil
1 clove of garlic, skinned and crushed
just over ¼ pint (⅝ cup) dry white wine
salt and pepper
1½ lb. courgettes (zucchini)
½ lb. tomatoes
pinch of dried chervil (optional)

Sauté the onions in the hot oil until soft but not coloured; add garlic, wine and a little seasoning. Wipe courgettes and discard a slice off each end. Cut remainder into rings. Skin and quarter the tomatoes, discarding the seeds. Add courgettes and tomatoes to the pan and cook gently, without covering, for 10 minutes. Cool quickly. Add a little chervil if liked (or add fresh chervil, if available, when serving).

To pack: Spoon into a polythene bag, set in a pre-former to shape it. Put in the freezer.

To freeze: When set in shape, remove from pre-former and overwrap with foil, or place inside another polythene bag, seal and label. Return the pack to the freezer.
To thaw: Allow 12–14 hours in the refrigerator or 6–8 hours at room temperature.
To serve: Add a further ½ lb. skinned, quartered and seeded tomatoes. Adjust seasoning if necessary. Sprinkle with chopped fresh chervil (if available and provided dried chervil was not included before freezing) or with chopped parsley.

UPSIDE-DOWN BEEF AND POTATO PIE

serves 4

3 oz. butter or margarine
4 oz. (2 cups) fresh white breadcrumbs
2 lb. old potatoes, peeled
salt and pepper
1 large onion, skinned and chopped
1 clove of garlic, skinned and crushed
6 gherkins, chopped
½ lb. button mushrooms, washed and sliced
1 lb. lean beef, minced
1 level tbsp. mild curry powder
1 level tbsp. flour

Line a 2½-pint ovenproof dish with kitchen foil, leaving enough foil to enclose the contents later. Brush lightly with butter or margarine.
Heat 2 oz. butter in a frying pan, add the breadcrumbs and fry, stirring, until golden. Place in the lined dish. Boil the potatoes until just tender; drain, mash and season with salt and pepper. Heat the remaining butter and fry the onion until golden. Add the garlic, gherkins, mushrooms, beef and curry powder and fry for 10 minutes, stirring frequently. Add the flour and mix well.
Arrange half the potatoes over the crumbs in the dish. Cover with the meat mixture and remaining potatoes. Press well down and cool quickly.
To pack: Seal foil over the top potato layer to enclose completely.
To freeze: Freeze rapidly until firm. Ease the foil pack from the dish and overwrap.
To use: Remove the overwrap and return the foil-wrapped food to the original dish. Open up the foil and cook the pie from frozen in the oven at 375°F. (mark 5) for about 1½ hours. To serve, invert on to a serving dish and garnish with tomato and parsley.

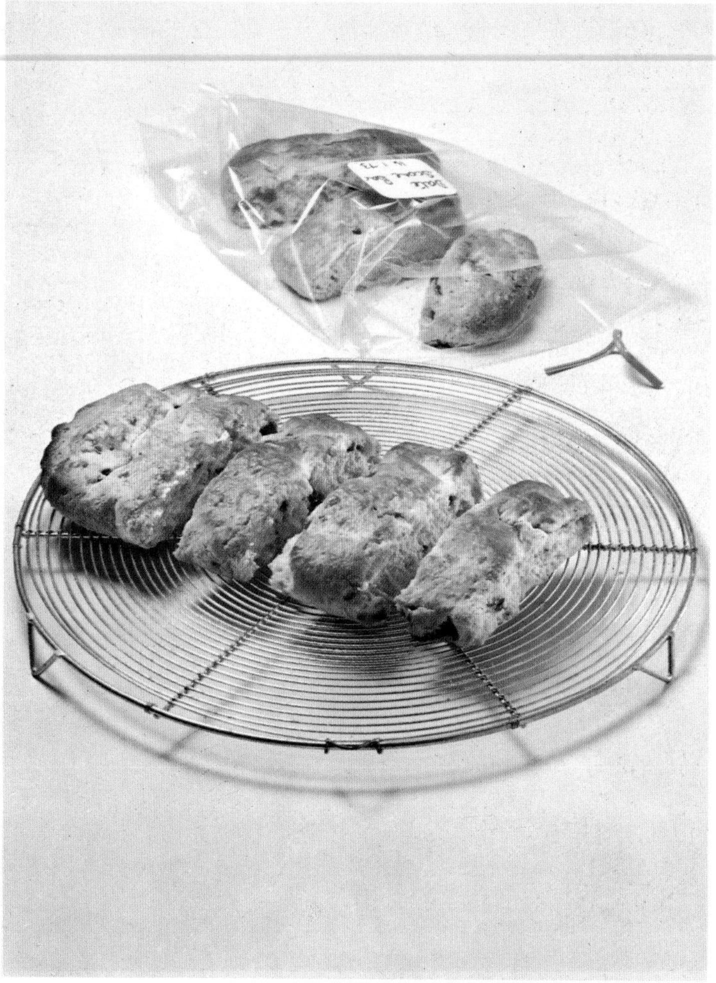

These date scone bars keep especially well in the freezer

BEEF EL DORADO

serves 4

2 small onions, skinned
4 young carrots, pared
3 level tbsps. cooking oil
1 lb. lean chuck steak, cubed
seasoned flour
½ pint (1¼ cups) light ale
½ level tbsp. black treacle
3 oz. (½ cup) sultanas
salt and pepper

Thickly slice the onions; cut the carrots into thin rings. Heat the oil and fry the onions and carrots for about 2 minutes; remove from the pan. Toss the meat in seasoned flour and fry it until lightly coloured. Return the vegetables to the pan, pour in the light ale, bring to the boil and add the treacle and sultanas. Place in an ovenproof dish, cover and cook at 325°F. (mark 3) for 1½ hours. Check seasoning. Cool quickly.
To pack: Spoon into a rigid foil container. Cover with lid and label.
To freeze: Freeze rapidly until solid.
To use: Remove the lid and cover loosely with foil. Reheat in the oven from frozen at 350°F. (mark 4) for about 1½ hours, until bubbling. Serve accompanied by natural yoghourt sprinkled with chopped parsley.

BEEF CURRY

serves 6

2 lb. best stewing steak
1 oz. (¼ cup) seasoned flour
2 oz. butter
½ pint (1¼ cups) beef stock
1 level tsp. tomato paste
salt and pepper

Trim the beef and cut it into even-sized pieces. Toss in the seasoned flour, then fry in the melted butter until brown on all sides. Stir in the stock and tomato paste and add a little seasoning. Bring to the boil, then pour into a casserole. Cover and cook in the oven at 325°F. (mark 3) for 1½ hours until fork-tender. Cool as quickly as possible.
To pack and freeze: Turn into 2 foil dishes, or freeze in a foil-lined casserole. Remove from pre-former, if used, overwrap. Seal and label.
To use: Thaw for 14 hours in the refrigerator. Place the meat in a saucepan containing 2 pints (5 cups) thawed curry sauce and heat gently. Test the seasoning and adjust if necessary. Alternatively place the thawed sauce and meat together in a casserole, cover and heat in the oven for 1 hour at 375°F. (mark 5). Serve with traditional side dishes and boiled rice.

CURRY SAUCE

makes 3 pints

4 oz. butter
1 tbsp. cooking oil
2 Spanish onions, skinned and chopped
2 cooking apples, peeled and chopped
3 oz. curry powder
2 level tsps. curry paste
2 oz. (½ cup) plain flour or cornflour
2 pints (5 cups) stock
3 tbsps. sweet chutney
2 level tbsps. tomato paste
juice of ½ a lemon

Melt the butter and oil in a pan, add the onions and apples and cook gently without browning for 5–8 minutes. Stir in the curry powder and paste and cook for a further 5 minutes, stirring occasionally, to bring out the full flavour. Add the flour or cornflour and cook for 1 minute, stirring all the time, before adding the stock. Bring to the boil, still stirring. Add the chutney, tomato paste and lemon juice, cover and cook gently for about ¾ hour. Cool quickly.
To pack: Put in heavy polythene bags inside pre-formers – 1 pint quantities are practical.
To freeze: Freeze quickly, then remove from the pre-former and overwrap with foil or place in a second polythene bag. Seal and label.
To use: Turn the sauce into a double saucepan or a heavy-based saucepan over gentle heat. Break up, using a wooden spoon, as the sauce thaws. Check the seasoning. Pour over chicken, meat, fish, etc. as desired.

NOISETTES OF LAMB

serves 6

2 best ends of neck of lamb (total weight approx. 5 lb.)

Ask your butcher to bone, trim, roll and string the best ends. Wipe the meat with a clean damp cloth, then cut each best end into 6, cutting between the strings at about 1¼–1½ in. intervals.
To pack: Place pieces of freezer paper between the noisettes so that they will separate easily before cooking. Cover in a double layer of foil.
To freeze: Overwrap, using a

olythene bag. Seal and label. 'reeze rapidly.

'o thaw: Place on a large plate nd allow to thaw for 12 hours in he refrigerator or 5 hours at oom temperature. Noisettes can e cooked from frozen.

'o cook: Unwrap, then season o taste and dot with butter. Brown he noisettes quickly on both sides nder a hot grill, then reduce the eat and cook for a further 10–15 ninutes if thawed, or 30 minutes f frozen. Baste frequently. They hould still be quite pink in the entre.

'lace some maître d'hôtel butter n each noisette and set on a roûte of fried bread. Garnish vith sprigs of parsley. Serve 2 oisettes per person.

)UCHESSE POTATOES

erves 10

lb. old potatoes, peeled and boiled
: oz. butter
: large egg
level tsp. salt
reshly ground black pepper
: level tsp. grated nutmeg

Sieve and mash the potatoes without milk, add the remaining ngredients and beat well. Line a aking tray with non-stick paper. Jsing a forcing bag fitted with a arge star nozzle, pipe onto the ray about 20 raised pyramids of otato, with a base of about 2 in.

'o freeze: Freeze uncovered until irm. Remove from freezer.

'o pack: Slide the potato pyranids off the tray on to foil lates or into containers. Cover vith polythene film, seal and label.

'o use: Grease some baking heets or line with kitchen foil, ransfer the frozen duchesse potato ortions to the trays, brush lightly vith egg glaze and put into a cold ven. Cook at 400°F. (mark 6) for 20–30 minutes or until heated nd lightly browned.

LEMON CRUMB PIE

erves 4–6

8 oz. gingernut biscuits
4 oz. unsalted butter
3 level tbsps. cornflour
$\frac{1}{4}$ pint ($\frac{5}{8}$ cup) water
juice and grated rind of 2 lemons
4 oz. ($\frac{1}{2}$ cup) sugar
2 eggs, separated

Crush the biscuits to give a fine crumb. Melt the butter and mix with the biscuit crumbs. Press the crumb mixture into an 8½-in. loose-bottomed French fluted flan ring to line the base and sides. Chill until firm. Blend the cornflour with the water in a saucepan, add the lemon juice and rind and bring slowly to the boil, stirring, until the mixture thickens and clears, then add the sugar.

Remove from the heat, beat in the egg yolks and return to the heat for a further 1–2 minutes. Pour into the crumb crust and leave until cold. Remove the flan ring from around the biscuits.

To pack and freeze: Place the pie on a baking sheet and freeze until firm; wrap in foil. Pack egg whites separately in a small, rigid plastic container. Cover, label and freeze.

To use: Replace flan ring. Leave the egg whites to thaw in the container for about 2¼ hours at room temperature, together with the lemon pie. Whisk the egg whites stiffly, whisk in 2 oz. caster sugar and re-whisk until stiff again. Fold in another 2 oz. sugar. Pile or pipe the meringue on top of the lemon filling.

Decorate with a few glacé cherries and some angelica leaves. Place the pie on a baking sheet and bake in the centre of the oven at 400°F. (mark 6) for 5–7 minutes to brown the meringue. Reduce the heat to 300°F. (mark 2) and cook for a further 10 minutes. Remove from the oven, leave in the metal case until cool, remove the tin and serve the pie with cream.

ICED STRAWBERRY MOUSSE

serves 4

$\frac{1}{2}$ lb. strawberries or $\frac{1}{4}$ pint ($\frac{5}{8}$ cup) purée
1 oz. ($\frac{1}{8}$ cup) caster sugar
4 egg yolks
$\frac{1}{4}$ pint ($\frac{5}{8}$ cup) double cream
lemon juice (optional)
2 egg whites

Hull the strawberries and put through a nylon sieve or purée in a blender. In a deep bowl over hot water whisk together the strawberry purée, sugar and egg yolks until thick. Remove from the heat and whisk from time to time while the mixture is cooling.

Half-whisk the cream until it just holds its shape; lightly fold it into the strawberry mixture. Add more sugar to taste, or sharpen with lemon juice. Fold in the stiffly whisked egg whites – these should look glossy but not whisked as far as the 'dry' stage.

To pack: Spoon the mixture into individual soufflé dishes or one large one. Cover tightly with foil.

To freeze: Freeze until firm. Overwrap in a polythene bag, seal, label and return to the freezer.

To use: Unwrap and put in the refrigerator 30 minutes before required.

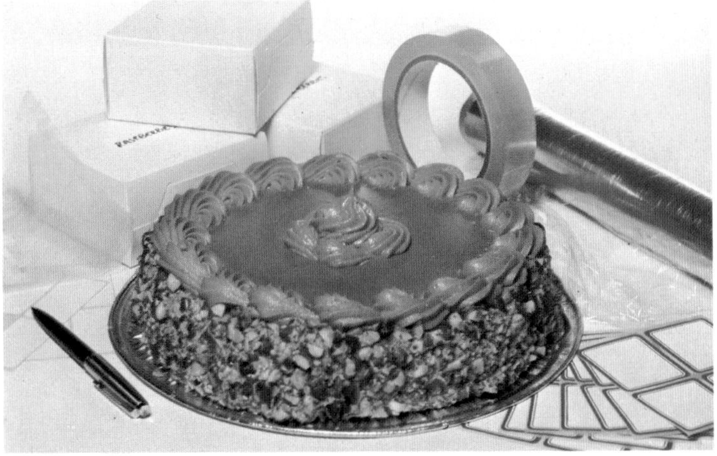

Hazelnut gâteau can be frozen complete with icing and decoration

HAZELNUT GATEAU

6 oz. butter
6 oz. ($\frac{3}{4}$ cup) caster sugar
3 large eggs
5 oz. ($1\frac{1}{4}$ cups) self-raising flour
1 oz. hazelnuts, ground

For icing:
12 oz. ($2\frac{3}{8}$ cups) icing sugar, sifted
3–4 tbsps. water

For decoration:
1 oz. butter
4 oz. ($\frac{5}{8}$ cup) icing sugar, sifted
a little top of the milk
24 whole hazelnuts

Lightly grease and base-line a moule-à-manqué cake tin 9½ in. in diameter. Cream the butter and sugar until light and fluffy. Beat in the eggs one at a time. Sift the flour over the surface and stir into the creamed ingredients, together with the ground hazelnuts. Turn the mixture into the prepared tin and level off. Bake in the centre of the oven or just above at 350°F. (mark 4) for about 40 minutes. Turn out and cool on a wire rack, narrow side uppermost.

Blend the icing sugar with enough water to give a coating consistency. Pour over the cake and, using a round-bladed knife, coat the surface evenly. Leave to set.

Beat the 1 oz. butter to a cream and gradually beat in the 4 oz. icing sugar, with just enough top of the milk to give a piping consistency. Using a large star nozzle, pipe 8 rosettes, one for each portion of cake. Top each rosette with 3 nuts.

To pack and freeze: Freeze unwrapped on a flat baking sheet until firm. Place carefully in a rigid container which protects the decoration and overwrap with polythene. If wished, cut the cake into portions and separate with waxed paper before placing cake in the container. Seal, label and return to the freezer.

To use: Remove the wrapping and allow to thaw 3–4 hours at room temperature if whole, 2–2½ hours if sliced.

DATE SCONE BAR

makes 8

8 oz. (2 cups) plain flour
$\frac{1}{2}$ level tsp. bicarbonate of soda
1 level tsp. cream of tartar
pinch of salt
2 oz. butter or margarine
1 oz. ($\frac{1}{8}$ cup) sugar
3 oz. ($\frac{5}{8}$ cup) dates, stoned
$\frac{1}{4}$ pint ($\frac{5}{8}$ cup) milk approx.

Sift together the dry ingredients. Rub in the fat to resemble fine breadcrumbs and add the sugar. Using kitchen scissors, snip the dates into small pieces and add to the mixture. Mix to a light dough with the milk. Roll out into an oblong approximately 12 in. by 4 in. Brush with milk and place on a greased baking sheet. Mark through into 8 bars, using the back of a knife. Bake near the top of the oven at 450°F. (mark 8) for about 15 minutes. Break apart, and cool on a wire rack.

To pack and freeze: Wrap immediately after cooling in foil or polythene, or pack in a rigid container. Overwrap, seal and freeze.

To thaw: Still in the wrappings, leave to thaw at room temperature for 1–1½ hours. Alternatively, place the bars, wrapped in foil, in the oven at 400°F. (mark 6) for about 10 minutes. Leave to cool on a rack or serve warm.

Packing beef curry for the freezer

COOKING IN A HURRY

IVER PATE DIP

rves 8–12

2 oz. soft liver sausage
lash of brandy or dry
  sherry
–2 oz. softened butter
lack pepper
rge pinch of mixed
  spice
ouble cream

ut all the ingredients except the
ouble cream into a bowl and beat
ith a fork until smooth and
reamy. (If you have a blender,
se that.) Add sufficient cream to
ake the pâté soft but not sloppy.
ransfer to a dish and serve on a
latter surrounded by crisps, sav-
ury biscuits and raw vegetables
or dunking. This makes a good
iller' for an impromptu party.

CREME ANDALOUSE

serves 3–4

10½-oz. can condensed tomato
  soup
4 medium onions, skinned
  and finely sliced
2 oz. butter
6½-oz. can pimiento (sweet
  red peppers), drained
2 oz. (¾ cup) cooked long
  grain rice
little stock or water (optional)
parsley

In a saucepan, dilute the soup
according to the directions on the
can. Fry the onions in butter until
well browned and stir into the
soup. Bring to the boil and reduce
the heat. Cover and simmer for
5 minutes.
Sieve half the can of pimiento into

the soup. Cover and simmer for a
further 5 minutes. Dice the remaining pimiento and, just prior
to serving, stir into the soup with
the cooked rice. Adjust consistency if necessary with hot water or
stock. Garnish with chopped
parsley.

SHERRIED CONSOMME

serves 3

15-oz. can consommé
2–3 tbsps. (¼ cup) dry sherry
lemon slices

Combine the consommé and the
sherry in a saucepan and heat
slowly to just below boiling point.
Pour into a warmed jug.
Serve in warmed wine goblets
with a spoon in each. Garnish with
lemon slices. This is an elegant
start to a dinner party.

PRAWN CELESTE

serves 4

7½-oz. can button mushrooms,
  drained
2 oz. butter
2 oz. (½ cup) flour
½ pint (1¼ cups) milk
6-oz. can cream (or ¾ cup fresh
  cream)
6-oz. can prawns
1–2 tsps. sherry
chopped parsley
fried bread cubes

Lightly cook the mushrooms in the
butter for 2–3 minutes. Stir in the
flour, cook for 2 minutes and
gradually add the milk and cream.
Bring to the boil, stirring constantly until the sauce has thickened. Season to taste.
Rinse the prawns in cold water,
then add to the sauce with the

sherry.

Reheat, sprinkle in the chopped parsley and serve with the fried bread cubes.

TOMATO AND TUNA EN GELEE

serves 4

½ pint (1¼ cups) tomato juice
1½ level tsps. powdered
   gelatine
2 7-oz. cans tuna
4 eggs, hard-boiled and sliced
lemon juice
salt and pepper
cress, to garnish

Heat the tomato juice and sprinkle the gelatine over. When dissolved leave to cool. Flake the tuna and add to the juice with 2 of the sliced hard-boiled eggs, a squeeze of lemon juice and plenty of seasoning. Pour into a 1 pint capacity ring mould and allow to set.

To serve, turn out of the mould, fill the centre with cress and surround with remaining hard-boiled eggs, chopped. Serve as a first course, or as a light lunch, accompanied by salad and crusty French bread.

CHICKEN AND ASPARAGUS SAUTE

serves 2

3 chicken leg portions
flour
1 oz. butter
1 tbsp. oil
10-oz. can condensed
   asparagus soup
6 tbsps. (⅜ cup) water
2 tomatoes, skinned and
   chopped
soy sauce
2-oz. can button mushrooms,
   drained
potato crisps, to garnish

Cut each chicken portion into 3, discarding skin if wished, and dust with unseasoned flour. Heat the butter and oil in a frying pan (preferably one with a lid). Brown chicken pieces quickly and evenly and put on one side.

Pour off most of the fat, stir in the soup, water and tomatoes. Return the chicken to the pan, cover and cook gently over a low heat until the chicken is tender–about 30 minutes.

Take out the chicken, arrange on a serving dish and keep warm. Add a few drops of soy sauce and mushrooms to the sauce, stir well and bring to the boil. Pour over the chicken and serve garnished with crisps.

BEEFEATER PIE

serves 6

pkt. of beef stew seasoning
   mix
½ pint (1¼ cups) water
2 level tbsps. dried sliced
   onion
1 level tbsp. dried marjoram
2 12-oz. cans corned beef
2 16-oz. cans baked beans
   with tomato sauce
2 3½-oz. pkts. instant mashed
   potato
2 oz. butter
salt and pepper
chopped chives

Mix together the seasoning and water in a saucepan until smooth. Add the onions and marjoram. Bring to the boil, then simmer. Cut the corned beef into 1-in. cubes and add to the sauce, with the baked beans. Mix well, cover and simmer gently.

Meanwhile make up the potatoes with water as directed on the packet. Beat butter and seasoning into the mashed potato. Turn the meat mixture into a casserole, spoon the potato over the top, fork up and brown under a hot grill. Sprinkle with chopped chives.

DEEP FRIED STEAK EN CROUTE

serves 4

2 oz. butter
4 4-oz. 'minute' steaks
1 lb. frozen puff pastry,
   thawed
5-oz. can pâté
1 egg, beaten
flour
2 15-oz. cans small whole
   carrots
chopped parsley
watercress
oil for frying

Melt 1 oz. butter in a frying pan and fry the steaks for 3 minutes, turning half-way through the cooking time. Roll out pastry to ⅛-in. thickness. Remove steaks from pan and lay them on a plate. Spread a quarter of the pâté onto one side of each steak. Position the meat on the pastry, leaving sufficient pastry between to cover each steak completely. Half-fill a deep frying pan with oil and heat to about 350°F. With a sharp knife cut a large circle of pastry round each steak. Brush pastry edge with beaten egg, dust lightly with flour and wrap pastry round the meat, securing it with a little more beaten egg. Pinch edges firmly together. Turn the parcels over and brush with egg. Roll out pastry trim-

Tomato and tuna en gelée–a starter or light lunch dish

mings, cut into strips and then into leaves and use to decorate each parcel.

Melt the remaining butter in a small saucepan. Open, drain and quarter the carrots. Cook them, tightly covered, in the butter for 6 minutes.

Lower the pastry parcels into the heated oil and cook for 4 minutes. Drain on absorbent paper. Sprinkle parsley over the carrots and garnish the steaks with watercress.

PAELLA

serves 4

½ level tsp. turmeric
4 oz. (½ cup) instant rice
1 chicken stock cube
2 oz. butter
2 medium onions, skinned

and chopped
8 oz. (1 cup) cooked chicken,
   diced
4 oz. (½ cup) fresh or frozen
   prawns
8-oz. pkt. frozen peas
5-oz. jar mussels, drained
salt and black pepper
4 tomatoes, skinned and
   quartered
small cos lettuce
juice of a lemon

Bring ½ pint (1¼ cups) salted water to the boil in a saucepan, remove from the heat, add turmeric and rice, mix well, cover tightly and leave to stand. Dissolve the stock cube in another pint (1¼ cups) water.

Melt the butter in a frying pan and gently sauté the onion. Add the chicken and prawns and slowly

An instant dinner party–delicious steaks, pâté and puff pastry

stir in the stock. Bring to the boil and allow to simmer for 2–3 minutes. Add the mussels and peas, season well and leave to simmer for a further 2–3 minutes. Add the tomatoes. Fluff the rice up with a fork and fold into the mixture in the frying pan using a spatula. Heat through and serve piping hot straight from the pan.

Serve accompanied by lettuce, seasoned with lemon juice and black pepper.

CURRIED CHICKEN CORNETS
serves 4

8-oz. bought puff pastry
beaten egg

For filling :
7½-oz. can of curry sauce
6 oz. cooked chicken, finely
**   diced**
1 tbsp. currants
1 tbsp. chopped almonds

Roll out the pastry to a rectangle approximately 16 in. by 6 in. and cut into strips ½ in. by 16 in. Brush with beaten egg and wind round cream horn cases, slightly overlapping, with the egg side outside. Place on baking sheets and bake near the top of the oven at 450°F. (mark 8) for about 10 minutes.

Carefully remove the horn cases by giving them a little twist and return the cases to the oven for a further 5 minutes at 400°F. (mark 6), until golden brown and crisp. Meanwhile, in a saucepan heat together the curry sauce, chicken, currants and almonds. When really hot, fill the warm pastry cases and serve.

CHOCOLATE NUT SUNDAE
serves 4

For sauce :
4 oz. plain (dark) chocolate
2 oz. butter
2 tbsp. milk
1 tsp. vanilla essence

vanilla ice cream
double cream, whipped
chopped walnuts

Melt the chocolate and butter in a basin standing in a pan of hot water. Stir in the milk and vanilla essence to make a smooth, creamy sauce.

Put a scoop of ice cream in each sundae glass and pour over the chocolate sauce. Pipe or spoon a whirl of cream on top and sprinkle with chopped nuts.

Chocolate nut sundae is a treat for all ages

Abricots à la crème, quick but delicious

LIQUEUR ICE CREAM

vanilla ice cream
liqueur – crème de menthe,
**   cherry brandy, apricot**
**   brandy, or Tia Maria**

Spoon the ice cream into sundae dishes. Trickle over it a little of the liqueur of your choice.

ABRICOTS A LA CREME
serves 4

15-oz. can apricot halves
2 level tsps. cornflour
4 tbsps. cointreau
¼ pint (⅝ cup) double cream
6 pistachio nuts (or almonds)

Drain the apricots, retaining the syrup, and arrange in 4 glasses. Keep back 4 halves for decoration. Sprinkle the cornflour into a small saucepan and blend to a paste with a little of the syrup. Add the remaining syrup, cointreau and 4 tablespoons of the cream. Bring to the boil over a medium heat, stirring constantly, and pour over the apricots. Allow to cool.

Place the nuts in a small basin, pour water over them and leave for 20 seconds. Drain, skin and halve them. Whip the remaining cream until it just holds its shape. Using a large vegetable nozzle, pipe cream in a whirl on each glass of apricots. Top each with an apricot half and stick three nut halves into each whirl of cream.

PEACH AND ALMOND UPSIDE-DOWN
serves 4

butter
½ oz. caster sugar
15-oz. can peach halves
½ oz. whole almonds, blanched
**   and browned**
6½-oz. pkt. sponge mix
1 level tsp. cornflour

Butter a 7½-in. round ovenproof dish. Sprinkle caster sugar around the dish, leaving any surplus in the base. Drain the peaches, reserving the syrup, and cut each in half again, vertically. Arrange with the almonds over the base of the dish. Make up the sponge according to the directions on the packet. Spoon the sponge mixture over the fruit, making sure it runs between the peaches. Bake at 375°F. (mark 5) for about 35–40 minutes, until golden brown and firm to the touch. Invert onto a serving plate and top with peach glaze made from ¼ pint (⅝ cup) syrup blended with the cornflour. Bring gradually to the boil, stirring continuously. Pour glaze over pudding.

COOKING IN A HURRY

FISH RAMEKINS

serves 3

6 tbsps. single cream
5½-oz. can pilchards in
**   tomato sauce**
1½ tbsps. lemon juice
salt and pepper
3 large eggs

Spoon 1 tablespoon of cream into
each of 3 ramekin dishes. Mash
the pilchards and divide between
the dishes and sprinkle with lemon
juice. Season to taste. Break an
egg into each dish and top with
remaining cream.
Bake at 350°F. (mark 4) for about

15 minutes until the egg is set.
Serve at once with Melba toast.

**BRISLING FRIED
PASTRIES**

makes about 24

**11-oz. pkt. frozen puff pastry,
   thawed**
2 3¾-oz. cans smoked brisling
mango chutney
2 eggs, beaten
5 oz. flaked almonds
oil for frying

Roll the pastry out into a rectangle
19 in. by 12 in. and cut in half
lengthwise. Drain the brisling and

lay in pairs side by side down the
centre of each strip of pastry. Dot
with a little chutney. Brush one
long edge of each piece of pastry
with egg, fold over and press the
edges well together. Cut into
pieces about 1½ in. long. Brush
each roll with beaten egg, then
toss in flaked almonds. Deep fry
in oil heated to 375°F. for about
3 minutes until crisp and brown.
Drain on absorbent kitchen paper
and serve at once.
These pastries are at their best
served straight from the pan, but
if this is not convenient they can
be kept warm in a hot oven.

VICHYSSOISE

serves 4

**1 large pkt. instant mashed
   potato**
**chicken stock, made from a
   stock cube**
1 level tsp. onion salt
cold milk
¼ pint (⅝ cup) double cream
salt and pepper
chives, chopped

Tip the potato mix into a larg
bowl. Gradually whisk in su
ficient very hot stock to give
fairly thick mash. Add the onio
salt. Still whisking, add enoug

old milk to thin the soup to the consistency of a thick white coating sauce. Gently stir in the cream (unwhipped). Season to taste. Serve chilled in individual bowls, garnished with chives.

AVOCADOS WITH CRAB DRESSING
serves 4

level tbsps. very thick
  mayonnaise
tsps. lemon juice
small clove of garlic,
  skinned and crushed
black pepper
oz. crab meat (fresh cooked
  or frozen)
ripe avocados
lemon

Mix together the mayonnaise, 1 teaspoon lemon juice, garlic and a little freshly ground black pepper. If using frozen crab meat, thaw and drain off excess moisture. Flake crab meat and fold through the mayonnaise until thoroughly mixed.
Cut round the fruit down to the stone, lengthways. Gently prise apart. Remove stone and rub the inside of the fruit with a little lemon juice to prevent discolouration, then fill the hollows with the dressing. Stand halves on small plates and garnish with quarters of lemon. Serve with thinly sliced brown bread and butter.

QUICK SOUPS
(CANNED AND PACKET SOUP VARIATIONS)

Oxtail and tomato
Use a can of each and add lemon juice or sherry to taste. Serve with grated cheese or toast.

Crab and asparagus
Drain and roughly chop a small can of crab meat and mix with a can of asparagus soup. Serve sprinkled with chopped parsley.

Quick mulligatawny
Make up a packet of French onion soup and simmer for 5 minutes. Add a can of oxtail soup with a bay leaf or a pinch of dried mixed herbs and 2 level teaspoons curry powder. Simmer for a further 10 minutes.

Chicken and almond
Fry 1 tablespoon each of finely chopped onion, parsley and blanched almonds in ½ oz. butter for 5 minutes. Add a can of cream of chicken soup and simmer for 10 minutes.

CANNED PHEASANT EN CASSEROLE
serves 4

4 oz. fried bacon, chopped
3-oz. pkt. thyme and parsley
  stuffing
2 oz. lard
3-lb. can whole roast
  pheasant in Burgundy jelly,
  or duck
3 level tbsps. cornflour
1 level tbsp. red-currant
  jelly
lemon juice to taste
1-lb. can small whole onions,
  drained
1 oz. butter
chopped parsley to garnish

Mix the bacon with the stuffing and add just enough water to give a fairly stiff consistency; leave to stand for 5 minutes. Shape into 20 balls, place in a small baking dish with the melted lard and put in the top of the oven at 425°F. (mark 7). Drain and joint the pheasant or duck, arrange in a large ovenproof casserole, cover and put in the centre of the oven for 15–20 minutes. Blend the cornflour with a little of the stock from the can, add to the remaining stock and bring to the boil.
Add the red-currant jelly and lemon juice. Simmer gently while frying the onions in the butter for 3–4 minutes, until coloured. When the bird is heated through (about 20–30 minutes), add the onions, pour the sauce over and top with the stuffing balls. Sprinkle with parsley.

OYSTER FRITTERS
serves 2

For fritter batter :
4 oz. (1 cup) plain flour
salt
¼ pint (⅝ cup) warm water
1 tbsp. cooking oil
1 egg white
oil for deep frying

3½-oz. can smoked oysters
6 oz. lean streaky bacon,
  about 8 rashers
1½ oz. butter
1 clove of garlic, skinned and
  crushed
chopped parsley
10½-oz. can asparagus
1 pkt. potato sticks

Sift the flour and a pinch of salt into a bowl. Mix together the water and oil and pour into the flour. Beat well.
Rind the bacon, lay the rashers on a wooden board and stretch them

Halving an avocado

by drawing the back of the blade of a knife along each one. Drain the oysters and roll each oyster in a rasher of bacon, securing with a cocktail stick. Heat the oil to 350°F. Whisk the egg white until stiff but not dry. Beat the batter again and pour it on to the egg white. Fold in with a tablespoon. Coat each bacon roll in the batter and deep fry for 5 minutes. Drain on absorbant kitchen paper. Meanwhile drain the asparagus and warm gently through in 1 oz. of the butter. Heat potato sticks in the oven.
Melt remaining ½ oz. butter in a small saucepan and add the garlic. Pour over the oyster fritters and sprinkle with chopped parsley.
Serve asparagus and potato sticks separately.

FRANKFURTER ROKA SALAD
serves 4

12-oz. can frankfurters,
  drained
12½-oz. can new potatoes,
  drained
4-fl. oz. bottle blue cheese
  dressing (such as Kraft
  Roka)
1 tsp. chopped parsley
2½-fl. oz. jar stuffed olives,
  drained and halved
1 lettuce, washed
paprika pepper

Cut the sausages into ½-in. pieces, halve the potatoes and mix well together in a bowl, with the dressing, parsley and olives. Arrange on a bed of lettuce on a serving dish and sprinkle with paprika .

Frankfurter Roka salad

An unusual mixture of canned fruits go into this salad

Flaming brandy and cherry pie filling make this special ice cream dish

Use canned pears to make this delicious dessert

ESCALOPES WITH MARSALA AND CHEESE

serves 4

4 veal escalopes
seasoned flour
2 oz. butter
2–3 tbsps. Marsala, sherry or Madeira
4 level tbsps. grated Parmesan cheese

Coat each escalope with seasoned flour and fry gently in the butter until just tender and golden (about 3 minutes on each side). Stir into the pan the Marsala (or sherry or Madeira) and sprinkle each escalope with 1 tablespoon cheese. Spoon some of the butter-wine mixture over, cover the pan with a lid and cook gently for a further 2–3 minutes, until the cheese melts.

PINEAPPLE CORN CRUNCH

serves 4

8½-oz. can crushed pineapple
7½-oz. can apple sauce
2 oz. golden syrup (see method)
1½ oz. butter
1½ oz. fresh, crisp cornflakes
¼ pint (⅝ cup) soured cream

Drain surplus juice from the pineapple and fold fruit through the apple purée. Divide between 4 sundae glasses.

To measure syrup and butter, place a small non-stick saucepan on the scale pan, note weight and in turn add the syrup and butter, totting up the weights. Over a low heat melt butter and then bubble the syrup for a few minutes. Cool. Pour the cool but not cold syrup over the cornflakes and toss until evenly coated.

Divide the soured cream between the glasses, spread over the apple purée and top with the butterscotch cornflakes. Serve soon after making.

TROPICAL FRUIT SALAD

serves 6

11-oz. can lychees
15-oz. can guava halves
15-oz. can crushed pineapple
1 lb. bananas, peeled
juice of 1 small lemon
6 fl. oz. ginger ale

Drain canned fruit well. Slice the bananas diagonally and mix all the fruit together in a large glass bowl. Pour over the ginger ale and chill. Serve with pouring cream and shortbread fingers.

RHUBARB VELVET

serves 4

¾ pint (2 cups) cold custard
14-oz. can rhubarb pie filling
grated rind of 1 orange
whipped cream and chocolate dots to decorate

Make the custard in the usual way with ¾ pint milk. Stir in the pie filling and orange rind. Spoon the mixture into glasses and chill. Top with cream and chocolate dots.

CHERRIES JUBILEE

serves 4

14-oz. can cherry pie filling
grated rind of 1 orange or lemon
a little brandy
4 portions vanilla ice cream

Heat the pie filling in a saucepan adding the grated orange or lemon rind. Just before serving, add a little brandy; ignite it and spoon the flaming cherries over the portions of ice cream.

STUFFED PEARS

serves 4

14-oz. can pear halves, drained
½ pint (1¼ cups) double cream
4 pieces crystallized ginger
8 glacé cherries
2 oz. nuts, chopped
1 jam Swiss roll

Whip the cream until it just holds its shape. Chop the crystallized ginger, glacé cherries and nuts. Mix with just enough cream to bind and fill the mixture into the pear halves.

Slice the Swiss roll and upturn a filled pear half on to each slice, coating each with whipped cream.

CREME MARRON

serves 4

½ pint (1¼ cups) double cream
6-oz. can sweetened chestnut purée
1 tbsp. coffee liqueur
1½ oz. marron glacé, chopped
2 egg whites, stiffly whisked
ratafia biscuits (small almond biscuits)

Reserve 2 tablespoons of cream for decoration and whip the rest. Combine the purée, liqueur and 1 oz. marron glacé. Fold into the cream, add egg whites and fold in evenly. Pile mixture into glasses and decorate with remaining cream and marron glacé. Chill and serve with ratafia biscuits.

DRESSED ARTICHOKE HEARTS
serves 3

14-oz. can artichoke hearts
¼ pint (⅝ cup) French dressing
12 black olives
parsley, chopped

Drain the artichoke hearts and marinade in the French dressing for 15 minutes. Drain most of the dressing off before serving the artichokes in individual dishes. Garnish with the olives and sprinkle with chopped parsley. Serve with brown bread and butter.

FRIED WHITEBAIT
serves 4

2 lb. whitebait
4 level tbsps. seasoned flour
deep fat for frying
1 lemon, for garnish

Wash the whitebait in a colander under cold running water. Drain the fish thoroughly and dry on absorbent kitchen paper. Toss half the fish in the seasoned flour, put them in the frying basket. Heat the fat to 375°F. Lower the fish into the fat and fry until crisp but still pale. Drain well on absorbent paper. Flour the remaining fish and repeat.

Reheat the fat and fry the fish again until crisp and golden brown. Drain well on fresh paper and serve at once, garnished with lemon slices and accompanied by brown bread and butter.

STEAK DIANE
serves 2

2 thin ('minute') steaks
salt and pepper
2 tomatoes, halved
3 tsps. Worcestershire sauce
1½ oz. butter
1 small onion, skinned and chopped
2 tsps. chopped parsley

Season the steaks. Place the tomatoes under a hot grill. Pour 2 teaspoons sauce into a frying pan, place it over a low heat and evaporate off; add 1 oz. butter and raise the heat. Add the onion and fry for 1 minute, then add the steaks and fry for 1 minute on each side. Place the steaks on a hot serving dish and sprinkle with parsley.

Melt the remaining butter in the pan, add the remaining 1 teaspoon Worcestershire sauce and mix. Pour the onion mixture over the steaks and garnish with the tomato halves.

SANDWICH STEAKS
serves 4

1 lb. finely minced steak
8 thin slices of cooked ham
French mustard
salt and pepper
lard

For anchovy butter :
2 oz. butter
2 tsps. anchovy essence

Divide the minced steak into 8 equal portions. Flatten each portion on a floured board with a round-bladed knife, until ¼ in. thick. Trim the ham to fit the steaks, spread each slice with mustard and sprinkle with salt and pepper.

Put a slice of ham on 1 steak and cover with another, to make a sandwich. Repeat to make 4 sandwich steaks. Grease the grill pan grid with lard, place the steaks on the grid and grill for about 3 minutes on each side.

Cream the butter and beat in the anchovy essence. Serve the steaks with a pat of anchovy butter on each.

Dressed artichoke hearts

COOKING IN A HURRY

BACON CHOPS
serves 4

4 rashers of back bacon or
    bacon chops, cut $\frac{3}{4}$ in. thick,
    rinded
cooking oil
I small cooking apple, cored
2 oz. shelled walnuts, chopped
2 oz. stoned raisins, chopped
juice of $\frac{1}{2}$ a lemon
$\frac{1}{2}$ oz. butter

Brush the lean surface of the bacon
with a little oil and place the chops
in a grill pan. Cook under medium
heat for 6 minutes on each side.
Grate the apple, without peeling,
and mix with the walnuts and
raisins; squeeze the lemon juice
over. Fry the nut mixture in the
butter over gentle heat, stirring
lightly all the time.
Serve the chops on the nut hash.

COD PROVENCALE
serves 4

4 cod cutlets (about 6 oz. each)
4 oz. butter
salt and pepper
2 onions, skinned and chopped
I green or red pepper
    (capsicum), seeded and
    chopped
2 level tbsps. tomato paste
2 level tbsps. flour
15-oz. can peeled tomatoes
dash of Worcestershire sauce
I level tsp. sugar
I pkt. instant potato (or I lb.
    potatoes, boiled and
    creamed)
approx. 6 tbsps. milk

Place the fish in a buttered grill
pan, dot with butter and season.
Grill for approximately 12
minutes, turning once and seasoning the second side when you
turn it.
Melt 2 oz. butter in a saucepan.
Fry the onion for 2–3 minutes,
add the pepper and continue to
fry gently for a further 3–4
minutes. Stir the tomato paste
and flour into the onion mixture,
then the tomatoes. Bring to the
boil, stirring all the time. Add a
dash of Worcestershire sauce and
the sugar. Continue to simmer.
Make up the instant potato, season
and beat in the remaining butter,
or beat the butter into creamed
potatoes. If too solid, add a little
milk. Spoon into a forcing bag
fitted with a star nozzle and pipe
round the edge of serving dish.
Arrange the fish in the centre of
the potato border. Stir the sauce
well and spoon it carefully over
the fish. Reheat under the grill for
I minute.

HERRINGS WITH LEMON CRUMBLE
serves 2

2 herrings
2 tbsps. cooking oil
2 $\frac{1}{2}$-in. slices day old bread
I oz. butter
grated rind and juice of $\frac{1}{2}$ a
    lemon
2 tbsps. chopped parsley
lemon wedges

Clean the herrings, cut off the
heads and fins, but leave on the
tails. Brush the fish with oil. Grill
for 8 minutes under a medium
heat, turning once.
Crumb the bread. Melt the butter
in a small saucepan, stir in the
breadcrumbs and cook over a
medium heat until golden brown.
Remove from the heat and add the
lemon rind, juice and parsley.
Put the breadcrumb mixture in a
serving dish and place the herrings
on top. Garnish with lemon.

CHINESE CHICKEN
serves 2

6 oz. ($\frac{3}{4}$ cup) long grain rice
2 oz. butter
8-oz. can pineapple pieces
I level tbsp. soft brown sugar
I level tbsp. cornflour
6 tbsps. water
2 tbsps. wine vinegar
2 tsps. soy sauce
10–12 oz. cooked chicken flesh
3 small tomatoes, skinned
    and quartered
I small green pepper
    (capsicum), seeded and
    sliced
salt and pepper
9$\frac{1}{2}$-oz. can bean sprouts
2 tsps. chopped parsley

Cook the rice in boiling, salted
water for 10–12 minutes, until
tender. Drain, add I oz. butter and
keep warm.
Meanwhile, drain the pineapple
syrup into a saucepan, mix the
sugar with the cornflour and blend
it into the syrup with the water,
vinegar and soy sauce. Cook until
thickened, stirring.
Cut the chicken into strips and
add to the bubbling sauce. Cover
with a tightly fitting lid and simmer. Add the tomatoes, sliced
pepper and pineapple. Cover and
simmer for a further 5 minutes.
Melt I oz. butter in a saucepan,
add the drained bean sprouts,
cover and heat for 2–3 minutes.
Make a ring of the rice on a serving
dish and spoon the chicken mixture into the centre. Serve the bean
sprouts separately, garnished with
chopped parsley.

Whitebait are very popular as a starter – quick to cook, too

APRICOT RICE MERINGUE
serves 4

2 eggs, separated
15$\frac{1}{2}$-oz. can creamed rice
15$\frac{1}{2}$-oz. can apricot halves,
    drained
3 oz. ($\frac{3}{8}$ cup) caster sugar

Beat the egg yolks and stir evenly
into the rice. Place in a small pan
and cook over a low heat until
thick. Bring almost to the boil, but
not quite. Turn into a pie dish.
Place the apricot halves over the
rice. Whisk the egg whites until
stiff, add about half the sugar and
whisk again until stiff. Fold in all
but I teaspoon of sugar. Spoon the
meringue over the fruit to cover
completely. Sprinkle with the
remainder of the sugar.
Place in the centre of the oven at
350°F. (mark 4) for about 15
minutes.
Serve warm or cold.

PEACH CONDE
serves 4

15-oz. can creamed rice
15-oz. can peach halves,
    drained
8 level tbsps. red-currant jelly
I tbsp. water
lemon juice

Divide the rice between 4 sund
glasses. Arrange the peach halv
on top of the rice, cut side dow
Heat the red-currant jelly wi
the water and lemon juice, sti
ring until smooth and somewh
thickened.
Pour over the peaches and lea
to cool before serving.

BRANDIED APRICOTS
serves 4

I lb. fresh apricots
$\frac{1}{2}$ pint (1$\frac{1}{4}$ cups) water
4 oz. ($\frac{1}{2}$ cup) sugar
thinly pared rind of I lemon
3 tbsps. brandy

Put the apricots into boiling wate
drain and remove the skins. Hal
them and remove the stones. P
the measured water, sugar an
lemon rind in a pan, dissolve th
sugar slowly and bring to the bo
Add the apricots and poach gent
for 5–10 minutes, until just so
Drain carefully.
Boil the syrup fast to reduce it
about one-third the quantit
strain it and stir in the brand
Pour this over the apricots an
chill.
For a really rich dessert, serve wi
whipped cream.

Apricot rice meringue; a real quickie, to serve hot or cold

COOKING IN A HURRY

Eggs are invaluable for a multitude of quick snacks. They are rich in protein, are available all the year round and remain cheap compared with meat and fish.

Except in the case of hard-boiled eggs, the more lightly an egg dish is cooked, the better. This applies particularly to fried and baked egg dishes and to omelettes, where cooking for too long makes the eggs tough.

HOT STUFFED EGGS
serves 4

4 eggs, hard-boiled
1½ oz. margarine
2 oz. mushrooms, wiped and chopped
1 onion, skinned and chopped
½-pint can tomato juice
1 level tsp. sugar
salt and pepper
2 level tsps. cornflour

Cut the eggs in half lengthwise and remove the yolks. Melt the margarine in a pan and lightly fry the mushrooms and onion in the hot fat for 5 minutes until golden brown. Put half the mixture in a basin. To the remaining mixture in the pan, add the tomato juice, sugar and seasoning; cook for 5 minutes.

Blend the cornflour to a smooth cream with a little water. Stir in a little of the hot tomato juice and return it to the pan. Bring to the boil, stirring until it thickens, and continue cooking for 1–2 minutes. Keep this sauce hot.

Meanwhile, mix the egg yolks with the onion and mushroom mixture in the basin and use to stuff the egg halves. Arrange the halves in a dish and pour the sauce over.

STUFFED ROLLS
serves 4

4 crisp dinner rolls
1 oz. butter
2 oz. mushrooms, wiped and sliced
3 tomatoes, skinned and chopped
1 small onion, skinned and grated
3 eggs
salt and pepper

Cut a slice from the top of each roll and scoop out some of the soft inside. Melt the butter, add the vegetables and lightly fry for 5–10 minutes, until soft but not coloured.

Whisk the eggs with some seasoning, pour into the pan and stir with a wooden spoon over a low heat until the mixture thickens. Pile it into the bread shells, replace the lids and place on a baking sheet. Cook in the centre of the oven at 400°F. (mark 6) for about 15 minutes, until the rolls are crisp and the filling thoroughly heated.

SCRAMBLED EGGS ARCHIDUCHESSE
serves 4

3 oz. butter
6 eggs, beaten
salt and paprika pepper
2–3 tbsps. cream
2 oz. cooked ham, chopped
1 oz. mushrooms, sliced and lightly fried
4 slices of fried bread
10-oz. can asparagus, drained

Melt the butter, add the eggs, seasonings and cream. Cook very slowly, stirring gently. As the mixture starts to thicken, add the ham and mushrooms. Serve on the slices of fried bread, topped with asparagus spears.

SCRAMBLED EGG NESTS
serves 4

4 tbsps. mashed potatoes
flour
bacon fat or dripping
2–3 eggs
salt and pepper
a little milk
a knob of butter
watercress or parsley for garnish

Shape the mashed potato into 4 flat cakes and flour them lightly. Fry in the bacon fat or dripping until golden brown on the underside. Turn the cakes over and hollow the centre of each slightly with the bowl of a spoon. Leave over a gentle heat to brown underneath.

Meanwhile, beat the eggs lightly

with salt and pepper, add the milk and cook very slowly in hot butter, stirring gently until lightly set. Fill the centres of the potato cakes with the scrambled egg and garnish with watercress or parsley.

PRAWN OMELETTE
serves 1

2 eggs
salt and pepper
1 tbsp. water
butter
2 oz. peeled shrimps or prawns, fresh or frozen and thawed
lemon juice

Whisk the eggs lightly, season and add the water. Place a small frying pan over gentle heat and when it is hot, add a knob of butter to grease it lightly. Pour the beaten eggs into the hot fat. Stir gently with the back of a fork, drawing the mixture from the sides to the centre as it sets and letting the liquid egg from the centre run to the sides. When the egg has set, stop stirring and cook for another minute until it is golden underneath.
Meanwhile, sauté the shrimps or prawns in a little butter with a squeeze of lemon juice. Place in the centre of the cooked omelette. Use a palette knife to fold over a third of the omelette to the centre, then fold over the other side. Turn on to a warmed plate with the folds underneath.

CHINESE OMELETTE
serves 4

½ lb. onions, skinned
4 bamboo shoots or sticks of celery, scrubbed
4 oz. mushrooms, wiped
1 clove of garlic, skinned
1 slice fresh ginger, if available
1 oz. long grain rice
1 tbsp. oil for frying
salt
2 tbsps. dry cider
2 tsps. soy sauce
½ pint (1¼ cups) stock or water
4 oz. peeled shrimps, fresh or frozen and thawed
4 eggs

Chop the vegetables, garlic and ginger finely and fry them with the rice in the oil, for a few minutes. Add the salt, cider, soy sauce and stock and cook for 10-15 minutes until the rice and vegetables are tender. Then add the shrimps. Beat the eggs, add 4 tablespoons water and salt to taste. Cook half the mixture as an omelette (see prawn omelette); pile half the

shrimp and vegetable mixture along the centre and fold in half. Repeat with the remaining egg and shrimp mixture. Serve any left-over filling separately. Each omelette will serve 2 people.

EGGS FRITURA
serves 4

1 green pepper (capsicum), seeded and blanched
2 oz. butter
½ an onion, skinned and chopped
4 tomatoes, skinned and chopped
salt and freshly ground black pepper
4 eggs
4 rounds of toast
butter
2 oz. Cheddar cheese, grated
parsley, to garnish

Chop the pepper, melt the butter in a frying pan and fry the pepper and onion. Add the tomatoes, plenty of salt and pepper and cook for 15 minutes.
Meanwhile poach the eggs. Spoon the vegetable mixture on to the buttered toast and place a poached egg on each portion. Sprinkle with grated cheese and grill quickly. Garnish with parsley.

EGGS A LA FLORENTINE
serves 4

1 lb. spinach
salt and pepper
1½ oz. butter
1 oz. (¼ cup) plain flour
½ pint (1¼ cups) milk
2½ oz. Parmesan or Cheddar cheese, grated
4 eggs
2-3 tbsps. single cream
tomato slices to garnish

Wash the spinach well, put it into a pan with a little salt and just the water that clings to the leaves. Cook for 10-15 minutes, until tender.
Meanwhile make a cheese sauce, melt 1 oz. butter in a pan, blend in the flour and cook over a gentle heat for 1 minute. Remove pan from heat, stir in milk and bring to the boil, stirring. Cook for 2 minutes. Stir in 2 oz. of grated cheese.
Drain spinach well, chop roughly, mix with ½ oz. butter and season. Put into an ovenproof dish. Poach the eggs lightly and place side by side on the spinach. Pour cheese sauce over spinach and eggs and sprinkle with remaining cheese. Put dish in the centre of the oven set at 375°F. (mark 5) and bake for

Chinese omelette, with bamboo shoots, mushrooms and prawns

10-15 minutes, until golden. Alternatively, brown under the grill. Garnish with tomato slices.

SHIRRED EGGS WITH CHICKEN LIVERS
serves 4

4 oz. chicken livers, sliced
butter
4 tbsps. tomato juice
4 eggs
salt and pepper
chopped parsley

Sauté the chicken livers lightly in a little butter and divide between 4 ramekins or individual soufflé dishes. Pour into each 1 tablespoon tomato juice, then slide in an egg. Sprinkle with salt and pepper and bake in the oven set at 350°F. (mark 4) for 15 minutes. Sprinkle with chopped parsley and serve.

CHEESY EGGS
serves 4-6

1 oz. butter
4 oz. mushrooms, wiped and sliced
salt and freshly ground black pepper
6 eggs
8 oz. mild Cheddar cheese, thinly sliced or grated

Melt the butter in a pan, sauté the mushrooms and season.
Put the whole eggs into boiling water, boil for 5 minutes. Break the shells lightly all over and peel carefully, holding the hot egg with a clean cloth or kitchen paper.
Place them in an ovenproof dish, spoon over the mushrooms and smother with cheese. Place under a hot grill until the cheese melts and starts to bubble.

BRAINS WITH EGGS
serves 2

2 sets of brains (lambs' or calves')
2 oz. butter or margarine
parsley, chopped
2-4 eggs, beaten
salt and freshly ground black pepper

Wash the brains and soak for an hour in cold water. Remove as much of the skin and membrane as possible.
Melt the butter in a pan and fry the brains until they look white and stiff. Add a little chopped parsley.
Pour the beaten eggs into the pan, season well and leave over gentle heat until the eggs are lightly set. Serve immediately.

Eggs à la florentine is a classic dish

COOKING IN A HURRY
USING A PRESSURE COOKER

A pressure cooker is an invaluable help, both when you need to produce a meal in a hurry and for other time-consuming cooking processes such as making stocks, boiling a fowl or preserving. This versatile piece of equipment will cook almost any meal in substantially less than the normal cooking time.

If you are buying a new pressure cooker, there are various models to choose from. If you generally cook for only 2–3 people, then an 8-pint model is big enough; for 4–6 people, you will need a larger, 10–13 pint model, or one with a domed lid. They are available with either single or 3-pressure control and you will certainly need 3 pressures if you are using the pan for preserving or for steaming

puddings. Whichever you have, do study the maker's instructions carefully.

There are certain rules which have to be followed when using all makes of pressure cooker. First, don't over-fill the cooker; it should never be more than two-thirds full with solid foods or half full with liquids, cereals or preserves. However, a model with a domed lid may be filled with solids to within 1–2 in. of the rim. Over-filling reduces the space for steam within the pan and will cause the safety valve to blow. (The safety valve is designed to blow if pressure rises above 20 lb., for instance if the cooker is over-filled, boils dry or the vent becomes clogged. If this happens, clean the vent thoroughly and check that there is the correct amount of liquid in the cooker

before replacing the lid and re-setting the valve.)

When cooking time is completed, it is very important to let the pressure drop back to normal before opening the pan – and whether you do this quickly or slowly depends on what you have been cooking. To reduce pressure quickly, hold the pan under cold running water. Lift the weight slowly to make sure there is no hissing before raising it completely and removing the lid. To reduce pressure slowly, leave the pan to cool at room temperature. Keep the cooker thoroughly clean, paying particular attention to the vent and rubber ring.

Stocks Remove the trivet. Break up the bones as small as possible, add to pan and add enough water to just cover the bones (e.g. 2 lb.

bones – $2\frac{1}{2}$ pints water). Add the required vegetables, herbs and seasonings. Bring to the boil without the lid, skim and put on the lid. Lower the heat and bring slowly to 15 lb. pressure; reduce the heat and cook steadily for 40–45 minutes (if using marrow bones, pressure cook for 2 hours). Allow pressure to reduce at room temperature.

Soups Follow any normal recipe and cook for the time given in your instruction book. If you wish to make a larger quantity than can be made by half filling the pressure cooker, make a strong soup and dilute with stock or milk after cooking. Don't over-season as pressure cooking concentrates flavour.

Stews and casseroles Again you can use any ordinary recipe, reducing the liquid if necessary to not more than 1 pint to 1–1½ lb. meat. Toss the meat in seasoned flour and brown it lightly in a little fat in the open pressure cooker without trivet before adding the liquid. Any additional thickening agent is best added after cooking.

Joints of meat may be boiled, pot roasted or braised.

Boiling is suitable for salt meats such as silverside or brisket, ham and bacon joints – particularly collar or flank – or boiling fowl.

For salt meats soak the joint overnight, drain off the water and put into the pressure cooker without the trivet, or cover the unsoaked meat with water, bring to the boil, lift out and throw away the water. Pour in enough fresh water to cover and add a small onion, a carrot and a stick of celery. When you have built up pressure, allow 15–20 minutes cooking time per lb.

To pressure cook a rather tough boiling fowl, rub the skin well with seasoning and place on the trivet. Add ½–¾ pint (1¼–1⅞ cups) water (depending on the length of cooking time) and cook for 10–12 minutes per lb. When it is cooked, placing the chicken in a hot oven for about 15 minutes gives a delicious, crisp, brown finish to the bird. Alternatively, brown the bird before cooking in hot fat with a selection of vegetables; cover the base of the pressure cooker with the cut vegetables, just cover them with water and lay the chicken on top; bring up to pressure and cook for 10 minutes per lb.

Pot roasting is a suitable method for less expensive cuts that are inclined to dry out when roasted in the oven – such as topside, rolled rib, fresh silverside or brisket. Rub some pepper (not salt) into the joint and brown it lightly all over in a little hot fat. Strain off the fat and add ½ pint (1¼ cups) hot liquid for a joint up to 3 lb., plus ¼ pint (⅝ cup) for each additional 2 lb. Never use less than ½ pint. Place the joint on the trivet. Cook for 12–15 minutes per lb., depending on the thickness of the joint.

For **braising**, prepare the meat and vegetables in the usual way, add the amount of liquid stated in the normal recipe and cook for 10–18 minutes per lb., depending on thickness.

Vegetables When you are preparing vegetables for cooking in the pressure cooker, make sure they are approximately the same size, or cut them into even-sized pieces. Always use the trivet when cooking vegetables – and you will find the separators supplied with the cooker are handy for lifting out the vegetables when cooking is completed. Sprinkle the salt sparingly on to the vegetables, rather than in the water, and never use more than ½ pint (1¼ cups) water, except for beetroot which requires 1 pint (2½ cups). Bring the cooker to pressure quickly and follow the manufacturer's directions for cooking time.

By using the separators or wrapping in foil you can cook several

Burgundy beef with ratatouille – both made in a pressure cooker

kinds of vegetable at the same time. Be sure to check the cooking times given in your instruction booklet before you do this – or else you will have some vegetables over-cooked and pulpy, while others aren't cooked at all! First put in those that require the longest cooking; after the necessary time has elapsed, reduce pressure, remove the lid and add the remaining vegetables. Bring the cooker up to pressure once more and continue to cook until all the vegetables are ready.

Puddings Pressure-cookers are invaluable for those marvellous winter warmers – steamed or boiled puddings. You can even cook your Christmas pudding in the pressure cooker – which will certainly save you being tied to the kitchen for the whole of a day!

A 1-pint sponge pudding should be allowed to steam without pressure for 15 minutes and then cooked at 5 lb. pressure for 25 minutes; reduce the pressure at room temperature. Check your manufacturer's instructions for precise cooking times for Christmas pudding and other different puddings.

All the recipes we have tested and give here were cooked in 8–12 pint pressure cookers. Whatever size cooker you have, remember to adjust the quantity of water so that it reaches the level of the trivet.

CELERY SOUP
serves 4–6

1 large head of celery, scrubbed
1 oz. butter
2 medium-sized onions, skinned and finely chopped
1 pint (2½ cups) chicken stock or 1 chicken stock cube dissolved in 1 pint (2½ cups) boiling water
salt and pepper
1 bay leaf
½ pint (1¼ cups) milk
2 level tbsps. cornflour
¼ pint (⅝ cup) cream

Chop the celery stalks, reserving a few of the leaves for decoration. Melt the butter in a pressure cooker, fry the celery and onion gently for 2 minutes and then add the stock and seasonings. Cover

and bring to 15 lb. pressure. Cook for 10 minutes, reduce pressure quickly and remove the bay leaf.

Purée in a blender or work through a coarse sieve and return to the heat in a clean saucepan. Blend together the milk and the cornflour and add to the saucepan. Bring to the boil, stirring all the time. Remove the pan from the heat and stir in the cream. Adjust the seasoning if necessary. Garnish with celery leaves.

CHICKEN LIVER PATE
serves 4–6

2 oz. lean bacon, rinded and roughly chopped
1 oz. butter
1 small onion, skinned and chopped
8 oz. chicken livers, washed and dried
4 oz. cooked chicken, chopped
1 chicken stock cube
4 tbsps. boiling water
salt and pepper
2 large eggs, beaten

Grease a 1½-pint pie dish. Heat the bacon rinds in a pan with the butter, add the bacon and onion and fry gently for 4 minutes. Discard the rinds. Add the livers and fry for 3 minutes. Remove the pan from the heat and add the chicken. Dissolve the stock cube in the boiling water. Either finely mince the liver mixture on its own or purée it in a blender with the stock. If minced, add the stock afterwards. Season with salt and pepper and mix in the beaten egg.

Put the mixture into the pie dish and cover with foil. Place on the trivet in the pressure cooker, and pour 1 pint (2½ cups) water round the dish. Bring up to 15 lb. pressure and cook for 20 minutes. Run it under cold water to reduce pressure quickly and leave to cool.

BURGUNDY BEEF
serves 4

2 tbsps. cooking oil
1 large onion, skinned and sliced
2 green peppers (capsicums), seeded and diced
1½ lb. chuck steak, trimmed and diced
4 oz. button mushrooms, washed and halved
¼ pint (⅝ cup) Burgundy
3 level tbsps. tomato paste
bouquet garni
salt and pepper

Heat the oil in the pressure cooker

nd fry the onions and peppers
ently for 4 minutes. Add the meat
nd fry lightly until it is sealed.
.dd the mushrooms, wine, tomato
aste, herbs and seasonings. Put
n the lid and bring up to 15 lb.
ressure. Cook for 10–15 minutes.
ool by the quick method, remove
he bouquet garni and serve at
nce, accompanied by ratatouille.

RATATOUILLE
erves 4

tbsps. cooking oil
oz. butter
tomatoes, skinned and
  chopped
large aubergine, washed
  and chopped
courgettes (zucchini),
  washed and sliced
green pepper (capsicum),
  washed and sliced
large onions, skinned and
  thinly sliced
clove of garlic, skinned and
  crushed
level tbsps. tomato paste
alt and pepper

Remove the trivet and heat the oil
nd butter in the pressure cooker.
.dd all the vegetables and season-
ags. Stir well, cover and bring up
o 15 lb. pressure. Cook for 4
ninutes. Reduce pressure quickly.
erve either hot or cold.

BARBECUED PORK
CHOPS
erves 4

lean spare rib pork chops,
  trimmed of fat
alt and pepper
tbsps. clear honey
tbsps. soy sauce
rounded tbsp. tomato
  ketchup
small clove of garlic,
  skinned and crushed
level tsp. dry mustard
uice of 1 large orange
uice of ½ small lemon
tbsps. vinegar
tbsp. cooking oil
small onion, skinned and
  chopped

Season the chops well. In a bowl,
nix together the honey, soy sauce,
omato ketchup, garlic, mustard,
ruit juices and vinegar.
Without the trivet, heat the oil in
he pressure cooker and fry the
hops quickly on both sides until
rown. Remove them from the
ooker. Drain off the excess fat
nd return the chops to the pres-
ure cooker together with the
auce mixture and onion.
over, bring up to 15 lb. pressure

The pressure cooker is useful for desserts – try this apricot caramel custard

Cherry layer pudding and winter fruit salad are 2 more quickies

and cook for 8 minutes. Reduce
from pressure quickly and serve
at once.

APRICOT CARAMEL
CUSTARD
serves 4

4 tbsps. apricot jam
4 large eggs
1 oz. (2 tbsps.) caster sugar
1 pint (2½ cups) milk
4 oz. (½ cup) granulated sugar
¼ pint (⅝ cup) and 4 tbsps.
  double cream
1 egg white
few drops vanilla essence

Butter a deep soufflé dish (6-in.)
and spoon the jam into the base.
Whisk the whole eggs, caster sugar
and milk together and strain the
mixture on top of the jam. Cover
the top of the soufflé dish with a

piece of greaseproof paper and
then with aluminium foil. Place on
the trivet in the pressure cooker,
pour round ½ pint water and add
a slice of lemon (this prevents the
cooker discolouring). Cover, bring
up to 15 lb. pressure and cook for
10 minutes. Allow pressure to
reduce slowly by leaving to stand
at room temperature. Allow to
cool.
Meanwhile, put the granulated
sugar and ¼ pint water in a pan
and dissolve over a low heat, stirring constantly. Bring to the boil
and boil until golden, then pour
the caramel on to an oiled baking
sheet and leave to cool.
Whip the cream and egg white
together until stiff and add a little
vanilla essence. Spread half the
cream mixture on top of the
apricot custard. Break up the cara-

mel with a rolling pin and sprinkle
over the custard. Pipe the remaining cream round the base.

WINTER FRUIT SALAD
serves 4

1 lb. (3 cups) mixed dried
  fruit
1 pint (2½ cups) boiling water
5 level tbsps. sugar
2 oz. (4 tbsps.) seedless raisins
4 slices of thinly pared
  orange rind

Wash and drain the fruit well.
Put it into a bowl and pour on the
boiling water; cover and leave for
10 minutes. Turn the contents of
the bowl into the pressure cooker
and add the sugar, raisins and rind.
Bring up to 15 lb. pressure and
cook for 10 minutes. Reduce pressure at room temperature.
Before serving, the juices can be
thickened with cornflour or arrowroot if wished.

CHERRY LAYER PUDDING
serves 4

½ oz. butter
2 oz. (⅓ cup) Demerara sugar
6 oz. (1½ cups) self-raising
  flour
pinch of salt
3 oz. suet, shredded
2 14-oz. cans cherry pie
  filling

Butter a 2-pint pudding basin and
sprinkle round 1½ oz. of the sugar.
Mix the flour with the remaining
sugar, salt and suet and add
enough cold water to make a soft
dough. Divide into 4 pieces of
graduating sizes. Roll out the
pieces individually, the smallest
to fit the base of the basin, the
largest to fit the top. Place the
smallest piece in the base.
Drain off most of the sauce from
the cherries and reserve. Put the
cherries and pastry in layers in
the basin, finishing with the largest
piece of pastry. Cover securely
with greaseproof paper.
In the pressure cooker, bring 1¾
pints (4¾ cups) water to the boil.
Place the basin in the cooker, on
the trivet, and fit the lid on.
Turn heat to high and wait until
the steam escapes freely from the
open vent. Lower the heat and
cook gently, with the vent still
open and steam puffing out gently,
for 15 minutes. Raise heat to high
and put on a 5-lb. weight. Bring
up to pressure and cook for 40
minutes. Reduce pressure slowly.
Serve hot with custard or with the
reserved cherry syrup thickened
with arrowroot.

QUICK CAKES AND COOKIES

CHOCOLATE CRACKLES
makes 12

8 oz. chocolate dots
1 oz. golden syrup
2 oz. butter
**2 oz. cornflakes or rice
    crispies**

Melt the chocolate dots with the golden syrup and butter over a very low heat, or put in a basin set over a pan of hot water. Fold in the cornflakes or crispies.
When well mixed, divide between 12 paper cases and leave to set.

TRUFFLE CAKES
makes 16–18

**4 oz. stale cake or cake
    trimmings**
4 oz. (½ cup) caster sugar
4 oz. (1 cup) ground almonds
apricot jam
sherry or rum to flavour
**chocolate vermicelli to
    decorate**

Rub the stale cake or cake trimmings through a fairly coarse

sieve and add the caster sugar, ground almonds and enough apricot jam to bind. Flavour as liked with sherry or rum.
Shape the mixture into small balls and leave to become firm. Sieve some apricot jam. Dip each ball into the jam and roll in chocolate vermicelli. When firm, put into small paper cases.

SHELL CAKES
makes 12–14

3 oz. butter
3 oz. (⅓ cup) caster sugar
½–1 egg, beaten
5 oz. (1¼ cups) plain flour
jam for filling
icing sugar for dredging

Grease 2 baking sheets.
Cream the butter and sugar until really light and fluffy. Beat in the egg (if the egg is small, use all of it). Fold in the flour and mix well. Place the mixture in a forcing bag fitted with a large star nozzle and pipe in small shell shapes on to the baking sheets.
Bake in the centre of the oven at

400°F. (mark 6) for 10–15 minutes, until just coloured. Cool on a wire rack.
To serve, sandwich together in pairs with jam and dredge with icing sugar.

TUTTI FRUTTI CUPS
makes 20

4 oz. butter or margarine
4 oz. (½ cup) caster sugar
2 eggs, beaten
4 oz. (1 cup) self-raising flour
grated rind of ½ lemon
1 oz. glacé cherries, chopped
**1 oz. flaked or chopped
    almonds**
2 oz. currants
2 oz. (⅓ cup) Demerara sugar

Cream the butter and sugar until light and fluffy. Beat in the eggs, one at a time. Gently beat in the flour and lemon rind. Divide between 20 paper bun cases (for a better shape, place the cases inside patty pans). Mix together the glacé cherries, almonds, currants and Demerara sugar and top each bun with a spoonful. Bake at

375°F. (mark 5) for 15–20 minute and leave to cool on a wire rack.

STRAWBERRY
SHORTCAKES
makes 12

8 oz. (2 cups) plain flour
2 level tsps. baking powder
2 oz. butter
1 oz. (2 tbsps.) caster sugar
1 egg, beaten
milk to mix
¾ lb. strawberries, hulled
caster sugar for berries
**¼ pint (⅝ cup) double cream,
    whipped**

Lightly grease a baking sheet.
Sift together the flour and bakin powder. Rub in the butter, add th sugar and mix to a stiff scon dough with the egg and a littl milk. Roll out to ½–¾ in. thick an cut out 12 rounds, using a 3-in plain cutter. Place on the bakin sheet and bake near the top of th oven at 450°F. (mark 8) for 7–1 minutes, until well risen an golden brown.
Crush ½ lb. strawberries ver

ghtly, adding a little sugar if
[d]esired. Beat the cream until light
[a]nd fluffy. While the shortcakes
[a]re still warm, split each in half and
[s]pread with crushed berries. Top
[w]ith whole berries and whipped
[c]ream.

[O]NE-TWO-THREE [B]ISCUITS
[m]akes about 9

[ ] oz. butter
[ ] oz. (2 tbsps.) caster sugar
[ ] oz. (¾ cup) plain flour
[s]ugar to dredge

[G]rease a baking sheet.
[C]ream together the butter and
[s]ugar. Work in the flour and knead
[li]ghtly to form a ball. Roll out
[c]arefully on a lightly floured sur-
[fa]ce – the mixture will be crumbly
[an]d needs knitting together be-
[t]ween rollings.
[S]tamp out rounds, using a 2¼-in.
[fl]uted cutter, or cut into fingers
[an]d mark in lines with a fork.
[B]ake in the centre of the oven or
[ju]st below at 300°F. (mark 1–2)
[fo]r about 25 minutes, until just
[li]ghtly tinged with colour. Cool on
[a] wire rack.
[T]o serve, dredge with caster sugar.

[M]ELTING MOMENTS
[m]akes about 24

[ ] oz. butter or margarine
[ ] oz. (⅓ cup) sugar
[li]ttle vanilla essence or
    grated lemon rind
[ ] egg yolk
[ ] oz. (1¼ cups) self-raising
    flour
[c]rushed cornflakes

[G]rease baking sheets.
[C]ream the fat and sugar and beat
[in] the flavouring and the egg.
[W]ork in the flour and mix to a
[sm]ooth dough. Wet the hands and
[di]vide the mixture into small
[b]alls. Roll these in cornflakes, put
[on] the baking sheet and bake in
[th]e centre of the oven at 375°F.
[m]ark 5) for 15–20 minutes. Cool
[o]n a wire rack.

[G]INGER NUTS
[m]akes about 24

[ ] oz. (1 cup) self-raising flour
[ ] level tsp. bicarbonate of
    soda
[1]–2 level tsps. ground ginger
[ ] level tsp. ground cinnamon
[ ] level tsps. caster sugar
[ ] oz. butter
[ ] oz. golden syrup

[G]rease 2 baking sheets.
[Si]ft together the flour, bicarbonate
[of] soda, ginger, cinnamon and

sugar. Melt the butter and stir in
the syrup. Stir this mixture into
the dry ingredients and mix well.
Roll the mixture into small balls,
place well apart on the baking
sheets and flatten slightly.
Bake just above the centre of the
oven at 375°F. (mark 5) for 15–20
minutes. Cool for a few minutes
before lifting carefully from baking sheets on to a wire rack.
Finish cooling, and store in an
airtight tin.

FLORENTINES
makes about 24

3½ oz. butter
4 oz. (½ cup) caster sugar
4 oz. almonds, chopped
1 oz. sultanas, chopped
1 tbsp. cream
1 oz. glacé cherries, chopped
1 oz. mixed peel, chopped
cooking chocolate

Line baking sheets with non-stick
paper.
Melt the butter, add the sugar and
boil together for 1 minute. Stir in
all the other ingredients except the
chocolate. When beginning to
cool, drop in small, well-shaped
heaps on the baking sheets, keeping them well apart to allow for
spreading – about 4 per tray. Bake
near the centre of the oven at
350°F. (mark 4) for about 10
minutes, until golden brown.
Remove from the oven and press
the edges to a neat shape with a
knife. Lift each florentine carefully
from the tray and cool on a wire
rack.
To finish, spread the smooth
underside of each with melted
chocolate. When this is beginning
to set, mark it in wavy lines with a
fork. Leave to harden, then serve.
The biscuits may be stored without the chocolate coating for up to
1 week. Place in an airtight container between sheets of non-stick
paper.

1-2-3 biscuits, ginger nuts, shell cakes and florentines

OVEN SCONES
makes 10–12

8 oz. (2 cups) self-raising flour
1 level tsp. baking powder
¼ level tsp. salt
1½ oz. butter or margarine
1½ oz. (3 tbsps.) sugar
2 oz. sultanas or currants
¼ pint (⅝ cup) milk

Sift the flour, baking powder and
salt into a mixing bowl. Cut the
fat into small pieces and add to the
flour. Rub in the fat with the
fingertips until no lumps are left
and the mixture looks like fine
breadcrumbs. Stir in the sugar and
the cleaned fruit, then add the
milk 1 tablespoon at a time,
stirring well with a round-bladed
knife until the mixture begins to
bind, making a light dough.
Using one hand, collect the mixture together and knead it lightly
to form a smooth, fairly soft
dough. Turn it out on to a lightly
floured board, form into a flat,
round shape and roll out 1 in.
thick. Cut into 2-in. rounds, put
on a baking sheet and brush the
tops with a little milk. Bake towards the top of the oven at
450°F. (mark 8) for about 10
minutes, until well risen and
golden. Cool on a wire rack. Serve
split and buttered on the same day.

DROP SCONES (SCOTCH PANCAKES)
makes 15–18

4 oz. (1 cup) self-raising flour,
    or 4 oz. plain flour sifted
    with a pinch each of
    bicarbonate of soda and
    cream of tartar
½–1 oz. (1–2 tbsps.) sugar
1 egg
¼ pint (⅝ cup) milk

Prepare a special griddle, a heavy
frying pan, or the solid hot plate
of an electric cooker, by rubbing
the surface with salt on a pad of

kitchen paper, wiping clean and
then greasing it very lightly. Just
before cooking the scones, heat
the griddle until the fat is 'hazing';
wipe the surface with paper.
Put the flour and sugar in a bowl,
add the egg and half the milk and
beat until smooth. Add the remaining milk and beat until bubbles rise to the surface. Spoon the
batter on to the heated griddle,
spacing well.
When the bubbles rise to the
surface, turn the scones with a
palette knife and cook for a further
½–1 minute, or until golden brown.
Place on a cooling rack and cover
with a clean tea towel until the
rest are cooked. Serve buttered.

GINGER AND DATE CAKES
makes 15–18

6 oz. (1½ cups) self-raising
    flour
pinch of salt
3 oz. butter or margarine
3 oz. (⅜ cup) caster sugar
2–3 oz. dates, chopped
1 oz. crystallized ginger,
    chopped
1 egg, beaten
milk to mix

Grease 18 patty tins.
Sift the flour and salt into a bowl
and rub in the fat lightly. Stir in
the sugar, dates and ginger, then
mix in the egg and milk to form a
stiff dropping consistency.
Place in spoonfuls in the patty tins
and bake just above the centre of
the oven at 375°F. (mark 5) for
15 minutes. Cool on a rack.

ROCK CAKES
makes 12

8 oz. (2 cups) plain flour
pinch of salt
2 level tsps. baking powder
½ level tsp. mixed spice
½ level tsp. ground nutmeg
2 oz. butter or margarine
2 oz. lard or cooking fat
4 oz. mixed dried fruit
4 oz. (⅔ cup) Demerara sugar
1 large egg, beaten
grated rind of ½ lemon
milk to mix

Grease 2 baking trays.
Sift together the flour, salt, baking
powder and spice. Rub in the fat.
Add the fruit and sugar, mix well.
Add the egg and sufficient milk to
give a stiff dough. Using 2 forks,
place the mixture in small rough
piles on the greased trays and
bake towards the top of the oven
at 400°F. (mark 6) for 15–20
minutes. Cool on a wire rack.

ixers take the arm ache out of food preparation. The most tiring processes – beating, whisking and mashing vegetables – become nothing more than a flick of the switch once your mixer is installed. Whether you have a small hand-held model or a full size one keep it out on the work surface, or hanging on the wall nearby, where it can become almost an extension of your own hands, to use automatically without thinking, at every possible opportunity. A large mixer particularly is cumbersome to lift and fit together and if it is tucked away out of sight in a cupboard you will tend not to use it as much as you might. If your hand model has a stand, keep that handy too.

You need no special recipes for a mixer, though you may have to adapt the method. A hand-held model will whisk or cream small quantities for any cake mixture, whisk the lumps out of sauces, whip cream, whisk up an omelette or cream potatoes without any effort at all. Follow the manufacturer's instructions regarding speeds but make sure that you do not over beat, especially when adding flour to a cake mixture, or whipping small quantities of cream. Also make sure that you do not overload the machine – some of the beaters are light-weight and cannot handle heavy fruit cake mixtures in large quantities. The large models usually have a variety of basic fitments (apart from the range of extra attachments) and a much wider variety of speeds, making it possible to mix small or large quantities for cakes, pastries and even bread. Cooking for a large family or for freezing, you can handle jumbo-size mixtures in a large mixer that would be extremely hard work by hand.

Whatever type of mixer you have, study the manufacturer's instructions before you use it, and do use the right type of beater at the correct speed. Never run a small mixer for more than 2 minutes without a break, or a large one for more than 5 minutes – this isn't as limiting as it sounds for everything is quicker with a mixer and it is only too easy to over-beat, over-whisk or rub-in for too long.

As a general rule, for whisking light mixtures such as meringues and sponges, use the top speed. Creaming fat and sugar or whipping cream is better done on a medium speed, or the mixture will

MIXER COOKING

splatter everywhere. If you're using the mixer instead of rubbing-in by hand, as with pastry or biscuit dough, use a very low speed.

Cake making is one of the main uses of a mixer. To give the best results, ingredients should be at room temperature, so remove eggs and butter from the refrigerator an hour or so before they are required (except in very hot weather or if you are using one of the luxury margarines). If the fat is too firm, cream it a little alone before incorporating the sugar, or warm the bowl and beaters before you start – but take care not to make the fat oily.

If the mixer has only one speed, it is better not to use it for folding in the flour; you can do this quite easily and quickly with a spatula and it really needs a very slow speed to do it successfully with the machine.

To judge the degree of beating, always test your mixture with a spoon if you are using a fine whisk. Mixer whisks are often so fine that the mixture tends to fall away too easily – giving the impression that more beating is required. Sometimes a creamed mixture or dough will climb too

far up the side of the bowl; if this happens, stop the mixer and scrape the mixture back into the bottom of the bowl with a spatula. If the head of a stand-held mixer is not adjustable, this may be necessary once or twice during creaming. With a hand-held mixer this is avoided by moving the whisk round the bowl slowly, much as you would a spoon. Choose a fairly straight sided bowl if possible.

Mixers can be pretty fierce, and it is often as well to start working for a moment or two at a low speed before switching to a higher one. Otherwise there is a tendency for the mixture to be thrown out of the bowl – this applies particularly to liquids such as cream, or to powders such as icing sugar. Another trick with icing sugar, when adding it to royal icing or to butter cream, is to cover the head of the mixer and/or the bowl with a cloth, to stop the powder flying about.

All your favourite baking recipes can be adapted to making in the mixer, but until you are used to using it, it will probably help to use some of our recipes that have been specially tested for suitability for mixers.

WHISKED SPONGES

These marvellously light sponge cakes are ideal to make with the help of your mixer. With no raising agent added, they rely on the amount of air you can beat into the mixture to give them that airy texture and it is essential to beat the eggs and sugar until they are really thick and creamy.

Here we give a basic recipe followed by flavouring variations which will help you to ring the changes – delicious cakes for weekend teas, a plain sponge to accompany ice cream for family supper, or an elaborate – yet not heavy – gâteau when you have guests for dinner.

The basic sponge will keep fresh for several days in an airtight tin or wrapped in foil, and this will be helped by the addition of some glycerine to the ingredients – teaspoons to a 3-egg mixture.

PLAIN WHISKED SPONGE

2 eggs
4 oz. (½ cup) caster sugar
4 oz. (1 cup) plain flour

Warm the bowl and beaters. Whisk the eggs and sugar at a fairly high speed until thick and leaving trail.

Sift the flour over the egg mixture and carefully fold it in, using metal spoon, until the flour is evenly distributed.

Grease an 8-in. sandwich tin and coat with equal quantities of flour and sugar. Pour in the sponge mixture and bake just above the centre of the oven at 350°F. (mark 4) for 25–30 minutes. When cooked, the sides of the cake should shrink slightly from the edge of the tin, and when you lightly press the top of the cake it should leave no impression.

PINEAPPLE SPONGE

a basic whisked sponge
15-oz. can pineapple rings
½ pint (1¼ cups) double cream
3 level tbsps. apricot jam
2 oz. (approx. ½ cup) walnut halves

Drain the pineapple, retaining the syrup. Split the cake in half and sprinkle each half with tablespoons of the syrup. Put the bottom half of the cake on a serving dish.

Beat the cream at medium speed until beginning to thicken. Chop of the pineapple rings and mix with 4 tablespoons of the cream. Use as a filling.

Put the apricot jam in a small

pan with 2 tablespoons of the pineapple juice. Bring to the boil, stirring, then simmer gently for 2 minutes. Brush this glaze over the top and sides of the cake. Finely chop all but 8 of the walnut halves. Using a small palette knife, press the chopped nuts round the sides of the cake. Decorate with remaining pineapple and reserved walnuts.

CHOCOLATE SPONGE

Add $\frac{1}{2}$ oz. cocoa with the flour. Dredge the cake heavily with icing sugar when cool.

LEMON SPONGE

Add the grated rind of a lemon with the flour.

ORANGE SPONGE

Add the grated rind of an orange with the flour.

OVEN SCONES

makes 10–12

8 oz. (2 cups) self-raising flour
1 level tsp. baking powder
$\frac{1}{4}$ level tsp. salt
$1\frac{1}{2}$ oz. margarine
$1\frac{1}{2}$ oz. sugar
2 oz. ($\frac{1}{2}$ cup) currants, washed
$\frac{1}{4}$ pint ($\frac{5}{8}$ cup) milk

Sift the flour, baking powder and salt into the mixing bowl. Cut the fat into small pieces and add. Beat on minimum speed until the mixture resembles fresh bread-crumbs. Add the sugar and currants. Add the milk slowly, still beating at a low speed until the mixture has the consistency of a soft dough.

Turn on to a lightly floured board, form into a flat, round shape and roll out to a 1-in. thickness. Cut into 2-in. rounds, put on to a greased baking sheet and brush the tops with a little milk. Bake near the top of the oven at 450°F. (mark 8) for about 10 minutes, until well risen and golden. Cool on a wire rack. Serve buttered. Any left over can be reheated under the grill the next day.

DUNDEE CAKE

8 oz. (2 cups) plain flour
1 level tsp. baking powder
pinch of salt
8 oz. butter
8 oz. (1 cup) caster sugar
4 large eggs
12 oz. sultanas, washed
12 oz. currants, washed
6 oz. chopped mixed peel
4 oz. small glacé cherries
grated rind of $\frac{1}{2}$ a lemon
2–3 oz. ($\frac{1}{2}$ cup) whole blanched almonds

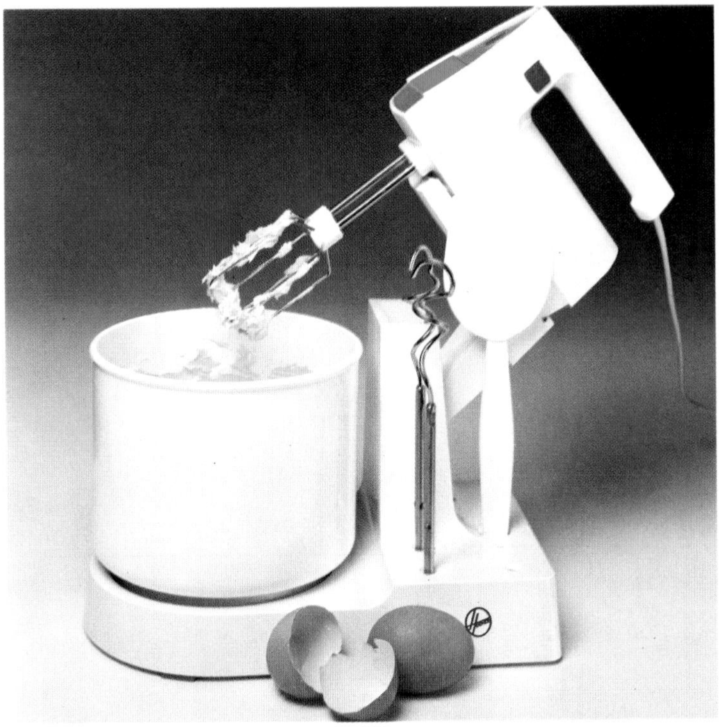

Creaming a cake mixture becomes easy with a mixer

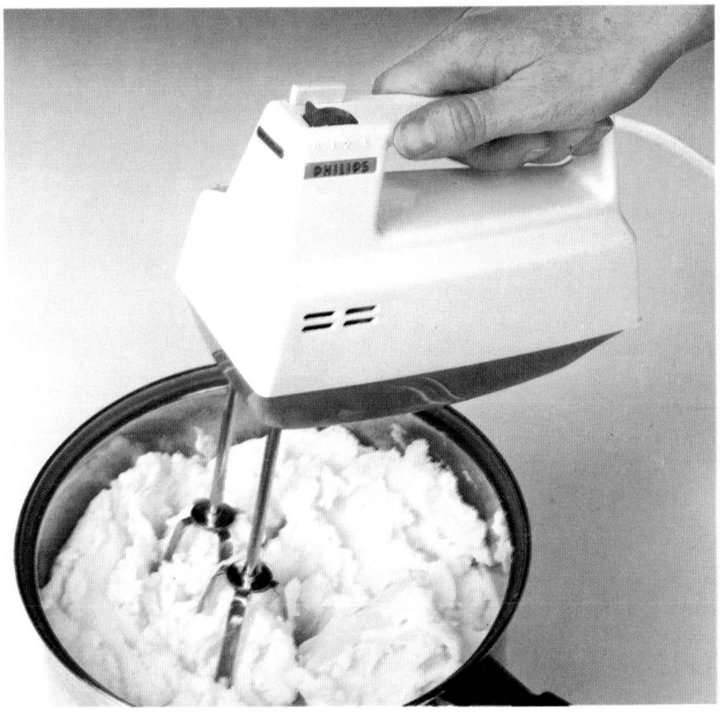

No more lumpy mashed potatoes if you make good use of your mixer

Sift together the flour, baking powder and salt; warm the mixer bowl and beaters. Cream the butter on minimum speed, add the sugar and beat together until light and fluffy (approximately 3 minutes). Break in the eggs one at a time, beating each until the mixture is fluffy.

Fold in by hand, or continue to use minimum speed and add the flour, fruit, peel, cherries and lemon rind. Chop 1 oz. of the nuts and add those.

Grease and line an 8-in. round cake tin. Turn the mixture into the prepared tin and level the surface with a palette knife.

Split the remainder of the nuts in half and arrange neatly over the cake, rounded side uppermost. Bake just below the centre of the oven at 300°F. (mark 2) for about $2\frac{1}{2}$ hours.

SWEET SOUFFLE OMELETTE

For each person:

2 eggs, separated
1 level tsp. caster sugar
2 tbsps. water
$\frac{1}{2}$ oz. butter

Add the sugar and water to the egg yolks, and beat lightly with a fork. Whisk the egg whites at top speed until really stiff. Melt the butter in an omelette pan over a low heat. Turn the yolks into the egg whites and fold in carefully, using a metal spoon. Make sure the pan is well lined with the melted butter and pour in the mixture.

Cook 1–2 minutes over moderate heat until the omelette is golden brown on the underside. Now place the pan under the grill until the omelette is browned on top. Don't over-cook, as this tends to make it tough. Loosen the omelette round the sides, make a mark across the middle, add the required filling and double the omelette over. Turn it gently on to a hot plate and serve at once.

SOUFFLE OMELETTE FILLINGS

Jam Spread the cooked omelette with warmed jam, fold it over and sprinkle with sugar.

Rum Add 1 tbsp. rum to the egg yolks before cooking. Put the cooked omelette on a hot dish, pour 3–4 tbsps. warmed rum round it, ignite and serve immediately.

Apricot Add the grated rind of an orange or tangerine to the egg yolks. Spread some thick apricot pulp over the omelette before folding it and serve sprinkled with caster sugar.

COFFEE CREAM

serves 4

3 level tsps. powdered gelatine
2–3 tbsps. water
$\frac{3}{4}$ pint ($1\frac{7}{8}$ cups) double cream
$\frac{1}{4}$ pint ($\frac{5}{8}$ cup) single cream
3 oz. ($\frac{3}{8}$ cup) caster sugar
3–4 level tsps. powdered coffee, dissolved in 2 tsps. hot water

Place the gelatine and water in a basin and stand this in a pan of hot water until the gelatine is dissolved. Put both kinds of cream into the mixer bowl and whisk at medium speed until you can see the trails left by the whisk. Fold in the sugar and coffee.

With the mixer at medium speed, pour the gelatine into the bowl in a thin, steady stream, taking care to avoid the mixture setting in lumps. Keep whisking until it is just on the point of setting. Pour quickly into a wetted $1\frac{1}{2}$-pint mould or 4 individual moulds. Leave to set in a cool place. Unmould just before serving.

BLENDER COOKERY

The electric blender deserves to be the most widely used of all kitchen gadgets. It cuts the time spent mixing and blending ingredients to a tiny fraction of that needed for traditional methods; in addition it will do most of the time-consuming chopping and grinding that are essential to good home cooking.

Breadcrumbs Cut off the crusts and drop the bread into the goblet, a piece at a time, through the feeder hole in the lid. For buttered crumbs, butter the bread slices first.

Biscuit crumbs Break the biscuits into 3–4 pieces each and feed them into the goblet through the feeder hole.

Nuts A blender will chop or grind nuts – add butter to make peanut, cashew or other nut butter.

Vegetables To chop cabbage, carrot and raw onion, half fill the goblet with water, cut the vegetable into manageable-sized pieces and add to the goblet. Blend until it is chopped as finely as you require. Drain off the water. (Some blenders will chop vegetables without added water, but follow the manufacturer's instructions and

chop only a small amount at a time.)

Sauces For a white sauce, put all the ingredients in the blender and switch on to high speed. When blended, turn into a saucepan and cook gently to thicken.

Soups Cook vegetables until soft, then purée in the blender. Add extra liquid and seasoning after blending. Be careful not to overcook the vegetables.

Fruit purées Soft fruits will purée without prior cooking, but harder fruits should be stoned, and cooked gently beforehand. Some fruit purées, e.g. raspberry, may need sieving through a fine nylon sieve afterwards to remove the seeds.

REMEMBER!

Do read the manufacturer's instructions carefully.

Do place the lid in position before switching on.

Do cut solid foods small.

Do begin with small quantities when using heavy and solid foods.

Do put liquids in before solids.

Do use the highest recommended speed for the smoothest results.

Don't overfill your blender. Most perform best when they are no

more than half-full.

Don't let it run for more than the recommended time (2–3 short bursts are better than 1 long one).

Don't let the motor race. If the mixture creeps up the side of the goblet, stop the motor and scrape the mixture down on to the blades.

Don't try to whip cream in your blender – it won't do it; nor will it extract juice or crush ice (unless specifically stated by the manufacturer).

Don't try to chop raw meat unless you have a high-powered blender, beat egg white, mash potato or cream fat and sugar.

COD ROE PATE
serves 6

1 thin slice white bread
8-oz. can cod roe
1 small potato, boiled
1 clove of garlic, skinned
few sprigs of parsley
juice of ½ lemon
1 tsp. cooking oil
salt and pepper
black olives, cucumber slices
   and lemon slices, to garnish

Crumb the bread. Add the cod roe and switch on to high speed until

mixed. Add the potato, garlic and parsley and switch to medium for a few seconds. Add the lemon juice, oil and seasoning and switch to high until blended.

Spoon into a shallow dish and garnish with olives, cucumber and lemon slices. Serve with crisp lettuce, gherkins and extra olives. Melba toast or hot toast fingers.

CREAM OF VEGETABLE SOUP
serves 6

1 lb. vegetables
2 oz. butter
½ pint (1¼ cups) white stock
salt and pepper
1 oz. (¼ cup) flour
1 pint (2½ cups) milk

Wash and trim the chosen vegetable. Roughly slice (except peas). Melt 1 oz. butter in a pan, add the vegetable and fry gently for minutes, without browning. Add the stock and simmer with the lid on for 10–15 minutes, until tender. Season to taste.

Meanwhile, make a white sauce using 1 oz. butter, the flour and the milk. Pour the vegetables and stock into the goblet and add the white

auce. Switch on to low speed for
few seconds, then to high until
mooth and creamy – about 2–3
minutes. Check the seasoning,
hen return to the pan and reheat
without boiling.
Note: Suitable vegetables are
nions, tomatoes, leeks, carrots,
elery, or frozen peas. With onion
nd tomato, use only ¼ pint (⅝ cup)
tock.

TUFFED TOMATOES
rves 6

slices bread without crusts
  (about 3 oz.)
large tomatoes
rashers back bacon, rinded
  and fried or grilled
small onion, skinned and
  roughly sliced
mall sprig of parsley
oz. Cheddar cheese, cubed
alt and pepper

Make breadcrumbs in the blender
nd turn them into a bowl. Cut a
mall round from each tomato at
he end opposite to the stalk.
coop out the centres and put in-
o the blender with the bacon,
nion, parsley, cheese and season-
ng. Blend until smooth and stir
nto the breadcrumbs.
ill each tomato shell with the
rumb mixture and bake in the
ven at 375°F. (mark 5) for 15–20
inutes, until the tomato cases
re beginning to soften.

AMILY MEAT LOAF
erves 6–8

oz. slice of white bread,
  with crusts removed
oz. onion, skinned and
  halved
clove of garlic, skinned
ind of ½ lemon, free of pith
large eggs
pint (1¼ cups) red wine
level tsp. dried sage
–1½ level tsps. salt
–½ level tsp. pepper
level tsp. dry mustard
tsp. Worcestershire sauce
ew sprigs of parsley
lb. lean beef, minced
lb. lean pork, minced
lb. veal or lean bacon,
  minced

Make breadcrumbs in the goblet;
ut to one side. Into the goblet put
nion, garlic, lemon rind, eggs,
ine, sage, seasonings and Wor-
estershire sauce. Switch on and
lend until the onion and garlic
re finely chopped. Add the pars-
y sprigs through the lid and
lend until roughly chopped.
n a large basin work together the

beef, pork, veal and breadcrumbs;
gradually add the mixture from the
blender. Turn it into a loaf tin,
cover with foil and cook at 325°F.
(mark 3) for 1½ hours.
Remove the foil and cook, uncovered, for a further 30 minutes.
Pour off the juices and thicken
them with a little cornflour, if
desired. Adjust seasoning before
serving.

JELLIED CHICKEN CREAM
serves 6

½ oz. powdered gelatine
¾ pint (1⅞ cups) chicken stock
1 small onion, skinned and
  quartered
12 oz. cooked chicken
2 stalks of celery, scrubbed
  and roughly chopped
6 stuffed olives
¼ pint (⅝ cup) double cream
¼ pint (⅝ cup) mayonnaise
sliced cucumber
watercress
3–4 tomatoes, sliced
1 onion, skinned and sliced

Dissolve the gelatine in a little of
the stock, in a small basin over a
pan of hot water. Add to the rest
of the stock and leave to cool.
Place the onion and 3 oz. of the
chicken in the goblet, turn on to
high speed for a few seconds until
roughly chopped. Empty into a
bowl and repeat until all the
chicken is chopped.
Place the celery and olives in the
goblet, switch to high until roughly chopped and add to the chicken.
Place the cream and mayonnaise in
the goblet, switch to high for a few
seconds and add the mixture to
the chicken. Mix well together and
season if necessary.
Pour a little chicken stock into the
base of a 1½-pint ring mould.
Arrange the sliced cucumber in
the base; pour over just enough
stock to cover and leave to set.
Slowly stir the remaining stock
into the chicken mixture. Spoon
into the ring mould and leave until
set. Do not over-chill.
Unmould, fill the centre with
watercress and surround with
tomato and onion slices.

BURGERBRAISE
serves 4

4 oz. white bread
12 oz. lean chuck steak
1 onion, skinned and quartered
pinch of mixed herbs
salt and pepper
flour
1 oz. lard
14-oz. can tomatoes, made up
  to ½ pint (1¼ cups) with water

Cod roe pâté is so simple in a blender

Use a high-powered blender for
this recipe.
Feed the bread through the top of
the blender to make crumbs. Put
them into a bowl.
Cut the meat into small pieces, put
into the goblet and switch on to
medium speed for a few seconds,
then to high for a further few
seconds. Put the meat into the
bowl with the breadcrumbs.
Place the onion in the goblet and
switch to high until finely chopped.
Add to the meat with the herbs and
seasoning, mix together until well
blended. Shape the mixture into 4
round flat cakes and toss them in a
little flour.
Melt the lard in a frying pan and
fry the burgers until they are
brown. Add the tomatoes, cover
and simmer for 25–30 minutes,
until thoroughly cooked.

PORK AND BACON LOAF
serves 8

1 lb. lean pork leg
1 lb. bacon joint, rinded
1 large carrot, peeled and
  roughly sliced
1 onion, skinned and
  quartered
¼ pint (⅝ cup) water or stock
1 level tsp. Italian seasoning
1 bay leaf
pepper
4 oz. white bread
1 egg, beaten

Cut the pork and bacon into pieces
and put in a casserole with the
carrot, onion, water or stock, seasoning, bay leaf and pepper. Cook
at 400°F. (mark 6) for 1½ hours.
Make breadcrumbs in the blender
and empty into a bowl.
Put half the contents of the cas-

Jellied chicken cream for a summer salad party

serole into the blender, and switch first to low then to high for about 1 minute, until the meat is finely ground. Add to the breadcrumbs and repeat with the remainder. Mix well together, check the seasoning and add sufficient egg to bind.

Turn the mixture into a greased loaf tin 9½-in. by 5¼-in. Cover with foil and return to the oven at 400°F. (mark 6) for a further 1½ hours. Cool slightly before turning out on to a serving plate.

This is excellent cold but can also be eaten hot.

FEATHER SPONGE

5 oz. (1¼ cups) plain flour
1 oz. (¼ cup) cornflour
6 oz. (¾ cup) caster sugar
2 level tsps. baking powder
½ level tsp. salt
3½ fl. oz. corn oil
3½ fl. oz. water
2 eggs, separated
whipped double cream and jam, for filling

Sift the flour, cornflour, 4 oz. (½ cup) sugar, baking powder and salt through a conical sieve straight into the goblet. Add the oil, water and egg yolks.

Switch on and blend to a batter. Whisk the egg whites in a large basin until foamy, add the 2 oz. sugar and whisk again until stiff. Lightly and evenly fold the batter mixture through the egg whites. Divide the mixture between 2 8-in. sandwich tins, lined with non-stick paper. Bake in the oven at 375°F. (mark 5) until well risen and spongy (25–30 minutes). Turn out carefully onto a wire rack and leave to cool. Sandwich with whipped double cream and jam.

LEMON LAYER SPONGE

1 large juicy lemon
2 large eggs, separated
6 oz. (¾ cup) caster sugar
2 oz. softened butter
2 oz. (½ cup) flour
½ pint (1¼ cups) milk

With a potato peeler thinly pare the lemon rind, free of white pith. Place in the goblet with the egg yolks, sugar, butter, flour, milk and 3 tablespoons lemon juice. Switch on and blend until smooth and rind is finely chopped. Whisk the egg whites in a large deep bowl and fold in the blended ingredients. Turn into a buttered 2-pint pie dish and bake in a bain marie at 350°F. (mark 4) for 40–50 minutes until golden and lightly set. Serve hot.

Try a blender cheesecake for an easy dessert

BAKED CHEESECAKE

8 oz. digestive biscuits
2 level tsps. caster sugar
4 oz. butter, melted
½ pint (1¼ cups) milk
1 tbsp. lemon juice
4 eggs
5 oz. (⅝ cup) caster sugar
2 level tbsps. flour
¼ level tsp. salt
1 lb. cottage cheese
icing sugar, for dusting

Lightly grease an 8-in. round loose-based spring-release cake tin. Crumb the biscuits with the sugar in the blender and mix into the melted butter. Press half the crumb mixture into the base of the tin.

Put the remaining ingredients (except icing sugar) into the goblet and mix until well combined. Pour over the crumb base.

Bake at 325°F. (mark 3) for 1–1¼ hours, until the centre is firm. Cool slightly until really firm and then cover with the remaining crumbs. Chill and remove from the tin.

Cut 6 strips of greaseproof paper, 1 in. wide; place these in a lattice pattern over the cheesecake and dust with icing sugar. Remove the strips of paper carefully.

APRICOT FOOL

serves 4

1 lb. apricots
¼ pint (⅝ cup) thick custard
caster sugar
¾ pint (1⅞ cups) double cream
toasted flaked almonds

Halve the apricots and stew for 10–15 minutes. Remove the stones and put the apricots into the goblet with the custard. Switch on and blend until smooth. Add sugar if desired. Lightly whip the cream in a deep bowl and lightly and evenly fold the apricot through. Chill and decorate with toasted flaked almonds.

BLENDER GINGERBREAD

10 oz. (2½ cups) plain flour
2 oz. (½ cup) cornflour
1 level tsp. bicarbonate of soda
1 level tsp. mixed spice
1 level tbsp. ground ginger
4 oz. (⅔ cup) soft brown sugar
3 oz. mixed peel, chopped
2 oz. crystallized ginger, chopped
3 oz. (2 tbsps.) treacle
¼ pint (⅝ cup) milk
¼ pint (⅝ cup) corn oil
1 egg

Grease an oblong cake tin, to measurement 10½ in. by 6½ in. b 2½ in. deep.

Sift together the flour, cornflou bicarbonate of soda and spices int a large bowl. Stir in the sugar mixed peel and crystallized ginge Put the treacle, milk, corn oil an egg into the blender and mi thoroughly. Pour into the sifte ingredients and beat well.

Transfer the mixture to the pre pared tin and bake in the oven fo about 1¼ hours at 350°F. (mark 4 until well risen and spongy to th touch.

QUICK APRICOT JAM

3 15-oz. cans apricot halves
1 lb. (2 cups) sugar
2 tbsps. lemon juice

Drain the apricots and put into th blender together with ½ pint (1 cups) syrup from the can, suga and lemon juice. Blend to a smoot purée. Turn the purée into saucepan and boil gently unt thick, pour into sterilized jars an seal in the usual way.

MAYONNAISE

makes ½ pint (1¼ cups)

2 egg yolks
½ level tsp. salt
¼ level tsp. dry mustard
¼ level tsp. pepper
¼ level tsp. sugar
½ pint (1¼ cups) olive oil
1 tbsp. vinegar or lemon juic

Ensure that all ingredients are a room temperature.

Place the yolks, seasoning an sugar in the goblet and switch t high for 10 seconds. With the spee at medium, gradually feed in th oil through the hole in the lid When all the oil is absorbed, ad the vinegar or lemon juice a medium speed and blend well.

Aspic mayonnaise: Dissolve pint (1¼ cups) aspic jelly and, whe cooled to the consistency of eg white, mix very gradually with pint (⅝ cup) stiff mayonnaise. Us for coating chaudfroid dishes.

Cream mayonnaise: Mix tablespoons mayonnaise and ¼ pin (⅝ cup) whipped cream. This i good with salads containing frui

Cucumber mayonnaise: Ski and finely dice a small cucumbe and mix into 2 tablespoons mayon naise. Good with fish salads, par ticularly crab, lobster and salmor

Piquant mayonnaise: Mix 1– teaspoons Worcestershire or chil sauce with ¼ pint (⅝ cup) mayon naise.

Poussins Marsala (page 210)

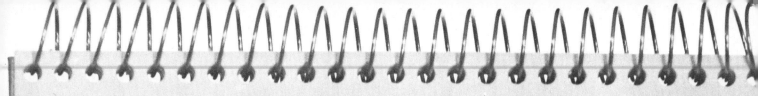

PLANNING A MENU

Planning daily menus for the family presents quite a problem for most people, without the extra thought of guests. There are the nutritional considerations to take into account, the personal likes and dislikes of the children, and the need for variety. You have to think of the time available for shopping and cooking, too. Cooking for guests takes just that little extra effort of planning. If anyone finds it no effort it is because her mind has learned to cope automatically with the groundwork, usually after much practice.

For a beginner it is important to accept your limitations, with regard to both cooking ability and circumstances. Unless you are lucky enough to have competent help for your dinner party, include only one course that is going to need serious on-the-spot concentration. Try to start with something that can either be bought or made a day or two in advance, like pâté. This will mean you can enjoy a pre-dinner drink with your guests and need vanish only at the last minute to prepare the toast. If the weather is cold, serve a hot soup made the day before and heated up at the last moment (a chilled soup in summer avoids even that!) Plan for a sweet that's simple too. There is no knowing how long the main course of a meal is going to take, and it is a pity to spoil it with worry about whether the next course is burning or boiling dry. Obvious dishes to avoid, unless you are absolutely confident of your skills and timing, are anything hit-or-miss like a hot soufflé, or anything fried. Mysterious pauses will have your guests every bit as worried as you are, wondering if they ought to offer to help.

For the inexperienced cook, the simplest solution is to choose as the main course a casserole that can be prepared entirely in advance. Potatoes baked in their jackets make a foolproof accompaniment, and you could offer a simple salad as a separate course. It is always best to choose vegetables that can wait happily for a few minutes while your guests catch up with them. Why sit wondering if the sprouts have gone soggy and yellow, when French beans, peas or carrots would have done equally well? And never risk trying out something new on an important occasion. If you want to branch into more exciting dishes, have a full 'dress rehearsal' with your family or some close friends who won't mind, the week before.

A good menu is a varied one. Give your guests cream of artichoke soup, veal à la crème and soufflé milanese and you'll have them all struggling to the sofa and falling asleep afterwards—the combined effect of a major assault on their digestive capacity and a certain boredom induced by cream in every course and a pale beigey colour predominating throughout. But if you serve a tomato salad before the veal and a tasty strawberry water ice with shortbread after, the effect will be quite different. If soufflé milanese remains your favourite dessert, serve steak and a fresh, green salad as the main course. The general principle is that a 'wet' course should follow a 'dry' one or vice versa and the same major ingredient should not feature in two courses. Texture is important and a menu that seems to be heading towards imbalance can often be redeemed by a simple touch, such as crisp croûtons with the soup or a salad instead of a cooked vegetable with the main course. A biscuit or a tiny helping of fresh fruit with a creamy dessert will often help. Flavour obviously needs considering because too much bland food is dull, whereas too much that is piquant is just impossible to eat. This is why a sharp hollandaise sauce is served with turbot, and a lemon sauce with a steamed sponge pudding. In reverse, it's why cream goes with a sharp flavoured apple pie, or rice is always served with curry.

Appearance, another vital factor, is one that is often overlooked. This can easily be improve by the moderate use of garnishes. A steak with chipped potatoes looks much more appetizing if set off with watercress and a grilled tomato and avoid any really anaemic-looking combination – creamed fish with marrow and potatoe for instance; serve carrots instead of marrow and use chopped parsley and perhaps som paprika pepper to make it look more attractive Consider the individual tastes of your guest and don't serve curry, tripe or any other fairl specialized taste without first checking tha they're going to like it. Be considerate in les obvious ways too—if you know one of you guests is shy, don't serve something that need to be eaten with blasé defiance of conventiona table manners (corn-on-the-cob and spaghett are prime offenders).

Having planned the menu, spend a little tim working out a rough timetable. Give yoursel time the day before to do any preparation tha can be done in advance—however simple th menu, if you leave everything till 2 hours befor the meal you will be rushed and flustered b the time the guests arrive. If you have chose a simple menu, give yourself a treat by doin the absolute minimum of cooking on the day you will enjoy the meal all the more.

Plan the shopping, too. Order anything lik fresh fruit that you cannot buy in advance, t avoid disappointment, and let your butche know if you want any special cut or boning ou done for you. He will appreciate not having t tackle a whole side of beef when the shop is fu on a Saturday morning.

All this planning is practical, and it has a additional psychological effect. A hostess wh knows she has all the details under control an that the work is progressing to schedule will b calm and relaxed on the day, able to take a littl more time over her own appearance. In the en she will win compliments from all angles!

EASY BUFFETS

Buffets for 12, 20 or 30 need be no effort
if you plan your menus carefully. Follow
our timetables for a really easy passage.

CHEESE AND WALNUT DIP
CELERY
FRENCH BREAD AND BUTTER
GLAZED BAKED GAMMON
PRESSED TONGUE
SALMON CUTLETS IN ASPIC WITH MAYONNAISE
GREEN SALAD
TOMATO AND ONION SALAD
NEW POTATOES IN FRENCH DRESSING
STRAWBERRY MERINGUE SLICE
PINEAPPLE CHIFFON FLAN

Timetable

The ham and tongue may be prepared 2–3 days before. The meringue layers and mayonnaise may also be made well in advance. Prepare the salmon, salad dressings and dip the day before and also the pineapple chiffon flans. On the day, finish off the sweets and make up the salads.

CHEESE AND WALNUT DIP

1 lb. Wensleydale or mild soft cheese
¾ pint (2 cups) top-of-the-milk
1 oz. onion, grated
tomato paste
salt and pepper
1½ oz. walnuts, finely chopped

With a fork, work the cheese until creamy, adding the milk a little at a time. Beat in the grated onion, tomato paste to taste and seasoning. Finally, fold in the chopped walnuts. Serve with crisps, crackers and pretzels.

GLAZED BAKED GAMMON

gammon joint, approx. 5 lb.
2 onions, skinned and quartered
2 carrots, peeled and quartered
1 bay leaf
4 peppercorns
about 20 cloves
3–4 tbsps. brown sugar

Weigh the gammon, then calculate the cooking time, allowing 20–25 minutes per lb. plus 20 minutes over. Cover the joint with cold water and allow to soak for about 1 hour. Drain and place the gammon in a large pan, skin side down;

cover with fresh cold water and bring slowly to the boil, skimming off any scum that forms. Time the cooking from this point.

Add vegetables, bay leaf, peppercorns and 3 cloves, cover the pan and simmer gently for half the cooking time, then drain and wrap in foil. Bake in the centre of the oven at 350°F. (mark 4) until ½ hour before the cooking time is complete. Raise the oven heat to 425°F. (mark 7). Undo the foil, peel away the rind from the gammon, score the fat into diamonds, stud with cloves and sprinkle the surface with brown sugar. Return

scum with a spoon. Add remaining ingredients. Bring to the boil again, reduce heat and simmer the tongue until thoroughly tender. Allow about 1 hour per lb.

When cooked, plunge the tongue briefly into cold water. Ease off the skin while tongue is still hot and remove the small bones from the back of the tongue. Return meat to the cooking liquid to cool.

When cold, curl the tongue into a round soufflé dish or deep cake tin lined with foil. The container used should be large enough to take the tongue, leaving a few gaps.

Check that the cooking liquid will

Strawberry meringue slice is a delicious way of making a little fruit go a long way

SALMON CUTLETS IN ASPIC

10 salmon cutlets – 6–8 oz. each
butter
2 lemons
5 bay leaves
salt and white pepper
1 pint (2½ cups) aspic jelly made from aspic jelly powder
home-made mayonnaise
cucumber and lemon for garnish

Liberally butter 10 pieces ⊙ kitchen foil large enough to en

the joint to the oven until the fat is crisp and golden.

Allow to cool for serving.

PRESSED TONGUE

1 salted ox tongue (2½–3 lb.)
8 peppercorns
1 carrot, peeled and sliced
1 onion, skinned and studded with 3 cloves
1 bay leaf

Wash the tongue, and allow it to soak for 24 hours if highly salted. Put the tongue into a saucepan, just cover with cold water, cover and bring to the boil. Remove any

set when cold. If it does not set to a firm jelly, either reduce by boiling fast or add a little gelatine. Just cover the meat with cool, strained cooking liquid. Press either with a heavily weighted plate, or a tongue press. Chill until the juices have jellied and turn out.

TOMATO AND ONION SALAD

Skin and slice 30 tomatoes and arrange in dishes. Sprinkle with finely chopped onion, season and pour over ½ pint (1¼ cups) French dressing. Sprinkle with chopped fresh parsley and marjoram.

velop each cutlet. Lay a thin slic⊙ of lemon and half a bay leaf on eac⊙ cutlet; season and seal in foil. Plac⊙ on baking sheets and cook in th⊙ oven at 325°F. (mark 3) for abou⊙ 20 minutes. Chill in the foil.

Unwrap and discard the bay leave⊙ and lemon. Turn the cutlets upsid⊙ down on a wire rack placed over ⊙ baking sheet. Meanwhile make u⊙ the aspic jelly. When on the poin⊙ of setting, spoon over the cutlet⊙ Garnish with cucumber and lemon⊙ Serve mayonnaise separately.

Note: An 8-oz. cutlet will giv⊙ portions. To serve one cutlet pe⊙ person choose those cut fro⊙

the tail end, weighing 5–6 oz.
To make 1 pint mayonnaise:
Mix 4 egg yolks with 2 level
teaspoons each salt, dry mustard
and sugar and 1 level teaspoon
pepper. Add 1 pint salad oil drop
by drop, stirring briskly all the
time, until the sauce is smooth
and thick. Gradually add 4 tablespoons white vinegar and mix.

STUFFED PEPPER SALAD

2 red and 2 green peppers
   (capsicums), approx. 1 lb.
6 oz. cottage cheese
6 oz. cream cheese
chives, chopped
1 small onion, skinned and
   chopped
salt and pepper
parsley, chopped
watercress

Cut away a thin slice from the
stem end of each pepper. Wash
and remove seeds. Beat together
the cottage cheese, cream cheese,
chopped chives and chopped
onion, seasoning and parsley. Stuff
the seasoned cheese mixture into
the peppers, press firmly and chill
for about ½ hour.
To serve, slice the peppers and
arrange in rows. Garnish with
watercress sprigs.

STRAWBERRY MERINGUE
SLICE
make 2

6 egg whites from large eggs
12 oz. (1½ cups) caster sugar
½ pint (1¼ cups) double cream
¼ pint (⅝ cup) single cream
¾–1 lb. strawberries, hulled

On each of 3 pieces of non-
stick paper, mark with a pencil a
rectangle 12 in. by 4 in. Place on
baking sheets. In a deep bowl,
whisk the egg whites until stiff.
Add half the sugar and whisk again
until stiff enough to stand in firm
peaks. Fold in all but 3 level teaspoons of the remaining sugar.
Spread a thin film of meringue
over one of the rectangles to cover
well. Using a plain ½-in. vegetable
nozzle in a fabric forcing bag, pipe a
trellis across the base. Divide the
remainder of the meringue between the other rectangles and
level off smoothly. Dust each layer
with a teaspoon of caster sugar.
Dry the meringues in the oven set
on its lowest setting for about 4
hours. Peel the paper away. When
cold, store in an airtight container.
Whisk together the creams until
just stiff enough to hold the shape
of the whisk. Slice half the strawberries. Layer meringue with

about two-thirds of the cream and
the sliced fruit. Press the top lightly then pipe rosettes of cream over
it and decorate with the remaining
strawberries.

PINEAPPLE CHIFFON
FLAN
make 2

For flan crust :
8 oz. sweetmeal biscuits
   (2 cups crumbs)
4 oz. butter, melted
1 oz. caster sugar

For filling :
4 tbsps. water
2 level tsps. powdered gelatine
3 large eggs, separated
6 oz. (¾ cup) caster sugar
15-oz. can crushed pineapple,
   drained, or fresh pineapple
   in season
grated rind and juice of 1
   lemon
8 oz. full fat soft cream
   cheese
whipped cream for
   decoration

Crush the biscuits and blend the
crumbs with the butter and sugar.
Use to make a shell in a 10-in.
loose-bottomed French fluted flan
tin.
Pour the water into a cup and
sprinkle the gelatine over. Beat
egg yolks and 2 oz. sugar until pale,
add pineapple, lemon rind and
juice. Turn into saucepan and
cook, without boiling, until thick.
Blend in the soaked gelatine and
then the cream cheese. Cool until
on the point of setting.
Whisk the egg whites stiffly and
gradually whisk in 3 oz. sugar.
When it stands in firm peaks, fold
in remaining 1 oz. sugar and the
pineapple cheese. When beginning
to set, pile into the biscuit shell
and chill. To serve, remove flan
ring, mark into portions and pipe
a whirl of cream on each portion.

MENU *serves 12*

**CHICKEN MILLE
FEUILLES
HAM ROYALE
GALA SALAD WHEEL
JACKET POTATOES
AUTUMN MOUSSE**

Timetable
*Make the pastry layers and the
chicken mixture for the mille
feuilles the day before, also
stuffing for ham royale. Finish
off the savouries and salads on the
day. The mousse is also best made
the same day, but may be made
early in the morning.*

A biscuit crumb case and a cheesy filling make this unusual flan

CHICKEN MILLE
FEUILLES
make 2

8 oz. frozen puff pastry,
   thawed
8 oz. full fat cream cheese
2 tsps. lemon juice
4 level tsps. thick mayonnaise
¼ level tsp. salt
freshly ground black pepper
12 oz. cooked chicken flesh
3–4 lettuce leaves, finely
   shredded
¼ lb. firm tomatoes

Roll out pastry into a rectangle
12 in. by 11 in. (¼ in. thick). Prick
well and place on a dampened
baking sheet. Divide equally into
3 crosswise and separate slightly.
Bake at 400°F. (mark 6) for 20–25
minutes until well risen. Cool on a
wire rack.
In a bowl, using either a rotary
whisk or an electric blender, blend
together the cheese, lemon juice,
mayonnaise and seasonings. Cut
the chicken flesh into small manageable pieces and add two-thirds
to the creamed cheese mixture.
Spread lightly over the 3 pastry
layers and sprinkle shredded lettuce on top. Slice the tomatoes
thinly, cut in half again and
arrange over the lettuce.

Layer up the pastry and chicken
to form a loaf, top with remaining
chicken and tomatoes. To serve,
cut into thick slices, with a really
sharp knife.

HAM ROYALE

6 oz. (¾ cup) long grain rice
1 sachet of saffron
1 bay leaf
1½ tbsps. olive oil
6 oz. cooking apple, peeled
   and cored
1½ oz. butter
6 oz. onion, skinned and
   finely chopped
2 level tsps. curry powder
6 tbsps. single cream
1 small lemon
salt and pepper
1½ lb. sliced ham
10-oz. can sweet red peppers,
   (pimientos) drained
black olives, stoned
parsley

Cook the rice until tender in
boiling salted water to which the
saffron and bay leaf have been
added. Rinse the cooked rice in
cold water, drain and remove bay
leaf. Tip rice into a basin, add the
oil and fork it through the rice to
coat the grains.
Chop the apple finely. Melt the

Ham royale – thinly sliced ham with curry flavoured rice

Serve this asparagus quiche warm

butter in a saucepan and add the apple and onion. Cover with a lid and cook over gentle heat for 5 minutes. Sprinkle the mixture with the curry powder and cook for 1 minute longer. Remove from heat. Pour in the cream then blend it into the rice with the grated rind of the lemon and 3 tablespoons juice. Season well with salt and freshly ground black pepper. Reserve 12 slices of ham. Dice the remainder with 3 of the red peppers and fork this through the rice. Leave the mixture to stand for an hour or so to 'marry' the flavours. Divide the mixture between the ham slices and roll them up. Decorate the rolls with the remaining peppers cut into strips, stoned black olives and parsley sprigs.

Handy hint

A curdled mayonnaise means you have added the oil too quickly, or the ingredients were not all at room temperature. If this happens, start with a fresh basin and another egg yolk. Add the curdled mixture very slowly, drop by drop, to the fresh yolk, whisking all the time. (As slowly as you *should* have done it the first time!) The mayonnaise should now blend smoothly.

Salads are a favourite at any buffet party. Try courgettes and rice

GALA SALAD WHEEL

For tomato cups :

12 even-sized, firm tomatoes
¼ pint (⅝ cup) soured cream
¼ pint (⅝ cup) mayonnaise
¾ lb. hard white cabbage, finely shredded
12 black olives, stoned

For devilled eggs :

12 eggs, hard-boiled
3–4 tbsps. mayonnaise
1½–2 level tsps. curry powder

For mixed salad :

1 head of celery
2 eating apples, peeled and cored
1 onion, skinned and halved
½ pint (1¼ cups) French dressing
2 medium lettuces
2 lb. cold cuts (e.g. 1 lb. rare roast beef, ½ lb. garlic sausage, ½ lb. pork roll)
cress and ½ cucumber, sliced or 1 whole cucumber

Cut a thin slice from each of the tomatoes at the end opposite the stalk. With a teaspoon, carefully scoop out pips and core and discard. Drain the tomato cases upside down. Fold the soured cream into the mayonnaise. Stir in the shredded cabbage. Pile coleslaw mixture into the tomatoes and top each with an olive. Keep covered until required.

Cut the hard-boiled eggs in half lengthwise and remove the yolks. Cream the yolks with 3–4 tablespoons mayonnaise and the curry powder. Pipe back into the whites. Cover until required.

Finely chop the celery and apples and slice the onion very thinly. Mix with the French dressing. Just before arranging the wheel, add the lettuce, roughly torn.

Pile the celery salad in a pyramid on a large flat platter with any remaining cabbage salad. Twist and fold the cold cuts and arrange over the salad. Tuck bunches of cress in between. Edge the platter with tomato cups, devilled eggs and sliced cucumber. Top the pyramid with a tomato cup. Serve extra French dressing separately.

AUTUMN MOUSSE

3 small cans evaporated milk, pre-chilled in cans
4 level tbsps. powdered gelatine
6 tbsps. water
1½ pints (3¾ cups) sweetened damson or plum purée
6 egg whites, whisked

In a large bowl, whisk the evapor-

ated milk until double its volume. Soften the gelatine in the water, in a basin standing in a saucepan of hot water. When it is dissolved, slowly whisk into the evaporated milk. Gradually fold in the fruit purée. Fold the egg whites into the fruit and milk mixture. Turn into 2 ring moulds or soufflé dishes and chill. Serve with thick pouring cream.

If you do not have an electric mixer, it will be easier to make this quantity of mousse in 2 lots.

MENU *serves 12*

TUNAFISH CREAMS
ASPARAGUS QUICHE
COLD ROAST CHICKEN
CABBAGE AND PINEAPPLE SALAD
COURGETTE AND RICE SALAD
STRAWBERRIES WITH MACAROONS

Timetable

Prepare pâté and quiches the day before and roast the chicken. (Do not put the quiches in the refrigerator—just keep in a cool place.) Carve the chicken, cover until ready to serve with plastic film. Prepare the salads and sweet on the day. To heat up the quiches, put them on baking sheets in the oven at 400°F. (mark 6) for about 15 minutes.

TUNAFISH CREAMS

¾ pint (2 cups) soured cream
4 tbsps. mayonnaise
salt and pepper
good dash of Worcestershire sauce
1 tbsp. chopped chives
4 tsps. capers, chopped
1 level tsp. finely grated onion
½ oz. powdered gelatine
4 tbsps. water
2 7-oz. cans tuna steak, drained and flaked
4 eggs, hard-boiled and chopped
3 firm tomatoes for garnish
parsley

Combine the soured cream, mayonnaise, seasonings, herbs and onion. Dissolve the gelatine in the water in a basin over a pan of hot water. Cool slightly and stir into the cream mixture; add the tuna steak and eggs and mix well.

Spoon into individual soufflé dishes and chill until set. To serve, garnish with tomato wedges and parsley.

SPARAGUS QUICHE

'or pastry :

o oz. ($2\frac{1}{2}$ cups) plain flour
ood pinch of salt
oz. butter or margarine
oz. lard
oz. ($\frac{1}{2}$ cup) Cheddar cheese, grated

'or filling :

8-oz. pkts. frozen asparagus spears, thawed, or 2 $7\frac{1}{2}$-oz. cans, drained
pint ($\frac{5}{8}$ cup) double cream
pint ($1\frac{1}{4}$ cups) single cream
alt and freshly ground black pepper
eggs, beaten
$\frac{1}{2}$ oz. Parmesan cheese, freshly grated

ift the flour and salt together and ub in the fats with the fingertips, ntil the mixture resembles fine rumbs. Stir in the cheese. With ne hand, collect the dough together and knead lightly to give a mooth dough. Roll out the pastry nd use to line 2 flan rings, 8 in. nd 9 in. diameter, placed on aking sheets.

'rim the asparagus from the nd opposite the head to fit the astry cases, cut up remaining ieces and place in the base of ach case. Arrange trimmed spears s the spokes of a wheel in each an.

Mix together the creams, salt and epper, eggs and Parmesan. Pour ver asparagus. Bake at 400°F. mark 6) for about 40 minutes ntil filling is set and pastry olden. Serve warm.

f this flan is stored in a re- rigerator, the pastry will go soft, o cover and store in a cool lace. Reheat in the oven at 400°F. mark 6) for 15 minutes.

:ABBAGE AND 'INEAPPLE SALAD

firm cabbage (e.g. Dutch or Savoy)
eating apples, peeled and cored
large can of pineapple pieces
sticks of celery, scrubbed and chopped
pint ($1\frac{1}{4}$ cups) mayonnaise
alt and pepper

Vash the cabbage, shred it and oak in really cold water for about 5 minutes to crisp it. Dice the pples.

Drain the cabbage and mix with ne drained pineapple, apples and elery. Season the mayonnaise well, our over and toss until every- hing is well coated.

Sherry-soaked macaroons, cream and strawberries – delicious

COURGETTE AND RICE SALAD

8 courgettes (zucchini)
8 oz. (1 cup) long grain rice
4 tomatoes
16 black olives
French dressing
fresh mint
4 tsps. chopped basil

Slice the courgettes, discarding a thin slice from the top and bottom, and cook (without peeling) in boiling salted water until just tender but still crisp. Drain well. Boil the rice, drain and allow to dry a little. Slice the tomatoes; stone and halve the olives. Mix the courgettes and olives with the rice, toss in the dressing and pile into a dish; surround with tomato slices. Spoon a little more dressing over the tomatoes and garnish with herbs.

FRENCH DRESSING

makes $\frac{1}{3}$ pint ($\frac{7}{8}$ cup)

Put 1 level teaspoon each of salt, dry mustard and sugar and $\frac{1}{2}$ level teaspoon pepper in a bowl with 4 tablespoons vinegar. Stir until well blended. With a fork, beat in 8 tablespoons salad oil. Beat again before using.

STRAWBERRIES WITH MACAROONS

This dessert is reminiscent of the traditional English trifle, but less substantial. It can be made in 1 large dish, but is more attractive in individual portions

3 3-oz. pkts. macaroons
6 tbsps. sherry
6 tbsps. fresh orange juice
$1\frac{1}{2}$ lb. fresh strawberries
icing sugar
$\frac{3}{4}$ pint (2 cups) double cream
3 tbsps. milk

Use twelve small, straight-sided glasses. Place a few macaroons in the base of each glass, reserving 12. Mix the sherry and orange juice and spoon over the macaroons. Leave to stand for about 1 hour to soften the macaroons. Reserve 12 of the best strawberries. Hull and slice the rest and divide between the glasses. Lightly dust with icing sugar. Whip the cream and milk together until it just holds its shape. Take the 12 reserved strawberries, split almost down to the stem end. Open them out and pipe in a rosette of cream. Pipe the remaining cream over the sliced strawberries. Top each glass with a split strawberry and a macaroon. Chill before serving.

MENU *serves 20*

QUICHE LORRAINE
RARE ROAST BEEF
PATE STUFFED CHICKEN
LES CRUDITES
WALDORF SALAD
GARLIC BREAD
MOUSSES AU CHOCOLAT
WINTER FRUIT SALAD

Timetable

Roast beef, stuff chicken but do not coat with crumbs, and make quiches the day before. Also prepare sweets. Coat and bake chicken, prepare salads and garlic bread on the day. Heat up quiches and garlic bread together just before serving.

QUICHE LORRAINE

make 2

8 oz. frozen puff pastry, thawed
6–8 oz. lean bacon rashers, rinded and chopped
6–8 oz. Gruyère cheese, thinly sliced
4 eggs, beaten
$\frac{1}{2}$ pint ($1\frac{1}{4}$ cups) single cream or creamy milk
salt and pepper

Roll out the pastry thinly and line a 10-in. plain flan ring or sandwich cake tin, making a double edge. Cover the bacon with boiling water and leave for 2–3 minutes, then drain well. Put into the pastry cases with the cheese. Mix the eggs and cream, season well and pour into the case. Bake towards the top of the oven at 400°F. (mark 6) for about 40 minutes until filling is set and pastry golden.

Handy hint

If you use a glass or earthenware flan case rather than a metal ring and baking sheet, the pastry on the bottom will take longer to cook. To overcome this, put a baking sheet in the oven when you light it and put the flan case on to the hot baking sheet. This helps to cook the underside of the pastry.

Pâté stuffed chicken – a soft, rich filling and a crisp outside

PATE STUFFED CHICKEN

20 chicken leg portions
2¼ lb. well seasoned liver pâté
6 eggs
6 tbsps. water
2¼ lb. fresh breadcrumbs
salt and pepper
8 oz. butter

Remove the chicken skin. Using a small, sharp knife, carefully work the flesh off the bone from the thigh downwards. Take care not to split the flesh. Stuff each chicken portion with pâté, pushing the filling in from the thigh end. Reshape the flesh and fasten well together, using wooden cocktail sticks. Leave in the refrigerator for at least 1 hour to firm up.

Remove cocktail sticks. Beat the eggs and water together. Dip the chicken joints one at a time in the glaze, coating them evenly, then coat with seasoned breadcrumbs. Pat the crumbs on well. Recoat with egg and crumbs on top of the first coating. Choose 2 ovenproof dishes large enough to take the chicken joints in a single layer. Divide the butter between the dishes and melt. Place the chicken in the hot butter. Bake uncovered at 350°F. (mark 4) for 30 minutes. Carefully turn the chicken over

and bake for a further 30 minutes. Raise the temperature to 400°F. (mark 6) and cook for a further 20 minutes until crisp and golden. Serve hot or cold.

LES CRUDITES

½ pint (1¼ cups) salad oil
4 tbsps. wine vinegar
4 tbsps. lemon juice
1 level tsp. caster sugar
1 level tsp. salt
1 level tsp. dry mustard
freshly ground black pepper
1 lb. tomatoes, skinned
**1 lb. pkt. frozen broad beans
  or shelled fresh**
**1 each, red and green
  peppers (capsicums),
  seeded**
1 lb. carrots, peeled
bunch of radishes
**1 lb. celeriac, peeled, or
  celery, scrubbed**
½ lb. salami, thinly sliced
black olives
chopped parsley

Whisk together the oil, vinegar, lemon juice, sugar and seasonings. Slice the tomatoes; cook the beans in boiling salted water and remove the outer skin if tough; thinly slice the peppers; coarsely grate the carrots; top and tail the radishes;

thinly slice the celeriac and cut into thin strips. Marinade each prepared vegetable separately in a little of the dressing, for a short time.

Arrange the vegetables separately in mounds, on 2 large platters, adding the sliced salami and black olives. Garnish with a little chopped parsley.

WALDORF SALAD

2 lb. crisp eating apples
lemon juice
2 level tsps. sugar
½ pint (1¼ cups) mayonnaise
1 head of celery, chopped
4 oz. (1 cup) walnuts, chopped
1 lettuce
few whole walnuts

Peel and core the apples, slice 2 and dice the rest; dip the slices in lemon juice to prevent discolouration. Toss the diced apples with 4 tablespoons lemon juice, the sugar and 2 tablespoons mayonnaise and leave to stand for about ½ hour. Just before serving, add the celery, walnuts and remaining mayonnaise and toss together.

Serve in a bowl lined with lettuce leaves and garnish with the apple slices and a few whole walnuts.

GARLIC BREAD

For each French loaf allow ½ lb. butter and 2 cloves of garlic, skinned and crushed.

Cut the loaves into thick slices, without completely separating the slices, so that the loaf appears to be hinged. Cream the butter with the garlic and spread between the slices. Wrap each loaf loosely in kitchen foil and place in the oven at 325°F. (mark 3) for 15 minutes. Raise the temperature to 450°F. (mark 8), take out the loaves, fold back the foil and return to the oven for a further 10 minutes to crisp.

MOUSSES AU CHOCOLAT

3 small oranges
3 tbsps. orange liqueur
**18 oz. Menier or plain (dark)
  chocolate**
6 oz. butter
9 large eggs, separated
6 oz. (¾ cup) caster sugar
**6 oz. plain (dark) chocolate
  for decoration**

Cut thin slices of peel, free from all traces of white pith, from one orange and half of another. Cut these into thin strips and blanch them in boiling water until tender. Remove, drain, then macerate them in the orange liqueur.

Melt the 18 oz. Menier chocola[te] in a basin over a pan of hot wate[r.] Cut the butter into small piece[s.] When the chocolate has melte[d,] remove it from the heat and mix [in] the pieces of butter. Put the eg[g] whites into a large bowl and chill [in] the refrigerator. Finely grate th[e] rind from the remaining orange[s.] Whisk the egg yolks with half th[e] sugar and the grated orange rin[d] until fluffy. Add the chocola[te] mixture slowly with 4 tablespoo[ns] orange juice and the liqueu[r] drained from the strips of orang[e] peel.

Stiffly whisk the egg whites, grad[u]ally adding remaining sugar. Fo[ld] the chocolate mixture even[ly] through the egg whites. Pour th[e] mousse into individual glasses an[d] chill.

Decorate with grated plain choco[c]late and the shredded orange pee[l.] If you do not have an electr[ic] mixer, you will find it easier t[o] make this quantity in 2 lots.

WINTER FRUIT SALAD

12 oz. (1½ cups) sugar
1½ pints (3¾ cups) water
rind and juice of 3 lemons
12 oz. prunes, stewed
12 oz. dried apricots, stewed
3 bananas, skinned and slice[d]
**6 oranges, skinned and
  segmented**
**3 grapefruit, skinned and
  segmented**

Make a syrup by dissolving th[e] sugar in the water over a gentl[e] heat; add the lemon rind, hea[t] gently and boil for 5 minute[s.] Add the lemon juice, strain th[e] syrup over the prepared fruit an[d] leave to cool.

Hot French bread with garlic butter is a tasty buffet filler

Formal Buffets

Enjoy entertaining at home—there's no
need to worry if you follow our menus
and timetables

Several days before: *Make florentine cornets and shortcake; store in airtight tins.*
Day before: *Stuff and roast turkey. Make galantine. Prepare salad vegetables. Make mayonnaise and salad dressings.*
In the morning: *Carve turkey. Make fruit salad.*
2 hours before: *Put potatoes to cook. Finish shortcake gâteaux. Make up prawn cocktails. Finish and dress salads.*

PRAWN COCKTAIL

2 lettuces, washed and
   shredded
1¼ lb. peeled prawns
cucumber slices, capers or
   lemon wedges to garnish

For dressing:
½ pint (1¼ cups) mayonnaise
½ pint (1¼ cups) tomato
   ketchup
½ pint (1¼ cups) single cream
salt and pepper
juice of 1 lemon or a few
   drops of Worcestershire
   sauce

Line 20 small glasses with the shredded lettuce. Mix together the dressing ingredients and combine the prawns with the dressing. Pile into the glasses and garnish.

COLD ROAST TURKEY

15-lb. turkey, dressed weight

For stuffing:
3 oz. bacon, rinded and
   chopped
6 oz. fresh white breadcrumbs
1½ tsps. chopped parsley
1½ oz. butter, melted
grated rind of 1 large lemon
12 oz. chestnut purée (see
   below)
salt and freshly ground
   black pepper
1–2 eggs, beaten

First prepare the stuffing. Fry the bacon gently in its own fat for 3–5 minutes, until crisp. Drain and add the breadcrumbs, parsley, butter, lemon rind and chestnut purée. Season well and bind with as much of the beaten egg as necessary.
Stuff the neck cavity of the turkey, wrap the bird in aluminium foil and cook in the oven at 450°F. (mark 8) for 4¼–4½ hours. Open the foil for the last 30 minutes of cooking time to allow the bird to brown.
Alternatively, wrap the bird in a large roasting bag or film and cook according to the manufacturer's instructions.
Served cold, the breast meat can be sliced and replaced on the carcass.

To make chestnut purée: Boil 1 lb. chestnuts for 2 minutes to soften the skins, remove them from the heat and peel them quickly while hot.
Simmer the peeled chestnuts in just enough milk to cover for about 40 minutes, until they are soft. Push them through a sieve or purée in a blender.
If you use canned chestnut purée, be sure to choose a type that is not sweetened.

PORK AND HAM GALANTINE

1½ lb. each lean raw pork and
   lean cooked ham
1½ level tbsps. finely chopped
   onion
¼ pint (⅝ cup) thick white sauce
2 eggs
pepper and salt
½ level tsp. each dried
   rosemary and savory
thinly cut rashers of back
   bacon, rinded
½ pint (1¼ cups) aspic jelly and
   sliced radishes, to garnish

Put the pork, ham and onion through the mincer twice. Blend with the white sauce, eggs and seasonings. Shape together into a roll about 3 in. diameter.
Scald a cloth (a double thickness of old white sheet is suitable), dredge with flour. Lay the rashers of bacon overlapping each other on the cloth. Lay the roll on the bacon and roll up the cloth so that the bacon covers the roll. Tie the ends of the cloth tightly with fine string or coarse thread.
Boil the roll gently in water with flavouring root vegetables, a little vinegar and salt for about 2½ hours.
Place a saucer or similar utensil in the base of the pan to prevent the roll coming directly in contact with the base.
Remove the roll and leave to cool under a board and weights, ensuring that the attractive pattern of the bacon is uppermost. When it is quite cold remove cloth and place galantine on a wire rack over a plate.
Make up the aspic and cool until it is the consistency of unbeaten egg white, spoon it over the meat. Repeat until the galantine is well glazed.
Garnish with slices of radish also dipped in aspic.

Prawn cocktail – a popular and refreshing start to a buffet meal

SALAD ROMANA

2 pkts. Italian dressing mix
2 tbsps. water
3 tbsps. cider vinegar
½ pint (1¼ cups) soured cream
1 firm white cabbage, finely
  shredded
4 oz. salted nuts, chopped
4 dates, stoned and chopped
2 apples, cored and chopped
2 level tsps. celery seeds
a little paprika pepper

Put the Italian dressing mix in a ½-pint screw-top jar, add the water and shake. Add the vinegar and soured cream and again shake very

MUSHROOM SALAD

1 lb. open mushrooms
2 tbsps. lemon juice or cider
  vinegar
⅓ pint (⅝ cup) salad oil
2 tbsps. finely chopped
  parsley
freshly ground black pepper
salt

Wash and dry the mushrooms, but do not peel; remove the stalks. Slice the mushrooms very thinly into a serving dish and add the lemon juice, oil, parsley and pepper. Marinade in the dressing for at least ½ hour and salt lightly just before serving.

FRUITS IN SYRUP

1 lb. (2 cups) sugar
1 pint (2½ cups) water
4 tbsps. orange liqueur
2 tbsps. lemon juice
8–12 peaches
1½ lb. white grapes
1½ lb. raspberries

FLORENTINE CORNETS
makes about 15

3½ oz. butter
4 oz. (½ cup) caster sugar
4 oz. almonds, finely chopped
1 oz. sultanas, chopped
1 oz. glacé cherries, chopped
1 oz. mixed candied peel,
  finely chopped
1 tbsp. top-of-the-milk or
  single cream

Melt the butter in a saucepan, add the caster sugar and boil together for 1 minute, stirring. Stir in the remaining ingredients. Cool the mixture for a few minutes and then

RASPBERRY SHORTCAKE GATEAU
make 2

10 oz. (2½ cups) plain flour
2 oz. ground rice
8 oz. butter
4 oz. (½ cup) caster sugar
finely grated rind of 1 lemon
2 oz. shelled walnuts, finely
  chopped
1 egg yolk
½ pint (1¼ cups) double cream
2 15½-oz. cans raspberries or
  loganberries, well drained,
  or 1 lb. fresh fruit
icing sugar

Place the flour, ground rice, butter, sugar and lemon rind in a bowl and rub in until the mixture resembles fine breadcrumbs. Add the walnuts and egg yolk and knead together to give a soft dough. Wrap in a polythene bag and chill for 30 minutes. Roll two-thirds of the dough into a rectangle 12 in. by 6 in. and place carefully on a baking sheet. Roll out the remainder, cut into 6 3-in. rounds with a fluted pastry cutter and cut each in half. Place on a baking sheet.
Bake at 350°F. (mark 4), allowing about 30 minutes for the rectangle and about 20 minutes for the semicircles, until light brown and firm. While still warm on the baking sheet, cut the rectangle in half lengthwise with a sharp knife. Cool. Wrap in foil to store.
Just before use, whip the cream until stiff and using a large rose vegetable nozzle, pipe two-thirds of the cream in a thick line down the centre of 1 walnut shortbread. Spoon most of the fruit over the cream, put the second piece of shortbread on top, press down lightly and pipe the remaining cream in whirls down the centre. Arrange the semi-circles along the cream and put a whole berry in between each.

A crisp shortcake forms the basis of this attractive raspberry gâteau

thoroughly. In a large bowl, toss together the cabbage, nuts, dates, apple and celery seeds. Pour the dressing over and mix thoroughly with a fork. Dredge lightly with paprika pepper.

Dissolve the sugar in the water, bring to the boil and boil for 5 minutes. Turn into a bowl, add the liqueur and lemon juice. Allow to cool.
Skin and halve the peaches and discard the stones. Keep the grapes whole and carefully remove the pips with the curved end of a sterilized hair grip.
Arrange the peach halves round a shallow dish, and pile the grapes and raspberries in the centre. Spoon over the sugar syrup and leave for at least 2–3 hours before serving, spooning the juices over from time to time.

drop it in small heaps on to baking sheets lined with non-stick paper; keep these heaps well apart, allowing only about 4–5 to each baking sheet.
Bake in rotation towards the top of the oven at 350°F. (mark 4) for about 10 minutes until golden and bubbling. Leave them on the sheets to cool until it is possible to handle them, then lift each one on a palette knife and roll round a cream horn tin. When cold, remove the tin by twisting.
These cornets will store in an airtight tin for 2–3 days. Separate the layers with non-stick paper.

Handy hint

When using powdered gelatine, always soak it in a little cold water for a few minutes to allow it to swell, then place the basin over a pan of hot water to dissolve the gelatine completely.

CHILLED MELON
SEAFOOD QUICHES
ROAST BEEF
PATE STUFFED HAM
CORNETS
DRESSED LEEKS
DRESSED MACARONI AND
MUSHROOMS
PLATTER SALAD
PEACH AND APPLE
SOUFFLE
GINGER CREAM TRIFLES

Day before: *Mix dry ingredients for pastry. Roast beef. Make ham cornets, cover and refrigerate. Make salad dressings and soufflé.*
In the morning: *Prepare salad vegetables but not apples. Prepare filling for quiches; add water and roll out pastry and line patty pans. Cut melon, cover and keep in a cool place, not refrigerator. Carve beef, arrange on serving platters; cover with polythene and keep in a cool place. Make ginger cream trifles.*
Before serving: *Fill and start to cook quiches 1 hour ahead. Arrange the salad platter and dress salads 1 hour before. Remove soufflé and ham cornets from refrigerator 30 minutes before serving.*

SEAFOOD QUICHES

12 oz. shortcrust pastry – i.e.
12 oz. (3 cups) flour, etc.

For filling:
4 oz. shelled prawns
4 oz. smoked salmon (freshly cut or canned)
1 pint (2½ cups) single cream
8 egg yolks
salt and freshly ground black pepper
2 tbsps. chopped parsley

Roll out the pastry and use to line 12 4¼-in. fluted patty pans. Roughly chop the prawns and cut the salmon into narrow strips; divide the fish equally between the uncooked pastry cases. Beat together the cream and egg yolks and season to taste (remember that the salmon is on the salt side). Add the chopped parsley.
Place the pastry cases on baking sheets and spoon in the filling. Bake in the oven at 400°F. (mark 6) for 10 minutes, then reduce the heat to 350°F. (mark 4) and cook for a further 20–25 minutes, until the pastry is beginning to colour and the filling is lightly set. Serve warm.

Spicy ginger cream trifles are simple to make

COLD ROAST BEEF

5 lb. sirloin of beef, boned and rolled

Roast the meat in the oven at 425°F. (mark 7) for 15 minutes per lb. and 15 minutes extra. Allow to cool.
To serve, slice thinly, fold each slice in half and arrange neatly on a meat dish.

PATE STUFFED HAM CORNETS

½ lb. thinly sliced, cooked ham (6 slices)
4 oz. butter
8-oz. can pâté with truffles
2 black olives
½ pint (1¼ cups) aspic jelly made from aspic jelly powder
watercress

Cut each slice of ham in half, to give 12 slices. Wrap each piece round a 4-in. long cream horn tin and place join side down on a baking sheet. Slip the sheet into a large polythene bag and leave in the refrigerator for 10 minutes to firm.
Cream together the butter and pâté until of a piping consistency. Spoon into a piping bag fitted with a star nozzle. Carefully remove the cream horn tins from inside the ham, 1 at a time, and pipe in the pâté. Place the cornets on a wire rack. Cut away 6 lengthwise segments from each olive and press a piece into the pâté in each cornet to decorate. Return the cornets to the refrigerator.
Make up the aspic jelly and when on the point of setting spoon over the ham cornets. Chill. Serve garnished with watercress.

DRESSED LEEKS

2½ lb. leeks
7 tbsps. salad oil
2 tbsps. cider vinegar
¾ level tsp. French mustard
1 oz. finely chopped onion
1½ level tsps. caster sugar
scant ½ level tsp. salt
freshly ground black pepper

Trim about half the green part from the leeks. Cut the remainder of the leeks into ⅛-in. slices and wash thoroughly in cold water. Drain, blanch in boiling salted water for 3–4 minutes, then cool quickly with cold water. Drain well.
Shake the remaining ingredients together in a screw-top jar, pour over the leeks and toss together.

DRESSED MACARONI AND MUSHROOMS

1 lb. quick-cooking macaroni
½ lb. button mushrooms
1 clove garlic, skinned and crushed
4 tbsps. lemon juice
2 tbsps. wine or cider vinegar
salt and black pepper
1 large red pepper (capsicum), seeded and chopped
1 large green pepper (capsicum), seeded and chopped
¼ pint (⅝ cup) thick mayonnaise
5 fl. oz. natural yoghourt
chopped parsley

Cook macaroni in boiling salted water. Drain and rinse under cold running water. Thinly slice the mushrooms and place in a bowl with the garlic, lemon juice, vinegar, salt and pepper. Leave to

marinade for 30 minutes, stirring frequently.
Blanch the peppers for 1 minute, rinse in cold water and drain. Blend together the mayonnaise and yoghourt; add to the mushrooms and mix well, then stir in the peppers. Toss through the macaroni until well coated in dressing. Turn into a serving dish.

PLATTER SALAD

½ lb. each red and green eating apples, wiped and cored
2 oz. walnuts, chopped
1 small head of celery, scrubbed and chopped
¼ pint (⅝ cup) lemon dressing (see below)
small punnet of cress
1 cucumber (or 2 small ridge cucumbers), sliced
bunch of radishes, washed and trimmed
1 lb. chicory, washed and sliced (optional)
chopped parsley and chives

Dice the apples and mix with the walnuts and chopped celery. Spoon over the lemon dressing and toss well. Arrange down the centre of a flat platter.
Wash and trim the cress and arrange down either side of the apple salad. Add the cucumber slices, sliced radishes and finally the chicory. Sprinkle the whole platter with the chopped herbs.
Lemon dressing: Thoroughly season 2–3 tablespoons salad oil with salt and pepper; blend well with a fork and whisk in 1 tablespoon lemon juice.

PEACH AND APPLE SOUFFLE

1¼ lb. cooking apples, peeled and cored
15½-oz. can peach slices
6 eggs, separated
10 oz. (1¼ cups) caster sugar
2 tbsps. lemon juice
5 level tsps. powdered gelatine
3 tbsps. water
2 tbsps. orange liqueur
¼ pint (⅝ cup) single cream
½ pint (1¼ cups) double cream
few frosted black grapes (see below)

Prepare a 2½-pint soufflé dish by tying a double band of greaseproof or non-stick paper round the outside of the dish, to stand 3 in. above the rim. Slice the apples into a pan and stew in 6 tablespoons syrup from the peaches until soft; cool. Sieve or purée in a blender with the drained peaches.

lace the egg yolks, sugar and emon juice in a bowl over a pan f hot water and whisk until very nick and creamy, when the whisk hould leave a trail. Remove from ne heat and whisk until cool. Dissolve the gelatine in 3 tablepoons water in a basin over a pan f hot water and cool slightly. Whisk the fruit purée into the egg nixture followed by the gelatine nd liqueur. Whisk the creams ogether until thick but not stiff nd fold into the mixture. Finally, tiffly beat the egg whites and old in. Turn into the prepared oufflé dish and chill until set.

Using a round bladed knife, remove the paper collar from the oufflé and decorate the top with rosted grapes.

To frost grapes: Dip the wiped rapes in egg white then coat horoughly with caster sugar and eave to dry.

GINGER CREAM TRIFLES
makes 12

pkts. soft sponge fingers
apricot jam
lb. stem ginger
bottle sherry
½ pints (3¾ cups) double cream, lightly whipped
oz. almonds, blanched and halved

Halve the sponge fingers and spread thickly with apricot jam. Sandwich together and cut into -in. pieces. Divide between 12 undae glasses. Finely chop the tem ginger, set aside one-third and mix the remainder with the ponge pieces. Pour about 2 tablepoons sherry into each dish and eave it to soak into the sponge. Spoon the cream over the sponge mixture and decorate with halved blanched almonds and the remaining ginger.

WEDDING MENU *serves 30*

CONSOMME INDIENNE
ROQUEFORT TOMATOES
SALMON AND MAYONNAISE VERTE
CUCUMBER CHARTREUSE
GREEN SALAD
POTATO SALAD LOAF
FRENCH BREAD AND BUTTER
STRAWBERRY NUT MERINGUES
WEDDING CAKE

In advance: *Make and ice cake (see recipe).*
Several days before: *Make*

Poached salmon is an impressive central display for a buffet

consommé and chill. Make meringues and store in airtight tin. Make mayonnaise and French dressing; store in a screw-top jar.
Day before: *Poach salmon. Make cucumber chartreuse and potato salad loaf. Make curry cream for consommé. Prepare salad vegetables. Hull strawberries and whip cream. Prepare the table, except for the food.*
In the morning: *Prepare Roquefort tomatoes. Dish up consommé and add topping. Unmould cucumber chartreuse and potato salad loaf, but keep covered. Finish strawberry nut meringues. Set foods out at last possible minute.*

CONSOMME INDIENNE
make 2 lots

5 pints (12½ cups) brown stock, cold
½ lb. lean beefsteak, e.g. rump
12½ fl. oz. (1½ cups) water
2 large carrots, peeled and quartered
2 large onions, skinned and quartered
a bouquet garni
2 egg whites
salt
5 tsps. sherry, optional
6 tbsps. chopped fresh herbs (chives, parsley and tarragon)
1 level tsp. curry powder
½ pint (1¼ cup) double cream, whipped
1 oz. flaked almonds, toasted

Remove any fat from the stock. Shred the meat finely and soak it in the water for 15 minutes. Put the meat and water, vegetables, stock

and bouquet garni into a large, deep pan; add the egg whites. Heat gently and whisk continuously with a balloon whisk until a thick froth starts to form.

Stop whisking and bring to the boil. Reduce the heat immediately and simmer for 2 hours. If the liquid boils too rapidly, the froth will break and cloud the consommé.

Scald a clean cloth or jelly bag, wring it out, tie to the legs of an upturned stool and place a large bowl underneath. Pour the soup through, keeping the froth back at first with a spoon, then let it slide out on to the cloth.

Again pour the soup through the cloth and the filter of egg white. Adjust seasoning and add a little sherry if required, to improve the flavour.

Stir in the fresh chopped herbs and leave the consommé to cool and set.

To serve, break up the jellied consommé and serve in individual dishes. Stir the curry powder into the whipped cream, spoon a little over each serving and sprinkle with toasted almonds.

ROQUEFORT TOMATOES

30 large, firm tomatoes, skinned
1 lb. cream cheese
12 oz. Roquefort or Stilton cheese
8 oz. celery, scrubbed and finely chopped
8 oz. walnuts, finely chopped
1 pint (2½ cups) double cream
salt and pepper
chopped parsley

Remove a slice from the round end

of each tomato. Carefully scoop out the core and seeds with the handle of a teaspoon. Leave tomatoes upside down to drain. Beat together the cheeses and stir in the celery and nuts. Lightly whip the cream, stir into the cheese mixture and adjust the seasoning.

Pile the cheese filling into the tomato cases and replace the 'lids'. Garnish with chopped parsley.

COLD POACHED SALMON

1 large salmon (or fresh tuna fish), scaled and cleaned, about 12 lb.
court bouillon (see below)
1 pint mayonnaise

Prepare the fish. Fill a fish kettle with just enough court bouillon to cover the salmon. Bring to the boil, lower in the salmon and boil gently for 10 minutes only. Remove the fish kettle from the heat, take off the lid and leave until cold.

To serve, arrange the fish whole on a long dish, garnished with radishes and cucumber, and serve the mayonnaise separately.

Alternatively remove the skin and coat the fish evenly with the mayonnaise, surrounding it with a garnish of salad vegetables.

COURT BOUILLON

1½ pints (3¾ cups) water
½ pint (1¼ cups) dry white wine
1 small carrot, peeled and sliced
1 small onion, skinned and sliced
1 small stalk of celery, scrubbed and chopped (optional)
1 tbsp. vinegar or lemon juice
a few sprigs of parsley
½ a bay leaf
3–4 peppercorns
2 level tsps. salt

Place all the ingredients in a pan, bring to the boil and simmer for about 30 minutes. Allow the liquid to cool and strain before using.

MAYONNAISE VERTE

watercress leaves
1–2 sprigs of fresh tarragon or chervil
a few parsley sprigs
thick mayonnaise
1 tbsp. double cream, lightly whipped

Chop the watercress leaves and herbs very finely. Just before serving, add the mayonnaise and cream.

CUCUMBER CHARTREUSE
make 2

2 lime jelly tablets
1–1½ pints (2½–3½ cups) hot water
½ pint (1¼ cups) cider vinegar
1 level tbsp. sugar
green colouring
1 lb. cucumber, peeled and diced
small tomatoes, skinned

Break up the lime jelly tablets and place in a 2-pint (5-cup) measure. Make up to 1½ pints (3¾ cups) with hot water and stir until the jelly has dissolved. Add the cider vinegar, the sugar and a few drops of green colouring and leave to cool until of the consistency of unbeaten egg white. Fold in the cucumber; when it is evenly suspended, pour the mixture into a 3-pint ring jelly mould. Leave in a cool place to set. To serve, unmould and fill the centre with tomatoes.

POTATO SALAD LOAF
make 3

1½ lb. potatoes, peeled and diced
6 oz. sliced ham roll
2 level tsps. powdered gelatine
1 tbsp. water
3 tbsps. salad cream
1 small onion, grated or finely chopped
3 gherkins or olives, chopped
1 tsp. chopped chives or parsley
salt and pepper
1 egg, hard-boiled

Line a loaf tin measuring 8½ in. by 4½ in. with greaseproof paper, letting the paper extend about 2 in. above the rim.
Cook the prepared potatoes in boiling salted water for about 10 minutes until just tender but not mushy. Drain. Rinse in cold water. Line the tin with slices of ham roll and dice the remainder of the meat.
Put the gelatine and water in a small bowl and stand it over a pan of hot water until dissolved. Mix the gelatine with the salad cream and pour over the potatoes. Add the onion, gherkins or olives, chives or parsley and seasoning. Mix well.
Place half the mixture in the ham-lined tin. Cover with diced ham, add the remaining potato mixture. Level the top and fold the paper over. Chill. Just before serving, unfold the paper, invert the loaf tin on to a serving dish and remove the paper. Decorate with sliced hard-boiled egg.

A loaf-shaped mould will add interest to a potato salad

STRAWBERRY NUT MERINGUES
makes 36

14 oz. (3 cups) icing sugar, sifted
6 egg whites
9 oz. almonds, blanched and finely chopped
almond essence
1 pint (2½ cups) double cream, whipped
36 large, whole strawberries, hulled

Line 2 baking sheets with silicone (non-stick) paper.
Put the icing sugar in a bowl with the egg whites and place over a saucepan of hot water. Whisk steadily with a rotary whisk or electric beater until the mixture forms stiff peaks.
Remove the bowl from the heat and stir in the nuts and a few drops of essence. Drop spoonfuls of the mixture on to the baking sheets and flatten with a palette knife into small discs about 2 in. across.
Bake in the oven at 300°F. (mark 1–2) for about 30 minutes, until the meringue is crisp on the outside and creamy in colour. Remove from the baking sheet and cool on a wire rack.
To serve, pipe a border of cream round each and place a large strawberry in the centre.

WEDDING CAKE
This recipe is for a 3 tier cake which will serve approximately 150 people.
For a small wedding a single tier is probably more practical;
a 12 in. cake serves approx. 100
an 8 in. cake serves approx. 30
a 6 in. cake serves approx. 20

For the bottom tier:
3 lb. 2 oz. currants
1 lb. 3 oz. sultanas
1 lb. 3 oz. raisins, stoned
12 oz. glacé cherries
1 lb. 13 oz. (7¼ cups) plain flour
3 level tsps. ground cinnamon
1½ level tsps. ground mace
grated rind of 1 lemon
1 lb. 12 oz. butter
1 lb. 12 oz. (4½ cups) light soft brown sugar
14 eggs, beaten
9 oz. mixed chopped peel
9 oz. (1½ cups) nibbed almonds
5 tbsps. brandy

For the 2 upper tiers:
1 lb. 8 oz. currants
10 oz. sultanas
10 oz. stoned raisins
7 oz. glacé cherries
1 lb. 2 oz. (4½ cups) plain flour
1¾ level tsps. ground cinnamon
1 level tsp. ground mace
grated rind of ¼ lemon
15 oz. butter
15 oz. (2½ cups) light soft brown sugar
8 eggs, beaten
4 oz. mixed chopped peel
4 oz. (⅔ cup) nibbed almonds
3 tbsps. brandy
a few drops of prepared gravy browning or a little home-made caramel (optional)

For finishing:
extra brandy
almond paste
decorations
royal icing

Make up and cook the bottom tier first, using a 12-in. round tin; prepare the mixture for the 2 upper tiers, divide between an 8-in. and a 6-in. round tin. Cook the 2 smaller cakes together.
Grease the cake tins and line with a double layer of greaseproof paper. Tie a double band of brown paper round the outside or put each tin in a slightly larger tin. Stand the tins on a layer of newspaper or brown paper for cooking. Wash and thoroughly dry the currants and sultanas (unless you are using pre-washed packaged fruit, in which case simply check it carefully.) Chop the raisins, quarter the glacé cherries.
Sift together the flour and spices. Add grated lemon rind. Cream the butter and gradually beat in sugar until light and fluffy. Beat in the eggs a little at a time. If the mixture shows signs of curdling, beat in 1–2 tablespoons flour. Fold in the rest of the flour and then the fruit, peel, nuts and brandy. If you wish, add to the smaller cakes a little gravy browning or caramel as they tend to be paler than the larger base.
Spoon the mixture into the prepared tins and level the surface. Using the back of a spoon, hollow out the centre of the cake slightly so that it will be level when cooked. At this stage the mixture may be left overnight. Cover lightly with a cloth, leave in a cool place but not in the refrigerator.
Bake on the lowest shelf in the oven at 300°F. (mark 1–2). Cook the 12-in. cake for about 8 hours, the 8-in. cake for about 3½ hours and the 6-in. cake for 2½–3 hours. Look at the cakes half way through the cooking time. If they seem to be browning too quickly, cover the top with a double thickness of greaseproof paper. With a large cake it is often wise to reduce the oven temperature to 275°F. (mark ½) after ⅔ of the cooking time.
Cool the cake for a short time in the tin and then turn on to a wire rack. When cold prick at intervals with a fine skewer and spoon some brandy evenly over the surface. Wrap completely in greaseproof paper and then in kitchen foil. Store for at least 1 month, preferably 2–3 months, in a cool, dry place before icing. After icing, wrap and store similarly, but for not longer than 2 months as a mould may form between the cake and the almond paste.
If one tier of the cake is kept for a later occasion such as a christening, remove the icing and almond paste and redecorate it for the second occasion. Directions for almond paste and royal icing are in the 'Cake Decorating' section.

SIT-DOWN LUNCHES

Lunch for 6-8 people is a tall order
if you are not prepared. Try some of
our planned menus, then branch out with
ideas of your own.

This page: Chilled prawn soup

MENU *serves 8*

TOMATO APPETIZERS
PORK CHOP BRAISE
VARIETY RICE
FRESH FRUITS AND
CHEESE
Wine – Hungarian Riesling

Timetable *for lunch at 1.00 p.m.*
Early: *Assemble ingredients and equipment.*
Skin and halve the tomatoes and arrange in dishes on the baking sheet, ready for baking. Divide 2 oranges into segments. Set out the fruit and cheese board.
11.30 *Start to cook pork.*
12.00 *Prepare rice and sauté mushrooms, keep hot. When chops are cooked, keep hot. Do not add mushrooms and orange segments.*
12.45 *Bake first course.*
1.00 *Stir mushrooms and orange segments into pork. Serve first course.*

TOMATO APPETIZERS

16 firm red tomatoes,
  skinned and halved
4 oz. Parmesan cheese,
  freshly grated
salt and freshly ground black
  pepper
dried basil
¼ pint (⅝ cup) cream

Arrange the tomato halves in 8 individual soufflé dishes and sprinkle with Parmesan, salt and pepper. Dust with basil and spoon the cream over the top.
Place on a baking sheet towards the top of the oven and cook at 375°F. (mark 5) for about 15 minutes. Serve hot.

PORK CHOP BRAISE

8 pork chops, approx. ¾ in.
  thick
2 level tbsps. flour
2 tbsps. cooking oil
4 tbsps. honey
½ pint (1¼ cups) water, boiling
¼ level tsp. ground cloves
4 oranges
2 onions, skinned and
  chopped
8 oz. mushrooms, sliced
2 oz. butter

Remove any excess fat from the chops and coat them in flour. Heat the oil in a large saucepan and fry the chops 2 at a time on both sides until golden brown. As each is browned, remove from the pan, drain on absorbent kitchen paper and keep warm.
Meanwhile, dissolve the honey in

Pork chop braise with variety rice

the water, stir in the cloves and the juice of 2 oranges.
When the chops are all browned, fry the onions in the oil until soft, drain off as much fat as possible and stir in any remaining flour. Add the honey mixture and stir well. Replace the chops, bring to the boil, cover and simmer for 45 minutes, or until really tender. Arrange chops on a serving dish and keep warm. If necessary reduce juices by boiling fast.
Meanwhile sauté the mushrooms in the butter. Peel the remaining oranges and divide into segments, free of membrane. Stir the mushrooms and orange into the chops 10 minutes before serving.

VARIETY RICE

12 oz. long grain rice
salt
3 oz. frozen peas
3 oz. frozen sweet corn
  kernels
freshly ground black pepper

Cook the rice in boiling salted water for about 12 minutes, or until tender. Meanwhile cook the frozen vegetables according to the directions on the packets.
Mix the rice and vegetables well together and season with pepper.

MENU *serves 6*

SMOKED SALMON WITH
BROWN BREAD AND
BUTTER
ESCALOPES DE VEAU AU
POIVRE ROSE
BOILED RICE AND
MUSHROOMS
GRAPEFRUIT SORBET
Wine – Alsace Sylvaner

Timetable *for lunch at 1.00 p.m.*
Day before: *Make the grapefruit sorbet.*
Early: *Assemble ingredients and equipment.*
11.00 *Slice smoked salmon and garnish with lemon wedges; leave covered with polythene film. Cut brown bread and butter. Leave covered.*
Bat out the veal and leave covered.
12.00 *Scoop sorbet into individual dishes and return to coldest part of refrigerator.*
12.30 *Start to cook veal (do not add cream); keep hot. Stir in the cream and reheat just before serving.*
Boil rice, drain and keep hot. Sauté mushrooms in butter and keep hot.
1.00 *Serve first course.*

ESCALOPES DE VEAU AU POIVRE ROSE

6 veal escalopes (approx. 5 oz.
  each)
1½ tbsps. cooking oil
1½ oz. butter
1½ level tbsps. flour
1½ level tsps. paprika pepper
3 bay leaves
1½ lemons
salt and freshly ground black
  pepper
4 fl. oz. (½ cup) double cream
watercress

Place each escalope between sheets of non-stick paper and bat out with a heavy knife or a meat bat. Nick the edges to prevent the meat contracting.
Heat the oil in a wide, shallow flameproof casserole; when hot add the butter. Coat the escalopes in the sifted flour and paprika. When the butter is sizzling, add the escalopes and quickly cook on 1 side only until golden brown. Remove the escalopes and drain off the fat, retaining the meat juices in the pan. Add to the pan the bay leaves, the thinly pared rind of ½ a lemon, 1½ tablespoon lemon juice, salt and pepper. Replace the escalopes, golden side uppermost, in the pan. Cover

192

Pecan stuffing for a party-roast chicken

lightly and simmer on top of the stove for 20 minutes.

Remove the escalopes and keep hot. Boil the pan juices fast to reduce to about 3 tablespoons, stir in the cream a little at a time and gently reheat. Do not boil. Replace the escalopes and garnish with watercress and lemon wedges.

GRAPEFRUIT SORBET

oz. (¾ cup) sugar
pint (1⅞ cups) water
½-fl. oz. can frozen grapefruit
   juice
egg whites
mint sprigs

Dissolve the sugar in the water. Bring to the boil and boil, un-covered, for 10 minutes. Turn the frozen juice into a bowl and pour in the sugar syrup; leave to cool. When cold, pour into a 1-pint capacity ice-cube tray and place in the ice making compartment of the refrigerator or in a freezer. Freeze to a slushy consistency.

Whisk the egg whites until thick and foamy but not dry. Fold into the grapefruit slush, return to the ice tray and freeze until firm.

Just before required, scoop into chilled glasses and decorate with a mint sprig. Serve with fan wafers.

MENU *serves 6*
**CHILLED PRAWN SOUP,
MELBA TOAST
ROAST CHICKEN WITH
PECAN STUFFING
BUTTERED COURGETTES
AND ROAST POTATOES
RED-CURRANT COMPOTE
AND CREME CHANTILLY
WITH BRANDY**
Wine – White Burgundy
(Pouilly Fuissé)

Timetable *for lunch at 1.00 p.m.*
Day before: *Make stuffing and compote. Store both in refrigerator.*
Early: *Assemble ingredients and equipment.*
Make soup, store in refrigerator.
Stuff and truss chicken. Prepare vegetables.
Remove crusts from bread and slice as thinly as possible for Melba toast.
11.00 *Put chicken to roast. When cooked, keep warm.*
12.00 *Start to roast potatoes. Whip and flavour cream. Take soup and compote out of refrigerator.*
12.30 *Cook courgettes. Make gravy for chicken.*
12.45 *Toast the bread.*
1.00 *Serve first course.*

CHILLED PRAWN SOUP

1 large can evaporated milk,
   chilled
4 tbsps. lemon juice
2 tsps. finely grated onion
1 level tsp. made mustard
2 tbsps. double cream
salt
6 oz. peeled prawns, finely
   chopped
3 tbsps. finely chopped
   parsley
paprika pepper

Combine the evaporated milk with the lemon juice, onion, mustard, cream and salt to taste. Gently

stir in the prawns and parsley. Pour into glasses or soup cups. Sprinkle the tops lightly with paprika and chill for at least 1 hour before serving.
Serve with Melba toast.

ROAST CHICKEN WITH PECAN STUFFING

4-lb. oven-ready chicken
melted butter or oil
salt and pepper

For stuffing :
heart and liver from the
   chicken
2 oz. fresh white breadcrumbs
2 oz. shelled pecans, chopped
   (or 1 oz. shelled walnuts,
   chopped)
1 egg, hard-boiled and
   chopped
pinch of ground nutmeg
pinch of ground mace
pinch of dried thyme
1 tbsp. chopped parsley
pinch of celery salt
2 oz. mushrooms, wiped
   and chopped
1½ oz. butter
1 small onion, skinned and
   chopped
2 tbsps. sherry
freshly ground black pepper

Place the heart and liver in a small saucepan, cover with water, simmer for 10 minutes, drain, finely chop or mince and cool. Add this mixture to the bread-crumbs, nuts, egg, spices, herbs and celery salt in a bowl. Sauté the mushrooms in half the butter for 3–4 minutes and add to the other ingredients. Fry the onion in the remaining butter and add to the bowl with the sherry. Season with pepper and mix well.
Wipe inside the chicken with a clean, damp cloth, stuff and truss. Brush with melted butter or oil and season.
Roast in the oven at 375°F. (mark 5) allowing 20 minutes per lb., plus 20 minutes. Serve with roast potatoes, courgettes and gravy made with chicken stock.

RED-CURRANT COMPOTE

1½ lb. ripe red-currants
10½ oz. (1⅓ cups) caster sugar
3 tbsps. water

Remove any stalks from the fruit. Put in a pan with the sugar and water. Shake the pan over gentle heat until the sugar has dissolved. Cool.
Divide the compote between 6 individual dishes and leave for about 2–3 hours, by which time the juice should have jellied.

CREME CHANTILLY WITH BRANDY

¾ pint (2 cups) double cream
caster sugar
2–3 tsps. brandy

Lightly whip the cream and sweeten to taste. Add the brandy and continue to whip until the cream just holds its shape.

MENU *serves 6*

CUCUMBER SWEET AND SOUR
SEAFOOD QUICHES
ENDIVE AND TOMATO SALAD
APPLE AND ORANGE BRISTOL
Wine – Rosé d'Anjou

Timetable *for lunch at 1.00 p.m.*
Day before: *Make pastry cases (do not bake), cover with polythene and keep in a cool place.*
Early: *Assemble ingredients and equipment. Prepare apple and orange Bristol, but do not decorate (prepare caramel). Slice cucumber and layer with salt. Prepare salmon and prawns, leave to marinade in the lemon juice in a covered bowl, in a cool place. Prepare salad and dressing.*
12.00 *Finish dessert.*
12.15 *Fill flans and cook. When ready, keep warm.*
12.30 *Combine cucumber and dressing. Toss salad.*
1.00 *Serve first course.*

CUCUMBER SWEET AND SOUR

1 large cucumber (or 2 small ridge cucumbers)
salt
1½ oz. onion, skinned
2 gherkins
1½ oz. sultanas
7½ fl. oz. (scant 1 cup) soured cream
1½ tbsps. lemon juice
¾ level tsp. caster sugar
a dash of Tabasco
freshly ground black pepper

Peel the cucumber and slice finely. Layer in a dish, sprinkling salt between the layers. Leave for a few hours.
Chop the onion, gherkins and sultanas and blend into the soured cream with the lemon juice, sugar, Tabasco and pepper. Drain the cucumber and dry on sheets of absorbent kitchen paper. Fold the cream mixture through the cucumber. Serve in individual dishes.

Individual seafood quiches make a tasty lunch

SEAFOOD QUICHES

For flan cases:
12 oz. (3 cups) plain flour
8 oz. butter
1 egg yolk
pinch of salt
¼ pint (⅝ cup) water

For filling:
6 oz. smoked salmon
1 pint prawns, shelled
1 tbsp. lemon juice
4 large eggs, beaten
¼ pint (⅝ cup) single cream
¾ pint (1⅞ cups) milk
salt and freshly ground black pepper
chopped parsley

Sift the flour and salt into a bowl. Rub in the butter until the mixture resembles fine breadcrumbs. Blend the egg yolk and water together. Stir into the rubbed-in ingredients. Knead the pastry lightly on a floured surface, divide into 6 and roll into pieces large enough to line 6 5-in. shallow flan cases. Line the pastry into the cases, prick the base of each with a fork and crimp the edges.
Using scissors, snip 1-in. pieces of salmon into a basin. Add the peeled prawns and sprinkle with lemon juice. Beat the eggs and whisk in the cream and milk. Season well.
Divide the salmon and prawns between the pastry cases and cover with the eggs and cream. Bake in the oven at 400°F. (mark 6) for 15 minutes. Reduce the temperature to 325°F. (mark 3) and cook for about a further 20 minutes. Sprinkle with chopped parsley before serving.
Garnish with a few whole prawns, if available.

ENDIVE AND TOMATO SALAD

1 endive (or a Webb's lettuce)
3 tomatoes, skinned and quartered
bunch of watercress, washed and trimmed
½ a small onion, skinned and chopped

For dressing:
1 tbsp. lemon juice
2 tbsps. salad oil
salt and freshly ground black pepper
a pinch of dry mustard
a pinch of sugar

Wash and roughly break up the endive or lettuce. Toss together the salad ingredients in a large bowl. Whisk together the ingredients for the dressing and spoon over the salad. Toss until the salad is evenly coated.

APPLE AND ORANGE BRISTOL

6¾ oz. (⅞ cup) caster sugar
½ pint (1¼ cups) water
6 dessert or cooking apples (or pears), peeled and cored
3 oranges
½ pint (1¼ cups) double cream, whipped

First make the caramel topping. Put 2 oz. of the caster sugar in a thick pan and heat gently until it becomes a light brown colour, taking care not to let it burn. Pour on to a greased tray, spreading it as thinly as possible, and leave to set. When cold, crush with a rolling pin.
Put the water and remaining sugar in a thick frying-pan, dissolve and bring to the boil. Quarter the

apples and put into the boiling syrup; cover and poach gently until just tender, then leave them to stand in the syrup until they become transparent.
Pare 5–6 very fine strips of rind free of white pith from 1 of the oranges, cut into fine shreds and put them in cold water. Bring to the boil and cook for 5–10 minutes until tender, then drain and dip into cold water.
Peel the oranges and divide into segments free of membrane. Arrange the apple and orange in a dish and pour a little of the syrup over them. Just before serving sprinkle with the strips of orange rind and the broken caramel. Serve with whipped cream.

MENU *serves 8*

PECHES FROMAGE
MIXED GRILL MAITRE D'HOTEL
SOUFFLE MONTE CRISTO
Wine – Claret (Médoc)

Timetable *for lunch at 1.00 p.m.*
Day before: *Prepare soufflé but do not decorate (do not soak ratafias yet). Make savoury butter.*
Early: *Assemble ingredients and equipment. Finish soufflé and leave out of refrigerator. Prepare pêches fromage and chill. Prepare ingredients for grill and put ready for cooking. Cut savoury butter into pats.*
11.30 *Cook matchstick potatoes, keep hot.*
12.00 *Cook mixed grill, keep hot. Remove pêches fromage from refrigerator.*
1.00 *Serve first course.*

PECHES FROMAGE

3 oz. Cheddar cheese, finely grated
1 oz. Parmesan cheese, finely grated
1 oz. softened butter
salt
cayenne pepper
1-lb. 13-oz. can peach halves, drained
1 lettuce
8 tomatoes, quartered (optional)
3 oz. Demi-sel cheese (soft cream cheese)
about ¼ pint (⅝ cup) single cream
paprika pepper

Blend together the Cheddar, Parmesan and butter and season with

194

lt and cayenne. Fill the cheese
mixture into the hollows in the
peach halves.

Arrange a lettuce leaf and a
quartered tomato on each plate
with an upturned, stuffed peach
half.

Beat the Demi-sel cheese in a small
bowl and gradually add the cream,
to give a coating consistency.
Spoon over the peach halves, to
mask. Dust with a little paprika
and chill.

MIXED GRILL MAITRE D'HOTEL

For maître d'hôtel butter :

oz. butter
tbsps. finely chopped parsley
lemon juice
salt and cayenne pepper

best end of neck lamb chops
lambs' kidneys
salt and pepper
tomatoes, halved
mushrooms, wiped and
   trimmed
salt and freshly ground
   black pepper
melted butter or oil
basil
lb. chipolata sausages
rashers bacon, rinded
watercress, for garnish

First blend together the ingredients for the maître d'hôtel butter.
Roll between 2 sheets of non-
stick paper to about ¼ in. thick and
chill. When firm, stamp out into
small rounds with a 1-in. cutter.
Heat the grill. Trim the chops,
halve and core the kidneys. Season
the chops, kidneys, tomatoes and
mushrooms and brush with melted
butter or oil.
Place the tomatoes (cut side up) in
the grill pan and sprinkle with
basil. Add the mushrooms, underside up. Put the grill rack in
position over the tomatoes and
mushrooms and put the chops on

it. Grill under full heat for 10–12
minutes, turning frequently. Remove chops and keep hot. The
juices from the meat will baste the
tomatoes and mushrooms without
need of further attention.
Prick the sausages, place the sausages and kidneys on the rack and
return to the grill. Cook under
medium heat for 14–16 minutes,
turning the food frequently. The
kidneys will probably be cooked
first, in which case remove them
and keep them hot. Replace them
with bacon rashers and cook for a
further 3–5 minutes.
Dish up the grill on 2 large platters,
garnished with watercress. Top
each chop with a pat of maître
d'hôtel butter.

SOUFFLE MONTE CRISTO

6 eggs, separated
3 oz. (⅜ cup) caster sugar
1 tsp. vanilla essence
¾ oz. powdered gelatine
3 tbsps. water
1 pint (2½ cups) double cream
4 large milk flake bars
2-oz. pkt. ratafias (small
   almond biscuits)
4 tbsps. Kirsch or maraschino

Tie a band of greaseproof or
non-stick paper round a 2-pint
soufflé dish, to stand 3 in. above
the rim of the dish.
Beat the egg yolks, sugar and
vanilla essence in a bowl over a pan
of hot water until thick and creamy
and the whisk leaves a thick trail.
Dissolve the gelatine in the water
in a small basin over a pan of hot
water. Stir into the soufflé mixture.
Cool until beginning to set.
Lightly whip three-quarters of the
cream. Whisk the egg whites until
stiff. Lightly crush the chocolate
bars. Whisk the yolk mixture again
and fold in the cream and egg
whites.
Place a straight sided tumbler or
jam jar in the centre of the prepared
soufflé dish and spoon the mixture
round the outside of the glass,
alternating it with layers of chocolate flakes, using about three-
quarters of the chocolate. Put in
the refrigerator to set.
Soak the ratafias briefly in the
liqueur. To serve, remove the
paper from round the soufflé, fill
the tumbler with warm water to
loosen it and remove it, gently and
quickly. Fill the hole with the
liqueur soaked ratafias.
Whip the remaining double cream
and pipe with a star vegetable
nozzle into 8 large whirls on top
of the soufflé. Decorate with the
remaining chocolate flakes.

Apple and orange Bristol, with a caramel decoration

WATERCRESS SOUP

For savoury butter :
1 oz. butter
paprika pepper
chopped chives

4 oz. butter
2 oz. (½ cup) plain flour
1¼ pints (3 cups) chicken or
   veal stock
½ pint (1¼ cups) milk
salt and freshly ground black
   pepper
3 oz. onion, skinned and
   chopped
2 bunches of watercress

Beat together 1 oz. butter, a little
paprika and a few chopped chives.
Roll out between sheets of non-

Peaches stuffed with cheese, as a first course for lunch

stick paper. Chill.

Melt 3 oz. butter in a pan and stir in the flour. Cook over gentle heat for 1–2 minutes. Remove from the heat and stir in all the stock and milk. Return to the heat and bring to the boil, stirring continuously. Simmer gently for 3 minutes; season well.

Sauté the onion in the remaining 1 oz. butter until soft. Wash the watercress and trim, leaving some of the stem. Chop roughly and add to the onion. Cover and cook for a further 4 minutes. Stir the sauté vegetables into the sauce and purée in a blender or pass through a sieve. Gently reheat, season to taste and ladle into preheated bowls. Stamp the butter into fancy shapes, using small decorative cutters, and float 1 pat on each bowl of soup. Serve pretzels separately.

BEEF GALANTINE

1 lb. blade-bone steak
¾ lb. gammon hock or knuckle
1 pig's trotter
½ an onion, skinned
2 carrots, scraped
1 tomato
sprigs of parsley
1–2 slivers of lemon rind
3–4 peppercorns
1 stick of celery, scrubbed
pinch of dried thyme or a
**   sprig of fresh thyme**
½ a clove of garlic, skinned
salt and pepper
1 tbsp. chopped parsley

For garnish :
2 tomatoes, skinned and
**   halved**
¼ pint (⅝ cup) aspic jelly,
**   made with aspic jelly**
**   powder**
2 eggs, hard-boiled and
**   halved**

Trim the beef of excess fat and coarse sinews, leave in large pieces. Rind the gammon and remove the bones. Wash and split the trotter. Place the beef, gammon and trotter in a pan with the onion, carrots, tomato, parsley, lemon rind, peppercorns, celery, thyme and garlic. Just cover with cold water. Cover the pan with a well fitting lid. Bring to the boil, skim and then simmer for about 2 hours until the meats are fork tender. Remove beef and gammon. Boil the cooking liquor, vegetables and bones in an open pan until reduced to ⅝ pint (1½ cups). Strain.

Mince or finely chop the meats, stir in the reduced liquor and chopped parsley and adjust the seasoning.

For the garnish, seed the tomatoes

Serve this sorbet in frosted orange cups

and remove the cores. Roughly chop and season the flesh. Arrange the tomatoes in the base of a 1½-pint capacity ring mould with the hard-boiled eggs and set with aspic. When set, spoon the beef mixture over. Chill until firm. Unmould for serving.

APPLE AND BRANDY POTS

3 level tsps. finely grated
**   orange rind**
9 tbsps. fresh orange juice
3 tbsps. brandy
3 lb. cooking apples
**   (preferably Bramleys),**
**   peeled and finely sliced**
6 level tsps. caster sugar
powdered cinnamon
½ pint (1¼ cups) double cream,
**   whipped**

Blend together the orange rind, juice and brandy. Tightly pack the apple into 6 individual soufflé dishes or ramekins and sprinkle 1 teaspoon caster sugar over each dish. Pour over the orange juice and brandy. Cover with buttered greaseproof paper, top each with a small weight and place on a baking sheet. Bake in the oven at 300°F. (mark 1–2) for 1½ hours. Serve warm, dusted with cinnamon and topped with whipped cream.

MENU *serves 6*

GLOBE ARTICHOKES WITH BUTTER
POT ROAST VEAL
BROCCOLI SPEARS AND CREAMED POTATOES
ORANGE SORBET CUPS
Wine – White Burgundy (Mâcon blanc)

Timetable *for lunch at 1.00 p.m.*
Day before: *Prepare the orange sorbet and chill the orange shells (if you do not have a separate ice making compartment or freezer, buy a good brand of sorbet on the day).*
10.30 *Assemble ingredients and equipment.*
Start to cook veal. When ready, keep hot.
Trim artichokes, prepare potatoes and broccoli.
12.00 *Pile sorbet into chilled shells and return to the coldest part of the refrigerator.*
12.15 *Cook artichokes. Put potatoes on to boil.*
Gently melt butter.
12.45 *Carve veal, thicken sauce and keep warm.*
Cook broccoli and keep vegetables warm.
1.00 *Serve first course.*

POT ROAST VEAL

3 lb. shoulder of veal, boned
**   and rolled**
salt and pepper
2 oz. butter
1 tbsp. cooking oil
1 small onion, skinned and
**   sliced**
6 small carrots, peeled and
**   sliced**
½ pint (1¼ cups) water
little dried thyme
cornflour

Wipe the meat and season we Melt the butter with the oil in frying pan. Lightly brown th meat all over. Transfer the meat a casserole and keep hot.

Fry the vegetables until brow add the water, bring to the bo and then pour round the meat the casserole. Add the thym Cover and cook at 350°F. (mark for about 2½ hours, until the me is tender.

Slice the meat and arrange on serving dish. Thicken the sau with a little cornflour and pou over the meat.

ORANGE SORBET CUPS

6–7 large oranges (see metho
6 oz. (¾ cup) sugar
¾ pint (1⅞ cups) water
3 tbsps. lemon juice
3 egg whites

Using a small, sharp, pointe knife, cut the tops off 6 orange with a zig-zag pattern and scoo out the flesh and membrane. Wor over a bowl to catch all the juic Discard the membrane. Wash th empty shells and put them, wit their lids, into the ice makin compartment of the refrigerato or in the freezer.

Dissolve the sugar in the wate over gentle heat, bring to the bo and boil for 5 minutes. Leave t cool.

Purée the orange pulp in a blende or sieve, and make up to ¾ pin (1⅞ cups) with juice from the extr orange, if necessary. Combine wit the syrup and lemon juice, pou into a polythene ice-cube tray an freeze until nearly firm – about hour.

Whisk the egg whites until stif but not dry. Turn the froze fruit mixture into a chilled bow break down with a spoon and fol in the egg whites. Return to th ice-cube tray and freeze until firm but still slightly soft in texture To serve, pack small spoonfuls orange sorbet into the chille shells and pile up well. Replac the lids and chill for up to 1 hour

Red-currant compote

INFORMAL BUFFET LUNCHES

MENU *serves 12*

LEMON CONSOMME
JELLIED CHICKEN PIE
HAM AND ASPARAGUS ROLLS
CUCUMBER SALAD
NEW POTATOES
GINGER MERINGUE CREAMS

Timetable *for lunch at 1.00 p.m.*
Day before: *Prepare consommé and chill.*
Make meringue cases and store in airtight tins.
Prepare salad dressings. Scrape potatoes; keep under water.
Assemble ingredients for chicken pie.
Early: *Assemble ingredients and equipment. Bake chicken pie, leave to cool. Combine yoghourt and flavourings and refrigerate.*
11.00 *Make up ham and asparagus rolls. Fill meringue cases.*
12.00 *Make cucumber salad. Cook potatoes, drain and cool.*
Set out foods on table.
12.45 *Spoon yoghourt over consommé and garnish.*

LEMON CONSOMME

3 10½-oz. cans concentrated consommé
4 tsps. dry sherry
grated rind and juice of 1 lemon
1 pint (2½ cups) natural yoghourt
fresh mint

Warm the consommé, sherry and lemon juice together. Pour into individual soup bowls and chill. Combine the yoghourt with the grated lemon rind and add a few leaves of mint.
Just before serving, remove the mint from the yoghourt and spoon it over the jellied consommé. Garnish each bowl of soup with fresh mint leaves.

JELLIED CHICKEN PIE

2 3-lb. oven-ready chickens
½ lb. lean streaky bacon, rinded and chopped
½ lb. onions, skinned and thinly sliced
½ lb. mushrooms, stalked and sliced
2 tbsps. chopped parsley
½ level tsp. mixed, dried herbs
salt and pepper
4 tbsps. water
8 oz. shortcrust pastry – i.e. made with 8 oz. (2 cups) flour, etc.
beaten egg to glaze

Ham and asparagus rolls, jellied chicken pie and cucumber salad

Skin the chickens, carve off all the flesh and cut into pieces. Layer the chicken, bacon, onions and mushrooms in a shallow ovenproof dish about 12 in. by 9 in. by 2 in. Sprinkle the layers with parsley, herbs and seasoning. Add the water.
Roll out the pastry and use to make a lid. Cut the pastry trimmings into leaves and use to decorate the top of the pie. Brush with the beaten egg. Cut a slit in the pastry lid, place on a baking sheet and cook in the oven at 350°F. (mark 4) for about 1½ hours. Allow to cool before serving.

HAM AND ASPARAGUS ROLLS

8-oz. pkt. frozen asparagus spears, cooked
1½ lb. cooked ham, thinly sliced
¼ pint (⅝ cup) mayonnaise
watercress
paprika pepper

Divide the cooled asparagus spears between the slices of ham. Roll up and arrange side by side on a serving dish. Spoon the mayonnaise down the centre, sprinkle with paprika pepper and garnish with watercress.

CUCUMBER SALAD

1 cucumber (or 2 small ridge cucumbers)
French dressing
paprika pepper
½ green pepper (capsicum), seeded and chopped

Wipe the cucumber, or peel it. Slice thinly. Put the cucumber in a dish, cover with the dressing and allow to stand in a cool place for about 15 minutes.
Sprinkle lightly with paprika and garnish with chopped green pepper.

GINGER MERINGUE CREAMS

6 large egg whites
12 oz. (1½ cups) caster sugar
½ pint (1¼ cups) double cream
¼ pint (⅝ cup) single cream
6 tbsps. finely chopped stem ginger

Line 2 baking trays with non-stick paper. Whisk the egg whites until stiff, whisk in half the sugar until the mixture becomes stiff again, then fold in remaining sugar. Spoon the meringue into 12 heaps on the prepared baking trays, keeping well apart. Make into flan shapes, hollowing out the centres with the back of a spoon. Dry out in the oven at 250°F. (mark ¼) for about 2½–3 hours. Peel off the paper and cool on a wire rack.
Whip the creams lightly together and fold in half the chopped ginger. Divide the ginger cream between the meringue shells and top with the remaining chopped ginger.

MENU *serves 12*

MELON AND PARMA HAM
DEEP FRIED CHICKEN DRUMSTICKS
TARTARE SAUCE
BURGUNDY BEEF GALANTINE
TOMATO AND WATERCRESS SALAD
FRENCH BREAD AND BUTTER
ROLLA TORTE

Timetable *for lunch at 1.00 p.m.*
Day before: *Make the Burgundy beef galantine.*
Egg and crumb the drumsticks, leave in a cool place. Prepare tartare sauce.
Make Rolla Torten and leave, covered, in a cool place.
Early: *Fry chicken joints, drain well, cover and leave in a cool place.*
Make up the salad, add French dressing if required.
Slice the galantine.
11.00 *Cut the melons and chill.*
12.00 *Remove melons from the refrigerator, add ham and lemon wedges. Set out the food on the table.*

MELON AND PARMA HAM

2 large cantaloup (rock) melons
1 lb. Parma ham, thinly sliced
lemon wedges for garnish

...t each melon into 6 portions
...d remove the seeds. Chill
...ghtly.
...ace a slice of Parma ham on
...ch portion of melon. Top with a
...edge of lemon and secure with a
...cktail stick.

...EEP FRIED CHICKEN ...RUMSTICKS

...e chicken drumsticks
...lt and pepper
...eggs, beaten
...readcrumbs
...l for deep frying

...eason the joints and dip each one
... the egg, then coat in bread-
...umbs. Leave the joints in a
...ol place for a while for the
...ating to 'set'.
...eat the frying oil to 375°F. and
...y the chicken joints, 2–3 at a time.
...hen golden brown, remove and
...ain on absorbent kitchen paper.
...llow to cool.
...rim the drumsticks with cutlet
...ills, which look pretty and give
...our guests something to hold, to
...revent their fingers becoming too
...icky.

...ARTARE SAUCE

... pint (⅝ cup) mayonnaise
...tsp. chopped tarragon and/or
... chives
...tsps. chopped capers
...tsps. chopped gherkins
...tsps. chopped parsley
...tbsp. lemon juice or
... tarragon vinegar

...Mix all the ingredients well and
...eave the sauce to stand for at
...east 1 hour before serving, to
...llow the flavours to blend.

...URGUNDY BEEF ...ALANTINE
...ake 2

... lb. chuck steak (in 1 piece)
... lb. back bacon rashers,
... rinded
...alt and pepper
... oz. butter
...tbsp. cooking oil
... large onion, skinned and
... sliced
... large carrot, peeled and
... sliced
... bay leaf
... level tsp. dried herbs
... pint (1¼ cups) red wine,
... preferably Burgundy
... lb. button mushrooms,
... wiped and sliced
... oz. powdered gelatine

...rim all the excess fat from the
...neat and discard. Lay the bacon
...ashers over the meat to cover it

completely and tie into a long roll
with string. Sprinkle the roll with
salt and pepper.
Heat 1 oz. butter and the oil in a
large flameproof casserole. Add
the meat and fry, turning until
sealed all over. Add the onion,
carrot, herbs, wine and ½ pint
(1¼ cups) water. Bring to the boil,
cover and cook in the oven at
350°F. (mark 4) for 3 hours.
Remove the meat from the pan
and leave until quite cold. Place
the stock in the refrigerator; when
it is cold, skim off the fat and
discard. Make the stock up to 1
pint (2½ cups) with water, if

A delicious spread for a buffet lunch

necessary.
Melt the remaining butter in a
frying pan and sauté the mushrooms; leave until cold.
Cut the meat into thin slices;
arrange half of these in a 3–4 pint
loaf tin, cover with the mushrooms, then the remaining sliced
meat.
Dissolve the gelatine in 2 tablespoons water in a basin held over a
pan of hot water, add to the stock
and mix well. Leave it to stand and,
when beginning to set, pour it over
the meat and mushrooms. Leave
until completely set.
To serve, unmould and slice.

ROLLA TORTE
make 3

⅛ level tsp. cream of tartar
pinch of salt
3 egg whites
5½ oz. (⅝ cup) caster sugar
1 oz. (¼ cup) ground almonds
1 oz. (¼ cup) cornflour

For filling and decoration:

3 oz. (⅜ cup) caster sugar
4 tbsps. water
2 egg yolks, lightly beaten
4–6 oz. unsalted butter
2 oz. chocolate dots
2 oz. toasted, flaked almonds
icing sugar

Draw 3 7-in. circles on non-stick
paper and place on baking sheets.
Add the cream of tartar and salt
to the egg whites and whisk until
very stiff.
Beat in two-thirds of the caster
sugar, 1 tablespoon at a time. Mix
together the remaining sugar, the
almonds and cornflour and fold
into the meringue mixture.
Using a forcing bag and a ¼-in.
plain vegetable nozzle, pipe the
mixture on to the papers, starting
at the centre of the circles and
working out to fill the marked area.
Take care to see that each ring of
meringue touches the next. Alter-

natively spread the meringue in
smooth layers with a palette knife.
Bake just below the centre of the
oven at 325°F. (mark 3) for about
30 minutes, until just coloured and
dry. Peel off the paper and cool on
a wire rack.
Meanwhile prepare the filling.
Place the sugar in a fairly large,
heavy-based saucepan; add the
water and dissolve the sugar over a
very low heat without boiling.
When completely dissolved, bring
to boiling point and boil steadily
for 2–3 minutes, or until a little of
the cooled syrup will form a thread
when pulled between your wetted
finger and thumb (225°F.). Place
the egg yolks in a deep bowl and
pour on the syrup in a thin stream,
whisking all the time. Continue to
whisk until the mixture is thick
and cold. Cream the butter and
gradually add the syrup and yolk
mixture.
Put the chocolate dots in a small
basin with 1 tablespoon water;
place over a pan of hot water and
leave to stand until the chocolate
is melted and smooth. Cool slightly
and beat into the butter mixture.
Sandwich the meringue layers
with chocolate filling and coat the
Torte round the sides. Decorate
the sides with flaked almonds and
dredge the top with icing sugar.
Leave the Torte in a cool place for
24 hours to mature before cutting;
the meringue layers should soften
a little.

MENU *serves 12*

**SMOKED HADDOCK AND
CHEESE FLAN**
**CHICKEN AND ALMOND
SALAD**
**AVOCADO AND TOMATO
SALAD**
GREEN SALAD
JACKET POTATOES
**ORANGE PRALINE
MOUSSE**

Timetable *for lunch at 1.00 p.m.*
Day before: *Bake flans; store,
covered, in a cool place but not the
refrigerator. Prepare ingredients
and dressings for salads (except
avocados); refrigerate separately.
Scrub the potatoes.
Prepare the mousse but do not turn
out (when preparing a mousse so
far in advance, line the tin with
non-stick paper to prevent
discolouration).*
Early: *Turn out mousse and
decorate.*
11.30 *Prick potatoes and put to
bake in the oven at 400°F.*

(mark 6). When cooked keep hot.
12.00 *Cut avocados and dress salads. Refresh the flans in the oven for a short time to re-crisp the pastry. Set out the food on the table.*

SMOKED HADDOCK AND CHEESE FLAN

make 2

For flan case :

5 oz. (1¼ cups) plain flour
pinch of salt
3 oz. butter or margarine
1 egg yolk
4 tsps. water

For filling :

½ lb. smoked haddock
¼ pint (⅝ cup) water
juice of ½ a lemon
1 oz. butter
1 small onion, skinned and finely chopped
2 oz. mushrooms, wiped and chopped
2 eggs
3 tbsps. single cream
4 oz. cottage cheese
salt and freshly ground black pepper
chopped parsley

Sift the flour and the salt together. Cut the fat into small pieces and add to the flour. Rub the fat into the flour with the fingertips, until the mixture looks like fine breadcrumbs. Add the egg yolk, blended with 2 teaspoons water; add more water if required to bind the dough. Knead lightly for a few seconds to give a firm, smooth dough. Put in a cool place to 'rest' for 15 minutes.

Roll out the pastry to ⅛ in. thick and use to line an 8-in. flan ring. Prick the base of the case, line with foil and bake blind in the oven at 400°F. (mark 6) for 15 minutes; remove foil and continue cooking for a further 5–10 minutes until the pastry is lightly browned. Cool. Poach the haddock in a pan with water and half the lemon juice. Drain the fish, discard the skin and bones and flake the flesh. Melt the butter in a pan, cook the onion for a few minutes then add the mushrooms and continue to cook for 3–4 minutes.

Combine the fish and vegetables and spread over the base of the flan case. Beat the eggs, add the cream, cheese and remaining lemon juice; adjust seasoning. Pour over the fish mixture.

Bake in the oven at 375°F. (mark 5) for about 35 minutes until set and golden. Garnish with chopped parsley. Serve hot or cold.

CHICKEN AND ALMOND SALAD

8 oz. stoned raisins
2¼ lb. cooked chicken meat
6 oz. almonds, blanched
½ an onion, skinned (optional)
¼ pint (⅝ cup) single cream
¼ pint (⅝ cup) mayonnaise
1 tbsp. lemon juice
3 tbsps. chopped parsley
salt and pepper
lettuce, washed and trimmed

Cover the raisins with boiling water, leave for 5 minutes and drain. Cut the chicken meat into chunks. Roughly chop the almonds and brown lightly under the grill. Grate the onion.

Mix the cream, mayonnaise, lemon juice and parsley. Adjust seasoning and combine with the raisins, chicken, almonds and onion in a bowl. Serve on a bed of lettuce.

AVOCADO AND TOMATO SALAD

3 avocados
juice of 1 lemon
2 small green peppers (capsicums), seeded and thinly sliced
6 tomatoes, skinned and sliced
2 onions, skinned and cut into wafer thin rings
French dressing
1 tbsp. chopped parsley

Cut the avocados in half lengthwise, using a stainless steel knife, and remove the stones. Peel and slice them; squeeze the lemon juice over to prevent discolouration.

Arrange the avocado on a large platter with the peppers, tomatoes and onion. Moisten with French dressing and garnish with chopped parsley.

Note : Whereas the peppers, tomatoes, and onions for this salad may be prepared well in advance, the avocado will discolour very quickly. Slice the avocados, therefore, only at the last minute.

An orange mousse, flavoured and decorated with praline

ORANGE PRALINE MOUSSE

make 2

4 oz. lump sugar
2 large juicy oranges
6 egg yolks
2 level tsps. cornflour
1½ pints (3¾ cups) milk
1 oz. powdered gelatine
6 egg whites

For praline :
4 oz. (½ cup) caster sugar

For decoration :
fresh orange segments
whipped cream
ratafia biscuits

Rub 2–3 sugar lumps over the skins of the oranges to extract the zest. Squeeze the oranges and if necessary add a little water to give

6 tablespoons juice.

Beat the egg yolks and blend wi[th] the cornflour. Put the sugar lump[s] in the milk and place over gent[le] heat; bring to just below boili[ng] point. Pour on to the egg yolk[s] stirring. Return the mixture to th[e] pan and cook gently, stirri[ng] occasionally without boiling unt[il] thickened.

Sprinkle the gelatine over t[he] orange juice, and leave in a sm[all] basin placed over a pan of h[ot] water until dissolved. Stir into t[he] custard until evenly mixed. Lea[ve] in a cool place until on the poi[nt] of setting.

Place the egg whites in a large deep bowl and beat with a rotar[y] whisk until stiff but not dry, the[n] quickly and evenly fold into th[e] custard with half the praline (se[e] below). Turn into an 8¼-in. spring release cake tin with a loose bas[e.] Leave in the refrigerator to set.

To serve, turn the mousse ou[t] carefully on to a flat plate. Decor[-] ate it with orange segments, whir[ls] of whipped cream, ratafia biscuit[s] and the remainder of the praline[.]

Praline

Place the caster sugar in a pa[n.] Dissolve very carefully over a lo[w] heat. Raise the heat and continu[e] to cook until golden brown. Quick[-] ly turn the caramel out on to [a] greased baking sheet. When co[ol] crush finely with a rolling pin.

HOT SUPPERS

Whether your supper is an after theatre meal or a casual alternative to dinner, dream up some hot, tasty snacks to fill your hungry family and guests. Start with our ideas and build your repertoire from there.

This page: Lasagne and jumbo prawn risotto

LASAGNE

serves 4

2 14-oz. cans tomatoes, drained
1 level tbsp. tomato paste
1 level tsp. dried marjoram
salt and freshly ground black pepper
1 lb. lean minced beef
4 oz. lasagne strips
1 oz. butter
1 oz. (¼ cup) flour
½ pint (1¼ cups) milk
6 oz. Cheddar cheese, grated
oil for glazing
4 oz. Mozzarella or Bel Paese cheese, sliced

Combine the canned tomatoes, tomato paste, marjoram, salt and pepper. Simmer in an open pan for 30 minutes. Add the mince and simmer for a further 25 minutes, still uncovered.

Cook the lasagne strips in a large pan of fast boiling, salted water for 10–15 minutes and drain.

In a small saucepan, melt 1 oz. butter, stir in the flour and gradually blend in the milk. Bring to the boil, stirring constantly. Remove from the heat add the Cheddar cheese and season.

Cover the base of an ovenproof dish (about 1½ in. deep) with strips of lasagne. Add alternate layers of meat and cheese sauce. Finish the final layer with strips of pasta placed diagonally across, with the sauces spooned between. Lightly oil the pasta to prevent it drying. Bake in the oven at 375°F. (mark 5) for about 30 minutes. Remove from the oven, add the slices of Mozzarella on top of the cheese sauce. Raise the temperature to 425°F. (mark 7) and return the lasagne to the oven until the cheese is golden and bubbling.

VEGETABLE FRICASSEE

serves 2

½ lb. courgettes
½ lb. firm tomatoes, skinned and sliced
3½ oz. butter
4 oz. onion, skinned and sliced
½ level tsp. dried thyme
2 level tbsps. flour
¾ pint (1⅞ cups) milk
4 oz. Cheddar cheese, grated
salt and pepper
2 oz. fresh brown breadcrumbs

Slice the courgettes and blanch in boiling salted water for 3 minutes; drain. Arrange all but a few slices of courgette and tomato in the base of a 2-pint flameproof dish. Dot with ½ oz. butter. Cover with foil

and keep hot under a low grill. Melt 2 oz. butter in a pan, add the onion and cook for about 2 minutes, until tender. Add the thyme and stir in the flour. Remove the pan from the heat, blend in the milk, return to the heat and bring to the boil, stirring. Add the cheese and season well.

Melt the remaining 1 oz. butter in a frying pan and add the breadcrumbs. Cook until well browned. Remove the foil from the vegetables, cover with cheese sauce and top with the crisp crumbs. Garnish with the remaining slices of courgette and tomato.

Top a vegetable fricassee with crisp fried crumbs

CHICKEN RAMEKINS

serves 2–4

4 oz. cooked chicken, minced
2 mushrooms, chopped
2 eggs, separated
2 tbsps. single cream
salt and pepper
½ oz. butter

Mix the chicken and mushrooms and bind with the egg yolks and cream; season to taste. Whisk the egg whites stiffly and fold into the chicken mixture. Divide between 4 buttered ramekins, place them on a baking tray and cook in the centre of the oven at 350°F. (mark 4) for 15–20 minutes.

OEUFS A LA MAISON

serves 2–4

4-oz. pkt. frozen peas
1 onion, skinned and finely chopped
4 tomatoes, skinned and chopped
⅛ level tsp. garlic salt
salt and freshly ground black pepper
3 large eggs
½ pint (1¼ cups) milk
parsley

Cook the peas according to the directions on the packet. Just before the end of the cooking time,

add the chopped onion and blanch for 1–2 minutes. Drain.

Divide the peas, onion and tomatoes between 4 individual ovenproof soup bowls or soufflé dishes. Sprinkle the salt and pepper over the top.

Place the eggs and milk in a bowl, beat with a fork to mix then strain over the vegetables. Place the dishes in a roasting tin with water to come half way up, and cook in the oven at 375°F. (mark 5) for about 40 minutes. Garnish with parsley and serve with crusty bread.

ROQUEFORT QUICHE

serves 4–6

4 oz. shortcrust pastry – i.e. made with 4 oz. (1 cup) flour etc.
3 oz. Roquefort or other blue cheese
6 oz. cream cheese
2 eggs, beaten
¼ pint (⅝ cup) single cream
1–2 level tsps. grated onion or 1 level tbsp. chopped chives
salt and pepper

Roll out the pastry and use to line a 7–8 in. flan case or metal pie plate. Place near the top of the oven at 425°F. (mark 7) and bake blind for 10 minutes, until the pastry is just set.

Cream the 2 kinds of cheese together and stir in the eggs, cream, onion or chives and seasoning. Pour into the pastry case, reduce the oven temperature to 375°F. (mark 5) and cook for about 30 minutes, until well risen and golden. Serve warm, with a green salad.

STUFFED GLOBE ARTICHOKES

serves 2–4

4 globe artichokes, trimmed
½ a small onion, skinned and finely chopped
2 mushrooms, washed and finely chopped
½ oz. butter
2 oz. cooked ham, chopped
2 level tsps. fresh white breadcrumbs
beaten egg to bind
salt and pepper

Cook the artichokes in boiling salted water for 20–40 minutes, according to size, until the leaves will pull out easily. Drain and remove the inner leaves and the chokes.

Lightly fry the onion and mushrooms in the butter for about 5 minutes, then add the other in-

Handy hint

If your eyes run when you are skinning onions, soak the onions in cold water for 30 minutes first. Alternatively hold them under cold water while skinning.

gredients, using enough beaten egg to bind the mixture. Season to taste, and spoon the mixture into the centres of the artichokes. Place them in a greased ovenproof dish, cover with greased greaseproof paper and bake in the centre of the oven at 375°F. (mark 5) for 10–15 minutes.

GREEN BEAN AND BACON FLAN
serves 4

For cheese pastry :

4 oz. (1 cup) self-raising flour
a pinch of salt
2 oz. butter, margarine or lard
2 oz. Cheddar cheese, grated
a little beaten egg or water

For filling :

4 tbsps. milk
2 oz. cheese, grated
4 eggs, beaten
salt and pepper
4 rashers streaky bacon, rinded
4 oz. cooked green beans

Sift together the flour and salt and rub in the fat until the mixture resembles fine crumbs. Stir in the cheese. Bind together with enough egg or water to give a firm but pliable dough. Roll out and use to line an 8-in. plain flan ring. Bake blind at 400°F. (mark 6) for about 10 minutes. Remove from the oven and reduce the temperature to 375°F. (mark 5).
Stir together the milk, cheese and eggs and adjust seasoning. Grill or fry the bacon until crisp, then cut into small pieces. Arrange half the bacon in the flan case and pour on a little of the egg mixture. Add the beans and the rest of the bacon and coat with the rest of the egg. Bake for about 30 minutes or until just firm. Serve hot or cold.

JUMBO PRAWN RISOTTO
serves 4

1 level tbsp. dried onion flakes
2 oz. butter
6 oz. (¾ cup) long grain rice
¼ level tsp. dried basil
¾ pint (1⅞ cups) stock
7-oz. can jumbo prawns
3 large eggs
2 tbsps. chopped parsley

Soak the onion flakes in a little water for several minutes, then drain. Melt the butter in a saucepan, add the onion and fry gently for 3 minutes. Stir in the rice and cook, stirring occasionally, for several minutes until the rice appears opaque.
Add the basil, stock and liquor from the prawn can; bring to the boil, cover and simmer for 25 minutes or until the rice is cooked and the liquid absorbed. Meanwhile, hard-boil the eggs, then chop. When the rice is cooked, stir in the prawns, egg and 1 tablespoon parsley. Adjust seasoning. Turn into a serving dish and garnish with remaining parsley.

TUNA AND SPAGHETTI CRISP
serves 4

4 oz. short-cut spaghetti
7-oz. can tuna steak, drained and flaked
½ pint (1¼ cups) white sauce
3 oz. cheese, grated
salt and pepper
1-oz. pkt. potato crisps

Cook the spaghetti in boiling salted water until tender, 8–12 minutes. Drain well and place in a bowl.
Add the drained and flaked tuna steak, the white sauce, cheese and seasoning. Mix well and transfer to a greased 2-pint casserole. Crush the crisps slightly and arrange on top. Bake for 20–30 minutes in the oven at 350°F. (mark 4).

STUFFED EGGS AU GRATIN
serves 4

15-oz. can celery hearts, drained
4 rashers streaky bacon, rinded
4 eggs, hard-boiled
4 oz. cheese, grated
¾ pint (1⅞ cups) white sauce
made mustard
4 slices white bread, crusts removed
butter, melted

Cut the celery hearts in thick slices and place in the base of a 2-pint casserole. Grill the bacon until crisp and crumble or chop it finely. Halve the eggs lengthwise and remove the yolks.
Cream the bacon and egg yolks together, fill the mixture into the egg whites and pair up the halves again. Place them on the bed of celery.
Mix most of the cheese into the white sauce, adding a little mustard to taste. Pour over the eggs. Dice the bread, dip in a little melted butter and spoon in a ring round the outer edge of the dish. Sprinkle the remaining cheese in the centre.
Place the dish under a low grill until the bread cubes are brown and the sauce bubbling.

Stuffed artichokes are a luxury supper dish

KROMESKI
makes 8

For fritter batter :

4 oz. (1 cup) plain flour
pinch of salt
1 tbsp. cooking oil
¼ pint (⅝ cup) warm water
1 egg white

For filling :

2 oz. butter
2 oz. (½ cup) plain flour
½ pint (1¼ cups) milk
1 egg yolk
1 tbsp. fruit table sauce
salt and pepper
4 oz. green peppers (capsicums), seeded and chopped
8 oz. cooked chicken, chopped
8 thinly cut rashers of back bacon, rinded
deep fat for frying

Sift together the flour and salt into a bowl. Make a well in the centre and pour in the oil and warm water; beat well. Allow to rest for 1 hour.
Melt the butter in a pan, remove from the heat, stir in the flour and cook for a few minutes without colouring. Gradually stir in the milk. Beat in the egg yolk and the table sauce and season well.
Blanch the chopped green pepper in boiling water for 1–2 minutes, drain and refresh in cold water. Drain again and add to the sauce with the chicken. Allow to cool.
Divide the mixture into 8 and shape into cork shapes on a floured board. Wrap each portion in a rasher of bacon, securing with wooden cocktail sticks.
Stiffly whisk the egg white and fold the batter through the white.

Supper Russian style, with kromeski

Use up left-over vegetables in a Spanish omelette

Dip the kromeski into the batter and deep fry in fat or oil heated to 375°F. for about 5 minutes until crisp and golden. Drain on absorbent paper. Remove the cocktail sticks. Serve really hot, with a savoury rice.

SAVOURY MERINGUE SLICES

serves 4

4 eggs, separated
4 rounds of buttered toast
salt and pepper
1 oz. Parmesan cheese, grated

Place an egg yolk on each round of toast. Whisk the egg whites until stiff, season the cheese and fold into the egg whites. Pile on to the toast and place under a low grill for about 10 minutes, until firm and golden brown.

Toast snacks are popular at supper time

PICK OF THE PANTRY PIZZA

serves 4

1 level tbsp. dried onion flakes
boiling water
8 oz. (2 cups) self-raising flour
1 level tbsp. powdered stock
1 level tsp. baking powder
2 oz. butter or margarine
milk and water to mix
15-oz. can pilchards in tomato sauce
8-oz. can tomatoes, drained
3 oz. cheese, grated
freshly ground black pepper
chopped parsley, optional

Soak the dried onion in boiling water for 5 minutes. Sift together the flour, powdered stock and baking powder.

Rub in the fat and mix to a firm scone dough with milk and water. Turn on to a floured board, knead lightly and roll to form a 9-in. round or, better still, press into a 9-in. flan ring.

Drain the onions and spread over the dough. Arrange the pilchards on top with the drained tomatoes and sprinkle with cheese. Season with pepper.

Bake in the oven at 425°F. (mark 7) for approximately 45 minutes. Cover with foil if necessary to prevent excessive browning. Serve hot from the oven, sprinkled with chopped parsley.

CHAKCHOUKA

serves 4

1 oz. lard
1 lb. tomatoes, skinned and sliced
¾ lb. potatoes, peeled and sliced
¼ lb. green peppers (capsicums), seeded and finely chopped
1 clove of garlic, skinned and crushed
salt and freshly ground black pepper
4 eggs

Melt the lard in a saucepan and fry the tomatoes and potatoes slowly for 20 minutes. Add the peppers and garlic, season and simmer for a further 15 minutes. Poach the eggs in gently simmering water for 3–4 minutes.

Turn the vegetables into a hot serving dish, drain the eggs and arrange them on top of the vegetables.

CURRIED SCRAMBLE

serves 2

1 small onion, skinned and chopped
fat for frying
1½ level tsps. curry powder
4 eggs
1 tsp. chopped parsley
3 tbsps. milk
salt and freshly ground black pepper
2 large slices buttered toast or 2–4 crumpets

Fry the onion in a little fat until soft but not coloured, then add the curry powder and fry slowly for 5 minutes.

Beat together the eggs, parsley, milk and seasoning. Add to the pan and cook gently, stirring constantly and lifting the egg from the bottom of the pan.

Serve on hot buttered toast or toasted crumpets.

STUFFED MUSHROOMS ON TOAST

serves 4

8 medium-sized mushrooms, wiped
1 small onion, skinned and finely chopped
½ oz. butter
3 tbsps. finely chopped cooked ham or bacon
5 level tbsps. fresh white breadcrumbs
1 oz. cheese, grated
1 tsp. chopped parsley
beaten egg to bind
salt and pepper
cooking oil
4 rounds of buttered toast

Remove and chop the stalks from the mushrooms. Lightly fry the stalks and the onion in the butter for 3–5 minutes, until soft. Add the ham or bacon, breadcrumbs, cheese and parsley and enough egg to bind them all together. Stir until well mixed and hot, season to taste. Brush the mushrooms with a little oil and put in a greased baking tin. Pile the filling into the mushrooms, cover with grease-proof paper or foil and bake in the centre of the oven at 375°F. (mark 5) for about 20 minutes. Serve on buttered toast.

CRAB TOASTS

serves 4

a little butter
1 oz. fresh white breadcrumbs
3½-oz. can crab meat, or fresh cooked crab meat
3 tbsps. top of the milk
salt and pepper
1 tbsp. sherry
4 slices of toast

Melt 1 oz. butter in a saucepan, add the breadcrumbs and flaked crab meat, mix well and stir in the top of the milk. Stir for a few minutes over the heat and season well, then pour in the sherry. Cut

Handy hint

To keep a sauce warm without allowing a skin to form, place a circle of buttered or damp greaseproof paper over it in the pan. Sprinkle a sweet custard sauce with caster sugar to prevent a skin forming.

the toast into triangles, removing the crusts, butter and pile high with the crab meat mixture.

SPANISH OMELETTE

serves 2

butter or oil for frying
1 small onion, skinned and chopped
2–3 mushrooms, wiped and sliced
1 cooked potato, diced
1 cap canned pimiento (sweet red pepper), chopped
small quantity cooked peas, beans or carrots
4 eggs
salt and freshly ground black pepper
chopped parsley

Put enough butter or oil in an 8-in. frying pan just to cover the base. Add the onion and sauté until soft but not coloured. Add the mushrooms and cook until tender. Add the potato, pimiento and cooked vegetables. Heat thoroughly.
Lightly mix the eggs, season and pour over the vegetable mixture, which should be bubbling. When just set, turn upside down on to a heated serving dish. Garnish with chopped parsley and serve at once.

MUSHROOMS IN PORT WINE

serves 2

1$\frac{1}{2}$ oz. butter
12 oz. button mushrooms, wiped and trimmed
4 thick slices of bread
2 tbsps. port wine
salt and freshly ground black pepper
oz. instant potato
2 tbsps. milk
pint ($\frac{5}{8}$ cup) double cream
heaped tbsp. grated Parmesan cheese

Melt 1 oz. butter in a saucepan; add the mushrooms, shake well to coat them and sauté gently.
Toast 2 slices of bread and grate the remaining slices into breadcrumbs. Cut the crusts off the toast and cut each slice into 2 triangles. Add the port to the mushrooms, season and continue to simmer.
Meanwhile, make up the instant potato with boiling water and stir in the milk and remaining butter. Spoon into a forcing bag and pipe with a large star vegetable nozzle round the edge of a flameproof serving dish.
Stir the cream into the mushrooms and continue to cook gently, stirring until the sauce thickens. Lightly brown the potato under the grill and spoon the mushroom mixture into the centre. Sprinkle with breadcrumbs and Parmesan and return to the grill until the cheese is golden brown. Garnish with the toast triangles and serve with salad.

KIDNEY TOASTS

serves 2

8 oz. calf's kidney or 4 sheep's or lamb's kidneys
4 oz. mushrooms, wiped
2 oz. butter
1 oz. ($\frac{1}{4}$ cup) flour
$\frac{1}{2}$ pint (1$\frac{1}{4}$ cups) stock
4 tbsps. single cream
1 tbsp. dry sherry
2 large slices white bread
butter
salt and pepper
chopped parsley

Remove the fat and skin from the kidneys, cut away the core. Cut the kidney into small pieces. Slice the mushrooms.
Melt the butter in a pan and sauté the mushrooms and kidney for about 5 minutes.
Stir in the flour and mix well. Gradually add the stock, stirring over gentle heat until thickened. Bring to the boil, reduce the heat, cover and simmer for about 20 minutes, or until the kidney is cooked.
Add the cream, then the sherry to the kidney mixture and reheat but take care not to boil. Adjust seasoning.
Prepare 2 slices of fresh hot toast and spread generously with butter. Stir some chopped parsley into the kidney mixture and spoon on to the toast.

SAUCISSES AU VIN BLANC

serves 2

$\frac{1}{2}$ lb. pork chipolata sausages
1$\frac{1}{2}$ oz. butter
2 oz. onion, skinned and finely sliced
4 oz. lean bacon rashers, rinded and diced
1 level tbsp. flour
$\frac{1}{4}$ pint ($\frac{5}{8}$ cup) chicken stock, made from a stock cube
2 tbsps. dry white wine
4-oz. pkt. instant potato
boiling water
salt and freshly ground black pepper
2 tbsps. milk
parsley for garnish

Twist each chipolata into two and separate with scissors. Melt $\frac{1}{2}$ oz. butter in a frying pan, add the sausages and fry gently for 2 minutes.
Remove the sausages from the frying pan, add the onion and bacon and fry for 2 minutes. Stir in the flour, stock and wine and blend well. Return the sausages to the pan, cover and simmer for 6 minutes.
Make up the instant potato with the boiling water, season well and stir in the milk and remaining butter.
Spoon potato into a forcing bag fitted with a vegetable star nozzle and pipe in whirls round a flameproof serving dish. Place under the grill to brown lightly.
Spoon the sausages and their sauce into the centre of the potato and garnish with parsley.
Serve with green beans or asparagus tips.

Use potted shrimps, peppers and cheese as a luxury pancake filling

SHRIMP PANCAKES

serves 2

For filling:
1 small green pepper (capsicum), seeded and diced
$\frac{1}{2}$ oz. butter
4 oz. potted shrimps
$\frac{1}{2}$ oz. flour
$\frac{1}{4}$ pint ($\frac{5}{8}$ cup) single cream
4 tbsps. milk
grated Parmesan cheese

For pancakes:
3 oz. ($\frac{3}{4}$ cup) plain flour
1 egg, beaten
$\frac{1}{4}$ pint ($\frac{5}{8}$ cup) milk and water, mixed
salt and freshly ground black pepper
lard for frying

Blanch the pepper in boiling water for 3 minutes; drain. Melt $\frac{1}{2}$ oz. butter in a frying pan, add the shrimps and heat gently. Stir in $\frac{1}{2}$ oz. flour, two-thirds of the cream, the milk and the pepper. Stir until thickened. Keep hot.
Sift the flour into a bowl, beat in the egg, milk and water and seasoning, and continue to beat well. Heat a knob of lard in a frying pan, spoon in 3 tablespoons batter, swirl round to coat the pan base and cook until golden underneath. Turn and cook the other side. Turn on to a hot tea towel and keep warm. Repeat with remaining batter, to make 4 pancakes.
Divide the filling between the pancakes and roll up each one carefully. Arrange on a hot flameproof serving dish. Pour the remaining cream over the pancakes, sprinkle with Parmesan cheese and brown under a hot grill.

CREAMED HAM AND ASPARAGUS

serves 6

2 10$\frac{1}{2}$-oz. cans condensed cream of chicken soup
1 medium-sized onion, skinned and finely chopped
2 tbsps. dry sherry
salt and freshly ground black pepper
$\frac{3}{4}$ lb. lean cooked ham or boiled bacon, diced
12-oz. can green asparagus tips, drained
4 oz. Emmenthal or Gruyère cheese, thinly sliced

Blend together the undiluted soup, onion and sherry. Adjust seasoning. Layer the ham and asparagus into a 2–2$\frac{1}{2}$ pint capacity ovenproof dish. Pour the soup mixture over. Top with slices of cheese and cook in the centre of the oven at 400°F.

(mark 6) for about 30 minutes. Serve with Melba toast or bread sticks.

QUICHE LYONNAISE
serves 4

4 oz. shortcrust pastry – i.e. made with 4 oz. (1 cup) flour etc.
1 large onion, skinned and chopped
2 tbsps. cooking oil
1 oz. butter
1½ level tbsps. flour
½ pint (1¼ cups) milk
4 oz. Cheddar cheese, grated
salt and freshly ground black pepper
4 eggs
parsley sprigs, for garnish

Roll out the pastry and use to line an 8-in. flan ring or tin. Bake blind in the oven at 400°F. (mark 6) for 15 minutes.

Fry the chopped onion in the oil until soft and evenly coloured. Drain off the fat and spread the onion over the base of the freshly baked flan case.

Melt the butter in a small pan, blend in the flour and cook for 2-3 minutes, without colouring. Blend in the milk and most of the cheese, reserving a little; bring to the boil, stirring, and season. Keep this sauce warm.

Poach the eggs in gently simmering water for 3-4 minutes. Drain well and arrange them on the onion, in the flan case. Coat with the cheese sauce, and sprinkle with the reserved grated cheese.

Place the flan under a pre-heated grill and brown quickly. Garnish with parsley sprigs and serve at once.

BUCK RAREBIT
serves 4

8 oz. Cheddar cheese, grated
1 oz. butter
1 level tsp. dry mustard
salt and freshly ground black pepper
3-4 tbsps. brown ale
4 eggs
4 large slices bread
butter

Place the cheese, butter, mustard, seasoning and ale in a thick-based pan and heat very gently until a creamy mixture is obtained. Meanwhile, poach the eggs and toast the bread.

Butter the hot toast generously. Pour the cheese mixture over the toast, put under a grill until golden and bubbling and top each slice with a poached egg.

Supper-time drinks are best served hot

HOT DRINKS FOR SUPPER TIME

HOT SPICED TEA
serves 6

3 whole cloves
½-in. stick of cinnamon
2 pints (5 cups) water
½ oz. tea
2 oz. (¼ cup) sugar
2½ fl. oz. (⅓ cup) orange juice
juice of 1 lemon
cinnamon sticks for serving

In a pan add the spices to the water and bring to the boil. Pour on to the tea in a bowl and allow to infuse for 5 minutes. Stir, add the sugar, stir again until dissolved and add the strained fruit juices. Place over a low heat and reheat but do not boil or even simmer. Strain and serve with cinnamon sticks.

CHINESE ORANGE TEA
makes 2¼ pints (5⅝ cups)

3 oranges
2 oz. (½ cup) flour
4 oz. (½ cup) sugar
2 pints (5 cups) water

Cut the oranges in half, scoop out the pulp and juice and place in a bowl. Gradually add some water to the flour to form a stiff dough, then roll into balls the size of tiny marbles and put on one side. Dissolve the sugar in 2 pints water in a large pan and bring to the boil, then drop in the flour balls and continue to boil until they float.

Add the orange pulp and juice, reboil for 30 seconds and serve the tea very hot.

BORGIA COFFEE
serves 3

pared rind of 1 orange
½ oz. finely ground coffee
½ pint (1¼ cups) water
½ pint (1¼ cups) milk
6 heaped tsps. drinking chocolate
4 tbsps. double cream, lightly whipped

Shred the orange rind into fine julienne strips and blanch in boiling water for a few minutes, until tender. Drain.

Use the coffee and water to make ½ pint black coffee (use an Espresso machine, filter, Cona, percolator or whichever method you prefer). Heat the milk in a small pan and whisk in the drinking

chocolate.

Combine the black coffee and the chocolate, divide between 3 mugs and top each with whipped cream. Decorate with shreds of orange rind.

EGG NOG
serves 1

1 egg
1 level tbsp. sugar
1 sherry glass of sherry or brandy
⅓ pint (⅞ cup) milk

Whisk the egg and sugar together and add the sherry or brandy. Heat the milk without boiling and pour it over the egg mixture; stir well and serve hot in a glass.

HOT SPICED PINEAPPLE CUP
makes about 1½ pints (3¾ cups)

2 15-fl. oz. cans pineapple juice
4 level tbsps. sugar
2 tbsps. lemon juice
4-in. cinnamon stick

Simmer all the ingredients together for 10 minutes, remove the cinnamon and pour the juice into glasses.

HUCKLE-MY-BUFF
serves 6

2 pints (5 cups) draught beer
6 eggs, beaten
2 oz. (¼ cup) sugar
grated nutmeg
brandy to taste

Heat 1 pint (2½ cups) beer with the eggs and sugar, but do not boil. Remove from the heat and add the remaining beer, a generous amount of nutmeg and brandy to taste. Serve in heatproof glasses.

Handy hint

To prevent dark rings forming round the yolks of hard-boiled eggs, cool the eggs quickly by cracking the shells and holding under cold running water until completely cold.

HOT SUPPER MENUS

SUPPER MENU *serves 6*
after the theatre

**BEEF AND PEPPER
CASSEROLE
GREEN SALAD
CRUSTY BREAD AND
BUTTER
GRAPE FLAN**

Timetable for supper at 11.15 p.m.
Early in the day: *Prepare the
salad ingredients and dressing but
do not mix. Store salads in the
refrigerator.*
*Make the grape flan, cool and
cover. Leave in a cool place (not
the refrigerator).*
*Prepare and cook the beef
casserole, discard bouquet garni but
do not add the reserved slices of
pepper. Cool quickly and leave in a
cool place.*
*If available, use automatic oven
timer to reheat casserole.*
10.45 *(on returning from theatre).
Add reserved pepper to casserole.
If automatic timer was not used,
put casserole in the oven at 400°F.
(mark 6) to reheat.*
*Serve drinks, crisps, nuts etc.
Slice bread and toss salad.*
11.15 *Serve supper.*

BEEF AND PEPPER
CASSEROLE

2 lb. chuck steak
2 oz. fat or oil
2 large onions, skinned and
   sliced
2 green peppers (capsicums),
   seeded and sliced
1½ oz. (⅜ cup) flour
1½ pints (3¾ cups) brown stock
2 tbsps. tomato paste
salt and freshly ground black
   pepper
bouquet garni

Cut the meat into 1-in. cubes. Heat
the fat or oil and fry the onions
until golden brown; remove and
place in a casserole. Reserve a few
slices of pepper and fry the rest
lightly. Add to the onions in the
casserole. Brown the meat in the
remaining fat, adding only a few
pieces at a time to the pan, so that
the fat remains really hot. When
the meat is well browned, transfer
to the casserole with the vegetables.
Add the flour to the fat remaining
in the frying pan, stir well and

Saucisses au vin blanc

A hot casserole and cold flan make a good choice for supper after the theatre

gradually stir in the stock and tomato paste. Bring to the boil, season and pour over the meat and vegetables in the casserole. Add the bouquet garni.

Cover and cook in the centre of the oven at 350°F. (mark 4) for 1–1½ hours; 20 minutes before serving add the reserved slices of pepper and return to the oven. Remove the bouquet garni before serving.

GREEN SALAD

For 6 people you will need 1 large lettuce, 1 bunch watercress, 1 head of chicory and 1 green pepper (capsicum). Wash and trim, slicing the chicory and pepper. Toss in French dressing.

GRAPE FLAN

For pastry :

4 oz. (1 cup) plain flour
a pinch of salt
3 oz. butter or margarine and lard, mixed
1 level tsp. caster sugar
1 egg, beaten

For filling :

½ pint (1¼ cups) milk
2 oz. (¼ cup) caster sugar
1 oz. (¼ cup) flour
2 level tsps. cornflour
1 large egg
1 tsp. grated orange rind
2 tsps. orange liqueur
¾ lb. grapes (black and white)
juice of 1 orange, strained
a little arrowroot

Sift the flour and salt together and rub in the fat with the fingertips, until the mixture resembles fine crumbs. Mix in the sugar. Add the egg, stirring until the ingredients begin to stick together; then with 1 hand, collect the mixture together and knead very lightly to give a firm, smooth dough. Roll out and use to line an 8½-in. fluted flan tin. Bake blind at 400°F. (mark 6) for 20 minutes. Allow to cool.

Heat the milk but do not boil. In a basin, blend together the sugar, flour, cornflour and egg. Stir in a little hot milk to give a smooth paste, return the mixture to the pan and stir until it thickens and just comes to the boil. Add the grated orange rind and the liqueur. Cool the orange custard and spoon into the pastry case. Cover the surface with buttered greaseproof paper to prevent a skin forming and leave until cold.

Halve and pip the grapes and arrange over the filling. Blend together the orange juice and arrowroot and brush this as a glaze over the grapes.

Soup and a warm quiche for a casual supper party

SUPPER MENU *serves 10 for an informal evening at home*

CREAM OF MUSHROOM SOUP OR CHILLED TOMATO JUICE
ONION QUICHE
PINEAPPLE AND PEPPER SALAD
FRENCH BREAD AND BUTTER
CHEESE BOARD

Timetable *for supper at 10.00 p.m.*
Day before: *Make the soup and refrigerate.*
Fry the croûtons, cool and store in an airtight container.
Bake the shortcrust flan cases.
Same day: *Slice the onions, sauté and keep in a covered bowl. Beat together the egg mixture and keep in a cool place. Prepare anchovies; keep covered.*
Prepare the cheese board and keep it covered.
Early in the evening: *Prepare the salad.*
9.30 *Fill the flan cases, decorate and bake.*
Put the soup to reheat.
Refresh croûtons in oven for a short time. Toss the salad.
10.00 *Serve supper.*

CREAM OF MUSHROOM SOUP

6 oz. butter
12 oz. onions, skinned and finely chopped
1 lb. button mushrooms, wiped and chopped
3 oz. (¾ cup) plain flour
3 pints (8½ cups) chicken stock, made from 4 stock cubes and 3 pints water
1 pint (2½ cups) milk
salt and freshly ground black pepper
¼ level tsp. garlic salt
lemon juice
fried croûtons

Melt the butter in a large pan and sauté the onions for 10 minutes, until soft but not coloured. Add the mushrooms, cover, and continue to cook for a further 5 minutes.

Stir in the flour and cook for 3 minutes, then slowly add the stock, stirring all the time. Bring to the boil and simmer gently for 20 minutes.

Add the milk and seasonings and lemon juice to taste. Simmer for a further 10 minutes. Do not boil after adding the milk. Garnish with croûtons of fried bread just before serving.

ONION QUICHE

12 oz. shortcrust pastry – i.e. made with 12 oz. (3 cups) plain flour etc.
4 oz. butter
2 lb. onions, skinned and sliced
4 eggs
2 oz. (½ cup) flour
¾ pint (1⅞ cups) milk
salt and pepper
2 2-oz. cans anchovies, drained
stoned black olives

Use the pastry to line 2 plain 8-in flan rings placed on baking sheets Bake blind at 400°F. (mark 6) fc 20 minutes.

Melt the butter in a frying pan an fry the onions until soft, takin care not to brown them. Divid the onions between the flans. Bea together the eggs, flour, milk, sa and pepper, then pour over th onions. Halve the anchovie lengthwise and arrange on top in criss-cross pattern and place black olive in each space. Bake i the oven at 350°F. (mark 4) fc 20–30 minutes, until set.

PINEAPPLE AND PEPPER SALAD

28-oz. can pineapple pieces
1 green pepper (capsicum), blanched, seeded and slice
¼ cucumber (or ½ a small ridge cucumber), diced
2 oz. sultanas
1 lettuce, washed and shredded
4 tbsps. French dressing

Drain the pineapple and reserv the juice. Mix the pineapple piece with the pepper, cucumber, sul tanas and lettuce.

Combine the French dressing an 2 tablespoons pineapple juice pour over the salad and toss we

Perfect Dinner Parties

Perfect dinner parties need planning. The menus here have been selected carefully to please the most discerning palate, without over taxing the energies of the cook-hostess. Follow the timetables and there will be no last minute flusters!

This page: A classic Boeuf Stroganoff

HARICOTS VERTS A LA TOMATE
BOEUF STROGANOFF
LEAF SPINACH AND BOILED RICE
TRANCHE AUX FRUITS
Wine – Claret
(Haut Médoc or St. Emilion)

Timetable *for dinner at 8.00 p.m.*
Day before: *Make flan case.*
5.00 *Collect ingredients and equipment. Fill flan.*
Beat and cut the steak and coat with seasoned flour. Prepare onions and mushrooms. Cook rice, drain and leave to cool. Wash and pick over spinach.
7.30 *Prepare first course. Put drained rice in a buttered casserole, cover tightly with a lid and place in warm oven to heat through. Boil spinach, drain and refresh.*
7.45 *Cook beef (add soured cream between courses); keep warm. Place roughly chopped spinach over a low light with a little butter.*
8.00 *Serve first course.*

HARICOTS VERTS A LA TOMATE

1 lb. French beans
½ lb. firm tomatoes
1½ oz. butter
1 bay leaf
sprig of thyme
salt and pepper

Top, tail and wash the beans. Plunge into boiling salted water, cover and cook for 5 minutes. Scald the tomatoes and remove the skins, then quarter them. Drain the beans in a colander, melt the butter in the pan over gentle heat and return the beans, with the tomatoes, bay leaf and thyme. Season with salt and freshly ground black pepper. Cover with a tightly fitting lid; if the lid is rather loose, place a buttered round of greaseproof paper under it to hold it tight. Simmer gently for about 15 minutes, shaking the pan occasionally.
Remove bay leaf and thyme before serving.

BOEUF STROGANOFF

1½ lb. rump steak
3 level tbsps. seasoned flour
2 oz. butter
1 onion, skinned and thinly sliced
½ lb. mushrooms, sliced
salt and pepper
½ pint (1¼ cups) soured cream

Tranche aux fruits, concealing a deliciously smooth pastry cream

Beat the steak, trim, cut into strips ¼ in. by 2 in. and coat with seasoned flour. Fry the meat in half the butter until golden brown – about 5–7 minutes. Cook the onion and mushrooms in the remaining butter for 3–4 minutes, season to taste and add the beef. Warm the soured cream and stir into the meat mixture. Serve with boiled rice and leaf spinach.

TRANCHE AUX FRUITS

For pâte sucrée :
6 oz. (1½ cups) plain flour
pinch of salt
1½ oz. caster sugar
3 oz. butter
2 tbsps. beaten egg
For pastry cream :
1 pint (2½ cups) milk
4 oz. (½ cup) caster sugar
2 oz. (½ cup) plain flour
½ oz. cornflour
2 large eggs
2 oz. butter
icing sugar
For filling :
12-oz. can pineapple pieces
11-oz. can mandarin oranges
8-oz. can cherries
For fruit glaze :
2 level tbsps. apricot jam
1 tbsp. water

Sift the flour and salt on to a pastry board or marble slab. Make a well in the centre and into it put the sugar, butter and egg. Using the fingertips of one hand, pinch and work the sugar, butter and egg together until blended. Gradually work in all the flour and knead lightly until smooth. Put the paste in a cool place for at least 1 hour, return to room temperature until

easy to roll out.
Roll out the pâte sucrée and use to line a 14-in. by 4½-in. by 1-in. flan frame (if your oven is small, use a square flan frame), placed on a flat baking sheet. Line with greaseproof paper, fill with dried beans and bake blind at 400°F. (mark 6) for about 25 minutes. Remove beans and bake for a further 5 minutes.
Heat the milk. Blend together the sugar, flour, cornflour and beaten eggs; stir in the milk. Return to the pan, heat gently, stirring until the mixture thickens and just comes to the boil. Stir in the butter. Cool. When nearly cold, spoon into the pastry case. Dust with icing sugar to stop a skin forming. Drain canned fruit thoroughly. Stone the cherries. Arrange fruit over pastry cream in tight panels. Bring jam and water to the boil. Bubble gently for 1 minute. Sieve and brush whilst warm over the fruit. Serve cold.

DRESSED CHICORY SPEARS
POUSSINS MARSALA
MUSHROOMS, FRENCH BEANS AND NEW POTATOES
APPLE BRULEE

Wine–Hock (Sichel's Blue Nun or Deinhard's Hanns Christoff Wein)

Timetable *for dinner at 8.00 p.m.*
Day before: *Make apple purée. Halve the poussins and refrigerate.*
5.00 *Collect ingredients and equipment. Prepare chicory and*

dressing. Prepare dessert and chill. Prepare vegetables.
6.30 *Start to cook poussins. When ready, transfer to flame-proof dish and keep warm. Prepare cheese topping.*
7.30 *Cook mushrooms and keep warm.*
7.45 *Cook beans and potatoes. Spoon cheese topping over poussins and place under hot grill. When ready return to oven to keep warm. Combine chicory and dressing.*
8.00 *Serve first course. Leave grill alight to finish off dessert between courses.*

DRESSED CHICORY SPEARS

1 lb. chicory spears
juice of 1 large lemon
1 egg yolk
salt and pepper
¼ pint (⅝ cup) oil
2 medium peppers, 1 green and 1 red

Cut the base off each head of chicory. Separate the leaves under cold running water and drain thoroughly. Toss in 3 tablespoon lemon juice. Beat the egg yolk with a pinch of salt and freshly milled pepper. Add the oil, a little at time, whisking continually. When thick, stir in the lemon juice drained from the chicory. Adjust the thickness to a stiff pouring consistency by adding a little warm water.
Divide the chicory between large goblets or balloon glasses. Just before serving, spoon over dressing and sprinkle with finely chopped red and green peppers.

POUSSINS MARSALA

3 poussins (approx. 1¾ lb. each), halved
2 oz. butter
¼ pint (⅝ cup) Marsala or sherry
¼ pint (⅝ cup) double cream
¼ level tsp. paprika
1 clove of garlic, skinned and crushed
4 oz. (1 cup) Cheddar cheese, grated
salt and pepper
chopped parsley
sprigs of rosemary, optional

Fry the poussin halves in butter for about 5 minutes, until golden brown. Remove from pan and drain off excess fat. Replace chicken joints flesh sides down. Pour over the Marsala or sherry. Top with a tightly fitting lid o

l and bubble gently for about
minutes or until the juices run
ear when the chicken flesh is
nctured with a fork.

eanwhile, whip the cream, fold
paprika, garlic and cheese.
ason. Transfer poussin halves
d juices to a flameproof dish
d spoon over the cheese topping.
ash under a fierce grill until the
eese melts and browns. Serve
rinkled with parsley.
arnish with rosemary sprigs and
rve with sauté mushrooms and
ench beans as accompanying
getables.

PPLE BRULEE

pint (2½ cups) thick apple
 purée
pint (⅝ cup) double cream
pint (⅝ cup) single cream
ated rind 1 orange
ft light brown sugar

urn cold purée into individual
ufflé dishes to give about 1 in.
epth of purée. Whisk creams
gether until light and fluffy, but
ot over-firm. Fold in the orange
nd and spread over the apple.
hill until just before required.
efore serving, cover with a thick
yer of sugar—about ¼–½ in.—and
ace under a hot grill to melt the
gar quickly. Serve when
ubbling.
ote : To prepare thick apple
urée, peel, core and slice 2 lb.
ooking apples. Cook with just
ough water to cover the bottom
the pan. When soft, reduce to
thick purée by boiling. Add
-4 oz. sugar and boil gently,
irring, for 5 minutes.

---

imetable for dinner at 8.00 p.m.
ay before: Make pâté and
ineapple granito.
30 Collect ingredients and
quipment. Start birds cooking.
repare potatoes for game chips.
lice pâté and put on individual
ates.
00 Scoop granito into pineapple
ell and leave in coldest part of
frigerator.
ook game chips (or heat packet

Dressed chicory spears make a refreshing starter

crisps) and celery; keep warm.
7.30 Carve birds and complete
casserole.
8.00 Serve first course.

PATE MAISON

½ lb. chicken liver
3 oz. lean pork or veal
2 oz. (1 cup) fresh white
    breadcrumbs
4 fl. oz. (½ cup) milk
salt and pepper
pinch of nutmeg
streaky bacon rashers, cut
    thinly and rinded
sprig of thyme
1 bay leaf
⅛ pint (⅓ cup) aspic jelly made
    from aspic jelly powder
½ tbsp. brandy

Mince the liver finely once and
the pork or veal twice. Soak the
breadcrumbs in milk. Season the
liver and pork with salt, pepper
and nutmeg. Stir in the breadcrumbs gently, otherwise the liver
will lose its colour.
Line a 1-pint terrine with very
thin slices of streaky bacon then
put in the liver mixture. Top with
more bacon and add the thyme
and bay leaf. Cover with a lid and
place in a roasting tin. Pour water

into tin to a depth of 1 in. Place in
the oven and cook at 325°F. (mark
3) for about 1½ hours.
Add a little melted aspic jelly and
the brandy 15 minutes before the
end of the cooking time. Remove
from the oven. When beginning
to cool, discard lid and place a
plate and a weight on top. Allow
to cool completely before covering
with remaining aspic.
Serve with crusty French bread.

CASSEROLE OF GAME

2 partridges or pheasants
    (dressed)
1 oz. butter
2 tbsps. oil
1 small onion, skinned and
    chopped
4 oz. veal, minced
4 oz. lean ham, minced
1 small cooking apple, peeled
    and sliced
1 clove of garlic, skinned and
    crushed
salt and pepper
1 bay leaf
4 tbsps. stock
¼ pint (⅝ cup) single cream
2 tbsps. brandy
lemon juice (optional)
¼ lb. button mushrooms
butter
watercress

Truss the birds and fry evenly
in the butter and oil until well
sealed and browned. Take out of
pan and set aside. To the pan add
the onion, veal, ham, apple and
garlic. Cook gently for 5 minutes.
Turn mixture into a casserole just
large enough to take the birds,
season and add the bay leaf. Place
the birds on top, breast sides
down, and pour over the stock.
Cook in the oven at 325°F. (mark
3) for about 1 hour until showing
signs of being tender. Remove from
the oven, discard the bay leaf,
turn birds over. Pour in cream.
Warm the brandy, ignite it and
add to casserole. Cover tightly and
return to the oven for ¾ hour.
To serve, carve the birds and
keep hot. Adjust seasoning in
gravy and sharpen if necessary
with lemon juice. Sauté the mushrooms in a little butter and add to
the gravy. Reheat but do not boil.
Spoon over the birds. Garnish with
watercress and serve accompanied
by game chips and braised celery.
Note : This method is also suitable
for duck. Use 1 3½-lb. oven-ready
duck, jointed into four; fry skin
side down until brown and drain
well on absorbent kitchen paper.
Pour off nearly all the dripping
from the pan, then continue as
for game. Before adding the cream,
again skim off as much fat as
possible.

PINEAPPLE AND
MARASCHINO GRANITO

1 medium pineapple
sugar to dredge
¼ pint (⅝ cup) water
8 oz. (1 cup) caster sugar
rind and juice of 1 lemon
2 tbsps. Maraschino liqueur
10 Maraschino cherries

Split the pineapple down the
middle and scrape the flesh and
juice into a bowl. Discard centre
core. Sprinkle the inside of the
pineapple with sugar and chill.
Make a purée of the fruit flesh and
juice in an electric blender. Add
water, sugar, lemon rind and juice
and bring to the boil. Boil for 5
minutes. Cool, then turn into a
freezing tray. Freeze until mushy.
Turn the pineapple mush into a
bowl, beat well and add the liqueur
and cherries. Return to home-
freezer or refrigerator and freeze
until firm.
To serve, scoop the pineapple
granito out of the tray and pile
into the chilled shell. This dish
looks particularly attractive on a
silver or stainless steel dish, in a
bed of ice cubes.

CHILLED CUCUMBER SOUP
BARBECUED LAMB
LEEKS, CARROTS AND CREAMED POTATOES
RASPBERRY CHEESE FLAN
Wine – Vin ordinaire (Bordeaux rouge)

Timetable *for dinner at 8.00*
Day before: *Make soup and chill.*
In the morning: *Make raspberry cheese flan.*
6.00 *Prepare barbecue sauce and put lamb to cook.*
6.30 *Whip cream and decorate flan.*
7.15 *Cook vegetables and keep warm.*
7.45 *Dish up meat and keep warm.*
8.00 *Serve first course.*

CHILLED CUCUMBER SOUP

1 small onion, skinned and sliced
1½ pints (3¾ cups) white stock
1 large or 2 small cucumbers
sprig of mint
1 level tbsp. cornflour
2–3 tbsps. cream
salt and pepper
green colouring

Simmer the onion for 15 minutes in a pan with the stock. Peel and chop the cucumber (saving a little for garnish), and add to the stock with the mint; simmer for about 20 minutes, or until the cucumber is cooked. Sieve the soup or purée in an electric blender, return it to the pan and reheat. Blend the cornflour with a little cold water to a smooth cream. Stir in a little of the hot soup, return the mixture to the pan and bring to the boil, stirring until it thickens. Cook for a further 2–3 minutes. Stir in the cream and re-season if necessary. Tint the soup delicately with green colouring, pour it into a large bowl, cover and chill. Serve with 2 or 3 slices of cucumber floating on top of the soup and serve cheese straws as an accompaniment.

BARBECUED LAMB

1 shoulder of lamb (approx. 3½ lb.)
1 level tsp. dry mustard
1 level tsp. ground ginger
salt and pepper
2 cloves of garlic, skinned and crushed
flour

A chilled cucumber soup makes a good start to a warm evening

For barbecue sauce :
4 tbsps. Worcestershire sauce
4 tbsps. brown table sauce
4 tbsps. mushroom ketchup
2 level tsps. sugar
1 tbsp. vinegar
1 oz. butter, melted
cayenne pepper and salt
¼ pint (⅝ cup) water
1 small onion, skinned and thinly sliced

Trim off any excess fat from the shoulder of lamb. Mix the mustard, ginger, salt, pepper and garlic well together and rub into the surface of the meat. Sprinkle the meat with flour and place it in a

> **Handy hint**
> To chop an onion, peel it keeping the root intact. Cut in half through the root. Holding the root end away from the knife, and using a sharp, pointed knife, cut down in even slices about ½ in. apart. Make a similar number of horizontal cuts, stopping just short of the root. Holding the onion firmly, cut down at rightangles to the previous cuts: the onion will then fall away in neat dice.

roasting tin. Blend the sauce ingredients well together, adding the sliced onion last, and pour over the meat.

Cook in the centre of the oven at 425°F. (mark 7) for 30 minutes, then lower the heat to 350°F. (mark 4) and continue to cook, allowing 27 minutes to the lb. Baste the joint with the sauce 2–3 times during the cooking, adding a little more water to the sauce if needed.

Serve with leeks and carrots.

RASPBERRY CHEESE FLAN

For rich flan pastry :
6 oz. (1½ cups) plain flour
salt (optional)
4 oz. butter or margarine
2 level tsps. caster sugar
1–2 egg yolks (according to size)
3–5 tsps. water

For filling :
3-oz. pkt. cream cheese
1 tbsp. milk
½ pint (1¼ cups) boiling water
½ 1-pint raspberry jelly tablet
8 oz. raspberries, fresh or frozen
double cream for decoration

Sift flour with a pinch of salt.

Lightly rub in the fat with t[he] finger tips. Add the sugar. Ble[nd] the egg yolks with 2–3 teaspoo[ns] water and add to flour with enou[gh] water to give a firm but plia[ble] dough.

Roll out to ⅛-in. thickness and u[se] to line a 9-in. plain flan ring, plac[ed] on a baking sheet. Make sure [no] air pockets are left between th[e] ring and the pastry. Trim th[e] pastry slightly above the edge [of] the flan ring to allow for shrink[k]age. Prick case with a fork, li[ne] with greaseproof paper, fill wi[th] dried beans to weigh the past[ry] down and bake blind at 400°[F.] (mark 6) for 15 minutes; remo[ve] the beans and paper and contin[ue] to bake until the pastry is light[ly] browned (5–10 minutes). Cool. Beat the cream cheese and mi[lk] together until smooth. Sprea[d] over the base of the flan case. Po[ur] boiling water over the jelly and s[tir] until dissolved. Add the rasp[-] berries and stir.

When jelly is beginning to se[t] pour into the pastry case. Leave [to] set. Just before serving, top wi[th] whipped cream.

AVOCADO WITH CHEESE DRESSING
POULARDE FARCIE ITALIENNE
BROCCOLI SPEARS AND NEW POTATOES
MALAKOFF TORTE
Wine – Red or White Chianti

Timetable *for dinner at 8.00 p.[m.]*
Day before: *Bone and stuff chicken. Prepare torte but do not decorate; keep in refrigerator. Make chocolate squares.*
5.45 *Collect ingredients and equipment. Put chicken to roast.*
6.30 *Decorate Malakoff Torte and return to refrigerator.*
7.30 *Prepare avocados. Cook vegetables and keep warm.*
7.45 *Dish up chicken and keep warm.*
8.00 *Serve first course.*

AVOCADO WITH CHEESE DRESSING

3 ripe avocados
a little lemon juice
2 oz. Roquefort or Stilton cheese
2 oz. cottage cheese

Halve each avocado lengthway[s] with a stainless steel knife, makin[g] a deep cut through the flesh up t[o] the stone and encircling the frui[t]

eparate the halves by gently
wisting them in opposite direc-
ons and discard the stones. Brush
e cut surface with lemon juice.
ice the Roquefort cheese and
ix with the cottage cheese. Care-
lly scoop out all the flesh from
e pear skins, dice it and combine
ith the cheese mixture. Pile the
ixture into the 'shells'.

OULARDE FARCIE TALIENNE

lb. chicken (oven-ready
  weight)
large orange
lb. lean pork
lb. lean streaky bacon, rinded
large clove of garlic, skinned
he chicken's liver
oz. onion, chopped
lb. pork sausage meat
level tsp. salt
reshly ground black pepper
level tsp. dried thyme
oz. cocktail gherkins
oz. butter
tbsps. thin honey
level tsp. powdered
  cinnamon

o bone the chicken, first cut off
he wings at the second joint and
he legs at the first. Then, using a
mall sharp knife, slit down the
entre of the back and work the
esh from the bones, gradually
rning it inside out and being
areful not to break the skin. The
gaments of the wing and leg
oints need to be severed and the
eg joints broken before the flesh
an be scraped off. Work round to
he breast bone and, after separ-
ting the flesh from it, remove the
arcass. (Most poulterers will bone
he bird for you if you prefer.
oned, the bird should weigh
bout 2½ lb.)

inely grate the rind of the orange.
Mince the pork, bacon, garlic, liver
nd onion into a bowl. Blend in
ausage meat, salt, black pepper,
hyme and ½ level teaspoon grated
range rind. Lay the boned
hicken, skin side down, on a
oard. Turn the wings inside out.
pread half the stuffing over the
ird and position 2 lines of gherkins
long its length. Force a little
tuffing into both legs and cover
he gherkins with the remainder.
Bring the sides together and sew
hem up using a trussing needle
hreaded with fine string. Sew
egs flat against body.
lace the bird in a small roasting
in. Melt the butter in a small pan,
dd remaining orange rind. Brush
ver the chicken and season.
Roast at 400°F. (mark 6) for about

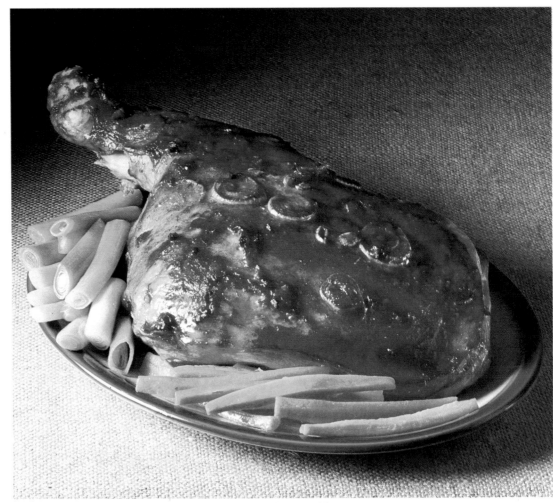

A shoulder of lamb and a tasty glaze for an economical party dish

1½ hours. Meanwhile, squeeze 6 tablespoons juice from the orange. Put this in the pan with the honey and cinnamon. Bring to the boil and bubble for 2 minutes. Pour juices from the chicken into the pan with the honey. Spoon orange and honey over chicken and return to the oven on the lowest shelf. Cook for a further 25 minutes, basting every 10 minutes so that it acquires a good glaze. Serve with broccoli spears and new potatoes.

MALAKOFF TORTE

8 oz. unsalted butter
6 oz. (¾ cup) caster sugar
1 egg yolk
1 tbsp. coffee essence
2 oz. candied peel, finely
  chopped
1 oz. nibbed almonds
2 oz. (½ cup) ground almonds
4 fl. oz. (½ cup) rum
4 fl. oz. (½ cup) water
3 pkts. Boudoir biscuits or
  sponge fingers
2 oz. plain (dark) chocolate
¼ pint (⅝ cup) double cream
2 tbsps. milk (optional)

Light oil an 8-in. cake tin. Cut 2 strips of greaseproof paper 1 in. by 16 in. and lay them across each other in the centre of the tin, or use a loose-bottomed tin. Line the base and the sides with paper. Cream the butter and sugar until pale and the sugar is only slightly gritty, beat in the egg yolk and coffee essence; fold in the candied peel and nuts. Blend the rum and water and pour into a flat dish. Crumple some kitchen foil and shape it into a collar to fit inside the base of the tin, leaving a small gap between the tin side and the foil to support the biscuits.

Soak the biscuits briefly in the rum but remove them before they soften. Place side by side round the outside of the tin in the gap left by the foil. Now carefully re-move foil by easing it up the sides of the tin. The biscuits will remain in position if they have been firmly wedged.

Soak sufficient biscuits, one at a time, to line the base of the tin. Spoon half the creamed filling in small amounts over the biscuit-lined base. Spread the mixture in an even layer with a spatula. Briefly soak more biscuits in the rum and layer over the filling. Spoon remaining filling over the biscuit layer and place the few remaining rum-soaked biscuits over the top. Cut the tips of the biscuits off where they extend

above the cake and embed the pieces into the surface. Chill the cake for at least 3 hours before serving.

Break the chocolate into a small bowl, place over a pan of hot, not boiling, water and allow to melt slowly. Ensure that no water bubbles into the chocolate. Line a baking tray with a sheet of non-stick paper (weighting down the paper at the corners if it comes off a roll). Pour the chocolate in a thin stream over the paper and spread to approximately $\frac{1}{10}$-in. thickness with a palette knife. Leave to cool until firm but not

Handy hint

When buying chicory, be careful to pick the whitest you can find. If there are traces of green at the tips, this indicates the chicory has been exposed to the light and will be exces-sively bitter.

213

brittle. To make the chocolate squares, dip a long knife into a jug of hot water, wipe dry and draw the knife through the chocolate at 1-in. intervals. Make cuts at right angles to the original cuts, 1 in. apart.

Whip the cream with the milk until stiff but still of a slightly floppy consistency.

Ease the torte away from the tin by pulling the strips of grease-proof paper. Place a serving plate over the tin and invert the whole thing. Remove tin and paper or ease out from loose-bottomed tin. With a forcing bag and large star vegetable nozzle, pipe large whirls of cream over the cake and top alternate whirls with a chocolate square.

MENU *serves 4*
TOMATO JELLY RINGS
PORK RAGOUT
CHOCOLATE SOUFFLE & TUILES D'AMANDES
Wine – Alsace Gewürztraminer

Timetable *for dinner at 8.00 p.m.*
In advance: *Make the tuiles d'amandes and store in an airtight tin.*
In the morning: *Make tomato jelly rings and leave in a cool place to set.*
Make soufflé but do not decorate with cream yet.
5.30 *Collect ingredients and equipment. Start pork cooking. Make stuffing balls. Prepare garnish for first course. Decorate soufflé.*
7.00 *Fry stuffing balls and keep warm. Turn out jelly rings and garnish.*
8.00 *Serve first course.*

TOMATO JELLY RINGS

1 lb. firm ripe tomatoes
2 small onions
1 small clove of garlic
1 bay leaf
1 tsp. peppercorns
1 level tsp. sugar
½ level tsp. salt
pinch of celery salt
pinch of grated nutmeg
1 level tbsp. powdered gelatine
1 tbsp. tarragon vinegar
3 tbsps. lemon juice
watercress

Scald the tomatoes, remove the skins; cut in quarters and remove the centres if tough. Chop the

Tomato jelly rings to serve as a first course at a dinner party

onions and crush the garlic. Put the tomatoes, onions, garlic, sugar, salts and nutmeg in a pan, add the bay leaf and peppercorns tied in muslin, and cook over a low heat until the onion is tender. Remove the muslin bag.

Dissolve the gelatine in 2 table-spoons water in a small basin over hot water. Work the tomato mixture in an electric blender, rub it through a sieve and turn into a measure. Add the vinegar and lemon juice and if necessary make up to 1 pint (2½ cups) with water. Add the dissolved gelatine, pour into wetted individual ring moulds and leave to set.

To serve, turn out moulds and garnish with watercress.

PORK RAGOUT

2 onions, skinned and sliced
2 oz. fat or oil
2 lb. shoulder of pork, boned and cubed
2 small green peppers (capsicums), de-seeded and sliced
2 cloves of garlic, skinned and crushed
¼ pint (⅝ cup) red wine
¼ pint (⅝ cup) stock or water
¼ level tsp. chilli powder
1 level tsp. celery salt
1 bay leaf
salt and pepper
1½ oz. long grain rice
3-oz. pkt. sage and onion stuffing mix

Cook the onions gently in the fat for about 5 minutes; remove from the pan and brown the meat in the remaining fat for 8–10 minutes; drain off any excess fat. Return the onions to the pan with the

peppers, garlic, wine, stock, chilli powder (a little at a time according to taste), celery salt, bay leaf and seasoning. Cover and simmer for 1½ hours, or until the meat is tender. Meanwhile cook the rice in boiling salted water for 15–20 minutes and drain well. Make up the sage and onion stuffing according to the directions on the packet, shape into 12 small balls and fry until pale golden brown – 3-4 minutes. Add to the meat with the rice just before serving.

CHOCOLATE SOUFFLE

3 large eggs, separated
3 oz. (⅜ cup) caster sugar
2 tbsps. water
2 level tsps. powdered gelatine
2 tbsps. water
3 oz. plain (dark) chocolate
1 tbsp. brandy
½ pint (1¼ cups) double cream

Prepare a 5-in. soufflé dish by tying a double piece of oiled

greaseproof paper around the dish extending 3 in. above the top. Whisk egg yolks and sugar with the water in a deep bowl over a pan of hot water, until thick and creamy. Remove from the heat and continue whisking until cool. Put the gelatine and water in a basin, stand this in a pan of hot water and heat gently until the gelatine is dissolved. Allow to cool slightly and pour into the egg mixture in a steady stream, stirring the mixture all the time. Melt the chocolate over a pan of hot water and stir the melted chocolate with the brandy into the egg mixture. Cool to the stage at which the mixture is nearly setting.

Lightly whip half the cream and fold into the chocolate mixture. Whisk egg whites in a clean bowl until stiff but not dry and quickly, lightly and evenly fold into the mixture. Pour the mixture into the soufflé dish and allow to set. Whip up the rest of the cream. When the soufflé is set, remove the paper and pipe 6–8 whirls of cream around the top and decorate with caraque or coarsely grated chocolate.

Note: To remove the greaseproof paper band, hold a knife in hot water then run it round the soufflé between the 2 layers of paper. This should loosen the paper sufficiently to allow you to peel it off easily.

TUILES D'AMANDES

These biscuits are called 'tuiles' because they resemble the old-fashioned curved roofing tiles

3 egg whites
6 oz. (¾ cup) caster sugar
3 oz. (¾ cup) plain flour
3 oz. flaked or nibbed almonds
3 oz. butter, melted

Using a rotary whisk and a large basin, whisk the egg whites until stiff and fold in the caster sugar, sifted flour and almonds. Mix well. Fold in the cooled melted butter. Place teaspoonfuls of the mixture on a greased baking sheet, keeping them well apart. Smooth out each one thinly with the back of a spoon, retaining the round shape. Bake at 375°F. (mark 5) for 8–10 minutes, until lightly browned. Use a palette knife to lift each one from the baking sheet and place it over a rolling pin, so that it sets in a curled shape. Allow a moment or two for the wafer to harden and then remove to a wire rack to cool. Store in an airtight tin and serve in glasses.

More Dinner Party Specials

More dinner party menus for small numbers, with wine suggestions and timetables. Make your dinners a pleasure for your friends and yourself.

esh pineapple in liqueur – irsch is a favourite choice

**PASTA HORS D'OEUVRE
SALTIMBOCCA ALLA
ROMANA
PETITS POIS A LA
FRANCAISE, CROUTONS
PRALINE BOMBE**
Wine – Red or white Chianti

Timetable *for dinner at 8 p.m.*
Day before: *Make bombe.*
*Prepare mayonnaise for hors
d'oeuvre.*
5.00 *Collect ingredients and
equipment. Prepare first course.
Prepare veal rolls ready for frying.
Fry croûtons; keep warm. Prepare
vegetables.*
7.45 *Cook main course and
vegetables; keep warm.
Unmould bombe on to chilled plate
and return to freezing compartment.*
8.00 *Serve first course.*

PASTA HORS D'OEUVRE

**4 oz. pasta shells
1 egg yolk
¼ pint (⅝ cup) corn oil
1 tbsp. vinegar
pinch of sugar
¼ level tsp. dry mustard
salt and freshly ground black
    pepper
1 tbsp. top of the milk
2 oz. onion, skinned and finely
    chopped
1 level tsp. tomato paste
4 oz. garlic sausage
4 oz. tongue, cooked
6 oz. crisp green apple, cored
    and finely diced
chopped parsley**

Cook the pasta shells until tender
in boiling salted water. Drain and
rinse under cold running water.
Make ¼ pint (⅝ cup) mayonnaise,
using the egg yolk, oil, vinegar,
sugar, mustard, salt and pepper.
Blend in the top of the milk, onion
and tomato paste.
Cut garlic sausage and tongue into
strips; toss with pasta and apple.
Fork through the mayonnaise.
Serve on individual plates garnished with chopped parsley.

SALTIMBOCCA ALLA
ROMANA

**8 thin slices of veal
lemon juice
freshly ground black pepper
8 fresh sage or basil leaves or
    1 level tsp. dried marjoram
8 thin slices prosciutto ham
butter
2 tbsps. Marsala
½-in. squares day-old bread,
    fried**

Ask the butcher to bat out the veal
to pieces about 4 in. by 5 in. Season with lemon juice and pepper.
Place a little sage, basil or marjoram in the centre and cover with
a slice of ham. Roll up and fix
firmly.
Melt the butter to cover the base
of a frying pan just large enough to
take the rolls in a single layer.
Gently fry the veal rolls until golden brown. Do not over-heat the
butter. Add the Marsala. Bring to
simmering point, cover the pan
and simmer gently until the rolls
are tender. Pour the juices over
and surround with fried croûtons.

PETITS POIS A LA
FRANCAISE

**¼ of a lettuce, washed and
    finely shredded
6 spring onions, halved and
    trimmed
a little parsley and mint, tied
    together
1½ lb. peas, shelled
¼ pint (⅝ cup) water
1 oz. butter
salt and pepper
2 level tsps. sugar
butter for serving**

Put all the ingredients except the
extra butter in a pan, cover closely
and simmer until cooked – about
20–30 minutes.
Remove the parsley and mint,
drain the peas well and serve with
a knob of butter.

PRALINE BOMBE

**4 oz. (½ cup) sugar
¼ pint (⅝ cup) hot water
4 egg yolks, beaten
4 oz. almond toffee, crushed
1 tsp. vanilla essence
a pinch of salt
½ pint (1¼ cups) double cream,
    whipped
1 pint (2½ cups) vanilla ice
    cream**

Put the sugar into a saucepan and
heat very gently until coffee-
coloured. Add the hot water, dissolve the caramel and cool.
Put the egg yolks in the top of a
double saucepan or in a bowl over
a pan of hot water and pour on the
caramel. Stir until the mixture
thickens.
Cool, add the crushed toffee,
vanilla essence and salt and fold
in the cream. Turn into empty ice
cube trays. Put in the ice-making
compartment of the refrigerator
set at coldest; freeze until half-set.
Chill a pudding basin or bombe
mould and line it to about 1-in.

thickness with the vanilla ice
cream. Fill the centre with the
half-frozen praline mixture and
finish off with more vanilla ice
cream. Press on lid of mould, or
cover basin with foil, and return
to the freezing compartment.
Turn out just before serving.

**CONSOMME
TOURNEDOS BEARNAISE
POTATO STICKS
APFELSTRUDEL**
Wine – Beaujolais

Saltimbocca alla romana is a traditional dish from Italy

Timetable *for dinner at 8 p.m.*
Day before: *Make apfelstrudel
and parsley butter.*
5.00 *Collect ingredients and
equipment.*
7.20 *Prepare béarnaise sauce and
keep warm in a bain-marie. Fry
bread croûtes lightly and keep
them warm.*
7.45 *Heat consommé and potato
sticks. Reheat apfelstrudel at
350°F. (mark 4).
Fry the tournedos, heat the
artichokes and keep them warm
without boiling. Garnish just before
serving.*
8.00 *Serve first course.*

CONSOMME

15-oz. cans consommé
salt and lemon juice

Heat the consommé gently in a
pan and add salt and lemon juice
to taste.

TOURNEDOS BEARNAISE

1½ tsps. chopped parsley
2 oz. butter, softened
3 7½-oz. cans artichoke
   bottoms
6 slices of bread, 3 in. square
6 tbsps. white wine vinegar
1½ tbsps. chopped shallot
6 peppercorns
1 bay leaf
sprig each of fresh tarragon
   and chervil
3 egg yolks
salt and pepper
½ level tsp. dried tarragon
½ level tsp. dried chervil
3 tbsps. cooking oil
6 tournedos, about ½ in. thick

Blend the parsley with 2½ oz. butter. Work into a pat, wrap in waxed
paper and chill until firm. Drain
the artichokes and rinse in cold
water. Simmer for about 7 minutes. Drain and keep warm.
Melt 3 oz. butter in a pan and fry
the bread on both sides until golden. Drain on absorbent kitchen
paper and keep warm.
Put the wine vinegar, shallot,
peppercorns, bay leaf, fresh tarragon and chervil in a saucepan. Boil
rapidly until reduced to about 1½
tablespoons. Cream the egg yolks
with about ½ oz. butter and a pinch
of salt in a basin standing over a
pan of hot water. Thicken slightly
over a gentle heat. Strain the herb
vinegar on to it and mix well. Add
4 oz. butter, piece by piece as the
mixture thickens, stirring continuously with a wooden spatula. Increase the heat slightly to thicken
the sauce. When all the 4 oz. butter
is added, adjust seasoning and add
½ level teaspoon each dried tarragon and chervil. Keep the sauce
just warm (not hot as it may
separate).
Heat remaining 2 oz. butter with
the oil in a heavy frying pan. Season the steaks with pepper and fry
quickly in hot fat for about 3 minutes on each side (less if you like
them rare, longer if you like them
well done). Place the fried croûtes
on a warmed serving dish and place
a steak on each. Arrange the artichoke bottoms between the steaks
on the dish and fill each with béarnaise sauce; just before serving top
each steak with a pat of parsley
butter.

APFELSTRUDEL

8 oz. (2 cups) plain flour
½ level tsp. salt
1 egg, lightly beaten
2 tbsps. oil
4 tbsps. lukewarm water
1½ oz. seedless raisins
1½ oz. currants
3 oz. (⅜ cup) caster sugar
½ level tsp. powdered
   cinnamon
2½ lb. cooking apples, peeled
   and grated
1½ oz. butter, melted
4 oz. (1 cup) ground almonds
icing sugar

Apfelstrudel is a universal favourite – always with cream

Put the flour and salt in a large
bowl, make a well in the centre and
pour in the egg and oil. Add the
water gradually, stirring with a
fork to make a soft, sticky dough.
Work the dough in the bowl until
it leaves the sides, turn it out on to
a lightly floured surface and knead
for 15 minutes. Form into a ball,
place on a cloth and cover with a
warmed bowl. Leave to 'rest' in
a warm place for 1 hour. Add the
raisins, currants, sugar and cinnamon to the apples and mix
thoroughly.
Warm the rolling pin. Spread a
clean old cotton tablecloth on the

table and sprinkle lightly with 1–2
tablespoons flour. Place the dough
on the cloth and roll out into a
rectangle about ⅛ in. thick, lifting
and turning it to prevent it sticking
to the cloth. Gently stretch the
dough, working from the centre to
the outside and using the backs of
the hands, until it is paper-thin
(traditionally it should be thin
enough to read through). Leave
to dry and 'rest' for 15 minutes.
Cut the dough into strips 9 in. by
6 in. Take each piece in turn, place
it on a damp tea towel, brush it
with melted butter and sprinkle
with ground almonds. Spread the

apple mixture over the dough,
leaving a ½-in. border uncovered
all round the edge. Fold the pastry
edges over the apple mixture, towards the centre. Lift the corners
of the cloth nearest you up and
over the pastry, causing the strudel
to roll up, but stop after each turn
to pat it into shape and to keep the
roll even. As each roll is completed
slide it on to a lightly buttered
baking sheet.
Brush the strudels with melted
butter and bake at 375°F. (mark 5)
for about 40 minutes, until golden
brown. Dust with icing sugar and
serve warm with cream.

MENU *serves 6*

MUSHROOMS A LA GRECQUE
DUCKLING WITH PINEAPPLE
MANGE-TOUT
PARISIENNE POTATOES
ICED ZABAIONE
Wine – Claret (Pauillac)

Timetable *for dinner at 8 p.m.*
Day before: *Make iced zabaione.
Prepare giblet stock for duckling.*
5.00 *Joint ducklings and start to
cook. Prepare mushrooms and chill.*
5.45 *Place casserole in oven. Cut
potato balls and trim mange-tout.*
7.45 *Add brandy and parsley to
casserole and keep warm.
Mange-tout (sugar peas) only take
about 5 minutes to cook in boiling
salted water. Start cooking potatoes.*
8.00 *Serve first course.*

MUSHROOMS A LA GRECQUE

1 onion, skinned and finely
   chopped
4 tbsps. olive oil
¼ pint (⅝ cup) dry white wine
bouquet garni
1 clove of garlic, skinned
salt and black pepper
1 lb. button mushrooms
½ lb. tomatoes, skinned and
   halved
chopped parsley

Sauté the onion in 2 tablespoons
oil until soft. Add the wine, bouquet garni, garlic and seasoning.
Wipe the mushrooms and seed the
tomatoes. Add to onion mixture
and cook gently, uncovered, for
about 10 minutes. Remove from
heat; cool.
Remove bouquet garni and garlic
and add the remaining oil if
required. Chill. Sprinkle with
chopped parsley.

Handy hint

When making a crushed
biscuit crust for a flan, place
the biscuits in a polythene
bag, or between sheets of
greaseproof paper wrapped
in a tea towel, before
crushing. This prevents both
mess and wastage.

Nasi goreng is a popular dish in Holland. It originated in Indonesia

DUCKLING WITH PINEAPPLE

2 3½-lb. ducklings
2 medium onions, skinned
4 cloves
flour
2 tbsps. corn oil
1½ oz. butter
1 level tbsp. ground ginger
2 tbsps. clear honey
15-oz. can pineapple pieces, drained
8 cocktail cherries, stoned
1 chicken stock cube
2 level tbsps. cornflour
juice of ½ a lemon
4 tbsps. brandy
chopped parsley

Put duck giblets in a pan with 1 onion, stuck with the cloves, and water to cover. Bring to the boil and simmer, covered, for ¾ hour. Strain and allow to cool. When cold skim off any fat.
Divide the ducklings into 4 portions each and remove the skin except from the wing joints.
Dredge the duckling joints with flour. Heat the oil and butter in a large, shallow pan and add the joints, flesh side down. Fry for 10 minutes until golden and then place in a casserole.
Finely chop the remaining onion, add to the juices in the frying pan and sauté. Add the ginger, honey, pineapple and cherries. Measure 1 pint (2½ cups) of the strained stock and add a crumbled chicken stock cube.
Blend the cornflour with a little pineapple juice, add with the stock and lemon juice to the pan juices. Bring to the boil, stirring. Pour over the duck, cover and cook in the oven at 325°F. (mark 3) for about 2 hours or until the duck is tender and cooked right through. Remove the excess fat from the surface of the casserole with a spoon or crumpled kitchen paper. Warm the brandy in a small pan, ignite and pour into the casserole while still flaming. Stir and sprinkle with chopped parsley. Serve the duckling straight from the casserole.

ICED ZABAIONE

6 egg yolks
6 oz. (¾ cup) sugar
9 fl. oz. Marsala

Beat the yolks to a cream and mix in the sugar and Marsala. Cook in a double saucepan, stirring continuously until the custard coats the back of a spoon. Pour into individual soufflé dishes, cool and freeze until firm.
Serve with crisp wafers or sponge fingers.

MENU *serves 4*

SALADE NICOISE
NASI GORENG
LEMON SORBET
To drink – Lager, chilled

Timetable *for dinner at 8 p.m.*
Day before: *Make lemon sorbet. (Unless you have a freezer or a refrigerator with a separate low temperature compartment it is wise not to try and keep the lemon sorbet overnight. In this case we suggest buying the sorbet mixture on the day.)*
5.00 *Collect ingredients and equipment.*
Prepare dressing and vegetables for salade niçoise and nasi goreng.
7.00 *Combine ingredients for salade niçoise.*
7.15 *Cook main course except for egg and tomato garnish and keep warm. Add egg and tomato at the last possible minute.*
8.00 *Serve first course.*

SALADE NICOISE

1 clove of garlic, skinned and cut in half
1 lettuce
6 oz. cooked French beans
1 green and 1 red pepper (capsicums), seeded and cut into thin rounds
2-oz. can anchovies, drained
1 large Spanish onion, skinned and finely sliced
6 tomatoes, skinned and quartered
½ cucumber (or 1 small ridge cucumber), peeled and thinly sliced
7-oz. can tuna steak, flaked
16 black olives
chopped chives
vinaigrette dressing (see below)
4 eggs, hard-boiled and quartered

Rub the inside of a salad bowl with the cut clove of garlic. Place in the bowl the smaller lettuce leaves and the heart, divided into quarters. Cut the French beans into pieces and add to the lettuce with the remaining ingredients except the eggs. Stir the dressing in very gently, just enough to make sure everything is glistening. Refrigerate for 30 minutes. Just before serving, add the quartered eggs.

VINAIGRETTE DRESSING

¼ pint (⅝ cup) salad oil
½ level tsp. dry mustard
¼ level tsp. French mustard
¼ level tsp. salt
little freshly ground black pepper
1 level tsp. sugar
2 tsps. lemon juice
4 tbsps. wine or cider vinegar
1 clove of garlic, skinned and crushed
½ small onion, skinned and finely chopped
1 level tsp. mixed chopped fresh herbs

Place all the ingredients in a screw-top jar and shake well.

NASI GORENG

4 oz. onion, skinned and chopped
1 clove of garlic, skinned and crushed
2 oz. butter
8 oz. (1 cup) long grain rice
½ level tsp. coriander powder
½ level tsp. caraway seeds
½ level tsp. chili powder
1 level tsp. curry powder
1 tbsp. soy sauce
1 lb. cold roast pork, diced
½ lb. freshly cooked peas
1 egg
2 tbsps. water
salt and pepper
tomato wedges

Fry the onion and garlic in the butter until soft but not coloured. Cook the rice in plenty of boiling salted water until cooked but still firm (about 12 minutes). Drain and rinse under cold water. Stir the spices and soy sauce into the onion and cook for 1–2 minutes. Stir in the meat, heat thoroughly; add the cooked rice, blending all the ingredients. When the meat and rice are thoroughly heated, add the peas.
Break the egg into a bowl, whisk lightly, add 2 tablespoons water and seasoning. Lightly grease the base of a frying pan and pour in the omelette mixture. When set, turn out on to a warm, greased baking sheet. Cut into strips.

A salt taste of the south in salade niçoise

Turn the nasi goreng into a serving dish. Decorate the top with a lattice of omelette. Garnish with tomato wedges.

LEMON SORBET

2 medium lemons
4 very large lemons
½ pint (1¼ cups) water
6 oz. (¾ cup) sugar

Thinly pare the rind from the smaller lemons, making sure it is free from all traces of white pith. Put in a pan with the water. Bring to the boil and simmer for 10 minutes. Cut the tops off the larger lemons and scoop out all the flesh. Squeeze the juice from this flesh and from the pared lemons. Strain the water to remove the rind and add to it 10 tablespoons of lemon juice and the sugar. Heat gently until the sugar has dissolved. Cool, then pour the mixture into ice-cube trays and place in the freezing compartment of the refrigerator. Chill lemon cases. Freeze the lemon mixture until it has almost set then turn it into a chilled bowl. Whisk well and pile into the 4 pre-chilled lemon cases. Return to the freezing compartment for a further 2–3 hours until firm. Cover with the lemon tops and serve at once.

MENU serves 4

COQUILLES ST. JACQUES
LAMB CUTLETS EN CROUTE
AVOCADO, TOMATO AND ONION SALAD
REMOULADE SAUCE
PINEAPPLE IN LIQUEUR WITH MACAROON STICKS
Wine – Claret
(Gloria St. Julien)

Timetable for dinner at 8 p.m.
Day before: Make macaroon sticks and store in an air-tight tin.
5.00 Collect ingredients and equipment. Prepare dessert. Wrap cutlets in pastry and place on baking sheet. Make salad dressing and prepare pepper, tomatoes and onion. Make rémoulade sauce.
6.00 Prepare scallops ready to grill. Keep cool. Cut bread and butter.
6.30 Cut avocado and combine salad ingredients, arrange as individual side salads.
7.45 Put cutlets en croûte in oven.
7.55 Turn down oven temperature. Brown scallops under grill.
8.00 Serve first course.

Lamb cutlets wrapped in pastry and served with salad

COQUILLES ST. JACQUES

8 large fresh scallops, or ½ lb. frozen, thawed
bouquet garni (parsley, bay leaf, thyme)
¼ pint (⅝ cup) dry white wine
¼ pint (⅝ cup) water
4 oz. butter
2 tbsps. lemon juice
2 oz. onion, skinned and chopped
4 oz. button mushrooms, wiped and chopped
1½ oz. (⅜ cup) flour
1 egg yolk
2½ fl. oz. (⅓ cup) double cream
salt and freshly ground black pepper
1 oz. fresh white breadcrumbs
watercress, for garnish
lemon wedges, for garnish
brown bread and butter, for serving

If using fresh scallops, first open the shells. Rest the hinge on a flat surface. Insert a sturdy small knife into the small opening to be found on either side of the shell just above the hinge. Prise open slightly, keeping the knife close against the flat shell to prevent mutilating the scallop, and sever the muscle attaching it to the shell. Discard the black sac and shell trimmings. Remove scallop, wash and polish the shells for later use. (If you are using frozen scallops, empty shells can usually be obtained from a fishmonger.)
Tip the prepared scallops into a pan, add the bouquet garni and pour over the wine and water. Bring to the boil, cover with a lid and simmer for 10–15 minutes until the scallops are tender when pricked.
Melt 1 oz. butter in a small pan with 1 tablespoon lemon juice and stir in the onion and mushrooms. Cover with a lid and cook gently without colouring for 10 minutes. Strain off juices and reserve.

Drain the scallops and remove the bouquet garni. Cut the scallops into bite-size pieces. Melt 1½ oz. butter in a pan, remove from the heat and stir in the flour. Return to the heat and cook for 1–2 minutes without colouring, stirring continuously. Stir in the stock from the scallops a little at a time, bring to the boil and simmer for 3 minutes.
Blend together the egg yolk and cream, add a little of the hot sauce, blend and pour back into the bulk of the sauce, whisking. Gently reheat the sauce but do not boil. Stir in the scallops, mushrooms and onion. Season to taste.
Melt 1½ oz. butter in a small pan and use a little to brush the insides of the scallop shells. Blend the remainder with the breadcrumbs. Off the heat, stir in 2 teaspoons lemon juice. Divide the scallops and sauce between the shells. Sprinkle with the crumbs and brown under a preheated grill. Garnish with watercress and lemon wedges. Serve with thinly sliced brown bread and butter.

LAMB CUTLETS EN CROUTE

8 oz. frozen puff pastry, thawed
1 oz. butter
1 clove of garlic, skinned and crushed
salt and freshly ground black pepper
4 lamb cutlets, trimmed
2 medium tomatoes, skinned and sliced
1 egg, beaten

Roll out the pastry into a strip 15 in. by 4 in.; leave to rest while preparing the cutlets.
Cream the butter, beat in the garlic and season to taste. Spread the garlic butter over one side of each cutlet and top with slices of tomato. Cut the pastry lengthwise into 4

narrow strips and brush with beaten egg. Use one strip to wrap round each cutlet; overlap each turn fractionally and keep the egg-glazed side uppermost. Place the pastry-wrapped cutlets on a baking sheet and bake in the oven at 450°F. (mark 8) for 10 minutes. Reduce the temperature to 350°F. (mark 4) and cook for about a further 20 minutes. Serve really hot.

AVOCADO, TOMATO AND ONION SALAD

For dressing:
4 tbsps. salad oil
2 tbsps. wine vinegar
½ level tsp. caster sugar
¼ level tsp. salt
¼ level tsp. dry mustard
¼ level tsp. Dijon mustard
freshly ground black pepper

1 avocado
juice of ½ a lemon
½ medium green pepper (capsicum), seeded and thinly sliced
2 tomatoes, skinned and sliced
1 small onion, skinned and thinly sliced
chopped parsley

To make the dressing, place all the ingredients in a screw-top jar and shake vigorously.
Cut the avocado in half lengthwise, discard the stone, peel and slice the fruit. Squeeze a little lemon juice over to prevent discolouration.
Combine the avocado with the pepper, tomatoes, and onion, moisten with dressing and garnish with chopped parsley.

REMOULADE SAUCE

¼ pint (⅝ cup) mayonnaise
1 tbsp. finely chopped mixed pickles
1 tbsp. made mustard

Combine all the ingredients and allow to stand a while for the flavours to mellow.

PINEAPPLE IN LIQUEUR

1 medium pineapple
Kirsch
caster sugar (optional)

Cut the pineapple into rings about ½ in. thick. Cut round the rings in a zig-zag pattern to remove all skin and eyes. Remove the core with an apple corer. Divide the rings between individual dishes or glasses and sprinkle each with a few drops of Kirsch.
Hand round caster sugar separately at the table.

MACAROON STICKS

1 egg white
2 oz. (½ cup) ground almonds
3 oz. (⅜ cup) caster sugar
¼ oz. ground rice
2 oz. plain (dark) chocolate, melted

Lightly whisk together the egg white, ground almonds, caster sugar and ground rice. Pipe in 2-in. lengths through a ¼-in. plain vegetable nozzle on to rice paper. Bake at 375°F. (mark 5) for 7–10 minutes, until tinged with brown. Allow to cool. When cold tear off the rice paper and drizzle with the melted chocolate.

MENU *serves 6*

CUCUMBER PORTUGAISE
TURBOT AU FOUR
BROCCOLI SPEARS
CREAMED POTATOES
STRAWBERRIES
ROMANOFF
Wine – White Bordeaux (Pouilly Fuissé)

Timetable *for dinner at 8 p.m.*
Day before : *Make feuilles royales. Prepare fish stock, strain and refrigerate.*
5.00 *Collect ingredients and equipment.*
Clean mussels. Bake fleurons, prepare orange garnish and prepare vegetables.
5.30 *Prepare cucumber portugaise.*
6.00 *Start to prepare dessert (decorate just before serving).*
7.15 *Start to cook main course. Leave fish and sauce to keep warm separately.*
7.50 *Finish off main course and keep warm.*
8.00 *Serve first course.*

CUCUMBER PORTUGAISE

2 large cucumbers (or 4 small ridge cucumbers)
4 oz. onion, skinned and finely chopped
4 tbsps. cooking oil
4 firm, ripe tomatoes, skinned and seeded
2 level tsps. tomato paste
2 tbsps. garlic vinegar
pinch of dried thyme
salt and freshly ground black pepper

Thinly pare the cucumbers using a potato peeler, then cut into 1-in. lengths. Cut each piece into quarters along the length. Remove the centre seeds with the point of a knife and discard. Plunge into

Strawberries Romanoff, topped with feuilles royales

boiling salted water for 5 minutes; drain and refresh under cold running water.
Sauté the onion in the oil until tender, add the diced tomatoes, tomato paste, vinegar and thyme. Blend the cucumber with the tomato. Season well and turn into a serving dish. Chill thoroughly. Serve with crusty bread.

TURBOT AU FOUR

4 oz. cod or fish trimmings
4 oz. onions, skinned and chopped
1 bay leaf
6 peppercorns
2 pints mussels
4 oz. butter
4 tbsps. dry white wine
6 cutlets of turbot (or sole or whiting), about 2½ lb.
2 oz. (½ cup) plain flour
8 oz. shelled shrimps
2 egg yolks
salt and freshly ground black pepper
1 tbsp. lemon juice
4 oz. Parmesan cheese, finely grated
1 orange
fleurons of puff pastry to garnish

Put the cod or fish trimmings in a

saucepan with 2 oz. chopped onion, the bay leaf and peppercorns. Cover with water and bring to the boil. Put the lid on the pan and simmer for about 1 hour. Top up with more water if necessary.
Meanwhile place the mussels in a large bowl under running water and scrape off any mud, barnacles, seaweed and 'beards' with a small sharp knife. Discard any that are cracked, open or loose (unless a tap on the shell makes them close). Rinse until there is no trace of sand in the bowl.
Melt 1 oz. butter in a pan, sauté the remaining chopped onion until soft. Add the wine and the mussels; cover and steam, shaking often, for about 5' minutes until the shells are open. Strain. Remove the mussels from their shells and discard the shells. Add the mussels and onion to the liquid in which they were cooked.
Lay the fish cutlets in 1 layer in a roasting tin or similar container and strain ¾ pint (2 cups) fish stock over them. Cover with a sheet of buttered kitchen foil and bake in the oven at 325°F. (mark 3) for about 20 minutes.
The fish when cooked should offer no resistance to a skewer inserted into the thickest part of the flesh,

close to the bone. Remove the cutlets from the stock and keep warm.
Strain the stock. Melt 3 oz. butter in a pan, stir in the flour and gradually add the strained stock. Stir in the shrimps and mussels in their liquid. Add a little of the hot liquid to the egg yolks, beat them and pour back into the sauce. Heat through, season to taste and add the lemon juice.
Coat the fish with the sauce, sprinkle with grated Parmesan and put under a hot grill until golden. Garnish with the fleurons and segments of orange.

STRAWBERRIES ROMANOFF

1 lb. strawberries, hulled
4 tbsps. port wine
1½ level tbsps. caster sugar
1½ tbsps. milk
7½ fl. oz. (scant 1 cup) double cream
vanilla sugar

For feuilles royales :
6 oz. (1¼ cups) icing sugar, sifted
1 egg white

Put aside 6 whole strawberries. Thickly slice the remainder and place in a bowl with the port and sugar. Turn lightly and leave to soak for at least 1 hour. Spoon the strawberries into individual glasses.
Add the milk to the cream with the vanilla sugar and whip until the cream just holds its shape. Spoon this mixture over the strawberries. Before serving, decorate with whole strawberries and feuilles royales.
To make feuilles royales, gradually stir the icing sugar into the egg white and beat well. Make a piping bag out of greaseproof paper, spoon in the royal icing and snip off the tip of the bag to allow the icing to flow through. Pipe the icing freehand into leaf shapes on kitchen foil, starting with the outline and then filling in the leaf itself. Allow to dry for about 1 hour then pipe in the centre vein.
Place the leaves on foil under a low grill for about 10 minutes, until dried out and tinged brown. The leaves should now come away from the foil easily. Turn them over and dry for a little longer. Cool on a wire rack.
Wrapped in foil, feuilles royales will store for up to 2 weeks. ●

DINNER PARTIES FOR SLIMMERS

You can't give a dinner party and expect to lose weight, but there is no need to add any. These menus are 'maintenance' meals– delicious and filling, but not too full of carbohydrates and calories

Grilled sole with grapes

A really refreshing start to a meal—frozen pineapple cocktail

Timetable *for dinner at 8.00 p.m.*
In the morning: *Make the frozen pineapple cocktail.*
5.00 *Collect ingredients and equipment. Make up the apricot yoghourt custard, cook and allow to cool. Meanwhile prepare the cabbage to the stage of placing half in the casserole. Scrape and slice carrots. Scrub even-sized potatoes.*

7.00 *Put potatoes in oven at 400°F. (mark 6). Grill chops, finish pork dish and place in oven (reduce temperature to 350°F., mark 4). Spoon pineapple cocktail into glasses, decorate and keep in refrigerator. Put carrots on to cook (when they are ready, drain, toss in butter and parsley and keep warm).*
8.00 *Serve first course.*

FROZEN PINEAPPLE COCKTAIL

16-oz. can crushed pineapple
**½ pint (1¼ cups) unsweetened
  orange juice**
**½ pint (1¼ cups) unsweetened
  grapefruit juice**
**¼ pint (⅝ cup) low calorie
  ginger ale**
**2–3 drops liquid sweetener
mint sprigs for garnish**

Mix together all the ingredients except the mint. Pour into an ice-cube tray and freeze.
When frozen, but not solid, spoon into stemmed glasses and garnish with the mint.

PORK CHOPS WITH CREAMED CABBAGE

**3 lb. cabbage, trimmed and
  shredded**
**salt and freshly ground
  black pepper**
**¾ pint (1⅞ cups) low fat
  natural yoghourt**
**6 pork chops, trimmed
cooking oil
sage**
3 tbsps. dry white wine
**1½ oz. (⅜ cup) cheese, grated
paprika pepper**

Plunge the shredded cabbage into boiling salted water; bring to the boil again and blanch for 3 minutes. Drain. Add the yoghourt and some pepper; toss the mixture together lightly.
Place half the cabbage in a shallow casserole, large enough to take the chops in a single layer.
Brush the chops with oil and grill until golden, turning. Arrange in a single layer on the cabbage and season lightly.
Add a sprinkling of sage and the wine to the grill pan drippings, stirring well to loosen any residue. Spoon the liquid evenly over the chops and cover with the remaining cabbage.
Cook in the oven at 350°F. (mark 4) for about ¾ hour. If there is too much liquid, drain it off and reduce it to the required amount by fast boiling in a separate pan; return it to the casserole. Just before serving, sprinkle the top with the cheese.
Garnish with a dusting of paprika. Serve with small jacket potatoes and carrot rings.

APRICOT YOGHOURT CUSTARD

**¾ pint (1⅞ cups) low fat
  natural yoghourt**
3 egg yolks, beaten
**6 oz. dried apricots, soaked
  overnight**

Beat the yoghourt and egg yolks together. Cut the apricots in half and arrange in the base of 6 oven-proof custard cups. Pour over the yoghourt mixture and stand cups in a baking tin with sufficient water to come half-way up. Cook in the oven at 325°F. (mark 3) for 15–20 minutes, until set.
Serve cold.

Timetable *for dinner at 8.00 p.m.*
In the morning: *Prepare the watercress. Cook to purée stage if serving hot or finish completely if serving cold. Make the apple fool and keep it in the refrigerator. Prepare the crown of lamb if you are doing this yourself.*
5.30 *Peel potatoes and par-boil; pare and dice carrots. Wrap the meat bones, fill the centre and put to roast.*
6.30 *Put potatoes in the oven to roast in hot dripping. (Slice melon, remove seeds and chill.)*
7.45 *Put carrots and peas on to cook. If serving soup hot, blend the yoghourt and yolks with the soup and put over a gentle heat.*
8.00 *Serve first course.*

WATERCRESS SOUP

**3 large bunches watercress,
  washed**
1½ oz. butter or margarine
3 spring onions, chopped
**1 chicken stock cube dissolved
  in 1½ pints (3¾ cups) water**
**7½ fl. oz. low fat natural
  yoghourt**
3 egg yolks
salt and pepper

Reserve a few sprigs of watercress for garnish, discard any coarse stems and chop the rest. In a large pan melt the butter and cook the spring onions until soft. Add the watercress and stock and bring to the boil. Push through a sieve or purée in a blender.
Return the soup to a clean pan. Beat together the yoghourt and egg yolks and gradually add to the soup. Adjust seasoning. Reheat, but do not boil. Serve hot or chilled, garnished with a few leaves of watercress.

GUARD OF HONOUR

**2 best ends of neck of lamb
  (6–7 cutlets each), approx.
  5lb. total weight**

Ask the butcher to chine 2 best ends of neck each with 6 to 7 cutlets. Remove the chine bone. With a sharp knife, cut through the

Pork chops with creamed cabbage are simple to make but tasty

...esh an inch or so from the end
...f the cutlet bones. Remove the
...at and meat from the bone ends
...nd scrape them clean. Interlace
...he best ends to form an arch, fat
...de out, then fasten together with
...ring. Cover the bone tips with
...il to prevent them burning.
...eason the fat with salt and pepper.
...lace in a roasting tin and roast in
...he oven at 350°F. (mark 4) for
...bout 1¼ hours.

...emove the foil and place on a
...erving dish.

...lternatively, ask the butcher in
...dvance to prepare the Guard of
...onour for you.

...PPLE FOOL

...large oranges
... pint (1¼ cups) fresh apple
**   purée (see below)**
... tsps. lemon juice
...–¼ level tsp. ground ginger
...accharin
...½ fl. oz. buttermilk
...level tsps. powdered
**   gelatine, dissolved in 3**
**   tbsps. water**
...egg whites

...alve the oranges, using a sharp-
...ointed, serrated knife and making
... zig-zag edge to each half. Care-
...lly remove the orange flesh,
...aking sure it is free of pith and
...embranes, and cut into small
...ieces. Clean out the orange halves.
...ix together the apple purée,
...mon juice, ginger and a little
...accharin to taste. Add the orange
...ieces and buttermilk and stir in
...e gelatine. Whisk the egg whites
...ntil stiff. When the apple mixture
... beginning to set, fold in the egg
...hites. Pile into the orange cases
...d top with a twist of fresh orange.
...o make ½ pint apple purée, peel
...d slice 1 lb. cooking apples and
...ok in very little water until soft.
...ieve or purée in a blender.

Handy hint

When using the juice only
of lemons or oranges, save
the rind. Grate it finely and
either dry in the oven and
store in an airtight jar, or
blend it with caster sugar
and store in an airtight jar
or keep in a tiny container
in the freezer.

MENU *serves 4*

**GRAPEFRUIT AND
ORANGE COCKTAIL
GRILLED SOLE WITH
GRAPES
CREAMED POTATOES
AND PEAS
CHEESE BOARD**
**Wine—White Loire
(Muscadet)**

Timetable *for dinner at 8.00 p.m.*
In the morning: *Make up the
mint freeze and put in the freezing
compartment.*
4.00 *Peel potatoes, leave in cold
water.*

*Trim the soles. Wash grapes and
parsley. Prepare the oranges and
grapefruit.*
*Put out the cheeses to allow time for
the flavours to develop – leave
covered.*
7.00 *Take out the mint freeze (if it
is solid, let it stand in the body of
the refrigerator to soften).*
*Complete the cocktail and leave in
the refrigerator. Skin grapes and
remove pips.*
*Put the potatoes on to cook in
boiling salted water.*
7.45 *Put the peas on to cook.
Cream the potatoes and keep them
warm. Grill the soles and keep
them warm; garnish just before
serving.*
*Drain peas, toss with butter and
keep warm.*
8.00 *Serve first course.*

GRAPEFRUIT AND
ORANGE COCKTAIL

For mint freeze :
1 tbsp. lemon juice
8½ fl. oz. low calorie lemonade
**2 tbsps. finely chopped fresh
    mint**

2 large grapefruit
2 oranges

Mix together the lemon juice,
lemonade and mint and pour into
an ice tray. Freeze until soft ice,
but not solid.
Meanwhile halve the grapefruit,
using a zig-zag cut to give a decorative edge. Remove the flesh from
the halves. Peel and segment the
oranges, remove the membranes
and cut into pieces.
Mix with the grapefruit, pile into
the grapefruit shells and top with
the mint freeze.

GRILLED SOLE WITH
GRAPES

4 lemon soles
cooking oil
salt and pepper
lemon juice
**grapes, parsley sprigs and
    lemon slices to garnish**

Remove any dark skin from the
fish. Brush each sole very lightly
with a little oil, sprinkle with salt
and pepper and grill. Squeeze the
lemon juice over the fish and serve
garnished with grapes, parsley
sprigs and lemon slices.

MENU *serves 6*

**CHILLED AVOCADO
SOUP
ITALIAN VEAL
CASSEROLE
GREEN SALAD
ORANGE POTS**
**Wine—Rosé
(Tavel)**

Timetable *for dinner at 8.00 p.m.*
In the morning: *Make the
orange pots and allow to chill.
Wash lettuce and other salad
ingredients, shake well, put in a
polythene bag and crisp up in the
refrigerator. Make up the salad
dressing.*
5.00 *Prepare the avocado soup.*
6.00 *Make up the casserole and
put in the oven at about 7.00.*
7.45 *Toss the salad. Pour soup
into bowls; garnish.*
8.00 *Serve first course.*

CHILLED AVOCADO SOUP

3 ripe avocados
juice of 1 lemon
15-oz. can consommé
**6 fl. oz. (¾ cup) low fat natural
    yoghourt**
salt and pepper
**chopped chives or spring
    onions for garnish**

Halve the avocados, scoop out the
flesh and pass through a nylon
sieve, using a wooden spoon.

Apple fool has an added zest when made with orange juice and served in the orange skins

Blend in the remaining ingredients, except the chives, and season well.

Alternatively, place all the ingredients (but not the chives) in an electric blender and set at high speed until the mixture is smooth. Serve chilled with a few chopped chives or chopped spring onions on top.

ITALIAN VEAL CASSEROLE

3 tbsps. cooking oil
2 lb. pie veal, trimmed and diced
salt and freshly ground black pepper
2 cloves of garlic, skinned and chopped
½ pint (1¼ cups) dry white wine
½ lb. tomatoes, skinned and chopped
4 level tsps. tomato paste
2 sprigs of rosemary
strip of lemon rind

Heat the oil in a frying pan. Add the meat, salt and pepper and continue cooking until the meat is golden brown – about 8–10 minutes. Add the garlic.

Stir in the wine, tomatoes, tomato paste, rosemary and lemon rind, and add just enough water to cover. Pour into a casserole, cover with a tightly fitting lid and cook in the centre of the oven at 350°F. (mark 4) for about 1 hour or until the meat is tender.

Remove the rosemary and lemon rind before serving.

ORANGE POTS

3 tbsps. orange juice
1½ tbsps. lemon juice
1½ level tsps. powdered gelatine
12 oz. cottage cheese
6 tbsps. buttermilk
liquid saccharin, optional
1 sliced orange, for decoration

Put the orange juice and lemon juice in a small bowl and sprinkle the gelatine on top. Stand the bowl in a pan of warm water and heat gently until the gelatine is dissolved.

Put the orange gelatine into a blender and add the cottage cheese and buttermilk. Blend until smooth. Adjust sweetness with a few drops of liquid saccharin if required. Divide the mixture between small soufflé dishes or dessert glasses. Chill.

Decorate with quarters of sliced orange shortly before serving.

Chicken Louisette is a delicious way to serve chicken in its own gravy

MENU *serves 6*

CRAB DIP PLATTER
CHICKEN LOUISETTE
HERBED RICE AND BROCCOLI
RASPBERRY DELIGHT
Wine – Alsace (Gewürz Traminer)

Timetable *for dinner at 8.00 p.m.*
In the morning: *Put the chicken wings out to thaw. Squeeze sufficient orange juice.*
4.00 *Pick over the raspberries. Wash in ice-cold water; drain on absorbent paper. Put into glasses (do not pour on orange juice until just before serving). Make the crab dip. Prepare the dunks and keep in polythene. Prepare the broccoli (if fresh) and the vegetables for the chicken.*
6.30 *Make up the chicken louisette, put in the oven at about*
7.00. *Arrange the crab dip platter.*
7.15 *Put the rice into fast boiling water with a teaspoon of mixed herbs.*
7.30 *Cook the broccoli. Drain rice and keep hot.*
7.45 *Drain broccoli, toss in butter and keep hot. Finish the chicken and keep hot.*
8.00 *Serve first course.*

CRAB DIP PLATTER

6 oz. canned crabmeat
¼ pint (⅝ cup) low fat natural yoghourt
salt and freshly ground black pepper
2 tomatoes, quartered
salad 'dunks' – celery, olives, asparagus, radishes, etc.

Combine the crabmeat and yoghourt; season, put into a small dish and chill. Place the dish on a larger platter, garnish with tomato quarters and arrange the dunks round it. Add cocktail sticks for the smaller items.

Handy hint

Almonds are best bought with their skins on and blanched as you need them—this way they are juicier. If you have only blanched almonds in your store cupboard, soak them in hot water for 30 minutes to make them plump and juicy again.

CHICKEN LOUISETTE

6 wing chicken joints, trimmed (allow to thaw if frozen)
salt and pepper
2 tbsps. cooking oil
1 medium onion, skinned and sliced
2 cloves of garlic, skinned and crushed
½ pint (1¼ cups) stock
½ pint (1¼ cups) dry white wine
bouquet garni
1 small (or ½ large) cucumber, peeled and thinly sliced
4 egg yolks
2 tbsps. milk
4 oz. lean cooked ham, chopped
parsley, chopped

Season the chicken joints and fr in the oil until evenly browned Pour off the excess drippings Add the onion, garlic, stock, win and bouquet garni. Bring to the boil, reduce heat, cover and sim mer until fork tender – about 4 minutes.

Discard the bouquet garni. Ad the cucumber and simmer for minutes. Arrange the chicke joints and vegetables on a hot dish

The perfect slimmers' dessert—orange pots are non-fattening, yet tasty and filling

Marinade the lamb cubes in the olive oil, lemon juice, seasoning and crushed garlic for at least 2 hours. Thread 8 skewers alternately with meat cubes, halved tomatoes, bacon rolls and whole mushrooms. If liked, a bay leaf or an onion quarter may be placed on each side of the meat pieces to give more flavour.

Brush with melted butter and cook under a low grill for 10–15 minutes, turning the kebabs about 3 times, until the meat is tender and cooked through.

Serve on plain boiled rice.

SPICED PEAR GRILL

1 lb. dessert pears, peeled and
   sliced
$\frac{1}{4}$ pint ($\frac{5}{8}$ cup) water
finely grated rind of $\frac{1}{2}$ lemon
small piece of cinnamon stick
artificial sweetener
2 oz. cornflakes
1 oz. butter

Poach the pears in the water until tender, with the lemon rind and the cinnamon. Add sweetener to taste. Drain the pears and place in a shallow flameproof dish, sprinkle with cornflakes and dot with butter. Place under a moderate grill for 5 minutes.

Serve while still hot and bubbling.

MENU *serves 8*

**SHRIMP COURGETTES
SWISS VEAL
NEW POTATOES AND
GREEN BEANS
STRAWBERRY SPONGE**
Wine – White Bordeaux
(Graves)

Timetable *for dinner at 8.00 p.m.*
In the morning: *Make the strawberry sponge and leave in the refrigerator. Make up the cheese dressing.*
Prepare the vegetables.
6.15 *Make the Swiss veal and put on to cook.*
7.00 *Blanch the courgettes, drain and cool.*
7.15 *Put the potatoes to cook. When ready, drain, toss in butter and keep hot. (Sprinkle the potatoes with chopped parsley before serving.) Fill the courgettes with shrimps and finish off.*
7.45 *Put beans to cook. When ready, drain and toss in butter. Remove the Swiss veal from the heat. Thicken the sauce, reheat and pour over the meat. Keep hot. Decorate the strawberry sponge.*
8.00 *Serve first course.*

---

keep warm.

Beat together the egg yolks and milk, add the liquor from the pan, return to the heat (in a double saucepan if possible) and heat very gently without boiling until the sauce thickens. Pour the sauce over the chicken and garnish with chopped ham and parsley.

RASPBERRY DELIGHT

1 lb. fresh raspberries
2 tbsps. orange juice
mint leaves

Divide the raspberries between 6 dessert glasses. Pour 1 tablespoon orange juice into each glass and chill. Serve decorated with mint leaves.

MENU *serves 4*

**APPLE-TUNA SALAD
MARINADED LAMB
KEBABS
BOILED RICE AND
GRILLED TOMATOES
SPICED PEAR GRILL**
Wine – Beaujolais

Timetable *for dinner at 8.00 p.m.*
In the morning: *Make up the marinade. Dice the lamb and leave*
to marinade during the day. Poach the pears. Make up the cheese dressing.
5.00 *Prepare the bacon, mushrooms, tomatoes, etc. for the kebabs. Make up the kebabs on skewers.*
6.30 *Make up the apple-tuna salad (the apple should not discolour if sufficient lemon juice is used).*
7.15 *Finish preparing the pears, but do not grill them.*
7.30 *Put rice on to cook.*
7.45 *Drain the rice; keep hot. Grill the kebabs and tomatoes and keep hot. (When the kebabs are cooked, leave the grill on a low heat and turn it up again shortly before the end of the main course. Then grill the pears.)*
8.00 *Serve first course.*

APPLE-TUNA SALAD

6-oz. can tuna
1 small green pepper
   (capsicum), seeded and
   chopped
4 medium red-skinned apples

For cheese dressing:
4 oz. cottage cheese
juice of $\frac{1}{2}$ lemon
salt and pepper

Drain and flake the tuna and mix with the pepper. Wash the apples, discard the core and scoop out the inside of each, leaving a $\frac{1}{4}$-in. wall. Chop the scooped-out apple and add to the tuna mixture.

Combine the cottage cheese, lemon juice and seasoning and sieve or blend until smooth and creamy. Add 1–2 tablespoons to the tuna mixture and mix thoroughly. Pile into the apple shells and chill. Serve the rest of the dressing separately.

MARINADED LAMB KEBABS

1 lb. lamb (taken from the
   leg), trimmed and cut in
   1-in. cubes
3 tbsps. olive oil
1 tbsp. lemon juice
salt and pepper
1 clove of garlic, skinned and
   crushed
4 small firm tomatoes, halved
8 rashers of streaky bacon,
   rolled up
8 even-sized button
   mushrooms, washed
a few bay leaves (optional)
2 small onions, quartered
   (optional)
melted butter

SHRIMP COURGETTES

8 small even-sized courgettes (zucchini)
7-oz. can shrimps, drained
1 tbsp. lemon juice
freshly ground black pepper

For cheese dressing :
4 oz. cottage cheese
juice of ½ lemon
salt and pepper

Remove a thin slice lengthwise from each courgette and scoop out the seeds. Blanch for 3–4 minutes in boiling water and cool. Fill with shrimps, add some lemon juice and sprinkle with freshly ground black pepper.

Make up the cheese dressing by combining the ingredients and sieving or blending until smooth and creamy. Use 2–3 tablespoons to top the shrimps, and chill before serving.

SWISS VEAL

4 lb. pie veal
seasoned flour
2 tbsps. cooking oil
8 oz. carrots, peeled and diced
8 oz. shallots, skinned and chopped
1 tbsp. lemon juice
½ pint (1¼ cups) stock
¼ pint (⅝ cup) dry white wine
bouquet garni
4 egg yolks, beaten
½ pint (1¼ cups) natural yoghourt
salt and pepper
parsley, chopped

Dust the veal lightly with the seasoned flour. Heat the oil and fry the veal until pale golden. Add the carrots, shallots, lemon juice, stock, wine and bouquet garni and simmer gently until the meat is tender – about 1¼ hours.

Alternatively, turn the mixture into a casserole and cook at 350°F. (mark 4) for about 1½ hours.

Blend the egg yolks with the yoghourt; add a little of the hot stock, then stir into the meat mixture and adjust the seasoning. Reheat gently without boiling, and serve sprinkled with chopped parsley.

STRAWBERRY SPONGE

1 oz. powdered gelatine
½ pint (1¼ cups) water
1 pint (2½ cups) strawberry purée, made from 2 lb. strawberries
2 egg whites
6 tbsps. evaporated milk
¼ lb. small whole strawberries, hulled

Chilled avocado soup is just right for a summer evening

Sprinkle the gelatine on top of the water in a small basin and leave to stand in a pan of hot water. When the gelatine has completely dissolved, add it to the puréed strawberries, stirring continuously and evenly until the mixture begins to thicken. When it is just starting to set and is the consistency of unbeaten egg white, add the egg whites and evaporated milk and beat until foamy, using either an electric mixer or a rotary whisk. Divide the mixture between 8 glasses and allow it to set.

Just before serving, decorate with small whole strawberries.

Handy hint

When baking bread, to test if a loaf is cooked, tap it underneath with your knuckles. If it is cooked it will sound hollow.

MENU *serves 4*

OYSTERS AU NATUREL
ORANGE-APPLE STEAK
FRENCH BEANS
GINGER FRUIT SALAD
Wine – With the oysters, White Bordeaux (Entre-deux-Mers With the main course, Red Burgundy (Nuits St. Georges)

Timetable *for dinner at 8.00 p.m.*
In the morning: *Make the ginger fruit salad. Leave in refrigerator.*
5.30 *Top and tail the beans. Mix together the stuffing for the steak.*
7.00 *Prepare brown bread and butter; cut up lemon wedges. Prepare bed of cracked ice for the oysters; keep frozen.*
7.30 *Put the beans on to cook. Prepare the steaks. Open the oysters and arrange on the serving dish. Drain the beans, toss in butter and keep warm.*
7.50 *Grill steaks and keep warm (remember that steaks will continue cooking while keeping warm, so be careful not to grill for too long).*
8.00 *Serve first course.*

OYSTERS AU NATUREL

Oysters are in season in Britain from September to April, the best are Whitstable or Colchester. In the southern hemisphere they are available all the year round

24 oysters

Scrub the oyster shells. Hold th deep half of the shell in the le hand (protected by a thick cloth and work the point of an oyste knife into the hinge between th shells to cut the ligament. Trir off the beard and any thread attached to the shell. Place ther on a bed of cracked ice – arrange so that the pointed end is toward the centre of the dish.

Serve with thin slices of brow bread and butter and lemo wedges. Have cayenne pepper o hand for those who like it.

ORANGE-APPLE STEAK

4 rump steaks, 1-in. thick
4 level tbsps. fresh breadcrumbs
2 tsps. coarsely chopped parsley
grated rind and juice of 1 orange
1 cooking apple, grated (do not peel)
1 oz. butter, melted
1 egg yolk
salt and pepper
cooking oil

Trim the steaks; using a shar knife, slit each one horizontall to within ½ in. of the edge and ope it out. Mix the breadcrumbs parsley, orange rind, apple, melte butter and egg yolk together season to taste.

Spread this mixture on one half o the steak, fold the other half ove brush with oil and grill for 3– minutes each side, depending o whether steaks are required rar or well done. Heat the orange juic and pour over the steaks.

GINGER FRUIT SALAD

2 apples, cored but not peele
2 apricots, peeled and stoned
1 orange, peeled and segmented
6 fl. oz. low-calorie ginger ale
2 bananas
2 tbsps. lemon juice
2 oz. green grapes

Dice the apples and apricots, ad the orange segments and ginge ale and leave to stand. Slice th bananas and mix with the lemo juice and grapes. Mix all the fruit and juices together and serve i individual glasses.

MAXI-MENUS FOR DINNER

Whether your dinner party is a family
occasion or something more formal, choose
a menu that is simple to prepare and
that will give you time to welcome your guests.

SMOKED TROUT WITH LEMON WEDGES
LAMB EN CROUTE
COURGETTES AND CARROTS
RUM GLAZED PEARS
CREME ST. VALENTINE
Wine–Loire (Pouilly-Fumé)

Timetable *for dinner at 8.00 p.m.*
Day before: *Marinade, stuff and cook leg of lamb; cool and store in refrigerator.*

In the morning: *Roll out pastry and wrap lamb; return to refrigerator. Prepare carrots.*

6.30 *Assemble ingredients and equipment. Start to cook pears, when cooked keep warm. Skin trout if wished (leave on the head and tail) and serve on individual plates. Make crème St. Valentine.*

7.15 *Put lamb en croûte in oven and make gravy.*

7.45 *Cook carrots; when ready, keep hot. Cook courgettes for about 10 minutes.*

8.00 *Serve first course.*

LAMB EN CROUTE

4½-lb. leg of lamb, boned
¼ pint (⅝ cup) red wine
1 lb. pork sausage meat
¼ lb. bacon rashers, rinded and chopped
½ oz. pistachio nuts, blanched and peeled
salt and freshly ground black pepper
1 oz. butter
½ lb. onions, skinned and sliced
sprig of fresh thyme or a little dried thyme
1 bay leaf
3 parsley stalks
1 clove of garlic, skinned and crushed
15-oz. can consommé
1 lb. bought puff pastry, thawed
2 eggs, beaten
1½–2 level tbsps. cornflour

Marinade the lamb in the wine for 2–3 hours, turning occasionally. Combine the sausage meat, bacon and nuts and season well. Take the meat out of the wine and dry on absorbent paper. Stuff the bone cavity with the sausage meat mixture. Sew up both ends of the joint with fine string.

Melt the butter in a large frying pan and brown the meat quickly on all sides. Transfer to a large casserole. Reheat the fat, add the onions, sauté and add to the cas-

A leg of lamb, stuffed and served 'en croûte' serves 10 easily

serole with the herbs, the marinade and the consommé. Cover and cook in the oven at 325°F. (mark 3) for 2 hours. Remove the meat from the casserole and cool quickly, reserving the juices.

Roll out the pastry to an oblong 20 in. by 10 in. Brush the meat surface with beaten egg and dust with flour. Place it in the centre of the pastry and make a parcel by folding the short pastry ends into the centre. Trim off the excess and brush the pastry with beaten egg. Bring together the long edges and seal with beaten egg. Place the croûte, join side down, on a baking sheet.

Roll out the pastry trimmings and cut some leaves to decorate. Place these on the croûte and brush again with egg. Place in the oven and bake at 450°F. (mark 8) for about 45 minutes. Cover with foil if the pastry is in danger of overbrowning.

To make the gravy, remove the fat from the cooking juices from the lamb by pressing a sheet of absorbent kitchen paper on to the surface. There should be 1–1¼ pints (2½–3 cups) of gravy. Thicken with 1½–2 level tablespoons cornflour and adjust seasoning.

CREME ST VALENTINE
serves 6

6 oz. cream cheese
4 large eggs, separated
¼ pint (⅝ cup) double cream
2–3 tbsps. coffee essence
3 oz. (⅜ cup) caster sugar
milk chocolate

Whisk together the cream cheese, egg yolks and cream until thick. Stir in the coffee flavouring. Whisk the egg whites until they stand in peaks, gradually adding the sugar. Pour the coffee cream over the whites, and fold through. Pour into 6 small glasses or sundae dishes and chill.

Decorate with curls of milk chocolate, pared from a block with a potato peeler.

RUM GLAZED PEARS
serves 6

6 large firm eating pears
juice and finely grated rind of 1 lemon
5 oz. (⅝ cup) granulated sugar
1 tbsp. rum
1 level tbsp. arrowroot
2 tbsps. cold water

Peel the pears thinly, keeping the stems intact. Dip in lemon juice to prevent discolouration. Sit the

pears in a single layer in a saucepan. Pour over the lemon juice, the grated rind and sufficient water to cover the pears to a depth of 1 in. Cover, bring to the boil and simmer for about 20 minutes until the pears are tender.

Meanwhile, place the sugar in a heavy based pan. Place over a medium heat and cook without stirring until the sugar caramelizes. Cool slightly. Remove the pears from the pan; gradually stir the poaching liquid and the rum into the caramel. Work with a wooden spoon to remove the caramel sediment from the base of the

Offer Crème St. Valentine and Rum Glazed Pears as alternative desserts

pan. Blend the arrowroot with the water and gradually add it to the sauce, stirring all the time. Bring to the boil.

Replace the pears in the sauce, cover and simmer for a further 15–20 minutes. Serve warm with whipped cream.

MENU *serves 12*

AVOCADO, GRAPEFRUIT AND SHRIMP COCKTAIL
CHICKEN WITH GINGER
BOILED RICE
STRAWBERRY TIMBALE
NORWEGIAN CREAM
Wine–White Burgundy
(Chablis)

Timetable *for dinner at 8.00 p.m.*
A few days before: Make meringue cases; store in an airtight tin.
In the morning: Prepare and cook custard for Norwegian cream. Hull strawberries. If wished fry chicken joints and get ready to put in oven; keep in refrigerator
6.00 Prepare grapefruit and dressing for cocktail. Start to cook chicken with ginger. Decorate desserts.
7.00 Prepare avocados and finish

cocktails.
7.30 Boil rice; when cooked, keep hot.
8.00 Serve first course.

AVOCADO, GRAPEFRUIT AND SHRIMP COCKTAIL

2 grapefruit
8 tbsps. salad oil
4 tbsps. wine vinegar
salt and pepper
caster sugar
1 level tsp. French mustard
3 ripe avocados
1 large lettuce, washed and well drained
1 pint (2½ cups) thick mayonnaise
12 oz. shelled shrimps or prawns, fresh or frozen and thawed

Peel the grapefruit with a sharp knife, removing all the pith, and divide into segments. Work over a bowl to catch the juice. Fork together the oil, vinegar, seasoning, a little caster sugar and the mustard.
Cut the avocados in half lengthwise, discard the stones and peel away the skin. Cut most of the flesh into small dice, but reserve half an avocado to cut 24 thin

slices to garnish. Toss the avocado in the grapefruit juice to prevent discolouration. Drain.
Shred the lettuce and toss in the dressing together with the avocado. Arrange in the bases of 12 medium-sized glasses. Lightly fold the shellfish through the mayonnaise and spoon over the avocado and lettuce. Garnish with slices of avocado and grapefruit.

CHICKEN WITH GINGER

6 tbsps. cooking oil
6 oz. butter
12 chicken joints
3 oz. (¾ cup) seasoned flour
3 large onions, skinned and sliced
1 level tbsp. powdered ginger
6 level tsps. French mustard
2¼ pints (5⅝ cups) chicken stock
6 tbsps. medium sherry
salt and freshly ground black pepper
¾ lb. button mushrooms, wiped and stalks removed

Heat the oil and half the butter in a frying pan. Toss the chicken joints in seasoned flour to coat and fry until evenly browned.
Drain from the fat and place in a large casserole. Reheat the fat, add

the onions and fry. Stir in any excess flour, ginger and mustard; cook for a few minutes. Off the heat, stir in the stock and sherry. Bring to the boil, stirring. Adjust seasoning and pour over the chicken.
In a clean pan, melt the remaining butter and quickly sauté the mushrooms; add to the casserole. Cover and cook in the oven at 325°F. (mark 3) for about 1½ hours. If preferred, strain off the juices and reduce a little by boiling; return to the chicken before serving.

STRAWBERRY TIMBALE
serves 6

4 egg whites
8 oz. (1 cup) caster sugar
½ pint (1¼ cups) double cream
¼ pint (⅝ cup) single cream
1 lb. strawberries, hulled and sliced

Draw an 8-in. circle on non-stick paper and place on a baking sheet. Whisk the egg whites until stiff and standing in peaks, add half the sugar, whisking continually until very stiff. Fold in the remaining sugar.
Spread some of the meringue mixture within the circle to form a base. Using a large star vegetable nozzle, pipe a circle of shell shapes to border the base. Pipe a circle of meringue just inside the shelled border, to form an interior wall. Pipe a similar double wall of shells in a circle on top, and complete the case by piping a final single border. This forms the timbale shape, with a deep hollow in the centre. Dry just below the centre of the oven at 300°F. (mark 1–2) for about 3 hours until crisp. Leave to cool on a wire rack. Remove the paper.
Whip the creams together until they just hold their shape. Layer the cream and two-thirds of the sliced strawberries in the meringue case. Decorate with the remainder of the strawberry slices.

NORWEGIAN CREAM
serves 6

6 oz. apricot jam
3 large eggs
1 level tbsp. sugar
few drops vanilla essence
¾ pint (1⅞ cups) milk
3 oz. plain (dark) chocolate
½ pint (1¼ cups) double cream, whipped

Cover the base of a 2-pint soufflé dish with the apricot jam. In a bowl, fork together 2 whole eggs, 1 egg yolk, the sugar and vanilla essence. Heat, but do not boil, the milk and pour on to the egg mixture, stirring. Strain on to the jam and cover the dish with foil. Stand the dish in a roasting tin with water to come half way up the dish and cook in the oven at 325°F. (mark 3) for about 1¾ hours, until the custard is set. Lift the dish from the tin and leave until quite cold.

Pare the block of chocolate with a potato peeler so that it forms curls. Cover the surface of the custard with about half the chocolate curls.

Whisk the remaining egg white until stiff and fold into about a third of the whipped cream. Spoon on to the chocolate. Pipe the remaining cream round the edge of the dish and fill the centre with the remaining chocolate curls.

This starter is simple, but looks luxurious

MENU *serves 8*

**FONDS D'ARTICHAUTS
CROWN ROAST OF PORK
WITH ORANGE RICE
BUTTERED CAULI-
FLOWER
FRUIT MERINGUE**
Wine Hock (Liebfraumilch)

Timetable *for dinner at 8.00 p.m.*
In the morning: *Prepare crown of pork and make stock; strain and cool Prepare flavouring vegetables for orange rice.
Make pastry base for dessert.*
5.00 *Assemble ingredients and equipment. Marinade artichokes and boil eggs. Finish dessert. Prepare cauliflower and keep covered.*
5.30 *Put pork to cook.*
6.00 *Make up first course.*
7.15 *Cook rice and keep warm.*
7.45 *Dish up and garnish pork. Make gravy. Cook cauliflower.*
8.00 *Serve first course.*

FONDS D'ARTICHAUTS

**6¼-oz. can artichoke bottoms, drained
juice of 1 lemon
2 tbsps. salad oil
salt and pepper
8 small eggs, hard-boiled
¼ pint (⅝ cup) thick mayonnaise
pinch of sugar
paprika pepper
lemon slices and parsley for garnish**

Marinade 8 of the artichoke bottoms for 1 hour in 1 teaspoon lemon juice, the oil, salt and pepper. Drain and arrange on serving dishes. Shell the eggs and slice off the bottoms so that they will stand. Place an egg upright on each artichoke bottom. Add the remaining lemon juice and sugar to the mayonnaise, spoon it into a forcing bag fitted with a small star vegetable nozzle, and pipe round the base of the artichokes. Dust with paprika. Garnish with lemon slices and parsley.

CROWN ROAST OF PORK WITH ORANGE RICE

**2 joints, 7 ribs from each side of a loin of pork
2 oz. lard, melted
salt and pepper
2 oz. butter
4 oz. celery, scrubbed and finely diced
4 oz. onion, skinned and finely chopped
¼ level tsp. curry powder
12 oz. (1½ cups) long grain rice
juice of 2 large oranges
6 oz. seedless raisins
1 level tbsp. finely grated orange rind
1 orange for garnish, sliced
1 tbsp. sherry**

For stock :

**1 onion, skinned and stuck with 5 cloves
1 carrot, peeled
1 stick celery, scrubbed
8 peppercorns**

Ask your butcher to skin the meat, remove the chine bones and trim the rib bones to an equal length. Keep the bone trimmings for the stock.
Score across both joints 1½ in. down from the bone tips. Remove the fatty ends and carefully scrape the bone tips free of flesh. Place the joints back to back, with the rib bones outermost. Sew the joint ends together using a trussing needle and fine string. Tie the string.
Place the crown in a roasting tin and tightly pack the cavity with foil to maintain the shape while cooking. Brush the outside of the meat with melted fat. Season. Cover the tips of the bones with foil to prevent charring. Place in the oven and roast at 425°F. (mark 7) for about 2¼ hours, basting frequently.
Meanwhile, place the bone pieces, meat trimmings, onion, carrot, celery and peppercorns in a pan. Cover with water and simmer for 2 hours, topping up with hot water when necessary. Strain and put aside.
Melt the butter in a large saucepan, add the diced celery and onion and sauté until tender. Stir in the curry powder and cook for 1 minute longer. Add the rice, 1¼ pints (3 cups) stock and the orange

```
Handy hint

When chopping glacé
fruits and candied peel, use
a wet knife to prevent
sticking, shaking off the
excess water first.
```

juice. Season well, cover and simmer for 20 minutes, until the rice is tender. Add raisins and orange rind, reheat gently.
Remove the foil from the pork crown and transfer meat to a serving plate.
Pour off the fat from the roasting tin. Add about ½ pint (1¼ cups) stock to the sediment and season well. Stir the sediment into the stock and add the sherry. Cook for 1 minute. Strain into a gravy boat. Spoon the orange rice into the centre of the crown and around the meat. Garnish with orange slices warmed in the oven.

FRUIT MERINGUE

**12 oz. bought puff pastry, thawed
1 tbsp. milk or 1 egg, beaten
1 large juicy lemon
7 oz. (⅞ cup) caster sugar
2 pears and 2 apples, peeled, cored and sliced
2 peaches, skinned, stoned and sliced
2 oranges, peeled and segmented
4 oz. black grapes, halved and pipped
15-oz. can pineapple pieces, drained
11-oz. can red cherries, drained and stoned
3 egg whites
3 oz. (⅜ cup) granulated sugar
a few glacé cherries, halved
angelica
1 oz. toasted, flaked almonds
1 lemon, sliced, for decoration (optional)**

Roll out the pastry to a 9-in. circle and place it on a wetted baking sheet. Brush with milk or beaten egg and prick it well. Stand the pastry in a cool place for 15 minutes, then cook in the oven at 450°F. (mark 8) for about 15 minutes, until well risen and golden brown. Allow to cool.
Thinly pare the rind from 1 lemon with the potato peeler. Put it in a small pan with the juice of the lemon and ½ pint (1¼ cups) water. Bring to the boil and continue boiling until the liquid is reduced by half. Strain, return to the pan and add 4 oz. (½ cup) caster sugar. Dissolve the sugar over gentle heat then bring back to the boil and continue boiling until the syrup is reduced by half. Allow to cool.
Place the pastry base on a baking sheet and top it with the fruit, arranged in layers to a height of 3–4 in. Flatten the top slightly. Spoon the lemon syrup carefully

ver the fruit, allowing it to run ırough to the pastry base.
Whisk the egg whites until stiff ut not dry, then whisk in the ranulated sugar a little at a time, naking sure the mixture is stiff etween each addition. Whisk in alf the remaining caster sugar a ttle at a time, then fold in the rest. poon into a forcing bag fitted ith a large star vegetable nozzle. Pipe the meringue in circles over ıe fruit and pastry until both are ompletely covered; smooth with flat bladed knife. Place in the ven at 200°F. (mark ¼) for 2–2½ ours until the meringue is firm ut not coloured. Cool, then trans- r to a serving dish. Decorate the ıeringue with halved glacé herries, strips of angelica and oasted almonds. Halve the lemon lices and arrange round the base f the meringue.

MENU *serves 12*

CHILLED CREAM OF SPINACH SOUP
SPICED ORANGE GAMMON
BROAD BEANS, CARROTS AND RICE
COFFEE CREAM RING
FRESH FRUIT SALAD
Wine–Claret (Pauillac)

Timetable *for dinner at 8.00 p.m.*
Day before: *Make soup; store in refrigerator. Prepare orange caramel glaze; store in refrigerator. Make choux ring and store in an airtight tin. Soak gammon.*
In the morning: *Make fruit salad. Prepare vegetables ready for cooking.*
.30 *Start gammon cooking. Finish coffee cream ring.*
.15 *Glaze gammon and heat remaining glaze. Cook rice and keep hot. When gammon is cooked, keep hot. Make croûtons.*
7.45 *Cook vegetables. Pour soup into individual cups and add cream.*
8.00 *Serve first course.*

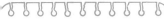

Handy hint

When reheating casseroles and stews, bring quickly to boiling point, then simmer for 15 minutes or for as long as necessary to heat through thoroughly. Keeping meat warm, but not boiling, for long periods may encourage the growth of fresh bacteria.

Baked gammon with an orange caramel glaze

CHILLED CREAM OF SPINACH SOUP

2 lb. spinach
4 oz. butter
2 onions, skinned and chopped
3 pints (7½ cups) chicken stock
½ level tsp. salt
freshly ground black pepper
1½ tbsps. lemon juice
2 bay leaves
1 oz. (¼ cup) flour
¼ pint (⅝ cup) single cream
croûtons of fried bread
grated cheese

Wash and drain the spinach and discard the stalks. In a large pan, melt 2 oz. butter and sauté the onion until soft but not coloured. Add the spinach and sauté for a further 5 minutes, stirring frequently. Add the stock, salt, pepper, lemon juice and bay leaves. Bring to the boil, cover and simmer for about 20 minutes. Discard the bay leaves and sieve the soup or purée in a blender.
In a clean pan, make a roux with the rest of the butter and the flour. Slowly add the soup, stirring. Bring to the boil and simmer for 5 minutes. Adjust seasoning. Turn into a bowl and chill. Just before serving, pour into soup cups and add a little cream to each cup. Sprinkle grated cheese on the croûtons and melt it under the grill. Hand round separately.

SPICED ORANGE GAMMON

6-lb. middle gammon joint
6 oz. butter
5 oz. (¾ cup) soft brown sugar
grated rind and juice of 3 oranges
5 tbsps. cider vinegar
½ level tsp. ground ginger
salt
freshly ground black pepper
2 whole oranges

Soak the gammon in cold water 2–3 hours. Drain and place skin side down in a large pan; cover with fresh water. Bring to the boil, skim off the scum, reduce the heat and cook for 55 minutes. Make sure that the joint is always covered with water, topping it up with fresh boiling water if necessary.
Drain the joint. Wrap it in foil and place in a roasting tin. Continue to cook in the oven at 350°F. (mark 4) for about 65 minutes.
Meanwhile, prepare the orange glaze. Melt the butter and sugar over a low heat. When the sugar is dissolved, raise the heat and cook until golden. Remove from the heat and add the rind and juice of the oranges, vinegar and ginger. Continue to heat gently, uncovered, for 7–10 minutes. Adjust seasoning.
Slice the whole oranges and poach in water to cover until the rinds are soft. Drain and add to the orange caramel. Continue to heat gently for a further 5 minutes to infuse the flavours.
About 20 minutes before the end of the cooking time, remove the gammon from the oven, unwrap the foil and strip off the rind. Coat the fat with a little of the orange glaze. Return it to the oven and raise the temperature to 425°F. (mark 7). Cook for a further 20 minutes.
Serve the gammon hot, with the rest of the glaze separately.

COFFEE CREAM RING

make 2

2½ oz. choux pastry, i.e. made with 2½ oz. (⅝ cup) flour etc.

For decoration:
2 oz. butter
2 oz. (⅓ cup) soft dark brown sugar
2 oz. mixed nuts, roughly chopped
½ pint (1¼ cups) double cream
1 tbsp. coffee essence

Lightly grease a baking sheet and dredge with flour. Upturn a 7½-in. cake tin on to it and with 1 finger, mark around the tin. Remove tin, leaving the guiding line.
Spoon the choux paste into a forcing bag fitted with a large plain nozzle and pipe it in a ring, just outside the marked circle on the baking sheet. Bake in the oven at 450°F. (mark 8) for 40 minutes, then lower the heat to 325°F. (mark 3) and bake for a further 15 minutes. If the ring starts to over-brown, cover with foil.
Cool the ring and split in half. In a small saucepan, melt the butter and sugar together over a low heat. When the sugar has dissolved, boil the syrup for 1–2 minutes and stir in the nuts. Drizzle the sauce over the top half of the choux ring.
Whisk the cream until it holds its shape; add the coffee essence. Spoon the cream inside the lower ring and top with the nut-encrusted ring.

FRESH FRUIT SALAD

For syrup:
4 oz. (½ cup) sugar
¼ pint (⅝ cup) water
2 tbsps. lemon juice
1 tbsp. orange liqueur

For salad:
2 eating apples, peeled and thinly sliced
2 pears, peeled and diced
2 oranges, peeled and segmented
2 large bananas, skinned and sliced

Dissolve the sugar in the water over a low heat, bring to the boil and boil for 2–3 minutes. Cool the syrup, then add the lemon juice and liqueur.
Mix all the fruits with the syrup. Serve chilled.

Potted shrimps are easily prepared a day in advance

MENU *serves 10*

POTTED SHRIMPS
ROAST SIRLOIN OF BEEF
ROAST POTATOES,
GLAZED CARROTS AND
GREEN BEANS
BERRIES WITH BRANDY
Wine–Burgundy (Morey
St-Denis or Chambertin
Clos de Bèze)

Timetable *for dinner at 8.00 p.m.*
Day before: *Prepare the potted shrimps.*

In the morning: *Prepare vegetables.*

5.30 *Start cooking beef.*
6.00 *Prepare berries with brandy. Whip the cream.*
Turn out the shrimps. Cut the bread and butter, cover and keep in a cool place.
7.00 *Put potatoes to roast, below the meat.*
7.45 *Cook carrots and green beans. Dish up beef and make gravy.*
8.00 *Serve first course.*

POTTED SHRIMPS

1¼ pints peeled shrimps
10 oz. butter, melted
ground mace
cayenne pepper
ground nutmeg
clarified butter
sliced cucumber and lemon

Heat the shrimps very slowly in the butter, without allowing them to come to the boil. Add seasonings to taste, then pour the shrimps into small pots or glasses. Leave them to become quite cold, then pour a little clarified butter over each.
To serve, turn out the shrimps on to individual plates, retaining the shape of the pots. Garnish with cucumber slices and twists of lemon. Serve with brown bread and butter.

ROAST SIRLOIN OF BEEF

Choose a joint about 7½ lb., on the bone. Roast in the oven at 425°F. (mark 7) for about 15 minutes per lb., plus 20 minutes extra.

BERRIES WITH BRANDY

2½ lb. small strawberries, hulled, or raspberries
6 tbsps. acacia honey
6 tbsps. brandy
1 pint (2½ cups) double cream, lightly whipped

Place the prepared fruit in a bowl. Blend together the honey and brandy and spoon over the berries. Turn the berries gently to coat them well. Chill for about 2 hours, stirring once or twice.
Serve with lightly whipped cream.

MENU *serves 8*

CHAMPIGNONS MARIE
ROAST STUFFED VEAL
BRAISED CELERY
HEARTS AND
CREAMED POTATOES
GRAPE DELIGHT
Wine-Claret (Château Haut-Brion)

Timetable *for dinner at 8.00 p.m.*
In the morning: *Stuff veal and return to refrigerator. Prepare potatoes, keep under water. Halve and pip grapes; store in refrigerator.*
5.00 *Assemble ingredients and equipment. Prepare all ingredients for first course but do not start to cook.*
5.30 *Start to cook veal.*
7.00 *Start to braise celery. Make up grape delight.*
7.30 *Cook mushrooms and make toast. Dish up mushroom mixture at the last minute. Cook potatoes. Keep vegetables hot.*
7.45 *Dish up veal and make gravy.*
8.00 *Serve first course.*

CHAMPIGNONS MARIE

1½ lb. button mushrooms, wiped and stalks removed
6 tbsps. cooking oil
4 shallots, skinned and finely chopped
4 level tbsps. fine, dry breadcrumbs
salt and pepper
2 tbsps. lemon juice
4 tbsps. chopped parsley

Quarter the mushroom caps and half of the stalks. Heat the oil in a thick frying pan and fry them for 10 minutes, until brown. Chop the remaining stalks finely, mix with the chopped shallots and add to the mushrooms in the pan. Fry for a further 2–3 minutes. Drain any excess fat from the pan and add the breadcrumbs. Stir over gentle heat.

Season and stir in the lemon juic and chopped parsley. Spoon int individual dishes to serve. Serv with hot toast fingers.

ROAST STUFFED VEAL

3½ lb. boned shoulder of veal
salt and freshly ground black pepper
½ lb. thin rashers streaky bacon, rinded

For stuffing :
3 oz. onion, skinned and finely chopped
4 oz. mushrooms, wiped and chopped
2 cloves of garlic, skinned and crushed
1 tsp. grated lemon rind
3 tbsps. chopped parsley
4 oz. fresh white breadcrumbs
6 oz. pork boiling ring, skinned and chopped
salt and freshly ground black pepper
1 egg
2 tbsps. melted butter

Cut through the veal and open out flat. Beat it lightly with heavy knife or meat bat until it a fairly even thickness. Seaso lightly.
Mix together the onion, mush rooms, garlic, lemon rind, parsley breadcrumbs, chopped pork ring salt and pepper. Add the egg an butter and bind the stuffing to gether. Pile it into the centre of th veal and fold each flap over it Tie with string.
Stretch the bacon rashers with th back of a knife, cover the mea completely with bacon and tie th rashers in place with string. Wra loosely in foil, weigh, and the place the joint in a roasting tin Place in the oven and roast a 425°F. (mark 7) for 35 minute per lb. Remove the foil for the las 30 minutes, to allow the meat t brown.
Serve with braised celery heart and creamed potatoes.

GRAPE DELIGHT

½ lb. black grapes, halved and pipped
½ lb. white grapes, halved and pipped
¾ pint (1⅞ cups) apricot yoghourt
3 egg whites

Turn the yoghourt into a bowl Whisk the egg whites until stif and fold into the yoghourt.
Layer the yoghourt and grape into glasses. Decorate with a few grapes on the top.

Grape delight – a light dessert after a rich meal

SAVOURIES

These are some of our favourite savouries. Pick the lighter ones for after dinner – the classics are angels and devils on horseback, anchovy toasts, Scotch woodcock, Welsh rarebit and chicken livers on toast.
Cook the more substantial recipes for snack meals such as lunch or supper.

DEVILS ON HORSEBACK
serves 4

4 blanched almonds
   (optional)
olive oil (optional)
salt (optional)
cayenne pepper (optional)
4 large, plump Californian
   prunes
2 thin rashers of streaky
   bacon
4 rounds of bread, about 2 in.
   in diameter
1 oz. butter
watercress

If you are using the almonds, heat the oil in a small pan and fry the almonds for 2–3 minutes, until they are golden brown. While they are still hot, toss them in salt and a very little cayenne pepper. Remove the stones from the prunes with a sharp knife and put the almonds in their place. Alternatively, simply remove the prune stones.
Cut the rind off the bacon and flatten and stretch the rashers with the back of a knife; cut each rasher in half and roll a piece round each prune. Secure with a cocktail stick or small wooden skewer. Cook under a medium grill, turning the rolls until all the bacon is golden brown.
Meanwhile, melt the butter in a frying pan and fry the rounds of bread for 2–3 minutes in the butter until golden. Put a grilled prune and bacon roll on each piece, garnish with watercress and serve at once.

ANGELS ON HORSEBACK
serves 4

4 rounds of bread, about 2 in.
   in diameter
1 oz. butter
2 rashers streaky bacon
4 oysters
a little cayenne pepper
lemon juice
watercress

Fry the bread in the butter until golden. Rind the bacon rashers and stretch them with the back of a knife blade and cut in half. Put an oyster in the middle of each piece of bacon, sprinkle with cayenne pepper and a squeeze of lemon juice and roll the bacon round the oyster. Secure each with a cocktail stick or a small wooden skewer.
Place a roll on top of each croûte of bread and bake towards the top of the oven at 400°F. (mark 6) for about 5 minutes, or until the bacon is lightly cooked. Serve at once, garnished with watercress.

CHICKEN LIVERS ON TOAST
serves 4

3–4 oz. chicken livers
seasoned flour
butter for frying
4 rounds of bread, about 2 in.
   in diameter
½ glass sherry or Madeira
1–2 oz. mushrooms, sliced
   (optional)

Wash and dry the chicken livers. Cut them in small pieces, using scissors, and coat with the seasoned flour. Melt a little butter in a small frying pan and fry the bread for 2–3 minutes until golden; remove it from the pan. Add more butter, put in the prepared livers and stir them over the heat until browned. Add the sherry or Madeira, mix well and cook slowly for 10–15 minutes.
Serve the livers on the croûtes of fried bread. If the mushrooms are used, sauté them before the livers;

when the livers are cooked, add the sauté mushrooms and adjust seasoning.

CHICKEN LIVER SAVOURY
serves 4

3-4 oz. chicken livers (or 1 pkt. frozen livers)
1 oz. butter
salt
cayenne pepper
1-2 tbsps. sherry or Madeira
a few mushrooms (optional)
½ oz. butter (optional)
8 fingers of fried bread
parsley (optional)

Wash and dry (or thaw) the chicken livers. Melt ½ oz. butter in a pan and cook the livers until browned–about 10 minutes. Sieve them. Mix to a paste with ½ oz. butter, season with salt and cayenne and add the Madeira or sherry. If the mushrooms are used, cook them lightly in about ½ oz. butter for 3–5 minutes. Spread the liver mixture on the fried bread and arrange the mushrooms (if used) on top, or garnish with parsley. Serve hot.

WELSH RAREBIT
serves 4

8 oz. Cheddar cheese, grated
1 oz. butter
1 level tsp. dry mustard
salt and pepper
3-4 tbsps. brown ale
4 small slices toast

Place the cheese, butter, mustard, salt, pepper and ale in a thick-based pan and heat very gently until a creamy mixture is obtained. Pour over the toast and put under a hot grill until golden and bubbling.

CHEESE FRITES
serves 4

2 egg whites
2 level tbsps. grated Parmesan cheese
salt
cayenne pepper
fat for deep frying
parsley or watercress to garnish

Whisk the egg whites stiffly and fold in the cheese and seasonings. Heat the fat to 350°F., or until a 1-in. cube of bread turns brown in 60 seconds. Drop in 1 tablespoon of the cheese mixture at a time and cook until golden brown –about 3 minutes. Drain well on crumpled kitchen paper and serve hot, garnished with watercress or parsley.

SOFT ROE SAVOURY
serves 4

12 herring roes
butter for frying
4 fingers of bread
salt and pepper
a squeeze of lemon juice
parsley

Wash the roes, dry them well and fry gently in a small pan in some butter for 8–10 minutes until golden. Remove them from the pan, wipe out the pan with kitchen paper, heat a little more butter and fry the bread fingers for 2–3 minutes until golden. Place the cooked roes on the fried bread, season, add a squeeze of lemon juice and garnish with a sprig of parsley.

SCOTCH WOODCOCK
serves 4

1 slice of bread from a large loaf
butter
2-oz. can anchovies, drained
½ oz. butter
2 tbsps. top of the milk
1 large egg
salt and pepper
pieces of canned pimiento (sweet red pepper) or paprika pepper, to garnish

Toast the bread, remove the crusts, butter the toast and cut it into triangles. Reserve 2 anchovy fillets for garnish, sieve the rest and spread on the toast triangles. Melt the butter in a saucepan. Whisk together the milk, egg and seasoning, pour into the pan and stir slowly over a gentle heat until the mixture begins to thicken. Remove from the heat and stir until creamy. Spread the mixture on top of the anchovy toast, garnish with thin strips of anchovy fillet and add pieces of pimiento or a sprinkling of paprika.

SCALLOPS AND BACON
serves 4

8 scallops, trimmed
salt and pepper
lemon juice
8 rashers of streaky bacon
tartare sauce

Sprinkle the scallops with salt, pepper and lemon juice. Remove the rind from the bacon, flatten and stretch with the back of a knife. Wrap 1 rasher round each scallop and secure with a cocktail stick. Grill under a moderate heat until cooked through–about 5 minutes on each side. Serve with tartare sauce.

Individual cheese soufflés make a tasty snack

CHEESE SOUFFLES
serves 4

1 oz. butter
½ oz. flour
¼ pint (⅝ cup) milk
3 oz. cheese, finely grated
3 eggs, separated
salt and pepper

Grease 4 individual soufflé dishes. Melt the butter in a pan, stir in the flour and cook for 2–3 minutes. Gradually stir in the milk and bring to the boil, stirring all the time. Cool slightly and add the cheese. Add the egg yolks 1 at a time, beating well, and season. Stiffly whisk the egg whites, fold these into the mixture and divide it between the soufflé dishes. Bake in the centre of the oven at 400°F. (mark 6) for about 25 minutes, until well risen.

MEXICAN FIRE
serves 4

½ oz. butter
1½ level tbsps. flour
¼ pint (⅝ cup) milk
salt and pepper
¼ level tsp. dry mustard
½ level tsp. chili powder
4 oz. Gruyère cheese, finely chopped
1 tbsp. chopped green pepper (capsicum), optional

Melt the butter, stir in the flour and cook for 2–3 minutes. Stir in the milk, gradually bring to the boil and stir until the sauce thickens; add the seasonings. Remove from the heat and add the cheese and the green pepper. Stir until the cheese has melted. Serve hot, with fried scampi (about 4–5 scampi per person).

Deep fried scampi with Mexican fire dip

CROQUE MONSIEUR
serves 4

2 oz. butter
8 large slices white bread
¼ lb. cooked ham, sliced
4 oz. Gruyère or Emmenthal
    cheese, sliced
8 gherkins

Butter the bread slices on 1 side only, and sandwich in pairs with a slice of ham and enough sliced cheese to cover. Toast each sandwich on both sides until evenly browned. Cut each in half crosswise and place a gherkin fan on each portion.

HAM FINGERS
serves 4

2 large slices of bread with
    crusts removed
butter for frying
3 oz. cooked ham, finely
    chopped
2 eggs, beaten
1–2 tbsps. milk
salt and pepper

Fry the bread in a little butter for 2–3 minutes, until golden; cut into fingers. Add more butter to the pan and fry the ham gently for 2–3 minutes. Whisk the eggs with the milk and seasoning, pour the mixture into the pan and stir slowly over a gentle heat until it begins to thicken. Remove from the heat and stir until creamy. Pile on the bread and serve hot.

EGGS EN COCOTTE
serves 4

2 rashers of bacon, chopped
4 eggs
salt and pepper
butter

Divide the bacon between 4 ramekins or individual soufflé dishes and bake towards the top of the oven at 350°F. (mark 4) for about 10 minutes, or until lightly cooked. Break an egg into each dish, sprinkle with salt and pepper. Put a few dots of butter on each and bake just above the centre of the oven for 7–10 minutes until the eggs are lightly set. Serve hot.

ANCHOVY TOASTS
serves 4

4 slices of bread
2 oz. butter
squeeze of lemon juice
8 fillets of anchovy, chopped
pepper
pinch of ground nutmeg
pinch of ground mace
parsley

Toast the bread and cut it into fingers. Melt the butter, add a squeeze of lemon juice, the anchovies, pepper, nutmeg and mace. Beat well and rub through a sieve. Spread this mixture on the fingers of hot toast and garnish with sprigs of parsley.
Similar savouries can be made with sardines or herrings.

CURRY PUFFS
serves 4

For pastry: (or use 7 oz. bought
    puff pastry, thawed)
4 oz. (1 cup) plain flour
pinch of salt
3 oz. butter or lard and
    butter, mixed
4 tbsps. cold water (approx.)
squeeze of lemon juice
beaten egg to glaze

Fluffy cheese boats are good after dinner or with evening drinks

For filling:
2 level tsps. curry powder
¼ pint (⅝ cup) thick white
    sauce
¼ pint picked shrimps or a
    4-oz. pkt. frozen shrimps,
    thawed

Sift together the flour and salt. Soften the fat by working it with a knife on a plate, and divide it into 4 equal portions. Rub 1 portion of the softened fat into the flour with the fingertips until it resembles breadcrumbs, and mix to a soft, elastic dough with the water and lemon juice.
On a lightly floured board, roll the pastry into an oblong 3 times as long as it is wide. Put another portion of the fat over the top two-thirds of the pastry in flakes, so that it looks like buttons on a card.

Fold the bottom third up and the top third down and turn it through 90°, so that the folds are now at the sides.
Seal the edges of the pastry by pressing firmly with a rolling pin. Re-roll as before and continue until all the fat is used up. Wrap loosely in greaseproof paper or polythene and leave to 'rest' in the refrigerator for 30 minutes.
Roll out the pastry thinly and cut into rounds, using a 1½-in. plain cutter. Stir the curry powder into the white sauce, roughly chop the shrimps and mix with enough sauce to bind. Put a little of this mixture into the centres of half the rounds of pastry. Moisten the edges with water and place another round of pastry on top of each to make a lid. Seal the edges and knock up.

Brush the puffs with beaten egg to glaze and bake towards the top of the oven at 450°F. (mark 8) for 10–15 minutes, until golden brown. Serve hot.

SHRIMPS IN ANCHOVY SAUCE
serves 4

For anchovy sauce:
¾ oz. butter
¾ oz. flour
½ pint (1¼ cups) milk or milk
    and fish stock, mixed
2 tsps. anchovy essence
salt and freshly ground black
    pepper
pinch of ground nutmeg

1 pint shrimps, shelled
chopped parsley
crescents of fried or toasted
    bread

Melt the butter in a small pan and blend in the flour. Cook over gentle heat for 2–3 minutes then remove from the heat and gradually stir in the liquid. Bring to the boil and cook for a further 1–2 minutes. Add the anchovy essence and season with salt, pepper and nutmeg.
Add the shrimps to the sauce and heat through. Divide the mixture between 4 individual dishes or scallop shells, garnish with chopped parsley and serve bordered with the crescents of fried or toasted bread.

FLUFFY CHEESE BOATS
serves 4

For shortcrust pastry:
4 oz. (1 cup) plain flour
pinch of salt
1 oz. lard
1 oz. margarine
4 tsps. water (approx.)

For filling:
1 oz. butter or margarine
1 oz. (¼ cup) flour
½ pint (1¼ cups) milk
4 oz. cheese, grated
salt and freshly ground black
    pepper
2 eggs, separated

Sift together the flour and the salt. Cut the fat into small knobs and add it. Using both hands, rub the fat into the flour with the finger tips until it resembles fine breadcrumbs. Add the water a little at a time, stirring with a round bladed knife until the mixture begins to stick together. With 1 hand, collect it together and knead lightly to give a smooth, firm dough. Wrap in greaseproof paper or polythene and chill for 15 minutes.
Roll out the pastry on a lightly floured board and use to line small boat-shaped moulds and patty tins. Bake blind near the top of the oven at 425°F. (mark 7) for 15 minutes, or until cooked but still pale in colour.
Melt the fat, stir in the flour and cook for 2–3 minutes. Remove from the heat and gradually stir in the milk. Bring to the boil and continue to stir until the sauce thickens. Remove from the heat and stir in 3 oz. cheese, the seasoning and egg yolks; pour into the pastry cases. Whisk the egg whites stiffly, spoon a little on to the top of each boat and sprinkle with the remaining cheese. Reduce the oven temperature to 350°F. (mark 4) and return the cases to the oven for about 10 minutes, or until the filling is heated through and the meringue is golden. Serve at once.

PETITS FOURS

A few petits fours are the perfect finish for a big dinner party. Serve them with the coffee, either at the table or after you have moved to easy chairs. These are the little details that make your guests feel really special!

Toffee grapes, marzipan toffees and chocolate rum truffles

ALMOND FOURS
makes 20–24

2 egg whites
6 oz. (1½ cups) ground almonds
3 oz. (⅜ cup) caster sugar
a few drops of almond essence
glacé cherries, angelica and toasted almonds, to decorate

Line 2 baking trays with non-stick paper or rice paper.
Whisk the egg whites until stiff and lightly fold in the ground almonds, sugar and almond essence. Place the mixture in a forcing bag fitted with a ½-in. star nozzle. Pipe out in small whirls on to the baking trays. Decorate each with a small piece of glacé cherry, angelica or toasted almond and bake in the oven at 300°F. (mark 2) for 15–20 minutes, until just beginning to colour.

BRANDY SNAPS
makes 10

2 oz. butter or margarine
2 oz. (¼ cup) caster sugar
2 oz. golden syrup (approx. 2 level tbsps.)
2 oz. (½ cup) plain flour
½ level tsp. ground ginger
1 tsp. brandy (optional)

Line 2 baking trays with non-stick paper and grease the handles of several wooden spoons.
Place the butter, sugar and golden syrup in a saucepan and heat slowly until the butter is melted (do not boil). Take off the heat and stir in the sifted flour and ginger and the brandy (if used). Place small teaspoonfuls of the mixture on the baking trays, spacing them

well apart to give plenty of room for spreading.
Bake in the oven at 350°F. (mark 4) for 8–10 minutes until golden brown. Bake them in rotation so that only 1 tray is ready at a time. Allow to cool for 1–2 minutes, then lift with a small palette knife and roll them round the spoon handles, with the upper surface of each brandy snap on the outside. When the biscuits have hardened enough to hold the shape, slip them gently off the spoon handles. (If the biscuits cool too much while still on the tray and become too brittle to roll, return the tray to the oven for a moment to soften them.)

COFFEE ECLAIRS
makes about 24

2½ oz. choux paste, i.e. made with 2½ oz. (⅝ cup) flour etc.

For filling and decoration:
½ pint (1¼ cups) double cream, whipped
coffee and chocolate glacé icing or melted chocolate

Put the choux paste into a forcing bag fitted with a plain round ½-in. diameter vegetable nozzle and pipe out on to a greased baking

tray, in fingers about 1½ in. long. Keep the lengths very even, cutting the paste off with a wet knife against the edge of the pipe.
Bake towards the top of the oven at 400°F. (mark 6) for about 35 minutes, until well risen, crisp and golden brown. Remove from the tin, slit down the sides with a sharp pointed knife to allow the steam to escape and leave on a wire rack to cool. When the éclairs are cold, fill with whipped cream, then ice the tops with coffee glacé icing. When the icing is set, pipe a trail of chocolate icing or melted chocolate over each using a small paper forcing bag.

COCONUT KISSES
makes about 1½ lb.

1 lb. (2 cups) granulated sugar
4 oz. powdered glucose
¼ pint (⅝ cup) water
6 oz. desiccated coconut
glacé cherries and crystallized violets, to decorate

Put the sugar, glucose and water into a pan and heat gently until the sugar has dissolved. Then boil to 240°F. (soft ball stage). Remove from the heat and stir in the coconut.

Form into small rocky heaps and place a small piece of glacé cherry or a crystallized violet on each. Leave on waxed paper to cool and harden.

TOFFEE GRAPES

¼ lb. each, black and white grapes
8 oz. (1 cup) sugar
½ pint (1¼ cups) water

Wipe the grapes clean and divide into pairs, keeping the stalks on. Dissolve the sugar in the water over gentle heat, then bring to the boil, and boil steadily until the syrup turns a pale caramel colour. Allow to cool a little, then dip the grapes in the caramel, holding them by the stalks. Leave on a greased plate or non-stick paper to harden, then pile in a glass dish to serve.
Note: Prepare about 1 hour before required. If wished, serve the grapes in individual paper cases.

MARZIPAN TOFFEES

almond paste trimmings
grated rind and juice of ½ a lemon
8 oz. (1 cup) sugar
½ pint (1¼ cups) water
whole blanched almonds, to decorate

Sharpen the almond paste with lemon rind and juice and roll into little balls. Dissolve the sugar in the water over gentle heat, then bring to the boil and boil steadily until the syrup turns a pale caramel colour. Remove from the heat and allow to cool slightly.
Hold each ball of marzipan on a skewer and dip into the caramel. Place on a greased plate or non-stick paper, decorate with blanched almonds and leave to harden.

CHOCOLATE RUM TRUFFLES
makes about 1 lb.

4 oz. plain (dark) chocolate
10 oz. (2¼ cups) icing sugar, sifted
4 oz. unsalted butter
rum
chocolate vermicelli

Place the chocolate in a small bowl over a pan of hot water until melted. In a bowl, beat together the chocolate, icing sugar and butter and add the rum, to taste. Form into small balls and roll in the chocolate vermicelli. Allow to harden for a few hours before serving. Serve plain or in small paper cases.

CHILDREN'S PARTY MENUS

Make the party fun for yourself as well as the children. Plan it in advance and save your energies for the day.

SAVOURY CHOUX BUNS
HOT DIGGETY DOGS
CHEESE PICTURES
ALASKA EXPRESS
GINGERBREAD MEN

Timetable *for preparing the food.*

Day before: *Bake choux buns but do not fill; bake gingerbread men; store both in airtight containers.*

In the morning: *Make cheese pictures, arrange and cover with polythene. Cook and stuff frankfurters, wrap in bacon and put ready for grilling; split and butter rolls.*
Slice Swiss roll for Alaska express and place on dish. Refresh, cool and fill choux buns.

Just before tea: *Grill and assemble hot diggety dogs. As tea is served finish Alaska express.*

Alaska express is a children's favourite

SAVOURY CHOUX BUNS

For choux pastry:
1½ oz. butter
¼ pint (⅝ cup) water
2½ oz. (⅝ cup) plain flour
2 eggs, lightly beaten

For filling:
4 oz. cream cheese
2 oz. butter
lemon juice
salt and freshly ground black pepper
chopped parsley

Melt the butter in the water in a small pan and bring to the boil. Remove the pan from the heat and add the flour all at once. Beat until the paste is smooth and leaves the side of the pan, forming a ball. Cool slightly, then gradually beat in the eggs.
Using a fabric forcing bag fitted with a ½-in. plain nozzle, pipe the mixture into about 24 walnut-sized balls on greased baking sheets. Bake in the oven at 400°F. (mark 6) for 15–20 minutes, until the buns are golden brown and cooked through.
Make a slit in the side of each bun to release the steam; if necessary, put them back in the oven to dry out; then cool on wire racks.
Beat together the cream cheese, butter, lemon juice, seasoning and parsley until smooth. Pipe into the hollow in each bun using a ½-in. plain nozzle. Pile the buns in a pyramid on a flat serving plate.

HOT DIGGETY DOGS

12 pairs frankfurters
4 oz. cottage cheese
chopped chives
12 rashers streaky bacon, rinded
24 long, soft rolls
butter

To cook the frankfurters, bring a large pan of water to the boil, turn off the heat and immerse the sausages in the water for about 5 minutes. Do not boil them or they will burst.
Slit the frankfurters lengthwise, almost to the ends, mix the cottage cheese well with the chives and fill the mixture into the split sausages.
Cut the bacon rashers in half and stretch each one with the back of the blade of a knife. Wrap each sausage spirally in a piece of bacon and fasten the ends with cocktail sticks. Grill until the bacon is crisp.
Split the rolls, leaving a hinge, and butter them. Just before serving, remove the cocktail sticks and place a hot, bacon wrapped sausage in each roll.
Serve hot diggety dogs with to-mato relish and sweetcorn relish in separate dishes.

CHEESE PICTURES

24 small slices bread
butter
24 slices cold luncheon meat
12 slices processed Cheddar or Cheshire cheese

Butter the bread and top each slice with a slice of luncheon meat. Trim the edges.
Using fancy biscuit cutters, cut the centres out of the processed cheese slices. Top half the slices of luncheon meat with the 12 fancy shapes, using the outsides of the cheese squares as 'frames' for the remaining 12 slices.

ALASKA EXPRESS

1 large chocolate Swiss roll
11-oz. can mandarin oranges
5 egg whites
10 oz. (1¼ cups) caster sugar
34-fl. oz. block vanilla ice cream
chocolate polka dots
1 individual chocolate covered roll
cotton wool

Cut the Swiss roll into 10 slices. Arrange 6 of the slices on a flat, oblong, ovenproof dish to form a rectangle. Spoon over 2 table-spoons mandarin juice from the can.
Whisk the egg whites until stiff, add half the caster sugar and whisk again until stiff. Fold in the re-maining sugar with a metal spoon. Spoon the meringue into a fabric forcing bag fitted with a large star vegetable nozzle. Place the block of ice cream on the Swiss roll slices and arrange all but 3 of the drained mandarins on top of the ice cream.
Quickly pipe the meringue over the ice cream to form an engine shape to completely enclose the roll.
Pipe meringue rosettes along the top and decorate with the reserved mandarins and polka dots. Place the engine in the oven, pre-heated to 450°F. (mark 8), for about 4 minutes, until golden. The meringue will be slightly crisp on the outside and soft inside.
Position the extra 4 slices of Swiss roll for wheels and use the small chocolate roll as a funnel with a puff of cotton wool for smoke. Serve at once.
Note: The Alaska express, com-plete except for wheels and smoke, can be packed in a rigid container and frozen. To serve, remove from the freezer 1 hour before slicing and keep in a cool place.

Sausage kebabs, with bacon rolls and cheese

GINGERBREAD MEN

12 oz. (3 cups) plain flour
1 level tsp. bicarbonate of
  soda
3 level tsps. ground ginger
4 oz. butter
4 oz. (1 cup) soft brown sugar
3 tbsps. golden syrup
1 egg, beaten
currants for decoration
white royal or glacé icing for
  decoration

Sift together the flour, bicarbonate of soda and ground ginger. Rub the butter into the sifted ingredients with the fingertips, add the sugar and mix well. Warm the syrup slightly and stir into the rubbed in mixture, with the egg, to give a pliable dough. Knead until smooth and roll out on a floured board to $\frac{1}{8}$-in. thickness. Draw a gingerbread man about $7\frac{1}{2}$ in. high and $4\frac{1}{2}$ in. broad on greaseproof or non-stick paper. Cut out the shape and use as a template. Place it on the dough and cut around it with a sharp-pointed knife. Carefully lift the men on to a greased baking sheet, keeping them well apart.
On to each man, put 3 currants for buttons and 3 more to represent his eyes and mouth.

Bake in the oven at 375°F. (mark 5) for 10–15 minutes, until evenly coloured. Cool on a wire rack. To decorate, outline the neck, sleeve ends and feet with piped white icing.

MENU *serves 12*

HOT SAUSAGES
POP CORN
CHICKEN PUFFS
DECKER SANDWICHES
CHEESE AND CHERRY HEDGEHOG
MONEY CAKE
STRAWBERRY AND ORANGE CUPS

Timetable *for preparing food.*
Day before: *Make and decorate the cake; store in an airtight container in a cool place.*
Cook the chicken puffs and store in a cool place.
Make the strawberry and orange cups but do not add cream and decoration.
In the morning: *Decorate the strawberry and orange cups.*
Twist the sausages and put in pan ready for cooking.
Make the sandwiches and chill.
1 hour before: *Make the hedgehog.*

Just before tea: *Refresh the chicken puffs in the oven at 350°F. (mark 4) for about 15 minutes.*
Cook sausages.
Cut sandwiches into fingers.

CHICKEN PUFFS

1 lb. cooked chicken meat
2 oz. butter or margarine
4 oz. onion, skinned and finely
  chopped
2 oz. ($\frac{1}{2}$ cup) flour
$\frac{1}{2}$ pint ($1\frac{1}{4}$ cups) milk
lemon juice
salt and pepper
13 oz. frozen puff pastry,
  thawed
beaten egg to glaze

Discard the skin from the chicken and cut the meat into small pieces. In a saucepan, melt the fat and add the onion; sauté until soft but not coloured. Stir in the flour and cook for 2 minutes. Off the heat, add the milk, stirring. Bring to the boil, reduce the heat and cook for 3 minutes, still stirring. Add the chicken, lemon juice and seasoning to taste. Turn into a bowl, cover closely with damp greaseproof paper and leave to cool.
Roll out the pastry very thinly and

cut out 24 4-in. rounds. Brush the edge of each round with egg. Put a teaspoon of the chicken mixture in the centre of each, fold the pastry over, seal and brush with more egg to glaze.
Place the puffs on baking sheets and cook in the oven at 400°F. (mark 6) for about 20 minutes, until puffed and golden. Serve warm rather than hot.

DECKER SANDWICHES

$1\frac{3}{4}$-lb. square sandwich loaf
  (preferably a day old)
butter

For first layer:
6 eggs, hard-boiled and sieved
4 oz. butter, softened
salt and pepper

For second layer:
2 $4\frac{3}{8}$-oz. cans sardines,
  drained
4-oz. can pimiento, drained
  and chopped
1 tbsp. lemon juice
salt and pepper

For third layer:
8 oz. pâté
2 gherkins, finely chopped
salt and pepper

For fourth layer:
$\frac{1}{2}$ lb. firm cream cheese
$\frac{1}{2}$ bunch watercress, chopped
salt and pepper

Remove the crusts from the loaf. Slice the loaf in half and cut each half into 12 slices, lengthwise. Mix the ingredients for the separate layers in individual basins. Butter and assemble the bread slices with different fillings, in 4 blocks of 6 slices. Wrap in foil and chill until required. Cut into fingers or small triangles.

MONEY CAKE

For Victoria sandwich cake:
4 oz. butter
4 oz. margarine
8 oz. (1 cup) caster sugar
4 eggs
6 oz. ($1\frac{1}{2}$ cups) self-raising
  flour
2 oz. cocoa

For butter cream:
8 oz. butter
1 lb. ($3\frac{1}{2}$ cups) icing sugar,
  sifted
4 tbsps. evaporated milk
a few drops of vanilla
  essence
2 oz. cocoa blended with a
  little water

For decoration:
foil-covered chocolate coins

Grease and line 3 8½-in. straight sided sandwich tins.

Cream the fats and sugar together until pale and fluffy. Add the eggs a little at a time, beating well after each addition. Sift together the flour and cocoa and fold half into the creamed mixture, using a metal spoon. Then fold in the rest of the flour and cocoa.

Divide the cake mixture between the tins and bake in the oven at 375°F. (mark 5) for 20–25 minutes. Turn out the cakes and cool them on a wire rack.

Meanwhile, make the butter cream. Cream the butter and gradually beat in half the icing sugar, with the evaporated milk and a few drops of essence. Then beat in the rest of the sugar. Divide the butter cream into 2 portions, and flavour half with the blended cocoa, mixing well.

When the cakes are cool, sandwich them together with white butter cream. Coat the top and sides with chocolate butter cream and decorate with the foil-covered chocolate coins.

STRAWBERRY AND ORANGE CUPS

6 medium oranges (6-8 oz. each)
1½ pkts. orange jelly
12 oz. cake crumbs
12 fresh strawberries, hulled
7 fl. oz. (⅞ cup) double cream, whipped
12 small chocolate peppermint or orange sticks

Halve the oranges and squeeze out the juice, without damaging the skins. Scrape out as much as possible of the white pith. Put the jelly tablets and orange juice in a measure and make up to 1½ pints (3¾ cups) with hot water. Stir to dissolve the jelly.

Soak the cake crumbs in ½ pint of the liquid jelly and divide amongst the orange halves. Chill until set. Leave the remaining jelly to set. When the jelly is set, chop it roughly and pile it on to the cake crumb base.

Pipe a whirl of cream into the centre of each 'cup' and place a strawberry in the centre. Decorate with a chocolate peppermint or orange stick.

FOR THE EXTRAS

You will need 1½ lb. chipolata sausages, each 1 twisted in half. Grill them, or bake in the oven, and spear with cocktail sticks.

Roundabout cake – allow a ribbon for each guest

Open bags of popcorn and serve it in small dishes.

For cheese and cherry hedgehog, use about ¾ lb. Cheddar cheese, cut into ½-in. cubes. Spear each cube on a cocktail stick with a stoned black cherry (about 1 lb.) and spike the sticks into a hard white cabbage. Or make small hedgehogs, using cooking apples instead of the cabbage.

MENU *serves 8*

SAUSAGE KEBABS
PINWHEEL SANDWICHES
SHOESTRING POTATOES
KNICKERBOCKER GLORIES
ROUNDABOUT CAKE
OWL COOKIES

Timetable *for preparing the food.*
Several days before: *Make roundabout cake but do not decorate; make owl cookies; store in airtight containers.*
Day before: *Divide the sausages, make bacon rolls and cut cheese cubes; store in separate polythene bags in refrigerator. Make jellies, leave in a cool place.*
In the morning: *Make sandwich rolls and refrigerate.*

Decorate cake.
Before tea: *Slice the pinwheel sandwiches, cook sausages and bacon and finish kebab arrangement. Make knickerbocker glories just before serving.*

SAUSAGE KEBABS

1 lb. pork chipolatas
¾ lb. streaky bacon rashers, rinded
½-¾ lb. Cheddar cheese
potato crisps

Twist each sausage in half and cut into 2 small sausages. Place in a baking tin and cook in the oven at 400°F. (mark 6) for about 30 minutes.

On a flat surface, stretch the bacon rashers with the back of a knife; cut each rasher in half and form into rolls. Place in a tin and cook in the oven until beginning to colour. Cut the cheese into cubes and spear with cocktail sticks. Spear the sausages and bacon rolls on sticks and spike all the kebabs into a cabbage, large apples or a long French loaf. Surround with potato crisps or shoestring potatoes.

The sausages and bacon are best eaten warm.

PINWHEEL SANDWICHES

1 large, square sandwich loaf (preferably a day old)
butter

For sandwich fillings:
mashed canned salmon and chopped cucumber, mixed
scrambled egg and chopped chives, mixed
cream cheese and diced tomatoes, mixed

Cut the loaf into slices lengthwise and trim off the crusts. Butter each slice right up to the edge.

> **Handy hint**
>
> Remove the syrup from glacé cherries before using them in a cake. Halve large cherries, place them in a sieve and rinse under cold running water. Dry them thoroughly on kitchen paper before using.

Owl cookies can be made well in advance

until pale and light-textured and beat in the sugar; add the beaten egg and vanilla essence.

Melt the chocolate in a small bowl over a pan of warm water; cool it slightly but keep it liquid, and add the bicarbonate of soda to darken it.

Add the dry ingredients to the creamed mixture and stir until evenly blended. Remove two-thirds of the dough to a floured board. Stir the melted chocolate into the remaining third.

Lightly shape both mixtures into sausage shapes. Chill in the refrigerator for ½–1 hour, until the dough is a rolling consistency. Divide the light-coloured dough into 2 portions and roll into an oblong 5 in. by 4 in. Divide the chocolate dough into 2 portions and roll each into a 5-in. sausage length. Place each chocolate roll on a piece of light dough and roll up. Leave both rolls in the refrigerator for a further 1–2 hours to firm. Cut into slices about ⅛–¼ in. thick.

To form the owl's head, place 2 circles side by side and press lightly together. Pinch the top corners of each head to form ears. Cut the almonds diagonally across and place a piece in the centre of each head, for the beak; place chocolate dots for the eyes. Bake the owls in the oven at 350°F. (mark 4) for 8–10 minutes. Remove carefully on to a wire rack to cool.

---

nd spread with the fillings. Roll each slice up like a Swiss roll. Wrap the rolls in polythene or oil and chill for several hours. ust before serving, slice the rolls cross into pinwheels and arrange n serving plates.

KNICKERBOCKER GLORIES

 pkt. red jelly
 pkt. yellow jelly
 5-oz. can peach slices, drained and chopped
 -oz. can pineapple, drained and chopped
 4-fl. oz. block vanilla ice cream
 fl. oz. (¾ cup) double cream, whipped
 glacé cherries

Make up the jellies as directed on ne packet and allow to set. When et, chop the jellies. Put small ortions of the chopped fruit in the ottom of tall sundae glasses and over this with a layer of red jelly. ut a scoop of ice cream on top nd add a layer of chopped yellow lly. Repeat the layers, finishing with layer of cream and topping ach with a cherry.

ROUNDABOUT CAKE

8 oz. butter
8 oz. (1 cup) caster sugar
4 eggs
8 oz. (2 cups) self-raising flour
juice of ½ a lemon

For filling:
8 oz. butter
12 oz. (2⅝ cups) icing sugar, sifted
juice of ½ a lemon

For decoration:
½ lb. orange and lemon slices
1 stick lemon rock
coloured ribbons

Grease 2 8-in. sandwich tins and line with paper to come a little way above the rim.

Cream the butter and sugar until light and fluffy. Add the egg a little at a time, beating well after each addition. Fold in half the flour using a metal spoon, then fold in the second half. Lastly mix in the lemon juice. Divide the mixture between the tins. Bake in the oven at 375°F. (mark 5) for about 25 minutes. Cool on a wire rack.

Make up butter icing by creaming the butter till fluffy then gradually add the icing sugar and lemon juice. Beat well.

Sandwich the cakes together with a little icing then spread the remainder over the top and sides. Place the cake on a silver board and draw a serrated scraper round the sides.

Using scissors or a sharp knife, cut the orange and lemon slices into little boys and girls. Arrange them round the sides of the cake. Fix the ribbons on to the stick of rock with icing, then press the rock into the centre of the cake. Arrange the ribbons so that each figure round the side is holding one.

OWL COOKIES

5 oz. (1¼ cups) plain flour
1 level tsp. baking powder
a pinch of salt
3 oz. butter
3½ oz. (½ cup) pale soft brown sugar
½ a large egg, beaten
a few drops vanilla essence
1 oz. cooking chocolate
a pinch of bicarbonate of soda
whole almonds, blanched
tiny chocolate dots

Sift together the flour, baking powder and salt. Cream the butter

---

Timetable *for preparing the food.*
Day before: *Make cake but do not decorate; store in an airtight container. Make sausage beehives; store in an airtight container in a cool place. Make up jelly for rabbit mousses.*

In the morning: *Decorate Jumbo the clown. Cut sandwiches and refrigerate, make dips. Prepare rabbit faces and ears.*

Just before tea: *Reheat sausage beehives if serving warm. Make rabbit mousses – if ice cream is used, do this at the last possible moment.*

SAUSAGE BEEHIVES

2 7½-oz. pkts. frozen
    shortcrust pastry, thawed
1 lb. sausage meat
1 egg, beaten

Roll out each piece of pastry into a
strip about 20 in. long by 2½ in.
wide. With a 2-in. cutter, stamp
out 2 rounds from each end of each
strip of pastry, making 8 altogether. Cut the remainder of each
strip into 4 long strips, each ½ in.
wide. Brush the pastry strips and
rounds with beaten egg. Divide
the sausage meat into 8 pieces and
shape each piece into a pyramid.
Place the pastry rounds on a
baking sheet; top each with a
sausage pyramid. Then, starting
at the base of the pyramid, coil a
pastry strip round the sausage
meat with the egg side outermost.
Slightly overlap each layer to make
it look like a beehive.
Brush the finished beehives with
beaten egg and bake in the centre
of the oven at 400°F. (mark 6) for
about 30 minutes until golden.

DIP-IN SALAD

2 large carrots
½ a small cucumber
2 sticks celery
6 tbsps. bottled salad cream
2 tbsps. sultanas
1 oz. peanuts

Peel the carrots and cut them
into chunky sticks, about 1½–2 in.
long. Cut the cucumber into sticks
about the same size, without removing the skin. Scrub the celery
and cut into pieces about 2 in.
long. Make small cuts down into
the celery to within ⅓ in. of one
end; leave the pieces in very cold
water for about 1 hour until the
ends start to curl.
Mix together remaining ingredients in a small bowl. Stand the
bowl on a plate and arrange the
vegetables round it, or serve
separately.

SANDWICH CHECKER-
BOARD

1 small white loaf
1 small brown loaf
butter
1 egg, scrambled with butter,
    milk and seasoning
5-oz. can tuna, drained and
    flaked
1 tsp. lemon juice
bunch of watercress

Cut 9 thin slices of bread from each
loaf and butter them. Make egg
sandwiches with the white bread.
Season the tuna with lemon juice

Jumbo the clown is fun to make as well as eat

and sandwich with brown bread.
Cut off all the crusts and cut each
slice into 4 squares (the 9th slice
in each case should be cut and
sandwiched to give 2 squares).
Cover a 10-in. square board with
foil or white paper and arrange alternating brown and white breads
to form a square. Garnish with
small sprigs of watercress.

CHIVE DIP

4 oz. cream cheese
2 tbsps. chopped chives
1 tbsp. cream or top of the
    milk

Blend all the ingredients to a soft
cream. Serve in a small dish,
surrounded with crackers.

RABBIT MOUSSES

2 oz. chocolate dots
12 marshmallows
6 individual block frozen
    mousses or individual dairy
    ice creams
6 plain chocolate finger
    biscuits
chopped jelly for decoration

Melt the chocolate dots in a small
bowl over a pan of hot water.
Stir with a teaspoon and then
spoon into a paper piping bag.

Dip a pair of kitchen scissors in
water and cut 6 of the marshmallows almost completely in half.
Snip off the very tip of the
chocolate filled bag and pipe rabbit faces on to the 6 whole marshmallows. Leave to set.
Unwrap the mousses or ice creams
and place side by side on a flat
dish. Decorate each with a rabbit
face, using the split marshmallows
for ears. Cut the chocolate biscuits
in half and position under the
faces, for legs. Decorate with
chopped jelly. If using mousses,
leave them to soften a little; if
using ice cream, serve at once.

Handy hint

Do not throw away stale
Cheddar cheese. Allow it to
dry out thoroughly, cut away
any mould and grate it. Store
in an air-tight container for use
in cooking.

JUMBO THE CLOWN

For cake :
8 oz. butter
8 oz. (1 cup) caster sugar
4 eggs, beaten
grated rind and juice of
    1 orange
8 oz. (2 cups) self-raising
    flour

For frosting :
3 egg whites
1 lb. 2 oz. (2¼ cups) caster
    sugar
pinch of salt
6 tbsps. water
pinch of cream of tartar
few drops of cochineal or
    orange colouring

For decorations :
1 ice cream cone
1 ping-pong ball
a length of orange ribbon
vermicelli

Grease and line 2 8-in. straigh
sided sandwich tins. Cream together the butter and sugar unti
light and fluffy. Gradually beat ir
the eggs, orange rind and juice
Sift the flour, fold it in to the
creamed mixture and mix well
Turn into the prepared tins and
bake in the centre of the oven a
350°F. (mark 4) for about 30
minutes, or until golden brown
Turn out carefully and cool on a
wire rack.
For the frosting, put the egg
whites, sugar, salt, water and
cream of tartar in a large bowl ove
a pan of hot water. Beat with a
rotary whisk or electric hand
mixer until the mixture thicken
enough to form peaks–approxi
mately 7 minutes. Colour with a
few drops of cochineal or orange
colouring; take care not to over
colour.
Sandwich the cakes together with
2–3 tablespoons of the frosting
Spread all but 2–3 tablespoons o
the remaining frosting over the
cake and, with a spoon handle
whirl it into a pattern.
Cut the ice cream cone, removing
the base for a collar. Fix this in the
centre of the cake. Paint a clown'
face on the ping-pong ball and fix
this to the collar; tie a bow round
with the ribbon.
Cover the top of the ice cream
cone with the frosting, peaking i
up and sprinkling with vermicelli
Attach it carefully to the 'face'
with the remaining frosting, to
make a tall clown's hat. Sprinkle
vermicelli on the cake round the
base of the collar to make a ruff
Serve the cake on a flat plate o
board.

sausage beehives and dip-in salad

Parties for Young Teenagers

Now is the time for you to leave the youngsters to themselves. If you have a suitable attic or spare room which you can hand over, they may even wish to decorate it to their own taste permanently.

Provide lots of food, preferably hot, plenty of soft drinks and 1 good punch or cup. They will enjoy organising the music and decor themselves, but be around in case advice is needed.

MENU *serves 8*

HAMBURGERS ON SAVOURY RICE
WHITE CABBAGE SALAD
ORANGE BAKED APPLES AND CREAM
MULLED CIDER

HAMBURGERS ON SAVOURY RICE

12 oz. (1½ cups) long grain rice
salt and pepper
4 oz. sultanas
4 tsps. chopped parsley
1 red pepper (capsicum), seeded and diced
1 green pepper (capsicum), seeded and diced
4 oz. cooked ham, chopped
stock
16 frozen hamburgers
olive oil

Boil the rice in salted water for 5 minutes, drain well and place in a large, shallow, ovenproof dish. Stir in the seasoning, sultanas, parsley, peppers and chopped ham; add just enough stock to cover. Brush the hamburgers with oil and place on top of the rice. Cover with greaseproof paper and cook at the top of the oven at 350°F. (mark 4) for 45 minutes.

WHITE CABBAGE SALAD

1½ lb. finely shredded crisp white cabbage
2 carrots, peeled and grated
1 eating apple, cored and cubed
1 small green pepper (capsicum), seeded and very finely chopped
1 level tbsp. chopped onion
2 level tbsps. caster sugar
1 tbsp. lemon juice
¼ pint (⅝ cup) soured cream
3 level tbsps. mayonnaise
salt and pepper
celery seeds

Baked apples, stuffed with orange butter and topped with fruit

Toss together the cabbage, carrot, apple, pepper and onion. Blend together the sugar, lemon juice, soured cream and mayonnaise. Check the seasoning.
Add the salad ingredients and lightly toss together; sprinkle with celery seeds.

ORANGE BAKED APPLES

8 large cooking apples, wiped and cored
4 oz. butter
4 oz. (½ cup) caster sugar
2 large oranges
½ pint (1¼ cups) double cream, whipped

Make a cut through the skin round the centre of each apple and place them in a large baking dish. Cream together the butter and sugar until pale and light. Grate

the rind from 1 of the oranges and squeeze out the juice; beat the rind into the butter, with as much juice as it will take. Fill this orange butter into the centres of the apples.
Pare the rind finely from the remaining orange, shred it and blanch in boiling water for 5 minutes. Meanwhile remove all the white pith from the flesh and chop the flesh roughly.
Bake in the oven at 350°F. (mark 4) for about 30 minutes. Top each apple with a spoonful of chopped orange and a few shreds of rind. Serve hot with whipped cream.

MULLED CIDER

makes 24 servings

6 in. of cinnamon stick
2 levels tsps. whole allspice
8 pints (20 cups) cider
8 oz. (1⅓ cups) Demerara sugar
1 orange, sliced
1 lemon, sliced
whole cloves

Put the cinnamon stick and allspice in a muslin bag. Heat the cider, sugar and spices in a saucepan and bring almost to boiling point. Remove the spices. Stud the centre of each fruit slice with a clove, float the slices on top of the mull and simmer gently for a few minutes.
Ladle the cider into tumblers or mugs – a spoon in the glasses will prevent them cracking.

MENU *serves 12*

BROWN ONION SOUP
POTATO MOUSSAKA
POOR MAN'S FONDUE
FRESH FRUIT
WHITE WINE CUP

BROWN ONION SOUP

2 tbsps. cooking oil
2 oz. butter
2 lb. onions, skinned and finely sliced
2 cloves of garlic, skinned and crushed
2 beef stock cubes
3 pints (7½ cups) boiling water
salt and pepper

Heat the oil and butter in a large pan and fry the onion over gentle heat for about 20 minutes, until soft but not coloured. Add the garlic, dissolve the meat extract in the boiling water, add to the pan, cover and simmer for 30 minutes. Adjust seasoning.

POTATO MOUSSAKA

4 oz. margarine
2 large onions, skinned and finely chopped
2 cloves of garlic, skinned and crushed
2 lb. cooked lamb, minced
2 beef stock cubes, dissolved in ½ pint (1¼ cups) boiling water
2 level tbsps. tomato paste
1 level tsp. dried oregano
salt and pepper
4 oz. lard
3 lb. potatoes, peeled and sliced
2 oz. (½ cup) flour
¾ pint (1⅞ cups) milk
pinch of ground nutmeg
2 egg yolks
2 oz. Cheddar cheese, grated
2 tomatoes, sliced

Melt 2 oz. margarine in a large pan, add the onion and fry for 5 minutes, until golden. Add the lamb and garlic, stir in the stock, tomato paste, oregano and season. Melt the lard in a large frying pan and fry the potato slices for about 10 minutes, or until golden. Drain off the fat. Melt the remaining margarine in a pan, stir in the flour and cook over gentle heat for 2 minutes. Remove the pan from the heat, stir in the milk gradually, then bring to the boil, stirring. Cook for 2 minutes. Stir in the nutmeg and season to taste. Beat in the egg yolks, one at a time. Cover the base of a large buttered casserole with a layer of potatoes

...d season. Spread half the meat ...ixture over the potatoes; top ...th half the remaining potatoes ...d half the sauce. Finish with ...yers of potatoes, meat and sauce. ...prinkle the cheese over the top ...d bake in the centre of the oven ...375°F. (mark 5) for 35 minutes. ...arnish with tomatoes.

...HITE WINE CUP

...esh fruit in season
...level tbsp. sugar
...tbsps. Kirsch or maraschino
...bottle medium-dry white
  wine
...bottle sparkling hock

...lice the fruit (strawberries, ...aches, apricots etc.) and place ...the bottom of a bowl. Sprinkle ...th sugar, pour on the liqueur ...d leave for 30 minutes. Pour on ...e still white wine and chill for a ...rther 30 minutes. Add the spark-...g wine and serve at once.

...OOR MAN'S FONDUE

...u may find it easiest to make
...is quantity in 2 pans

...clove of garlic, skinned and
  cut in half
...oz. butter
...level tbsps. flour
...pint (2½ cups) medium
  sweet cider
... lb. Cheddar cheese, grated
...lb. Gruyère cheese, grated
...lt and pepper
...level tsp. grated nutmeg

...ub the halves of garlic round the ...des and base of a large flame-...oof pan—this will impart just ...e faintest garlic flavour. Melt ...e butter in the pan, stir in the ...our and cook for 1–2 minutes. ...our the cider slowly into the flour ...ixture and bring to the boil, ...irring all the time. Simmer for ...minutes.
...tir the grated cheeses into the ...uce and heat gently until it ...elts. Season lightly with salt, ...epper and nutmeg.
...ransfer the pan to a table heater ...r serving, so that it remains hot ...roughout. Serve with a basket-...l of French bread cut into small ...bes.

CREAM OF CELERY AND TOMATO SOUP

12 oz. onions, skinned and
  sliced
6 oz. butter
3 lb. celery, scrubbed and
  sliced
3 lb. tomatoes, skinned and
  sliced
4 pints (10 cups) chicken stock
1 level tsp. sweet basil
salt and freshly ground black
  pepper
4 oz. (1 cup) flour
2 pints (5 cups) milk
chopped parsley

Potato moussaka is a good filler for young people

Fry the onions gently in 2 oz. butter in a large pan, for 5 minutes. Add the celery and cook for a further 5 minutes.
Add the tomatoes, chicken stock and basil, season well and bring to the boil. Reduce the heat, cover the pan and simmer for about 45 minutes. Sieve, or purée in a blender.
Make a roux by melting the remaining butter in a clean pan and stirring in the flour. Cook over a low heat for 2–3 minutes, remove from the heat and add the milk slowly, stirring until well blended.
Gradually add the vegetable purée, bring to the boil, adjust seasoning and simmer for a further 15 minutes.
Sprinkle in the chopped parsley just before serving.

STUFFED JACKET POTATOES

12 large potatoes, of even
  sizes
cooking oil

For curried egg filling :
4 eggs, hard-boiled and
  shelled
4 oz. onion, skinned and
  chopped
1 oz. butter
1 level tsp. curry powder
4 oz. cooking apple, peeled
  and diced
salt and freshly ground black
  pepper

For bacon filling :
2 oz. onion, skinned and
  chopped
1 oz. butter
6 oz. bacon rashers, rinded
  and chopped
½ level tsp. marjoram
1 tbsp. milk
salt and freshly ground black
  pepper
4 oz. cheese, grated

Wash, scrub and dry the potatoes. Prick with a fork and brush with oil, then place on baking sheets and cook in the oven at 350°F. (mark 4) for about 1½ hours.
For the first filling, sieve 2 of the eggs, fry the onion in the butter until soft but not coloured; add the curry powder and apple and fry for a further 5 minutes, then add the sieved egg.

Cut lids from the tops of 6 of the potatoes when they are cooked and scoop out the centres, leaving a wall of skin. Mix the soft potato with the curried mixture and season well. Replace the mixture inside the potato shells and garnish with the remaining 2 eggs, sliced. Serve with mango chutney.
For the second filling, fry the onion in the butter until soft but not coloured, and set aside. Add the bacon to the pan and fry until crisp. Stir in the marjoram.
Scoop out the centres from the remaining 6 potatoes, cream the soft potato with the milk, add the onion and bacon and season well. Refill the potato cases. Top with grated cheese and keep warm in a low oven. Brown under a hot grill just before serving.

HOT DOGS

2 lb. chipolata sausages
1 lb. streaky bacon rashers,
  rinded (optional)
32 long, soft, hot-dog rolls
butter

Grill the sausages alone, or wrap each one first in a piece of streaky. Split the rolls lengthwise, leaving a hinge, and butter them. Insert a sausage in each and serve with sweet corn relish, apple sauce, tomato relish or mild mustard.

WINTER FRUIT SALAD

juice of 6 large lemons
3 lb. bananas, skinned and
  sliced
1½ lb. black grapes, pipped
1½ lb. white grapes, pipped
3 1-lb. cans pineapple slices,
  drained
12 tangerines, peeled and
  segmented
1½ pints (3¾ cups) water
12 oz. (2 cups) brown sugar
3 tbsps. Kirsch
3 trays of ice cubes
¾ pint (2 cups) single cream
  or 34 fl. oz. block vanilla
  ice cream

Pour the juice of the lemons into a bowl. Add the bananas, grapes, quartered pineapple slices and tangerines. Turn the fruit lightly in the juice. Make up the water to 2¼ pints (5⅝ cups) with the juice from the can of pineapple.
In a saucepan, heat the liquid with the sugar until dissolved, then reduce to 1½ pints by boiling rapidly. Cool until there is no steam, then pour over the fruit. Chill, add the Kirsch, and just before serving add the ice cubes. Serve with cream or ice cream.

245

Sweet and sour meat balls with buttered noodles

MENU *serves 8*

WEST AFRICAN BEEF CURRY
BOILED RICE
SAMBALS
CHICKEN, RICE AND CORN SALAD
FRUIT SALAD
MERINGUE SHELLS
SHANDY

WEST AFRICAN BEEF CURRY

4 lb. chuck steak
2 oz. ($\frac{1}{2}$ cup) flour
$\frac{1}{4}$ level tsp. paprika pepper
$\frac{1}{4}$ level tsp. cayenne pepper
$\frac{1}{4}$ level tsp. chilli powder
corn oil
1 lb. onions, skinned and chopped
2 level tbsps. desiccated coconut
4 level tbsps. curry powder
2 level tbsps. curry paste
1 clove of garlic, skinned and crushed
a few drops of Tabasco sauce
2 pints (5 cups) stock

Trim the steak and cut it into serving-size pieces. Toss in the flour seasoned with the paprika, cayenne and chilli powder, using just enough flour to coat the steak thoroughly. Heat 3 tablespoons oil in a large saucepan and fry the onions until evenly browned. Add the coconut, curry powder, curry paste, garlic, Tabasco and stock; bring to the boil.

In a large frying pan, heat enough oil to just cover the base and fry the meat a little at a time, until sealed and brown. Add the drained meat to the curry sauce, cover and simmer until the meat is tender – about 2 hours. As sambals, serve sliced fruits and raw vegetables, desiccated coconut and pappadums.

CHICKEN, RICE AND CORN SALAD

4-lb. chicken, cooked
6 tbsps. French dressing
$\frac{1}{2}$ pint (1$\frac{1}{4}$ cups) lemon mayonnaise
2 tbsps. lemon juice
2 tbsps. single cream
salt and pepper
12 oz. (1$\frac{1}{2}$ cups) cooked long grain rice
2 11-oz. cans sweet corn kernels, drained
2 green peppers (capsicums), seeded and finely diced
1 large lettuce

Strip the chicken flesh off the bone and cut into 1-in. pieces. Toss the meat in French dressing. Put the mayonnaise, lemon juice, cream and seasoning in a bowl. Gently fold in the chicken, rice, corn and green peppers. Adjust seasoning.

Line a large salad bowl with torn lettuce leaves and pile the chicken salad in the centre.

MENU *serves 12*

SWEET AND SOUR MEAT BALLS
NOODLES
DUTCH APPLE PIE
VERANDAH PUNCH

SWEET AND SOUR MEAT BALLS

3 lb. minced beef or pork
2 cloves of garlic, skinned and finely chopped
4$\frac{1}{2}$ oz. (1 cup) plain flour
2 oz. fresh white breadcrumbs
3 egg yolks
3 oz. lard
salt and pepper

For sauce :

9 oz. (1$\frac{1}{8}$ cups) caster sugar
12 tbsps. cider vinegar
12 tbsps. soy sauce
4$\frac{1}{2}$ level tbsps. cornflour
1$\frac{1}{2}$ pints (3$\frac{3}{4}$ cups) water
3 green peppers (capsicums), seeded and sliced
1$\frac{1}{2}$ lb. tomatoes, skinned and quartered
3 11-oz. cans crushed pineapple, drained

In a large bowl, mix together the meat, garlic, 1$\frac{1}{2}$ oz. flour, the breadcrumbs, salt and pepper. Bind with the egg yolks and form into balls (this quantity should make about 50–60 balls). Toss the meat balls in remaining flour.

Melt the lard and fry the balls for 20 minutes, in batches, turning frequently during cooking. Keep each batch hot when cooked.

Meanwhile prepare the sauce. Place the sugar, vinegar and soy sauce in a pan. Blend the cornflour with a little of the measured water and add to the pan with the remaining water. Bring to the boil, stirring, and simmer for 5 minutes. Blanch the pepper and add with the tomatoes and pineapple and simmer for 5–10 minutes.

When the meat balls are cooked divide them between 2–3 large pans, pour the sauce over them and simmer gently for 3 minutes. Serve in large dishes with noodles.

DUTCH APPLE PIE
make 3

1$\frac{1}{2}$ lb. cooking apples, peeled and quartered
4-6 tbsps. water
4 oz. ($\frac{2}{3}$ cup) soft brown sugar
1 level tbsp. cornflour
$\frac{1}{2}$ level tsp. salt
1 level tsp. powdered cinnamon
2 tbsps. lemon juice
1 oz. butter
$\frac{1}{2}$ level tsp. vanilla essence
6 oz. (1$\frac{1}{2}$ cups) plain flour
1 level tsp. salt
1 oz. lard
2 oz. butter
milk to glaze

Simmer the apples with the water until soft. Mix together the sugar, cornflour, salt and cinnamon and add to the cooked apples. Stir in the lemon juice and cook, stirring, until fairly thick. Remove from the heat, stir in the butter and vanilla essence and cool.

Sift the flour and salt into a bowl. Rub in the lard and butter with the fingertips until the mixture resembles fine breadcrumbs, then add enough cold water to make a stiff dough.

Roll out half the dough and use it to line a 7-in. pie plate, preferably metal; put the apple mixture in the pastry case. Roll out the remaining pastry to make a lid. Damp the edges of the pastry base, cover the pie with the lid and press the edges well together. Knock up and scallop the edges. Brush the top of the pie with milk to glaze and bake in the centre of the oven at 425°F. (mark 7) for 10 minutes. Reduce the heat to 375°F. (mark 5) and cook for a further 20 minutes, until the pastry is golden.

Serve hot or cold, with whipped cream.

VERANDAH PUNCH

2 large juicy oranges
3 thin-skinned lemons
$\frac{1}{4}$ pint ($\frac{5}{8}$ cup) sugar syrup
$\frac{1}{2}$ pint (1$\frac{1}{4}$ cups) freshly made tea
3 6-fl. oz. bottles ginger ale, well chilled
3 6-fl. oz. bottles soda water, well chilled
ice cubes and slices of orange to decorate

Squeeze out the fruit juices and mix with the sugar syrup and tea. Cool, then strain into a bowl and chill.

Just before serving, mix in the ginger ale and soda water. Add the ice cubes and sliced orange.

Verandah punch is ideal for a teenage party

Christmas

Turkey and Christmas pudding must form the centre of most families' traditional meal, but there's more to it than that. Here are some recipes both old and new to try.

ROAST TURKEY

To help you calculate what size turkey you need, use this chart:

Turkey (oven-ready weight)	Servings
6–8 lb.	6–10
8–12 lb.	10–20
14–16 lb.	20–40

It's useful to know that a 10-lb. turkey yields about 2 lb. 12 oz. white meat and about the same amount of dark meat. As a straight roast meal, with trimmings, this will serve 8, plus a further 4 servings as cold cuts and should leave you enough for a réchauffé dish as well.

Approximate cooking times for the quick oven method using foil wrap, at 450°F. (mark 8) are:

6–8 lb.	2½ hours
8–10 lb.	2½–2¾ hours
10–12 lb.	2 hours 50 minutes
12–14 lb.	3 hours
14–16 lb.	3–3¼ hours
16–18 lb.	3¼–3½ hours

If wished, open the foil for the last 30 minutes and cover the bird with rinded bacon rashers. Turn the bird about half-way through the cooking time so that it cooks evenly.

To check if the turkey is cooked, pierce the deepest part of the

the bird ready 30 minutes before serving. When ready, lower the oven temperature and keep the bird warm.

If you wish to use the slow oven method, don't wrap the bird in foil, but if it just about fills the oven it is wise to protect the legs and breast. Approximate cooking times for this method, at 325°F. (mark 3) are:

6–8 lb.	3–3½ hours
8–10 lb.	3½–3¾ hours
10–12 lb.	3¾–4 hours
12–14 lb.	4–4¼ hours
14–16 lb.	4¼–4½ hours
16–18 lb.	4½–4 hours 50 minutes

1 tablespoon lemon juice and sage. Season well.
Bind together with the giblet stock.

NUT STUFFING

2 oz. shelled walnuts
1 oz. cashew nuts
1 oz. shelled Brazil nuts
2 oz. butter
2 small onions, skinned and finely chopped
¼ lb. mushrooms, wiped and finely chopped
pinch of dried herbs
1 tbsp. chopped parsley
6 oz. fresh white breadcrumbs
1 large egg, beaten
giblet stock to moisten, optional
salt and freshly ground black pepper

Finely chop the nuts. Melt the butter and sauté the onion for 5 minutes until soft but not coloured. Add the finely chopped mushrooms and sauté for a further 5 minutes.

Toss together the nuts, herbs and breadcrumbs. Stir in the mushroom mixture with the beaten egg and, if necessary, moisten with stock. Season to taste.

MUSHROOM AND BACON STUFFING

6 oz. fresh white breadcrumbs
1 tbsp. chopped parsley
½ level tsp. dried thyme
1 clove of garlic, skinned and crushed
2 oz. butter
4 oz. onion, skinned and chopped
¼ lb. streaky bacon rashers, rinded and chopped
¼ lb. mushrooms, wiped and chopped
salt and freshly ground black pepper
egg yolk
giblet stock (optional)

In a mixing bowl, mix together the breadcrumbs, parsley, thyme and garlic.

Melt the 2 oz. butter in a frying pan and fry the onion until soft but not coloured. Stir in the bacon, cook for a further 3–4 minutes, then add the mushrooms and mix well. Combine with the breadcrumb mixture.

Season well with salt and pepper and bind the ingredients together with egg yolk and a little stock if necessary.

A tasty risotto makes a change on Boxing Day

If your turkey is frozen, make sure it arrives in good time. Remove it from the container, cover with muslin and leave it to thaw, preferably in the refrigerator, for 2–3 days. If refrigerator space is not available store in the coldest possible place.

To prepare the bird for the oven, first remove the giblets and use them to make a stock for the gravy. Wipe the turkey inside, then put in the stuffing. Most people use 2 kinds of stuffing in a turkey, 1 at the neck end and 1 at the vent. Allow about ½ lb. stuffing to each 5 lb. of turkey; do not stuff too tightly. Brush the skin with melted butter or dripping and season with salt, pepper and lemon juice. Either put it in a roasting tin and cover with foil or use plastic film roasting wrap or bag.

thigh with a skewer. If the juices are colourless, the bird is ready; if tinged pink, cook it a little longer. Calculate the cooking time to have

Handy hint

Stuffings are best made with fresh breadcrumbs. If only dry crumbs are available, soak in a little milk or stock for 1 hour and squeeze out the excess moisture before use.

CELERY STUFFING

4 oz. onion, skinned and finely chopped
2–3 celery sticks, scrubbed and finely diced
2 oz. butter
4 oz. cooking apple, peeled and cored
6 oz. fresh white breadcrumbs
juice and finely grated rind of 1 small lemon
2 level tsps. dried sage
salt and freshly ground black pepper
3 tbsps. concentrated giblet stock

Fry the onion and celery in the butter until transparent. Finely dice the apple, add to the pan and fry a little longer. Stir in the breadcrumbs with the lemon rind,

CRANBERRY SAUCE

6 oz. (¾ cup) sugar
½ pint (⅝ cup) water
1 lb. fresh cranberries,
    washed, or frozen
    cranberries, thawed
a little sherry

Gently heat the sugar with the water in a pan until the sugar dissolves. Add the cranberries and cook uncovered over a medium heat for about 10 minutes; allow to cool. Add sherry to taste before serving.

CRANBERRY AND BACON BALLS

makes 16–20

6 oz. onion, skinned and
    finely chopped
4 oz. streaky bacon, rinded
    and chopped
1 oz. butter
4 oz. fresh cranberries,
    washed
2 oz. shredded suet
1 level tsp. dried thyme
finely grated rind of 1 orange
6 oz. fresh white
    breadcrumbs
1 level tsp. salt
freshly ground black pepper
1 large egg, beaten
orange juice

Fry the onion and bacon in the butter until tender. Add the cranberries and cook until the cranberries 'pop'. Cool a little, then add the suet, thyme, orange rind and breadcrumbs. Fork through to blend evenly; adjust the seasoning. Stir in the egg and enough orange juice to moisten. Form the mixture into balls.

Heat some lard or dripping to give ¼-in. depth in a baking tin and cook the stuffing balls at 400°F. (mark 6) for about 20 minutes.

TURKEY RISOTTO

serves 4

6 oz. onion, skinned and finely
    chopped
2 oz. butter
½ lb. lean bacon rashers,
    rinded and diced
8 oz. cooked turkey meat,
    diced
½ lb. button mushrooms,
    wiped and sliced
1 small green pepper
    (capsicum), seeded and
    sliced
8 oz. (1 cup) long grain rice
celery salt
freshly ground black pepper
4 tbsps. white wine
1 pint (2½ cups) turkey stock
tomato wedges for garnish

Fry the onion in the butter until tender, add the bacon and cook a little longer.

Add the cooked, diced turkey, mushrooms, pepper, rice and seasonings, stir well and pour in the wine and stock.

Bring this mixture to the boil, stirring gently, and turn into a casserole. Cover tightly and cook in the oven at 325°F. (mark 3) for about 35 minutes, until the stock is absorbed and the rice is fluffy and tender.

Turn on to a hot serving dish and serve garnished with tomato wedges.

Traditional Christmas pudding with a fluffy brandy flavoured sauce

TURKEY CRANBERRY SALAD

serves 4

6 level tsps. powdered
    gelatine
¼ pint (⅝ cup) water
4 tbsps. lemon juice
7-oz can whole berry
    cranberry sauce
½ pint (1¼ cups) turkey stock
¼ tsp. Tabasco sauce
5 level tbsps. lemon
    mayonnaise
2 tsps. finely chopped onion
2-3 sticks celery, scrubbed
    and chopped
1 small green pepper
    (capsicum), seeded and
    diced
1 red-skinned eating apple,
    diced
12 oz. cooked turkey, diced

Sprinkle 3 level teaspoons gelatine over the water in a bowl and dissolve it over a pan of hot water. Add 2 tablespoons lemon juice and the cranberry sauce. Stir thoroughly. Pour into a 1½-pint mould and leave to set.

Place the turkey stock in a saucepan, sprinkle the remaining gelatine over the surface, dissolve over a low heat but do not boil. Add the Tabasco sauce and remaining lemon juice, pour into a bowl and leave to cool. Gradually whisk in the mayonnaise. When beginning to set, fold in the onion, celery, pepper, apple and turkey.

Adjust seasoning. Spoon the turkey mixture on to the cranberry layer and leave to set.

To serve, unmould and accompany by coleslaw and French bread.

TURKEY BROTH

serves 4

6 oz. carrot, scraped and
    coarsely grated
6 oz. onion, skinned and
    finely chopped
1 oz. butter
1½ pints (3¾ cups) strong
    turkey stock
1 bay leaf
2 oz. small pasta
2 oz. fresh celery leaves,
    washed and roughly
    chopped

Fry the carrot and onion in the butter until soft–about 10 minutes. Pour in the stock and add the bay leaf and pasta. Bring to the boil, cover and simmer for 30 minutes. Discard the bay leaf, adjust seasoning and add the celery leaves.

Served with grated cheese and hunks of bread, this is almost a meal in itself.

ROAST GAMMON

serves 10

4 lb. gammon joint
4 oz. (⅔ cup) Demerara sugar
cloves
2 tbsps. honey
2 tbsps. orange juice
glacé cherries, canned
    apricots, drained or sliced
    oranges

Soak the gammon for several hours in cold water, then drain. To calculate the cooking time, allow 20–25 minutes per lb. and 20 minutes over. Place the joint in a pan, skin side down, cover with water and add half the sugar. Bring slowly to the boil and remove the scum. Reduce the heat and simmer, covered, for half the calculated cooking time. Top up with extra boiling water when necessary.

Drain the joint, carefully strip off the rind and score the fat into squares, then stud with cloves. Blend the remaining sugar, honey and orange juice and spread over the joint. Place it in a roasting tin and roast at 350°F. (mark 4) for the rest of the cooking time. Baste two or three times during cooking and, 20 minutes before the end of the cooking time, raise the temperature to 425°F. (mark 7). Serve hot; garnish with apricot halves and glacé cherries impaled on cocktail sticks or with slices of orange.

CHRISTMAS PUDDING

serves 6–8

6 oz. (1½ cups) plain flour
1 level tsp. mixed spice
½ level tsp. grated nutmeg
4 oz. apple, peeled and cored
3 oz. fresh white breadcrumbs
4 oz. shredded suet
4 oz. stoned raisins, chopped
8 oz. currants, cleaned
8 oz. sultanas, cleaned
3 oz. (½ cup) Demerara sugar
grated rind of 1 lemon
grated rind of 1 orange
2 eggs, beaten
⅓ pint (⅞ cup) brown ale

Grease a 2-pint pudding basin. Sift together the flour, mixed spice

and nutmeg. Dice the apple and add to the flour, along with the breadcrumbs, suet, dried fruit, sugar, lemon and orange rind. Mix the ingredients well. Gradually stir in the beaten eggs and ale and stir thoroughly. If possible, leave to stand overnight.
Turn the mixture into the prepared basin, then cover with greased greaseproof paper and kitchen foil or a pudding cloth. Tie the foil or cloth firmly in place with string.
Either place the bowl in a pan with water half-way up the sides and, after bringing to the boil, reduce heat and boil gently for about 6 hours, or place in a steamer and cook for 8 hours. A piece of lemon in the water will prevent discolouration of the pan. Top up with more boiling water at intervals.
To store, leave the greaseproof paper in position, but re-wrap with fresh foil or pudding cloth. On the day, reboil for about 3 hours.

EASY CHRISTMAS PUDDING

makes 2

4 oz. (1 cup) plain flour
1 level tsp. cinnamon
$\frac{1}{2}$ level tsp. grated nutmeg
4 oz. fresh white breadcrumbs
2 oz. ($\frac{1}{3}$ cup) soft brown sugar
grated rind of 1 lemon
4 oz. glacé cherries, chopped
2 oz. nibbed almonds
3 lb. ready-made mincemeat
3 eggs, beaten

Grease 2 1-pint pudding basins and place a circle of greaseproof paper in the bases.
Sift together the flour, cinnamon and nutmeg into a large bowl. Add the breadcrumbs, sugar, lemon rind, cherries and almonds, mix together and stir in the mincemeat and eggs. Mix the ingredients well together with a wooden spoon.
Divide the mixture evenly between the 2 basins. Cover tightly with greased greaseproof paper and kitchen foil or pudding cloths. Tie the foil or cloths firmly in place with string.
Place in a saucepan with water half-way up, bring to the boil, reduce heat and simmer for about $4\frac{3}{4}$ hours. Top up with boiling water when necessary.
To store, leave greaseproof paper in position but cover with fresh foil or pudding cloths.
To reheat, boil gently for about 2 hours.

FLUFFY SAUCE

2 oz. butter
4 oz. ($\frac{7}{8}$ cup) icing sugar, sifted
2 eggs, separated
2 tbsps. brandy
$\frac{1}{4}$ pint ($\frac{5}{8}$ cup) double cream

Cream together the butter and icing sugar. Beat in the egg yolks and then gradually beat in the brandy. Add the double cream. Place in a double saucepan and cook over a gentle heat until the mixture is the consistency of thick custard. Beat the egg whites until stiff but not dry. Pour the custard mixture on to the egg whites, whisking all the time. Return to the double pan to keep warm. Stir before serving.

Snowman cake for the children

Handy hint

When adding strong colourings and flavourings to food, dip a skewer into the bottle and shake drops off the end of the skewer into the food.

RUM BUTTER

8 oz. butter (preferably unsalted)
4 oz. ($\frac{2}{3}$ cup) soft light brown sugar
2–3 tbsps. rum
icing sugar

Cream the butter in a bowl with a wooden spoon and beat in the sugar.
When the mixture is soft, slowly beat in the rum to taste. Pile into the bowl in which it is to be served and chill.
Just before serving, dredge with icing sugar.

MINCEMEAT

makes about 6 lb.

12 oz. currants, cleaned
8 oz. sultanas, cleaned
12 oz. stoned raisins, cleaned
4 oz. cut mixed peel
$\frac{3}{4}$ lb. firm, hard cooking apples, peeled and cored
1 lb. ($2\frac{2}{3}$ cups) soft light brown or Demerara sugar
1 lb. shredded suet
1 level tsp. grated nutmeg
$\frac{1}{2}$ level tsp. powdered cinnamon or mace
grated rind and juice of 1 lemon
grated rind and juice of 1 small orange
$\frac{1}{3}$ pint ($\frac{7}{8}$ cup) brandy

Roughly chop the prepared fruit, peel and apples. Combine with the sugar, suet, spices, lemon and orange rind and juice and brandy and mix all the ingredients together thoroughly. Cover the mincemeat and leave overnight.
Next day stir the mincemeat well and put into jars. Cover as for jam. Store in a cool, dry, well ventilated place and allow to mature for at least 2 weeks before using.
Note: 1 oz. finely chopped sweet almonds may be added to each 1 lb. of mincemeat just before use.

MINCE PIES

makes 20

12 oz. shortcrust pastry – i.e. made with 12 oz. (3 cups) flour
$\frac{3}{4}$ lb. mincemeat
icing sugar, sifted

Grease 20 $2\frac{1}{2}$-in. patty tins.
Roll out the pastry about $\frac{1}{8}$ in. thick. Using a 3-in. fluted cutter, cut out 20 rounds for the base and then cut 20 smaller rounds with a $2\frac{1}{4}$-in. fluted cutter, re-rolling as necessary.
Line the patty tins with the larger rounds and two-thirds fill with mincemeat, using a teaspoon. Damp the edges of the smaller rounds and place in position. Make a small slit in the top of each and bake towards the top of the oven at 400°F. (mark 6) for about 20 minutes until light golden brown.
Serve pies warm or cold, lightly dusted with icing sugar. If preferred, the tops may be brushed with a little milk before baking, to glaze them.

YULE LOG PUDDING

serves 6

1 oz. crystallized ginger
3 oz. glacé cherries
1–2 tbsps. brandy
1 oz. blanched almonds
1 pint ($2\frac{1}{2}$ cups) custard
$\frac{1}{4}$ pint ($\frac{5}{8}$ cup) double cream, whipped
1 egg white

Cut the ginger and cherries into small pieces and soak in the brandy for 30–60 minutes.
Chop the nuts roughly. Put the custard into the freezing compartment of the refrigerator, set at its coldest, or a home freezer and leave until half frozen.
Add the fruit, nuts and whipped cream to the custard. Stiffly beat the egg white, fold it into the mixture and freeze until almost set, then beat well.
Pour the mixture into a wetted loaf tin and freeze hard. Turn out, cut into slices and decorate.

CHRISTMAS CAKE

8 oz. stoned raisins
8 oz. sultanas
8 oz. currants
4 oz. chopped mixed peel
4 oz. (1 cup) ground almonds
4 oz. glacé cherries,
    quartered
8 oz. (2 cups) plain flour
1 level tsp. mixed spice
pinch of salt
8 oz. butter
6 oz. (1 cup) soft light brown
    sugar
4 large eggs
1½ tbsps. brandy

Grease and line an 8-in. round cake tin.

Check the raisins to make sure all stones are removed; cut large ones in half. Clean the sultanas and currants. Mix the raisins, sultanas, currants, peel, almonds and cherries together.

Sift the flour, spice and salt. Cream the butter until soft, add the sugar and beat until light and fluffy. Beat in the eggs one at a time. Fold in the dry ingredients, adding the fruit and brandy last. Turn the mixture into the prepared tin. Stand it in a larger tin or line the outside with brown paper. Place on a baking sheet lined with brown paper.

Bake in the lower part of the oven at 300°F. (mark 1–2) for about 3½ hours. Cool on a wire rack. If wished, baste with a little more brandy before storing. Wrap in foil or put in an airtight tin and store in a cool, dry place. Decorate not more than 1 week before Christmas.

SNOWMAN CAKE

8 oz. butter or margarine
8 oz. (1 cup) caster sugar
4 large eggs
8 oz. (2 cups) self-raising
    flour
1 oz. (¼ cup) cocoa
2 tbsps. hot water

For decoration :
2 egg whites
1 lb. 2 oz. (4 cups) icing sugar,
    sifted
1 tbsp. glycerine
1 tsp. lemon juice
4 oz. bought marzipan
few drops red colouring
coloured sweets

Grease a ¾-pint and a 2-pint ovenproof pudding basin. Line the bases with greased greaseproof paper.

Cream the butter and sugar until light and fluffy, then beat in the eggs one at a time. Fold in the

No need to pipe elaborate decorations on the Christmas cake—icing 'snow' is just as pretty

Home-made mincemeat, with almonds and a little brandy, makes the best mince pies

251

flour. Blend the cocoa with the hot water and stir into the mixture. Fill both basins two-thirds full and put them in the centre of the oven at 350°F. (mark 4). The smaller one will take 40–45 minutes, the larger about 1 hour 15 minutes. Turn out and cool on a wire rack. Brush the loose crumbs off both cakes and place the larger one on a silver board.

Roughly beat the egg whites in a basin, beat in the icing sugar a little at a time with a wooden spoon. Add the glycerine and lemon juice. The icing should be soft but firm enough to hold the shape of peaks. Using a palette knife, spread the icing over the cake to cover completely and rough up into soft peaks. Place the small cake on top and cover with icing in the same way. Leave to set.

Meanwhile, add a few drops of colouring to the marzipan, roll out fairly thinly into a circle and shape into a brimmed hat. When the icing is nearly set, place the hat in position and put the coloured sweets in place to make the eyes, nose and buttons. When the icing is firmly set, secure a coloured ribbon round the snowman's neck to make a scarf.

MARZIPAN AND RAISIN TRUFFLES

makes about 24

8 oz. plain (dark) chocolate
6 oz. seedless raisins
1 tbsp. rum or coffee liqueur
8 oz. ready-made marzipan
1 tsp. coffee essence
3 oz. chocolate vermicelli drinking chocolate

Melt half the chocolate in a basin over hot water. Add the raisins and rum or liqueur. Blend thoroughly and, when firm enough, shape into 24 small balls. Chill.

Knead the marzipan until pliable, and work in the coffee essence. Roll

Handy hint

1 tbsp. oil added to the water when cooking pasta prevents the pasta sticking together and also improves the flavour.

out to about ¼ in. thick and stamp out 24 rounds, using a 2-in. plain cutter. Shape the marzipan round the chocolate and raisins to form balls.

Melt the remaining chocolate in a basin small enough to give a good depth, over hot water. Dip each ball in the chocolate, drain a little, then coat half of them with chocolate vermicelli. Leave the rest to dry on non-stick paper, then roll them in drinking chocolate.

Serve in small paper cases.

CHRISTMAS PRESERVES

After Christmas, some special preserves will add to the pleasure of meals. These make good presents, too, if made in attractive jars.

SPICED ORANGE RINGS

8 thin-skinned oranges
1½ pints (3¾ cups) water
1½ lb. (3 cups) sugar
½ pint (1¼ cups) white distilled vinegar
¼ oz. whole cloves
1½ sticks of cinnamon
6 blades of mace

Wipe the oranges, cut into ¼-in. slices and discard the pips. Place the sliced oranges in a pan, cover with water, cover the pan and simmer the contents for about 40 minutes, or until the peel is soft. Make a syrup by dissolving the sugar in the vinegar, add the spices and boil for 3–4 minutes.

Drain the oranges, place in a shallow pan and cover with vinegar syrup. Simmer, covered, for 30–40 minutes, until the orange slices

Christmas preserves—rich or spicy—for cold meats

look clear. Remove from heat and leave in the syrup for 24 hours. Drain the orange rings and pack them into sterilized jars. Cover the fruit with the syrup. Do not seal at once, but keep topping up with syrup for the next 3–4 days; then cover as for pickles.

Leave to mature if possible for at least 6 weeks.

BRANDIED PEACHES

1 lb. fresh peaches
8 oz. (1 cup) sugar
approx. ¼ pint (⅝ cup) brandy or Cointreau

Skin the peaches by plunging them into boiling water, then gently peeling off the skins. Halve the peaches and remove the stones. Make a light syrup by dissolving 4 oz. (½ cup) sugar in ½ pint (1¼ cups) water and poach the peaches gently for 4–5 minutes. Remove from the heat, drain and cool, then arrange the fruit in small jars.

Add the remaining sugar to the syrup and dissolve it slowly. Bring to the boil and boil to 230°F.; allow to cool. Add an equal quantity of brandy or Cointreau to the syrup, pour over the peaches and seal with preserving skin.

SPICED CRAB APPLES

6 lb. crab apples
1½ pints (3¾ cups) water
2–3 strips lemon peel
1 lb. (2 cups) sugar
¾ pint (1⅞ cups) wine vinegar
1 stick cinnamon
1–2 whole cloves
3 peppercorns

Wash and trim the crab apples, then simmer in the water with the

lemon peel until just tender; remove from the heat.

Place the sugar and vinegar in a pan and add 1½ pints (3¾ cups) of the liquid from the fruit. Tie the spices in muslin and add to the liquid. Heat gently to dissolve the sugar, then bring to the boil and boil for 1 minute. Remove the pan from the heat and add the crab apples. Simmer gently until the syrup has reduced to a coating consistency – 30–40 minutes. Remove the spices after 30 minutes. Place the fruit in small jars, cover with syrup and seal with preserving skin.

SPICED PEARS

14 oz. (1¾ cups) sugar
¾ oz. salt
2 pints (5 cups) water
6 lb. small, hard pears, peeled and cored
2 pints (5 cups) white vinegar
2 sticks cinnamon
¼ oz. whole cloves

Dissolve 2 oz. (¼ cup) of the sugar and the salt in the water and bring to the boil. Cut the pears into quarters and add to the boiling water; remove the pan from the heat, cover and allow to cool.

Boil together the vinegar, remaining sugar and spices. Remove the pears from the water and drain, then place them in the syrup and bring to the boil. Take from the heat, allow to cool and bring back to the boil. Repeat this process 3 times.

Finally allow to cool and place the pears in small sterilized jars. Pour the syrup over them, retaining the surplus, but do not seal. Top up each day for the next days, or until no more syrup is absorbed. Cover with preserving skin.

BRANDIED PINEAPPLE

1 large can (1 lb. 13 oz.) pineapple pieces
3 cloves
2-in. stick cinnamon
¼ pint (⅝ cup) brandy or Kirsch

Drain the juice from the pineapple and put it into a saucepan. Add the cloves and cinnamon and simmer gently until of a syrupy consistency. Add the pineapple pieces and simmer for a further 10 minutes. Remove from the heat and add the brandy or Kirsch. Leave to cool.

Pack the fruit in a wide-necked bottle, pour in the syrup and seal with preserving skin.

EASTER

Warm hot cross buns on Good Friday,
Easter bread for Sunday breakfast,
simnel cake and Easter biscuits for
tea. In between, all children love a
chocolate egg.

HOT CROSS BUNS

makes 12

1 lb. (4 cups) plain strong bread flour
1 oz. fresh baker's yeast or 1 level tbsp. dried yeast
1 level tsp. caster sugar
¼ pint (⅝ cup) milk
¼ pint (⅝ cup) water, less 4 tbsps.
1 level tsp. salt
½ level tsp. powdered mixed spice
½ level tsp. powdered cinnamon
½ level tsp. grated nutmeg
2 oz. (¼ cup) caster sugar
2 oz. butter, melted and cooled but not firm
1 egg, beaten
4 oz. currants
1-2 oz. chopped mixed peel

For glaze:

2 tbsps. milk
2 tbsps. water
1½ oz. (3 tbsps.) caster sugar

Flour 2 baking sheets. Place 4 oz. (1 cup) of the measured flour in a large mixing bowl. Add the yeast and caster sugar. Warm the milk and water to about 110°F., add to the flour and mix well. Set aside in a warm place until frothy – about 20 minutes for fresh yeast, 30 minutes for dried yeast.

Sift together the remaining 12 oz. (3 cups) flour, the salt, spices and 2 oz. (¼ cup) sugar. Stir the butter and egg into the frothy yeast mixture, add the spiced flour, fruit and peel, then mix. The dough should be fairly soft.

Turn it out on to a lightly floured board and knead until smooth. Place the dough in a lightly greased polythene bag, close and leave at room temperature until doubled in size – about 1–1½ hours. Turn risen dough on to a floured surface and knock out the air bubbles. Knead again.

Divide the dough into 12 pieces and shape into buns. Press down hard at first on the table surface, then ease up as you turn and shape the buns. Arrange the buns well apart on the floured baking sheets, place inside lightly greased polythene bags, close and allow to rise at room temperature for 45 minutes (only 30 minutes if the dough has had an initial rising). Make quick slashes with a very sharp knife, just cutting the surface of the bun in the shape of a cross.

Bake just above the centre of the oven at 375°F. (mark 5) for 15–20 minutes. Brush the hot buns twice with glaze. Leave to cool.

Buy an Easter egg mould and make your own chocolate eggs

SIMNEL CAKE

1 lb. ready-made almond paste
8 oz. (2 cups) plain flour
pinch of salt
½ level tsp. grated nutmeg
½ level tsp. powdered cinnamon
8 oz. currants, cleaned
4 oz. sultanas, cleaned
3 oz. chopped mixed peel
4 oz. glacé cherries, quartered
6 oz. butter
6 oz. (¾ cup) caster sugar
3 eggs
milk to mix, if required
1 egg white

Grease and line a 7-in. round cake tin.

Roll out one-third of the almond paste into a round slightly smaller than the cake tin.

Sift together the flour, salt and spices. Mix together all the fruit. Cream the butter and sugar until pale and fluffy and beat in each egg separately. Fold in the flour, adding a little milk if necessary to give a dropping consistency. Fold in the fruit.

Put half the mixture into the prepared tin and place the round of almond paste on top. Cover with the rest of the mixture, spreading it evenly. Bake in the oven at 300°F. (mark 1–2) for 2½–3 hours, until the cake is a rich brown and firm to the touch. Cool on a wire rack. It is not possible to test this cake with a skewer as the almond paste remains soft and may give a false impression. From the remaining almond paste, shape 11 small balls, then cut the rest into a round to fit the top of the cake. Brush the top surface of the cake with egg white, place the almond paste in position and smooth it slightly with a rolling pin. Pinch the edges into scallops with finger and thumb. Score the surface into a lattice with a knife, brush with egg white, arrange the almond paste balls round the top of the cake and brush these with egg white.

Put under a moderate grill until light golden brown.

EASTER BISCUITS

makes 15–20

3 oz. butter or margarine
2½ oz. (⅜ cup) caster sugar
1 egg, separated
6 oz. (1½ cups) self-raising flour
pinch of salt
1½ oz. currants
½ oz. chopped mixed peel
1-2 tbsps. milk or brandy
little caster sugar

Grease 2 baking sheets.

Cream the butter and sugar and beat in the egg yolk. Sift the flour with the salt and fold into the creamed mixture, with the currants and finely chopped mixed peel. Add enough milk to give a fairly soft dough, cover and leave in a cool place to become firm.

Knead lightly on a floured board and roll out to about ¼ in. thick. Cut into rounds, using a 2½-in. fluted cutter. Put on the baking sheets, well spaced, and cook in the oven at 400°F. (mark 6) for about 20 minutes, until lightly coloured. After 10 minutes baking, brush the biscuits with egg white and sprinkle with sugar.

Cool on a wire rack.

EASTER BREAD

1 oz. yeast
½ pint (1¼ cups) warm milk
1 lb. (4 cups) plain strong bread flour
6 egg yolks
6 oz. (¾ cup) sugar
2 oz. butter, melted
4½ oz. candied fruit, chopped

Dissolve the yeast in the milk, mi with half the flour and leave in warm place to start to work.

Beat the egg yolks and suga together and when the dough ha risen, mix them in, with th melted butter. Add the remainin flour and the candied fruit.

Beat the mixture well, leave t rise again and form it into plaite loaves. Place on a baking sheet prove for 20–30 minutes an bake at 450°F. (mark 8) until we risen and browned – about 30–4 minutes.

EASTER EGG CAKE

3½ fl. oz. corn oil
juice of ½ a lemon, made up to 3½ fl. oz. with water
2 eggs, separated
5 oz. (1¼ cups) plain flour
1 oz. (¼ cup) cornflour
2 level tsps. baking powder
5 oz. (⅝ cup) caster sugar
grated rind of 1 lemon

For decorating:

jam or lemon curd
8 oz. almond paste
6 oz. glacé icing, tinted
ribbon and sugar flowers
chocolate glacé icing
chicks or small eggs, optiona

Grease an oblong tin measurin 9 in. by 5 in. by 3 in.

Whisk together the corn oil, lemo juice and the egg yolks. Si together the dry ingredients. Ad to the liquid, with the grate lemon rind, then beat to give smooth, slack batter. Beat th egg whites stiffly and fold in. Tur the mixture into the tin and bak in the oven at 375°F. (mark 5) fo 50 minutes. Cool on a wire rack Use a sharp knife to cut it into th shape of an egg. Slice it throug lengthwise and sandwich wit jam or curd. Brush the outsid with sieved jam and cover wit rolled out almond paste, mouldin it into shape with your hands.

Leave on a wire rack to dry over night, then coat with tinted glac icing. When this is complete dry and set, place the cake on board and tie a ribbon round it Decorate with sugar flowers, pip a nest of chocolate glacé icing an add the chicks or eggs.

ANNIVERSARY SUPPERS

There are no traditional anniversary dishes, but a celebration of this importance merits something special.

Day before: *Wash the salad ingredients and pack them in polythene in the refrigerator to keep crisp. Make up the salad dressing, keep it in a screw-top jar. Cook the beans.*
Make the gâteaux and leave them in the refrigerator.
Make the mousse, but do not leave it in the mould overnight if it is a metal one.
In the morning: *Make up the fruit salad.*
hours before: *Turn out the mousse and garnish. Turn out the gâteaux and decorate.*
hour before: *Prepare the gammon and put it on to cook. Boil the rice. Toss the salads.*

PRAWN AND SALMON MOUSSE

oz. aspic powder
pint (⅝ cup) hot water
oz. peeled prawns
8-oz. cans red salmon
tbsps. lemon juice
salt and freshly ground black pepper
oz. powdered gelatine
pint (2½ cups) double cream
large egg whites
few extra prawns to garnish, optional

Dissolve the aspic powder in the hot water and pour 3 tablespoons of it into the base of a 4-pint ring mould. Leave to set. Arrange the prawns on the set aspic and gently pour over the remaining aspic; leave to set.

Coffee brandy gâteau and sunshine fruit salad for an anniversary

Drain the salmon, reserving the juice, and discard the skin and bones. Mash together the fish, fish juice and lemon juice; or use an electric blender. Season well. Put the gelatine in a bowl with 8 tablespoons cold water and stand it over a pan of hot water until completely dissolved. Whip the cream until thick and stiffly whisk the egg whites. Fold the gelatine and cream into the fish mixture, then lightly fold in the egg whites. Turn the mixture into the ring mould and leave in the refrigerator to set.
To serve, turn out the mousse on to a flat plate and garnish, if wished, with a few whole prawns.

GAMMON SLICES WITH PEACHES

2 oz. butter
3 tbsps. cooking oil
1 oz. (2 tbsps.) caster sugar
12 gammon rashers, rinded
1-lb. 15-oz. can peach halves
2 tbsps. vinegar
1 level tsp. mustard powder
salt and freshly ground black pepper

Heat the butter and oil in a large frying pan and add the sugar. Fry the gammon rashers, approximately 3 at a time, on both sides until golden brown. Remove them from the pan and place in a large shallow casserole, or use 2 if more practical.
Drain the peaches, reserving the juice. Fry them lightly on both sides, and add to the casserole. Pour the reserved juice into the frying pan with the vinegar and mustard and bring to the boil. Simmer until slightly thickened,

season well, and pour the syrup over the peaches and gammon. Cook in the centre of the oven at 400°F. (mark 6) for about 30 minutes.
Serve hot with boiled rice, mixed with halved almonds, and mixed salad and French beans in vinaigrette dressing.

COFFEE BRANDY GATEAU
make 2

6 oz. butter
6 oz. (¾ cup) caster sugar
3 large eggs
2 tbsps. coffee essence
1 tbsp. brandy
12 trifle sponge fingers
¼ pint (⅝ cup) double cream, whipped
chopped walnuts

Line the base of an 8-in. loose base cake tin with non-stick paper.
Cream the butter and sugar together until light and fluffy and the sugar has lost its grittiness. Beat in the eggs, one at a time. Beat in the coffee essence and brandy. Cut the sponge cakes in half, lengthwise. Arrange 8 pieces in the base of the prepared tin. Pour in half the coffee mixture. Cover with a further 8 sponge pieces, then pour in the remaining coffee mixture. Arrange the rest of the sponge pieces on top.
Press down well. Cover with a small plate, put a weight on the plate. Leave in the refrigerator for about 3 hours, until set.
Shortly before serving, run a round-bladed knife round the edge of the tin. Turn the gâteau out on to a plate, cover the top with cream and pipe the remaining cream round the top and base of the

gâteau, using a large star vegetable nozzle.
Cluster a few chopped walnuts in the centre.

SUNSHINE FRUIT SALAD
make 2

4 oz. (½ cup) caster sugar
½ pint (1¼ cups) water
juice of ½ lemon
1 medium-sized melon (cantaloup)
3 oranges
3 grapefruit
½ lb. strawberries
2 tbsps. Grand Marnier

Make the syrup by dissolving the sugar in the water over a gentle heat and boiling for 5 minutes; allow to cool, then add the lemon juice.
Halve the melon, discard the pips and scoop out the flesh. Chop it roughly. Remove the skin and pith from the oranges and grapefruit, and cut into segments. Discard the hulls from the strawberries and cut the fruit in half.
Put all the fruit into the syrup, add the Grand Marnier and leave to stand for 2–3 hours in a cool place before serving.

Day before: *Prepare crawfish but do not slice.*
Marinade meats.
Make sponge flan cases; when cold store in polythene bags.
In the morning: *Prepare salad dressing.*
Cook cutlets.
Prepare soured cream dip.
Finish the cherry flans and make the tutti frutti ratafia.
1½ hours before: *Cook the meats and arrange on skewers.*
1 hour before: *Arrange crawfish and garnishes.*
Before serving: *Spoon juices over meat.*
Add dressing to salad.

CRAWFISH TAILS WITH TARRAGON DRESSING

12 crawfish tails, fresh or
    frozen
2 limes or lemons
2 tbsps. tarragon vinegar
½ pint (1¼ cups) salad oil
thinly pared rind of 1 lemon
2 eggs, hard-boiled
sprigs of parsley
salt and freshly ground black
    pepper
sugar to taste

Cook fresh crawfish tails by placing
in cold salted water, bringing to
the boil and cooking for 10 minutes. To cook frozen crawfish,
plunge while still frozen into boiling salted water and cook for about
8 minutes. Plunge into cold water
to cool.

Slit the soft undershell of each
with scissors and peel away. Ease
out the meat in one piece. Slice
thickly and return to the shells.
Garnish with wedges of lime or
lemon.

Put the remaining ingredients into
a blender and mix until creamy (or
chop the parsley, roughly chop the
eggs and whisk with the remaining
ingredients in a basin until
creamy).

Serve on a platter with salads such
as tomatoes and coleslaw, onions
and sweet peppers, marinaded
mushrooms and cucumber.

CRUMBED LAMBED CUTLETS

½ lb. fresh white breadcrumbs
4 oz. streaky bacon, rinded
    and cooked until crisp
2 oz. onion, skinned and
    chopped
a sprig of parsley
thinly pared rind of 1 lemon
salt and freshly ground black
    pepper
12 lamb cutlets, trimmed
2 eggs, beaten
6 tbsps. cooking oil

Put the breadcrumbs in an electric
blender with the bacon, onion,
parsley, lemon rind and seasoning.
Blend until well mixed. Turn the
mixture on to a plate. Dip each
cutlet into the egg, then coat with
the seasoned crumbs, pressing the
crumbs in well. Chill.

Divide the oil between 2 roasting
tins and add the cutlets, turning
them in the oil so that both sides
are covered. Cook in the oven at
400°F. (mark 6) for about 45 minutes, until the meat is tender. Drain
and cool on kitchen paper.

To serve, put a cutlet frill on the
end of each bone.

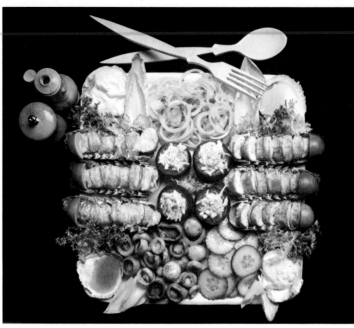

A special salad for a celebration supper

BEEF AND PORK SKEWERS

2½ lb. topside of beef
2½ lb. middle leg of pork
½ pint (1¼ cups) red wine
6 tbsps. corn oil
2 level tsps. dried rosemary
1 level tsp. dried sage
freshly ground black pepper

Cut the beef and pork into large
pieces. Place in separate dishes
each with ¼ pint (⅝ cup) wine, turn
well and leave covered in a cool
place for several hours or overnight.

Drain the meats, add 3 tablespoons oil and the rosemary to the
beef, and 3 tablespoons oil and the
sage to the pork. Turn each to
distribute the oil and herbs.
Season with pepper.

Place in baking tins or dishes and
cook in the oven at 400°F. (mark 6)
for 1 hour, then reduce to 350°F.
(mark 4) for 30 minutes. Baste
frequently with the pan juices, add
a little of the wine marinade and
turn the meat 2–3 times during
cooking.

When tender, skewer the meats
and keep hot. Reduce the juices by
rapid boiling, adjust seasoning and
spoon over the meats.

Serve with the soured cream and
garlic dip.

SOURED CREAM AND GARLIC DIP

½ pint (1¼ cups) soured cream
2 cloves of garlic, skinned
    and crushed
salt and freshly ground black
    pepper

Mix the soured cream and the
garlic, and season to taste.

CONFETTI SALAD

1½ large cucumbers (or 3
    small ridge cucumbers)
1½ lb. firm tomatoes, skinned
    and halved
¾ lb. young carrots, scraped
bunch of radishes, trimmed
celery seed dressing

Cut the unpeeled cucumbers in
¼-in. slices and then cut each slice
into sticks. Remove the seeds from
the tomatoes and cut the flesh into
strips.

Slice the carrots in rings and cut
into sticks as for the cucumber.
Slice the radishes thinly.

Combine these ingredients in a
large bowl. Add enough French
dressing, made with lemon juice
and flavoured with celery seeds, to
moisten.

TUTTI FRUTTI RATAFIA

serves 6

3 oz. ratafias
3 oranges
½ lb. strawberries, (fresh or
    frozen, thawed), hulled and
    sliced
2 oz. (¼ cup) Demerara sugar
¼ pint (⅝ cup) soured cream
long shred coconut, toasted

Divide half the ratafias between 6
individual dishes. Peel the oranges,
removing all the white pith; divide
into segments. Place on top
of the ratafias.

Layer up the strawberries, sugar
and soured cream on top of the
oranges, using half of each. Repeat
the layers with the remaining ingredients, finishing with a layer of
soured cream. Chill for 1 hour
before serving and decorate with
toasted, shredded coconut.

CHERRY FLAN

serves 6–8

For flan case :
2 eggs
2 oz. (¼ cup) caster sugar
2 oz. (½ cup) plain flour

For filling :
14-oz. can cherries
¼ pint (⅝ cup) cherry juice (if
    necessary made up with
    water)
2 level tsps. arrowroot
3 tbsps. red-currant jelly
½ pint (1¼ cups) double
    cream, lightly whipped

Grease an 8½-in. sponge flan tin
Place a round of greased grease
proof paper on the raised part o
the tin to prevent sticking.

Put the eggs and sugar in a larg
bowl, stand it over hot water an
whisk until the mixture is light an
creamy and thick enough to sho
a trail when the whisk is lifted
Remove from the heat and whis
until cool.

Sift half the flour over the whiske
mixture and fold in very lightly
using a tablespoon. Add the re
maining flour in the same way
Pour the mixture into the flan ti
spread it evenly with a palette kni
and bake above the centre of th
oven at 425°F. (mark 7) for abou
15 minutes. Loosen the edge care
fully, turn the flan case out on to
wire rack and leave to cool.

Drain and stone the cherries an
place in the sponge flan case
Blend the cherry juice and arrow
root together and add the red
currant jelly. Pour into a saucepa
bring to the boil and cook until
thickens – about 3 minutes. Allo
to cool but not become quite col
then use to glaze the cherries.
Serve with lightly whipped crea

PATE FLEURONS
makes about 50

14 oz. bought puff pastry,
 thawed
beaten egg to glaze

For filling:
4¼-oz. tube liver pâté
2 oz. butter

Roll out the pastry thinly and, using a 1½-in. fluted round cutter, stamp out as many rounds as possible.

Brush with beaten egg and fold over into semi-circles. Place on a baking tray and leave in a cool place for 30 minutes. Brush with beaten egg and bake in the oven at 400°F. (mark 6) for about 15 minutes.

With a sharp knife, cut almost through the pastry to allow steam to escape. Leave to cool on a wire rack.

Combine the liver pâté and butter and beat well, or use an electric blender. Spoon the pâté into a forcing bag fitted with a No. 8 star icing nozzle. Pipe in a shell shape down the centre of each fleuron.

CHEESE OLIVES
makes 30

8 oz. full fat soft cream
 cheese
35 stuffed olives
chopped walnuts

Cream the cheese until well blended.

Using about 1 heaped teaspoon cheese for each, roll the cheese round the olives to enclose them completely. Lightly toss in chopped walnuts. Chill for about 1 hour. Just before serving, cut in half with a sharp knife.

HARE TERRINE

1 hare, boned and filleted
1 medium-sized carrot,
 scraped and grated
1 medium-sized onion,
 skinned and grated
1½ lb. pork sausage meat
4 egg yolks
11 oz. raisins
4 tbsps. stock
salt and pepper
bacon rashers, rinded

Reserve the best pieces of hare and mince the remainder. Mix the minced hare with the carrot, onion, sausage meat, egg yolks, raisins, stock and seasonings. Line a terrine with overlapping bacon rashers and fill with alternate layers of sausage mixture and hare fillets. Wrap the bacon over the top to cover and bake in the oven at 350°F. (mark 4) for about 2½ hours. Pour off most of the fat and leave to cool. Serve thickly sliced.

SALMON RICE SALAD
make 2

12 oz. (1½ cups) long grain rice
2 8-oz. cans salmon
1 lb. tomatoes, skinned and
 chopped
8 tbsps. finely chopped chives
5 tbsps. double cream
12 tbsps. mayonnaise
2 level tsps. celery seeds
grated rind of 2 lemons
salt and pepper
lettuce and radishes

Cook the rice in boiling salted water and allow to cool. Drain the salmon, remove the skin and bones and flake the fish; add the salmon, tomatoes and chives to the rice. Whip the cream, fold into the mayonnaise and add the celery seeds, with the lemon rind and seasoning. Fold in the rice mixture and press into a 4-pint ring mould. When set, turn out on to a plate lined with lettuce and garnish with sliced radishes.

COFFEE CREAM FLAN
make 3

8 oz. digestive biscuits
3 oz. butter, melted
2 eggs, separated
3 oz. (⅜ cup) caster sugar
1½–2 level tbsps. instant coffee
4 tbsps. water
2 tbsps. Tia Maria
2 level tsps. powdered
 gelatine
¼ pint (⅝ cup) double cream
1 tbsp. milk
36 hazelnuts, toasted and
 skinned

Coffee cream and nuts for a delicious flan

Crush the digestive biscuits, blend with the melted butter and use them to line a 10-in. French fluted loose-bottomed flan case, or an 8-in. deeper fluted flan ring placed on a plate. Press crumbs well on to the base and up the sides. Chill the flan case.

Whisk the egg yolks and sugar in a deep bowl until thick and creamy. Blend together the instant coffee, 2 tablespoons water and the liqueur and gradually whisk into the egg mixture.

Dissolve the gelatine in the remaining 2 tablespoons water, in a basin held over a pan of hot water, and add to the coffee mixture. Mix thoroughly and leave in a cool place to set. When this is beginning to set, fold in the stiffly whisked egg whites. Turn into the flan case and chill.

Before serving, whisk together the cream and milk until light and just thick enough to pipe. Pipe 12 whirls of cream round the flan edge and top each with three toasted hazelnuts.

BANANA AND MANDARIN CHARTREUSE

2 lemon jelly tablets
1 orange jelly tablet
juice of 1 orange
juice of 1 lemon
2 11-oz. cans mandarin
 oranges
2–3 bananas
lemon juice

Place the broken up jelly tablets in a large bowl. Pour over 1 pint (2½ cups) boiling water. Stir until dissolved.

Pour the fruit juices into a 2-pint measuring jug, add syrup from the mandarins and make up to 1¼ pints (3⅛ cups) with cold water. Strain and add to the hot liquid. Spoon enough jelly into a 3-pint fancy jelly mould to cover the base; allow to set.

Slice the bananas thinly, dip them in lemon juice. If the mandarins are large, slice them horizontally. Dip the fruit in a little jelly and arrange banana and mandarins alternately in the base of the mould.

The cake is the centre of the Christening meal

Leave to set.

Cover the fruit with more jelly and leave to set, then coat the sides of the mould with jelly. To help it set quickly, rotate the mould at an angle over a shallow dish containing water with ice cubes added. Arrange orange and banana alternately round the sides; allow to set. Layer the sides and middle alternately with fruit and then jelly. Chill until firm for at least 2 hours.

To serve, unmould and serve with pouring cream.

OPEN SANDWICHES

Danish rye bread, sold in a packet, makes a firm-to-handle base. The butter on the bread provides a useful anchor for the topping, so be generous. Choose both fillings and garnishes with an eye for colour.

Here is a selection of toppings:
Slices of tomato with a good-sized piece of crab, garnished with cottage cheese and black olives.
Slices of salami topped with stuffed olives and tomato slices.
Slices of hard-boiled egg and a sardine, with a few slivers of tomato and stuffed olive.
Luncheon meat topped with a spoonful of potato salad, a few rings of raw onion and slices of radish.
A slice of strong blue cheese, with rings of green pepper (capsicum) and a black olive on top.
A few prawns, with a slice or two of hard-boiled egg.
A slice of luncheon meat, garnished with tomato, cucumber, cottage cheese and a black olive.

ORANGE TEABREAD
make 2

2 oz. butter
6 oz. (¾ cup) caster sugar
1 egg, beaten
grated rind of ½ orange
2 tbsps. orange juice
2 tbsps. milk
8 oz. (2 cups) plain flour
2½ level tsps. baking powder
pinch of salt

Tasty snacks to serve with pre-lunch drinks

Grease and bottom-line an 8-in. by 4¼-in. loaf tin (top measurement).
Beat the butter, add the sugar and beat again until well mixed. Gradually beat in the egg until smooth and creamy. Slowly add the orange rind and juice; don't worry if the mixture curdles. Lightly beat in the milk alternately with sifted flour, baking powder and salt.
Turn the mixture into the tin. Bake in the centre of the oven at 375°F. (mark 5) for 40–50 minutes. Turn out and cool on a wire rack. Make 1–2 days before required and wrap in kitchen foil to store. Slice and spread with honey and cream cheese spread or butter.

ALMOND GINGERBREAD

2 oz. flaked almonds
12 oz. (3 cups) plain flour
½ oz. ground ginger
1 oz. stem ginger, chopped
3 oz. lard
3 oz. (½ cup) soft light brown sugar
12 oz. (¾ cup) golden syrup
4 fl. oz. (½ cup) water
1 egg, beaten
1½ level tsps. bicarbonate of soda

Grease a 3½-pint plain ring mould. Sprinkle the almonds in the base. Sift together the flour and ginger, add the stem ginger.
Gently heat together the lard, sugar, syrup and half the water, making sure it does not boil. Stir the syrup into the flour, add the egg and beat well. Dissolve the bicarbonate of soda in the remaining water, pour into the mixture and stir thoroughly.
Bake at 325°F. (mark 3) for about 50 minutes, until well risen and spongy to the touch. Turn out and cool on a wire rack, nut side uppermost.

COFFEE WALNUT GATEAU
make 3

For sponge cakes:
6 large eggs
6 oz. (¾ cup) caster sugar
5 oz. (1¼ cups) plain flour
1 oz. (3 tbsps.) cornflour
1 tbsp. glycerine

For crème au beurre:
3 egg yolks
4 oz. (½ cup) caster sugar
¼ pint (⅝ cup) milk
1 level tbsp. instant coffee
6–8 oz. butter
3 tbsps. coffee liqueur

For topping and decoration:
3 oz. walnuts, finely chopped
8 oz. (1¾ cups) icing sugar
1 level tsp. instant coffee
2 tbsps. hot water
sugar coffee beans

Grease 2 9½-in. sandwich tins, line the bases with greaseproof paper and sprinkle with caster sugar.
Break the eggs into a deep bowl. Add the sugar and whisk with an electric mixer or rotary whisk until the mixture is thick and pale and leaves a trail when the whisk is lifted out.
Sift the flours twice, then tip half the flour into the sieve and shake it on to the surface of the egg mixture. Fold in quickly with a metal spoon. Spoon glycerine in a thin stream over the surface, sieve in the remaining flour and fold in until no pockets of flour are left. Pour the mixture quickly into the cake tins. Bake in the oven at 375°F. (mark 5) for about 30 minutes.
Meanwhile, whisk together the egg yolks and caster sugar until light and creamy. Bring the milk and coffee to the boil. Pour the milk into the whisked sugar and yolks, stirring. Return to the pan and cook over a gentle heat, stirring all the time until the mixture thickens.

Remove from the heat and coo[l] stirring occasionally. Beat th[e] butter until light and cream[y.] Pour the cold coffee sauce in [a] thin stream into the butter, bea[t]ing all the time. Store in a cool (n[ot] cold) place until required.
Sprinkle the sponges with coff[ee] liqueur and sandwich with on[e]-third of the coffee crème au beurr[e.] Coat the sides with another thir[d.] Press the chopped walnuts on [to] the sides of the cake with a sma[ll] palette knife. Spoon the remainin[g] crème au beurre into a forcing ba[g] fitted with a medium size st[ar] vegetable nozzle. Pipe stars roun[d] the edge, touching each other.
For the glacé icing, beat togeth[er] the icing sugar and coffee blende[d] with 2 tablespoons hot water. Ad[d] a little more water if necessary [to] give a thick, flowing consistenc[y.] Pour into the centre of the cak[e,] tilting the plate slightly so that t[he] top is evenly coated. Before t[he] icing sets, burst air bubbles with [a] fine skewer or pin. Decorate ed[ge] of the cake with sugar coffee bean[s.]

CUP CAKES

4 oz. butter or margarine
4 oz. (½ cup) caster sugar
2 eggs
4 oz. (1 cup) self-raising flou[r]
grated rind of 1 small orang[e]

For decoration:
4½ oz. chocolate dots
1½ oz. butter
4 tbsps. top of the milk
3 oz. icing sugar, sifted
butter cream

Line about 30 deep bun pans wi[th] paper cases – use 2 cases to sto[p] over-browning.
Cream together the fat and sug[ar] until light and fluffy. Beat in th[e] eggs a little at a time. Sift the flo[ur] and lightly beat it in with th[e] orange rind. Half fill each of th[e] paper cases with the mixture an[d] bake just above the centre of th[e] oven at 375°F. (mark 5) for abou[t] 12 minutes, until well risen an[d] golden. Cool on a wire rack an[d] remove the second paper case.
Melt the chocolate, butter an[d] milk in a small bowl over h[ot] water. Beat in the icing sugar. A[s] the mixture cools and thicken[s,] spoon a little over about half th[e] cakes, to come level with the pape[r] cases. Leave to set. Pipe a whirl [of] butter cream in the centre of eac[h] cake. Slice the top off each of th[e] remaining cakes and cut it into [2,] pipe a butter cream rosette in th[e] centre of the cake and replace to[ps] as wings. Dust with icing sugar.

PICNIC MENUS

Summer or winter, given good weather, a picnic is always fun. Our menus offer a variety of foods that are far removed from the usual sandwich.

POTTED SMOKED SALMON
FRIED SALAMI CHICKEN
ITALIAN CAULIFLOWER SALAD
STUFFED FRENCH LOAF
JELLIED BEETROOT AND APPLE SALAD
DANISH BAKED FRUIT SALAD

POTTED SMOKED SALMON

2 3-oz. pkts. full fat soft cheese
finely grated rind of 1 lemon
2 egg yolks
½ pint (1¼ cups) double cream
salt and freshly ground black pepper
cayenne pepper
1 clove of garlic, skinned and crushed
6 oz. smoked salmon trimmings
4 tbsps. finely chopped parsley
2 oz. fresh white breadcrumbs
2 oz. butter

Put the cheese, lemon rind, egg yolks and cream in a small bowl. Place the bowl over a pan of hot water and cook until smooth and thick. Remove from the heat. Season with salt, pepper, cayenne pepper and garlic.

Chop the smoked salmon finely and add to the cheese mixture with the chopped parsley and breadcrumbs.

Spoon into 6–8 individual soufflé dishes or ramekins until about two-thirds full. Melt the butter and pour a little into the top of each dish. Chill until firm.

FRIED SALAMI CHICKEN

12–16 chicken drumsticks, skinned
4–5 oz. salami, skinned and sliced (2 slices per joint of chicken)
3–4 large eggs, beaten
⅔ large white loaf made into breadcrumbs
oil for deep frying
15-oz. can grapefruit segments, drained
¼ cucumber (or ½ small ridge cucumber) sliced

Make an incision to the bone along 1 side of each drumstick and loosen the flesh around the bone. Place 2 slices of salami around the bone, pull the chicken flesh together and secure with cocktail sticks.

Dip the salami-filled chicken first into beaten egg, then breadcrumbs and pat the crumbs in well. Repeat the egg and breadcrumb process to give a good coating.

Deep fry in hot oil (360°F.) for 7–10 minutes, until golden brown and cooked through. Drain on absorbent kitchen paper and cool. Pack the drumsticks in several plastic boxes with the drained grapefruit segments and cucumber slices.

ITALIAN CAULIFLOWER SALAD

1 medium-sized cauliflower
7 anchovy fillets, cut into small pieces
10 ripe olives, stoned and sliced
1 tbsp. bottled capers
1 tbsp. minced shallot or onion
freshly ground black pepper
3 tbsps. olive oil or salad oil
1 tbsp. wine vinegar

Wash and trim the cauliflower and

Fried salami chicken is as good cold as hot

STUFFED FRENCH LOAF

1 French loaf
5 sticks celery, scrubbed and chopped
a little butter
4 oz. cream cheese
milk
salt and freshly ground black pepper

Cut off the top of the loaf at a slight angle, so that you remove the top and part of the inside. Scoop out some of the inside to make room for the filling. Mix the celery, butter, cream cheese, milk and seasoning and pile this filling into the loaf. Replace the top.

Wrap the stuffed loaf in foil until required at the picnic. To serve, cut the loaf into 2–3 in. slices.

break into small florets. Cook in 1 in. of boiling water for about 10 minutes, or until tender but still crisp.

Drain thoroughly, cool and chill. Place the chilled cauliflower, anchovy fillets, olives, capers and shallot in a bowl.

Shake the oil and vinegar together in a screw-top jar. Toss the salad very gently in the dressing and serve in a salad bowl.

JELLIED BEETROOT AND APPLE SALAD

1 pkt. red jelly
½ pint (1¼ cups) boiling water
¼ pint (⅝ cup) vinegar
2 tbsps. lemon juice
1 lb. cooked beetroot
2 eating apples
2 oz. shelled walnuts

Break up the jelly tablet, place in a basin and dissolve it in th boiling water.

When dissolved, mix together th vinegar and lemon juice, make u to ½ pint (1¼ cups) with cold wate and add to the hot jelly liquid.

Peel and slice or dice the cooke beetroot; peel, core and slice th apples. Place the walnuts in th base of a 2-pint ring mould an add the beetroot and apple i layers.

Pour on the liquid jelly and leav in a cool place to set. To serv unmould on to a flat plate an garnish.

DANISH BAKED FRUIT SALAD

6 oz. dried prunes
6 oz. dried apricots
6 bananas, quartered
a few raisins, stoned
4 tbsps. thin honey
¾ pint (1⅞ cups) fresh orange juice
grated rind of 1 lemon

Soak the prunes and apricots i warm water for several hours, c overnight. Butter a large, fl. ovenproof dish and arrange th fruit on it. Add the honey to th orange juice and mix it wel then pour it over the fruit. Sprinkl the lemon rind over the frui Bake in the centre of the oven a 350°F. (mark 4) for about 3 minutes. Cool. Serve with pourin cream.

HAM AND CHEESE ROLLS
CURRIED KIPPER SALAD
PARTY CHICKEN MOULD
CABBAGE SALAD
LEEK AND TOMATO SALAD
BREAD STICK
CHERRY AND ALMOND PIE

CURRIED KIPPER SALAD

2 7-oz. pkts. kipper fillets (or
  15 oz. other smoked oily
  fish, boned)
6 tbsps. mayonnaise
3 level tsps. curry powder
3 tsps. vinegar
4 oz. cooked long grain rice
1 lb. tomatoes, skinned and
  sliced
4 sticks celery, scrubbed and
  sliced
salt and pepper
watercress for garnish,
  optional

Cook the kippers as directed on the packet. Skin them and cut into fingers. Mix the mayonnaise, curry powder and vinegar together. Stir in the kippers, rice, tomatoes and celery. Blend well and adjust the seasoning with a little salt and pepper. Pile into a plastic box. Take watercress sprigs along for a garnish, if wished.

PARTY CHICKEN MOULD

1 a cooked chicken
3 eggs, hard-boiled
1 pint (1⅛ cups) well seasoned
  aspic jelly, made from
  aspic jelly powder and a
  dash of sherry
cooked peas

Cut the chicken into small pieces, removing all the bone and skin. Slice the eggs neatly. Wet a 2-pint ring mould with straight sides and coat with aspic jelly. Set the peas round the base.
Dip each slice of egg in aspic jelly and position them round the side of the mould; leave in the refrigerator for a few minutes to set firmly. Fill up the mould with chicken and pour in the rest of the aspic. Leave in a cool place to set. Unmould just before leaving and carry in an insulated container.

CABBAGE SALAD

1 small white cabbage
1 onion, skinned and chopped
3 tbsps. French dressing
1 level tsp. caraway seeds
1 level tsp. dried marjoram

Trim the cabbage, remove the outer leaves, then wash and shred it. Place it in a bowl and pour boiling water over it. After 10 minutes, drain and rinse under cold running water to cool. Drain the cabbage well and transfer it to a plastic box with a lid and add the chopped onion.
Make the French dressing, adding the caraway seeds and marjoram. Put the dressing into a screw-top jar and pour it over the salad at the picnic.

LEEK AND TOMATO SALAD

4 young tender leeks, washed
4 small tomatoes, skinned
1 lettuce
1 level tsp. chopped basil
1 level tsp. chopped chervil
3 tbsps. French dressing

Slice the white part of the leeks very finely. Cut the tomatoes into sections. Wash and drain the lettuce. Put the lettuce, leeks and tomatoes into a plastic container and sprinkle on the basil and chervil. Put the French dressing in a separate container and put the lid on firmly. Pour the dressing over the salad at the picnic.

CHERRY AND ALMOND PIE
make 2

12 oz. shortcrust pastry, i.e.
  made with 12 oz. (3 cups)
  flour etc.
raspberry jam
2 oz. ground almonds
2 oz. (¼ cup) caster sugar
1 large egg, beaten
¾ lb. cherries, stoned
caster sugar for dredging

Roll out the pastry and use half to line a 7-in. foil pie plate. Spread raspberry jam over the base.
Blend together the ground almonds, sugar and egg and spread

Handy hint

To make Melba toast, toast bread from a thin sliced loaf on both sides, cut off the crusts and slice into 2 with a sharp knife (this is easier after toasting); open out and toast the insides.

This is an elegant salad for a garden lunch

half this mixture over the jam. Add the cherries and cover with the remaining almond mixture. Cover the pie with a lid made from the remaining pastry and seal the edges. Decorate with leaves cut from the pastry trimmings.
Bake in the oven at 375°F. (mark 5) for 30–40 minutes. Cool and dredge with caster sugar.

PICNIC MENU *serves 8*

MIXED MEAT PATE OR MEAT LOAF
EGG AND VEGETABLE FLAN
GOLDEN SLAW
FILLED BEETROOTS
FRENCH BREAD AND BUTTER
PINEAPPLE SOUFFLES

MIXED MEAT PATE

6–8 oz. bacon rashers, rinded
4 oz. lambs' liver, chopped
4 oz. lean raw pork, chopped
4 oz. sausage meat
1 oz. fresh white
  breadcrumbs
1 tbsp. milk
1 small onion, skinned and
  finely chopped
a little beaten egg
1 small glass of brandy
salt and pepper
good pinch of ground nutmeg
8 oz. cold roast chicken, duck
  or game, sliced

Line a 7-in. round cake tin with kitchen foil leaving enough to cover the top later.
Stretch the bacon rashers with the back of a knife and use them to line the cake tin. Mix together

A mixture of fresh and dried fruits for the Danish fruit salad

the liver, pork, sausage meat, breadcrumbs, milk, onion, egg, brandy and seasoning. Fill the tin, starting with a layer of sliced meat and alternating with layers of the forcemeat mixture. Cover with foil, place the tin in a roasting tin with water to come half way up and cook in the oven at 325°F. (mark 3) for about 2½ hours.

Remove from the oven, cover with a plate, put a weight on top and chill overnight.

To pack, turn out of the tin, wrap the extra foil over the top and slip the pâté into a plastic bag.

MEAT LOAF

8 oz. stewing veal
8 oz. lean stewing beef
8 oz. lean bacon, rinded
4 oz. onion, skinned
2 oz. carrot, peeled and grated
4 oz. tomatoes, skinned and chopped
8 level tbsps. thyme and parsley stuffing mix
1 level tsp. salt
freshly ground black pepper
1 egg, beaten

Put the veal, beef, bacon and onion through the mincer twice. Combine this mixture with the remaining ingredients.

Place the mixture on a piece of kitchen foil and shape it into a loaf about 3 in. by 7 in. Wrap it neatly, place it in a baking dish or loaf tin and cook in the oven at 350°F. (mark 4) for 1¼ hours; open the foil and cook for a further 1¼ hours.

When cold, wrap in fresh kitchen foil or pack in a large plastic box. At the picnic, garnish with a few slices of tomato before serving.

EGG AND VEGETABLE FLAN

4 oz. shortcrust pastry–i.e. made with 4 oz. (1 cup) flour etc.
1 oz. butter
1 oz. (¼ cup) flour
½ pint (1¼ cups) milk
3 oz. cheese, grated
salt and pepper
3 eggs, hard-boiled and sliced
1 pkt. frozen mixed vegetables

Roll out the pastry and use it to line a 7-in. flan ring or case. Bake blind at 400°F. (mark 6) until lightly browned. Cool. This can be done a day ahead.

Melt the butter, stir in the flour and cook for 2–3 minutes. Remove

A pâté covered with bacon rashers always looks attractive

the pan from the heat and gradually stir in the milk. Bring to the boil and continue to cook, stirring, until the sauce thickens and is cooked. Stir in the cheese and season to taste.

Arrange the sliced eggs in the cooled flan case, retaining 2–3 slices for garnishing. Cook the frozen vegetables according to the directions on the packet, mix them with the cheese sauce, cool a little and spoon into the flan case. Leave until cold. Garnish with the remaining slices of egg just before packing.

Cover the flan with kitchen foil, but be careful not to stand anything on top of it. Slice it, as required, at the picnic.

GOLDEN SLAW

1 small Savoy cabbage
4–6 oz. Gruyère cheese, cut in thin strips
½ lb. red-skinned apples, cored and chopped
¼ pint (⅝ cup) mayonnaise
1 level tbsp. made mustard
1 level tsp. sugar
salt and pepper

Wash the cabbage well. Curl back the outer leaves, cut round the base of the heart and scoop out the

heart, to leave a 'bowl'. Finely shred the cabbage heart and put in a basin with the cheese and apples. Combine the mayonnaise with the mustard, sugar and seasoning and toss the salad in this dressing until the ingredients are well coated. Spoon into the scooped-out cabbage 'bowl' and pack in kitchen foil or a plastic bag.

FILLED BEETROOTS

8 small cooked beetroots
salt and pepper
2 tbsps. lemon juice
8 sticks of celery, scrubbed and chopped
2 oranges, peeled and chopped
2 tsps. horseradish sauce
2 level tsps. sugar
French dressing

Peel the beetroots. Trim the base of each so that it will stand firmly and hollow out the centre to form a cup. Season with salt and pepper and sprinkle with lemon juice. Mix the celery and orange and fill the beetroot cups. Add the horseradish sauce and sugar to the French dressing, mix well and spoon over the beetroots. Wrap each one separately.

PINEAPPLE SOUFFLES

15-oz. can crushed pineapple
4½ level tsps. gelatine
4 large eggs, separated
3 oz. (⅜ cup) caster sugar
2 tbsps. whisky
¼ pint (⅝ cup) single cream
¼ pint (⅝ cup) double cream
frosted grapes for decoration

Drain the crushed pineapple. Reserve 2 tablespoons juice and place it in a small bowl. Sprinkle over the gelatine and dissolve over a pan of hot water.

Whisk the egg yolks, sugar and whisky in a large basin over a pan of hot water until they are thick and pale. Remove from the heat and add the crushed pineapple. Add a little of this mixture to the gelatine, mix well and pour it back into the soufflé mixture, whisking. Leave to cool, whisking from time to time.

Whisk the creams lightly together. Fold the cream into the cool, but not set, pineapple base. Whisk the egg whites until stiff but not dry, pour the pineapple cream base over the whites and fold in lightly. Divide the mixture between the chilled soufflé dishes and put in a cool place to set. When set, decorate with frosted grapes.

Use frozen mixed vegetables for this tasty flan

APPETIZER SOUP

3½ pints (6¼ cups) water
2 beef stock cubes
2 chicken stock cubes
2 15-oz. cans tomatoes
2 medium-sized onions,
 skinned and chopped
3 oz. carrots, peeled and
 thinly sliced
4 stalks of celery, scrubbed
 and cut into ½-in. lengths
6 peppercorns
1 level tsp. dried sage
salt and freshly ground black
 pepper
grated Parmesan cheese to
 garnish

Put the water into a saucepan, then add the stock cubes, tomatoes, onion, carrot, celery, peppercorns and sage. Mix well, bring to the boil, cover and simmer gently for 1 hour. Adjust seasoning. Pour while still hot into a warmed, wide-necked vacuum jug. Take the Parmesan in a separate container, to sprinkle on each serving.

RAISED BACON AND EGG PIE

For hot water crust :

1 lb. (4 cups) plain flour
2 level tsps. salt
4 oz. lard
7 fl. oz. (⅞ cup) milk or water
beaten egg, to glaze

For filling :

2 lb. bacon joint, cooked
1 egg, lightly beaten
2 level tbsps. tomato paste
3 tbsps. chopped parsley
freshly ground black pepper
3 eggs, hard-boiled
½ pint (1¼ cups) aspic jelly,
 made from aspic jelly
 powder

Sift the flour and salt into a basin and put in a warm place. Melt the lard and add the liquid. Bring to the boil and pour the mixture into the flour. Mix to a paste quickly, using a wooden spoon, turn it on to a floured board and knead until the dough is smooth and free from cracks.

Cut off a quarter of the dough and put aside. Use the rest to line a 7-in. round cake tin; take care to keep the pastry warm while it is being moulded or it will crack.

Divide the cooked bacon joint in half. Mince one half and mix the meat with the beaten egg, tomato paste, parsley and pepper to make a forcemeat. Chop and mix the remaining bacon and 2 of the cooked eggs.

Line the pastry with the forcemeat. Fill the centre with the chopped bacon and eggs, placing the remaining hard-boiled egg in the centre.

Roll out the remaining piece of pastry to make a lid. Cover the pie and press the edges together to form a rim and scallop it. Make a cut in the centre to allow steam to escape and decorate the pie with leaves cut from the pastry trimmings. Brush with beaten egg. Bake the pie in the centre of the oven at 425°F. (mark 7) for 30 minutes. Reduce the temperature to 350°F. (mark 4) and cook for a further 15 minutes, Carefully remove the pie from the tin and allow to cool.

Make up the aspic jelly and when it is on the point of setting, pour it into the pie through the hole in the centre of the lid. Chill to set the jelly completely. Pack in foil.

PORK LOAF

1 lb. raw lean pork, cubed
1 lb. raw lean ham, cubed
1 tbsp. finely chopped onion
¼ pint (⅝ cup) thick white
 sauce
1 egg, beaten
salt and pepper
pinch of rosemary
thinly cut rashers of back
 bacon, rinded
vinegar

Mince the pork, ham and onion twice. Blend these very thoroughly with the white sauce, egg, seasoning and rosemary and place the mixture on a sheet of kitchen foil. Form it into a loaf shape and cover with the rashers of bacon.

Fold the foil over and seal the edges tightly. Place in a large pan of boiling water with a little vinegar and salt added and boil gently for 2½ hours. (A saucer placed on the base of the pan will prevent the foil coming directly into contact with the metal.)

Remove the loaf from the pan, leave to cool and remove the foil. Pack in fresh foil for carrying.

CHICORY SALAD

4 heads chicory (or 2 heads
 celery), trimmed
12 black olives, stoned
2 tbsps. vinegar
2 tsps. honey
2 onions, skinned and finely
 chopped
4 tbsps. salad oil
2 tbsps. lemon juice
pinch each of sugar and salt

Cut the chicory (or celery) into fine slices. Mix in the olives. In a screw-top jar, shake together the vinegar, honey, onions, oil, lemon juice, sugar and salt. Pack the salad and dressing separately and toss together just before serving.

TOMATO COLESLAW

¾ lb. white cabbage, quartered
 and washed
1 red pepper (capsicum),
 seeded
4 tomatoes, skinned
½ cucumber (or 1 small ridge
 cucumber)
8 fl. oz. (1 cup) thick
 mayonnaise
4 tbsps. soured cream
2 tsps. clear honey
2 tsps. tomato ketchup
salt and freshly ground black
 pepper
juice of 1 lemon

Shred the cabbage finely and slice the pepper, tomatoes and cucumber. Beat the mayonnaise with the remaining ingredients and toss the salad ingredients in this dressing. Pack in a plastic container.

SUMMER PUDDING
make 2

1 lb. soft fruits (raspberries, currants, blackberries etc.)
sugar
thin slices of white bread, crusts removed

Stew the fruit gently with sugar and water as necessary, keeping it as whole as possible. Line a plastic pudding basin with bread and fill it with alternate layers of fruit and bread, retaining some of the juice. When the last layer of fruit is in the basin, pour the remaining juice over and cover the surface with a slice of bread. Cover the pudding with a plate and press this down with a heavy weight. Leave overnight, in the refrigerator.
Remove the weight and plate and cover the basin with a lid or foil for carrying. Turn out before serving with cream.

PICNIC MENU *serves 12*

COURGETTE AND CARROT SOUP OR CHILLED VEGETABLE JUICE
PICNIC SANDWICH BOX
SALMON RICE
FENNEL AND GRUYERE SALAD
COFFEE AND VANILLA MILK JELLY

COURGETTE AND CARROT SOUP

4 oz. butter or margarine
1 lb. carrots, pared and thinly sliced
1 lb. courgettes, trimmed and thinly sliced
½ level tsp. dried thyme
2 bay leaves
4 pints (10 cups) chicken stock
4 level tsps. tomato paste
6 level tbsps. instant potato powder
salt and freshly ground black pepper
chopped parsley

Melt the butter in a large saucepan. Add the carrots and courgettes with the thyme and bay leaves.
Cover and sauté, shaking the pan occasionally, for 10 minutes. Pour

A plastic mould is ideal for a picnic jelly

the stock into the pan, add the tomato paste and stir, bringing to the boil. Cover and simmer for about 30 minutes.
Add the potato, stir and bring back to the boil; adjust seasoning. Pour into a vacuum flask and garnish with chopped parsley when serving.

PICNIC SANDWICH BOX
make 2

1 small uncut Bloomer loaf
3 oz. butter, melted
½ lb. pork sausage meat
¼ lb. cooked ham, finely chopped
¼ lb. cooked tongue, finely chopped
2 oz. onion, skinned and chopped
2 eggs
¼ pint (⅝ cup) milk
salt and freshly ground black pepper
2 eggs, hard-boiled and halved

Cut horizontally across the loaf, two-thirds of the way up. Remove the lid, gently ease away the bread from around the crust edge of both pieces and make 4 oz. of it into breadcrumbs.
Brush the cavity of the loaf and lid with some of the melted butter. Combine the sausage meat, ham, tongue, breadcrumbs and onion. Beat together the raw eggs and the milk and combine with the forcemeat.
Place one-third of the mixture down the centre of the loaf. Arrange the halved hard-boiled eggs lengthwise on top and pack round with more forcemeat. Top with the lid.
Tie the loaf up like a parcel with string and brush all over with the remaining melted butter. Place on a baking sheet and bake in the oven at 400°F. (mark 6) for 15 minutes. Cover with foil and

continue cooking for another 45 minutes.
Unwrap, remove the string and cool on a wire rack. Pack in fresh foil. Cut into thick slices for serving.

SALMON RICE
make 2

8 oz. (1 cup) long grain rice
2-oz. can anchovy fillets, drained
milk
3 tbsps. corn oil
1 tbsp. wine vinegar
1 tbsp. lemon juice
1 level tsp. French mustard
salt and freshly ground black pepper
3 oz. onion, skinned and finely chopped
2 level tbsps. chopped parsley
7½-oz. can pink salmon
1 small ripe avocado
extra lemon juice

Cook the rice in boiling salted water until tender and rinse it in cold water to cool it quickly. Drain well.
Separate the anchovies, cover with milk and leave to soak for 30 minutes.
Whisk together the oil, vinegar, lemon juice and mustard. Season

```
Handy hint
```

When frying fish or sauté potatoes in butter, put 1 tablespoon cooking oil in the pan before adding 2 oz. butter. This doesn't affect the flavour, but helps to stop the butter burning too quickly.

well with salt and pepper and fork this dressing through the rice with the onion, parsley and drained, chopped anchovies. Discard the dark skin and bone from the salmon and flake the flesh. Lightly fold it through the rice but take care not to break down the salmon too finely. Pack in a rigid plastic container.
To serve, cut the avocado in half lengthwise and discard the stone. Peel and slice it and toss in lemon juice to prevent discolouration. Use the avocado slices to garnish the salad.

FENNEL AND GRUYERE SALAD

2 fennel roots
8 oz. Gruyère cheese
freshly ground black pepper
lemon and oil dressing

Shred the fennel finely and cut the cheese into slivers.
Mix the fennel and Gruyère, season well with freshly ground black pepper and pack in a plastic box.
Take the dressing separately and pour over the salad at the picnic.

COFFEE AND VANILLA MILK JELLY
make 2

2 oz. (¼ cup) caster sugar
¼ pint (⅝ cup) strong coffee
¾ pint (1⅞ cups) milk
8 level tsps. powdered gelatine
4 tbsps. water
vanilla pod

Add 1 oz. sugar to the coffee and ¼ pint (⅝ cup) of the milk.
Dissolve half the gelatine in 2 tablespoons water in a basin over a pan of hot water, then add the coffee and milk mixture.
Pour one third of this jelly into a picnic jelly mould and put in a cool place to set (keep the rest warm so that it does not set).
Infuse the vanilla pod in the remaining milk for a short time, then make a jelly with this and the remaining sugar, gelatine and water. Pour half this vanilla jelly on to the set coffee jelly and put into a cool place to set. Repeat the layers, finishing with the coffee jelly.
Transport the jelly in an ice-box, if possible, and unmould at the picnic.

BARBECUE MENUS

Eating out of doors adds a zest to any appetite, and what better way to entertain friends on a summer evening than to have a barbecued meal in your own garden? Salads, sauces and vegetable accompaniments can all be prepared beforehand in your kitchen, and you'll find that most men enjoy being in charge of the barbecue — which leaves you free to enjoy yourself. Choose simple menus with desserts that can be cooked either in foil in the charcoal embers or in a pan on the grill.

MENU *serves 8*

TANDOORI CHICKEN
PAPPADUMS
MELON AND BANANA SALAD
SLICED TOMATOES AND GHERKINS
BOILED RICE
PEACHES WITH BUTTERSCOTCH SAUCE

TANDOORI CHICKEN

8 chicken joints
salt and pepper
7½ fl. oz. (1 cup) plain yoghourt
1½ level tsps. chilli powder
pinch of ground ginger
pinch of ground coriander
1 large clove of garlic, skinned and crushed
juice of 1½ lemons
3 tbsps. melted butter

Remove any protruding bones from the chicken joints, wipe and season with salt and pepper. Combine the yoghourt with the chilli powder, ginger, coriander, garlic, lemon juice, 1 level teaspoon black pepper and 2 level teaspoons salt. Mix well and add the chicken pieces. Leave to stand for 3–4 hours, turning several times. Remove the chicken from the marinade, shaking off as much of the liquid as possible, then pour a little melted butter over each chicken joint. Place the joints on the barbecue grid and brown them quickly on all sides. Remove the

chicken and place each joint on a piece of kitchen foil, about 15 in. square. Fold over the sides of the foil, making a double join in the centre, and make a double fold in each end of the foil to seal.
Place each packet on the grid and cook for a further 20 minutes, turning once during the cooking time. Heat the spicy marinade and serve separately.
Serve with pappadums and melon and banana salad.

PAPPADUMS

These savoury wafer-like biscuits are usually bought, as they are not easy to make at home. Stored in an airtight tin they will keep for several months. White pappadums are fairly mild, red are very hot.

allow 1–2 pappadums per person

Choose a frying pan considerably larger than the raw biscuit. Heat a little fat to a high temperature, then fry the pappadums one at a time for about 20–30 seconds. Keep them flat by holding down with a flat draining spoon; when

crisp, drain and serve hot.

MELON AND BANANA SALAD

2 ripe cantaloup melons
8 bananas
lemon juice

Cut the melons in half, scoop o the seeds and discard. Remove th skin and cut the melon flesh in cubes. Peel the bananas and sli thinly. Turn in lemon juice prevent browning, then mix th melon and bananas together.

PEACHES WITH BUTTERSCOTCH SAUCE

2 oz. butter
2 15-oz. cans peaches, draine
soft brown sugar

Melt the butter in a frying pa over the barbecue and add th peaches, cut side up. Fill th centre of each with some so brown sugar. Simmer gently unt the sugar melts and runs into th butter to form a sauce.
Serve with pouring cream.

FOIL-ROASTED CORN COBS

12 corn cobs
4 oz. butter
freshly ground black pepper

Remove the husks and silks from the cobs. Mix together the butter and a generous amount of pepper. Spread some butter on each cob. Put the cobs on individual squares of kitchen foil, bring the sides together, with a double fold in the centre and make double folds at each end to seal completely. Cook at the sides of the barbecue grid for 25–30 minutes, turning occasionally.

HAMBURGERS

2 lb. lean beef, finely minced
2 level tsps. mixed herbs
salt and pepper
melted butter or oil for
  coating
2 onions, skinned and sliced
12 soft round buns, split
  in half

Mix together the meat, herbs and seasonings. Shape into 12 flat rounds and brush with a little melted butter or oil. Grill over the barbecue for 6–10 minutes, turning them once (the cooking time depends on whether you like them rare, medium, or well done). Meanwhile, fry the onion rings in a pan in a little fat until soft and lightly coloured. Place the buns, split side down, on the grill and toast for 2–3 minutes.
To serve, top each hamburger with a few onion rings and put between 2 toasted bun halves. Wrap it in a paper napkin. Serve a selection of relishes separately.

HOT DOGS

12 frankfurters
12 long soft rolls

Grill the frankfurters over the barbecue and put inside a split roll. Add some mustard, tomato sauce or relish. Wrap one end in a paper napkin and serve hot.

TOMATO SAUCE

1 rasher bacon, rinded
1 lb. tomatoes, chopped
2 onions, skinned and sliced
2 oz. butter
bouquet garni
1 pint (2½ cups) stock
salt and pepper
2 level tsps. sugar
½ oz. (1½ level tbsps.) flour
milk to mix

Dice the bacon and put the tomatoes, onions and bacon in a pan with the butter; cook with the lid on for about 10 minutes, shaking frequently.
Add the herbs, stock, seasoning and sugar and simmer gently, uncovered, for 30 minutes. The mixture should now be pulpy and well reduced.
Sieve the mixture, return it to the pan and bring to the boil. Blend the flour with a little cold milk, add to the pan and bring to the boil, stirring constantly. Cook for 2–3 minutes and adjust the seasoning.

Hamburgers and hot dogs are traditional barbecue fare

Handy hint

To remove the fat from gravy place a double thickness of absorbent kitchen paper on the gravy and press lightly. The paper will soak up a little of the gravy and all of the fat. Alternatively use a bulb-type gravy syphon.

Serve hot or cold with the hot dogs and hamburgers.

CREAMY MUSTARD SAUCE

¼ pint (⅝ cup) soured cream
2 level tbsps. prepared
  mustard
1 tbsp. minced onion
¼ level tsp. salt
⅛ level tsp. pepper

Mix all the ingredients together in a pan and heat gently for a few minutes.
Serve warm with the hot dogs and hamburgers.

HOT-WEATHER GREEN SALAD

1 lettuce
large bunch of watercress,
  optional
1 large cucumber (or 2 small
  ridge cucumbers), peeled
12–15 spring onions, skinned
French dressing
1 tbsp. white wine

Wash the lettuce and watercress, discarding stems and coarse outer leaves.
Slice the peeled cucumber and spring onions very finely. Mix all the ingredients together in a bowl and add the French dressing and wine.

APPLE AND TOMATO SALAD

4 dessert apples, peeled and
  cored
1 lb. tomatoes, skinned and
  sliced
French dressing
mustard and cress to garnish,
  optional

Dice the apples and put in a bowl with the tomato slices. Add enough salad dressing to coat and garnish with mustard and cress, if wished.

Stuffed apples, baked in the oven or in the embers

BARBECUE SAUCE

4 tbsps. Worcestershire sauce
4 tbsps. brown table sauce
4 tbsps. mushroom ketchup
2 level tsps. sugar
1 tbsp. vinegar
1 oz. butter, melted
cayenne pepper
salt
¼ pint (⅝ cup) water
1 small onion, skinned and
    thinly sliced

Blend all the ingredients together, adding the onion last. Be very sparing with the cayenne pepper. Pour the sauce over the meat to be cooked and baste frequently while it is cooking.

LAYERED COLESLAW

1 small head of white cabbage
½ a cucumber (or 1 small
    ridge cucumber)
1 large green pepper
    (capsicum)
2 onions, skinned
bunch of radishes

For golden dressing :
½ pint (1¼ cups) mayonnaise
½ level tsp. salt
⅛ level tsp. pepper
⅛ level tsp. paprika
2 level tsps. sugar
2 tbsps. vinegar
2 tbsps. milk
2 level tsps. prepared mustard
2 egg yolks

Finely shred the cabbage. Score the cucumber from end to end with the prongs of a fork. Slice the cucumber very thinly. Wash and seed the pepper and cut into fine rings; cut the onion into wafer thin rings. Prepare and wash the radishes and slice very thinly.

Arrange about a quarter of the cabbage in a salad bowl; on this arrange the cucumber in a layer, cover with another quarter of the cabbage, then a layer of green pepper rings; next cover with more of the cabbage, then a complete layer of onion rings. Finally, heap the remaining cabbage in the centre. Arrange radish slices round the outside of the salad.

Combine the mayonnaise for the dressing with the remaining ingredients and whisk until well blended. Pour the dressing over the salad.

CHICORY AND ORANGE SALAD

3 large heads chicory (or
    1 head celery)
3 large oranges
French dressing

Remove the root and outer leaves of the chicory, wash (or scrub and trim the celery) and cut into chunks. Peel the oranges and divide into segments. Mix the two together in a bowl and sprinkle with French dressing.

STUFFED BAKED APPLES

8 medium-sized cooking
    apples
6 tbsps. water
mixture of currants, sultanas,
    chopped dried apricots,
    mixed peel or glacé fruits
Demerara sugar
butter

Wipe the apples and make a shallow cut through the skin round the middle of each. Core the apples and stand them in an ovenproof dish. Pour the water round and fill each apple with the fruit mixture. Sprinkle a little sugar over the apples and top each one with a knob of butter.

Bake in the centre of the oven at 400°F. (mark 6) for ¾–1 hour until the apples are soft.

Alternatively, wrap individual apples in foil (omitting the water) and bake in the embers of the barbecue.

FISH CHOWDER

6 rashers of lean bacon,
    rinded and chopped
3 onions, skinned and sliced
3 lb. fresh haddock, cooked
    and flaked
3 14-oz. cans tomatoes
6 potatoes, peeled and diced
1½ pints (3¾ cups) fish stock
salt and freshly ground black
    pepper
3 bay leaves
6 cloves
¾ pint (1⅞ cups) milk
chopped parsley

Fry the bacon until the fat runs add the onion and fry until clear Add the fish, tomatoes and potatoes, with the stock and seasonings, and simmer gently for about 30 minutes. Add the milk and remove the bay leaves and cloves then reheat gently. Serve in mugs with a little chopped parsley sprinkled on top.

MIXED KEBABS

For the marinade :
2 parts olive oil
1 part wine vinegar
garlic, skinned and crushed
few peppercorns

lean, tender steak, cubed
sausages, halved
button mushrooms, wiped
small tomatoes, whole, or
    large tomatoes, quartered
rashers of lean bacon, rinded
button onions, skinned and
    par-boiled
a few bay leaves

Marinade the steak for a few hours. Thread a selection of the ingredients on to skewers (allow 2 skewers per person) and refrigerate them until required.

Brush them with melted butter and grill over the barbecue, basting and turning regularly.

BANANES AU CARAMEL

12 oz. (1½ cups) sugar
6 tbsps. water
12–15 bananas (according to
    size), peeled

Choose bananas which are slightly under-ripe. Using a strong, deep frying pan, dissolve the sugar in the water over a low heat. Bring to the boil and bubble until the syrup is lightly coloured. Lay the bananas in the sauce and spoon the caramel over them until they are coated.

Cook for about 10 minutes on top of the barbecue grill. Serve the bananas with the caramel poured over them.

Mix steak with sausages and bacon for tasty kebabs

EASY WEEKENDS

Weekend guests become part of your family for a short time – yet somehow they seem to merit more than family treatment!

iver and bacon provençale

Make a change from every-day bacon and eggs

BREAKFAST

A good breakfast goes a long way towards keeping your guests happy for the rest of the day. It may be a meal they don't bother with at home, and the sheer luxury of having someone else prepare it is bound to make them appreciate your efforts. Most of the dishes in our menus can be prepared all at once, and then kept hot in the oven or on a hot tray.

MENU 1

**CEREAL or
ORANGE WAKE ME UP
PLAIN OMELETTE
PRUNE AND BACON ROLLS
GRILLED TOMATOES
TOAST
MARMALADE**

Home-made muesli is wholesome and different from packet cereals

ORANGE WAKE ME UP

For each person :
**juice of 1 orange
1 tbsp. clear honey
1 egg**

Place all the ingredients in an electric blender and switch on for 30 seconds. Alternatively whisk with a rotary whisk until thoroughly blended.

PRUNE AND BACON ROLLS

**prunes
streaky bacon rashers
prepared mustard**

Soak the prunes (allow 2 prunes for each rasher of bacon) overnight in enough water to cover. Drain and stone them. (Alternatively, use well drained canned prunes.) Rind the bacon and

stretch with a knife. Cut each rasher in half and spread with mustard. Roll one piece round each prune, place on small skewers and grill until the bacon is cooked.

MENU 2

**YOGHOURT
MIXED SALAD OF DRIED
FRUITS – PRUNES,
APRICOTS, APPLES,
PEARS
FINNAN HADDIE or
BACON
MUSHROOMS
ROLLS
HONEY**

FINNAN HADDIE

serves 4 ; these are smoked haddock named after the Scottish fishing village of Findon, near Aberdeen

**2 finnan haddock (or smoked
cod fillets), total weight
approx. 1½ lb.
1 pint (2½ cups) milk
2 oz. butter
2 oz. (½ cup) flour
chopped parsley
salt and pepper
2 eggs, hard-boiled**

Place the fish skin side up under a hot grill for a few minutes – this makes skinning very simple. Peel the skin off and cut the fish into 8 pieces. Poach in milk for about 15 minutes until tender. Drain off the milk into a measure and make up to 1 pint with more milk if necessary. Melt the butter in a pan, stir in the flour and gradually blend in the measured milk. Flake the fish, removing any bones, and add to the sauce with the chopped parsley, salt and pepper. Bring to the boil. Pour into individual serving dishes and garnish each with wedges of hard-boiled egg.

> **Handy hint**
>
> Soured cream is not the same as fresh pasteurized cream that has gone 'off'. It is specially treated to give a fresh, sharp flavour. If a recipe calls for soured cream and you have none available, add a little lemon juice to fresh cream.

MENU 3

**FRUIT JUICE or
HONEY MUESLI
BREAKFAST GRILL –
Kidneys, bacon, sausages,
grilled tomatoes
POACHED EGGS
TOAST
BRAN MUFFINS**

HONEY MUESLI

serves 4–6

**4 oranges
grated rind of ½ lemon
4 eating apples, wiped
2 tbsps. sultanas
1 banana, peeled and sliced
2 level tbsps. ground almonds
2 level tbsps. rolled oats
1 tbsp. clear honey
4 tbsps. single cream
1 red eating apple, cored
2 tbsps. lemon juice
black and white grapes,
pipped**

Squeeze the juice from 2 of the oranges into a large bowl. Add the grated lemon rind. Grate the apples into the juice, discarding the core. Add the sultanas, banana, almonds, oats, honey and cream. Turn into a serving dish.
Divide remaining 2 oranges into segments. Slice the red apple and dip it into the lemon juice to prevent discolouration. Decorate the muesli with alternate slices of orange and apple and a few grapes. Serve chilled.

BRAN MUFFINS

makes 20

**7 oz. (1¾ cups) plain flour
1 level tsp. salt
6 level tsps. baking powder
4 oz. ready-to-eat bran
1 pint (2½ cups) milk, less
6 tbsps.
4 tbsps. soft butter
4 level tbsps. caster sugar
2 eggs, beaten**

Grease 20 2½-in. diameter deep muffin tins. Sift the flour, salt and baking powder together. Soak the bran in milk for 5 minutes. Meanwhile, beat the butter and sugar until light; add the egg and stir until smooth. Add the bran mixture and stir. Add the flour and stir until only just mixed, no longer. Fill the muffin tins two-thirds full and bake in the centre of the oven at 400°F. (mark 6) for 25 minutes, or until well browned. Turn out on a wire rack. To serve, split rather than cut open, and butter.

WEEKEND LUNCHES

Nobody expects a 3-course meal twice a day, but you probably feel you want to offer something a little more organised than your usual family Saturday lunch. These menus are quick and easy to prepare, even for a full house.

MENU *serves 4*

LIVER AND BACON
PROVENCALE
BUTTERED NOODLES
GREEN SALAD
ICE CREAM CAKE

Slice the liver into long, thick strips, coat with flour and fry in oil until golden brown. Place in a casserole.

Add the bacon and onions to the frying pan and cook until golden. Stir in any flour left over from coating the liver. Add the tomatoes, marjoram, bay leaf and Worcestershire sauce. Stir in the stock, season well, place in the casserole. Cover with a tightly fitting lid and cook in the oven at 300°F. (mark 2) for about 1½ hours. Serve with a green salad and noodles cooked in boiling salted water, drained and tossed in butter and pepper.

MENU *serves 4*

DEVILLED GAMMON WITH PINEAPPLE
SPINACH, CREAMED POTATOES
DOUBLE CRUST BLACK-CURRANT PIE

DEVILLED GAMMON WITH PINEAPPLE

2 12-oz. gammon rashers
4 level tbsps. dry mustard
6 oz. light, soft brown sugar
8-oz. can pineapple rings
8 maraschino cherries

area with a piece of kitchen foil. Each rasher will serve 2 people. Serve with spinach and potatoes. *Note :* If the gammon tends to be salty, leave it to soak in cold water for an hour before cooking, then pat it dry.

DOUBLE CRUST BLACKCURRANT PIE

For shortcrust pastry :
6 oz. (1½ cups) plain flour
a pinch of salt
1½ oz. lard
1½ oz. margarine
6 tsps. water (approx.)
milk, to glaze

1–1½ lb. blackcurrants
4 oz. (½ cup) sugar
1 level tbsp. flour

First make the pastry. Mix the flour and salt together. Cut the fat into small pieces and add to the flour then, using both hands, rub the fat into the flour with the fingertips, until the mixture looks like fresh breadcrumbs. Add the water, stirring with a round-bladed knife until the mixture begins to stick together. With one hand, collect it together and knead lightly for a few seconds, to give a firm, smooth dough. Divide the pastry in 2, and use half to line a 7-in. pie plate. String, pick over and wash the fruit and mix it with the sugar and flour. Fill the lined pie plate with the fruit mixture and roll out the remaining pastry to form a lid. Damp the edges of the pastry on the dish and cover with the lid, pressing the edges well together. Scallop the edges, brush the top with milk and bake towards the top of the oven at 425°F. (mark 7) for 10–15 minutes, until the pastry is beginning to brown. Reduce the temperature to 350°F. (mark 4) and continue cooking for a further 20–30 minutes, or until the fruit is soft. Serve with cream, ice cream or custard.

Double crust blackcurrant pie to finish a Saturday lunch

LIVER AND BACON PROVENCALE

lb. lambs' liver
oz. (½ cup) flour
tbsps. cooking oil
lb. lean streaky bacon rashers, rinded and chopped
lb. onions, skinned and chopped
4-oz. can tomatoes
level tsp. dried marjoram
bay leaf
tbsp. Worcestershire sauce
pint (2 cups) stock
salt and pepper

ICE CREAM CAKE

7-in. sponge sandwich cake
jam (e.g. cherry or black-currant)
a block of ice cream
¼ pint (⅝ cup) double cream, whipped

Split the sponge cake and spread one half with jam. Cover with ice cream, piling it up in the centre. Cut the other half of the cake into wedges and arrange round the cake so that they open at the centre to show the ice cream. Fill the gaps between the wedges with cream, piping or spooning it in place.

Trim the rind from the gammon rashers and snip the fat at intervals. Mix together the mustard, sugar and 8 tablespoons syrup from the can of pineapple. Lay the gammon on the grill rack, spread evenly with some of the sugar mixture and cook under a medium grill for 15 minutes, basting every 5 minutes with the pan drippings.

Turn the gammon, spread with remaining sugar mixture and cook for a further 15 minutes. Place 2 pineapple rings and 4 cherries on each rasher; baste, and cook for a further 5 minutes. If the fat shows signs of over-browning, cover the

Handy hint

When browning meat in fat, choose a large, deep pan to prevent splashing the cooker and yourself with fat.

Herrings Normandy style – cheap and quick to prepare

A huge toasted sandwich will satisfy tea-time appetites

MENU serves 4

**HERRING FILLETS
NORMANDY STYLE
GRILLED TOMATOES,
CHIP POTATOES
FRESH FRUIT
CHEESE BOARD**

HERRING FILLETS
NORMANDY STYLE

**4 herrings (or 1 lb. oily fish)
seasoned flour
2 tbsps. cooking oil
2 oz. butter
2 eating apples
juice of ½ lemon
pepper
chopped parsley**

Bone the fish and cut in halves down the centre. Dip fillets in seasoned flour and fry in the oil and 1 oz. butter until crisp and golden on each side; keep warm. Wipe pan out with absorbent kitchen paper.

Peel and core the apples and cut each into 8 pieces, then add the rest of the butter to the pan and sauté the apple until tender but still in whole pieces. Add the lemon juice and a dusting of freshly ground pepper (with a little more butter if needed). Arrange the fillets in a dish, overlapping each other, spoon the apple mixture over and sprinkle with chopped parsley.

TEAS

Tea-time at the weekend may be anything from toast and muffins round the fire, to a quick mouthful of something in the kitchen. If you have guests, you may find they do not want tea, but something must be available for the hungry types. Even those who don't bother at home will probably develop a healthy appetite when they see some of your goodies.

Handy hint

Aluminium pans will go black when in contact with boiling water for long periods. To prevent this, add a little vinegar to the water (e.g. when boiling eggs or steaming) or a little lemon juice (e.g. when boiling rice). If vinegar or lemon juice would spoil the flavour of the food being cooked, boil up a fresh pan full of water afterwards with a little vinegar added.

TOASTED TEAS

are ideal in winter, particularly if dinner is to be late. Your guests will be grateful for one of these snacks if they have spent the afternoon walking briskly in the snow – if they have just dozed in front of the fire, try some tempting pastries instead! Toasted sandwiches usually need a knife and fork for eating.

Apart from the recipes given here you can also serve traditional crumpets and muffins from your local bakery – toast these on a long fork in front of the fire.

TRIDENT TOASTED
SANDWICHES

serves 4–6

**2 large eggs, hard-boiled
4 oz. strong Cheddar cheese, grated
7-oz. can tuna steak, drained and flaked
5 sweet pickled onions, chopped
4 level tbsps. mayonnaise
juice of ½ lemon
few drops Tabasco sauce
salt and freshly ground black pepper
1½ oz. butter
12 slices from a large, white, medium-sliced loaf**

Either chop the hard-boiled eggs or place in an egg slicer and cut in both directions. Combine the egg, cheese, tuna, pickled onions, mayonnaise, lemon juice, Tabasco, salt and pepper. Melt the butter in a small pan and brush it on to one side of each of the slices of bread. Place 6 of the slices, butter side down, on a board. Spread each with ⅙th of the filling, and top with another slice of bread, butter side up. Grill under a medium heat on both sides until golden. Cut in half and serve.

SMOKED ROE SALAD

serves 4

**1 lemon
¼ pint (⅝ cup) mayonnaise
few drops Tabasco sauce
salt and freshly ground black pepper
4 slices white bread from a medium-sliced white loaf
butter
1 small lettuce
3 large eggs, hard-boiled
½–¾ lb. smoked cod's roe
paprika pepper**

Blend the juice from ½ the lemon into the mayonnaise, add a few drops of Tabasco and adjust the seasoning.

Toast the bread until golden brown on both sides. Cool a little and butter liberally whilst still crisp. Lay 3 or 4 lettuce leaves on each slice of toast and spoon the mayonnaise down the centre.

Slice the eggs and position overlapping down one side of the toast. Slice the roe and position down the opposite side. Take 4 slices from the remaining ½ lemon, make a cut into the centre of each slice, twist and place on top. Dust the egg with paprika pepper.

PIZZA BAMBINI

serves 4

**4¼-oz. pkt. mixed salami-cervelat-ham
6 anchovy fillets
4 oz. Lancashire cheese, grated
4 round soft rolls
butter
½ lb. firm tomatoes, skinned and thickly sliced
1 small, firm green pepper (capsicum), seeds removed**

Roughly chop the meat and anchovy fillets. Combine with the grated cheese.

Halve the rolls and toast until golden on both sides, butter and spoon the cheese mixture on to each half. Spread evenly. Top each with a thick slice of tomato and grill under a medium heat until the cheese bubbles and browns. Garnish with thin rings of green pepper. Serve in paper napkins.

BEANS AND BACON
SANDWICH

serves 4

**4-oz. can baked beans in tomato sauce
8 rashers streaky bacon, rinded
horseradish sauce
prepared mustard
8 slices white bread, from a ready-sliced loaf
butter**

Heat the beans gently through in a small pan. Fry or grill the bacon until crisp, and then crumble on to a plate. When hot, mix the beans with a little horseradish sauce, to taste, and mustard, and stir in the crumbled bacon.

Toast the bread on both sides, butter and spread with the bean filling, as for an ordinary sandwich. Alternatively, butter the bread, untoasted, fill with the bean mixture and place each sandwich buttered side out in a special toasted sandwich cooker.

272

SANDWICHES

Sandwiches are the easiest to eat if you don't want to sit down to a table with a knife and fork. Ring the changes with different types of bread—white, brown, wholemeal, granary, rye and so on—and slice it very thinly and butter it well. Fillings need to be well-flavoured; anything very delicate is muted to the point of tastelessness when encased in a double layer of bread.

For some unusual sandwich fillings, try the following mixtures:

Shrimp, chopped celery, shredded pineapple and mayonnaise.

Cream cheese, chopped walnuts and stoned raisins or dates.

Chopped tongue, chopped hard-boiled egg, mayonnaise and a pinch of curry powder.

Flaked, canned crabmeat, chopped avocado and mayonnaise.

Minced chicken, minced ham and finely chopped pineapple.

Cream cheese, chopped celery and chopped green pepper (capsicum).

CAKES

A large cake is always welcome at tea-time, either on its own or with sandwiches. These two are among our favourites.

BRANDY, ORANGE AND SULTANA CAKE

This is a moist cake and keeps well for 2–3 weeks after baking.

1½ lb. sultanas
2 medium oranges
¼ pint (⅝ cup) brandy
8 oz. (1 cup) caster sugar
8 oz. butter
4 large eggs
8 oz. (2 cups) plain flour
2 oz. (½ cup) self-raising flour

The day before baking, place the sultanas in a deep bowl. Grate the rind from the oranges, add to the sultanas with the juice squeezed from the oranges (about ¼ pint) and the brandy. Stir well. Leave for at least 12 hours to plump up, stirring occasionally. Grease an 8-in. round cake tin and line with 2 layers of greased greaseproof paper. Tie a band of brown paper round the outside of the tin.

Cream the butter and sugar, beat in the eggs one at a time and lightly beat in the sifted flours. Fold in the fruit and all its juices.

Turn the mixture into the prepared tin and bake in the centre of the oven at 325°F. (mark 3) for about 3 hours. If the top of the cake appears to be getting too brown towards the end of the cooking time, cover with greased grease-

Cream horns are a real weekend luxury – make the horns in advance

proof paper. To test whether the cake is cooked, insert a hot skewer into the centre of the cake. It should come out perfectly clean. If any cake mixture is sticking to it, the cake requires longer cooking. Turn out and cool on a wire rack. Store in an airtight tin.

WALNUT BUTTER CAKE

3 oz. unsalted butter
2 oz. (½ cup) plain flour
½ oz. cornflour
3 large eggs
4 oz. (½ cup) caster sugar
4 oz. shelled walnuts, finely chopped
coffee butter cream or glacé icing, optional

Grease and flour a 9-in. diameter (3¼-pint) tube cake tin.

Heat the butter gently until melted, remove from heat and let stand till any sediment settles. Sift the flour and cornflour together. Put the eggs and sugar in a large bowl, stand this over a saucepan of hot, not boiling, water and whisk until light and creamy. The mixture should be stiff enough to retain the impression of the whisk for a few seconds. Remove from the heat and whisk until cool.

Pour the tepid but still flowing butter round the edge of the mixture. Lightly fold in the butter until most of the fat is worked in. Re-sift half the flour over the surface of the mixture and fold in lightly. Fold in remaining flour and nuts. Pour the mixture into the prepared tin and bake in the centre of the oven at 375°F. (mark 5) for about 20 minutes.

Serve plain or decorated with coffee butter cream or glacé icing.

PASTRIES

Introduce a touch of luxury into the weekend, without hard labour. The pastry cases can be made a day or two in advance and stored in an airtight tin. Fill them the day you intend serving them.

TARTLETTES AUX FRUITS

makes 6

For pâte sucrée:
4 oz. (1 cup) plain flour
pinch of salt
2 oz. (¼ cup) caster sugar
2 oz. butter at normal room temperature
2 egg yolks

For crème pâtissière:
2 egg yolks
2 oz. (¼ cup) caster sugar
¾ oz. plain flour
½ oz. cornflour
½ pint (1¼ cups) milk
1 egg white
vanilla essence
icing sugar, for dredging

15-oz. can black cherries
¼ pint (⅝ cup) cherry juice
1 level tsp. arrowroot
¼ pint (⅝ cup) double cream
4 tbsps. single cream

Sift together the flour and salt on to a pastry board. Make a well in the centre and into it put the sugar, butter and egg yolks. Using the fingertips of one hand, pinch and work the sugar, butter and egg yolks together until well blended. Gradually work in all the flour and knead lightly until smooth. Put the paste in a cool place for at least 1 hour to relax. Have ready 4½-in. shallow patty tins. Roll out the pastry and use it to line the tins. Bake blind at the

top of the oven at 375°F. (mark 5) for 15–20 minutes. Turn out on a wire rack to cool.

Make up the crème pâtissière a day in advance to save time. Cream the egg yolks and sugar together until really thick and pale in colour. Beat in the flour and cornflour and add a little cold milk to make a smooth paste. Heat the rest of the milk in a saucepan until almost boiling and pour on to the egg mixture, beating well all the time.

Return the mixture to the saucepan and stir rapidly over a low heat until it boils. Whisk the egg white until stiff. Remove the custard mixture from the heat and fold in the egg white. Return the pan to the heat, add a few drops of vanilla essence and cook for a further 2–3 minutes. Leave to cool, dredged lightly with icing sugar to prevent a skin forming.

Before serving, spread a layer of crème pâtissière over the base of each tart. Drain the cherries (reserving the juice) and stone them. Blend ¼ pint of the juice with the arrowroot, pour into a saucepan, bring to the boil and cook until it thickens (about 3 minutes). Allow to cool.

Whip the 2 creams together and pipe round the pastry cases. Arrange the cherries in the centre and spoon the thickened juice over.

CREAM HORNS

makes 8

8 oz. frozen puff pastry, thawed
1 egg, beaten
raspberry jam
¼ pint (⅝ cup) double cream
4 tbsps. single cream
icing sugar to dredge

Roll out the pastry to a strip 26 in. by 4–4½ in. Brush with beaten egg. Cut 8 ½-in. ribbons from the pastry with a sharp knife. Wind each round a cream horn tin, glazed side uppermost. Start at the tip, overlapping ⅛ in. all the way, and finish neatly on the underside. The pastry should not overlap the metal rim. Place on a damp baking sheet, with the joins underneath. Bake near the top of the oven at 425°F. (mark 7) for 8–10 minutes, until golden. Cool for a few minutes.

Carefully twist each tin, holding the pastry lightly in the other hand, to ease off the case. When cold, fill the tip of each horn with a little jam. Whip together the two creams and fill the horns. Dust with icing sugar.

*Dinner when you have weekend
guests has to be fairly informal,
since you are not free yourself
to make elaborate preparations
in the shops or kitchen.*

MENU *serves 4*

**AVOCADO AND MELON
COCKTAIL
ROLLED STUFFED
BREAST OF LAMB
SAUTE POTATOES AND
BROCCOLI WITH
BROWNED ALMONDS
ANANAS GLACE**

AVOCADO AND MELON COCKTAIL

**2 charentais (1 cantaloup)
 melons
4 avocados
lemon juice
¼ watermelon, optional
fresh mint, to garnish**

Cut the charentais (or cantaloup) melons in half and discard the seeds. Scoop out as much of the flesh as is practical with a small vegetable baller and retain the skins. Cut the avocados in half lengthwise, remove the stones and scoop out the flesh with the same size baller. Sprinkle the avocado balls with lemon juice to prevent discolouration. Cut open the watermelon and cut out the flesh in the same way.

Pile the melon and avocado balls into the charentais melon skins and top with a sprig of mint. Chill for up to 30 minutes before serving. *Note:* The melon balls can be prepared 1–2 hours in advance, but the avocado should be left as near as possible to the time of serving.

ROLLED STUFFED BREAST OF LAMB

**3 lb. breast of lamb, boned
salt and pepper
4 oz. lean veal
3 oz. lean bacon
1 onion, skinned and finely
 chopped
1 oz. butter
3 oz. fresh white breadcrumbs
1 large mushroom, washed
 and chopped
1 level tsp. finely chopped
 parsley
cayenne pepper
ground mace
1 egg, beaten
milk, optional**

Spread the boned out joint flat on a board, sprinkle with salt

Refreshing and simple to make – avocado and melon cocktail

and pepper and rub the seasonings into the meat.

Pass the mixed veal and bacon twice through a mincer, then beat them well in a bowl. Lightly fry the onion in a little of the butter, until soft but not coloured. Add to the meat. Add the breadcrumbs, mushroom, remaining butter, and parsley; season with salt, pepper and a very little cayenne and mace. Lastly, bind with the beaten egg. Mix well, and if the mixture is too stiff add a little milk.

Spread the veal forcemeat over the lamb and roll the meat up loosely to allow the stuffing to expand during cooking. Tie the roll in several places with fine string, to hold its shape. Weigh it and calculate the cooking time, allowing 27–30 minutes per lb. plus 27 minutes. Place the meat in the roasting tin, putting it on a grill grid or meat trivet if it is fatty, and cook in the centre of the oven at 350°F. (mark 4) for the calculated time.

Remove the strings and serve sliced fairly thickly, accompanied by a thickened gravy. Any stuffing left over can be cooked in a separate small dish and served with the joint.

ANANAS GLACE

**2 small or 1 large pineapple
4 tbsps. Kirsch
2 oranges
2 pears
2 tbsps. lemon juice
12 glacé cherries
2 oz. piece crystallized citron
 peel, sliced
1 block vanilla ice cream**

Cut the pineapple into halves lengthwise and scoop out all the flesh. Take care not to damage the shells. Remove the core and cut the rest of the flesh into cubes. Put these into a basin with the Kirsch. Chill the pineapple shells. Peel the oranges, removing all the white pith, and divide into segments, discarding the membrane. Add the oranges and any juice to the pineapple. Peel, core and slice the pears and dip them into the lemon juice before adding to the other fruit together with the glacé cherries and citron peel. Chill for at least 2 hours.

Pile the fruit and juice into the pineapple shells and top with scoops of ice cream.

MENU *serves 6*

**FLORIDA COCKTAIL
CARBONNADE OF BEEF
RUNNER BEANS,
CREAMED POTATOES
PEAR AND ALMOND PIE**

FLORIDA COCKTAIL

**3 large juicy grapefruit
6 oranges
caster sugar
sherry, optional**

Cut the grapefruit in half across the centre and divide them into segments using a small sharp knife or a curved grapefruit knife. Divide the pieces between 6 small sundae glasses, pouring any juice over. Peel the oranges, removing all the white pith and again divide into segments, add to the grapefruit in the glasses, with their

juice. Dust with caster sugar an[d] add a dash of sherry for the adult[s.] Serve chilled.

CARBONNADE OF BEEF

**3 lb. lean stewing steak, cut
 into ½-in. cubes
salt and pepper
3 oz. fat or oil
4 oz. lean bacon rashers,
 rinded and chopped
2 oz. (½ cup) plain flour
¾ pint (2 cups) beer
¾ pint (2 cups) stock or water
3–4 tbsps. vinegar
1½ lb. onions, skinned and
 chopped
2 cloves of garlic, skinned an[d]
 chopped
bouquet garni**

Season the meat and fry a little at [a] time in the fat or oil until brown[,] about 5 minutes for each batch[.] Add the bacon and continue cook[-] ing for a few minutes. Remov[e] the meat and bacon from the pa[n] stir in the flour and brown lightl[y.] Gradually add the beer, stock an[d] vinegar, stirring continuously unt[il] the mixture thickens. Fill a cas[-] serole with layers of meat, bacon[,] onion and garlic. Pour the sauc[e] over and add the bouquet garn[i.] Cover and cook at 300°F. (mark 2[)] for about 4 hours. Add a littl[e] more stock while cooking, if th[e] sauce seems very thick. Remov[e] the bouquet garni before serving[.]

PEAR AND ALMOND PIE

**13-oz. pkt. frozen puff pastry,
 thawed
2 lb. cooking pears
4 tbsps. brandy
2 oz. butter
6 oz. (1½ cups) ground
 almonds
8 oz. (1 cup) caster sugar
1 level tsp. ground cinnamon
1 egg, beaten
a little sugar
½ pint (1¼ cups) double cream**

Carefully peel and core the pear[s.] Cut them lengthwise into eighths and lay them in the base of [a] round, shallow, 11-in. pie dis[h.] Pour the brandy over them and do[t] with the butter cut into sma[ll] pieces. Mix together the almonds[,] caster sugar and cinnamon an[d] spoon evenly over the fruit. Ro[ll] out the pastry and cover the dis[h.] Trim and crimp the edges an[d] decorate with pastry leaves cu[t] from the trimmings. Glaze wit[h] beaten egg and stand the pie in [a] cool place for about 20 minutes, t[o] prevent shrinkage when cooking[.] Bake at 425°F. (mark 7) for 1[5]

...inutes, then reduce heat to ...75°F. (mark 5) for a further ...5–30 minutes, until the pastry ... well risen and golden brown. ...prinkle with a little granulated ...ugar 5 minutes before end of ...ooking time and return to the ...ven. Serve hot or cold with lightly ...hipped cream.

HOT STUFFED TOMATOES
WIENER BEEF BRAISE
BLACKCURRANT STREUSEL

HOT STUFFED TOMATOES

- even-sized tomatoes
- ½ oz. ham, chopped
- ½ tsps. chopped onion
- oz. butter
- tsp. chopped parsley
- tbsps. fresh white breadcrumbs
- salt and pepper
- level tbsps. grated cheese, optional

Cut a small round from each tomato at the end opposite the stalk, and scoop out the centres. Lightly fry the ham and onion in the butter for 3 minutes. Add the parsley, breadcrumbs, salt and pepper, cheese if used and the pulp removed from the tomatoes. Fill the tomato cases with this mixture, pile it neatly on top, put on the lids and bake at 400°F. (mark 6) for about 15 minutes.

WIENER BEEF BRAISE

- ½ lb. buttock steak (thick-flank or topside), cut in 12 thin slices
- 2 small frankfurters
- oz. dripping
- medium onions, skinned and chopped
- carrots, peeled and cubed
- large turnip (swede), peeled and cubed
- sticks celery, scrubbed and sliced
- pint (2 cups) beef stock, made with a cube
- salt and pepper
- ½ lb. potatoes, cooked and creamed
- level tsps. cornflour

Beat the sliced beef with a rolling pin. Roll each slice round a frankfurter and tie with fine string or cotton.
Melt half the fat and brown the beef rolls on all sides. Remove the rolls from the pan and add re-

maining fat; sauté the vegetables until the fat is absorbed. Place the beef rolls on top, pour on the stock and season with pepper. Bring to the boil, cover, reduce heat and simmer for about 2 hours until the meat is tender.
Lift the beef rolls out and arrange in a ring of creamed potato. Keep hot. Strain the cooking liquid, thicken it with the cornflour and check the seasoning. Pour sauce over the beef rolls.

BLACKCURRANT STREUSEL

- 6 oz. (1½ cups) plain flour
- 4 oz. butter
- 2 oz. (¼ cup) caster sugar
- 1 lb. blackcurrants
- 4 oz. (½ cup) sugar
- ½ pint (1¼ cups) double cream, whipped

For topping:
- 3 oz. (¾ cup) plain flour
- 3 oz. butter
- 3 oz. (⅜ cup) caster sugar

Sift the flour, rub in the butter and then add the caster sugar. Knead the mixture until it forms a dough. Press the dough out to fit a cake tin 8 in. by 10 in. by 1½ in. deep. Wash and top and tail the blackcurrants, mix with the sugar and strew over the base. To make the topping, sift the flour, rub in the butter very lightly. Add the sugar but do not knead. Sprinkle this crumble mixture over the blackcurrants.
Cook at 375°F. (mark 5) for approximately 1 hour, until a golden brown. Allow to cool a little then turn out of the tin. Serve warm or cold, cut into squares and topped with cream.

Cheese topped gammon with peas lyonnaise for an informal dinner

EGG MAYONNAISE
CHEESE TOPPED GAMMON
LYONNAISE PEAS, SAUTE POTATOES
GALETTE JALOUSIE

EGG MAYONNAISE

- 4 eggs, hard-boiled and shelled
- a few lettuce leaves
- ¼ pint (⅝ cup) mayonnaise
- chopped parsley or paprika pepper

Cut the eggs lengthways into halves or quarters. Wash and drain the lettuce and put on individual plates. Serve the eggs on the lettuce, cut side down; coat with the mayonnaise and garnish with parsley or paprika.

CHEESE TOPPED GAMMON

- 4 gammon rashers (about 6 oz. each)
- a little melted butter
- 2 green eating apples
- 6 oz. Cheddar cheese, thinly sliced

Rind the gammon and snip the fat in four or five places on each rasher. Line the grill pan with foil and lay the rashers side by side on the foil. Grill for 4–5 minutes, turning halfway through cooking time. Wipe and core the apples, but do not peel; slice thinly across in rounds. Lay the apple slices over the gammon.
Brush a little melted butter over the apple slices and continue grill-

ing for 2–3 minutes. Lay the cheese slices over the apple and return to the grill for a further 1 minute.

LYONNAISE PEAS

- 2 oz. butter
- 2 large onions, skinned and finely sliced
- 1-lb. pkt. frozen peas
- salt

Melt the butter in a small pan, add the onion and cook over gentle heat for 3 minutes. Meanwhile, bring a pan of salted water to the boil, add the peas and cook for 3 minutes. Drain the peas and mix with the onion.

GALETTE JALOUSIE

- 8 oz. frozen puff pastry, thawed
- 1 egg, beaten
- ½ lb. jam or thick apple purée
- 1 egg white, beaten
- caster sugar

Roll out the pastry into a strip 18 in. by 4 in. Cut into 2 portions, one 2 in. shorter than the other. Roll out the smaller piece to the same size as the larger. Place this piece on a dampened baking sheet. Brush a border ½ in. wide at the end of each strip with beaten egg. Spread the jam or purée over the centre of the pastry. Fold the thicker strip of pastry in half lengthwise. Using a sharp knife, cut across the fold at intervals to within ½ in. of the edge. Unfold the pastry and lift it carefully on to the portion on the baking sheet. Press the edges well together and knock up with a knife.
Bake in the centre of the oven at 425°F. (mark 7) for about 20 minutes. Remove from the oven, brush with egg white, dredge with caster sugar and return to the oven for a further 5 minutes to frost the top.

Handy hint

To cook a perfect omelette, you need the pan evenly heated. Place the pan on a very gentle heat to ensure that it is heated evenly right to the edges. When the pan is ready for the mixture it will feel comfortably hot to the back of your hand about 1 in. from the surface. Add the butter or oil when the pan is ready.

FONDUE BOURGUIGNONNE

A meat fondue is a pleasant Swiss way of giving an informal dinner party for 6–8 people. It entails very little by way of preparation by the hostess, and what has to be done can all be done well in advance. In fact the guests cook their own meat in a pot at the table, which adds to the interest of the evening.

You need a fondue set consisting of a flameproof pot over a spirit burner, and a set of long handled forks. If you have no fondue set you could improvise with an electric table cooker – but the atmosphere won't be quite the same. The traditional meat fondue pots are copper or iron; there are also some attractive stainless steel pots available.

Allow 6 oz. good frying steak per person, cut into 1-in. cubes. Fill the pot two-thirds full with cooking oil (corn oil is suitable) and heat on your ordinary cooker to 375°F., using a frying thermometer for accuracy. Transfer the pot to the spirit burner or a table cooker that will keep the oil at just the correct temperature (the oil should not smoke or spit as this indicates a dangerous heat, but it must be hot enough to seal the meat quickly, so that the fat is not absorbed). It helps to have a second pot of oil heated so that the first can be replaced when the temperature of the oil begins to drop.

Place a plate of raw steak and a long handled fork in front of each person and equip them with a second fork with which to eat the meat (if they use the same forks as those on which the meat is cooked someone will get a nasty burn). Each person impales a piece of steak on the long handled fork and puts it into the oil until it is cooked. It is then transferred to the cold fork and dipped into one of the sauces on the table.

HOLLANDAISE SAUCE

2 tbsps. wine or tarragon vinegar
1 tbsp. water
2 egg yolks
3–4 oz. butter
salt and pepper

Put the vinegar and water in a small pan and boil until reduc

about 1 tablespoon; cool lightly. Put the egg yolks in a basin and stir in the vinegar. Put over a pan of hot water and heat gently, stirring all the time, until the egg mixture thickens (never let the water go above simmering point).

Divide the butter into small pieces and gradually whisk into the sauce and add seasoning to taste. If the sauce is too sharp add a little more butter - it should be slightly piqu-ant, almost thick enough to hold its shape and warm rather than hot when served.

TARTARE SAUCE

¼ pint (⅝ cup) mayonnaise or salad cream
1 tsp. chopped tarragon or chives
2 tsps. chopped capers
2 tsps. chopped gherkins
2 tsps. chopped parsley
1 tbsp. lemon juice or tarragon vinegar

Mix all the ingredients well, then leave the sauce at least 1 hour before serving, to allow the flavours to blend.

TOMATO MAYONNAISE

Blend ¼ pint (⅝ cup) mayonnaise with tomato paste to taste.

CURRY MAYONNAISE

Blend ¼ pint (⅝ cup) mayonnaise with a little curry powder to taste.

HORSERADISH SAUCE

Mix whipped double cream with horseradish relish to flavour.

SIDE DISHES

Chopped banana
Sliced gherkins
Sliced olives
Green salad
Salad vegetables – tomato wedges, cucumber slices, whole small rad-ishes, carrot sticks.

PARTY PLANNERS' CHECK LIST

Countdown

A MONTH BEFORE

What sort of party will it be? You've a good idea of the numbers by now and have probably decided more or less what to serve, but now you must finalize your ideas.

Food and drink

Order wine and/or spirits from the off licence preferably on 'sale or return'. If you have a freezer, you can start cooking for your party now. Pastry cases, meringues, sauces and pâtés can all be made and packed carefully away.

Extras

Glasses – check if your wine merchant will loan them. If not, compare the price of hiring or buying cheap ones. Will you need extra chairs – china – loudspeakers for your record-player? There's sure to be a firm locally which hires these out.

THE WEEK BEFORE

All replies will be in by now, and you'll be able to confirm your drinks and glasses orders, as well as anything else you may be hiring. Make a hair appointment for the day of the party, and lash out on a manicure as well.

Non-freezer owners can make meringues and pâtés – both keep happily for up to 5 days. Buy the 'nibblers' – olives, peanuts, crisps, etc. and check you have everything you need in the store-cupboard. Order meat, fish and any special fruit. Make a complete list of other foods you will need, not forgetting coffee, tea and soft drinks.

Order the flowers. Buy in a stock of cigarettes (make sure you have plenty of ashtrays to go round). Buy a quantity of paper napkins and whatever covering you plan to use for the table. Check the linen is all clean and re-iron during the week if necessary. Check your serving dishes and hire or borrow any extras necessary. Buy some candles.

THE DAY BEFORE

Clean the house thoroughly. Put away superfluous or precious ornaments to prevent damage. Move furniture away from main traffic areas, but don't let your main room get too bare.

Take food out of the freezer. Prepare pastry and pie fillings. Make up fruit salad (except for bananas) and leave to mature. Order extra milk and cream. Make sure the drink is delivered. Make up the salad dressings; prepare salad stuffs and vegetables as much as possible; cut garnishes. Make up a lot of extra ice cubes – keep them in polythene bags.

Check that you have tissues, cotton wool, safety pins and so on for your women guests. Arrange the flowers. Make up the spare bed – there's always someone who's left at the end. Check that you have enough cutlery – borrow some from a friend if it's too late to hire any. Clean any silver. Collect the meat, fish and green groceries. Don't forget extra bread.

ON THE DAY

Remember it's your party and you should enjoy it as well. Clear your dressing table and put out hair spray, tissues, pins and so on for your women guests. A needle and thread might also come in useful. When the family has finished in the bathroom have a tidy-up and put out fresh soap and several guest towels. A clean glass, with drinking water, aspirins and Alka Seltzer would probably be welcome. And don't forget your hairdresser's appointment!

Do as much of the cooking as possible as early as possible. If you're having cold roast meat, this will give your husband a chance to carve it during the afternoon. If anything has a tendency to dry out – wrap it in self-clinging plastic film. Put out the nibblers at the last moment. If you're making a cold wine cup do it in the early afternoon to give it time to mellow. Rice or pasta can be cooked early and reheated by plunging into hot water for 5 minutes if necessary.

Set out the china, glass and cutlery (don't forget to leave room for last-minute serving dishes). Try to arrange your buffet so that you achieve a flow of traffic round the room. Put out *plenty* of ash trays; put out some of the cigarettes, but keep a couple of packets in reserve for late-night desperation. Make sure your record-player and speakers are all functioning properly. Make a note of local all-night taxi services and put it near the phone. Leave yourself time to have half an hour's relaxation – even if it's in the bath.

CATERING QUANTITIES

APPROXIMATE QUANTITIES FOR BUFFET PARTIES

	1 portion	24-26 portions	Notes
Soups: cream, clear or iced	$\frac{1}{3}$ pint	1 gallon	Serve garnished in mugs or cups
Fish cocktail: shrimp, prawn, tuna or crab	1 oz.	1$\frac{1}{2}$ lb. fish 2—3 lettuces 1$\frac{1}{2}$ pints sauce	In stemmed glasses, garnished with a shrimp or prawn
Meat with bone	5 oz.	7—8 lb.	Cold roasts or barbecue chops
boneless	3—4 oz.	5—6$\frac{1}{2}$ lb.	Casseroles, meat balls, sausages, barbecue steaks
Poultry: turkey	3—4 oz. (boneless)	16 lb. (dressed)	
chicken	1 joint (5—8 oz.)	6 2$\frac{1}{2}$—3 lb. birds (dressed)	Serve hot or cold
Delicatessen: ham or tongue	3—4 oz.	5—6$\frac{1}{2}$ lb.	Halve the amounts if making stuffed cornets
pâté for wine-and-pâté party	3—4 oz.	5—6$\frac{1}{2}$ lb.	Half the amount if pâté is starter course
Salad vegetables lettuce cucumber tomatoes white cabbage boiled potatoes	$\frac{1}{6}$ 1 in. 1—2 1 oz. 2 oz.	3—4 2 cucumbers 3 lb. 1$\frac{1}{2}$ lb. 3 lb.	Dress at last minute for winter salads for potato salads
Rice or pasta	1$\frac{1}{2}$ oz. (uncooked)	2 lb.	Can be cooked a day ahead, reheated in 5 min. in boiling water
Cheese (for wine-and-cheese party)	3 oz.	4$\frac{1}{2}$—5 lb. of at least 4 types	You'll need more if you serve a cheese dip too
Cheese (for biscuits)	1—1$\frac{1}{2}$ oz.	1$\frac{1}{2}$—2 lb. cheese plus 1 lb. butter 2 lb. biscuits	Allow the larger amounts for an assorted cheese board

SAVOURIES AND SWEETS

	Ingredients	Portions	Notes
Sausage rolls	1$\frac{1}{2}$ lb. shortcrust or flaky pastry 2 lb. sausage meat	25—30 medium or 50 small rolls	Pastry based on 1$\frac{1}{2}$ lb. flour, $\frac{3}{4}$—1 lb. fat
Bouchées	1 lb. puff pastry 1 pint thick white sauce 10 oz. prepared filling	50 bouchées	Pastry based on 1 lb. flour, $\frac{3}{4}$ lb. butter. Fillings: chopped ham, chicken, egg, mushrooms, shrimps
Cheese straws	$\frac{1}{2}$ lb. cheese pastry	100 cheese straws	$\frac{1}{2}$ lb. flour, $\frac{1}{4}$ lb. fat, $\frac{1}{4}$ lb. cheese
Meringues	6 egg whites 12 oz. caster sugar $\frac{3}{4}$ pint whipped cream	50 (small) meringue halves	2 halves per head with cream 1 half with fruit and cream, or ice cream
Jelly	2$\frac{1}{2}$ quarts	25	
Trifle	4 pints custard 25 sponge fingers 1 large can fruit	25	Decorate with cream, glacé cherries, chopped nuts, angelica
Fruit salad	6$\frac{1}{2}$ lb. fruit 3—4 pints sugar syrup 1$\frac{1}{2}$ pints cream	25	Can be prepared a day ahead and left submerged in syrup but bananas should be added just before serving

CATERING QUANTITIES

QUANTITIES FOR PARTY DRINKS
Rough guide only, as drinking habits vary.

BUFFET PARTIES
Allow for each, 1—2 shorts and
3—6 longer drinks plus coffee.
Reckon a half-bottle of wine
per person.

DINNER PARTIES
One bottle of table wine is
sufficient for 4 people.

DROP-IN-FOR-DRINKS
Reckon on 3—5 short drinks
each and 4—6 small savouries
besides the usual olives
and nuts.

DRINKS BY THE BOTTLE
Sherry and port and straight
vermouths give roughly 12—16
glasses. In single nips for
cocktails, vermouths and spirits
give just over 30 a bottle.
Reckon 16—20 drinks of spirit
from a bottle when serving them
with soda, tonic or other
minerals. Liqueurs served in
proper glasses—30 portions.
A split bottle of soda or tonic
gives 2—3 drinks. A 1-pint can of
tomato juice gives 4—6 drinks.
Dilute a bottle of fruit cordial with
7 pints water for 20—25 drinks.

APPROXIMATE COFFEE AND TEA QUANTITIES

	1 Serving	24–26 Servings		Notes
Coffee				
ground, hot	$\frac{1}{3}$ pint	9–10 oz. coffee 6 pints water	3 pints milk 1 lb. sugar	If you make the coffee in advance strain it after infusion. Reheat without boiling. Serve sugar separately
ground, iced	$\frac{1}{3}$ pint	12 oz. coffee 6 pints water	3 pints milk sugar to taste	Make coffee (half sweetened, half not), strain and chill. Mix with chilled milk. Serve in glasses
instant, hot	$\frac{1}{3}$ pint	2–3 oz. coffee 6 pints water	2 pints milk 1 lb. sugar	Make coffee in jugs as required. Serve sugar separately
instant, iced	$\frac{1}{3}$ pint	3 oz. coffee 2 pints water	6 pints milk sugar to taste	Make black coffee (half sweetened, half not) and chill. Mix with chilled creamy milk. Serve in glasses.
Tea				
Indian, hot	$\frac{1}{3}$ pint	2 oz. tea 8 pints water	$1\frac{1}{2}$ pints milk 1 lb. sugar	It is better to make tea in several pots rather than one outsize one
Indian, iced	$\frac{1}{3}$ pint	3 oz. tea 7 pints water	2 pints milk sugar to taste	Strain tea immediately it has infused. Sweeten half of it. Chill. Serve in glasses with chilled creamy milk
China	$\frac{1}{3}$ pint	2 oz. tea 9 pints water	2–3 lemons 1 lb. sugar	Infuse China tea for 2 or 3 minutes only. Put a thin lemon slice in each cup before pouring. Serve sugar separately

STORAGE

Foods such as meat, fish, dairy produce, fruits and vegetables are all perishable and if they are kept too long the action of bacteria, mould and enzymes (called micro-organisms) will make changes in them so that milk will sour, fats go rancid, meat, fish and eggs decompose and fruits and vegetables discolour and go mouldy. The lower the temperature, the less micro-organism activity there will be, so that the best way to store perishable foods is in a refrigerator at a steady temperature of 35°F.—45°F. The next best thing is a cool larder where the temperature does not exceed 50°F.

Bacon, cheese, eggs and fats should really be bought at least once a week – or twice a week in hot weather if a refrigerator is not available. Meat, fish, poultry, soft fruits, green and salad vegetables should, ideally, be purchased as you need them – preferably not too much at a time.

In the store cupboard (in covered containers)
Flour
Plain, self-raising	Up to 6 months
Wheatmeal	2–3 months
Wholemeal	Up to 1 month
Cake mixes (unopened)	Up to 6 months

Raising agents
Baking powder, bicarbonate of soda, cream of tartar	2–3 months
Dried yeast	Up to 6 months

Cereals
Cornflour, custard powder	Up to 12 months
Dried vegetables—pearl barley, lentils, peas, etc.	Up to 12 months

Oatmeal	Up to 1 month
Rice, sago, tapioca	Up to 12 months

Nuts
Whole almonds, walnuts	Up to 1 month
Ground almonds, coconut	Up to 1 month

Jams and bottled goods
Gravy browning	Up to 12 months
Sauces	Up to 6 months
Salad oil	Up to 18 months
Pickles and chutneys	Up to 12 months
Lemon curd, bought	2–3 months
home-made	Up to 1 month
Jams and mincemeat	Up to 12 months
Mayonnaise, salad cream (bought)	Up to 12 months
Vinegar	At least 2 years

Cans
Fish, meat, fruit and juices	Up to 12 months
Ham	Up to 6 months

Sugars
Granulated, caster, cubes	Up to 12 months
Icing, brown	Up to 1 month

Syrups
Golden syrup, treacle	Up to 12 months
Honey	Up to 6 months

Dried fruit
Currants, sultanas, raisins	2–3 months
Prunes, figs, apricots	2–3 months
Candied peel, glacé cherries	2–3 months

Miscellaneous
Dried milk, whole	Up to 1 month
skimmed	2–3 months

Jellies and gelatine	Up to 12 months
Breakfast cereals	Up to 1 month
Tea	Up to 1 year
Coffee (beans)	Up to 1 month
(ground)	1 week
Soups (including condensed)	Up to 12 months
Vegetables (including tomato juice and purée)	Up to 12 months
Evaporated milk	6–8 months
Condensed milk	4–6 months
Cocoa, drinking chocolate	Up to 12 months
Packet soups	Up to 12 months

Herbs, spices and seasonings
Allspice, bay leaves, cloves, celery seeds, cinnamon, dried herbs, ginger, mace, mixed spice, curry powder	Up to 6 months
Curry paste, mustard, pepper	Up to 12 month
Salt	Up to 6 months (or longer if perfectly dry)

Colourings and flavourings
Flavouring essence	Up to 12 month
Block chocolate or polka dots	Up to 1 month
Colourings	Up to 12 month
Silver balls, vermicelli and other decorations	Up to 1 month

Note: Many of these items will keep longer than the recommended times if t packaging is not disturbed. In particular, mc canned goods will keep for years if the tin not exposed to damp that will cause it rust. However, it is advisable to turn o your storecupboard 3 or 4 times a year, as to ensure a regular turnover of stock.

In the refrigerator	How to store	Time
Milk produce		
Fresh milk	In the bottle or carton. If in a jug, keep covered	3—4 days
Milk puddings, custards, etc.	In a covered dish	2 days
Yoghourt	Leave in the original container	7 days
Fats		
Butter, margarine, lard, etc.	Leave in original wrapping and store in the special door compartment	2—4 weeks
Cheese		
Hard and blue cheeses	Wrapped in the original pack, in polythene, or foil	1—2 weeks
Cream cheese	Keep in a covered container, or wrap in polythene or foil	5—7 days
Poultry		
Whole, fresh birds	Draw, wash, dry and wrap in polythene or foil. Remove wrappings from ready-to-cook poultry	2—3 days
Cooked birds	Cool and refrigerate straight away. Remove any stuffing and wrap or cover with polythene or foil	2—3 days
Frozen birds	Leave in the original wrapping and put while still frozen into the frozen food compartment	Depends on star rating (refer to manufacturer's instructions) 2—3 days in main cabinet
Cooked and made-up poultry dishes	Cool quickly and refrigerate in covered dish or container	1 day
Meat		
Joints	Rinse off any blood and wipe dry. Cover lightly with polythene or foil (do not seal tightly) and refrigerate straight away	3—5 days
Steaks, chops, stewing veal		2—4 days
Smoked hams, sliced bacon		1 week
Offal and mince		1—2 days
Cooked meats		
Joints	Wrap in foil or polythene or leave, covered, in the dish they were cooked in. Alternatively, store in any covered container	3—5 days
Casseroles, made-up dishes		2—3 days
Fish		
Raw	Cover loosely in polythene or foil	1—2 days
Cooked	Cover loosely in polythene or foil, or place in covered container	2 days
Eggs		
Fresh in shells	Small end down	About 2 weeks
Yolks	Covered with water if whole	2—3 days
Whites	In a covered container	3—4 days
Hard-boiled in shell	Leave uncovered	Up to 1 week
Fruit and vegetables		
Soft fruits	Clean and store in a covered container	1—3 days
Hard and stone fruits	Lightly wrapped, or in the crisper	3—7 days
Bananas	*Never refrigerate*	
Salad vegetables	Wash and dry; store in crisper, plastic container or wrap lightly in polythene	4—6 days
Greens	Prepare ready for use. Wrap lightly or place in the crisper	3—7 days

OPERATION RESCUE

If something goes wrong when you're cooking – be it for a family supper or a formal dinner – the essential rule is don't panic. Take a good look at the dish in question – taste it – and think what can be done to save it. If the flavour is wrong, it can often be saved (see our specific examples). If there's time, use it as the base for another dish altogether (if necessary, give your guests another drink to keep them happy). If the result looks a disaster, but the flavour is fine, change its appearance – cover it up with sauce, for instance, or turn a collapsed cake into a delicious trifle. Whatever you do, don't serve something that looks a failure – it will make you feel bad and embarrass your guests. If you've under-calculated badly on quantities, serve an extra variety of vegetable – or try to serve another course (be inventive – see what you have in the store cupboard by way of canned soups, or hors d'oeuvre). Be sure you always have some cans of attractive vegetables available –
French beans, asparagus or artichoke hearts.

SWEETS

To eke out a scanty sweet course

Top each serving with a portion of bought ice cream.

If a chocolate cake turns out rather too moist

Call it a pudding and serve it hot with a fluffy sauce.

If homemade biscuits crumble badly

Use them to make a biscuit crumb flan case.

If the top of a fruit cake gets burnt

Cut if off and use a well-flavoured almond paste to disguise it.

If apples or pears stew unevenly

Some fluffy and some still hard? Put them in the blender and purée to make a fool.

If a jelly won't set

Put in a warm place to complete melt, then add more dissolve gelatine and place in the colde part of the refrigerator. If yo haven't time to wait any longe turn it into a jelly trifle, wit sherry-soaked sponge on the bo tom, fruit and cream.

If meringues break as you li them from the baking sheet

Meringue shells can be served o top of fruit and cream if the piece are large enough. A mering gâteau can usually be stuck to gether and suitably disguised wit large quantities of whipped crea and fruit or grated chocolate.

If your custard sauce curdle

Whip in 1–2 level teaspoons cor flower per pint; continue cookin

If a pastry flan case breaks

Put 4 tablespoons jam in a sma pan, boil and brush well into t broken edges. Press together an brush over the join again wit more jam. Allow to cool befor filling.

If your sponge cake turns out a thin, flat, biscuity layer
Cut into fancy shapes with a biscuit cutter and sandwich together with jam and cream.

If your cake rises unevenly
Level the top, turn it over and ice the bottom.

If a cake breaks up as you take it out of the tin
It can often be disguised as a hot pudding, with custard sauce or fruit.

If a cake sinks in the middle
Cut out the centre and decorate with fruit, cream or butter cream. If it is a heavy fruit cake, cut out the centre and turn into a ring cake, decorating with almond paste and royal icing if you wish.

SAUCES

If a sweet sauce is too sickly
Add some lemon juice to give it zest. This is also a good ploy with puddings generally which are too bland.

If a sauce turns lumpy
Whisk with a rotary whisk, purée in a blender or press through a fine sieve.

If a savoury sauce lacks flavour but will not stand more salt and pepper
Add lemon juice (especially good with sauces for fish).

If French dressing tastes too oily
Add more salt and a splash of vinegar or lemon juice.

If mayonnaise curdles
Start again with a fresh egg yolk in a clean basin and add the curdled mixture slowly to it – the whole should then blend properly.

MEATS, POULTRY AND FISH

If a chicken is over-cooked (flesh falls apart, skin breaks)
Cut into pieces and mix with the vegetables instead of serving separately. Dish up on a bed of buttered noodles or rice.

If fish breaks up
Mix it with rice to make a kedgeree, or serve in piped potato nests, or allow it to cool, flake it and make up a fish salad.

If a curry sauce is too hot
Add yoghourt, soured cream, milk, lemon juice or potato, or a combination of these.

If a casserole is too spicy
Add a few tablespoons of cream or milk.

If a casserole has too much liquid
Work together butter and flour in the proportion 1 oz. butter to ½ oz. flour with a fork and stir into the hot liquid in small pieces until the sauce is the desired consistency. Continue to cook a little longer.

SOUPS

If a soup is too salty but not too thick
Add a small quantity of instant mashed potato.

VEGETABLES AND FRUIT

If your potatoes – or other vegetables – boil dry
Cut off the burnt part and remove whatever is salvageable to another pan. If necessary, add more boiling water, or toss in butter and season well.

If creamed potatoes are lumpy
Purée in a blender with plenty of butter, salt and pepper.

If rice is overcooked and soggy
Rinse in a colander with cold running water to stop it cooking any further. Cool any other vegetables similarly, drain and mix together as a rice salad, using French dressing to moisten.

If soft fruits are damaged
Cut off the damaged parts and purée the remainder for use as a fruit sauce with ice cream.

If jam won't set
Small quantities of runny jam can be used as fruit sauce for hot puddings or ice cream. ●

COOK'S TOOLS

It's difficult to be a successful cook without the right equipment. By that, we don't mean that you should go to your nearest big store and spend the month's housekeeping money in the kitchen gadget department! It simply means that if you *are* going to buy a piece of kitchen equipment, make sure it's something that is really useful—and that it's well made. It's far better to spend a little more and buy something that's going to last, rather than buy a cheap version that will break the first time it has something tough to cope with. And if you're buying bakeware—cake tins and so on—do consider the easy clean type; they are well worth the extra money in time- and temper-saving. To give you an idea, we have assembled a variety of pieces that we consider essential basic equipment and photographed them all together.

Scales
Colander
Forcing bag and nozzles
Pie plate
Swiss roll pan
Rolling pin
Flour dredger
Loaf pan
Deep cake pan
Sandwich pan
Cooling tray
Tongs
Set of non-stick saucepans and frying pan
Measuring jug
Peppermill
Set of mixing bowls
Lemon squeezer
Kitchen scissors

15 Sieve
16 Mouli grater
17 4-sided grater
18 Set of kitchen knives
    Skewers
    5-hour timer
    Chopping board
19 Egg beater
20 Whisk
21 Hand-held electric beater
22 Set of measuring spoons
23 Garlic crusher
24 Corkscrew
25 Wall-fixed can opener
26 Egg and tomato slicer
27 Potato peeler
28 Corer
29 Rubber spatula

30 Set of wooden spoons
31 Pastry brush
    Yorkshire pudding tin
    Bun pan
In addition, you will probably find the following very useful to have in your kitchen:
Metal basting spoon and draining spoon
2- or 3-pronged kitchen fork
Palette knife
Butter spreader (a small palette knife)
Deep fat fryer (or a collapsible wire basket to fit your largest saucepan)
Omelette pan
Set of flan rings
Jelly moulds
Mincer
Spare baking sheets to fit your oven
Assortment of casserole dishes

CALORIES AND CARBOHYDRATES

	Grammes of carbohydrate per oz.	Calories per oz.
FRUIT		
Apples	3·5	13
Apricots, raw	1·9	8
dried	12·3	52
Bananas	5·5	22
Blackberries	1·8	8
Blackcurrants	1·9	8
Cherries	3·4	13
Damsons	2·7	11
Gooseberries, ripe	2·6	10
Grapes, black	4·4	17
white	4·6	18
Grapefruit	1·5	6
Lemons	0·9	4
Melons	1·5	7
Olives in brine	trace	30
Oranges	2·4	10
Peaches	2·6	11
Pears	3·1	12
Plums	2·7	11
Prunes	11·4	46
Raisins	18·3	70
Raspberries	1·6	7
Rhubarb	0·2	1
Strawberries	1·8	7
Sultanas	18·4	71
Tangerines	2·3	10
VEGETABLES		
Artichokes, globe	0·8	4
Asparagus	0·3	5
Avocados	0·7	25
Beans, broad	2·0	12
butter	4·9	26
French	0·3	2
haricot	4·7	25
runner	0·3	2
Beetroot	2·8	13
Broccoli	0·1	4
Brussels sprouts	0·5	5
Cabbage, raw	1·1	7
cooked	0·2	2
Carrots, raw	1·5	6
cooked	1·2	5
Cauliflower	0·3	3

	Grammes of carbohydrate per oz.	Calories per oz.
Celery, raw	0·4	3
cooked	0·2	1
Chicory	0·4	3
Cucumber	0·5	3
Leeks, cooked	1·3	7
Lentils	5·2	27
Lettuce	0·5	3
Marrow, courgettes (zucchini)	0·4	2
Mushrooms, raw	0·0	2
fried	0·0	62
Onions	0·8	4
Parsley	trace	6
Parsnips	3·8	16
Peas, boiled	2·2	14
dried, cooked	5·4	28
Potatoes, old	5·6	23
new	5·2	21
chips	10·6	68
crisps	14·0	159
Pumpkin	1·0	4
Radishes	0·8	4
Seakale	0·2	2
Spinach	0·4	7
Spring greens	0·3	3
Swedes	1·1	5
Tomatoes, raw	0·8	4
Turnips	0·7	3
Watercress	0·2	4
NUTS		
Almonds	1·2	170
Brazils	1·2	183
Chestnuts	10·4	49
Coconut, desiccated	1·8	178
Peanuts	2·4	171
Walnuts	1·4	156
MEAT AND POULTRY		
Bacon, back	0·0	169
streaky	0·0	149

	Grammes of carbohydrate per oz.	Calories per oz.
Beef, topside, roast	0·0	91
sirloin, roast	0·0	109
silverside	0·0	86
corned	0·0	66
Chicken, roast	0·0	54
Duck, roast	0·0	89
Ham, boiled	0·0	123
Heart	0·0	68
Kidney	0·0	45
Lamb, chop, grilled	0·0	80
leg, roast	0·0	100
Liver, calf, fried	0·7	74
ox, fried	1·1	81
Luncheon meat, canned	1·4	95
Pork, leg, roast	0·0	90
chops, grilled	0·0	92
Rabbit, stewed	0·0	51
Sausages, fried	4·5	81
Tongue, sheeps', stewed	0·0	84
Tripe	0·0	29
Turkey, roast	0·0	56
Veal, roast	0·0	66
FISH		
Cod, steamed	0·0	23
Crab	0·0	36
Haddock	0·0	28
Hake	0·0	30
Halibut	0·0	37
Herring	0·0	54
Kippers	0·0	57
Lemon Sole	0·0	26
Lobster	0·0	34
Mackerel	0·0	53
Oysters	trace	143
Plaice	0·0	26
Prawns	0·0	30
Salmon, canned	0·0	39
fresh	0·0	57
Sardines, canned	0·0	84
Shrimps	0·0	32
Sole	0·0	24

	Grammes of carbohydrate per oz.	Calories per oz.
SUGARS, PRESERVES		
Chocolate, milk	15·5	167
plain	14·9	155
Chutney, tomato	11·0	43
Glacé cherries	15·8	137
Honey	21·7	87
Ice cream	5·6	56
Jam	19·7	74
Jelly, packet	17·7	73
Lemon curd	12·0	86
Marmalade	19·8	74
Mars Bar	18·9	127
Sugar	29·6	112
Syrup, golden	22·4	84
Treacle	19·1	73
MILK PRODUCTS, etc.		
Butter	trace	226
Cheese, Cheddar	trace	120
Edam	trace	88
blue	trace	103
Gruyère	trace	132
Cream, double	0·6	131
single	0·9	62
Milk, whole	1·4	19
skimmed	1·4	10
Yoghourt, low-fat	1·4	15
Eggs	trace	46
Margarine	0·0	226
Lard	0·0	262
Oil	0·0	264
CEREAL PRODUCTS		
All-Bran	16·5	88
Arrowroot	26·7	101
Bread, Hovis	13·5	67
malt	14·0	71
Procea	14·3	72
Cornflakes	25·2	104

	Grammes of carbohydrate per oz.	Calories per oz.
Cornflour	26·2	100
Energen rolls	13·0	111
Flour, 100%	20·8	95
85%	22·5	98
80%	22·9	99
75%	23·2	99
Macaroni, boiled	7·2	32
Pearl barley, cooked	7·8	34
Oatmeal porridge	2·3	13
Puffed wheat	21·4	102
Rice, polished	8·4	35
Ryvita	21·9	98
Sago	26·7	101
Semolina	22·0	100
Shredded Wheat	22·4	103
Spaghetti	23·9	104
Tapioca	27·0	102
Weetabix	21·9	100
Salt	0·0	0
Pepper	19·3	88
BEVERAGES		
Bournvita	19·2	105
Bovril	0·0	23
Cocoa	9·9	128
Coffee with chicory essence	16·1	63
Coffee, infusion	0·1	1
Lemonade	1·6	6
Marmite	0·0	2
Tea, infusion	0·0	1

ALCOHOL BY THE GLASS: BEERS	Calories
Brown ale, bottled (½ pint)	80
Draught ale, bitter ,,	90
Draught ale, mild ,,	70
Pale ale, bottled ,,	90
Stout, bottled ,,	100
Stout, extra ,,	110
Strong ale ,,	210

	Calories
CIDERS	
Dry (½ pint)	100
Sweet ,,	120
Vintage ,,	280
TABLE WINES	
Beaujolais (glass, 4 fl.oz.)	76
Champagne ,,	84
Chianti ,,	72
Graves ,,	84
Médoc ,,	72
Sauternes ,,	104
FORTIFIED WINES	
Port, ruby (glass, 2 fl.oz.)	86
Port, tawny ,,	90
Sherry, dry ,,	66
Sherry, sweet ,,	76
SPIRITS, 70° PROOF	
Whisky, Gin, Vodka, Rum (1 fl.oz.)	63
LIQUEURS	
Bénédictine (glass, 2–3 oz.)	69
Crème de Menthe ,,	67
Anisette ,,	74
Apricot brandy ,,	64
Curaçao ,,	54
COGNAC	
Brandy (pony, 1 oz.)	73

Herbs and Spices

	Meat	Fish	Poultry, game	Soups	Vegetables
Basil *Use sparingly*	Lamb, pork, veal, beef casseroles	Shrimps, white fish		Many soups, especially tomato	Tomatoes, broad beans
Bay	Kebabs, marinades for beef, casseroles	Baked or casseroled fish	Marinades	As a background seasoning, remove before serving	
Chervil *Use generously*	Chervil butter for veal cutlets	Crab	Fricassees, rub into chicken before roasting/grilling	Herb soup	Chervil butter fo peas, tomatoes, aubergines
Chives *According to taste*	Hamburgers, meat loaves, garnish for casseroles	Fish cakes, fish stuffings	With dishes containing tomatoes	Garnish for vegetable soups, especially vichyssoise	Garnish to potatoes, other vegetables
Dill *Use carefully*	Lamb and rich pork dishes, beef and chicken ragoût	All fish dishes, especially salmon, crab, mackerel	Creamed chicken, add a spray to roasting pan	Fish, pea, tomato and bean soups	With delicate vegetables
Garlic *Use judiciously*	Continental cookery, pasta, sauces, casseroles	Use sparingly in most fish dishes	Together with other robust flavours	Most soups	Ratatouille
Marjoram *Use judiciously*	Veal, lamb, pork, sausages, liver	Salt fish, shellfish	Stuffings, rub unstuffed chicken, duck before roasting	Onion, potato, lentil, pea soups	Tomatoes, peas, carrots, spinach, mushrooms
Oregano *Use judiciously*	Veal, lamb, pork, sausages, liver	Many fish dishes	Stuffings	Onion, potato, lentil, pea soups	Tomatoes, peas, carrots, courgett spinach, mushro
Parsley *Use freely*	Stuffings, casseroles	Fish cakes, stuffings	Stuffings	Garnish for any soup	Parsley butter, n potatoes, celery
Rosemary *Use sparingly*	Roast lamb, tripe, kidneys, marinades	Marinades for salmon, eel, mackerel	Sprinkle lightly inside before roasting; stuffings	Minestrone	Sauté potatoes, beans (cassoule spinach, tomatoe
Sage *Use carefully*	Stuffing for pork		Stuffing for duck, goose, turkey	Robust chicken, turtle, mushroom soups; fish chowder	
Tarragon *Use carefully*	Marinades, steak, casseroles	Many fish dishes	Classic Tarragon Chicken, chicken liver pâté, hare		
Thyme *Use very carefully*	Stuffings, gravies, sausages	All types of fish	Stuffing for chicken, rabbit; jugged hare	Thick soups	Tomatoes, sauté vegetables
Allspice *ground* Spicy-sweet, mild	Pot roasts, meat balls, baked ham, beef stews	Boiled fish, oyster stews		Broths	Add a little to tomatoes, cream potatoes, carrots
Cayenne *ground* Hot, pungent	Use sparingly in meat dishes and gravies, mince	Shellfish	Chicken dishes	All soups	Baked beans, vegetable curries aubergines
Celery seeds *whole* Slightly bitter	Casseroles	Most fish dishes		Meat soups	
Chillies *whole* Spicy, hot	Mexican dishes		Excellent in a chicken pie filling		Use sparingly (crushed) in tomato dishes
Cinnamon *stick or ground* Sweet, spicy	Ham glaze, pork				
Cloves *whole or ground* Strong and spicy	Ham, tongue		Poultry and game casseroles, marinades	Beef, tomato, bean, pea, beetroot soups	Pumpkin, spinac
Curry *powder* Strong and spicy	Casseroles, left-over meat dishes, meat loaves	Shellfish, devilled fish	Chicken	Mulligatawny, apple, tomato soups	Vegetable curries
Ginger *root or ground* Hot, rich, aromatic	Curries	Many fish dishes	Duck, rub into the flesh of chicken and brush with butter		
Mace *blade or ground* Sweet, softly spicy	Meat stuffings, mince dishes, veal, lamb chops, pâté	Potted shrimps, fish dishes with sauces	Chicken à la King	Cream of chicken soup	Mashed potato, creamed spinach
Mustard *seed or ground* Hot, pungent	Beef, ham, bacon, frankfurters, cold meats			Cream of celery, lentil, mushroom, chicken soups	
Nutmeg *whole or ground* Sweet, spicy	Veal, meat loaves	Fish cakes, croquettes	Chicken		Spinach, carrots, beans
Paprika *ground* Colourful, mild	Lamb, pork, veal, mince dishes, goulash	Shellfish	Chicken	Cream soups, chowders	Beans, potatoes, cauliflower
Pepper *whole or ground* Strong	Most meat dishes	Most fish dishes	Most poultry and game dishes		Most vegetable dishes
Saffron *powder* Mildly spicy, golden colour	Oriental cooking	Spanish cod dishes	Chicken, rabbit	Bouillabaise, chicken, turkey	Rice
Turmeric *powdered* Aromatic, slightly bitter	Curries	Fish kedgeree, fish stew			Rice dishes

...lads and ...ad dressings	Cheese	Eggs	Sauces	Preserves	Baked goods	Other uses
...en, tomato, rice ...ds		Fines herbes or tomato omelette	For pasta, rice			
			Infuse in milk for béchamel sauce			Rice pudding
...st salads, ...nch dressing	Excellent with cream cheese	Fines herbes omelettes and soufflés	Most lightly seasoned sauces, béarnaise, green			
...salads and ...ssings	Cottage and cream cheeses	Scrambled eggs, soufflés, fondue	In savoury white and herb sauces, mayonnaise			
...st salads, soured ...am dressing, ...cado	Cream cheese and other dishes	Egg mayonnaise	Dill sauce with pike, eel	Pickled cucumber		In egg sandwiches, dill tea
...nch dressing	Pizza	Pickled eggs	Use sparingly in many sauces especially for pasta			
...een, chicken ...ds	Cottage and cream cheeses	Egg based quiches, omelettes	Cheese sauces			Pizza, tomato juice cocktail
...een and chicken ...ds	Cottage and cream cheeses	Egg based quiches, omelettes	Cheese sauces			Pizza
...st salads	Most cheese dishes	Fines herbes omelettes and other dishes	Sauces for ham, chicken, fish			
	Cottage and cream cheeses		Apple jelly, jams			Herb tea, fruit salads, wine/cider cups, vegetable cocktail
	Many cheese dishes					
...paragus, chicken ...ds; soured ...am dressing		Tarragon pickled eggs	Béarnaise, hollandaise, mousseline, tarragon			Tomato and fish cocktails, sandwich spread, aspic glaze
...any salads	Most cheese dishes, cheese herb bread	Many egg dishes				Lemon thyme in fruit salads, liqueurs
...uit salads	Cottage cheese	Egg dishes with sauce	Tomato and barbecue sauces	Pickles, chutneys, relishes, mincemeat	Fruit cakes, rice puddings, apple pies, poached fruit	Ingredient in mixed spice
...ocktail sauce for ...awns			Use sparingly in sauces for fish			Ingredient in curry powder
...lads and ...essings, coleslaw	Cream cheese as a sandwich spread			Pickles, chutneys	Bread	
			Tomato sauce for pasta, also meat sauces	Pickles	Cakes, pies	
		Egg nog		Pickles, mincemeat	Fruit cake, milk pudding, pumpkin pie, Christmas fare	Mulled wine (stick), cinnamon toast (ground)
			Bread, apple, cranberry sauces	Chutneys, mincemeat, bottled sauces	Fruit cake, apple and pear pies	Mulled wine
...ayonnaise		Curried eggs	For shellfish, chicken, eggs, meat	Chutneys, pickles		
				Fruit chutneys	Cakes, biscuits	With melon (ground), stewed fruit (root)
	Welsh rarebit or other cheese dishes		For fish and vegetables	Chutneys, pickles	Fruit cakes, pies, cherry pie, chocolate	Tomato juice
...ench dressing, ...ayonnaise	Strengthens the flavour of cooked cheese	Stuffed eggs	For meat, fish, barbecues	Pickles		Sandwiches
		Scrambled eggs	Cheese sauce		Cakes, pies, puddings, doughnuts	Milk, egg nog, puddings
...ressings, coleslaw	Cream cheese	Devilled eggs	Cream sauces			
...ost dressings and ...lads	Many cheese dishes	Many egg dishes	Most sauces	Most preserves		
...ce salads, ...afood, chicken	Cream cheese		Veal and fish sauces		Buns, cakes	Risotto, paella
		Devilled eggs, creamed eggs	Adds colour and flavour to white sauces	Pickles, relishes	For colouring cakes	Ingredient of curry powder

HANDY CHARTS
EVERYDAY MEASURES

OVEN TEMPERATURES

Electric	Gas
250°F.	mark $\frac{1}{4}$
275°F.	mark $\frac{1}{2}$
300°F.	mark 1–2
325°F.	mark 3
350°F.	mark 4
375°F.	mark 5
400°F.	mark 6
425°F.	mark 7
450°F.	mark 8
475°F.	mark 9

IMPERIAL/METRIC CONVERSIONS

Capacity
(ml. = millilitre(s))

$\frac{1}{4}$ pint	= 142 ml.
$\frac{1}{2}$ pint	= 284 ml.
1 pint	= 568 ml.
$\frac{1}{2}$ litre	= 0.88 pints
1 litre	= 1·76 pints

Mass
(g. = gramme(s))

1 oz.	= 28.35 g.
	(25 g. is a working equivalent)
2 oz.	= 56.7 g.
4 oz.	= 113.4 g.
8 oz.	= 226.8 g.
12 oz.	= 340.2 g.
1 lb.	= 453.6 g.
	(450 g. is a working equivalent)
1 kilogramme	= 2.2 lb.

HANDY EQUIVALENTS

Spoon measures are level, based on a 15 ml. tablespoon.

Flour, cornflour, cocoa, custard powder	1 oz.	3 tbsps.
Dried fruit	1 oz.	2 tbsps.
Sugar, rice	1 oz.	2 tbsps.
Breadcrumbs (fresh)	$\frac{1}{4}$ oz.	$1\frac{1}{2}$ tbsps.
Breadcrumbs (dry)	$\frac{1}{4}$ oz.	1 tbsp.
Syrup and treacle (using a warmed spoon)	$1\frac{1}{2}$ oz.	1 tbsp.

AUSTRALIAN CUP MEASURES

1 cup = 8 fl. oz.

Almonds (whole)		6 oz.	1 cup
(ground)		4 oz.	1 cup
Biscuit crumbs		4 oz.	1 cup
Breadcrumbs (dry)		3 oz.	1 cup
(fresh)		2 oz.	1 cup
Cheese (grated)		4 oz.	1 cup
Cream		4 fl. oz.	1 cup whipped
Dried fruit		1 lb.	3 cups
Flour		1 lb.	4 cups
Golden syrup or treacle		1 lb.	1 cup
Rice		8 oz.	1 cup
Sugar	(brown)	6 oz.	1 cup
	(caster)	1 lb.	2 good cups
	(icing)	1 lb.	$3\frac{1}{2}$ cups
	(granulated)	1 lb.	2 cups

GLOSSARY OF COOKING TERMS

spic jelly Savoury jelly used for tting and garnishing savoury shes.

u gratin Food coated with a uce, sprinkled with breadcrumbs nd sometimes grated cheese) d browned under the grill. sually served in the dish in hich it has been cooked.

ain marie A flat, open vessel, lf-filled with water, which is pt at a temperature just below oiling point; used to keep sauces, c. hot without further cooking. lso a baking tin half-filled with ater in which custards and other g dishes stand whilst cooking to revent over-heating.

Making a sauce in a bain marie

aking Cooking in the oven by ry heat. The method used for ost cakes, biscuits and pastries, d for many other dishes.

aking blind Baking pastry apes without a filling. Line the an case or pie dish with pastry d trim. Line with greaseproof aper and fill with haricot beans, ce or stale crusts of bread. Or ess kitchen foil into the pastry se and omit beans etc. When astry has set, remove the grease-roof paper or foil and return to e oven to dry out.

arding Covering the breast of oultry or game birds with pieces fat bacon to prevent it drying t during roasting.

asting Moistening meat, poultry game during roasting by spoon-g over it the juices and melted t from the tin, to prevent the food drying out.

Beating Agitating an ingredient or mixture by vigorously turning it over with an upward motion so as to introduce air; a spoon, fork, whisk or electric mixer may be used.

Béchamel A rich white sauce, one of the four basic types of sauce.

Binding Adding a liquid, egg or melted fat to a dry mixture to hold it together.

Blanching Treating food with boiling water in order to whiten it, preserve its natural colour, loosen the skin or remove a flavour which is too strong. Two methods are:–

1. To plunge the food into boiling water; used for skinning tomatoes or to prepare vegetables for freezing.

2. To bring it to the boil in the water; used to whiten veal and sweetbreads or to reduce the saltiness of kippers or pickled meat.

Blending Mixing flour, cornflour and similar ground cereals to a smooth cream with a cold liquid (milk, water or stock) before a boiling liquid is added, as in the preparation of soups, stews, or gravies.

Boiling Cooking in liquid at a temperature of 212°F. (100°C.). The chief foods that are boiled are vegetables, rice, pasta and suet puddings; syrups that need to be reduced are also boiled. Meat, fish and poultry should be simmered–fast boiling makes them shrink, lose flavour, and toughen.

Bouquet garni A small bunch of herbs tied together in muslin and used to give flavour to stews, etc. Usually consists of a sprig of parsley and thyme, a bay leaf, 2 cloves and a few peppercorns.

Braising A method of cooking either meat or vegetables which is a combination of roasting and stewing. A casserole or pan with a tightly fitting lid is used to prevent evaporation. The meat is placed on a bed of vegetables (a mirepoix), with just sufficient liquid to cover the vegetables and to keep the food moist.

Brining Immersing food (mainly meat or fish which is to be pickled and vegetables which are to be preserved) in a salt and water solution.

Browning 1. Giving a dish (usually already cooked) an ap-petising golden brown colour by placing it under the grill or in a hot oven for a short time.

2. Preparing a dish for stewing or casseroling, by frying to seal and colour.

Caramel A substance obtained by heating sugar syrup very slowly in a thick pan until it is a rich brown colour. Used for flavouring cakes and puddings and for lining pudding moulds.

Casserole A baking dish with a tightly fitting lid, used for cooking meat and vegetables in the oven. The food is usually served straight from the dish. May be 'ovenproof' (for oven use only) or 'flameproof' (suitable for use on top of the stove and in the oven).

Chaudfroid A jellied sauce with a béchamel base, used for masking cold fish, poultry and game.

Chining Severing the rib bones from the backbone by sawing through the ribs close to the spine. Used on joints such as loin or neck of lamb, mutton, veal or pork.

Use a special saw for chining

Chopping Dividing food into very small pieces. The ingredient is placed on a chopping board and a very sharp knife is used with a quick up-and-down action.

Clarifying Clearing or purifying fat from water, meat juices or salt.

1. Butter or margarine–Heat the fat gently until it melts, then continue to heat slowly without browning until all bubbling ceases (this shows the water has been driven off). Remove from the heat and allow to stand for a few minutes until the sediment has settled. Pour the fat off gently. It is not usually necessary to strain the fat through muslin.

2. Dripping–Melt the fat and strain into a large basin to remove any big particles. Then pour over it 2–3 times as much boiling water, stir well and leave to cool; the clean fat will rise to the top. When it has solidified, lift it off, dab the underside dry and scrape off any sediment.

Coating 1. Covering food which is to be fried with flour, egg and breadcrumbs, batter, etc.

2. Covering food which is cooked or ready to serve with a thin layer of mayonnaise, sauce, etc.

Coddling A method of soft-

boiling eggs: they are put into a pan of boiling water, withdrawn from the heat and allowed to stand for 8–10 minutes.

Compôte Fruit stewed in a sugar syrup and served hot or cold.

Consistency The term used to describe the texture of a dough, batter, etc.

Creaming The beating together of fat and sugar to resemble whipped cream in colour and texture, i.e. until pale and fluffy. This method of mixing is used for cakes and puddings containing a high proportion of fat.

Crimping 1. To remove the skin in strips from cucumber and similar foods, to give the finished slices a ridged appearance.

2. To decorate the double edge of a pie or tart or the edge of a short-

Use thumbs and fore-fingers to crimp the edge of a pastry case

bread by pinching it at regular intervals, giving a fluted effect.

Croquettes A mixture of meat, fish, poultry or potatoes, bound together and formed into various shapes, then coated with egg and breadcrumbs and fried in deep fat.

Croûte A large round or finger of toasted or fried bread, about ¼ in. thick, on which game and some entrées and savouries are served.

Croûtons Small pieces of bread which are fried or toasted and served as an accompaniment or garnish to soup.

Curd 1. The solid part of soured milk or junket.

2. A creamy preserve made from fruit–usually lemons or oranges–sugar, eggs and butter.

Dariole A small, narrow mould with sloping sides, used for setting creams and jellies and for baking or steaming puddings, especially castle puddings. Also used to prepare English madeleines.

Devilled Food which has been grilled or fried with sharp, hot seasonings.

Dough A thick mixture of un-cooked flour and liquid, often combined with other ingredients. As well as the usual yeast dough, it can also mean mixtures such as pastry, scones and biscuits.

Dredging The action of sprinkling food lightly and evenly with flour, sugar, etc. Fish and meat are often dredged with flour before frying, while pancakes, etc. may be dredged with fine sugar to improve their appearance. A pierced container of metal or plastic (known as a dredger) is usually used.

Dripping The fat obtained from roasted meat during cooking or from small pieces of new fat that have been rendered down.

Dropping consistency The term used to describe the texture of a cake or pudding mixture before cooking. To test, fill a spoon with the mixture and hold it on its side – the mixture should fall in 5 seconds, without jerking the spoon.

Egg-and-crumbing A method of coating fish, cutlets, rissoles, etc., before they are fried or baked. Have a beaten egg on a plate and some breadcrumbs on a piece of kitchen paper; dip the food in the egg and lift out, letting it drain for a second or two. Transfer it to the crumbs and tip the paper until the food is well covered. Press in the crumbs, then shake the food to remove any surplus.

Entrée A hot or cold dressed savoury dish consisting of meat, poultry, game, fish, eggs or vegetables, served complete with sauce and garnish.

Escalope A slice of meat (usually veal) cut from the top of the leg. Escalopes are generally egg-and-crumbed and fried.

Espagnole A rich brown sauce, one of the four basic sauces.

Farce, forcemeat Stuffing used for meat, fish or vegetables. A farce is based on meat, bacon, etc. while the basic forcemeat is made from breadcrumbs, suet, onion and herbs.

Fillet A term used for the under-cut of a loin of beef, veal, pork or game, for boned breasts of poultry and birds and for boned sides of fish.

Fines herbes A combination of finely chopped herbs. In practice, the mixture is usually parsley, chervil, tarragon and chives, and it is most commonly used in omelettes. When fresh herbs are used one can add enough to make the omelette look green, but when dried ones are used, ½ level teaspoon of the mixture is plenty for a 4-egg omelette. For other dishes, the blend is sometimes varied.

Flaking Breaking up cooked fish into flakes with a fork.

Folding in (Sometimes called cutting-and-folding). Combining a whisked or creamed mixture with other ingredients so that it retains its lightness. It is used for certain cake mixtures and for meringues and soufflés. A typical example is folding dry flour into a whisked sponge cake mixture. Important points to remember are that the mixture must be folded very lightly and that it must not be agitated more than absolutely necessary, because with every movement some of the air bubbles are broken down. Do not use an electric mixer.

Fricassee A white stew of chicken, veal or rabbit.

Frosting 1. A method of decorating the rim of a glass in which a cold drink is to be served. Coat the edge with whipped egg white, dip into caster sugar and allow to dry. **2.** An icing, especially of the American type.

Iced and creamy desserts look good in a frosted glass

Frying The process of cooking food in hot fat or oil. There are two main methods:
1. Shallow frying A small quantity of fat is used in a shallow pan. Used for steak, chops, sausages, fish steaks and white fish, which need only sufficient fat to prevent them sticking to the pan. Made-up dishes such as fish cakes can also be shallow-fried, but need enough fat to half-cover them. In most cases the food requires coating.
2. Deep frying The food is cooked in sufficient fat to cover it completely. Used for batter-coated fish, whitebait, chipped potatoes, doughnuts and made-up dishes such as croquettes and fritters.
A deep pan and a wire basket are needed, with fat to come about ¾ up the pan; clarified beef fat, lard and cooking oil are suitable. The fat must be pure and free from moisture, to avoid spurting or boiling over, and it must be heated to the right temperature or the food will be either grease-sodden or burnt. If the fat is strained into a basin,

jug or wide-necked jar and covered, it may be stored in a cool place for further use. A frying thermometer should always be used with oil for deep fat frying.

Galantine White meat, such as poultry or veal, which has been cooked, rolled and pressed. Sometimes glazed or finished with toasted breadcrumbs.

Garnish An edible decoration, such as parsley, watercress, hard-boiled egg or lemon added to a savoury dish to improve the appearance and flavour.

Glaze Beaten egg, egg white, milk, etc. used to give a glossy surface to certain sweets and to savouries such as galantines. The meat glaze used for savouries is home-made meat stock reduced by rapid boiling. Stock made from a cube cannot be treated this way.

Grating Shaving foods such as cheese and vegetables into small shreds. Foods to be grated must be firm and cheese should be allowed to harden.

Grilling Cooking food by direct heat under a grill or over a hot fire. Good quality, tender meat (steak, chops), whole fish (herring, trout) and fish cutlets are the foods most generally cooked in this way. Some cooked dishes are put under the grill to give them a brown top surface or to heat them through before they are served.

Grinding The process of reducing hard foodstuffs, such as nuts and coffee beans, to small particles by means of a food mill, grinder or electric blender.

Hors d'oeuvre Small dishes served cold, usually before the soup, as an appetiser. Hors d'oeuvre are generally small and piquant.

Infusing Extracting flavour from spices, herbs, etc. by pouring on boiling liquid and then covering and allowing to stand in a warm place.

Jardinière A garnish of diced, mixed, spring vegetables, plus green peas, cauliflower sprigs, etc.

Julienne A garnish of fine strips of mixed vegetables.

Kneading Working a dough firmly, using the knuckles for bread-making, the fingertips in pastry-making. In both cases the outside of the dough is drawn into the centre.

Knocking up Preparing a pastry edge ready for crimping. Hold a round bladed knife parallel with the pastry and knock against the knife, to open up the pastry in ridges.

Larding Inserting small strips of

fat bacon into the flesh of gar birds, poultry and meat befo cooking, to prevent it drying o when roasting. A special lardi needle is used for the process.

Liaison A thickening agent, su as flour, cornflour or arrowroo which is used for thickening binding sauces and soups.

Lukewarm Moderately warr approximately 100°F. (38°C.).

Macedoine A mixture of fruits vegetables cut into evenly siz dice, generally used as a decor tion or garnish. Alternatively, t fruits may be set in jelly.

Marinade A seasoned mixture oil and vinegar, lemon juice wine, in which food is left for given time. This helps to soft the fibres of meat and fish and ad flavour to the food.

Masking 1. Covering or coating cooked meat or similar dish wi savoury jelly, glaze or sauce. **2.** Coating the inside of a mou with jelly.

Ice helps to set the thin layer of jelly quickly

Meringue Egg white whiske until stiff, mixed with caster sug and dried in a cool oven till cris

Mincing Chopping or cutting in very small pieces with a knife o more commonly, in a mincer.

Mixed herbs These most con monly consist of a blend of drie parsley, tarragon, chives, thym and chervil, but other variation may occur in certain recipes.

Mirepoix A mixture of carro celery and onion, often includin some ham or bacon, cut into larg pieces, lightly fried in fat and use as a 'bed' on which to braise mea

Noisettes Neatly trimmed roun or oval shapes of lamb, mutton o beef, not less than ½ in. thick.

Panada A thick binding sauc (using 1 oz. fat and 1 oz. flour t ¼ pint liquid) made by the rou method and used for bindin croquettes and similar mixtures.

Parboiling Part-boiling; the foo is boiled for part of the norma cooking time, then finished b some other method.

Paring Peeling or trimming, especially vegetables or the rind of citrus fruits.

A potato peeler makes paring a lemon easy

Petits fours Very small fancy cakes, often iced, and almond biscuits, served at the end of a formal meal.

Piping Forcing cream, icing or butter out of a forcing bag through a nozzle, to decorate cakes etc. Also used for potatoes and meringues. The bag may be made of cotton, nylon or plastic.

Poaching Cooking in an open pan at simmering point with sufficient seasoned liquid to cover. Used in egg, fish and some meat dishes.

Pot-roasting Cooking meat in a saucepan with fat and a very small amount of liquid; it is particularly good for small and less tender cuts.

Pulses Dried beans, peas, split peas and lentils.

Purée Fruit, vegetable, meat or fish which has been pounded, sieved or pulverised in an electric blender (usually after cooking), to give a smooth pulp. A soup made by sieving vegetables with the liquor in which they were cooked is also called a purée.

Raspings Fine crumbs made from stale bread; used for coating fried foods and for au gratin dishes. The bread is first dried in a cool oven and then crushed.

Réchauffé Reheated leftover foods.

Reducing Boiling a liquid in an uncovered pan in order to evaporate it and give a more concentrated result. Used especially when making soups, sauces, or syrups.

Refreshing 1. After cooking vegetables, pouring cold water over them to preserve the colour; they are then reheated before serving.
2. Crisping up already-cooked pastry in the oven.
3. For home-freezing, plunging partly-cooked or blanched vegetables and meat into ice-cold water immediately after removing from the heat.

Rendering Extracting fat from meat trimmings by cutting them up small and heating in a cool oven (300°F., mark 1) until the fat has melted out, or boiling them in an uncovered pan with very little water until the water is driven off and the fat is melted; the fat is then strained into a basin.

Rennet An extract from calves' stomachs. It contains rennin and is used for curdling or coagulating milk for junket and for cheese-making.

Rissoles Small portions of minced meat enclosed in rounds of pastry and folded to form a semi-circle, then egg-and-crumbed and fried in deep fat. The term is now loosely applied to a round cake of a meat or fish mixture, egg-and-crumbed and fried.

Roasting In its true sense, roasting means cooking by direct heat in front of an open fire. Thus rôtisserie cooking is true roasting, but the modern method of cooking in a closed oven is really baking. Only good quality poultry, and the best cuts of meat, should be cooked in this way.

Roux A mixture of equal amounts of fat and plain flour cooked together to form the basis for a sauce and for thickening sauces and stews.

Rubbing in Incorporating fat into flour; used when making shortcrust pastry, plain cakes and biscuits, when a short texture is required. Put the fat in small pieces in the flour, then rub it into the flour with the fingertips.

Rusks Fingers or slices of bread dried in a slow oven.

Salmi A ragoût or stew, usually of game.

Sauté To cook in an open pan over a strong heat in fat or oil, shaking the pan to make whatever is in it 'sauter' or jump, to keep it from sticking. The pan used should be heavy, wide and shallow. This may be used as a complete cooking method or as the initial cooking before finishing in a sauce.

Scalding Pouring boiling water over food to clean it, to loosen hairs (as from a joint of pork) or to remove the skin (as on tomatoes or peaches). The food must not be left in the boiling water or it will begin to cook.

Scalloped dishes Food (often previously cooked) baked in a scallop shell or similar small container; it is usually combined with a creamy sauce, topped with breadcrumbs and surrounded with a border of piped potato.

Scalloping A means of decorating the double edge of the pastry covering of a pie. Make close horizontal cuts with a knife round the edge of the pie, giving a flaked effect (see **knocking up**) then, with the back of the knife, pull the edge up vertically at regular intervals to form scallops. Traditionally these should be close together for a sweet pie and wider apart for a savoury one.

Scoring To make shallow, parallel cuts in the surface of food in order to improve its flavour or appearance or to help it cook more quickly (e.g. fish).

Searing Browning meat quickly in a little fat before grilling or roasting.

Seasoned flour Used for dusting meat and fish before frying or stewing. Mix about 2 level tablespoons flour with about 1 level teaspoon salt and a good sprinkling of pepper. Either pat it onto the food or dip the pieces in the flour and shake them gently before cooking.

Shredding Slicing a food such as cheese or raw vegetables into very fine pieces. A sharp knife or coarse grater is generally used.

Sieving Rubbing or pressing food (e.g. cooked vegetables) through a sieve; a wooden spoon is used to force it through.

Sifting Shaking a dry ingredient through a sieve or flour sifter to remove lumps and aerate it.

Simmering Keeping a liquid just below boiling point (approximately 205°F. or 96°C.). First bring the liquid to the boil, then adjust the heat so that the surface of the liquid is kept just moving or 'shivering'; continuous bubbling indicates the temperature is too high.

Skimming To take fat off the surface of stock, gravy or stews, or scum from other foods (e.g. jams) while they are cooking. A piece of absorbent kitchen paper or a metal spoon may be used.

Steaming An economical method of cooking food in the steam from rapidly boiling water. There are several ways of steaming, according to the equipment available.

Steeping The process of pouring hot or cold water over food and leaving it to stand, either to soften it or to extract its flavour and colour.

Stewing A long, slow method of cooking in a liquid which is kept at simmering point; particularly suitable for coarse-fibred foods. The liquid is served with the food, so that flavour is not wasted.

Stock The liquid produced when meat, bones, poultry, fish or veg-etables are simmered in water with herbs and flavourings for several hours, to extract their flavour. Stock forms the basis of soups, sauces and stews and many savoury dishes.

Sweating Cooking a food (usually a vegetable) very gently in a covered pan with melted fat until it exudes juices. The food should not colour.

Syrup A concentrated solution of sugar in water, prepared by boiling and used in making water ices, drinks and fruit desserts.
Golden syrup is a by-product of sugar refining.
Maple syrup is extracted from the North American sugar maple.

Tammy To strain soups, sauces, etc. through a fine woollen cloth.

Tepid Approximately at blood heat. Tepid water is obtained by adding 2 parts cold water to 1 part boiling.

Thickening Giving body to soups, sauces or gravies by the addition of flour, cornflour or arrowroot.

Trussing Tying or skewering a bird into a compact shape before cooking.

Vol-au-vent A round or oval case made of puff pastry and filled with diced meat, poultry, game or fish in a well-flavoured sauce.

Whipping or whisking To beat air rapidly into a mixture:
1. By hand, using an egg beater or whisk.
2. By rotary beater.
3. By electric beater.

Whisk eggs and sugar over gentle heat for best results

Zest The coloured part of orange or lemon peel containing the oil that gives the characteristic flavour. To obtain zest, remove the rind very thinly, with no pith, by grating, or use a zester. If it is required for a sweet dish, you can rub it off with a lump of sugar.

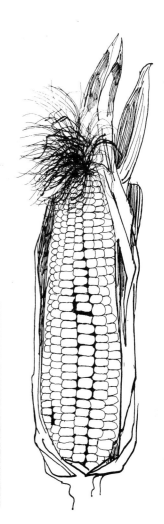

E F G

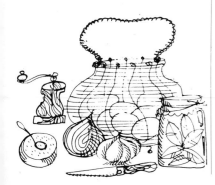

H I J K

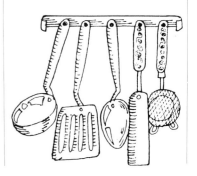

L M N

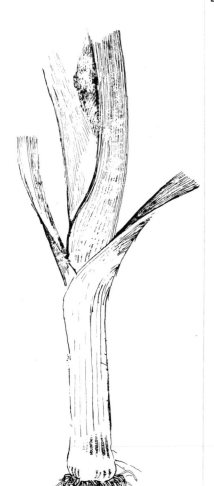

R   S

T U V

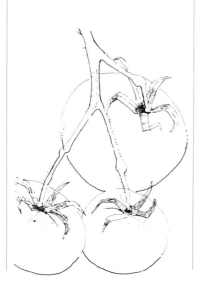

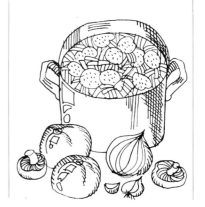

W Y Z

We wish to thank the following companies for the loan of accessories for photography:

Bosch ; Bourne and Hollingsworth ; Casa Pupo ; Civil Service Stores ; Collets Chinese Art Gallery ; Cona ; Craftsmen Potters' Association ; Cucina ; Dartington : David Mellor ; Denby ; Design and Crafts , Farnham ; Divertimenti ; Domecq ; Elizabeth David ; Garrards ; Grants of St James ; Gratnel ; Habitat ; Heal's ; Henry's ; Hoover ; John Lewis ; Kenco ; Kenwood ; Langley London ; Loon Fung Supermarket ; Macdonald Imports and Exports, Exeter ; Melita ; Midwinter ; Optima ; Philips ; Presents, Farnham ; Prestige ; Robert Carrier Cookshop ; Robert Jackson ; Robinson and Cleaver ; Rosenthal ; Russell Hobbs ; Selfridges ; Shaplans ; Staines Kitchen Supplies ; Tiarco ; Viners ; Wedgwood ; Wilson and Gill.